*New Beacon Bibl

EXODUS
A Commentary in the Wesleyan Tradition

H. Junia Pokrifka

BEACON HILL PRESS
OF KANSAS CITY

Beacon Hill Press of Kansas City
PO Box 419527
Kansas City, MO 64141
www.BeaconHillBooks.com

ISBN 978-0-8341-3560-4

Printed in the United States of America

Cover Design: J.R. Caines
Interior Design: Sharon Page

Unless otherwise indicated all Scripture quotations are from the Holy Bible, New International Version® (NIV®). Copy-right © 1973, 1978, 1984, 2011 by Biblica, Inc.™ Used by permission. All rights reserved worldwide. *Emphasis indicated by underlining in boldface quotations and italic in lightface quotations.*

The following version of Scripture is in the public domain:

The King James Version (KJV)

The following copyrighted versions of Scripture are used by permission:

The Holy Bible, English Standard Version® (ESV®). Copyright © 2001 by Crossway Bibles, a publishing ministry of Good News Publishers. All rights reserved.

The New American Standard Bible® (NASB®), copyright © 1960, 1962, 1963, 1968, 1971, 1972, 1973, 1975, 1977, 1995 by The Lockman Foundation. *Emphasis indicated by italic.*

The NET Bible® (NET), copyright © 1996-2016 by Biblical Studies Press, L.L.C., http://netbible.com. Scripture quoted by permission. All rights reserved.

The New Jerusalem Bible (NJB), copyright © 1985 by Darton, Longman & Todd, Ltd. and Doubleday, a division of Random House, Inc. Reprinted by permission.

The New JPS Hebrew-English Tanakh (NJPS), © 2000 by The Jewish Publication Society. All rights reserved.

The New King James Version® (NKJV). Copyright © 1982 by Thomas Nelson, Inc. All rights reserved.

The New Revised Standard Version Bible (NRSV), copyright © 1989 National Council of the Churches of Christ in the United States of America. All rights reserved. *Emphasis indicated by italic.*

Library of Congress Cataloging-in-Publication Data
Names: Pokrifka, H. Junia, 1965- author.
Title: Exodus / H. Junia Pokrifka.
Description: Kansas City, MO : Beacon Hill Press of Kansas City, 2018. |
   Series: New Beacon Bible commentary | Includes bibliographical references.
Identifiers: LCCN 2017040026 | ISBN 9780834135604 (pbk.)
Subjects: LCSH: Bible. Exodus—Commentaries.
Classification: LCC BS1245.53 .P64 2018 | DDC 222/.1207—dc23 LC record available at
https://lccn.loc.gov/2017040026

The Internet addresses, email addresses, and phone numbers in this book are accurate at the time of publication. They are provided as a resource. Beacon Hill Press of Kansas City does not endorse them or vouch for their content or permanence.

10 9 8 7 6 5 4 3 2 1

DEDICATION

To my beloved husband, Todd
with deepest gratitude for sacrificial love and support

To our dearest sons, Daniel and Immanuel
with deepest gratitude for affection and laughter

COMMENTARY EDITORS

CONTENTS

GENERAL EDITORS' PREFACE

The purpose of the New Beacon Bible Commentary is to make available to pastors and students in the twenty-first century a biblical commentary that reflects the best scholarship in the Wesleyan theological tradition. The commentary project aims to make this scholarship accessible to a wider audience to assist them in their understanding and proclamation of Scripture as God's Word.

Writers of the volumes in this series not only are scholars within the Wesleyan theological tradition and experts in their field but also have special interest in the books assigned to them. Their task is to communicate clearly the critical consensus and the full range of other credible voices who have commented on the Scriptures. Though scholarship and scholarly contribution to the understanding of the Scriptures are key concerns of this series, it is not intended as an academic dialogue within the scholarly community. Commentators of this series constantly aim to demonstrate in their work the significance of the Bible as the church's book and the contemporary relevance and application of the biblical message. The project's overall goal is to make available to the church and for her service the fruits of the labors of scholars who are committed to their Christian faith.

The *New International Version* (NIV) is the reference version of the Bible used in this series; however, the focus of exegetical study and comments is the biblical text in its original language. When the commentary uses the NIV, it is printed in bold. The text printed in bold italics is the translation of the author. Commentators also refer to other translations where the text may be difficult or ambiguous.

The structure and organization of the commentaries in this series seeks to facilitate the study of the biblical text in a systematic and methodical way. Study of each biblical book begins with an ***Introduction*** section that gives an overview of authorship, date, provenance, audience, occasion, purpose, sociological/cultural issues, textual history, literary features, hermeneutical issues, and theological themes necessary to understand the book. This section also includes a brief outline of the book and a list of general works and standard commentaries.

The commentary section for each biblical book follows the outline of the book presented in the introduction. In some volumes, readers will find section ***overviews*** of large portions of scripture with general comments on their overall literary structure and other literary features. A consistent feature of the commentary is the paragraph-by-paragraph study of biblical texts. This section has three parts: **Behind the Text**, **In the Text**, and **From the Text**.

The goal of the **Behind the Text** section is to provide the reader with all the relevant information necessary to understand the text. This includes specific historical situations reflected in the text, the literary context of the text, sociological and cultural issues, and literary features of the text.

In the Text explores what the text says, following its verse-by-verse structure. This section includes a discussion of grammatical details, word studies, and the connectedness of the text to other biblical books/passages or other parts of the book being studied (the canonical relationship). This section provides transliterations of key words in Hebrew and Greek and their literal meanings. The goal here is to explain what the author would have meant and/or what the audience would have understood as the meaning of the text. This is the largest section of the commentary.

The **From the Text** section examines the text in relation to the following areas: theological significance, intertextuality, the history of interpretation, use of the Old Testament scriptures in the New Testament, interpretation in later church history, actualization, and application.

The commentary provides **sidebars** on topics of interest that are important but not necessarily part of an explanation of the biblical text. These topics are informational items and may cover archaeological, historical, literary, cultural, and theological matters that have relevance to the biblical text. Occasionally, longer detailed discussions of special topics are included as **excursuses.**

We offer this series with our hope and prayer that readers will find it a valuable resource for their understanding of God's Word and an indispensable tool for their critical engagement with the biblical texts.

Roger Hahn, Centennial Initiative General Editor
Alex Varughese, General Editor (Old Testament)
George Lyons, General Editor (New Testament)

ACKNOWLEDGMENTS

My love for the book of Exodus goes back to my student years at the University of St. Andrews, where I wrote my Ph.D. thesis on the attributes of God as revealed in Exod 34:6-7 and some of its echoes under the guidance of Christopher Seitz. Since then, my interest, research, and reflection on the book has only widened and deepened as I have taught a course on the book at Azusa Pacific University since 2001. On a personal level, I feel that I have lived out the basic storyline of the book—from oppression to deliverance to intimacy with God. My life has been profoundly influenced and shaped by its theological messages. This volume, therefore, is a product of more than two decades of meditation and teaching.

Words of gratitude are in order. I am deeply grateful for Beacon Hill Press for inviting me to contribute to the New Beacon Bible Commentary series. I also thank them for their extreme patience and grace, which they extended to me through several extensions on the submission deadline. I am also thankful for the administration at APU for granting a reduced teaching load in the fall of 2012. Paula Miller at APU deserves special recognition for proofreading the entire volume and for her encouraging words. My heartfelt gratitude goes to Alex Varughese, professor emeritus of Biblical Literature at Mount Vernon Nazarene University and a general editor for this commentary series. I thank him not only for his editorial work but also for his insights and ideas, which appear especially in the From the Text sections.

I am extremely grateful to my mom for her prayers that God would receive glory in and through this commentary. The sweet hours with my two boys filled most of my staple break times during the years of writing this volume. I could not have enjoyed writing it without them.

Todd—my husband, my theologian, and my pastor—has walked and talked with me throughout all my writing projects, including this one. He read the entire volume and contributed innumerable, invaluable theological insights, ideas, and comments. I could not have completed this work without him.

I praise my Father in heaven, my Lord Jesus Christ, and the Holy Spirit for giving me understanding and the words to write when I often felt poor in spirit and bereft of insight. All glory is due to his name. "May these words of my mouth and this meditation of my heart be pleasing in your sight, Lord, my Rock and my Redeemer" (Ps 19:14).

—Junia Pokrifka

ABBREVIATIONS

With a few exceptions, these abbreviations follow those in *The SBL Handbook of Style* (Alexander 1999).

General

→	see the commentary at
AD	anno Domini (precedes date)
BC	before Christ (follows date)
ca.	circa
ch	chapter
chs	chapters
cm	centimeter(s)
ed.	edition, editor
e.g.	*exempli gratia*, for example
esp.	especially
etc.	*et cetera*, and the rest
fem.	feminine
ff.	and the following ones
g	gram(s)
HB	Hebrew Bible
Heb.	Hebrew
i.e.	*id est*, that is
kg	kilogram(s)
km	kilometer(s)
L	liter(s)
lb	pound(s)
lit.	literal or literally
LXX	Septuagint
m	meter(s)
masc.	masculine
mi	mile(s)
MS(S)	manuscript(s)
MT	Masoretic Text (of the OT)
n(n).	note(s)
n.d.	no date
n.p.	no pages
NT	New Testament
OT	Old Testament
oz	ounce(s)
pl.	plural
r.	reigned
sg.	singular
v(v)	verse(s)
vol(s).	volume(s)

Modern English Versions of the Bible

ESV	English Standard Version
KJV	King James Version
NASB	New American Standard Bible
NET	New English Translation
NIV	New International Version
NJB	New Jerusalem Bible
NJPS	Hebrew-English Tanakh
NKJV	New King James Version
NRSV	New Revised Standard Version

Print Conventions for Translations

Bold font	NIV (bold without quotation marks in the text under study; elsewhere in the regular font, with quotation marks and no further identification)
Bold italic font	Author's translation (without quotation marks)

Behind the Text: Literary or historical background information average readers might not know from reading the biblical text alone

In the Text: Comments on the biblical text, words, phrases, grammar, and so forth

From the Text: The use of the text by later interpreters, contemporary relevance, theological and ethical implications of the text, with particular emphasis on Wesleyan concerns

Ancient Sources

Old Testament

Gen	Genesis
Exod	Exodus
Lev	Leviticus
Num	Numbers
Deut	Deuteronomy
Josh	Joshua
Judg	Judges
Ruth	Ruth
1—2 Sam	1—2 Samuel
1—2 Kgs	1—2 Kings
1—2 Chr	1—2 Chronicles
Ezra	Ezra
Neh	Nehemiah
Esth	Esther
Job	Job
Ps/Pss	Psalm/Psalms
Prov	Proverbs
Eccl	Ecclesiastes
Song	Song of Songs/ Song of Solomon
Isa	Isaiah
Jer	Jeremiah
Lam	Lamentations
Ezek	Ezekiel

Dan	Daniel
Hos	Hosea
Joel	Joel
Amos	Amos
Obad	Obadiah
Jonah	Jonah
Mic	Micah
Nah	Nahum
Hab	Habakkuk
Zeph	Zephaniah
Hag	Haggai
Zech	Zechariah
Mal	Malachi

(Note: Chapter and verse numbering in the MT and LXX often differ compared to those in English Bibles. To avoid confusion, all biblical references follow the chapter and verse numbering in English translations, even when the text in the MT and LXX is under discussion.)

New Testament

Matt	Matthew
Mark	Mark
Luke	Luke
John	John
Acts	Acts
Rom	Romans
1—2 Cor	1—2 Corinthians
Gal	Galatians
Eph	Ephesians
Phil	Philippians
Col	Colossians
1—2 Thess	1—2 Thessalonians
1—2 Tim	1—2 Timothy
Titus	Titus
Phlm	Philemon
Heb	Hebrews
Jas	James
1—2 Pet	1—2 Peter
1—2—3 John	1—2—3 John
Jude	Jude
Rev	Revelation

Apocrypha

Bar	Baruch
Add Dan	Additions to Daniel
Pr Azar	Prayer of Azariah
Bel	Bel and the Dragon
Sg Three	Song of the Three Young Men
Sus	Susanna
1—2 Esd	1—2 Esdras
Add Esth	Additions to Esther
Ep Jer	Epistle of Jeremiah
Jdt	Judith
1—2 Macc	1—2 Maccabees
3—4 Macc	3—4 Maccabees
Pr Man	Prayer of Manasseh
Ps 151	Psalm 151
Sir	Sirach/Ecclesiasticus
Tob	Tobit
Wis	Wisdom of Solomon

Josephus

Ant.	*Jewish Antiquities*

Greek Transliteration

Greek	Letter	English
α	alpha	a
β	bēta	b
γ	gamma	g
γ	gamma nasal	n (before γ, κ, ξ, χ)
δ	delta	d
ε	epsilon	e
ζ	zēta	z
η	ēta	ē
θ	thēta	th
ι	iōta	i
κ	kappa	k
λ	lambda	l
μ	mu	m
ν	nu	n
ξ	xi	x
ο	omicron	o
π	pi	p
ρ	rhō	r
ρ	initial rhō	rh
σ/ς	sigma	s
τ	tau	t
υ	upsilon	y
υ	upsilon	u (in diphthongs: au, eu, ēu, ou, ui)
φ	phi	ph
χ	chi	ch
ψ	psi	ps
ω	ōmega	ō
ʽ	rough breathing	h (before initial vowels or diphthongs)

Hebrew Consonant Transliteration

Hebrew/ Aramaic	Letter	English
א	alef	ʼ
ב	bet	b
ג	gimel	g
ד	dalet	d
ה	he	h
ו	vav	v or w
ז	zayin	z
ח	khet	ḥ
ט	tet	ṭ
י	yod	y
ך/כ	kaf	k
ל	lamed	l
ם/מ	mem	m
ן/נ	nun	n
ס	samek	s
ע	ayin	ʻ
ף/פ	pe	p; f (spirant)
ץ/צ	tsade	ṣ
ק	qof	q
ר	resh	r
שׂ	sin	ś
שׁ	shin	š
ת	tav	t; th (spirant)

BIBLIOGRAPHY

Aldred, Cyril. 1998. *The Egyptians*. 3rd ed. London: Thames & Hudson.

Alexander, Patrick H., et al. 1999. *The SBL Handbook of Style*. Peabody, MA: Hendrickson Publishers.

Allen, James P. 2002. The Speos Artemidos Inscription of Hatshepsut. *Bulletin of the Egyptological Seminar* 16:1-17.

Alter, Robert. 2004. *The Five Books of Moses: A Translation with Commentary*. New York: Norton.

Averbeck, Richard E. 2003. Sacrifices and Offerings. Pages 706-33 in the *Dictionary of the Old Testament: Pentateuch*. Edited by T. Desmond Alexander and David W. Baker. Downers Grove, IL: InterVarsity Press.

Barth, Karl. 1956. *Church Dogmatics*. Vol. VI.1: *The Doctrine of Reconciliation*. Edinburgh: T&T Clark.

_____. 1957. *Church Dogmatics*. Vol. II.1: *The Doctrine of God*. Edinburgh: T&T Clark.

Berlin, Adele, and Marc Zvi Brettler. 2004. *The Jewish Study Bible*. Oxford: Oxford University Press.

Braaten, Carl E., and Christopher R. Seitz. 2005. *I Am the Lord Your God: Christian Reflections on the Ten Commandments*. Grand Rapids: Eerdmans.

Bruckner, James K. 2008. *Exodus*. New International Biblical Commentary. Peabody, MA: Hendrickson Publishers.

Brueggemann, Walter. 1994. Exodus. Pages 675-982 in vol. 1 of *The New Interpreter's Bible: General Articles, Genesis, Exodus, and Leviticus*. Edited by Leander Keck. Nashville: Abingdon Press.

Cassuto, Umberto Moshe David. 1967. *A Commentary on the Book of Exodus*. First English ed. Jerusalem: Magnes Press, Hebrew University.

Childs, Brevard S. 1974. *The Book of Exodus: A Critical, Theological Commentary*. Philadelphia: Westminster Press.

Clarke, Adam. 1831. *Commentary on the Bible*. N.p. http://sacred-texts.com/bib/cmt/clarke/exo020.htm.

Cochrane, Arthur C. 1962. *The Church's Confession under Hitler*. Philadelphia: Westminster Press.

Durham, John I. 1987. *Exodus*. Word Biblical Commentary. Waco, TX: Word Books.

Enns, Peter. 2000. *The NIV Application Commentary: Exodus*. Grand Rapids: Zondervan.

———. 2003. Exodus Route and Wilderness Itinerary. Pages 272-80 in the *Dictionary of the Old Testament: Pentateuch*. Edited by T. Desmond Alexander and David W. Baker. Downers Grove, IL: InterVarsity Press.

Erlich, C. S. 2005. Philistines. Pages 782-92 in the *Dictionary of the Old Testament: Historical Books*. Edited by Bill T. Arnold and H. G. M. Williamson. Downers Grove, IL: InterVarsity Press.

Fretheim, Terence E. 1991. *Exodus*. Louisville, KY: Westminster John Knox Press.

———. 2003. Exodus, Book of. Pages 248-52 in the *Dictionary of the Old Testament: Pentateuch*. Edited by T. Desmond Alexander and David W. Baker. Downers Grove, IL: InterVarsity Press.

Gardiner, Alan H. 1909. *Admonitions of an Egyptian Sage*. Leipzig: J. C. Hinrichs.

Hamilton, James M. 2010. *God's Glory in Salvation through Judgment: A Biblical Theology*. Wheaton, IL: Crossway.

Hamilton, Victor P. 2011. *Exodus: An Exegetical Commentary*. Grand Rapids: Baker Academic.

Hoffmeier, James K. 1996. *Israel in Egypt: The Evidence for the Authenticity of the Exodus Tradition*. New York: Oxford University Press.

Hugenberger, Gordon P. 1998. *Marriage as a Covenant: Biblical Law and Ethics as Developed from Malachi*. Grand Rapids: Baker Books.

Jacob, Benno. 1992. *The Second Book of the Bible, Exodus*. Translated by Walter Jacob. Hoboken, NJ: KTAV.

Lienhard, Joseph T. 2001. *Exodus, Leviticus, Numbers, Deuteronomy*. Ancient Christian Commentary on Scripture. Edited by Thomas C. Oden. Downers Grove, IL: InterVarsity Press.

Meyers, Carol. 2005. *Exodus*. The New Cambridge Bible Commentary. New York: Cambridge University Press.

Milgrom, Jacob. 1990. *Numbers: The Traditional Hebrew Text with the New JPS Translation*. Philadelphia: Jewish Publication Society.

Moltmann, Jürgen. 2001. The Liberation of the Future and Its Anticipations in History. Pages 265-90 in *God Will Be All in All: The Eschatology of Jürgen Moltmann.* Edited by Richard Bauckham. Minneapolis: Fortress Press.

Noth, Martin. 1962. *Exodus: A Commentary.* Philadelphia: Westminster Press.

Propp, William H. C. 1999. *Exodus 1—18.* The Anchor Yale Bible. New Haven, CT: Yale University Press.

_____. 2006. *Exodus 19—40.* The Anchor Yale Bible. New Haven, CT: Yale University Press.

Provan, Iain W., V. Philips Long, and Tremper Longman III. 2003. *A Biblical History of Israel.* Louisville, KY: Westminster John Knox Press.

Redford, Donald B. 2003. *The Wars in Syria and Palestine of Thutmose III.* Boston: Brill.

Richter, Sandra L. 2008. *The Epic of Eden: A Christian Entry into the Old Testament.* Downers Grove, IL: IVP Academic.

Ryken, Philip G. 2005. *Exodus: Saved for God's Glory.* Wheaton, IL: Crossway Books.

Sanders, John. 1998. *The God Who Risks: A Theology of Providence.* Downers Grove, IL: InterVarsity Press.

Sarna, Nahum M. 1996. *Exploring Exodus: The Origins of Biblical Israel.* New York: Schocken Books.

———. 2004. *Exodus.* The JPS Torah Commentary. Ebook. Scholar pdf ed. Skokie, IL: Varda Books. https://publishersrow.com.

Shaw, Ian, ed. 2000. *The Oxford History of Ancient Egypt.* New York: Oxford University Press.

Stuart, Douglas K. 2006. *Exodus: An Exegetical and Theological Exposition of Holy Scripture.* The New American Commentary. Nashville: Broadman & Holman.

Van Dam, C. 2003. Priestly Clothing. Pages 643-46 in the *Dictionary of the Old Testament: Pentateuch.* Edited by T. Desmond Alexander and David W. Baker. Downers Grove, IL: InterVarsity Press.

Walton, John H. 2003. Exodus. Pages 258-72 in the *Dictionary of the Old Testament: Pentateuch.* Edited by T. Desmond Alexander and David W. Baker. Downers Grove, IL: InterVarsity Press.

Wesley, John. 1980. Sermon XLIV, "The Use of Money," in *Sermons on Several Occasions.* 14th impression. London: Epworth Press.

———. 1990. *Wesley's Notes on the Bible.* Compiled and edited by G. Roger Schoenhals. Grand Rapids: Zondervan.

———. *John Wesley's Notes on the Bible.* Wesley Center Online and Wesleyan Heritage Publishing. http://wesley.nnu.edu/john-wesley/john-wesleys-notes-on-the-bible/.

Wright, Christopher J. H. 2006. *The Mission of God: Unlocking the Bible's Grand Narrative.* Downers Grove, IL: InterVarsity Press.

TABLE OF SIDEBARS

EXODUS

INTRODUCTION

A. The Significance of the Book of Exodus

The English title of the book—Exodus—comes from the name the Greek (LXX) translators gave it (*exodos*; "going out," "departure"; see Heb 11:22), which was retained by the Latin translation. The Greek or English title emphasizes one of the major themes of the book, namely, the Israelites' deliverance from Egyptian bondage. The Hebrew title is *wĕʾēlleh šĕmôt* ("and these are the names"), the first two words in the Hebrew text, or simply "Shemot" (*šĕmôt*; "names"), even as the book begins with a list of the names of the sons of Jacob. The Hebrew title emphasizes the book's literary and theological continuity with the book of Genesis.

The book of Exodus records the foundational events of Israel's history, including the Exodus from Egypt, the making of the covenant and giving of the law on Mount Sinai, the breaking and renewing of the covenant, and the construction of and God's presence in the tabernacle. These events are foundational for understanding God, the people of God, and the covenant that binds them together. As such, these stories provide a key for understanding the rest of the Israelites' life with God as witnessed in the OT.

(1) The book of Exodus is intricately related to the ancestral history found in the book of Genesis. Genesis provides a prologue to the inauguration of the covenant made in Exodus. Exodus carries forward key themes from the ancestral history of Genesis. The divine predictions of the Israelites' migration to a foreign land, their preceding life as oppressed foreigners in Egypt, and their departure from that land (Gen 15:13-14) are fulfilled in Exodus. In addition, God's promises to Abraham concerning a nation, blessings, and fame (Gen 12:1-3) begin their fulfillment in Exodus. The promise of the possession of the promised land (Gen 13:14-17; 15:16, 18-21) also moves toward fulfillment. In these ways, Exodus provides the essential continuation of the story of divine election, redemption, and revelation that begins in Genesis (see Fretheim 2003, 249-50).

(2) Exodus is also closely linked to the three remaining books of the Pentateuch, which is concerned with ritual legislations for ensuring the abiding presence of God (Leviticus), the journey to the promised land and the people's readiness to take possession of it (Numbers), and the people's covenant faithfulness as a condition for conquest and lasting possession of the land (Deuteronomy).

The rest of Israel's history is decisively influenced by the events recorded and interpreted in Exodus. The gracious events of the Exodus and the formation of the covenant at Sinai shape the Israelites' identity as a redeemed, priestly kingdom. The nation Israel is called to be a mediator between God and the Gentile nations. As a mediating nation, their covenant faithfulness ensures blessings for both Israel and the nations, but rebellion results in curses and the exile of Israel.

Exodus is formative in Israel's understanding of God's identity and character. God is thereafter known as "I am the LORD your God, who brought you out of Egypt" (20:2). God is also known as the one who is merciful and just (see the paradigmatic self-revelation of God in 34:6-7, following the golden calf incident). Israel's ongoing confession of faith, therefore, includes the proclamation of his great deeds and his unique attributes.

The book of Exodus shapes Israel's cultic and religious life. Through the signs and wonders, God proves that there is only one true God and that God *is* Yahweh. Israel, thus, must be a monotheistic people. In addition, Exodus gives extensive revelation concerning the acceptable worship and the true, abiding presence of God. More broadly, Exodus inspires the prayer life of God's people. Many psalms are composed to memorialize God's historical deeds and indelibly etch them into the conscience of the people (see Pss 77; 78; 81; 99; 105; 106; 114; 135; 136). The events of the Exodus become the paradigm of divine salvation from powerful enemies and, thus, the basis for trust and praise in times of trouble.

(3) The book of Exodus is also important in the NT. Especially, there is a significant connection between the role of Moses as the lawgiver and covenant mediator and the role of Jesus Christ as the fulfiller of the law and the new covenant mediator.

Moses and the law of Moses have the highest level of authority among the Jews of Jesus' day. As a good Jew, Jesus also upholds the law of Moses (Matt 5:17-20) and teaches the correct interpretations and applications of Moses' laws (e.g., Matt 5:21-48; Mark 10:3-12; 7:10-15). Rightly interpreted, the law continues to provide divine standards of truth and conduct for Jesus, his parents, and his disciples (Matt 5:17-20; 22:24, 36-40; Mark 1:44; 12:19, 26; Luke 2:22; 16:29-31; John 7:22-23; Acts 6:14; 7:53; Jas 2:8-12).

At the same time, the NT writers attest to the superiority of Jesus Christ over Moses and Moses' deliverance, laws, sacrifices, covenant, reconciliation, and tabernacle (John 1:17-18; 9:28-33; Acts 13:39; Rom 10:1-13; 2 Cor 3:3-18; Heb 3:1-6; 7:17—10:18).

Jesus declares that Moses testifies concerning him (Luke 24:27, 44; John 5:46; see also John 1:45; Acts 3:21-23; 7:37; 28:23). Indeed, Moses and his deeds provide several important types for Christ and his work (e.g., the bronze serpent in John 3:14; the manna in John 6:32-38; the water from the rock in 1 Cor 10:4). Jesus Christ is seen as the one who fulfills the hidden intentions of God expressed in various key events and themes recorded in Exodus.

Moreover, the Christian community, emerging from this Christ event and experiencing the coming of the Holy Spirit at Pentecost, also recalls Exodus texts and themes as means to understand its own identity, ethics, and mission. As Fretheim states, "Drawing upon virtually every existing interpretative means available to them," the NT writers use "Exodus texts as a vehicle for interpreting and proclaiming God's act in Jesus" (2003, 257). In sum, without the book of Exodus, the rest of the Bible would crumble, losing one of its constitutive pillars of history and law.

B. The Prophet Moses

The book of Exodus also provides a kind of biography of Moses, the mediator of the old (Sinai) covenant, which is completed by the rest of the Pentateuch. Moses, no doubt, is the greatest prophet of the OT (Deut 34:10-

12). His life and ministry are unsurpassed by anyone except Jesus Christ, who "has been found worthy of greater honor than Moses . . . the Son over God's house" (Heb 3:3, 6).

Moses was born to the tribe of Levi (Exod 2:1-2). He was rescued from Pharaoh's genocidal decree and adopted by Pharaoh's daughter (1:22—2:10). He likely received a royal education (languages, math, politics, law, and architecture) useful for his later ministry (Acts 7:22). After killing an Egyptian (Exod 2:12-15), Moses spent forty years in Midian as a refugee (Acts 7:23, 30). During that time, Moses lived as a humble shepherd. He was likely exposed to his father-in-law's duties as a high priest during that time.

Moses experienced theophany ("appearance of God") in a burning bush (Exod 3:2-5). He heard the audible voice of God, speaking from the burning bush. He was commissioned by God to deliver the Israelites out of Egypt (v 10). Moses was a spokesman for God, not eloquent (4:10), but mighty in word and deed (Acts 7:22). Moses received and transmitted divine revelation of God's identity (Exod 3:15), his name (3:14; 34:5 ff.), and his character (33:18-19; 34:6-7). He demonstrated divine power, supremacy, and judgment over political and religious powers through signs and wonders (chs 7—14; 12:12). He led the Israelites out of Egypt.

As a covenant mediator, Moses gave and taught the law of God (chs 19—24) and renewed the covenant the Israelites break (chs 32—34). Moses was an effective intercessor and diverted total destruction of Israel on at least two occasions (32:7-14; Num 14:10-20). Moses spoke "face-to-face" with God and reflected the glory of God (Exod 34:29-35).

Moses governed Israel and established Israel's judicial and administrative structure (18:19-24). Moses performed priestly duties until the Aaronic priesthood was established (e.g., 24:6-8). Moses led the Israelites in successful military campaigns (Num 21:21-35).

Moses, unfortunately, failed to trust and obey God completely at the waters of Meribah at Kadesh (Num 20:1-13). Consequently, Moses was not allowed to enter the promised land. Moses experienced an unusual death and receives a burial by God (Deut 34:5-7).

In the biblical narrative, Moses holds a unique place. As a covenant mediator, who is a prophetic, priestly, and kingly leader of Israel, Moses is considered a type of Jesus Christ in the Christian tradition.

C. Authorship

Traditionally both Jews and Christians held Moses as the author of the book of Exodus. The modern Documentary Hypothesis sought to identify various sources behind the final text, but due to its highly speculative nature and ultimate theological fruitlessness, it has been largely replaced by other approaches. While some critical scholars presuppose the basic assumptions of the Documentary Hypothesis, there have been a growing number of works (especially from the 1970s) that emphasize the literary and theological unity of the book of Exodus.

The entire book is narrated with Moses in the third person. There are also a few traces of editorial hands, such as the insertion of Aaron's genealogy in ch 6 and other editorial comments throughout the book (e.g., 9:31-32; 11:3; 16:36; 30:13). Most critical scholars view the book as a compilation of oral and literary traditions about Israel's origins in the thirteenth century BC that were reworked during various periods in Israel's history. There is also some consensus among critical scholars that the book was given its final form during the Babylonian exile or soon thereafter by a priestly redactor.

There are, however, several pieces of internal biblical evidence that support the view that Moses wrote the bulk of the material found in the book of Exodus, a traditional view maintained by conservative Jewish and Christian scholars. Several passages allude to Moses' writing activities (17:14; 24:4; 34:1, 27-28), mostly related to the laws given by God. That Moses was actively writing in his lifetime also supports the idea that he wrote even the narrative portions of the book of Exodus. Joshua 8:31 refers to "the Book of the Law of Moses," according to which Joshua builds an altar to Yahweh on Mount Ebal. This passage attests to the existence of at least a written body of laws by the time of Joshua.

Whatever the exact history of writing, compilation, editing, and transmission of the book of Exodus, this commentary affirms the divine revelation and inspiration of the book; also, the book in its present canonical form is the focus of this commentary. We also affirm the ongoing divine illumination of this inspired text to promote the obedience and the love of God and the love of neighbor that the Bible as a whole demands (Matt 22:36-40). This position partly reduces the significance of identifying the exact author, authorial intention, and original audience (see Enns 2000, 21-23). God has spoken and continues to speak in authoritative and life-giving ways through Exodus to the church all throughout the world.

D. Historical Context

I. Historical Setting

For those critical scholars who view the book of Exodus as an exilic or a postexilic product of priestly writers, the question of historical setting and date of the great events of the book is largely irrelevant. However, for the millions of faithful readers of the Bible from around the globe, this question, while not central to faith, is still an important one.

There are two main theories about the date of the exodus, the traditional view that it takes place in the mid-fifteenth century BC, and the more recent view that it occurs in the thirteenth century BC (see Provan, Long, and Longman 2003, 131-32). The pivotal text for dating the exodus is 1 Kgs 6:1, which places the exodus 480 years prior to "the fourth year of Solomon's reign over Israel." The fourth year of Solomon's reign is datable to 966 BC, but the two views interpret the 480 years in different ways. The proponents of both views cite volumes of available archaeological and textual data (see Enns 2003, 258-72, and Hoffmeier 1996). However, since our historical and archaeological knowledge of the ancient world is still at an elementary level, we wish to avoid arguments from silence or conclusions drawn from lack of evidence. Rather, we prioritize the Bible's own testimony in establishing the possible historical setting for the past events recorded in Exodus.

This commentary favors a literal reading of the 1 Kgs 6:1 passage, which supports the earlier fifteenth-century date for the exodus. This view finds striking correlations between the chronology of the Bible (established on internal data) and Egyptian "low chronology" (for a comparison of Egyptian chronologies, see Enns 2003, 261; also see Shaw 2000, 480-87).

a. Late Date

The thirteenth-century view interprets the 480 years symbolically as twelve generations of 40 years. Each generation is understood to have lasted only about 25 years. This interpretation then grants only 300 years between the exodus and the beginning of the temple construction (see Provan, Long, and Longman 2003, 131-32).

In this view, Ramesses II (r. 1279-1213 BC) is understood as the pharaoh of the oppression and also of the exodus. The Merenptah Stele refers to the military campaign of his son Merenptah (r. 1213-1203 BC) in Canaan against the Israelites; therefore, Merenptah cannot be the pharaoh of Exodus without entirely eliminating the forty-year wilderness wandering. In this view, the reference to the city of Rameses in Exod 1:11 is a nonanachronistic reference to the new capital, constructed under Ramesses II. He rebuilt the old city of Avaris and modern Qantir two kilometers north of it. Ramesses II annexed the two cities and made the site his new capital, naming it Pi Rameses, which means "House of Rameses" (Shaw 2000, 292-93).

The proponents of the later date support it with the claim that there is no undisputed archaeological evidence for the Israelites' settlement in Palestine until the late thirteenth century. However, since the late date is tenable only if one alters much of the Bible's own testimonies, it is an undesirable view.

b. Early Date

Proponents of the early date view Ahmose I (r. ca. 1550-1525 BC; → Figure 1 below) as the most likely candidate for the pharaoh of the oppression. He founded the Eighteenth Dynasty by expelling the Hyksos and destroying their capital at Avaris (see Provan, Long, and Longman 2003, 131-32; Aldred 1998, 148-49; Shaw 2000, 197-206).

Avaris and Hyksos

The city of Avaris, identified as modern Tel el-Dab'a (see Provan, Long, and Longman 2003, 131-32), was occupied from the Twelfth Dynasty of Egypt until the end of the Hyksos period in 1550 BC. There is compelling evidence that the term "Hyksos" is a corrupted form of the Egyptian *Hyk-khase* ("rulers of foreign lands"; see Aldred 1998, 142; Shaw 2000, 174). The term *Hyk-khase* is confirmed in the late Old Kingdom in Egypt, referring to foreign rulers, including the Semitic chieftains of Syria and Canaan. A number of historical and archaeological findings support the view that the Israelite elders or "chieftains" governed their own tribal people in Egypt (for discussion of the Semitic rulers in Egypt between the Thirteenth and Seventeenth Dynasties, see Aldred 1998, 142-45; also see Hoffmeier 1996, 62-68). Notable evidence includes the presence of multiple pharaohs ruling concurrently between the Thirteenth and the Seventeenth Dynasties, many of whom bear West Semitic names (Shaw 2000, 175).

After successfully driving out the Semitic (probably largely Israelite) rulers and their military elites, Ahmose I enslaved and exploited (rather than expelling or massacring) the remaining people of Israel and other foreigners, following the usual practice of the ancient Near East. Ahmose I engaged in massive construction projects, including a pyramid. Ahmose I had two daughters; one of these princesses would have been the daughter of Pharaoh who rescued Moses (2:5-10). Of the various successors of Ahmose I, Thutmose I (r. 1506—1493 BC) and Hatshepsut (r. 1479-1458 BC) were ambitious builders of temples and other large-scale building projects. It is likely that oppression of the Hebrews and their forced labor to complete the building projects continued during the reign of these pharaohs.

As for the pharaoh of the exodus, Thutmose III (r. 1479-1426 BC) is the candidate most compatible with the biblical and external data (see Provan, Long, and Longman 2003, 132). He was the stepson and nephew of Hatshepsut and a co-regent with her until her death. Archaeological evidence suggests that Thutmose III is the one who initiated the reconstruction of Avaris (later renamed Pi Rameses) as a store city. This supports the view that the reference to Rameses in 1:11 is a case of anachronism. Scarabs from Thutmose III and his successor Amenhotep II (r. 1426-1400 BC) have been found in Pithom, another store city the Israelites were forced to build. Thutmose III, with his massive expansionist military campaigns, turned Egypt into an international superpower by the thirty-first year of his reign. Interestingly, there is an interruption in campaigning for sixteen to eighteen months from the middle of his thirty-first regnal year through his thirty-second year (see Redford 2003, 220). If we take Solomon's 480 years literally, then the middle of the thirty-first regnal year of Thutmose III's reign (end of 1448 BC or beginning of 1447 BC) would be when Moses and Aaron would have confronted him. The end of the following regnal year (March/April of 1446 BC) would be the time of the exodus and the drowning of Pharaoh's impressive army of horse-drawn chariots in the Red Sea.

Thutmose III's eldest son, Amenemhet, the anticipated heir to the throne, died around the time of the exodus (between years twenty-four and thirty-five of the reign of Thutmose III [1454-1443 BC], between the year when Amenemhet was last mentioned and the year when Amenhotep II was born). Amenemhet would be the "firstborn" of the pharaoh of the exodus, who was struck dead in the tenth plague (12:29).

Amenhotep II (r. 1426-1400 BC) would be the pharaoh during the last two decades of the Israelites' wilderness period (1427-1406 BC) and also the beginning of the Israelites' conquest of Canaan. He made a few military expeditions into Syria and Palestine (Walton 2003, 261) but focused on domestic affairs, with the one possible exception of Nubia.

During the reign of Thutmose IV (r. 1400—1390 BC), there is no evidence of proven warfare in Palestine (Shaw 2000, 250; Walton 2003, 261). However, the Canaanite kings in the Amarna letters might indicate that Thutmose IV exerted Egyptian control in a few key Palestine posts. After his time, however, territory in Canaan was lost to the Habiru, according to the Amarna letters (Walton 2003, 261). The term "Habiru"/"Apiru" is used in relation to nomadic people, mentioned in various ancient Near Eastern sources. The Israelites, emerging out of their forty-year-long nomadic life in Kadesh Barnea, certainly would have earned such a title.

During the reign of Amenhotep III (r. ca. 1390-1352 BC), Egypt was engaged in virtually no military activity, except for south of Egypt and Nubia. The time of Thutmose IV and Amenhotep III, therefore, provide for the Israelites a window of time in which to conquer and settle in the promised land.

A few notable challenges to this view deal with the extent of Egyptian military control in Canaan and the lack of conclusive archaeological evidence for the late fifteenth-century and early fourteenth-century widespread destruction and conquests of Canaan. Some scholars claim that the Egyptians controlled Canaan and that the Israelites could not have been in Canaan prior to Ramesses II's time. However, detailed study shows that the Egyptian activity and control in Canaan from the thirty-third year of Thutmose III is rather incomplete and nominal. Even if the Egyptians were still exerting control in a few cities along the coastal plain and the northern and southern tip of Canaan, their influence did not necessarily pose a problem for the Israelite conquest and settlements in Transjordan and the central hills (see Walton 2003, 263-66).

Hoffmeier notes that the current prevailing conquest model of widespread destruction is not sustainable, based on the current archaeological evidence and the biblical textual evidence (1996, 24-44, esp. 33-36). There is much harmony between archaeological records and the textual records but disharmony between the records and the conquest model. First of all, Provan, Long, and Longman (2003, 167-68) make the important distinction between subjugation (by destroying the kings and the military forces), which the Israelites fulfilled (Josh 18:1; 23:1), and occupation (by driving out the remaining peoples), which they did not complete (13:1, 13; 15:63; 16:10; 17:12; 18:2-3; 23:4-7, 12-13) until David's time. Second, the Bible itself makes no claims to a widespread violent destruction of all the Canaanite cities. In fact, Joshua mentions that only three cities—Jericho (Josh 6:24), Ai (8:19-20, 28), and Hazor (11:11)—were destroyed by fire (for a discussion of some of the issues with these sites, see Hoffmeier 1996, 4-14; Walton 2003, 266-70). Joshua 11:12-14 makes it explicit that the Israelites completely destroyed the peoples living in Canaanite cities but did not burn any of the cities themselves. The cities were rather divided up among and occupied by the tribes. Thus, Josh 24:13 states, "So I gave you a land on which you did not toil and cities you did not build; and you live in them and eat from vineyards and olive groves that you did not plant." These verses indicate that the Israelites inherited "the material culture of the Canaanites," so this detail may explain the absence of evidence of a violent destruction of Canaan in the Late Bronze Age (Hoffmeier 1996, 44).

Israel and Moses	Year (BC)	Pharaohs	
		Hyksos Pharaohs of Lower Egypt	Pharaohs of Upper Egypt
		Khamudi (r. 1555-1540)	Kamose (r. 1555-1550)
The defeat of Khamudi, the last of the Asiatic Hyksos or "foreign rulers," and enslavement of the Israelites by Ahmose I	ca. 1540		Ahmose I (r. 1550-1525)
Moses' birth and rescue (80 years before the call)	1527	Amenhotep I (r. 1525-1506)	
		Thutmose I (r. 1506—1493) Princess Hatshepsut's birth (1507)	
Moses' flight (at 40) Moses in Midian	1487	Thutmose II (r. 1493-1479)	
		Hatshepsut (r. 1479-1458)	

Moses' return (at 80)	1447	Thutmose III (r. 1479-1426)
Exodus; 480 years before the fourth year of Solomon's reign (1 Kgs 6:1), datable to 966; 430 years after Jacob's migration Israel in the wilderness	1446	Thutmose III's eldest son Amen-emhet's death (between 1454 and 1443) Amenhotep II's birth (1443)
Israel in the wilderness Beginning of the conquest	1405	Amenhotep II (r. 1426-1400)
Conquest and settlement		Thutmose IV (r. 1400—1390)
Conquest and settlement		Amenhotep III (r. 1390-1352)

Figure I: Timeline
(See Shaw 2000, 484-85. Note that the above approximate dates are disputed.)

2. Historicity

Besides questions about the historical setting and dating of the events of the exodus, questions also arise regarding the degree of historicity of the events recorded in the book of Exodus, including those that are obviously supernatural. The biblical text, while not conforming to modern criterion of historical writing, is a trustworthy witness to the history and acts of the living God. The recorded stories are truthful and faithful testimonies of the Israelites who experienced and witnessed firsthand the mighty acts of God. These accounts are, therefore, historically true, stating what happened, and theologically true, interpreting and presenting what happened in light of God's central purposes for his covenant people and other nations. The narrative meaningfully connects Israel to the God of their ancestors and instructs and invites their future generations to know, love, and serve this God well. The book establishes the foundational parameters of this covenant relationship, which decisively shapes the theology, ethics, and spirituality of God's people in Scripture and in postbiblical history.

E. Geographical Issues

There are two main topics associated with locations that attract much discussion—Mount Sinai and the Red Sea. Locating these sites would powerfully support the authenticity of the events of the book of Exodus and the history of the Israelites' ancestors (Enns 2003, 277). Such a discovery would also provide important clues for reconstructing the exodus itinerary.

As important as these sites are, one must be wary of making claims, as very little archaeological evidence is available, and the findings remain tentative and elusive. Such archaeological inquiry is also complicated by the change of climate, waterways, and hills of the region (Provan, Long, and Longman 2003, 133). Other challenges involve the changed borders, either due to conquests and displacements or its fluid nature due to the nomadic lifestyle of various people groups related to the Israelites' desert itinerary. These events took place more than three thousand years ago with specific sites and memories destroyed or changed or buried deep beneath vast, forbidding terrains. Ultimately, the sites may be archaeologically unrecoverable. Therefore, we prioritize the biblical texts' own witness to Israel's experiences, by putting them first.

1. The Location of Mount Sinai

a. The Biblical Data

(1) According to 3:1, Moses led the flock to the back side (*'aḥar*, "back side" or "behind") of the wilderness (of Sin, perhaps). This verse gives the impression that there were mountains between Jethro's Midianite tribal territory and Mount Horeb. It is normal for the desert dwellers (such as the Midianites) to travel long distances to graze their herd in fresh pastures.

(2) Judges 8:24 states that the Midianites were Ishmaelites. Genesis 25:18*a* asserts that the descendants of the Ishmaelites "settled in the area from Havilah to Shur, near the eastern border of Egypt, as you go toward Ashur." The Ishmaelites lived near or in the presence of "all the tribes related to them" (v 18*b*), namely, the Israelites, Edomites, Amalekites, Moabites, and Ammonites. The Amalekites, who attacked the Israelites at Rephidim (Exod 17:8), appear to have lived in the same region, "Havilah to Shur" (1 Sam 15:7).

(3) Exodus 19:1 reports that the Israelites arrived at Mount Sinai "on the third new moon" (ESV), which means on the first day of the seventh week after they left Egypt. Providing for the Sabbath day rest and other longer camps and considering the slow travelers (see Deut 25:18; → Behind the Text for Exod 17:8-16), any site out of the Sinai Peninsula poses a challenge due to their distance from Goshen.

(4) Deuteronomy 1:2 states that Horeb/Sinai was an eleven days' journey to Kadesh Barnea "by the Mount Zeir road." This editorial information probably does not refer to a massive group of migrants traveling with young and old along with livestock. Rather, it likely refers to an average adult's travel distance. Thutmose III's expedition records his army traveling 150 miles (240 km) in ten days (Hoffmeier 1996, 198). The eleven-day journey for an adult would then be about 165 miles (265 km). Numbers 33:15-36 records twenty-one camping stations between Sinai and Kadesh. The long itinerary shows that the Israelites journeyed at a much slower pace, perhaps due to adverse conditions (see Deut 1:19; 8:15) and slow travelers.

(5) Numbers 10:11-12 reveals that the Israelites "traveled from place to place" from Sinai until they came into the Desert of Paran, where Kadesh Barnea is located (it is noteworthy that some mistakenly read this passage as indicat-

ing that Paran immediately follows Sinai). Kadesh Barnea traditionally has been identified with Petra (in modern Jordan) near Jabal Haroun ("Mount Aaron") and Wadi Musa ("Valley of Moses"), which is compatible with the Bible's description of its location (unlike the modern suggestion of Ain el-Qudeirat).

(6) Deuteronomy 1:19 indicates that the Israelites left Sinai, going "through all that vast and dreadful wilderness" on their way "toward the hill country of the Amorites." In other words, they crossed a vast wilderness after the Red Sea and not before. Deuteronomy 8:15 describes that wilderness as a "thirsty" land with "no water" but with "fiery serpents and scorpions" (ESV).

(7) The Apostle Paul located Mount Sinai in Arabia, which, in the first century, included the Sinai Peninsula.

b. The Proposed Sites

(1) *Edom Sinai.* Some have interpreted Judg 5:4-5 as identifying Mount Sinai with Mount Seir in Edom. But the poetic text simply invokes the God ("One") of Sinai as active in delivering Israel in a new setting. Likewise, in Deut 33:2, Yahweh who came from Sinai is said to also have revealed himself from the region of Seir, where the Israelites began their militant march toward the promised land (Deut 2:1-3, 24-25). Two factors—the Edomites' hostile stance against the Israelites for setting foot on their territory in Num 20:14-21 and God's warning concerning the Edomite territory in Deut 2:1-8—suggest that Mount Sinai could not have been Mount Seir. The Israelites would not have been allowed to camp in their territory (by God or by the Edomites) for a whole year. Also there is no "vast and dreadful wilderness" (8:15) to cross or place for twenty-one camping sites between Mount Seir and Petra.

(2) *The North-West Saudi Arabia site with the Nuweiba or the Straits of Tiran crossing.* There are many challenges to this site, including the sheer distance from Rameses to Midian Sinai (some 380 mi / 620 km through Nuweiba or 460 mi / 740 km through the Straits of Tiran), which the Israelites could not have traveled in a mere six weeks. Also according to Exod 15:22, the Israelites went into the wilderness of Shur after crossing the Red Sea. However, the suggested crossing points are extremely far from the Desert of Shur.

(3) *South of the Sinai Peninsula.* The earliest Christian traditions designated Mount Serbal as Mount Sinai with a monastery being built in the early fourth century. In the sixth century, the monastery at Mount Serbal moved to Jebel Musa. The move was motivated by Josephus' writing that named Mount Sinai as the "the highest of all the mountains thereabout" (*Ant.* 2.12.1), an assertion that may have no historical basis.

Mount Serbal, therefore, remains as the most attractive site for Sinai among the suggested sites and is most compatible with the biblical witness. It is about 240 to 250 miles (380 to 400 km) from Pi Rameses to the mountain base (reasonable for a six-week journey). Although we do not know the Israelites' exact route through the wilderness, the distance from the eastern side of the mountain to Kadesh Barnea or Petra could be about 165 to 185 miles (270 to 300 km), which would require an eleven- to twelve-day journey for an average adult. Jethro's Midianite territory was likely in the Desert of Shur by the front side (as opposed to the "backside" mentioned in 3:1 [KJV]) of the Wilderness of Sin. The Amalekites living in the Desert of Shur descended upon the Israelites at Rephidim (a station before Horeb). The description of the wilderness as "vast and dreadful" (Deut 1:19) is appropriate for southern Sinai.

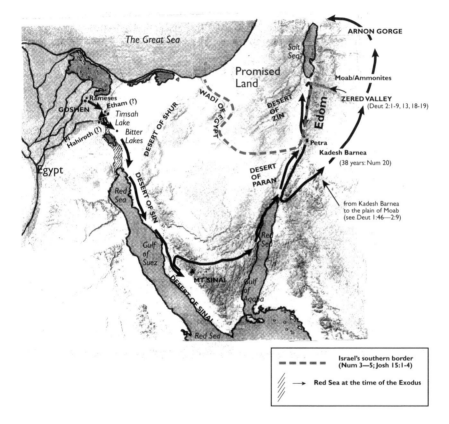

Figure 2: Map of Kadesh Barnea and the Exodus route

2. The Red Sea

a. The Biblical Data

While the issues involved in identifying the *yam sûp* (Red Sea) that the Israelites crossed (Exod 13:18; 15:4, 22) are complex, the biblical witness can guide us in our process of elimination.

(1) God in 14:2 directs the Israelites to camp near Pi Hahiroth ("mouth of the gorges/canals"; → 14:1-2) between Migdol ("fortress," "tower," perhaps

35

a fortified city with a watchtower) and the Red Sea (*yam sûp*; → *sûp* at 2:3). Pi Hahiroth is the third station from Rameses, which implies that it is not too far from Rameses.

(2) From Rameses, the Israelites traveled explicitly away from the "road through the Philistine country" and directly toward the Red Sea (13:17-18).

(3) The Israelites were supposed to make "a three-day journey into the wilderness to offer sacrifices to the LORD" (3:18; 5:3; 8:27 [23 HB]). However, they made a turn from "the edge of the desert" (13:20) and camped at a place where they appeared to be "wandering around the land [of Egypt] in confusion, hemmed in by the desert" (14:3). In other words, they did not go far into the Desert of Shur, which is where the Midianites and Amalekites lived (Gen 25:18).

(4) The Israelites were in the Desert of Shur upon crossing *yam sûp* (Exod 15:22). Pi Hahiroth most likely lay west of "the edge of the desert" (13:20) of Shur, in the eastern edge of the Delta region.

(5) Seven campsites—Marah (15:23), Elim (15:27), by the Red Sea (Num 33:10), Desert of Sin (Exod 16:1), Dophkah (Num 33:12), Alush (Num 33:12), and Rephidim (Exod 17:1)—are mentioned between the Red Sea and Mount Sinai. The Israelites are in the Desert of Sin exactly one month after the exodus (16:1). This implies that the Red Sea crossing is close to the date of the exodus.

(6) In many texts, *yam sûp* clearly refers to the modern Gulf of Aqaba (23:31; Num 14:25; 21:4; Deut 1:40; 2:1; 1 Kgs 9:26).

(7) Exodus 10:19 states that the westerly wind carried the swarms of locusts out of Egypt and into *yam sûp*. This *yam sûp* most likely refers to the Gulf of Suez.

(8) The widely accepted literal meaning of *sûp* is "reed" and *yam sûp* "Sea of Reeds." Apparently, there are reeds and rushes that thrive in salt waters, as found in the Gulf of Suez (see Hoffmeier 1996, 209).

Another possibility is to read *sûp* as *sôp*, "the end" (see Hoffmeier 1996, 205), and *yam sûp* as referring to the body of water that ends, such as an "inlet" (of a river [→ 2:3, 5] or a "gulf," such as Suez or Aqaba). This reading might explain why both gulfs are referred to as *yam sûp* in the Bible.

b. The Proposed Waters

(1) The Gulf of Aqaba (at Nuweiba, some 280 mi / 450 km from Rameses; or the Straits of Tiran, 320 mi / 520 km) as the Red Sea that the Israelites crossed is unlikely, since it is too far from Rameses and the Desert of Shur. The fact that Pi Hahiroth is the third station mentioned does not necessarily imply that Pi Hahiroth was a three-day journey from Rameses. However, it does imply that the crossing cannot be at a place that would require the Israelites two to three months to reach.

(2) The very reedy Lake Menzaleh or Lake Ballah or any other lake in the northeast region of the Delta is an unlikely choice, since these lakes are too close to and lie in the same direction as the "road through the Philistine country" (see Cassuto 1967, 156; → 13:17).

(3) The third view, first proposed by Jerome in the late fourth century and further promoted by recent scholars, is that the Bitter Lakes was part of the Gulf of Suez at the time of the exodus (see Hoffmeier 1996, 207-10). Archaeological, historical, and geological evidence show that the head of the Gulf of Suez was the present saltwater Bitter Lakes or Lake Timsah (see Hoffmeier 1996, 164-72). The gradual receding of the Red Sea and accumulation of the Nile silt over millennia dried up the head of the gulf, altering its boundaries to the present location. In this view, the crossing point could be anywhere from Bitter Lakes or Lake Timsah to north of the present Gulf of Suez. This view does not pose any apparent contradiction with the biblical data, representing an attractive possibility.

F. Literary Features and Structure

The book of Exodus is composed of a mixture of genres (narratives, laws, instructions, poetic hymns, and genealogy), which are woven into an over-arching salvation-historical narrative. Interpretation, therefore, involves reading a passage appropriate to its genre while paying attention to its literary and theological context provided by the story-centered canonical final form of the book.

For example, the law codes found in Exodus are understood in light of ancient Near Eastern law codes (which help to elucidate some distinct feature of this genre). In addition, they are read in light of the narrative that regards God as the source of law (and not merely a human king or lawgiver) and God's abiding presence as the purpose of the law.

The structure of the book of Exodus is basically threefold. The first part focuses on the Israelites' oppression and mighty deliverance from Egypt (1:1—15:21). The second part focuses on their testing and journey in the desert (15:22—18:27). The third part concerns their time at Mount Sinai (19:1—40:38) where God makes a covenant with the Israelites and grants his indwelling presence (see Enns 2000, 3). Aside from this basic threefold division, various subdivisions mark the book of Exodus:

   I. Egypt (1:1—15:21)
     A. The Setting (1:1-22)
     B. The Rise of the Leader of Israel (2:1—7:13)
     C. The Mighty Acts of Judgments and the Exodus (7:14—15:21)
  II. In the Wilderness (15:22—18:27)
  III. At Mount Sinai (19:1—40:38)

A. Covenant at Mount Sinai (19:1—24:18)
B. Instructions for the Tabernacle (25:1—31:18)
C. The Golden Calf: False Presence (32:1—34:35)
D. Construction of the Tabernacle and the Real Presence (35:1—40:38)

G. Hermeneutical / Interpretive Issues

Christian interpretation of the book of Exodus must address a number of hermeneutical questions related to the extent of continuity between the covenant relationship between God and Israel found in the book and the new covenant relationship between God and Christians found in the NT. How do the old and new covenants relate to each other? More specifically, does the old covenant law apply to the new covenant church? If so, to what extent and in what ways does it apply (see Enns 2000, 19, 458-68)? Answers to these questions inform the interpretative conclusions presented in this commentary and their application to the contemporary church in the From the Text sections.

Within the range of positions found in orthodox Christian biblical interpretation of the OT, this commentary emphasizes more than most the continuity of the revelation and covenantal structures of the old and new covenants. For example, I emphasize that the God of the NT is one and the same as the God revealed in the book of Exodus (→ From the Text for Exod 3:1-10, 24:1-18, 25:31-40, 33:12-23, and 34:5-7; → In the Text for 3:11; and → "Divine Sin-Bearing / Removing" sidebar in 34:7*b*). Both old and new covenants are marked by similar covenantal structures (e.g., gracious divine initiative of salvation and covenant relationship, moral/legal requirements, and blessings and curses). Of course, there are elements of discontinuity between the old and new covenants (especially laws related to cultic rituals and theocratic structures). However, even the seemingly irrelevant covenantal elements often reveal aspects of God's being and character that remain relevant to the people of God today.

Following the majority of Christian theological interpreters, including those in the Wesleyan tradition, then, I emphasize the ongoing moral force and pedagogical value of many of the laws of Israel. For example, the Decalogue has abiding relevance or normative force for Christians. Moreover, many other laws (sometimes called "moral laws," although the designation does not easily identify a distinct group of laws) remain applicable to Christians today by providing authoritative guidance. This approach somewhat contrasts with certain Christian traditions, such as Lutheranism, which has historically denied the moral use of the law, affirming only its evangelical and civic uses.

From a Wesleyan perspective, no one is able to keep the law adequately by unaided human moral effort. Christians, however, can receive the sanctifying and empowering grace of the Holy Spirit for obedience and holiness to the greater glory of God. Therefore, the members of the church can be hopeful that they can fulfill the moral obligations of the new covenant to love God and to love their neighbors as they love themselves, which Jesus articulated as the summary of the law (Matt 22:36-40).

A polemic against what may be called Marcionism and neo-Marcionism indicates a significant undercurrent of this commentary. Marcion was a second-century son of a bishop who argued that the Father of Jesus Christ was not the same being as the God of the OT and that the OT (plus many "Jewish" portions of the NT) was to be rejected. Despite the early church's valiant attempts to oppose Marcion's teachings, some of his views took root, persisted, and even flourished in Christian circles, especially since the advent of modernity. One aspect of neo-Marcionism brings a constellation of doubts about the supposedly flawed moral character of the God of Israel, with an accompanying tendency to emphasize how the NT God is supposedly quite different in character (more merciful and gracious, it is said). Such distortions provide breeding grounds for antinomianism and an accompanying distortion of the Christian doctrines of grace (sometimes called "hypergrace"). In a variety of ways, this commentary seeks to correct such misunderstandings.

The precise extent and manner in which the features, revelations, and laws of God's covenant with Israel should or should not be applied to the new covenant church is a thorny issue that can only be met with both careful and prayerful exegesis of particular passages and with the correlative development of a biblical theology. The exegetical reflections in this commentary join many other worthy Christian attempts to take up these tasks.

H. Theological Themes

Exodus treats a number of important theological themes, many of which are especially relevant to the Wesleyan tradition of theological reflection. These themes are developed in more depth in From the Text sections throughout the commentary. Therefore, only a brief overview of the major themes that unfold with the narrative is needed here. I present these themes in the order in which they emerge as key elements of the book's narrative.

I. The Supreme Ruler and Judge

God is absolutely sovereign over history, individuals, nature, and over false gods. That God is sovereign over human history is implicitly present in the Israelites' prosperity in Egypt and their continued population explosion even under the cruel oppression of Pharaoh (1:7-12). God harnesses his great power to judge Egypt, the most powerful kingdom on the earth at the time, and to deliver his people from the inferior power of Egypt. God's sovereignty is also evident in the manner in which the history-altering deliverer of Israel is rescued and raised by Pharaoh's daughter. The moment when Pharaoh thinks he has complete control over the Israelites is precisely the time when God uses Pharaoh's own schemes to fulfill divine plans for the Israelites.

God's sovereignty over individuals extends to lesser-known figures, such as the midwives Shiphrah and Puah (1:15-21), whose lives are sovereignly protected from the bloodthirsty pharaoh. God is also sovereign in his appointment and empowerment of the covenant mediator Moses. God freely chooses individuals and makes them "usable," despite their foibles and limitations. Thus, God remains supreme even in his choice to partner with and depend on human emissaries to accomplish his work and purposes.

God also shows his sovereignty over those who exalt themselves over God and actively oppose him, such as Pharaoh. Through the plagues, Pharaoh is exposed as a finite and flawed human being who cannot control even his own heart's attitude. In addition, the tenth plague shows God's sovereignty over life and death. Those who submit to God's sign of grace live, but those who do not must die.

God demonstrates his absolute sovereignty over nature and false gods through the plagues (→ 12:12). The forces of nature bow to God's supremacy and lordship over them as God musters them as a means of punishment of the powerful kingdom of Egypt. Through the plagues, the false gods of Egypt, which are fashioned in the image of the created things, are exposed as empty and powerless creations of religious, but misled, human beings.

The way the plague narrative portrays God's sovereignty over humans, both the obedient and the disobedient, is significant for theological reflection. These events show how God's ruling actions are compatible with human responsibility and choices.

2. The God of Salvation

One of the great themes of the book of Exodus is God's deliverance of the people of Israel from slavery in Egypt. God delivers the people in a holistic manner from all that hinder them from trusting, worshipping, and communing with him and from enjoying the blessed life that he offers.

To understand God's redemptive work adequately, then, we need to grasp its comprehensive character. God's salvation of the Israelites includes the political, economic, social, and spiritual aspects of their lives (see Wright 2006, 268-72). We must resist the tendency to neglect some of these dimensions in favor of others.

Much of historic Christianity has spiritualized the exodus. This follows certain NT passages that interpret God's deliverance of the Israelites from the Egyptian slavery as a type of Christ's salvation for those who believe, delivering them from bondage to sin and death. We cannot deny the truth of this typological fulfillment, but we must also affirm that overcoming socioeconomic and political injustice and oppression remains one of God's fundamental concerns and that Christ's victory over sin and death includes a victory over social and structural evils.

Conversely, in the politicizing interpretation that marks some expressions of liberation theology or liberation hermeneutics, there is a contrasting emphasis on God's will to resist political and economic injustice and oppression. At times, the claim is made that God is at work wherever people struggle against such oppression, regardless of the ethicality of the means by which the oppression is resisted. While a strong biblical case can be made that God is, indeed, on the side of the victims of oppression and injustice, a politicizing approach can neglect the spiritual dimensions of the exodus as a model for salvation.

In addition, understanding the exodus in terms of God granting formal freedom from oppression for the sake of Israelite self-determination is also inadequate. God is not focused on simply freeing the Israelites from political repression and physical slavery. Rather, God delivers God's people from bondage to the evil tyrant, so that they might serve God who is good (→ Exod 4:22, 23; 6:6-8; Wright 2006, 269-72, 284-86; Stuart 2006, 35-36). They are freed from Pharaoh for another, one who is infinitely worthy of their service and worship. Those physical, political, and economic freedoms find their ultimate value only when the liberated people worship God and enter into loving communion with him and with one another.

God's redemptive work with Israel is comprehensive and holistic. The redemption history of the book of Exodus is a model for what God ultimately wants for all peoples and nations (Wright 2006, 282-88). God desires that the full extent and depth of his glorious work with Israel would be made available to those who are in similar situations as the ancient Israelites in Egypt.

3. The God of Testing

When God rescues the Israelites from Egypt, he plans to make a covenant with them and dwell among them. Before this happens, however, God tests his delivered people in the wilderness. Divine testing in order to "see whether [Israel] will follow [his] instructions" (16:4) is an important theme found in the journey from Egypt to Sinai (15:22—18:27).

God's testing takes different forms. God tests the people through situations that restrict life's essentials, such as food and water (see 15:22-25). God does not create harsh situations for them, but he does lead them through the conditions that are unfavorable to life. The people must trust God to provide for them. At other times, God tests them through the opposite circumstance of abundance (of manna and quail, as in ch 16). The people must obey God's commands and resist the temptation to save or hoard.

In whatever the circumstance, God's desire is to create a people who will trust and obey him, for these are the essential qualities necessary for a thriving covenant relationship with him. Yet the people of Israel often fail to trust and obey God; they typically distrust God and grumble against him and his leaders (15:24; 16:2-3, 8, 20, etc.). The exodus narrative shows that in spite of their failure to trust Yahweh and obey his commands and decrees, Yahweh remains faithful. God not only provides for his people but also grants them a covenant relationship with him. Divine faithfulness in the face of human failure indicates that human righteousness cannot be the basis for a covenant relationship with God. The covenant must be founded essentially on God's grace.

However, even after the covenant relationship is formed, God continues to test his people, so that they may have the fear of God with them to keep them from sinning and to inspire them to trust and obey God (see 20:20; Deut 8:2-3, 16; 13:3-4 [4-5 HB]).

4. The God of Covenant Relationship and Partnership

Based on God's gracious initiative in the redemption of the Israelites from Egypt and gracious testing and provisions in the wilderness, God makes his covenant relationship with them explicit on Mount Sinai. While rooted in God's sovereign, redemptive, and gracious acts, the covenant requires the response of the people to be complete. God is not looking merely for those who will observe and benefit from his work, but for covenant partners who will partner with him in his work in the world as his faithful, priestly people (Exod 19:6).

The Israelites are, therefore, called to certain covenantal responsibilities, the covenant stipulations. Disobedience will result in judgment and rejection, but obedience ensures continued blessing and the maximal fulfillment of God's promises to and purposes for them. The free and responsible moral decisions of the Israelites carry great significance and shape their future. God does not control their responses, but rewards them either with judgment or blessing.

In some sense, then, Yahweh takes a risk in entering into covenant relationship with Israel, for God invests much in people who could bring either a good or a bad return on this divine investment.

Chapters 32—34 represent a "bad return" on God's investment of love and presence. With the golden calf incident, there is a crisis in the covenant between God and the rebellious Israelites. The faithful God desires to maintain a covenant relationship with the people whom he has chosen in Abraham. But since God is a holy God, he cannot dwell with an unholy, rebellious people. Thus, important questions emerge: How can a holy God have a covenant relationship with his unholy people? How can God commune with them without utterly destroying them?

In the book of Exodus, the solutions to these questions are found in God's prior choice to be in covenant relationship with the descendants of Abraham (32:13-14), in the intercession by the covenant mediator who has God's favor and friendship (32:11-14; 33:11—34:10), and in the establishment of true worship that includes a sacrificial system (the tabernacle). Moses' intercession causes God to adjust the divine intentions or declared actions. The apparent invitation of human friends into the divine council and the allowance of human intercession to shape human history are consistent with the divine election of and covenant with Abraham and his descendants to be the instrument of God's blessing to all nations (Gen 12:2-3). Ultimately, it points to the restoration of the original intention for humans to be divine representatives on earth (1:26-28), having dominion and shaping divine history.

In Exodus, then, the future of the earth and its people is dependent not only on God but also partly on the covenantal, priestly agency of Moses and Israelites. Instead of doing everything alone, God sovereignly and voluntarily unites himself to human agents whom God appoints to carry out his works and purposes.

The ideal, fully restored model of divine-human partnership is realized in Jesus Christ, the true Moses and true Israel. The divine "self-emptying" (*kenosis* [Phil 2:7]) and the eternal Son's assumption of humanity in Jesus Christ is the supreme expression of the divine-human partnership. In Christ is the perfect unity of divine and human will and work.

5. The God Who Gives Laws

One aspect of God's role as a God of covenant is God's role as lawgiver. For God's people to be conformed to God's will and purposes, they must be shaped and challenged by laws that affect every area of their lives. The comprehensive legal righteousness that we find in the book of Exodus is a clear expression of Israel's "ethical" monotheism. There is no autonomous region of life over which God does not have the right to address and hold the people accountable. Just as God's liberation of his people is comprehensive—including the spiritual, the political, and the social—so also the guidance and accountability provided by the law is comprehensive. There is, therefore, no possibility in Israel of establishing right relationship with God simply through religious rituals of worship, without the individuals and the community living ethically.

Law can function to guide people into right paths (see Stuart 2006, 44-45) and also to hold them accountable when they fail. Both of these functions are necessary for understanding and reinforcing the need for God's grace and forgiveness among his people.

The laws found in Exodus, however, do not represent the fullest ideals of divine law and justice. Rather, they represent a conjunction of God's ideals for human life before him and God's accommodation to the weakness of fallen human culture. The laws elevate the level of ethics and true worship above what is found in laws of the surrounding ancient Near Eastern cultures, but allow for improvements that will emerge in later revelations and clarifications of God's will through the prophets and ultimately in the new covenant. As such, the laws of Exodus exemplify the patient manner in which God moves his people toward his will and purpose. On one hand, God does not expect them to change overnight. But on the other hand, God does not simply leave them as they are, as products of their time and cultural context. The Sinai laws do not leave them with "Egypt" in them, nor do they expect the people to have already arrived at the fullness of their destiny, the fullness of God in them. The guidance and accountability that the laws of Exodus provide are resources for a people on a journey away from their "old life" in Egypt and toward their new life in the promised land.

6. The God of Mercy and Justice

Exodus contains some of the fullest and most fundamental revelations about the divine character in the Bible. In this book, God's character can be summarized in the claim that God is both merciful and just. God's character is revealed both through divine action (beginning with the great exodus event, which becomes a paradigm for redemption and judgment in the OT) and through divine words, especially the self-declarations of divine attributes uttered in the aftermath of Israel's idolatry and apostasy (see Exod 33:19 and 34:6-7). While terms such as "holiness" and "love" could be used to describe God's character in Exodus, the attributes of mercy and justice are closer to the linguistic, narrative, and conceptual world of this book. Mercy, and the closely related concepts of grace, patience, and compassion, is the predominant "face" of God that Israel comes to know in the events and revelations recorded in this book.

However, Yahweh's abundant mercy is not without justice, which is expressed in judgment or punishment upon those who resist God, whether the Israelites' enemies or the Israelites themselves (32:25-28, 33, 35; 33:3). So strong is the emphasis on Yahweh's judgment in Exodus that some commentators have suggested that divine punishment can sometimes be divorced from divine mercy and even be unjust and without limits. However, careful reflection on both the larger themes and details of the book show that this is not the case. Rather, there is no mercy without justice and no justice without mercy.

In the plague narratives, the intense judgments that fall on Egypt in the form of the plagues are not capricious but clearly purposeful. They are for the merciful and just purpose of the deliverance of the Israelites from oppression and into the service of the one true God. Moreover, the divine judgments have the merciful intent that the Egyptians and their leader (7:4-5; 8:20-22 [16-18 HB]), together with the Israelites (6:7), would truly know God (consider the use of the repeated phrase "that you would know that I am the LORD"). Such knowledge of Yahweh would ultimately lead mercifully to the salvation of the Egyptians.

In the crisis narrative in chs 32—34, divine judgments concern primarily the Israelites. After the golden calf incident, God threatens to destroy the Israelites and start afresh with Moses (32:9-10), which would be within the appropriate limits of justice as defined by the covenant laws. In this dire context, divine freedom is expressed in God's choice not to destroy the Israelites against the strict legal requirement of the covenant. Thus, the crucial new revelation in 33:19 and 34:6-7 is that where human sin demands destruction and the covenant contract requires strict justice, God, in sovereign power and freedom, grants life and forgiveness instead. God's freedom is emphatically *not* a freedom to punish unjustly or without limit, but a freedom to forgive and grant life in lieu of the destruction demanded by divine holiness in the face of sin. Of course, lest the people take God's grace for granted, God punishes the Israelites in a limited manner (32:26-28, 35). The punishment also serves to purify the people.

In this light, we might say that God's punishment toward both the Israelites and their enemies (like Egypt) is measured and reasonable, but God's grace is unlimited and transrational. Of course, there is an ultimate rationale for divine mercy, namely, the mysterious depths of God's own merciful character and saving purpose for the creation.

I conclude this section with two observations about the paradoxical conjunction of God's merciful forgiveness and his just judgments in Exodus and other parts of Scripture. (1) When one asks how God can both forgive and punish at the same act, part of the answer is found in God's own "bearing" of the wickedness, rebellion, and sin (→ 34:7b, "forgiving wickedness, rebellion and sin"), which allows for a just (rather than arbitrary) reduction or tempering of deserved divine punishment. Divine forgiveness (through divine sin-bearing) can involve the reduction of divine punishment but may not always remove punishment entirely.

(2) The conjunction of forgiveness and punishment may also refer to the disciplinary nature of much punishment. Of course, from the perspective of the individual within the sinful nation who is struck down (as by the Levites in 32:27 ff. or by the plague in 32:35), Yahweh's avenging would seem retributive and final rather than disciplinary. However, from the corporate or national perspective, partial punishment serves a disciplinary and purifying purpose, which is essential for God's continued presence among his people. Divine discipline not only demonstrates God's righteousness that judges and punishes sin but also emphasizes God's unmatched mercy that finds ways to continue his covenant relationship with sinners.

7. The God of Presence and Indwelling

It is not accidental that the book of Exodus concludes with the glory of God filling the tabernacle and the cloud of God covering it (40:34-38). This is the destination toward which the entire narrative moves. This is the goal of redemption and of the supreme expression of covenant relationship. This is what the testing of God's people and their obedience to his law (especially laws concerning the tabernacle and its atoning forms of worship) make possible. God desires to manifest his glorious presence to his people and dwell in communion with them. The tabernacle allows God to be present with his people and they with him. Once the real and visible presence of God is given to the Israelites, they must attentively follow his presence to reach their God-intended destination (40:36-38).

Yet God's presence in the tabernacle and the cloud, despite its tangible and powerful quality (see 40:35), is nonetheless limited (see Stuart 2006, 40; see 40-44). It is not everywhere among the Israelites nor is it accessible to every Israelite at all times. There are barriers to a full encounter with God's presence, which is marked more by mediacy than immediacy. Even Moses, who reportedly speaks with God "face to face" (33:11), could only see God's "back" (→ 33:20-23), or hear his name (attributes) being proclaimed (34:6-7). The mediated and symbolic character of Israel's relationship with God's presence points ahead to fuller and perhaps immediate encounter with God's presence that only the new covenant would make possible. Jesus Christ and the Holy Spirit provide the true and full mutual indwelling between God and his people toward which Exodus strains and points.

COMMENTARY

I. IN EGYPT: EXODUS 1:1—15:21

Overview

Israel's liberation from the powerful, oppressive nation of Egypt is one of the most riveting stories in the OT. The first part of the book of Exodus (1:1—15:21) narrates that powerful story. The great story of deliverance starts with a list of the names of the ancestors of Israel and a brief historical summary of the growth of the Israelite migrants in Egypt (1:1-7), connecting it to the ancestral stories found in the book of Genesis as their continuation. The brief introduction is followed by a report of the rise of Egyptian oppression of the Israelites, setting the stage for the subsequent two sections of the book: the rise of the leader of Israel, Moses (2:1—7:13), and Yahweh's mighty acts of judgment of Egypt and the deliverance of the Israelites from the Egyptian oppression (7:14—15:21).

A. The Setting (1:1-22)

1. Connection with the Past (1:1-7)

BEHIND THE TEXT

The story of Exodus starts with a mundane list of names. Yet it is this list of name-giving ancestors of Israel that meaningfully connects the stories of Exodus to the ancestral stories of Genesis, which lay both literary and theological foundations for what follows them.

The ancestral stories in Genesis end with the fulfillment of the first of God's covenant promises to Abraham as found in Gen 15—a migration of his descendants to a foreign country, their bitter enslavement, God's punishment of the oppressing nation, their emancipation after four hundred years in a foreign land, and finally, their reentry into the promised land (vv 13-16). Joseph's final words in Gen 50:24, "God will surely come to your aid and take you up out of this land," appear to treat future oppression and deliverance as an expected occurrence and anticipate the latter.

The book of Exodus begins the story when all those who first migrated to Egypt are gone. Nothing is told of the time between the death of Joseph and the onset of the Egyptian oppression, other than the bare minimum: the death of the migration generation (1:6) and the phenomenal explosion of Israel's population (v 7). The exponential growth of the Israelites is evidence of God's past and ongoing faithfulness to his covenant promises to Abraham. Yahweh's faithfulness to Israel's ancestors provides a theological anchor through the stories of the Egyptians' diabolic treatment of the Israelites in Egypt.

IN THE TEXT

a. Jacob's Sons in Egypt (1:1-6)

■ 1 The opening phrase **These are the names** constitutes the title for the book of Exodus in the Hebrew Bible. This verse echoes Gen 46:8 and takes us to the time when Jacob's clan migrated to and settled in Egypt, in the region called Goshen, also known as "the district of Rameses" (47:11).

■ 2-4 The list of the names follows the order found in Gen 35:23-26, rather than that of 46:8-24, placing the sons of Jacobs' wives in order of their seniority ahead of the sons of the maids. Thus, the sons of Leah—**Reuben** ("Behold a son!"), **Simeon** ("heard"), **Levi** (probably "attached one," i.e., to God), **Judah** (most likely short for "May God be praised"), **Issachar** ("wage, reward"), and **Zebulun** ("elevated, lordly") are followed by the son of Rachel—**Benjamin** ("son of the *right hand*," i.e., the south). Further, the list includes the sons of Rachel's maid Bilhah—**Dan** ("judge") and **Naphtali** ("wrestler")—and of

Leah's maid Zilpah—**Gad** ("fortune") and **Asher** ("blessing"; see Propp 1999, 128-29). The name **Israel** ("God strives" or "persists") refers to Jacob but also to the people of Israel, the population derived from Jacob's clan.

■ **5** This verse acknowledges that **Joseph** ["increase"] **was already in Egypt** when **Jacob** migrated there. In such a fashion, the reader is reminded of the Joseph story: his enslavement, his imprisonment, and his exaltation as a ruler of Egypt. The number **seventy** alludes to Gen 46:27 and refers to the total number of Jacob's **descendants** at the time of Jacob's move to Egypt. Accordingly, seventy descendants include Joseph, his two sons (Manasseh and Ephraim) born in Egypt, Jacob's daughter Dinah (v 15) and granddaughter Serah (v 17), but it excludes the two deceased sons of Judah, all of whom are listed in Jacob's genealogy (vv 8-24). The number seventy might be literal and/or symbolic of perfection and completeness. Understood symbolically, it may simply mean that the entire family of Jacob settled down in Egypt and that no one was left behind in Canaan.

■ **6** We are told that **Joseph** and **all** of the immigrant **generation died**.

b. Multiplication of the Israelites in Egypt (1:7)

■ **7** This verse reports that the **Israelites** flourished and became exceedingly **numerous**, apparently under divine blessing. The expressions **fruitful**, **multiplied greatly**, and **the land was filled** are allusions to God's initial blessing of humankind in the first chapter of Genesis: "Be fruitful and increase in number; fill the earth" (1:28). This creational blessing is reaffirmed to Noah (8:17; 9:1, 7) and then to **Abraham**, **Isaac**, Jacob, and, indirectly, to Joseph (see 17:6; 22:17; 26:22; 35:11; 41:52). The matriarchs and the patriarchs of Israel struggled with barrenness at times. Yet their descendants evidently multiplied greatly in the fertile land of the Nile. The repeated reference to the phenomenal explosion of Israel's population indirectly emphasizes God's ongoing faithfulness. It also sets the stage for the appalling story of Egyptian ill-treatment and the near genocide of the Israelites.

Even with a supernatural proliferation of population, it may have taken many generations before the Israelites reached a population large enough to pose a perceived threat to the national security of Egypt (Exod 1:9-10).

FROM 🞉 THE TEXT

Although God's presence is not explicit in this narrative, the signs of God's work are evident. Curiously, the text does not mention God, causing some to speak of the conspicuous absence of God here and of the progress of human life and history apart from God's direct involvement. Even in this seemingly mundane three-hundred-year period, however, there is at least one undeniable factor that points to the presence of God among his people, namely, the supernatural explosion of Israel's population.

Genesis 3 indicates that human rebellion brought about alienation from God, hostility of the serpent, and frustration in procreation (such as the barrenness experienced by the matriarchs; see Gen 11:30; 25:21; 29:31). Therefore, any extraordinary deviation from the fallen norm (such as a barren woman having a child or a population increasing at an abnormally high rate) must be viewed as resulting from divine intervention, overcoming the hostile serpent that inhibits the multiplication of God's people (3:15). In other words, the Israelites grew phenomenally, not simply because of God's covenant of blessing with Abraham ("I will make you into a great nation" [Gen 12:1]) but also from the active, present, life-giving work of God in their midst, however implicit.

In a similar way, we Christians may not always find God's presence to be obvious, but we can discern signs of his presence among us. In particular, where there is supernatural fruitfulness—perhaps on a spiritual level—it is a sign of God's presence and work among and through his people.

2. Oppression of the Israelites (1:8-22)

a. Enslavement of the Israelites (1:8-14)

BEHIND THE TEXT

Obviously a significant period of time elapsed between the death of Joseph and the beginning of the oppression. According to Exod 12:40, the Israelites lived in Egypt for 430 years. Galatians 3:17 reports 430 years as the time between the Abrahamic covenant and Mosaic law. Perhaps the Galatians passage takes the number 430 from Exod 12:40 and loosely applies it to the period from the end of the patriarchs to the giving of the law at Mount Sinai. The number 400 in Gen 15:13 and Acts 7:6 is probably a round number. The passages of Gen 15:13 and Acts 7:6 speak of the entire time in Egypt as a time of affliction, perhaps in a very broad sense of their being aliens in a foreign land.

The precise duration of the oppression that the early chapters of Exodus describe is difficult to determine. However, we need to allow for a sufficient time for the expansion—albeit a rapid expansion—of the Israelites' population from a mere seventy or so to the size of a nation. In addition, the timeline must include at least a decade to allow for Pharaoh's diabolical campaigns against the Israelites and eighty years for Moses' birth, flight, and return to Egypt (see Exod 7:7; Acts 7:23, 30; → Introduction, Figure 1). The onset of the enslavement, thus, is best placed close to the last quarter of those 430 years. In this unit, the Israelites' fortune is quickly reversed as the king of Egypt treats them as a formidable threat to Egypt's national security.

(1) The Rise of an Oppressive Egyptian King (1:8-10)

■ **8** Long after his death, the legends of a former foreign slave named Joseph and the benefits of his rule probably lived on in Egypt's culture. This history probably allowed the Israelites to flourish and live in relative peace for a time. However, the rise of an Egyptian ruler **to whom Joseph meant nothing** indicates a sudden change in the Israelites' fortune. The phrase **new king** may indicate the founding of a new dynasty (Durham 1987, 7). In particular, it highly likely refers to the establishment of the Eighteenth Dynasty by an ethnically Egyptian ruler, after a long period of Semitic (*Hyk-khase*; "rulers of foreign lands," popularly known as Hyksos) rule (→ Introduction). The expression **came to power** suggests that the enmity against the Israelites resulted from a change of rulers rather than from a gradually developed policy against the people. Some suggest that the text refers to the ruler of **Egypt** as **king**, and not pharaoh, because he was one of the Hyksos. However, this interpretation does not stand, since he is called Pharaoh in the same chapter (vv 11, 19, 22).

■ **9-10** These verses depict the pharaoh who oppressed the Israelites as a fearful and insecure ruler. He breathes fear into his people and instigates hostility against Israel (v 9). He does so by presenting Israel as a formidable enemy, an imminent threat to Egypt's national security, unless a shrewd policy of homeland security is implemented against the Israelites. The goal of this policy was to prevent the Israelites from becoming **even more numerous** (v 10) and powerful than they already were. Pharaoh entertains the possibility that the Israelites will join the enemies of Egypt **if war breaks out**.

The phrase **leave the country** is more literally *rise from the ground* (*we'ālâ min hā'āreṣ*), which implies a rise from a humble status to flourish. The NIV rendering indicates a departure or escape from the land. However, there is no indication in the narrative that the Israelites wanted to leave Egypt at this point. Thus, the translation "leave the country" is clearly influenced by the wider contextual concern with Israel's emancipation from Egypt. The Hebrew idiomatic expression recurs in Hos 1:11 [2:2 HB], and in both verses the phrase "flourish and take possession of the land" fits the context well. Pharaoh's fear was that Israel would join in a fight against the Egyptians, take possession of the land, and gain dominance over Pharaoh and Egypt once again.

(2) The Oppression (1:11-14)

■ **11** The phrase **they put slave masters** indicates that the Egyptians agreed with Pharaoh and instituted the program of enslavement of the Israelites. The goal of **forced labor** was twofold: (1) the subjugation of the enslaved population under the hard labor, which would result in a drastic decrease in their population, and (2) the expansion and growth of the urban centers of the oppressive empire. The Israelites were forced to build **Pithom and Rameses as store cities for Pharaoh**. The word "build" (*bānâ*) could mean to build from scratch or to rebuild and expand. In either case, the Israelites were exploited for a monumental task of constructing or expanding large cities. The Septuagint renders the "store cities" *poleis ochuras*, "strong cities" or "fortified cities." The same Hebrew expression is used of certain garrison cities of Solomon (in 1 Kgs 9:19 and 2 Chr 8:4, 6) and of Jehoshaphat (in 2 Chr 17:12) and refers to military bases with weapons and supply storehouses. The building of enormous military storehouses, silos, and military camps at the city of Avaris during the reign of Ahmose I fits well with the biblical description here.

Pithom, mentioned only once in the Bible, is commonly identified with Per-Atum ("house of Atum"), about sixty miles northeast of Cairo. Tum or Atum was the sun god of Heliopolis ("sun city"), ancient Egypt's primary place of sun worship.

The term "Rameses" first appears in Gen 47:11 in "the district of Rameses" in reference to the area where Jacob's clan settled. Accordingly, Rameses (district) is identified as the departure point for the exodus of Jacob's descendants in Exod 12:37 and Num 33:3, 5. In these texts, Rameses is another name for Goshen, where Jacob's clan settled during Joseph's lifetime. The use of the name Rameses in Joseph's era (Gen 47:11) is probably anachronistic. The reference to the name Rameses in this verse is also best understood as yet another incident of anachronism. The text reflects the updating of the name by the editor of Exodus in a later date after Avaris (the capital of Egypt during the Hyksos period) was rebuilt and annexed to Pi Rameses (→ Introduction).

■ **12** The purpose of Pharaoh's oppression is mysteriously thwarted: **the more they were oppressed, the more they multiplied and spread**. Instead of decreasing, the population grew more aggressively than ever. Apparently, the God of Abraham was at work behind the scenes, continuing to fulfill his promise to make Abraham's descendants innumerable (Gen 22:17). However, this supernatural explanation is not available to Pharaoh and his people. The inexplicable outcome generates in Pharaoh and his people feelings of **dread** and defeat, leading to unrestrained, ruthless treatment of the Israelites.

■ **13-14** The repeated expressions **ruthlessly** (v 13) and **harsh labor** (v 14) convey a terrible intensification of the oppression. Apparently, the Egyptians showed no regard for the humanity of the Israelites; they totally exploited the Israelites, demanded hard manual **labor** for extensive architectural projects and agricultural **work in the fields**, and made their lives utterly **bitter**.

The political, social, and economic realities present in this text cannot be overlooked. The world portrayed in this text is a world in which the powerful engage in oppressive and ruthless ways to make the lives of the powerless bitter and miserable. It is important to note that the oppressor rationalizes its policy of brutality and oppression in this text as a national security measure. The political agenda of Egypt in this text includes the utilization of the slave labor force for the economic advantage of the empire. Human history has witnessed and continues to witness dictators and nations undertaking such oppressive and inhumane actions, disguised as legitimate policies for the preservation of certain political, economic, social, or religious ideologies. We also witness corporate empires building enormous wealth through child labor, marginal wages, and deplorable working conditions in different world areas. The biblical text strongly criticizes and condemns brutality and exploitation of all kinds in which certain groups of people are focused on their self-preservation at the expense of other groups, often the powerless and the marginal in the world.

The text also conveys a spiritual reality consistent with biblical theology. *Although God's people are persecuted, God enables them to grow and spread their story and message.* Pharaoh and his oppression illustrate the attempt of evil forces in the world to resist and thwart God's plans and purposes and persecute his people. The people of God have known persecution throughout their history, and they continue to be persecuted in many parts of the world because of their faith in Jesus Christ. Persecution has not impeded the growth of the church; the church continues to grow, particularly in world areas where persecution is intense. The text reminds its readers that no empire or power in the world can hinder or overcome God's good and gracious plans and purposes for his creation that he intends to fulfill through his people. The writer of Revelation anticipates and announces God's victory over all evil forces: "Hallelujah! Salvation and glory and power belong to our God . . . Hallelujah! For our Lord God Almighty reigns" (Rev 19:1*b*, 6*b*).

b. Pharaoh's Genocidal Campaign (1:15-22)

The time frame of Pharaoh's first measure against the Israelites is unclear from the text. However, since the forced labor was for the purpose of completing large building projects and fieldwork and since there was sufficient time to observe extraordinary population growth, the text must cover at least two decades. During this time, Pharaoh experiences a painful failure of his policies. Unfortunately, "a new Pharaoh cannot afford to be wrong" (Durham 1987, 9), so he grows even more cruel and savage than before.

IN THE TEXT

(1) Pharaoh's Edict and the Midwives' Disobedience (1:15-21)

■ **15** The narrative at this point introduces the **midwives** and their involvement in the story of Israel in Egypt. Pharaoh devises a secret plan to use the **Hebrew** midwives to reduce the Israelite population (vv 15-16). The Hebrew midwives (*hāmeyalledôt hā'ibrîyōt*) can equally mean "the midwives to the Hebrews," as the Greek has, which allows for the possibility that the midwives were Egyptian. This understanding could more easily explain Pharaoh's plan to have the midwives kill the Hebrew male infants. Yet the midwives' fear of God (in contrast to the rest of the Egyptian population) is one of several reasons for the conclusion that the midwives were Hebrews (see Jacob 1992, 18). **Shiphrah** (from *šāpar*; "be pleasing, beautiful, bright, clear"; Job 26:13; Ps 16:6) and **Puah** ("girl"; Sarna 2004, 7) were probably the head midwives who oversaw and trained the many other midwives (mentioned in Exod 1:19) who served the large Hebrew population. It is important to note that the text names these two heroic midwives; they are remembered and celebrated. The ruthless and tyrannical Pharaoh remains without a name in the Israelite history as someone not worthy of any honor or memory as far as the Israelites are concerned.

The Israelites are often called Hebrews in Israel's early history. Some claim that the Israelites rarely called themselves Hebrews, as it was the outsiders' designation for them. It is true that outsiders used this term (Gen 39:14, 17; 41:12; Exod 1:16; 2:6; 1 Sam 4:6, 9; 13:19; 14:11; 29:3). However, the predominant use of the term "Hebrews" in the OT is by the Israelites themselves (who are narrators or speakers) in reference to themselves (Gen 14:13; 40:15; 43:32; Exod 1:15, 19; 2:7, 11, 13; 5:3; 1 Sam 13:3, 7; 14:21; Jonah 1:9). Yahweh also addressed the Israelites by this name (Exod 21:2; Deut 15:12; Jer 34:9, 14) and even identified himself as "the LORD, the God of the Hebrews" (Exod 3:18; 5:3; 7:16; 9:1, 13; 10:3). This Israelite self-designation survives into the NT times, even as Paul called himself "a Hebrew of Hebrews" (Phil 3:5; also see 2 Cor 11:22).

■ **16** Pharaoh's order to the head midwives is not public, but private. It is likely that Pharaoh commanded them to instruct all the other midwives under them to **kill** the Hebrew male babies as the mother gave birth by squatting **on the delivery stool** (lit. "two stones"). The midwives are to verify the sex of the child. Although the royal decree, **if . . . a boy, kill him; but if . . . a girl, let her live**, conveys an appearance of some compassion toward female infants, it remains a calculated attempt to wipe out the future of this ethnic group.

■ **17** Verses 17-19 report the midwives' disobedience to Pharaoh. The (head and assistant) **midwives** fear **God** more than the murderous **king of Egypt** and his punishments. The fear of God restrains the midwives from becoming agents of evil. In the mind of the biblical Hebrews, fear of God is one's recognition of and commitment to live under God's sovereign authority over creation. He alone has authority over life-and-death issues. The text thus portrays these women as courageous individuals who refused to do what the king of Egypt, the most powerful ruler in the world, **had told them to do**. The royal decree falsely claims and presupposes Pharaoh's authority over life-and-death matters. The midwives' action of defying the royal decree and letting the **boys live** displays their rejection of the claims of Pharaoh and Egypt. Their defiance is an act of civil disobedience based on strong theological convictions. By defying Pharaoh, they continued their calling to save and assist life and to participate in the creational purpose of God. They understood that life belongs to God and not to Pharaoh. Therefore, the text remembers their names, celebrates their memory, and indirectly commends their civil disobedience as an act of faithfulness to God.

■ **18** Throughout this narrative, the tradition maintains an unflattering view of Pharaoh and Egypt, which is clearly evident in vv 18-19. **The king** clearly understands what happened; **the midwives . . . let the boys live** (vv 17, 18). However, Pharaoh only interrogates the head midwives and does not punish them. Perhaps Pharaoh is restrained by God's unseen protection over the women. Perhaps he is fearful that punishment of midwives who are agents of life may tarnish his reputation.

■ **19** The head midwives' answer in v 19 is rather elusive; it supports the idea that Pharaoh's order is to feign stillbirth. Their claim of the **vigorous** physical condition of the **Hebrew women** is bold and perhaps intended to show that the life-giving power of God is at work among the Hebrews against the royal decree. Their response, **Hebrew women . . . give birth before the midwives arrive**, further indicates the futility of Pharaoh's claim of power over the life of the Hebrew infants. The head midwives' response implies that the midwives refused to kill the boys and make it look like a stillbirth. To what extent Pharaoh accepted their explanation is unclear, but he clearly abandons his plan. With their wise answer, the head midwives silenced Pharaoh, the sovereign ruler over Egypt, preserved their own lives, and ensured ongoing protection of the Hebrew boys. "This is ironic, of course, for no king worth his scepter would have considered the response satisfactory, let alone from midwives" (Fretheim 1991, 34). The supreme ruler of Egypt and his power is no match for the wisdom and cleverness of the lowly Hebrew midwives who feared God.

■ **20-21** In vv 20-21, God rewards the midwives for fearing **God** and honoring life. God protects the midwives so that they flourish in their profession, and the Israelites continue to multiply and grow, becoming **even more numerous** than before (v 20). God also blesses (perhaps all) the midwives, who were apparently unmarried women, by giving them **families of their own**, husbands and children (v 21). Since an unmarried and childless status was a great shame in their culture, establishing a family was one of the greatest rewards God could give them.

(2) Pharaoh's Genocidal Decree (1:22)

■ **22** In v 22, when his previous efforts fail, Pharaoh orders **all his people** to throw into the Nile *every boy that is born*. Although not explicit, Pharaoh's intention to throw (*hišlîk*; "throw down," "cast," "hurl") *every* boy is unquestionably limited to **Hebrew** boys. Without doubt, Pharaoh implies infanticide, rather than simply abandoning the babies allowing for the possibility of their rescue and adoption. As Fretheim observes, if successful, the command would result in "genocide within a few generations" (1991, 35).

Whereas the text states that the Israelite population supernaturally grew faster and mightier than ever before in Pharaoh's previous campaigns against the Israelites, there is no such report made in this case. Pharaoh (Ahmose I, according to the early date view) probably enjoyed some measure of success under this new decree, perhaps until the year of his death (→ Introduction, Figure 1). That the genocidal command is given to **all his people** implies that all Egyptians became involved in brutality and their ruler's murderous plot and bloodshed. The Israelite tradition would have seen in this decree Pharaoh's signing of his own family's death warrant (Fretheim 1991, 35).

Ironically, God later uses the Nile as a means of punishment of Egypt, by turning the river to blood. In addition, the place of drowning Hebrew boys soon becomes the very place where the future deliverer of Israel is rescued. This order sets in motion a series of events that ultimately leads to Yahweh's decree of the death of every firstborn in Egypt including "the firstborn son of Pharaoh" (11:4-5).

FROM THE TEXT

God continues to call people into civil disobedience like that of the Hebrew midwives whenever leaders and their policies oppose God's justice and the sanctity of life. The midwives feared God more than they feared their own death at the hands of a tyrant. Their godly resistance of Pharaoh's barbarous policy is a case of civil disobedience. They submit to God's righteous ways by upholding life; they resist a diabolic ruler, and God delivers them and blesses them. Of course, not all who resist evil powers, policies, or cultural forces to pursue God's righteousness enjoy immediate divine deliverance or reward. Often, there are heavy prices to be paid, even the cost of one's life. However, it is precisely when the godly seek the establishment of God's justice and righteousness more than personal security that evil is eventually overcome. This model shows the power of nonviolent resistance that people such as Martin Luther King celebrated and embodied in the twentieth century.

Despite the admirable personal risk that the midwives took to preserve life, Christian commentators have long questioned their actions, particularly their willingness to lie to Pharaoh. Augustine's tentative conclusion is that the midwives' lying was wrong but that God mercifully pardoned that transgression in light of the "act of mercy" they performed in letting the boys live (Lienhard 2001, 4). But perhaps even the lie itself was morally warranted in this situation, given the importance of preserving innocent life from the wicked intents of Pharaoh, which called for shrewdness. Surely, not all lies are equally wrong (even as murder, accidental homicide, and killing in self-defense are distinguishable). There is a difference between bearing a false witness to condemn the innocent (which breaks the covenant) and the justifiable acts of lying to protect oneself (as David does in 1 Sam 21:13 [14 HB]) or others (as the midwives do here).

Is Pharaoh singularly bloodthirsty and savage? Is he unique in disguising and promoting barbarous policies as necessary for national and personal security? No, there are certainly "pharaohs" and "pharaoh systems" in contemporary society. Yet Amos still cries out to us to break off the passive tolerance that allows the unrighteous to set the currents of our society. Even today, God is still looking for those who, like the midwives, will actively promote justice until it runs down like torrential waters and righteousness flows like a mighty river in our midst (see Amos 5:24)—a passage that M. L. King famously quoted in his "I Have a Dream" speech in 1963.

The text is also a powerful testimony to the life-giving power of God at work in the midst of the death-decreeing empire of Pharaoh and similar powers in the world. God preserves the lives of the Hebrew infants through the agency of the midwives; moreover, he blesses the midwives with children. Pharaoh decrees death, but God decrees life. The powerful Pharaoh attempts to thwart God's creation purpose; God utilizes the powerless and insignificant midwives to promote life. The church hears in this text the challenge to be God's agency to promote life wherever the power of death is at work in our world. In particular, the church needs to be Shiphrah and Puah, daring to rescue children who have lost parents and home and who are maimed by war and violence.

B. The Rise of the Leader of Israel (2:1—7:13)

Overview

With Israel's bloodthirsty enemy raging against them (1:22), this section focuses on God's long-term solution to Israel's plight—the birth and preparation of a leader of Israel who will confront Pharaoh with signs and wonders and bring the Israelites out of Egypt.

The narrative slowly builds to Moses' first confrontation with Pharaoh (with no accompanying signs), which proves detrimental to the Israelites. The leader Moses becomes discouraged, and Yahweh's words of assurance are to no avail. Toward the end of this section, Moses' worst fears (as voiced at the time of his call) seem to come true, and he is fully convinced of his ineffectiveness as a leader. However, this section ends on a positive note, with Yahweh's recommissioning of the leaders and confirmation of the leaders' authority over Pharaoh. It nicely leads to the subsequent section (beginning with 7:14), in which the tides turn for Moses. Moses' status as a leader is thoroughly vindicated when Yahweh releases his supreme authority and mighty acts of judgment through Moses.

The section is comprised of the following subsections, which narrate from Moses' birth to his recommissioning as leader: the birth narrative of the chosen leader Moses (2:1-10), the humiliation and exile of the leader (2:11-25), the theophany and the call of the leader (3:1—4:28), the return and testing of the leader (4:18—5:23), and the reaffirmation and recommissioning of the leader (6:1—7:13).

I. The Birth of the Leader: Moses (2:1-10)

BEHIND THE TEXT

The text does not reveal to what extent Pharaoh and his people carried out their genocidal campaign. Instead, the narrative focuses on a particular Hebrew mother and her infant son, Moses. This story is marked by a remarkable irony: a daughter of Pharaoh ensures the safety of the future deliverer of Israel from the hands of the tyrant king.

The question of the identity of Pharaoh and the daughter of Pharaoh in this text is subject to speculation. A number of conservative scholars have suggested the famous queen Hatshepsut (1507—1458 BC) as the most probable candidate for the daughter, with her father Thutmose I (r. 1506—1493 BC) as the king who made the policy to drown Hebrew boys. However, this view does not harmonize with the early dating for the onset of the enslavement or the exodus. Rather, Ahmose I is most likely the pharaoh, not only of the enslavement but also of the infanticide. This would also mean that one of his daughters would be the daughter of Pharaoh in 2:5-10. Moses was probably born during the reign of Ahmose I, long before Hatshepsut's birth. In this view, Amenhotep I, Thutmose I, Thutmose II, Hatshepsut, and Thutmose III would be the many pharaohs involved in the oppression (→ Introduction, Figure 1).

The precise identity of the pharaoh or the Egyptian princess is in the end irrelevant to the interpretation and theological meaning of the text. Instead, the fact that the daughter of the murderer was precisely the one who saved Moses is an important detail. Her act, born out of compassion (rather than defiance), changed the destiny of the greatest nation and one of the lowliest peoples of that time.

In the ancient world, including the ancient Near East, there are many parallels of heroes being spared at birth in unusual ways. In some of these tales, the baby hero, usually a royal boy, is placed in water and found by someone else who raises him (see Propp 1999, 155-58). The most compelling parallel to the Moses story is the Legend of Sargon, which is probably from the eighth century BC. In this case and some other parallels, the royal son is raised by commoners yet later becomes king. However, in Moses' case, nearly the reverse is true; he is a commoner but is adopted and raised as a royal son in the context of the royal court and later faces a season of humiliation.

IN THE TEXT

a. The Birth of and Rescue Plan for Moses (2:1-4)

■ **1-2** The narrative portrays the Hebrews as participating in God's creation purposes by bringing forth children even in the midst of the decree of death issued by Pharaoh. Verse 1 begins with the report of a marriage in the **tribe of Levi**, which would have taken place well before Pharaoh's genocidal decree. The genealogical record identifies the husband as Amram and the wife as Jochebed (6:20). While the text (with the repeated use of the *waw* consecutive "and") gives the impression that the woman conceived and **gave birth to** her first **son** immediately after her wedding, there is a significant time lapse between vv 1 and 2. Two other children, Miriam (2:4; 15:20) and Aaron (4:14), were already part of the household at the time of Moses' birth. Perhaps Aaron, who was only three years older than Moses (7:7), narrowly escaped infanticide due to the Hebrew midwives' faithfulness. This verse reports the birth of the couple's third child, who was born after Pharaoh had issued his genocidal decree. This son remains without a name in the narrative at this point.

Verse 2 reports the mother's evaluation of her son and her decision to save him from the decree of Pharaoh. She **saw** him as a **fine** [*ṭôb*; "good, healthy, beautiful"] **child**. The Hebrew term for "good" (*ṭôb*) is repeatedly used in Gen 1 to describe God's evaluation of his creation. The term is also used as a summation of the manifold divine character, translated as "goodness" in Exod 33:19. As such, the term "good" here refers to more than mere physical condition or appearance. It is also theological, hinting at the boy's special destiny to bring the goodness of God into the lives of the oppressed Israelites. Determined to save her son, the mother **hid him for three months**.

■ **3** In v 3, the mother takes an extraordinary measure to save her son when **she could hide him no longer** from prying eyes and ears, presumably due to the ever-increasing activity and sound of the baby (Stuart 2006, 88). Jochebed makes a small **ark** (*tēbat*) or papyrus boat (also mentioned in Job 9:26 and Isa 18:2) with the resilient, tall, and lightweight stems of **papyrus** reeds (*gōme'*) and waterproofs it with **tar and pitch**. Presumably the ark was made in the same manner the ancient Egyptians made the crescent-shaped papyrus boats out of bundled-up papyrus reeds that were waterproofed with some form of tar. It most likely was not an oval or rectangular wicker basket with a lid, as popular biblical illustrations often portray it. A reed boat (unlike a small basket) would not only be secure on a **riverbank** but would have sufficient visibility for the boy to be discovered and saved.

The Hebrew term *tēbat*, used only for Noah's ark in the Bible, brings out a clear thematic parallelism. In both instances one who is "saved and destined to bring salvation to others is to be rescued from death by drowning" (Cassuto 1967, 18-19). The one carried in the ark is under special divine protection and care.

In Exod 2:3, the mother places (*śîm*; "put," "set," "lay") **the child in** the boat and puts (*śîm*) it **among the reeds** [*sûp*] **on the bank of the Nile**. The precise meaning of *sûp* is debated. However, the suggestion that the Hebrew *sûp* refers to reeds or marshes or seaweed (Jonah 2:5 [6 HB]), derived from an Egyptian word for reeds or rushes, is widely accepted and popularly held as its literal meaning (for a fuller discussion on the term *sûp*, see Hoffmeier 1996, 203-10). Another suggestion is to read the term as a noun, *sôp* ("end"; Enns 2003, 276; see Hoffmeier 1996, 205; see "end" of the earth in Dan 4:11 [8 HB], "end" of the gorge in 2 Chr 20:16). This reading suggests the end or extremity of a body of water or an inlet or a gulf.

The repeated use of the term *śym* points to the mother's careful placement of the ark to secure its position. The ark is decidedly *not* abandoned to haphazardly travel downstream in the crocodile-infested Nile in the vague hope that a good-willed Egyptian will find and rescue it. The mother no doubt trusted the baby to God's care but used her intelligence to ensure the safety of the child and the visibility of the ark.

■ **4** The ark is stationary on the riverbank, as its vigilant watcher is. **His sister**, likely Miriam (first mentioned by name in 15:20), stations herself **at a distance**, so as to "not arouse suspicions that the child [is] not really abandoned" (Sarna 2004, 8). It is likely that her mother gave her the task **to see what would happen** to the infant. Would he survive or perish? Perhaps the mother's hope was that her son would be discovered and be saved by the princess (who apparently is expected to arrive at this particular location for her bath [v 5]; see Durham 1987, 16). The presently "abandoned" status of the ark dictates against the interpretation that the mother intended the Nile to be a long-term hideout, where the mother would continue to care for the infant.

b. The Rescue and Naming of Moses (2:5-10)

■ **5** Verse 5 reports the discovery of the ark by Pharaoh's daughter when she went *to the hand* [*yād*; "arm" or "hand," that is, rivulet] *of* the Nile, perhaps a safe and secluded place along or at the end of a branch of the river **to bathe**. The mother of the child must have observed the location and the bathing time of this particular princess. As the mother perhaps hoped and prayed, the princess sees *the ark* and sends **her female slave to get it**.

■ **6** Verse 6 continues the noteworthy actions of the princess; she **opened it . . . saw the baby . . . and she felt sorry for him** who *wept bitterly* (*bākâ*, a term usually used with adults). The cry of the infant evokes not only the distress caused by the baby's painful separation from his mother but also stresses the dreadful decree that will seal the child's fate unless some miraculous intervention takes place. The (adult-like) bitter wailing of an apparently abandoned Hebrew baby immediately arouses deep compassion (*ḥāmal*; "feel compassion," "feel pity for") in the princess. Her statement, **This is one of the Hebrew babies**, is saturated with maternal tenderness and a will to save the child, rather than a heartless rejection ("Throw him in the Nile!"). The princess's response to the child anticipates the response of Yahweh to the cry of the Israelites later in the narrative (see 2:23-24; 3:7).

■ **7** In 2:7, the **sister** of the infant (presumably Miriam) emerges from hiding and suggests a Hebrew woman **to nurse the baby**. Miriam is careful not to expose the boy's connection to herself or the Hebrew wet nurse. The Hebrew verb "to nurse" (*yanaq*) is used four times in vv 7 and 9 to emphasize the pivotal role nursing plays in Moses' life. On the one hand, nursing is required for physical survival, health, and growth. On the other hand, nursing and nurture by his own mother are essential for the formation of his identity as a Hebrew, rather than as an Egyptian prince.

■ **8** The princess listens and urgently commands the girl, **Yes, go**; in other words, "Do as you have said at once." The Hebrew for **girl** (*'almâ*) refers to "a girl of a marriageable age," "a young woman," or "a virgin" (also in Gen 24:43 and Isa 7:14). Thus, Miriam is probably around fourteen or fifteen years old. She gets the baby's mother, and the mother and the baby are reunited. The mother's life-and-death undertaking is rewarded as she hoped and perhaps even believed.

■ **9** Pharaoh's daughter orders the woman, not knowing that she is the infant's mother, to **take this baby and nurse him** for her (Exod 2:9). The princess promises to pay the woman for nursing the infant. She acts independently and with compassion; however, the narrator's reference to her as **Pharaoh's daughter** clearly is an attempt to portray her as a member of the oppressive regime. Her decision to hire a wet nurse means that the child will be under the religious and cultural influence of his mother and at the same time under the protection of the very power that decreed his death. He will grow up with the awareness of his own ethnic and family heritage and relationships, including his relation to his sister and his brother.

■ **10** Verse 10 does not make it clear when the mother took her son to Pharaoh's daughter. Most scholars agree that the phrase **when the child grew older** means when he was weaned (see Gen 21:8). In the ancient world, children were weaned at around three and a half to four years old. The Egyptian princess adopts the child as her son and gives him the name *Mōšeh* (**Moses**).

The origin and etymology of the name Moses is not clearly known to us. This verse indicates that the name *Mōšeh* (Moses) was given to Israel's greatest leader by the daughter of Pharaoh. The etymology of the name is often linked to the statement of Pharaoh's daughter: **I drew him out** [*māšâ*; "to draw out"] **of the water**. However, it is most likely that the name she gave the infant she rescued and adopted as her son was an Egyptian name *Mose* (means "son"), which is found in Egyptian records as part of a personal name, as in Ahmose or Thutmose, and rarely as a personal name by itself. Some scholars think that in this verse, the Egyptian *Mose* is transliterated into Hebrew *Mōšeh*, which means "one who draws out." As a result, a Hebrew wordplay is created between *Mōšeh* and the Hebrew root *māšâ* ("to draw out"). The Hebrew wordplay makes the princess appear to be an expert in Hebrew language, giving the baby a Hebrew name and the Hebrew explanation for the name (Propp 1999, 152-53). However, that is highly unlikely. Perhaps there is a link between the child becoming her son and the name *Mose* or Son. In other words, her explanation has to do with the *mother-son* relationship that she established not only by her rescue of the child but also by the name she gave him. That is, he is Son (*Mose*) not because he was drawn out of the water but because *she* (and no other) found him, which made *her* the sole rightful owner and adopter of the child. She is emphatic that it is **because I drew him out** that he is *Mose*. As such, the Egyptian name *Mose* or Son expresses the princess's firm resolve to establish and seal Moses' high legal and social standing in Egypt so as to make him virtually untouchable, especially by Pharaoh's barbarous decree against the Hebrew boys.

Once the Egyptian name and explanation are transliterated and translated into Hebrew by a clever and playful mind, an etymological connection is created between the name *Mōšeh* ("one who draws out") and the verb *māšâ* ("to draw out") in the princess's explanation. Accordingly, the emphasis is shifted from the princess and her legal rights over Moses to Moses' fate as one drawn out of the water and one who, in turn, will "draw" the people of Israel out of the water of the Red Sea.

God often works in ironic ways to overturn and subvert the plans of those who oppose him. The narrative of Moses' birth and his rescue is full of irony. Out of all the Egyptians, none other than Pharaoh's own daughter unwittingly saves and secures the life of Israel's future deliverer. Another irony in the narrative is that the royal princess listens to the suggestion of a little Hebrew girl, who in the narrative is the one with wisdom that the royal family lacks. The wisdom of the Hebrew girl promotes life, and she imparts that wisdom to the royal family. Moreover, the very regime that ordered the death of Hebrew infants pays for the services of this Hebrew infant's mother to preserve her son's life and help him grow up! The adoption of the infant by the daughter of Pharaoh as her son is the greatest irony in this narrative. Pharaoh orders the eradication of Israel's future warriors, but the future deliverer of Israel grows up in his palace, under his and his daughter's protection. The royal house of Pharaoh that decreed the savage genocide becomes the very instrument of protection of the future opponent of that very house.

Throughout the narrative women play a role in the preservation of life. The midwives, the mother, the sister, the princess—all are involved in saving lives. While Pharaoh is focused on eliminating the perceived male threats, the "female saviors" plot to frustrate his efforts (Propp 1999, 153-54). As Fretheim states, these women "are actively engaged on the side of life against a ruler who has shown himself to be capable of considerable brutality. Bucking a male-dominated system, they risk their lives for the sake of life" (1991, 39). These ironies in the story speak of Yahweh's marvelous ability to use unlikely people to subvert and overturn the will and plans of Pharaoh and others like him in unexpected and creative ways.

Texts like these lead us to trust in God's resourcefulness and sovereign power when we are faced with circumstances that appear insurmountable and contrary to God's ideals. They also speak of the ways God often works that subvert the goals of the rich and powerful. They also challenge us to become actively engaged in life-giving, life-supporting, and life-preserving activities in our death-filled world. Who knows, perhaps a future leader might emerge from among the innocent victims of violence, rescued by the people of God.

2. The Humiliation and Exile of the Leader (2:11-25)

As is typical in biblical narratives, the story at this point makes a great leap from Moses' birth in the preceding subsection to his adulthood. In this subsection, Moses flees to Midian and eventually marries a Midianite woman (on Zipporah, → From the Text for 18:1-12). His precise age is uncertain, but the book of Acts places him at forty years of age when he visits his fellow Israelites (Acts 7:23). Exodus 7:7 (and Acts 7:30) states that Moses is eighty when he returns from Midian.

The ancestry of the Midianites is traced to Midian, son of Abraham's third wife, Keturah (Gen 25:1-4). The exodus narrative indicates peaceful relations between the Hebrews in Egypt and the Midianite tribe associated with Jethro, who became Moses' father-in-law. Jethro's Midianite tribe lived on the front side of the Wilderness of Sin, with Mount Horeb / Sinai on the "backside" (Exod 3:1 KJV) of that wilderness. Other Midianite tribes appear to have occupied the area east of the lands of Edom and Moab to the north (see Gen 25:4-6; Num 22). Numbers 31:8, which names five of the kings of Midian whom the Israelites defeated, indicates that the Midianites were made up of many tribes, like other nations at the time. Other Midianite tribes, together with Moabites, hired Balaam to curse the Israelites (Num 22—25). From that incident, we may surmise that the relationship between the Israelites and the Midianites was hostile. During the time of Judges, the Midianites were one of Israel's formidable enemies (Judg 6—7).

Reuel, elsewhere called Jethro, is Moses' ḥōtēn (which is always translated into "father-in-law" in all versions [Exod 3:1; 4:18; 18:1]). In Judges, Hobab and "the Kenite" are also called Moses' ḥōtēn (Judg 1:16; 4:11). There are different explanations for this variation. Some suggest that Moses' father-in-law had multiple names. Others believe that the texts reflect different sources, referring to the same person by different names. Still others suggest that Reuel was the grandfather and all other names (Jethro, Hobab, and the Kenite) were for Zipporah's father. A more plausible explanation is as follows: (1) The Hebrew term ḥōtēn probably refers not only to the "father-in-law" but also to other male relatives by marriage, such as "father-in-law," "grandfather-in-law," "brother-in-law," and "son-in-law" (see Gen 19:12, 14), for which there are no distinct terms in biblical Hebrew. (2) Reuel ("friend of God") is a proper name, used only in relation to his immediate family members, that is, his seven daughters (Exod 2:18) and his son Hobab (Num 10:29). Other individuals had this name: Esau's son (Gen 36:4, 10, 13, 17); a Benjamite (1 Chr 9:8) and, probably, a Gadite (Num 2:14; the NIV reads "Deuel," but many MSS read "Reuel"). (3) Jethro is an honorific title, meaning "His excellency" (Sarna 2004, 11). This title is attached only to "Moses' father-in-law" and used exclusively in relation to Moses as Moses' father-in-law (Exod 3:1; 4:18; 18:1, 2, 5, 6, 9, 10, 12, 27). (4) Hobab is Reuel's son and Moses' ḥōtēn or brother-in-law (Num 10:29). Hobab is also the name-giving ancestor of the Kenites (Judg 4:11), thus he is called the Kenite (Judg 1:16). Hobab goes with Moses to live in Canaan (Num 10:33), whereas his father Reuel goes back to Midian (Exod

18:27). If we assume the integrity of the text, then Hobab and Reuel cannot be the same person.

This subsection consists of three units: Moses in Goshen (2:11-14), Moses in Midian (vv 15-22), and Yahweh's explicit response to the cries of the Israelites (vv 23-25).

IN THE TEXT

a. Moses in Goshen (2:11-14)

■ **11** The narrative of Moses continues in v 11 without giving any indication of his age; the term **grown up** perhaps refers to adulthood. He goes **out** presumably to the site where the Israelites were subjected to intense forced labor (→ 1:13-14). The repeated expression **his own *brothers*** conveys Moses' strong identification with the Israelites. The book of Hebrews interprets his going out to his own people as a public declaration of his refusal "to be called the son of Pharaoh's daughter" and a decision "to be ill-treated with the people of God" rather than "to enjoy [Egypt's] fleeting pleasure" (Heb 11:24-25 NET). If Moses is around forty years of age at this time, one can speculate that his decision to identify himself with his own people and thus potentially give up his privileged life in the court does not come about easily or swiftly. However, when he seeks out his own people, he breaks out of the royal life he is used to and displays the deepest empathy for their suffering **at their hard labor**.

The statement **he . . . watched them** refers to more than mere glancing (which is what Moses does before killing the Egyptian in the next verse); it is a prolonged observation. In this case, the observation is mixed with indignation at injustice, passion for justice, and compassion for the oppressed. In this way, Moses' watching can be seen as an extension of Yahweh's own watching of his people's suffering. Apparently, Moses' emotions are stirred up when he sees injustice being done by an **Egyptian** who is **beating** [*nākâ*; "smite," "strike," "kill"] **a Hebrew, one of his own people**. Propp observes that an Egyptian man beating is "a stereotypical scene in Egyptian art" (1999, 163).

■ **12** Verse 12 indicates that Moses' action was calculated and premeditated. He decides to take justice into his own hands, waits for an opportune moment, and kills (*nākâ*) **the Egyptian**. The book of Acts, however, interprets Moses' killing as a form of defense and vengeance on behalf of the defenseless (Acts 7:24). In this view, Moses is carrying out an appropriate form of capital punishment on a cruel slave master who regularly beat the Israelites (see Fretheim 1991, 42-43). Interestingly, the term *nākâ* is also used in relation to the plagues, with which God *strikes down* Egypt (Exod 3:20; 7:17, 20, 25; 8:16, 17 [7:17, 20, 27; 8:12, 13 HB]; 9:15, 25; 12:12, 13, 23, 29). As such, Moses' "smiting" may be seen as an "execution of divine justice against Egypt" (Enns 2000, 79). That said, Moses' action demonstrates his emotional bond with his people and against the oppressors. Moses' action of hiding the corpse **in the sand** to effectively cover up his action further indicates his knowledge of the Egyptian legal system and the punishment for the murder of an Egyptian citizen.

■ **13-14** The theme of Moses' concern for justice continues in vv 13-14. His attempt to intervene in the fighting between **two Hebrews** (v 13) results in the exposure of his own crime. His question, **Why are you hitting** [*nākâ*] **your fellow Hebrew?** indicates a judicial role he plays in this conflict. He identifies the guilty party and wants to resolve this conflict in a peaceful manner. His intervention, however, is not welcome. The guilty party's rhetorical questions, **Who made you ruler** [*śar*; "prince, ruler, chieftain"] **and judge over us? Are you thinking of killing me . . . ?** (v 14) reflect a total rejection of Moses and his concern for the end of violence against the Israelites. This angry Israelite rejects and mocks any notion that Moses is their advocate and defender. His condemning rhetorical question doubly charges Moses with intent to kill him and of the actual killing of an Egyptian.

b. Moses in Midian (2:15-22)

■ **15** The narrative does not state how **Pharaoh** came to hear of what **Moses** did; v 14 might indicate that many in the Israelite community had knowledge of Moses killing an Egyptian. Presumably, eventually it became a matter of public knowledge. Pharaoh attempts **to kill Moses**, to carry out punishment against a murderer according to the Egyptian legal system. But Moses escapes to a certain part of **Midian**. Hebrews 11:27 interprets his narrow escape as an act of faith, done without fear of Pharaoh, but with hope, perhaps of one day returning to Egypt to help his people. Whatever hope he may have, after his escape, he soon finds himself far away from the land of his birth and from his own people.

Somewhere in Midian, Moses **sat down by a** certain **well**. In Genesis and in this text, a well is a significant place of life-altering meetings. By a well in the desert, Hagar met "the angel of the LORD" (Gen 16:7; see vv 7-14). By a well, Abraham's steward had a divinely arranged appointment with Rebekah, Isaac's future wife (24:15). By a well, Jacob met his future bride Rachel (29:9). And in this instance, as Moses sits by a well, another divinely arranged appointment is about to happen.

■ **16-17** Exodus 2:16-22 reports Moses' encounter with the **seven daughters** (v 16) of a Midianite **priest** named Reuel, his marriage to Zipporah, and the birth of his first son. The narrative again portrays Moses' concern for justice and intolerance for cruelty; in v 17, when some malicious **shepherds** drive the daughters of the Midianite priest **away** from the well, **Moses** comes **to their rescue** and draws water for them and **their flock**. In ancient times, a well was a place of sustenance for all and often conflicts arose because of shortage of water. The well-being of a community depended on people sharing the water supply.

■ **18-19** The father's amazement at his daughters' early return (v 18) and the report of their rescue from the **shepherds** by **an Egyptian** (v 19) suggests that male shepherds frequently troubled them. Moses, on the other hand, is a hero who acts to right the wrong done against the helpless and the weak by the strong and the powerful. The daughters recognize Moses as an Egyptian, probably due to his distinctively Egyptian attire and hairstyle.

■ **20-21** The father sends the girls, who failed to extend hospitality to the stranger who came to their rescue, back to the well to **invite him** to his home (v 20). Travelers through the desert often enjoyed the hospitality of Bedouin shepherds in ancient times, which included food and lodging. Moses accepts Reuel's invitation to stay with him (v 21). At some point, Reuel finds Moses worthy enough to be the husband of **his daughter Zipporah** (means "a bird") and gives her to Moses **in marriage**. It is likely that there was some kind of marriage contract between Reuel and Moses; ch 3 opens with the report of Moses tending the flock of his father-in-law. Moses may have consented to give his service as a dowry for his bride.

■ **22** The report of the birth of **Gershom** immediately follows the announcement of Moses' marriage. However, given the apparent young age of Moses' sons at the time of Moses' return to Egypt, Gershom's birth is best placed toward the last decade of Moses' stay in Midian (→ 4:20; see Isaac who was forty when he married Rebekah and sixty when she gave birth to Esau and Jacob [Gen 25:20, 26]). The meaning of the boy's name (**Gershom**; *gēršōm*) is elusive although it is popularly linked to the verb *gāraš* ("drive away," "banish"), used earlier of the shepherds (Exod 2:17). Whatever its precise meaning, Moses' own explanation for the name, **I have become a foreigner [*gēr*] in a foreign land**, provides a phonetic wordplay for the name as it sounds like a combination of *gēr* ("foreigner") and *šām* ("there"). Moses is a foreigner to Egypt, living in a foreign land of Midian. Moses appears to be lamenting his double foreigner status. His permanent residency is now attached to his family in Midian, and as a fugitive, his return to Egypt remains an impossibility.

c. The Cries of the Israelites (2:23-25)

■ **23-25** These verses provide a transition from Moses' long life as a fugitive in Midian to his call to be a deliverer of his people. Verse 23 draws attention back to the Israelites' intense misery in **Egypt**. The expression **During that long period** refers to the period between Moses' escape from Egypt and his encounter with **God** at Horeb (ch 3). Verse 23 of ch 2 draws attention to three matters that took place during that time: (1) the pharaoh(s) who sought to kill Moses **died** (→ 4:19 and Introduction, Figure 1) and a new pharaoh came into power in Egypt (2:23), but there was no change for the enslaved Israelites as the new regime continued to keep them under its tyrannical power by coercion and threat; (2) **and** [the conjunction omitted in the NIV; see the NET] the Israelites continued to **cry out for help**. The narrative does not state that the cry of the Israelites was directed to God, although one can well imagine it was; it is simply the cry for help, cry of despair, cry of the oppressed who cannot help but cry out for help; and (3) most significantly, God paid attention to them and their intense suffering, which is implied by the expression **their cry for help . . . went up to God**.

In vv 23-25, the God of Israel whose presence and faithfulness have been in the background comes to the forefront of Israel's history. Verse 23 mentions God for the first time in ch 2 (he is mentioned only briefly in ch 1). These verses say something significant about God. Though the cry of the Israelites is not explicitly directed to God, he hears their cry. The verbs **heard**, **remembered**, **looked**, and **was concerned** do not imply that Yahweh previously turned a deaf ear, forgot, ignored, or did not care. Rather the focus is on God's impending active and history-altering response to the cry of an oppressed and powerless people; God responds with great empathy, compassion, and power, as the subsequent narrative shows.

FROM THE TEXT

Often, those who are great leaders of God's people are those who have lived out and participated in the life experiences of those whom they are called to serve. Moses in this narrative is the embodiment of the enslaved Israel in Egypt. Moses was among those infants in Egypt who were decreed by Pharaoh to die. He witnessed the hardship and daily struggles of his people. After forty years of prominence, privilege, and luxury as a prince in the Egyptian court, he experienced forty years of obscurity as an alien and lowly shepherd in the Midian desert. These life experiences taught him to be a leader in touch with his people. These experiences also taught him to be a humble leader. Humility, as seen later in Moses' life, is truly a mark of great leaders. The Israelite tradition remembers him as a leader "more humble than anyone else on the face of the earth" (Num 12:3).

Great leaders of God's people are those who are passionate about justice and righteousness in the world. Throughout ch 2, Moses is the embodiment of justice; his passion to make things right for the oppressed results in his exile from the life of luxury he enjoyed in Egypt. Even in a foreign land, he demonstrates his passion for making things right for the oppressed and the harassed. The tradition of Israel portrays Moses in this narrative as a leader who reflects the true nature of Israel's God. In the end, it is God's passion to save the oppressed that brings him to the scene of oppression and cry for help. In that sense, the narrative, though brief and lacking details, reminds us that wherever there is cry for help, God is motivated to move and act to bring an end to oppression and suffering in the world. As the exodus narrative reminds us, God does not deliver the oppressed alone in a single-handed divine act; he does this in full cooperation with human agency, those who respond to his call to participate with him in delivering the oppressed from oppressive powers.

3. Theophany and the Call of the Leader (3:1—4:17)

Overview

In these two chapters, Yahweh makes explicit his plans to punish Egypt, deliver the Israelites, and bring his people into the promised land. Yahweh appears to Moses and calls him into this new function (3:1-10). Yahweh reveals his divine name and his identity and character (vv 11-22) and empowers Moses for the task (4:1-17). Moses responds to Yahweh's call with reluctance and resistance, but he eventually accepts. Here, Yahweh reveals that he does not act alone but primarily through a human agent such as Moses, who becomes a leader and deliverer. As with Yahweh himself, Moses also moves from a place of obscurity in Midian to a place of prominence and visibility in Pharaoh's court, which is not only his previous home but also the greatest center of political power in the ancient Near East at the time.

a. A Theophany and a Commission (3:1-10)

BEHIND THE TEXT

In previous chapters, Yahweh is behind the scenes. From this point on, Yahweh is explicitly present. The narrative begins with a theophany (divine manifestation); theophanies occur again when the Israelites meet Yahweh on Mount Sinai (19:16-19). The theme of visible divine self-manifestation, especially through the person of "the angel of the LORD" (3:2), has precedence in God's encounters with the patriarchs in Genesis (16:7-11; 22:11, 15 [10, 14 HB]; see 15:17; 18:1-33). Beginning with this chapter, theophany plays a special role in the book of Exodus and its theology.

Exodus 3:1-10 is the first unit within the larger call narrative that extends from 3:1 to 4:17. The call narrative makes it abundantly clear that it is Yahweh who initiates a special relationship with Moses and who also equips him for his calling. Yahweh's call does not appear rooted in any special abilities or worthiness in Moses. However, his call to deliver an oppressed people comes to a person, who in the past demonstrated a great passion for justice in human relationships, particularly justice for the oppressed (see 2:11-13, 17).

IN THE TEXT

(1) Theophany (3:1-6)

■ 1 Verse 1 sets the scene for the theophany that will follow. It appears that Moses' service as a shepherd for his father-in-law started as a form of a dowry.

However, the text does not clarify whether these years of service as a shepherd were voluntary or contractual and obligatory. Reuel is referred to by his honorific title **Jethro** (→ Behind the Text for 2:11-25).

While carrying out his mundane job of **tending the flock, Moses** comes **to Horeb**, to the "backside" (KJV; *'aḥar*, also "behind") of the **wilderness** (probably Wilderness of Sin). This gives the impression that the mountains of the Wilderness of Sin lay between Jethro's Midianite tribal territory and Mount Horeb (see 16:1).

Horeb ("desert") in this verse, which is called **the mountain of God**, refers to Mount Sinai (see 33:6; 1 Kgs 19:8, in which Mount Sinai is called Mount Horeb). In many texts, Horeb is just another name for Sinai (Exod 17:6; Deut 1:2, 6, 19; 4:10, 15; 5:2; 9:8; 18:16; 29:1 [28:69 HB]).

■ **2-3** The theophany narrative in Exod 3:2 begins with the report of the appearance of **the angel of the LORD** to Moses. The Hebrew for **appeared** (*wayyērā'*) literally means "presented himself" or "allowed himself to be seen." So the emphasis is not on Moses' ability to see but on God's will to reveal himself to one who normally cannot see him. Yahweh's self-manifestation to Moses on the mountain of God foreshadows the theophany to the entire people of Israel at Mount Sinai (19:16-19).

"The Angel of the LORD"

3:2-4

"The angel of the LORD" most likely refers to the Lord in a visible form. "The angel of the LORD" is usually used interchangeably with the Lord himself (see Gen 16:7, 9, 11; 22:11, 15), as is the case in the present text. In the history of Christian interpretation, some have identified "the angel of the LORD" with the preincarnate Christ. Whether the visible form of Yahweh can be identified with the preincarnate Christ is an issue that Scripture does not address directly. Some might hold that understanding the OT theophany as a visible manifestation of God the Son is consistent with the NT understanding of the Son as the "image" or "radiance" of God the Father (as in Col 1:15 and Heb 1:3).

Unlike Genesis, in which the angel of the Lord appears in human form, **the LORD** in this instance manifests himself as **flames of fire from within a bush** (Exod 3:2). A similar visual manifestation of God is also found in the wilderness when his divine presence is manifested as fire in a pillar of cloud (13:21-22; 40:38) and like a consuming fire from the cloud-covered mountaintop (24:17). Flames of fire that burn from the midst of a bush without consuming it capture Moses' attention (**Moses saw**) in 3:2. This unusual phenomenon prompts him to investigate: **I will go over and see** (v 3).

■ **4** The second part of the narrative (vv 4-6) reports Yahweh's introductory speech, which begins with **God** calling Moses by name: **Moses! Moses!** The repetition of Moses' name suggests urgency, as when the angel of the Lord cried out Abraham's name at the sacrifice of Isaac ("Abraham! Abraham!" [Gen 22:11]). It is a direct call as when the Lord visited Samuel in the middle of the night ("Samuel! Samuel!" [1 Sam 3:10]). Moses' answer to the call is immediate: **Here I am**. He utters "the standard, spontaneous, unhesitating response to a call" (Sarna 2004, 12). This response indicates one's readiness to serve the one who calls; with this response, the narrative makes explicit the "theological dimension" of Moses' existence, which is implicit in his birth narrative (see Brueggemann 1994, 712).

■ **5** The boundary that Yahweh sets, **Do not come any closer . . . the place where you are standing is holy ground**, conveys the reality of God's holy presence. The holy presence of God demands a respectful distance; Moses is drawn into the sphere of God's holiness, but he is still a finite and sinful human being who needs to be aware of and recognize the incomparable holiness of God. Moses dare not encroach further. Even the ground is transformed and becomes **holy** (*qādaš* means "to set apart"). The presence of the Holy God transforms otherwise "common, unholy ground into extraordinary, holy ground" (Hamilton 2011, 49), set apart to God and God's purposes. Yahweh's instruction, **Take off your sandals**, emphasizes respect, humility, and submission required of the one who stands in the holy presence of God (see also Josh 5:15). Approaching God in reverence protects Moses from the fiery, holy presence of God, while allowing him to remain near. Later, the Israelite priests minister barefoot in the tabernacle and temple (see Exod 28, which prescribes no footgear for the priests).

■ **6** God's self-identity is the focus of his speech in v 6. The divine self-introduction (**God of your father . . . Abraham . . . Isaac . . . Jacob**) reveals to Moses that the God who speaks to him is the same God whom his ancestors worshipped (3:6, 15, 16; 4:5). The possessive pronoun (**your**) connects Moses to the patriarchs of Israel, to their God, and to their covenant with Yahweh. Yahweh is by implication the God of the patriarchs and the God of Moses.

Verse 6 of ch 3 concludes with Moses' deferential response to God's presence and his self-introduction. His initial curiosity and fascination with the "strange sight" (v 3) completely vanishes. The magnitude of the encounter with a living God whom his ancestors worshipped is simply terrifying and overwhelming to Moses. Thus, he hides **his face** in fear of looking at God and perhaps even of being looked at by him. Later, Moses is emboldened by his many encounters with Yahweh and requests to see Yahweh's glory, which Yahweh grants to some extent (→ 33:18, 19).

(2) The Commission of Moses (3:7-10)

■ **7** In vv 7-9, Yahweh states his reason for the theophany, which is the salvation of the Israelites through Moses. The God of the past, whose presence has been implicit thus far, now explicitly responds to the cries of his **people** in the present (v 7). The verbs used of Yahweh indicate his responsiveness to human misery (→ 2:24-25).

■ **8** The expression **I have come down** refers to the manifest presence of Yahweh and his sovereign involvement in human history that decisively alters course (see the coming of the Christ [John 1:9-18] and the coming of the Holy Spirit [Acts 1:5-8; 2:2-47]). The explicit purpose of Yahweh's advent is to **rescue** his people **from the hand of the Egyptians**. The metaphor **hand** here (and also in 14:30; 18:9-10) refers to Egyptian power. Elsewhere, "hand" is used of Yahweh's supreme power and/or mighty judgments (3:19; 7:4, 5; 13:3, 9, 14, 16) that work salvation for his people. Yahweh's power is often extended through the "hand" of a human agent, such as Moses (4:4; 8:5-6 [1-2 HB]; 9:22-23; 10:12-13, 21-22; 14:16, 21, 26-27) or Aaron (7:19; 8:5, 16-17 [1, 12-13 HB]). (→ 3:19 and 6:1 for military force as the referent of the "hand.")

The coming of Yahweh will bring freedom from bondage and a new life in a **land** of abundance. Yahweh's promise to Abraham in Gen 15:18-21 includes ten nations in the land, indicating the utmost boundaries of the land to be granted to his descendants. Only six of those nations appear in this text, which is the most prevalent list in the Bible (Exod 3:8, 17; 33:2; 34:11; Deut 20:17; Josh 9:1; 11:3; 12:8; Judg 3:5; see Neh 9:8). Other lists name five nations (Exod 13:5; Num 13:29; 1 Kgs 9:20; 2 Chr 8:7) or seven with the Girgashites as one of the "seven nations larger and stronger than you" (Deut 7:1; Josh 3:10; 24:11).

From the original list of ten, the Kenizzites and the Kadmonites are not attested outside Gen 15:19; perhaps they were displaced or destroyed by other people groups before Moses' time. Deuteronomy 2:9-11 indicates that the Moabites drove out the Rephaites and occupied their territory. Under Moses' leadership, the Israelites destroyed the last of the Rephaites (King Og of Bashan) and took possession of their land in the Transjordan (Deut 3:11-12; also see Num 21:33-35).

■ **9** Verse 9 sums up the reason for the theophany; Yahweh has heard **the cry of the Israelites**; he has seen **the way the Egyptians are oppressing them**. What prompts Yahweh to act is the suffering of a slave community; he cannot turn a deaf ear to their cry for help.

■ **10** Here we find the purpose of Yahweh's appearance to Moses. Yahweh who introduces himself as the God of the ancestors and the God who has come down to rescue his people commissions Moses to deliver the **Israelites** from oppression. The words **go, I am sending you . . . to bring my people . . . out of Egypt** are heard for the first time in the biblical tradition. Yahweh who responds to human suffering demands human agency and cooperation to accomplish his work of salvation.

God's theophanies in Horeb and in Bethlehem have striking similarities. In the theophany to Moses, God appears in and through a burning bush, without destroying its created properties. It shows that God is able to meet with Moses and use him as a deliverer without utterly consuming him. The theophany at Horeb anticipates the coming of Jesus Christ. In the incarnation of Christ, Mary's womb remains and functions as a normal womb, yet conceives and gives birth to a God-human. The divine is within the human without altering or destroying the human. Furthermore, mysteriously, the finite physical being of Jesus of Nazareth is united with the eternal divine nature of the Son of God: "in Him all the fullness of Deity dwells in bodily form" (Col 2:9 NASB). The physical being remains intact, but it is transformed into a perfect vehicle for the divine work of salvation. Partly inspired by these parallels, some church fathers regarded the burning bush as a type either of Mary's womb or of the human body of Jesus (Lienhard 2001, 10-11). Whether it is God meeting Moses from the fire of the burning bush or being incarnate in Jesus Christ, God stoops down to save those in unbreakable bondage. He sees the misery, hears the cry, and shows concern for those who suffer by coming down to rescue them. Ultimately, as Moltmann states, "God comes to his creation and, through the power of his righteousness and justice, frees it for his kingdom, and makes it the dwelling place of his glory" (2001, 265).

b. Revelation of the Divine Name (3:11-22)

BEHIND THE TEXT

In this unit, Moses raises two objections to Yahweh's call, based on his feelings of inadequacy as a leader (3:11) and his doubts about the Israelites' validation of the authenticity of his encounter with God (v 13). Yahweh graciously responds to Moses in his long speech, assuring him of Yahweh's identity as the God of the Israelites' ancestors, his commitment to fulfill his covenant promises, and his sovereign power over human superpowers (vv 12, 14-22). The revelation of the divine name occupies a significant place in this unit.

The Divine Name Yahweh

Yahweh reveals his name to Moses in Exod 3:14. The name Yahweh is a modern reconstruction of the four consonants *yhwh* (called the Tetragrammaton). The reconstructed name Yahweh is widely accepted and used (→ v 14; for a detailed discussion of the divine name, see Stuart 2006, 120-22; Meyers 2005, 57-59). In early Judaism, in the effort not to use God's name in vain (see 20:7), the name *yhwh* was pronounced only on the Day of Atonement. The rest of the time when the Scripture was read, *yhwh* was typically substituted with *'ădōnāy*,

"Lord" (and *'ĕlōhîm*, "God," when *'ădōnāy* precedes *yhwh*). Consequently, the pronunciation of *yhwh* was quickly lost after the destruction of the temple in AD 70. Later, the Masoretes (AD 500—1000) placed the vowels of the word *'ădōnāy* (and *'ĕlōhîm*) with the consonants, yielding *yehōwāh* (and *yĕhōwîh*). The English "Jehovah" comes from a transliteration of *yehōwāh*.

IN THE TEXT

■ **11** Moses' first objection to God's call and commission reveals his recognition of the overwhelming and difficult nature of the task of delivering Israel from **Egypt** and **Pharaoh**. His rhetorical question, **Who am I?**, conveys his unworthiness, unpreparedness, inadequacy, and perhaps his fear. In other words, Moses says: "I am nothing!" Perhaps his self-doubt traces back to his past crime and his long life in humiliation as a fugitive. Much later in Israel's history, David also utters these words to Yahweh: "Who am I?" (2 Sam 7:18). However, David's "Who am I?" expresses not only genuine humility and modesty before **God** but also profound acknowledgment of Yahweh's power and faithfulness in exalting David above his enemies and his favor in granting him an eternal covenant (2 Sam 7:18-22). In contrast, Moses' "Who am I?" in this situation betrays Moses' doubt and lack of awareness of God's sovereign power and presence with him.

■ **12** Yahweh's response to Moses' objection has several parts. It begins with an assurance of his presence with Moses: **I will be with you**. This is an extraordinary statement about God's willingness and commitment to be with and use a faulty human vessel for his purposes. The human agent is inadequate, but Yahweh is mighty and more than adequate. This assurance is followed by a **sign** that will prove to Moses the identity and the trustworthiness of the one who is sending him to **Egypt**. Moses will accomplish the mission and bring the Israelites to **Horeb**, the very place of Moses' encounter with Yahweh, and here they will **worship** Yahweh. As far as Yahweh is concerned, the mission is an accomplished fact; what Yahweh wills will be fulfilled.

■ **13** **Moses** responds **to God** with a second objection in v 13. The concern of Moses shifts to God's identity, which he raises in a roundabout way. Instead of asking directly, Moses puts the question of the identity of God in the mouth of the **Israelites**. He wants to know what answer he should give should the Israelites challenge the authenticity of his commission with the test of his knowledge of the **name** of the God of their ancestors. The name implies identity and character, and "in the case of someone giving orders, official authorization" (Alter 2004, 321).

■ **14** Yahweh's response to **Moses** is also indirect. Yahweh gives Moses a rather elusive name: **I AM WHO I AM** (*'ehyeh 'ašer 'ehyeh* [the verb *hāyâ* means "to be"] is repeated twice in this statement). Yahweh then instructs Moses to tell the Israelites that **I** AM is the God who sent him to them. As mysterious as it is, by revealing his name, Yahweh shows his desire to be known and to have a covenant relationship with humans, to be called upon and to respond. While the LXX and Masoretic text read, **I** AM (*ego eimi* and *'ehyeh* respectively), the archaic Canaanite causative *'ahyeh* ("I cause to be") is likely the original reading. The related name *yahweh* ("LORD") is thought to be a short form of the third-person causative of "to be" (early *hwh*, late *hyh*), thus, "He causes to be" (Stuart 2006, 121). When God speaks of himself, he says, "I cause to be," and when we speak of him, we say, "He causes to be."

The name **I** AM WHO **I** AM or *I CAUSE TO BE **what I cause to be*** reveals Yahweh as the Creator of all that exists and the Sovereign Lord of human history. Therefore, the divine name is given as a reliable and trustworthy revelatory deposit of what is to come: the plagues, the deliverance, and the possession of the promised land, which are listed in subsequent verses (vv 17-22). While the meaning of the name cannot be exhausted, the unfolding human history will continue to reveal who Yahweh is and compel the nations to worship Yahweh (see Childs 1974, 76).

It is significant that Jesus applied to himself (the Greek version of) the name **I** AM (in John 6:35, 48; 8:12, 58; 9:5; 10:9, 11; 11:25; 14:6; 15:1), blatantly claiming his equality and unity with Yahweh.

■ **15** Exodus 3:15-22 represents a basic summary of what is to come, from Moses' first encounter with the Israelite elders to the last plague. In v 15, Yahweh again identifies himself as the same **God** whom the ancestors worshipped (vv 6, 15, 16; see 4:5). Yahweh is not a new God but the God who has already acted on behalf of the Israelites' ancestors and who made a covenant with them. He establishes this name as his eternal **name** (**my name forever**) by which all future generations will **call** him. Calling the name of Yahweh means engaging in the act of worship. Implied here is the promise that the one who is being called upon, the object of worship, will respond to those who call his name.

■ **16** Verses 16-22 sum up Yahweh's words to the **elders of Israel** that he entrusts with Moses. Here we find Yahweh laying before Moses a series of actions that begins with a meeting with the elders. The elders represent the traditional leadership of Israel. They were the rulers or chieftains of the Israelite tribal communities.

Moses' second action is to convince the elders that the God of their ancestors **appeared** to him and to communicate to them Yahweh's word. Yahweh's speech to the elders begins with his past and present relationship with Israel: **I have watched over you** [lit. *I have indeed visited* (*pāqōd pāqadtî*) **you**] **and have seen what has been done to you in Egypt**. In wider biblical usage, Yahweh's visit (*pāqad*) may bring covenant blessings (as was the case for Sarah and Hannah, who each became pregnant and had a child [Gen 21:1-2; 1 Sam

2:21]). It may bring divine punishment for sin (thus translated into "I will punish" in Exod 32:34). Divine visitation of Israel is for the purpose of their deliverance and salvation, because Yahweh has seen the Egyptians' cruel treatment and oppression of Israel. In the exodus narrative, Yahweh's visit means both severe judgment for Egypt and redemption for Israel. *I have indeed visited you* perhaps is a fulfillment of Joseph's words, "God will surely come to visit you" (see Gen 50:25).

■ **17** Yahweh's speech concludes with a reiteration of his past promises and his commitment to fulfill them. The promise to **bring** the Israelites **out of** their **misery in Egypt** may be an allusion to God's speech to Abram in Gen 15:13-14. Yahweh's visitation is for the purpose not only of delivering Israel from Egypt but also of bringing them in to Canaan, **a land flowing with milk and honey**. It is precisely in these "bringing out" and "bringing in" activities of Yahweh that Israel will experience the faithfulness of God to his promises and his presence with them.

■ **18** Moses' third action is to recruit the **elders** to **go** with him and speak to **the king of Egypt**. Yahweh assures Moses that **the elders of Israel will listen** to him. The purpose of the delegation's meeting with Pharaoh is to seek permission for a **three-day journey into the wilderness to offer sacrifices to Yahweh our God**. It is important to note here the slave community's claim of its God and its plan to worship its God. It is possible to view this as a challenge to the established religious claims of Egypt. Three days is neither how long they will be gone from Egypt nor how long it will take them to get to their destination of Mount Sinai (see 19:1). Whether a literal or idiomatic expression, "three days" appears to be a diplomatic approach to persuade someone who is unlikely to grant any kind of leave.

■ **19** Yahweh warns Moses of Pharaoh's resistance: "The king of Egypt will not let you go, no, not by a mighty hand" (KJV). The NIV and other versions interpret the **mighty hand** to be Yahweh's, given that the majority of its occurrences clearly have Yahweh's power as the referent (e.g., 13:3, 9, 14, 16; 32:11). However, in Num 20:20, "with a mighty hand" (lit.) clearly refers to a show of strong (military) force. The phrase **a mighty hand** here likewise refers to the strong military force, but not of Yahweh or Egypt, but of Israel (→ Exod 6:1 for Pharaoh's civil and military force as the referent of a "mighty hand"). Of course, the Israelites' military force (however mighty) is significantly weaker than that of Pharaoh's.

■ **20** The fourth plan of action does not involve Moses, but only Yahweh. Yahweh announces that he will **stretch out** his hand and **strike *down*** the **Egyptians**, which will cause Pharaoh to release the Israelites. The Hebrew terms for **stretch out** (*šālaḥ*) and **strike *down*** (*nākaḥ*; also used in 2:12-13) are used to convey the release of God's power.

■ **21** Not only will Yahweh compel Pharaoh to release the Israelites, but also he will **make the Egyptians favorably disposed toward** his **people**. They **will not go empty-handed** but with "a token of compensation for the years of forced labor" (Bruckner 2008, 47). This may indicate that, according to God's just character, punishment of the Egyptian oppressors is not sufficient to right their wrongs. Rather, a measure of restitution is needed, partly supplied by the Egyptians yet mostly supplied by God's future establishment of the Israelites in the promised land.

■ **22** Verse 22 describes the final plan of action; **every woman** is to ask her neighbor **for articles of silver and gold and for clothing**. The intent of this action is to **plunder the Egyptians**. The command to ask for silver and gold is given to both men and women in 11:2 and is carried out by both in 12:35. They will give whatever the Israelites demand. Like a victor in battle, the Israelites will **plunder** or strip the defeated people. There will be nothing left in Egypt for the Israelites to look back to (which makes their frequent "nostalgia" in the wilderness absurd). The **neighbor** (*šākēn*; also "inhabitant") does not necessarily indicate next-door family, but resident Egyptians who live near Goshen. The resident neighbors are differentiated from **any woman living in her house** (lit. "a woman sojourner" or "a woman foreign lodger"); they are most likely foreigners taking refuge under the protection of the Israelites (by either living in an Israelite household or living in Goshen).

FROM THE TEXT

God calls Moses to a task that is humanly impossible, but God promises to be with Moses to accomplish that task in and through him. When God calls Moses, he resists God's call. As far as Moses is concerned, the chance for failure is 100 percent. In this context, God's promise, "I will be with you," is not a general affirmation of God's omnipresence or even God's special presence given to all people of God. As important as these theological affirmations of divine presence are, what Moses needs and thus what God promises is God's powerful presence that will perform mighty signs and wonders in and through Moses (which begins to fulfill in 4:1-9). Nothing less than an explicit and overwhelming demonstration of power will bring the decisive victory that the Israelites need.

These observations shed light on Christ's famous promise to his disciples, "I am with you always, to the very end of the age" (Matt 28:20), which concludes his Great Commission. According to John, the post-cross/resurrection/ascension Christ comes to be with his disciples forever through the arrival of the Holy Spirit (John 14:16-18, 23). This particular coming of the Holy Spirit also is for the special empowerment of the disciples for the task of fulfilling the Great Commission (see Luke 24:49). Just like "I will be with you," "I am with you always" is not an assertion of divine omnipresence or a reference to the special saving knowledge and grace given to all believers. The promise refers to the powerful presence of the triune God that empowers the disciples of Christ to do the works of God that no human beings can do on their own. This special, empowering presence of Christ is also promised to his followers in any age, who obey the call to preach the gospel, make disciples of all nations, and teach them to obey all of Jesus' commands.

c. Empowerment of the Leader (4:1-17)

BEHIND THE TEXT

In this unit, Moses continues to doubt about whether he can carry out the divine call and raises two more objections, but Yahweh continues to respond graciously. Yahweh gives Moses three signs to perform (4:1-9) that will demonstrate Yahweh's superiority over the magicians and gods of Egypt and inspire faith and hope in the Israelites. Despite the powerful signs, however, the chosen leader is unwilling and Yahweh has to overcome Moses' reluctance with divine anger and a gracious provision of an assistant, namely, Moses' brother Aaron (vv 10-17).

IN THE TEXT

(1) The Sign of the Rod (4:1-5)

■ 1 This unit begins with Moses' third objection to God's call and commission. The concern he expresses here is that the Israelites will not **believe** (*'āman*; "put trust in," "believe," "have faith," "rely upon") and **listen** (*šāmaʿ*; "hear," "listen to," "obey") to him. The term *'āman* is used five times in this unit (vv 1, 5, 8 [twice], 9) and comes with the nuance of trusting, rather than merely believing theoretically (Stuart 2006, 128). It is possible that Moses is expressing here his own doubt in Yahweh's assurance given in 3:18.

■ 2-4 In 4:2-9, Yahweh responds to Moses' third objection with a series of signs (v 9) aimed to reassure Moses that his mission will be successful and that the Israelites will believe in the authenticity of his commission. The narrative here refers to these actions as signs, though they also belong to the category of wonders or miracles. The first sign involves Moses' **staff** or **rod**, which for a shepherd is a "familiar possession and constant practical tool" (Alter 2004, 325). Due to Moses' reference to "the staff of God in my hands" in 17:9, some suggest that it was not the staff that **Moses** was carrying, but a new staff given by God. However, the power is not inherently resident in the staff but in Yahweh who transforms a shepherding tool into an instrument of divine power. The sign of a staff turning into a **snake** and the snake turning back into a staff has a dual purpose. Moses does not believe in himself or in the assurance of

Yahweh; he attempts to hide his doubt by castigating the Israelites as people who will not believe. The sign aims to make both Moses and the Israelites believe in Yahweh's power to save them and his presence with them.

The sign of the rod/snake is significant in an ancient Egyptian context. The rod represents kingly power and authority. The snake on Pharaoh's head-dress represents "divinely protected sovereignty" and serves as "a menacing symbol of death dealt to the enemies of the crown" (Sarna 2004, 17). As such, Moses' rod/snake represents Yahweh's authority, power, and supremacy over Pharaoh and the gods of Egypt. And as such, Moses' rod/snake later devours those of the Egyptian magicians (7:12).

■ **5** The report of the first sign concludes with the explicit reason for the sign—**that they may believe that _Yahweh_, the God of their fathers . . . has appeared** to Moses. The context of this sign makes it clear that Moses is included among the doubting Israelites. **That they may believe** is the consistent purpose of signs in the biblical narrative (see 10:1-2; Num 14:11; Dan 4:2-3 [3:32-33 HB]; Mark 16:17-20; John 20:30-31).

(2) The Sign of the Hand (4:6-7)

■ **6** As in the case of the first sign, the sign of the leprous hand is also intended to produce faith in Moses and the doubting Israelites. The Hebrew root for "to be leprous" (ṣrʿ) is used for a wide variety of infectious dermatitis and may mean "to have a skin disease" or "to be diseased of skin." Although the Hebrew root (ṣrʿ) is usually mistranslated into "leprous," the biblical description of the symptoms of this skin disease (ṣāraʿat, e.g., Lev 13—14) does not match the symptoms of leprosy (now known as Hansen's disease). The description like **snow** probably relates to **whiteness** from an open sore, wetness from oozing, or flakiness from crusting or some combination thereof. Whatever the exact nature of the skin condition Moses experiences, the point is clear; Yahweh is sovereign over skin diseases, to inflict and to heal them (see Stuart 2006, 131). Skin diseases in the Bible are consistently a punishment for hubris (Num 12:1-12; 2 Kgs 5:22-27; and 2 Chr 26:16-21), which would fit the context here in which Pharaoh will arrogantly resist Yahweh. Various skin diseases plague Egypt later in the exodus narrative, which the Egyptian magicians fail either to duplicate or to heal.

■ **7** The sign also includes Yahweh's immediate restoration of the skin on Moses' hand. In the exodus narrative, the infected and healed hand anticipates Yahweh's sovereign power not only to instantly inflict plagues but also to instantly remove them. This sign, therefore, may be seen as a token of the various judgments to come upon the Egyptians.

(3) The Sign of the Water (4:8-9)

■ **8-9** These verses suggest the difficulty of inspiring faith in a doubting community. The fact that Yahweh continued to give signs to the Israelites suggests that Moses himself remained skeptical of his ability to convince the Israelites or to persuade them to have trust in Yahweh. He hopes that if the **first sign** failed to inspire faith in him and Moses, the **second** one might work (v 8). Yahweh knows the reality of the conditions of the people of Israel; he knows not only their suffering but also their skepticism and resistance to the good news of their deliverance. So he remains patient with them and graciously gives them a third sign. However, this sign can be performed only after Moses' return to Egypt. Moses needs to wait to perform this sign; there are no practice runs. He needs to trust that Yahweh will be faithful and will enable him to perform this sign and thus prove himself as a trustworthy God. The sign of **water from the Nile** turning to **blood** is powerful (v 9), for it accuses and condemns the Egyptians for committing the horrific crime of infanticide in the Nile. It also demonstrates Yahweh's total control over the Nile, the main source of Egypt's prosperity. For the Israelites, the sign will speak volumes of coming divine vindication.

(4) Provision of a Speaker (4:10-17)

EXODUS

4:10-12

■ **10** Verses 10-17 deal with Moses' final objection to his call and commission. In v 10 he complains that he is not an **eloquent** speaker, that is, literally *I am not a man of words* either **in the past** or in the present. Some commentators have interpreted the expression, **slow of speech and** *slow of* tongue (*ûkebad lāšôn*), as a reference to a speech impediment, such as stuttering, and others to lack of fluency (Sarna 2004, 18). The latter is more likely. The expression *kebad lāšôn* ("difficult language" [most versions]) occurs in Ezek 3:5-6 and is used as a parallel expression to "obscure speech," both referring to foreign language. A similar expression in reference to foreign language occurs in Isa 33:19. Moses is likely referring to his loss of fluency in the Egyptian and Hebrew languages due to living in a foreign land for some forty years (Exod 7:7; see Acts 7:30). He is saying, "I am of difficult speech and a difficult language," or simply, "I speak a foreign language" (i.e., the Midianite language). If so, Moses is drawing attention to his lack of qualifications as God's spokesperson as he is no longer fluent in either the Egyptian or Hebrew languages, and he is a man of few words.

■ **11-12** Yahweh's response to Moses' objection in v 11 begins with a series of rhetorical questions that emphasize his sovereignty over all creation and its conditions, wholesome or imperfect: **Who gave . . . Who makes . . . Who gives?** The obvious response is, **Is it not I, the LORD?** This text indicates that Yahweh gives both positive abilities and negative disabilities. Logically, then, Yahweh can easily overcome or make up for any imperfection within his creation, including Moses' lack of fluency in the languages and eloquence of speech required for the mission. Moses' objection, however, does not prompt Yahweh to release him from his commission; instead, Yahweh commands Moses, **Now** go (v 12). Yahweh also promises to **help** Moses **speak** and **teach** him **what to say**; here we find the source of the prophetic speech. Moses' commission is to be a prophet for Yahweh; the words of Moses and the authority of his speech originate from Yahweh.

■ **13** Moses responds to Yahweh's command with a final plea to **send some- one else** to accomplish this monumental task. He has no more excuses; he is simply unwilling to go.

■ **14** Verses 14-17 describe Yahweh's angry response to Moses. The burning **anger** of Yahweh **against Moses** in v 14 indicates that his patience has exhaust- ed. Unlike Yahweh's anger that burns against the idolatrous Israelites, which threatens to destroy them (see 32:9-10), here Yahweh's anger is constructive in that its purpose is to inspire the fear of the Lord and persuade Moses to accept the call (together with Yahweh's alternate plan). The fear of the Lord will also help Moses withstand the lesser fury of the murderous king of Egypt.

It appears that Yahweh alters his original plan to accommodate Moses' reluctance by letting Moses' brother **Aaron the Levite** serve as Moses' spokes- person (4:14-16). Yahweh knows that Aaron **can speak well** (or, lit. *He speaks and speaks*) for better or for worse (see his smooth explanation for the golden calf he makes in 32:22-24). **He is already on his way to meet** Moses to accom- pany Moses on his return to Egypt (see 4:27); apparently Yahweh appeared to and called Aaron to join Moses in the mission prior to the call of Moses. Aaron at the time is eighty-three years old, three years senior to Moses (7:7).

■ **15-16** Verses 15-16 describe the prophetic role of both Aaron and Moses. Presumably, Moses will remain the only direct recipient of God's prophetic message. Moses will be like **God to him** (v 16), relaying God's words to Aaron who will, in turn, speak to the people. Yahweh promises to **help** both Aaron and Moses (v 15). Thus, the main issue at stake is not a human ability to speak but the endowment of divine words and empowerment to deliver the message with divine authority.

■ **17** The narrative ends with Yahweh's instruction to Moses to take his **staff** and **perform the signs with it**. The purpose of this instruction is perhaps to remind Moses that he is still Yahweh's primary messenger and that the com- mission has not been transferred to Aaron. Aaron's role as Moses' mouthpiece, in fact, diminishes during the plagues. While Aaron initiates the first three plagues (7:19-20; 8:5-6, 16-17 [1-2, 12-13 HB]), Moses performs the sixth plague (9:10) and addresses Pharaoh directly and performs the signs in the seventh to ninth plagues (9:23; 10:13, 22).

FROM ◉ THE TEXT

God not only calls his people to partner with him in his redemptive mission but also equips, enables, and empowers them to carry out his work in the world.

In this narrative, Moses understands the enormous risk and challenge of what he is being called to do; so he attempts to escape his calling by making excuses and raising objections. Moses has no fame or qualifications or family heritage in this narrative; he has lost whatever credibility or claim he had when he escaped Egypt as a fugitive. However, God responds to Moses with reassurance, promises him resources he could rely on, and even seemingly adjusts his plan to accommodate Moses' weaknesses. God remains resolved to use as his spokesperson a feeble, fearful, and insecure person who lacks self-esteem and self-worth. Moses is God's choice and God is going to empower him and use him whether Moses likes it or not.

The text reminds us to be intentional and deliberate when confronted by the divine call. Those who understand the massive responsibility that comes with God's call will neither trivialize it nor see it as an opportunity for fame and popularity. They will reflect and ponder over it, even raise objections, and come to terms with it only after they experience the compelling power of the call. Though Moses initially resisted the call, in the end he emerges in the exodus narrative as a fully resolved, fully committed spokesperson for God who is fully aware of all the risks and challenges ahead of him. Later prophets of Israel saw in this call narrative a pattern for their call and service to Yahweh.

God is sovereign over all things and has the power to mend and heal anything that has "gone wrong" in creation. This narrative includes a bold affirmation of God's absolute sovereign rule over creation (4:11). Taken literally, one may see here a God who gives the deaf, mute, and blind their disabilities, which they may see as a product of divine will. If so, why does Jesus treat them as symptoms of being "harassed and helpless, like sheep without a shepherd" and why does he with compassion heal them and all the other "disease and sickness" (Matt 9:36, 35)?

There are three helpful responses to these kinds of questions that are hinted at in this passage and made explicit elsewhere in the Bible.

(1) Isaiah's analogy of God as the potter and humans as mere clay in the potter's hands (Isa 29:16; 45:9) puts us in a place of utter humility and awed reverence before God. It is especially so since God cuts down ruthless, haughty eyes and mocking mouths, while filling with joy those who are humble and needy, giving sight to the blind and hearing and speech to the mute (Isa 29:18-21). Paul's rebuke, paraphrased here, "Who are [we], mere creatures, to talk back to God, the Sovereign Creator?" (Rom 9:20-22), also silences all arguments. God is absolutely sovereign and righteous in allowing or even ordaining some conditions and events that are difficult to understand or accept (such as the hardening of the more righteous Israel for the sake of the salvation of the undeserving Gentiles). The absolute righteousness of God in all his mysterious ways is implicit in God's address to Job (Job 38—39).

(2) In the wider literary context in which God displays his absolute prerogative and sovereign power over all things (creation, creatures, atmosphere, and nations), the rhetorical questions in Exod 4:11 might not be making a theological statement that God specifically ordains handicaps. Rather, v 11 simply might be making the point that since God is supremely powerful (even able to make people deaf, blind, and mute), God is more than able to make Moses eloquent and fluent. No handicap or deficiency is inevitable or incurable. This seems to be exactly the point made by the instant restoration of the skin-diseased hand in the second sign God gives to Moses (v 7). In this line of thought, God's absolute sovereignty over his creation needs to be understood not in philosophical terms of unrestrained independent power to do whatever one pleases, but rather in theological terms of authority and power to overcome all that is evil (even handicaps); this includes God's compassion and grace to heal and restore all to glorious wholeness.

(3) God uses human disabilities and weaknesses for the glory of God. The repeated purpose statement for God's action in the exodus is that they "will know that I am the LORD." Accordingly, God accomplishes his goals by means of Moses, an inarticulate man who is full of doubts. As Paul testified, God's "power is made perfect in weakness" (2 Cor 12:9). Even when weakness looks as hopeless as a man who has been born blind, God can heal it and do so to display his own glorious works (see John 9:2-3). The people around the world are "harassed and helpless, like sheep without a shepherd" (Matt 9:36), but with the coming of Jesus, who is full of compassion, "the blind receive sight, the lame walk, those who have leprosy are cleansed, the deaf hear, the dead are raised, and the good news is proclaimed to the poor" (11:5). This is the full, redemptive will of God. Accordingly, where there is "harassment," the real challenge is not figuring out why it happened or who caused it, but availing ourselves to God to be his instrument of salvation, deliverance, and healing and bring glory to God's name.

4. The Testing of the Leader (4:18—5:23)

Overview

In this important subsection, Moses makes the transition from life in exile in Midian to life as a deliverer of Israel in Egypt (4:18-31). The leadership of Moses, however, is severely tested, and the reluctant leader becomes a failed and discouraged leader by the end of this subsection (5:1-23). The initial failure and demoralization become an important opportunity for Yahweh's display of his compassionate nature and his power and authority over Pharaoh in the next subsection (6:1—7:13).

a. Return of the Leader (4:18-31)

BEHIND THE TEXT

In this unit, Moses obediently responds to the call given in Sinai by leaving Midian to return to Egypt. Following the Lord's gracious assurance of his safety in Egypt, Moses takes his family and starts his journey to Egypt (4:18-20). During the journey, the Lord reminds Moses of his call, the challenge he will face in Egypt, and the ultimate outcome (vv 21-23). Then the narrative focuses on a strange event that takes place at a lodging place, which highlights the covenantal obedience and readiness of the leader (vv 24-26). After the ordeal at the lodging, Moses and Aaron reunite (vv 27-28). The unit ends with their arrival in Egypt and their acceptance by the elders of Israel (vv 29-31).

IN THE TEXT

(I) The Beginning of the Journey (4:18-20)

■ **18** Midian is the scene of this segment of the narrative. Verse 18 reports Moses' return to Midian and his request to **Jethro** for permission to leave for **Egypt**. It appears that **Moses** does not reveal the true reason for his leaving. It is also possible that Moses never revealed his true past in Egypt, both the privileges and the crime (Alter 2004, 329). Jethro does not ask any questions but simply gives his blessing to Moses with the customary farewell statement: *Go in peace*.

■ **19** Verse 19 is a reiteration of Yahweh's command to Moses to **go back to Egypt**; he does not want Moses to stay in Midian. The NIV assumes that this verse points to a past event. Yahweh assures Moses that **all those who wanted to kill** him **are dead**. This expression likely refers to the pharaoh of 2:15 and his successor (→ Introduction, Figure 1) who tried to search out and kill Moses.

■ **20** Perhaps because the news made him less apprehensive, **Moses** leaves for **Egypt**. Moses takes **his wife**, Zipporah, and two **sons** with him on his journey to Egypt. The name of the firstborn, Gershom, is mentioned in 2:22, but the second son's name, Eliezer, is not mentioned until 18:4, perhaps because he does not play any crucial role in the narrative. Moses puts **them on a donkey**. The Hebrew for **donkey** is very likely a collective noun (the LXX has "donkeys"). Possession of many donkeys may indicate that Moses has acquired some personal property (perhaps through the compensation he received from Jethro for his labor). Moses' shepherd's **staff** in his hand is referred as **the staff of God**; this may be the tradition's recalling that Moses is only a vehicle for the display of Yahweh's power in this narrative.

(2) Yahweh's Plan for Pharaoh (4:21-23)

■ **21** Yahweh's speech to Moses in vv 21-23 takes place while Moses and his family are on the way to Egypt. Verse 21 indicates that Yahweh has already empowered Moses to **perform before Pharaoh all the wonders**. But Yahweh reveals for the first time that he **will harden** (*ḥāzaq* in causative; "make strong," "strengthen," thus implying "make stubborn") Pharaoh's **heart** so that Pharaoh will resolutely resist Yahweh's demand to **let the people go** (→ 7:1-7 for more detailed discussion on hardening). As Moses confronts him, Pharaoh will become more stubborn than he already is as the king of Egypt. This is probably the last news Moses wanted to hear from Yahweh.

■ **22** Verses 22-23 sum up Yahweh's words that Moses is to convey to Pharaoh. The speech to Pharaoh in these two verses contains three announcements to Pharaoh. The first announcement, **Israel is my firstborn son**, emphasizes Israel as the first people group with whom Yahweh made a covenant. Yahweh is Israel's God, and Israel is Yahweh's special chosen people. In Deut 32:18, Moses speaks of Yahweh as the Rock that gave birth to Israel and brought it forth through labor. Announcing to **Pharaoh** Israel's identity as Yahweh's firstborn son is nothing short of a declaration of war against the enslaving nation.

■ **23** Yahweh's second announcement deals with Yahweh's demand to Pharaoh; since Israel his son is destined to **worship** (*'ābad*, lit. "serve") Yahweh, he demands Pharaoh to **let** his **son go**. The **firstborn** in the ancient world is "regarded as being naturally dedicated to God" and has "certain cultic prerogatives and obligations" (Sarna 2004, 19). The third announcement reveals the consequence of Pharaoh's refusal to let Yahweh's son go and worship his God. Detaining Yahweh's firstborn son to serve Pharaoh and his Egyptian gods and compelling their forced labor grossly violate Yahweh's right over Israel. Yahweh declares the punishment for detaining his son; **I will kill your firstborn son**. Yahweh will punish Pharaoh and Egypt until Yahweh's firstborn son is set free (the exodus) and out of the reach of Egypt's oppressing power (the Red Sea crossing). Moses is told beforehand not to expect victory until the killing of Pharaoh's firstborn son (who represents all firstborns of Egypt; → "firstborn" in 11:5).

(3) Near Death at a Lodging (4:24-26)

■ **24-26** This story takes place **at a lodging place on the way** (v 24). It is difficult to interpret the episode due to unspecified pronouns or pronominal suffixes (**him** or "his") in vv 24 and 25 and an enigmatic expression **bridegroom** [*ḥātān*] **of blood** (v 26). The NIV and many other versions interpret Moses as the referent of the pronouns in **the LORD met *him* and was about to kill him** (v 24) and **touched *his* feet with it** (v 25).

The most widely accepted interpretation is that Yahweh seeks to kill Moses (perhaps through a destroying angel) for his failure to circumcise his sons (e.g., Childs 1974, 102). In this view, Zipporah, accurately discerning the cause of and the remedy for the near death of Moses, quickly acts to save her husband. Being familiar with the procedure of **circumcision** (commonly practiced by Semites and Egyptians), Zipporah circumcises her son. She subsequently touches Moses' "feet" (euphemism for genital organs) with the **foreskin** and the blood on him averts his death. She calls him "bridegroom of blood" because she delivers him from death and acquires him a second time as her bridegroom, as it were, through blood (Cassuto 1967, 60-61).

Others suggest Gershom as the referent of the pronoun, which is more likely. Like the above view, the main cause for the death threat is the failure to circumcise Moses' sons. While all uncircumcised males are to be cut off from Israel (Gen 17:14), the destroyer (as in Exod 12:23) specifically targets the firstborn (in the middle of the night as in the tenth plague). The reason for this action is that in the wider context of the exodus narrative, only the firstborn of the household of the uncircumcised is destroyed. Zipporah's circumcising and "touching" (*nāgaʿ* [v 25]) Gershom's own "feet" with the bloody foreskin turns away the destroyer from Gershom in the same manner in which the blood of the Passover lamb "put" (*nāgaʿ* [12:22]) on the doorframe turns away the destroyer from the houses of the Israelites (Sarna 2004, 21).

Sarna suggests rendering *ḥātān* (translated "bridegroom" in English versions) into "circumcised (and so) protected," based on the meaning of the Arabic and Akkadian stem *htn* (2004, 21). The whole phrase then reads, "You are now circumcised [and so] protected for me by means of the blood—the blood of circumcision." Incidentally, the Greek translates *ḥātān* into *peritomē* ("circumcision"), supporting Sarna's view. One major weakness of this interpretation is that it entirely leaves out Moses and leaves unexplained the reason that Zipporah, rather than Moses, performs the circumcision rite. Perhaps Moses was slow not only of speech but also of decision-making and responding.

One curious element is that Zipporah and the two sons are not mentioned again until 18:2-7, when Jethro brings them back to Moses to reunite them. It is implied from the text in ch 18 that, at some point, Moses sent away Zipporah and his sons, presumably to return to Jethro. Some commentators suggest that it is this "attack" on Gershom that prompted Moses to send them to her father's house for their own safety (→ 18:2 and Behind the Text and From the Text for 18:1-12).

(4) Reunion of Leaders (4:27-28)

■ **27-28** Verses 27-28 narrate another important episode in the journey from Midian to Egypt. **Aaron's** journey **into the wilderness** and meeting with Moses **at the mountain of God** takes place at the command of Yahweh (v 27). The narrative also preserves the primacy of Moses by reporting Aaron's journey to meet Moses. If the arrangement of the stories in this chapter is chronological, then the lodging place (of vv 24-26) lies between Jethro's Midianite territory and Mount Sinai. There is no mention of Moses' family, so we may presume that he traveled alone from the lodging place. The text here is brief and to the point; the brothers greet each other and Moses immediately gives Aaron his task by sharing with him **everything *Yahweh* had sent him to say** and about the **signs** Yahweh **commanded him to perform** (v 28). Obviously, the text presents this meeting as the fulfilment of Yahweh's promise that Aaron would meet him and serve him as his spokesperson (4:14-16).

(5) Acceptance of Leaders in Egypt (4:29-31)

■ **29-31** Moses and Aaron have a successful initial meeting with the Israelite **elders**, the tribal leaders of Israel. The focus of the text is on Aaron's role; he functions as Moses' spokesperson by conveying to the elders **everything *Yahweh* had said to Moses** (v 30). Aaron also performs **the signs before the people**, and the signs accomplish their purposes, as the people believe (although short-lived) Aaron and Moses. The initial mission of Moses is to bring the elders and thereby Israel to faith in Yahweh. The narrative ends with a report of the act of worship on the part of the elders (and Israel). What prompts worship is the word about Yahweh's present visitation (→ "visited" in 3:16) of his people and the impending acts of deliverance from the oppression, which is implied by the use of the term "visited" (as the text literally reads, ***and when they heard that Yahweh visited the children of Israel and had seen their affliction***; the NIV translation is too weak and misses the point).

FROM THE TEXT

Our obedience to all that God requires is necessary to the fulfillment of the divine mission. Though we cannot solve all the difficult interpretive issues in 4:24-26, it is possible to conclude that Moses' failure to obey the ordinance of circumcision is a key issue in this narrative. God is prepared to bring judgment on Moses or his son, but Zipporah's mediation averts the danger. Israel's survival depends on God's mercy and the mediation and obedience of God-chosen human agency (such as Zipporah in this narrative and Moses in the later stories) who embrace the divine mission in the world. Jesus models this obedience when he says to John the Baptist, who attempts to deter him from baptism: "Let it be so now; it is proper for us to do this to fulfill all righteousness" (Matt 3:15). Matthew's Gospel focuses on Jesus' perfect obedience to all the demands of God's righteousness. It is then not surprising to find in Jesus' final words to his disciples in Matthew's Gospel the emphasis on obedience: "Go and make disciples of all nations, . . . teaching them to obey everything I have commanded you" (28:19-20). All disciples are called to comprehensive obedience, even as Moses was. Only in such obedience, which is ultimately possible by the grace of

God, are God's people able to do his work in his way and with his blessing (to paraphrase a statement of the missionary Hudson Taylor).

The final segment of the narrative clearly suggests that God's people worshipping him is a powerful public act that displays their faith in God and proclaims to the world that God is the sovereign authority over all creation. Faith is generated in Israel by the display of powerful signs, but worship takes place at the hearing of the word about the God who visits his people and sees their affliction. Yahweh, the giver of life, is quite the opposite of the unfeeling and murderous Pharaoh who lives in a death-filled world. The Israelites embrace the new rule of the caring, compassionate, and delivering God and worship him. In the context of the exodus story, Israel's worship of God is "an act of enormous political courage" (Brueggemann 1994, 719).

We cannot ignore the tremendous "political" dimension of Christian worship that takes place in many parts of the world where Christians are persecuted. Whenever and wherever Christians gather to worship God in the name of Jesus Christ and in the presence of the Holy Spirit, they proclaim to the world of "pharaohs" that their allegiance is not to the oppressive powers of this world but to the God of all creation who redeems and restores it.

b. Initial Failure (5:1-23)

BEHIND THE TEXT

In the previous unit, Moses and Aaron are initially received by the Israelites with enthusiasm and faith. But in this unit, events turn for the worse. Moses' initial meeting with Pharaoh is disastrous. Instead of the freedom that they hoped for (5:1-3), they experience strong opposition (vv 4-5) and the intensification of oppression (vv 6-18). As a result, the Israelites become extremely resentful toward Moses and Aaron (vv 19-21), and Moses, in turn, expresses profound disappointment in Yahweh (vv 22-23).

Various features of this chapter—such as the concept of religious festivals to honor deities, the use of straw to make bricks, and the work quotas for the slaves—match well what we know from nonbiblical, historical, and archaeological sources about the ancient Near East and ancient Egypt in particular.

IN THE TEXT

(1) Moses' First Audience with Pharaoh (5:1-5)

■ 1 Verse 1 reports the meeting of **Moses and Aaron** and their message to Pharaoh from Yahweh. Apparently, the elders are not part of the delegation (in contrast to 3:18), or the text simply focuses on the key leaders only. Verse 1 introduces the message from Yahweh in the messenger style form also found in the prophetic literature (**This is what the LORD, the God of Israel, says**).

The announcement of Yahweh as the God of Israel suggests a rejection of Pharaoh's claim over the enslaved community. Yahweh does not make a request or bargain, but commands the sovereign ruler of Egypt, **Let my people go**. At the outset, with this command from Yahweh, the narrative anticipates a conflict between two rival authorities who have claims over Israel. Israel is Yahweh's firstborn. Thus, enslaving Israel is tantamount to stealing from Yahweh. Pharaoh must relinquish all his claims over the people of Israel. The enslaved community belongs to Yahweh (**my people**). Pharaoh must submit to Yahweh's claim over Israel. In 3:18, Yahweh instructs Moses (and the elders) to make a request to Pharaoh for "a three-day journey into the wilderness" to worship Yahweh. Here in 5:1, Yahweh himself states the purpose of Israel's journey from Egypt. He wants his people to **hold a festival** (*ḥāgag*) or a festive feast to him (**to me**) **in the wilderness**. Unfortunately, the Israelites dedicate a festival to a golden calf at Mount Sinai (→ 32:5-6).

■ **2** As expected, in 5:2, Pharaoh remains stubborn with his claim over Israel. **Who is Yahweh . . . ?** is a rhetorical question, a way of saying that Yahweh is nothing. His retort betrays his feeling of infinite superiority and contempt over Yahweh. He regards himself as a god over Egypt. No one gives him orders, especially not the God of his slaves. Pharaoh's statement, **I do not know Yahweh**, reiterates his contempt over Yahweh. Pharaoh regards himself sovereign over the Israelite community. He does not acknowledge any claim made by any god over a people he owns and exploits under his sovereign will; he insists that he is the final authority over everything and everyone in Egypt. He, and not Yahweh, determines the destiny of the slave community; he **will not let Israel go**. Yielding to the demand of Yahweh means yielding to the rule of Yahweh; by his defiant refusal to Yahweh's demand, Pharaoh insists on Yahweh's yielding to his claim over Israel.

■ **3** The dumbfounded leaders' response to Pharaoh appears to be a mixture of what Yahweh commanded them to say and their own addition. Yahweh's words (concerning the "three-day journey," → 3:18) likely represent a diplomatic approach, whereas Aaron's words (**he may strike us**) are an ill-conceived threat to Pharaoh that noncompliance will result in his loss of the slaves because Yahweh will strike down his own people in captivity.

■ **4-5** In Pharaoh's response to Moses and Aaron, the focus shifts from the theological issue of vv 1-3 to a more pragmatic economic matter. Pharaoh indicates that a three-day journey from Egypt means shutdown of work in Egypt, which means loss of productivity and revenue and prosperity for Egypt. He blames Moses and Aaron as participants in a plot to slow down the economy of Egypt (**why are you taking the people away from their labor?**). As far as he is concerned, economic growth through uninterrupted labor trumps all other interests, including religious loyalties and theological interests. His answer to the pressing theological interest of the slave community is simple and in the economic interest of the empire: **Get back to your work**. He accuses Moses and Aaron of **stopping** the slaves **from working**. Work must come first and foremost; all other interests will have to wait.

(2) Intensification of Oppression (5:6-18)

■ **6** Pharaoh's response to Moses and Aaron continues in vv 6-9 with a cruel decree he issues **that same day**, the day they conveyed to him a decree issued by Yahweh. Pharaoh's order aims to intensify the hardship of the slave community by making their work unbearable, while his empire continues to enjoy economic gain from the abused slaves. Pharaoh issues the order to those who are **in charge of** the slaves, which includes Egyptian **slave drivers** who manage the Israelite **overseers** who, in turn, supervise the **people** and their work. The Hebrew term for overseer (*šōṭēr*) derives from a root meaning "to write" or "to keep record." The Greek thus has "scribe, keeper of records" (*grammateus*). The overseers probably were those who kept records of the slave population and their work production. Ancient Egypt probably had a well-organized administrative structure, which included supervisors recruited from the slave community who enforced the policy. The narrative suggests that the Israelites were faced with a systemic evil, which left them with no hope of freedom from the powerful grip of the Egyptian empire and its economic system that perpetuated slavery and promoted cruelty.

■ **7-9** The policy itself is found in vv 7-9. No more **straw** (v 7) for the slaves to make the required **quota** of bricks (v 8); make the same number of bricks by your own straw! Work hard and don't listen to lies. Straw comes from the long stems of threshed cereal plants. Straw in sunbaked mud bricks makes them much stronger than the bricks without straw. Since Pharaoh was trying to build two storage cities, all straw was likely gathered, bundled, and stored at the time of harvest.

Pharaoh is convinced that his slaves are idle; thus, he calls them **lazy** no less than three times (here and also twice in v 17). Fretheim sees this kind of deception to be "typical of oppressors" (1991, 84). Pharaoh is also convinced that the Israelites' request for a furlough to worship Yahweh is nothing more than a display of their laziness. He is determined to discredit Moses and Yahweh and render their words **lies** or false promises by the hardship he imposes on Israel (v 9). Pharaoh dismisses the idea that Yahweh the God of the Israelites has power to save. He appears to believe that by keeping the slaves busy with their hard work, they will not have time to listen to false promises. Underlying this decree is Pharaoh's claim of his uncontestable power and his presumptive thinking that no power in the world can save the oppressed community from his power.

■ **10-14** Verses 10-14 show the full force of Pharaoh's decree. This segment begins with the announcement of Pharaoh's decree by the **slave drivers** and the **overseers** to the Israelites (v 10; → v 6). The introductory formula of Pharaoh's command, ***Thus says*** **Pharaoh**, makes clear the intent of Pharaoh's decree; Pharaoh seeks to delegitimize and annul Yahweh's decree (see ***Thus says Yahweh*** in v 1). Pharaoh contests the authority of Yahweh to issue a demand to Pharaoh; he perceives himself as a power greater than Yahweh.

Pharaoh's words in vv 10*b*-11 reveal his power and control over the Israelites; he refuses to give them the straw needed for brickmaking. Pharaoh's malicious new policy, **Get your own straw wherever you can find it** (v 11), is to force the Israelites to do double duty, to collect the straw and still meet the brick quota.

Verses 12-14 describe the increased hardship of the Israelites. The slaves spend their time collecting **stubble to use for straw** (v 12), which results in the loss of time from brickmaking. Stubble is the short, stiff stem from hay that remains in a field after harvesting. Collecting stubble involves "tedious hand pulling and cutting," which means difficult, time-consuming, and even futile work (Stuart 2006, 165). The loss of time and productivity lead to the harassment of the Israelites by **the slave drivers** (v 13); the slave drivers also **beat the Israelite overseers** (v 14), perhaps for not working their fellow Israelites more ruthlessly to fill the quota.

■ **15-16** In vv 15-16, **the Israelite overseers** make a daring attempt to confront Pharaoh and accuse him of his unjust policy (v 15). The overseers are caught in the middle between Pharaoh's new policy, which must be implemented, and their fellow Israelite slaves who may have been suspicious of them for collaborating with Egypt. They ***cry out*** (*ṣāʿaq*; → 2:23) to Pharaoh concerning the slave drivers' mistreatment and the new policy's unreasonableness.

The NIV translation of the final phrase, **the fault** [*ḥāṭāʾ*; "to go wrong," "sin," "miss the mark"] **is with your own people** (5:16), does not follow the MT (*wĕḥāṭāʾt ʿammekā*), which is difficult to interpret. The NIV places the blame on the slave drivers (**your own people**). However, most commentators emend the Hebrew text (into *wĕḥāṭāʾtā lĕʿammekā*, following the LXX reading, "you have sinned against your people"). The emendation makes the final statement a bold accusation: ***and you wrong your people*** (see the NRSV, "You are unjust to your own people"; see Childs 1974, 93). The overseers identify themselves as Pharaoh's people, even as they complain that Pharaoh has sinned against them.

■ **17-18** Pharaoh pays no attention to the protests of the overseers (vv 17-18) but reiterates his view that the Israelites are **lazy**. Apparently, Pharaoh is convinced that the Israelites will seek any excuse to get out of work, including the claim of their religious duty to **sacrifice to the Lord** (v 17; → v 8). Therefore, Pharaoh maintains his policy concerning straw and demands the slaves to **get** to work and produce their full quota of bricks (v 18). He is determined to keep the slaves under his tight control and continue his oppressive policies. Pharaoh will not let the slaves go and sacrifice to Yahweh.

(3) Discouragement (5:19-23)

■ **19-21** Verses 19-21 report the overseers' response to Pharaoh's rejection of their appeal. They blame Moses and Aaron for Pharaoh's inflamed cruelty. Pharaoh has succeeded in discrediting Moses and Aaron and making their words seem like deceitful promises. Whatever faith and hope they first had (4:31) is all but gone. They want God to **judge** Moses and Aaron and to punish them (5:21). The people accuse Moses: *you have made our smell (of breath) odious in the eyes of Pharaoh*. The overseers' mixed metaphor (smell/eyes) communicates a sense of disgust and hate that they felt from Pharaoh.

■ **22-23** Moses turns to Yahweh with his complaint and accuses Yahweh of bringing **trouble on** his **people** (v 22). Moses resents the fact that the Yahweh-initiated mission of making a demand on **Pharaoh** in Yahweh's **name** made conditions worse for the people. He expresses his deep disappointment in Yahweh for not having rescued his people from Pharaoh **at all** (v 23). The cruel oppression that has been endured for so long is now intensified, producing a deeply felt, bitter resentment toward Yahweh. Moses' reactions show that he falsely and naively hoped that the rescue would be immediate and trouble-free. It appears that Moses has not paid attention to Yahweh's earlier warning about Pharaoh's stubbornness and the need to compel Pharaoh with many signs and wonders (3:19-20), culminating with the death of his firstborn son (4:23).

FROM THE TEXT

Pharaoh and Egypt are not unique but are paradigmatic of powerful governments, empires, or groups everywhere that prey upon the poor and weak and take advantage of them. Tragically, virtually all human civilizations in history have been marked by the oppression, enslavement, and exploitation of human beings. In our world today, oppression and exploitation of the poor take place in the form of political and economic policies by governments that often support the wealthy and powerful corporations that require their employees to produce their daily quota under unsafe working conditions in sweatshops for meager wages. The wealthy treat the poor and weak at home and abroad merely as a cheap labor supply. Modern-day pharaohs (wealthy nations, corporations, and individuals), like pharaohs of Egypt, are primarily concerned about their wealth, power, and dominance. The rich seldom pay attention to the plight of the poor. They are more focused on high productivity driven by the ideology of consumerism. We live in a world where the rich become richer and the poor become poorer; inordinate and insatiable greed of the wealthy for more and more drives the poor into greater misery and hopelessness.

Those who live in the United States or in other powerful nations in the world cannot afford to simply spiritualize the meaning of the oppression in this text (or many other biblical texts), but must reckon with the fact the nations of the emerging majority world actually see and experience the wealthy nations in the world much like the Israelites did Egypt. The text challenges its readers to see in the narrative the potentially oppressive nature of the economic and foreign policies of all wealthy nations that guarantee dominance and affluence of the wealthy at the expense of the poor and weak around the world. The narrative accuses, rebukes, and warns the oppressive systems in the world. At the same time the narrative focuses on God's concern for justice; God pays attention to the cry of the oppressed, and God is engaged in the world to bring about changes and freedom to the oppressed through spiritual, social, and political processes. In the exodus narrative changes come through the agency of Moses and Aaron and even the overseers who are bold to confront Pharaoh and charge him with sin against his own people.

Christian readers of this narrative cannot escape from their responsibility to stand in solidarity with the poor around the world. First of all, the text calls the church to genuinely repent for her inaction, apathy, and failure to speak for the oppressed in the world. In addition, the text invites the church to cry out to God on behalf of the oppressed and the poor for freedom and justice. Further, the text reminds the church to be involved in rescuing the oppressed from their bondage in which she is complicit.

Thankfully, this narrative is not the end of story. Moses and Aaron and Israel persist in voicing their protest against Pharaoh. They are not dissuaded by opposition, temporary setbacks, and failures; the church must do no less in our contemporary situations of exploitation and oppression of the poor for whom there is no voice other than the voice of the people of God.

5. Reaffirmation of the Leader (6:1—7:13)

Overview

The last subsection (4:18—5:23) ends with the leader Moses' bitter complaint against Yahweh, after the failed attempt at setting his people free. The hope of deliverance that Moses and the people had shatters in the face of the blatant injustice of Pharaoh's recent decrees. At that moment, it appears to them that Pharaoh is prevailing over Yahweh. On the other side of the Red Sea, however, the Israelites will be able to see the big picture. They will marvel at Yahweh's power along with his wisdom and purposes for Israel, Egypt, and all nations of the earth for all generations. However, Yahweh's power and purposes are yet to be revealed (progressively), and they are not available to

Moses or to the people. Yahweh's being, power, and ways (that allow so much injustice to prevail, often for a long time) remain mysterious and frustrating to them.

In this context, Yahweh, in this subsection, responds to their discouragement, complaints, and unbelief. The subsection is comprised of three units: Yahweh's reassuring words to Moses and the people and their rejection (6:1-12), Moses' self-rejection and authentication of Moses' and Aaron's leadership through their genealogy (6:13-30), and Yahweh's recommissioning of Moses and Aaron with the demonstration of their authority and power over Pharaoh (7:1-13).

a. Reassurance (6:1-12)

BEHIND THE TEXT

Yahweh's response is gracious. The tone of Yahweh's words is full of understanding and compassion. Yahweh reassures Moses that he knows how to deal with Pharaoh; God will deliver the people after all. Yahweh's encouraging words are composed of divine declarations of his power, identity, and faithful, compassionate character (6:1-5) along with Yahweh's promises to the Israelites (vv 6-8). Yahweh also gently urges Moses to speak to Pharaoh again (vv 10-11). However, Moses and the demoralized Israelites are unable to trust in Yahweh's words (vv 9, 12).

IN THE TEXT

(1) Divine Power, Identity, and Character (6:1-5)

■ 1 In vv 1-5, Yahweh speaks to Moses and reiterates his plan to deliver Israel and reminds him of his past and present relationship with Israel. Yahweh tells Moses to just watch and **see what** Yahweh **will do to Pharaoh**. The result of Yahweh's mighty acts will be that (more literally) *with a strong* [ḥāzāq] *hand, he* [Pharaoh] *will let them go; with a strong hand, he will drive them out of his land*. The NIV adds *my*, making the **mighty hand** Yahweh's. Since the phrase "strong/mighty hand" is used in reference to civil and military power (→ 3:19; see Num 20:20), the strong hand in this verse is best understood as belonging to Pharaoh and as referring to his use of military power. This view is supported by the report in Exod 12:33 of the Egyptians *exerting power* (ḥāzaq; NIV: "urged") upon the people of Israel to hurry them out of Goshen. Pharaoh also chases the Israelites with his military force, driving them into the Red Sea, out of Egyptian reach (14:8-9, 23).

■ 2 Yahweh's self-declaration of his identity **I am the LORD** is repeated in vv 6 and 8 and frames the divine speech, which recapitulates the essential message of 3:6-20. The all-sufficiency of Yahweh's name and presence is not yet made evident to Moses or to the Israelites, but they will soon have a personal and overwhelming experience of it.

■ **3** In v 3, Yahweh discloses his intention to make his **name** and identity as LORD . . . **fully known**. The ancestors knew Yahweh more as *ēl šadday* (**God Almighty**).

Ēl Šadday

The translation of the Hebrew *ēl šadday* into **God Almighty** is etymologically unsupported. The divine epithet is best understood as deriving from the Hebrew *šad*, which means "breast." The divine epithet occurs by itself ("Almighty" [NIV]) or with *ēl* (e.g., Gen 17:1; 28:3; 35:11; 43:14; 48:3; 49:25; Num 24:4; Ruth 1:20; Ps 91:1). As such, the divine name *šadday* is associated with the divine blessing of fertility, fruitfulness, and multiplication, expressed as "blessings of heaven" (ESV), "blessings of the deep," and "blessings of the breast and womb" in Gen 49:25. For the patriarchs and matriarchs of Israel who struggled with barrenness, knowing Yahweh as the supreme God is inextricably tied to their experience of Yahweh as *ēl šadday*, one who bequeaths supernatural fertility. Their descendants undoubtedly continue to experience Yahweh as *ēl šadday* throughout their sojourn in Egypt and even under Egyptian oppression.

But Yahweh would now be known as the Redeemer of Israel, even as the declaration "I am the LORD your God, who brought you out of Egypt" will preface the Decalogue and other covenant texts of Israel (see Exod 20:2).

The statement **but by my name the LORD I did not *reveal* to them** can equally be translated into a rhetorical question; ***and* by my name the LORD, *did I not reveal* to them?** Given the statement in Gen 4:26, the clear cases of Yahweh declaring his identity ("I am the LORD") to the patriarchs **Abraham** and **Jacob** (Gen 15:7 and 28:13), and numerous cases where the patriarchs refer to God by the name "the LORD" (e.g., 24:3; 26:22; 27:20; 28:16), the translation into a rhetorical question is more desirable. Also, it is not without significance that Moses' own mother is named Jochebed (→ Exod 6:20), which means "Yah[weh] is glory."

6:3

However, the NIV translation **fully known** well conveys the implicit meaning of the text, since "to know" has a varied semantic range, from having an acquaintance to having a deeper experiential, intimate relationship. The patriarchs had limited revelation of Yahweh's character and power, but the exodus community is about to experience them in unprecedented ways. The range of meaning of the term "to know" is, in fact, found in the plague narrative itself. The text shows that Pharaoh, Moses, the Egyptians, and the Israelites knew Yahweh in varying degrees, but their knowledge of him was limited. Thus, one of the express purposes of the plagues and the exodus is to make Yahweh known to Pharaoh, Moses, Egypt, Israel, and indeed to all the nations of the earth from generation to generation. In other words, the knowledge of

Yahweh will exponentially increase for Egyptians and Israelites alike due to the new revelation of Yahweh through the events of the exodus.

■ **4** Yahweh declares his faithfulness to his **covenant** promises in v 4. The name "the LORD" is the **covenant** name, by which Yahweh established his covenant with the patriarchs **to give them the land of Canaan** (see Gen 15:7). Yahweh's reference to the unrealized covenant promise is to indicate that this moment is the time for its fulfillment. Through the experience of conquering the land through the incontestable power of Yahweh, the Israelites will come to know more fully the reality of the name Yahweh.

■ **5** Yahweh declares his compassionate nature. As in Exod 2:24, hearing the Israelites' cry signifies that Yahweh's focused attention is on them. Yahweh's remembering of the **covenant** signals the beginning of the divine fulfillment of the long-standing covenant promises given to Abraham (in Gen 15) and confirmed to other ancestors.

(2) Reaffirmation of Yahweh's Promises (6:6-8)

■ **6-8** The proclamation **I am the LORD** both introduces and concludes the seven declarations (in vv 6-8) of what the Lord will do for Israel in fulfillment of the covenant promises confirmed with that name: **I will bring you out, I will free you, I will redeem you, I will take you as my own, I will be your God, I will bring you to the land**, and **I will give it to you**. The Israelites will experience the Lord's deliverance from Egyptian bondage, adoption as God's **people**, and settlement in the promised **land**.

The expression **mighty acts of judgment** (v 6) refers to all of the plagues but especially to the last act of judgment (killing of the firstborn of Egypt and judging "all the gods of Egypt" [12:12]), which will bring decisive victory and the exodus.

The three verbs in 6:7, to **take**, to **be** someone's, and to **know** are sometimes used in relation to marriage, pointing to a firm and mutual covenant relationship between Yahweh and his people.

(3) The Israelites' and Moses' Discouragement (6:9-12)

■ **9** In v 9, perhaps strengthened by his encounter with Yahweh, **Moses** returns to the Israelites to relay Yahweh's words to the **Israelites** and encourage them. The proclamation "I am the LORD" (v 8) commands belief in Yahweh's sovereign power and covenant faithfulness over and against the present discouraging situations. However, the Israelites are unable to **listen** to Moses, as their initial hope of deliverance has been dashed under more cruel bondage and **harsh labor** than before—triggered by Moses' initial failed confrontation of Pharaoh.

■ **10-12** The Israelites' discouragement and failure to pay attention to Moses do not deter Yahweh from his mission (v 10); instead he reissues his command to Moses to deliver his demand to **let the Israelites go out of his country** (v 11).

Moses, however, is also dejected and doubtful. His sentiment is that his mission to Pharaoh is doomed to failure. If his own people do **not listen** to him, it seems highly unlikely that **Pharaoh** would (v 12). Moses believes his failures are based on his lack of fluency and eloquence in speech (→ 4:10) or simply his ineffective communication. The NIV's **faltering lips** in the Hebrew is "uncircumcised lips." As "uncircumcised hearts" devise iniquity (Lev 26:41) and uncircumcised (NIV: "closed") ears rebuff God's words (Jer 6:10); so perhaps Moses thinks his uncircumcised lips render powerless God's message. Moses' claim that his speech is powerless will become irrelevant as divine power supports the message he delivers (from Exod 7). Presently, however, Moses responds to Yahweh's urging with doubt and inaction.

FROM THE TEXT

The text reminds readers of God's resolute resistance to oppressive powers in the world. In this text, Yahweh remains relentless in his covenant promise to his people and unyielding in his demand to the oppressive power of Egypt. One may wonder why he did not make things right for Israel in a quick and decisive action as soon as he saw the suffering of his people. Israel's response to Moses and Moses' response to God originated out of the fact that they did not see his work, but only heard his words. Suffering continued in the absence of any noticeable work of God on behalf of the suffering community.

How do we know God is at work in the world, in the midst of increasing violence against and oppression of the poor or the powerless? We find in this text the beginning of the process of God's work to deliver the oppressed; he speaks, he reminds, he remembers, he authorizes, he demands—all leading to deliverance. The road to the fulfillment of God's promise may be bumpy at times, even hazardous and dangerous, but the promise maker in this text is also the promise keeper.

Between promise and fulfillment, the people of God must walk "by faith, not by sight" (2 Cor 5:7); this means believing that God can do what is impossible. The people of God in any age often face an apparent gulf between the words of God and the situations of life. However, demoralizing circumstances in life open new ways to *see* God's work and new opportunities to experience his power to save (see Exod 5:22—6:1). This faith is more than wishful thinking; it is faith rooted in the promises of God that inspire imagination of God's people in the dawning of a new era for them. In that sense, they already *see* God at work through their eyes of faith. God's word thus energizes God's people to remain hopeful in the midst of despair and hopelessness; hope reminds us of God's plans and purposes that are often difficult for us to understand (Isa 55:8-9). Finally, hope challenges us to see what is otherwise unimaginable and even incomprehensible.

b. Genealogy (6:13-30)

BEHIND THE TEXT

Instead of addressing Moses' doubts and objections, the narrative digresses to the genealogy of Moses and Aaron. The introductory (6:13) and concluding summaries (vv 26-27) frame the genealogy and function to connect the Moses and Aaron of the exodus narrative to the Aaron and Moses of the Levitical Priestly genealogy. The placement of the genealogy here authenticates Moses' Israelite (and not Egyptian or Midianite), Levitical Priestly origin. It perhaps counters any doubts cast on the legitimacy and effectiveness of his leadership.

The genealogy is extremely abbreviated. Levi's son Kohath is named in Jacob's genealogy (Gen 46:11). The text makes it clear that Amram and Jochebed were Moses' parents (not ancestors). Moses is 80 years old at the time of his commission (Exod 7:7), and the Israelites lived in Egypt for 430 years (12:40-41). If we allow age 40 as the age when a Hebrew man typically married and had children (see Isaac in Gen 25:20-21, Esau in Gen 26:34-35, and Moses in Exod 2:21-22), then there are approximately nine generations from the time of Kohath to Moses. The text abbreviates those generations.

The names do not indicate successive generations. Rather, the genealogy provides Aaron's tribe (Levi, one of three named in 6:14-16), Aaron's clan (Kohath, one of three named in vv 17-19), Aaron's families (vv 20-25). In this way, the genealogy focuses on the tribe of Levi and, in particular, on the Aaronides. No doubt, the genealogy anticipates or reflects the elevated status of the Levites (32:26-29; Num 3:12-51), the distinguished priesthood of Aaronides, and the preeminent high priesthood of Aaron (Exod 28; Lev 9; Num 3:1-10). The genealogy ends with Aaron's grandson Phinehas, which may testify to its early date (the wilderness period).

Similar to the previous unit, this unit ends with Moses' self-doubt and rejection as one speaking with "faltering lips" (Exod 6:30).

IN THE TEXT

(1) Introduction and Aaron's Tribe (6:13-16)

■ **13** This introduction to the genealogy briefly summarizes the preceding narratives of Yahweh's self-revelation and Moses' call and mission (3:1—6:12).

■ **14** Verses 14-16 name Aaron's tribe, Levi. **Their families** is literally *the house of their fathers*. The referent of the possessive "their" is Moses and Aaron. The term "house" may refer to a tribe, a clan, or a family. Here, it refers to the tribe, a unit made up of **clans**.

In order for readers not to mistake Levi as the firstborn, his elder brothers (Reuben and Simeon) are mentioned before him in order of seniority, as found in Gen 46:8-11. This way of presenting Levi's tribe underscores the fact that the "house" of Levi belongs to a nation, descending from one single ancestor.

■ **15** The acknowledgment of Simeon's intermarriage with a Canaanite woman in the genealogy here (also Gen 46:8) most likely reflects a measure of esteem (see the foreign women honored in the genealogy of Jesus in Matt 1:1 ff.) rather than disfavor as in the patriarchal narratives (Gen 24:3; 26:34-35; 27:46; 28:1, 6, 8; 38:2). The disapproved Canaanite wife of Judah (Gen 38:2) is omitted in Jacob's genealogy in Gen 46:8, which creates a stark contrast with those who are included. Honor is undoubtedly what is intended with the inclusion of the two other women in this genealogy: Jochebed, the mother of Aaron and Moses (Exod 6:20), and Elisheba, Aaron's wife (v 23).

■ **16** The sons of **Levi** are **Gershon** ("exiled one"), **Kohath** ("assembly"), and **Merari** ("bitterness"). Their inclusion in Jacob's more complete genealogy in Gen 46:11 suggests that they are literal sons (not descendants) of Levi. They were the heads of the Levitical clans who served in the tent of meeting. The members of those clans and their duties are listed in Num 3:17-39 and 4:4-33.

Unlike most other people listed in the genealogy, Levi's years are counted (**137 years**) because Aaron and Moses directly descend from him. Kohath's and Amram's years (133 and 137 years respectively) are also listed for the same reason (Exod 6:18 and 20). The remarkable longevity of the fathers (in comparison to 70 or 80 years noted in Ps 90:10) would partly explain the astonishing proliferation of the Israelites noted in Exod 1.

(2) Aaron's Clan (6:17-19)

■ **17-19** Verses 17-19 focus on the three Levitical **clans, Gershon, Kohath** (v 18), which is Aaron's clan, and **Merari** (v 19). Their **sons** are named; however, given the abbreviated nature of the genealogy, the term **sons** in vv 17-19 are best interpreted as descendants.

One of the descendants of **Kohath** is **Amram**, who is identified as Aaron and Moses' father (v 20). There is a huge gap from the generation that migrated into Egypt (Kohath) to the generation of oppression (Amram and all the other **sons** named in vv 17-19).

(3) Aaron's Families (6:20-25)

■ **20** Verses 20-22 name Aaron's parents' children as well as Aaron's uncles' children. **Amram** ("exalted people") and **Jochebed** (*yôkebed*; "Yahweh is glory") are named as Aaron and Moses' parents. Jochebed is identified as Amram's **father's sister** (*dôdâ*; "aunt" elsewhere refers to the wife of a "father's brother" [Lev 18:14] or "uncle's wife" [Lev 20:20 ESV, NJPS, NRSV]). Since the generations between Kohath and Amram are left out from the genealogy,

6:15-20

Amram's *dôdâ* is not Kohath's sister, who is long dead, but Amram's unlisted father's sister. Consanguineous marriage is prohibited in Lev 18:12, 14 and 20:19. Since this marriage precedes the Mosaic law, however, their marriage did not violate any covenant stipulations. Jochebed is the first name in the Bible to appear with a shortened form of the divine name Yahweh (*yô-*).

Since **Aaron** is older than **Moses**, Aaron is listed first in the genealogy. This list reverses the usual order of the names ("Moses and Aaron" [Exod 4:29; 5:1, 4, 20]) in the narrative, which reflects the spiritual and functional superiority of Moses over Aaron.

■ **21-22** Uzziel's sons **Mishael** ("who is what God is") and **Elzaphan** ("God has protected") are noted in Lev 10:4 for carrying out the body of Nadab and Abihu (Aaron's sons) from the sanctuary.

■ **23** This verse names Aaron's nuclear family. Aaron's wife is a prominent Judahite woman **Elisheba** ("my God is an oath"), **daughter of Amminadab** ("my people are noble") and **sister of Nahshon** (probably "enchanter"). Nahshon was the commanding leader of the tribe of Judah (Num 2:3). He was the ancestor of King David and appears in the genealogy of Jesus Christ (Matt 1:4). Elisheba's four sons are named. In the covenant-making narrative, **Nadab** ("noble") and **Abihu** ("my father is he" or "he is [like] my father") are named along with Moses and Aaron as prominent leaders who had the privilege of seeing God on Mount Sinai (Exod 24:1, 9). All four sons were ordained as priests (28:1 ff.). Nadab and Abihu, however, offered an "unauthorized fire" at the tabernacle and were executed by the Lord (Lev 10:1 ff.). They apparently died childless and **Eleazar** ("God has helped") and **Ithamar** ("land of palms") continued the priestly line (Num 3:4).

■ **24** This verse names Korah's nuclear family. **Korah** ("bald") was Aaron's cousin and rival and just as distinguished as Aaron and Moses in his genealogical lineage. However, Korah led a large-scale revolt against Moses and Aaron and was destroyed by Yahweh, along with all his rebels (Num 16). The sons of Korah—**Assir** ("prisoner"), **Elkanah** ("God has redeemed/possessed"), and **Abiasaph** ("my father has gathered")—presumably did not participate in that insurrection and did not die (Num 26:11). King David employed the **Korahites** as temple musicians who ministered with music before the tabernacle (1 Chr 6:32 [17 HB]; also see 1 Chr 6:33-38 [18-23 HB]; 2 Chr 20:19). Accordingly, many psalms are attributed to them (Pss 42; 44—49; 84; 85; 87; 88). The Korahites also served as guards of "the thresholds of the tent" (1 Chr 9:19), managers of the storehouses, and gatekeepers (1 Chr 26:1-20).

■ **25** This verse names Aaron's son's family. This verse highlights **Eleazar** and his son, probably because the high priesthood was passed down to Eleazar and to his line (→ Exod 28:1 and on 29:29-30). **Putiel** is not mentioned elsewhere in the Bible, but the text seems to assume that he was well known. The name is a mixture of Egyptian and Hebrew, meaning "the one whom God gave" (see the Egyptian name Potiphera, meaning "the one whom the Re gave" [Gen 41:45]). **Phinehas** is Egyptian, meaning "the dark-skinned one." By demonstrating uncompromising zeal for Yahweh, Phinehas and his descendants were rewarded with a covenant of a permanent priesthood (Num 25:1-18).

Exodus 6:25 ends with the indicator that **the heads of the Levite families** are now named.

(4) Summary and Moses' Discouragement (6:26-30)

■ **26-27** This editorial-concluding summary confirms that **this Aaron and Moses** whom Yahweh sent to **Egypt** were the **same** Aaron and Moses found in the genealogy of Levi.

The term **divisions** (Heb. "army, hosts") is a military term employed for organizing the **Israelites** into military regiments for an orderly departure from Egypt (12:41, 51), an encampment in the wilderness (Num 1:52), and a military march to the land of Canaan (Num 10:28). Thus, the translation "armies" (KJV, NJB) or "troop by troop" (NJPS) is preferable.

■ **28-29** In Exod 6:28-30, the narrative resumes with an exchange between Yahweh and **Moses**, which might be a recapitulation of the previous conversation in vv 10-12 (where the narrative ends before the genealogy). Despite Pharaoh's previous rejection of Yahweh's words, Yahweh here commands Moses to deliver the message to Pharaoh. Yahweh acts as if his words will have an impact on Pharaoh.

■ **30** Whether or not a new conversation, this unit ends with Moses' doubts based on his lack of fluency, eloquence, and persuasiveness (originally mentioned in 4:10 and revisited in 6:10-12). As far as Moses is concerned, it is a futile mission with a guaranteed disastrous outcome. Moses' deep-seated self-doubt is finally overcome in the next unit with his recommissioning.

FROM THE TEXT

Biblical genealogies resist our individualism and remind us of God's purposes for the corporate people of God. In our individualistic contemporary world, we often struggle to find the significance of biblical genealogies. Why are these texts in the inspired Scripture? What is their abiding significance? The answer to these questions can be found in the concept of "corporate solidarity" in the Bible. Specifically, God calls individuals to have solidarity with the particular family lines that he has chosen and blessed. That is, God does not view individual Israelites as a set of separate individuals but as people whose identities and destinies are constituted by their relationships with one another and with their ancestors. In this genealogy, particular attention is given to tracing the origin of Aaron and Moses within the Levitical line. Establishing their ancestry legitimizes their origins, calling, and leadership. In the wider context of the book of Exodus, their Levitical lineage in part authenticates the various roles they fulfill and in turn foreshadows the election and consecration of the Aaronides as priests.

The NT also includes genealogies (e.g., Matt 1:1-17; Luke 3:23-38). Just as Israelite genealogy bolstered the authority of Aaron and Moses, these NT genealogies validate Jesus as standing in the line of promise that extends from Adam to Abraham to David. Jesus Christ is who he says he is, for he is not an impostor.

The biblical genealogies also play important roles for those who are adopted into the spiritual family of Jesus Christ (Rom 8:15-16). Without need for lineage by blood, God is our heavenly Father (Matt 6:9), Jesus is our eldest Brother (Rom 8:29), and Abraham is our spiritual father (Gal 3:29; 4:28-31). Therefore, the genealogies of the Bible remind us of our membership in a spiritual family that extends through the millennia and across the continents. Grasping this corporate reality of our identity helps to overcome the individualism that is endemic in Western cultures today. We are who we are not as individuals in isolated relationships with God. Rather, our individual identity is intricately related to and derives from the multigenerational, multiethnic, and multicultural body of Christ, the church, which is grafted into Israel (see Rom 11:17-24).

Correct understanding of our spiritual roots and lineage also helps to overcome sectarianism and promote unity and solidarity with other spiritual "tribes" belonging to the same family of Jesus Christ. As with the Israelite tribes, clans, and families, our destiny is inextricably linked with the destiny of others. We are equipped and empowered by God to fulfill our Christian calling, not apart from other Christians, but with them and through them. Therefore, we are called to mutually honor and love all brothers and sisters of various traditions within the body of Christ.

c. The Recommission (7:1-13)

(1) Recommissioning of the Leaders (7:1-7)

BEHIND THE TEXT

After reluctantly accepting Yahweh's call, Moses continually questioned his call, unable to overcome his self-doubt (6:12, 30). Here, Yahweh completely halts Moses' disputes through a recommissioning, giving a higher authority than before (7:1-7). The recommissioning likely involves not just Yahweh's reassuring words but also Yahweh's Spirit that renews and strengthens Moses' heart (see 1 Sam 10:6, 9; 11:6 for the Spirit of God changing Saul's heart from timid to fearless). Moses evidently remains trusting and faithful throughout the plague narratives, the point of which is summarized in Exod 7:6-7.

Yahweh's words of reassurance consist of the following: Moses will now confront Pharaoh's illegitimate power over Israel with his divinely renewed authority over Pharaoh (7:1) through Aaron, who will be Moses' prophet (vv 1-2); Yahweh will use the hardness of Pharaoh's heart to multiply acts of judgment and deliver the Israelites out of Egypt (vv 3-4); through these events, Egyptians will acknowledge the supremacy of Yahweh (v 5).

The subunit ends with a summary statement of Moses and Aaron's obedience and a report of their ages at the time of their recommissioning (vv 6-7).

IN THE TEXT

(a) Yahweh's Reassurance to Moses (7:1-5)

■ **1-2** In vv 1-2, Yahweh promotes both Moses and Aaron. In v 1, Yahweh responds to Moses' self-rejection and dejection (see 6:12, 30) and elevates his status. Earlier, Moses was to be like a god to Aaron (4:16), but now, Moses is **made . . . like God** even **to Pharaoh** (7:1). With divine authority and power over the king of Egypt, Moses will issue commands to Pharaoh. Some interpret the Hebrew term for God (*'ĕlōhîm*) used here as referring to a human judge acting on Yahweh's behalf (also in 21:6; 22:8-9 [7-8 HB]; to human kings as God's representatives in Pss 45:6 [7 HB]; 82:6). But *'ĕlōhîm* as God best fits both the literary and theological contexts (→ the translation of *'ĕlōhîm* into "judges" in Exod 21:6).

In harmony with the elevation of Moses, Aaron—earlier appointed Moses' **prophet** (*nābî'*) to their own people—is now commissioned to be Moses' prophet to **Pharaoh**. A prophet is one who speaks for God and represents God. Aaron is given that function in 7:1-2; Yahweh speaks to Moses; Moses speaks to Aaron; Aaron speaks to Pharaoh.

■ **3** In v 3, Yahweh gives a strong warning against any optimism for quick results. On two occasions, in 4:21 and here in 7:3, Yahweh informs Moses that he will harden Pharaoh's heart. Accordingly, the motif of Pharaoh's stubborn heart is found with each plague. The text does not present Yahweh as hardening Pharaoh apart from or in contradiction to Pharaoh's own will and character. Instead, Yahweh is only said to harden Pharaoh's heart (in the sixth and eighth through tenth plagues, Red Sea) that is already proven to be incorrigibly stubborn and self-hardening (in the first to fifth and seventh plagues).

■ **4** Yahweh also warns Moses that despite numerous "signs and wonders" (v 3), Pharaoh **will not listen** to him (v 4). What prompts Yahweh to act in judgment against Egypt and Pharaoh is Pharaoh's resolute stubborn resistance to Yahweh's demand. Through **mighty acts of judgment**, Yahweh promises to lead Israel out of Egypt (→ 6:6-8).

■ **5** Verse 5 states the twofold purpose of Yahweh's mighty acts. (1) **The Egyptians will know** that he is **Yahweh**; they will experience and acknowledge

Yahweh's supreme authority and power over all creation and all nations. (2) Israel will experience deliverance from Egypt. He will indeed **bring** his people **out** from the land of their slavery and bondage (vv 4-5). Israel will know (experience and acknowledge) Yahweh as a delivering God.

(b) The Leaders' Obedience and Age (7:6-7)

■ **6** Verse 6 represents an editorial summary of the plague narrative that is about to begin. **Moses and Aaron** act on divine initiative and successfully complete their mission.

■ **7** Moses and Aaron begin their mission at an age that comes at the end of a long lifespan (Ps 90:10; Isa 23:15), and astonishingly they live for some 40 more years (Num 33:39; Deut 34:7). Moses apparently maintained visual acuity, mental faculties, and physical vitality until the time of his death at age 120 (Deut 34:7). Other leaders of Israel known to have lived long are Caleb, who at age 85 boasted of his vitality and vigor (Josh 14:10-11), and Joshua, who presumably remained youthful like Caleb and lived to age 110 (Josh 24:29).

FROM THE TEXT

The texts in which God hardens Pharaoh's heart indicate a divine confirmation of prior human sinfulness, not an arbitrary instigation of sinful actions. The motif of hardening Pharaoh's heart begs for further reflection as it can raise the suspicion that all human resistance to God is generally divinely willed and caused. Yahweh's predictions of his own hardening action in 4:21 and 7:2-4 do not indicate when the divine act of hardening occurred. Only later texts shed light on the question of whether it preceded or followed Pharaoh's hardening of his own heart.

Upon closer analysis, it appears that the condition of Pharaoh's heart is described by three separate phases. In the beginning of the plague narrative, the text simply describes Pharaoh's heart as being hardened, resolute, and unyielding, without saying who hardened it (7:13, 14, 22, 23; 8:19 [15 HB]; 9:7). In this way, Pharaoh's character is portrayed from ch 5 and onward as already set in stone, presumably due to his arrogance, status, and power. In the middle (mostly in the second through seventh plagues), Pharaoh is said to willfully harden his own heart (8:15, 32 [11, 28 HB]; 9:34-35), making it increasingly calloused against severer plagues. In the last phase (sixth, eighth through tenth, the Red Sea), God is described as hardening Pharaoh's heart (9:12; 10:1, 20, 27; 11:10; 14:4, 8, 17). If there is any danger of Pharaoh's will weakening due to the severest of punishments, Yahweh hardens Pharaoh's heart to ensure his continued resistance until the complete fulfillment of God's divine purposes.

In his comment on 4:21 in his notes on the Bible, John Wesley says that it is as if God is saying, "I will harden his heart—After [Pharaoh] has frequently hardened it himself, willfully shutting his eyes against the light, I will at last permit Satan to harden it effectually" (*Wesley's Notes on the Bible*, Wesley Center Online). The text of Exodus does not clarify whether Satan is involved but does confirm Wesley's view that it is only after Pharaoh hardened his own heart that God hardened it. Although the text does not resolve the mystery of the relationship between divine sovereignty and human responsibility, God's eventual hardening of Pharaoh can be understood as a form of wrath or judgment in which God gave him over to his own sinful tendencies, which, in turn, led to his destruction (as with all humanity in Rom 1:24, 26, 28). Careful study of Exodus underlines that Pharaoh was responsible for his own sinful actions, a point that the Wesleyan tradition has consistently stressed in the treatment of humanity's relationship with God.

Of course, not every Bible scholar agrees with this interpretation. Hamilton claims that in 7:13 and 7:22 Yahweh hardened Pharaoh's heart as predicted earlier, even before Pharaoh is said to harden his own heart in ch 8 (2011, 87). But since the text clearly names God as the subject of the verb "to harden" when it is God who hardened Pharaoh's heart, the texts in ch 7 are better interpreted as saying that Pharaoh was being unyielding because he already was arrogant and stubborn.

Regardless of whether one is Calvinistic/Reformed or Arminian/Wesleyan in forming a theological interpretation of the text, both sides agree that Pharaoh's story provides an instructive paradigm for the hardness of the sinful human heart that, apart from God's grace, afflicts all humanity. Accordingly, the incorrigibly stubborn heart is not a condition unique to Pharaoh and his officials. Despite the numerous experiences of Yahweh's supernatural power and mercy, the Israelites hardened their hearts on countless occasions in the wilderness. Not only that, in their persistent rebellion, the Israelites ultimately rejected Yahweh, most notably in creating the golden calf at Sinai (ch 32) and in the rebellion at Kadesh (Num 14), which brought Yahweh's judgment on them.

Later biblical texts also mention the hardening of the human heart, some explicitly attributing it to God (e.g., Isa 63:17; John 12:40; Rom 9:18) while others do not (Rom 11:7, 25; see Isa 6:8-10; Mark 4:10-12; Luke 8:9-10; 2 Cor 3:14). A closer look at each of these cases reveals that the hardening of Israel resulted from Israel's persistent resistance to God, which yielded Yahweh's withdrawal of favor (or exile or temporary rejection), producing, in turn, a growing stubbornness.

The examples of Pharaoh and the Israelites (in the exodus, the exile, and in Jesus' day) give us a strong warning not to harden our own hearts (1 Sam 6:6; Ps 95:8). As the author of Hebrews admonishes: "Today, if you hear his voice, do not harden your hearts as you did in the rebellion" (Heb 3:15; 4:7). This admonition warns of the possibility of God rejecting rebellious Christians. More positively, it indicates that even if we do have a "hard" heart (whatever the root cause), we can choose to submit to God and avert severe divine judgment (even as the Philistine lords chose to do, surprisingly enough [1 Sam 6:6]). We must choose to bend our will to that of Yahweh, not only when chastised (like Pharaoh under the plagues) but also ideally even in the absence of such discipline or judgment.

(2) The Leaders' Authority over Pharaoh (7:8-13)

BEHIND THE TEXT

Having been recommissioned and encouraged by Yahweh, the leaders begin the demonstration of Yahweh's power. Earlier, Moses and Aaron performed signs before the elders of Israel to prove that Yahweh sent them (4:29-31). Now, they perform a sign before Pharaoh and his officials (7:8-10) to show they are not simply exaggerating as Pharaoh had charged earlier (5:9). The impressive signs, however, do not move Pharaoh's stubborn heart. Yet the signs speak for themselves that the authorized representatives of Yahweh have authority over Pharaoh and any false gods believed to protect his throne.

IN THE TEXT

(a) A Sign for Pharaoh (7:8-10)

■ **8-9** Yahweh tells **Moses and Aaron** in vv 8-9 what to do before **Pharaoh**; he anticipates that Pharaoh will test the power and authority of Yahweh; he will ask Moses and Aaron to **perform a miracle** in order to test Yahweh's power and authority and thereby the power of his spokespersons. Yahweh initially gave the sign of the staff to Moses (4:3-4) who was then commanded to perform the sign (4:17). However, since Aaron is appointed Moses' prophet to Pharaoh, to speak and act on Moses' behalf, Aaron is to perform the signs before Pharaoh and the Egyptians.

■ **10** Verse 10 reports the response of Moses and Aaron. Aaron performs the first sign before Pharaoh. According to Yahweh's words (7:9), Aaron's **staff** becomes **a snake**. The Hebrew term for **snake** here (also in vv 10 and 12) is *tannîn* rather than the usual term for snake (*nāḥāš*) used in 4:3. The word *tannîn* is variously translated into "serpent," "monster," or "great sea creature" elsewhere in the NIV (e.g., Deut 32:33; Job 7:12; and Ps 148:7 respectively). While this word may suggest a greater miracle occurring here than in the Exod 4:3 episode, both terms, more plausibly, refer to a cobra (→ 4:3), the symbolic protector of the Egyptian monarchy. The Egyptian magicians' rods also become snakes (*tannînim* [7:12]), making the comparison and contest between the snake (*tannîn*) of Aaron and the snakes (*tannînim*) of the magicians (rather than the comparison between *nāḥāš* and *tannîn*) the focal point here.

(b) The Counterfeit and the Second Sign (7:11-12)

■ **11** In v 11, Pharaoh responds to the power of Yahweh demonstrated by Moses and Aaron. Instead of acknowledging Yahweh's power and yielding to his demand, Pharaoh attempts to counter Yahweh's power by **secret arts** performed by the top **Egyptian** religious personnel (**wise men, sorcerers, magicians**). The Egyptian **magicians** were diviner priests and learned scribes, "whose skills included expertise in magic and dream interpretation" (Sarna 2004, 29). *Targum Pseudo-Jonathan* on the Pentateuch names the magicians as Janis (Jannes [NIV]) and Jambres (2 Tim 3:8 also makes an allusion to them as ones who opposed Moses). The contest between Yahweh's two prophets and all of Pharaoh's servants recalls the story of Joseph and anticipates that of Daniel, both of whom had true revelation and understanding from Yahweh and prevailed over all the sages, astrologers, sorcerers, and magicians of Egypt and Babylonia respectively. The secret arts may have included a trick that Egyptian snake charmers today still use, namely, temporarily paralyzing the serpent and turning it into a rodlike state and then reviving it. Yahweh sends his spokespersons to perform miracles; Pharaoh summons his religious personnel to perform secret arts that have the semblance of a miracle. There is a contest between Yahweh and Pharaoh, between the God of the oppressed and Pharaoh the oppressor. However, Yahweh's unmatched power will soon shatter the notion that a human ruler can contest his Creator.

■ **12** Verse 12 reports the success and defeat of Pharaoh's magicians. **Aaron's staff** (apparently acting on its own) swallows up **their staffs**—a clear indication that Aaron is not using secret arts as the magicians are. This second sign signifies Yahweh's superiority and ultimate victory over Pharaoh. Yahweh will render all Egyptian gods/goddesses utterly powerless (→ 12:12).

(c) Pharaoh's Defiance (7:13)

■ **13** As Yahweh anticipated and warned Moses and Aaron, this ominous sign makes little impression on the proud and stubborn heart of Pharaoh. The king of Egypt **would not listen to them** and launches a titanic struggle: Yahweh versus Pharaoh and all his gods (12:12).

FROM THE TEXT

Despite the ongoing presence of counterfeits and false gods, God will one day be vindicated as the only God worthy of worship and allegiance. In today's world, we face both genuine signs of God's presence and work and deceptive counterfeits. Sometimes, the counterfeits are the cheap equivalent of the magicians' tricks described in this text, while at other times they are more subtle and profound. Although it is not always easy to discern truth in the present moment, the Bible testifies that the time will come when the overwhelming superiority of the one true God over all other gods will be revealed. God's superiority is one of the main points of the first half of Exodus and also a key theme of the NT. As anticipated by the resurrection of Jesus Christ, God will one day act in judgment and glorious self-revelation that will undercut and expose the claims of all would-be gods. This action will cause "every tongue" to confess and "every knee" to bow, whether joyfully or grudgingly, in recognition of the lordship of Jesus and his Father (Phil 2:10-11; see Isa 45:23; Rom 14:11). All people will come to know, in the words of Exodus, that "I am Yahweh!"

C. The Mighty Acts of Judgment and the Exodus (7:14—15:21)

Overview

Yahweh responds to Pharaoh's stubbornness with "mighty acts of judgment" (7:4) and delivers his people out of Egypt. This judgment and deliverance narrative starts with the plagues and ends with the destruction of the entire Egyptian military at the Red Sea (13:17—15:21).

The judgment of Egypt and the deliverance of the Israelites serve as Yahweh's legal actions, as a righteous Judge, against Pharaoh and Egypt. Yahweh judges the Egyptians for their inhumane treatment of the Israelites and for contesting Yahweh's legal right over Israel. Yahweh judges and overcomes the proud ruler and powerful nation and delivers the Israelite people from bondage. During the long process of humbling Pharaoh with the plagues, Yahweh's promise to Abraham—"I will punish the nation they serve as slaves, and afterward they will come out with great possessions" (Gen 15:14)—gives the Israelites assurance of the favorable final outcome. Abraham and Sarah's own history of temporary settlement in Egypt, the near jeopardy of Yahweh's promises, Yahweh's intervention through punishment of the pharaoh's house, their departure from Egypt with increased wealth, and their reentry into the land of Canaan also foreshadow and anticipate Israel's own Exodus with great wealth and entry into and occupation of the promised land.

This section consists of three subsections: the nine plagues (7:14—10:29), the exodus from Egypt after the tenth plague and the Passover (11:1—13:16), the final act of judgment of the Egyptians and the deliverance of the Israelites at the Red Sea (13:17—15:21). After this section, the Israelites become completely free from Egyptian bondage and oppression, ready for their new life with Yahweh.

1. The Nine Plagues (7:14—10:29)

Overview

The literary structure of the plague narrative is noteworthy. The phrase "The LORD said to Moses" heads the narrative of each plague (7:14; 8:1, 16, 20 [7:14, 26; 8:12, 16 HB]; 9:1, 8, 13; 10:1, 21; 11:1). In addition, the plague narrative is structured with elaborate symmetry (Sarna 2004, 30). The first nine plagues form three triads, each triad having a symmetrical structure. The first plague of each triad has Yahweh's command to Moses, "Go to Pharaoh in the morning" and to Pharaoh, "Let my people go, so that they may worship me" (first plague [7:15-16]; fourth [8:20 (16 HB)]; and seventh [9:13]). The second plague of each triad has the same command to Pharaoh as the first plague of the triad, plus an additional threat of the impending plague in the event of Pharaoh's refusal: e.g., "If you refuse to let them go" followed by the announcement of the consequential punitive act of Yahweh (second [8:1-2 (7:26-27 HB)]; fifth [9:1-3]; eighth [10:3-4]). The third plague of each triad lacks any direct confrontation of Pharaoh. Yahweh commands Aaron or Moses to perform the sign without giving any warning to Pharaoh (third [8:16 (12 HB)]; sixth [9:8]; ninth [10:21]). Its description is also brief.

Furthermore, the first triad has Yahweh commanding Moses, "Tell Aaron," and Aaron carrying out the divine act of judgment (7:19-20; 8:5-6, 16-17 [1-2, 12-13 HB]). In the second triad, Yahweh directly executes the first two (8:24 [20 HB]; 9:6) and Moses performs the third (9:10), effectively transitioning from the ruling pair, Aaron and Moses, to Moses no longer depending on Aaron. In the last triad, Moses addresses Pharaoh directly and performs all three acts of judgment (9:23; 10:13, 22). Yahweh, of course, carries out the last act or the tenth plague.

Thematic inclusion is also evident. The first and last plagues involve blood. The first plague indicts Egypt's bloodguilt for murdering Hebrew babies and the last extracts blood payment for the same crime.

There are four stated purposes of the plagues: (1) to judge and punish Egypt for the Israelites' enslavement and murder (e.g., Gen 15:14; Exod 6:6; 7:4); (2) to break down Pharaoh's arrogant resistance to Yahweh and self-claimed divine status by exposing the Egyptian gods' impotence (e.g., 12:12; Num 33:4; Ps 82:1); (3) to deliver the Israelites out of Egypt (e.g., Gen 15:14-15; Exod 7:2, 4); and (4) to make known that Yahweh is the supreme God to all relevant parties—Moses, the Israelites, Pharaoh, the Egyptians, and other peoples of the present and future generations (6:9; 7:17; 8:10 [6 HB]; 9:14). The first three purposes serve the supreme fourth purpose, the self-revelation of Yahweh by which Yahweh is glorified.

Accordingly, the ten plagues address the all-important theological question, "Who is Yahweh?" Although this question is Pharaoh's defiant retort to Moses in Exod 5, God answers the question for the benefit of all. Each plague comes with specific self-revelation of who Yahweh is, summarized as follows: Yahweh is the Redeemer of the Israelites and their only God (6:7; see 16:6, 12; 20:1; 29:44-46); Yahweh is supreme (7:5, 17; 10:2; see 14:4, 18); Yahweh is matchless, unequaled, and unique (8:10 [6 HB]; 9:14; see 15:11-16 and 18:11);

Yahweh is sovereign over Egypt, the earth, and all creation (8:22 [18 HB]; 9:29; 10:13-15, 21-23); Yahweh alone is God, thus judging all false gods and false religion (12:12); and Yahweh distinguishes Israel from Egypt and other nations, for he alone delivers his people (7:5; 8:23 [19 HB]; 11:7). The ultimate purpose of the knowledge of Yahweh is the exclusive service, obedience, and worship of Yahweh, not only for the Israelites but also for the Egyptians and all other people.

Plagues and the Ipuwer Papyrus

Some scholars have noted possible parallels between the account of the ten plagues and portions of the Ipuwer Papyrus that contain poems. The dating of the original composition is debated, but the extant copies of the Ipuwer Papyrus date to the thirteenth century BC. The content appears to lament multiple events perhaps from many centuries, rather than a single event, such as the collapse of the Old Kingdom and the threats of the Asiatics within the Delta. The content appears to lament events that are already familiar to those of Ipuwer's time through oral or scribal traditions. Some of the lines lament the entire land of Egypt becoming like desert and "barbarians from abroad" coming to Egypt when Egypt is entirely desert (3, 1), foreigners taking over Egypt (4, 1), the land being "deprived of the kingship by a few lawless men" (7, 4), and "the tribe of desert" becoming "Egyptians everywhere" (1, 9). These lines seem to parallel the migration of Jacob's clan during the great famine in Egypt and their eventual domination of the Delta. Further, other poetic lines seem to parallel the language or themes of the plague narrative: for example, "the river" that "is blood and pestilence is throughout the land, blood is everywhere, death is not lacking" (2, 3); "the river is blood" and men "thirst after water" (2, 9); the servants are plundering the masters (1, 1); "towns are destroyed and the Upper Egypt has become an empty waste" (2, 11). Although most Egyptologists regard it as unlikely that both the biblical narrative and the Ipuwer Papyrus refer to the same historical event, there are no compelling reasons for their position. Some of the lines in the papyrus appear to use language drawn from the Egyptian cultural memory of the events of the plagues and the Israelite Exodus (somewhat comparable to the Song of Moses in 15:1-18).

Some suggest that the first six plagues involve a "domino effect" in which one seamlessly leads to the next. But purely naturalistic explanations and the domino-effect view are not ultimately tenable (→ Behind the Text sections below). Many hold the view that the first nine plagues are extreme (perhaps divinely intensified) natural phenomena known to happen in the region. Although there are some intensified natural phenomena and natural processes of cause and effect involved in the plagues, the texts focus on "the supernatural and not the natural and the 'normal'" (Provan, Long, Longman 2003, 128).

The ten plagues come as diseases or disasters that strike Egypt over a period of about a year. Psalms 78:43-51 and 105:27-36 give abbreviated versions with different contents, numbers, and orders of the plagues, perhaps taking poetic license.

a. The First Plague: Blood (7:14-25)

BEHIND THE TEXT

The unit 7:14-25 represents the first of three triads of plagues. Consistent with the pattern, it begins with Yahweh's command to Moses, "Go to Pharaoh in the morning . . . say to him, '. . . Let my people go, so that they may worship me'" (vv 15-16). Unlike the warning sign (of the serpent) previously given, the plague is a punishment from Yahweh and brings an adverse effect on all of Egypt.

The proponents of the natural explanation for the plagues see this first plague as one caused by an extreme flooding of the Nile during its annual flood season (beginning in June and peaking in September) with an excessive amount of red sediment from the mountains to the south turning it deep red like blood. They hold that large quantities of sediments and algae and/or bacteria washed down from the mountains decreased oxygen levels, eventually killing fish and producing a foul stench.

However, the ancient Egyptians called the river Ar (meaning "black"), due to the rich black silt the annual inundation brought to the Nile Valley (known as "the black land"). This makes the "bloody" red sediment theory unlikely. The theories about the red sediments from either the Blue Nile that originates in Ethiopia or the White Nile that originates from Rwanda are highly speculative. Furthermore, the Egyptian annual Nile flooding was an important natural cycle, which fertilized the farming land (until 1970, when the High Dam at Aswan put to an end to the annual flooding of the Nile). Without the annual flooding of the Nile, there would have been famine. If the first plague was a mere intensification of the much-needed and celebrated annual flooding of the Nile, it would have hardly been perceived as an act of judgment or an ominous sign from the God of creation. I suggest that, just like the last plague, this first plague was wholly supernatural, completely beyond natural explanation.

IN THE TEXT

■ **14** Verse 14 announces the reason for the first plague. Like all the plagues, this plague account begins with the phrase **the LORD said to Moses**. This repeated phrase, which functions much like a unit heading, underlines how Yahweh initiated each plague, rather than the notion that nature took its natural course. The diagnosis that **Pharaoh's heart is unyielding** is foreseen and is not a surprise. Pharaoh's blatant refusal to comply (**he refuses** [v 14]; "you have not listened" [v 16]) serves as a just occasion for Yahweh to begin acts of judgment. In this way, Pharaoh is encouraged to make the connection between his noncompliance and the plagues. The Egyptians are judged not only for their past cruelty and ongoing oppression but also for their leader's present resistance to Yahweh.

■ 15 In vv 15-19, Yahweh commands Moses to **confront** Pharaoh and announce the plague as Yahweh's judgment intended to compel Pharaoh to acknowledge Yahweh. Yahweh sends Moses and Aaron to meet Pharaoh **as he goes out to the river**; the fourth plague also mentions the river as the place of confrontation. Water is an important commodity and the source of life for Egyptians. Some speculate that Pharaoh went out to the river to check the water level during the seasonal floods. Others suggest it was for worship of the deified Nile for its annual inundation, which provided rich fertilization of the farmland. However, since this plague probably did not involve flooding (→ v 25), **morning** bath would be the best explanation.

■ 16 The announcement to Pharaoh in v 16 includes Pharaoh's guilt of resisting Yahweh, **the God of the Hebrews**, whose will for his people is for them to **worship** (*'ābad*, also "serve") him. The Hebrews are not to serve Pharaoh as slaves but to serve Yahweh as his treasured, holy people. However, this idea is preposterous to Pharaoh, who has not **listened** (*šāma'*, also "obey") to Moses thus far.

■ 17 The purpose of this first act of judgment is to make Yahweh's identity known to Pharaoh. The **Nile**, which the **Egyptians** deify as their life source, will turn **into blood**. It will be so when Moses' **staff** strikes **the water**, making it impossible to miss the supernatural nature of the plague.

■ 18 The effects of the plague on **the river** are detrimental. The **fish** [part of their staple food (Num 11:5, 22)] **will die**. The water **will stink**. As such, the plague is a major confrontation with their worship of the **river**. The statement about the water being undrinkable for the **Egyptians** seems to suggest that the Israelites themselves will continue to have clean water.

■ 19 Yahweh instructs Moses to let Aaron perform the sign by taking the **staff** and stretching **out** his hand [→ "hand" in 3:8] **over** the Nile. This verse suggests that *all* **waters of Egypt** in **streams**, **canals**, **ponds**, **reservoirs** (that is, gathered or collected waters), and **vessels of wood and stone** spontaneously changed when Aaron struck the Nile.

■ 20-21 Verses 20-21 describe the plague itself. Moses and Aaron obediently carry out Yahweh's commands, and the **Nile** changes into **blood** and all the devastation follows as foretold. Some scholars insist that the **water** did not actually change **into blood** (no more than the moon became blood in Joel 2:31 [3:4 HB]). According to them, it only appeared to be like blood due to an extreme amount of red silt (see "the water looked red—like blood" owing to the early morning sun in 2 Kgs 3:22). Besides other challenges to a naturalistic explanation (→ Behind the Text above), the following factors support a more literal and supernatural interpretation of the text. (1) The plague takes place the moment Aaron's staff strikes **the water**, not as a gradual increase of red color during a flood season (Exod 7:20). (2) Blood is **everywhere**, even in water containers in Egyptian households (vv 19, 21). (3) In 4:30, Aaron successfully performed a miniature version of this miracle in sight of the Israelite elders. There was neither flooding nor secret arts involved. It was a purely supernatural miracle that inspired faith in the extremely oppressed people. (4) While the literary context and the poetic-prophetic genre justify a figurative interpretation of passages such as Joel 2:31 [3:4 HB] ("The sun will be turned to darkness and the moon to blood"), nothing in the present text demands a nonliteral interpretation. (5) The literal interpretation allows the plague to function as a dramatic act of divine poetic justice. It makes explicit Egypt's bloodguilt, foreshadowing the ultimate punishment by the death of the firstborn of Egypt.

■ **22-23** The **magicians** respond by successfully performing their **secret arts**, perhaps empowered by some demonic supernatural force (vv 22-23). They effectively remove any reason **Pharaoh** had for taking **this to heart**. The end result is that **Pharaoh's heart became hard** (that is, more than it was already), just as predicted (also in 7:13; 8:15, 19 [11, 15 HB]). This report warns the Israelites to neither naively expect Pharaoh's quick surrender nor to lose hope in Yahweh's ultimate victory in the face of Pharaoh's continued resistance.

■ **24** Verse 24 indicates that the plague affected **all the Egyptians** who **dug along the Nile** to get fresh underground **water**, which evidently was not contaminated by either the blood or the dead fish. Although no specific statement is made about Yahweh making a distinction between the Egyptians and the Israelites, it is understood. Presumably, water sources for the Israelites (existing wells, containers, and reservoirs) remained fresh.

■ **25** Verse 25 reports the duration of the plague. The expression *seven days were filled* likely refers to the completion of the plague since the number seven symbolizes completeness. Others suggest that "seven days" mark when the next plague is stated. But this suggestion is unlikely. Given that the blood plague is followed by the plague of frogs (the proliferation of which requires clean water), it is more reasonable to assume that at the end of the blood plague came the annual Nile flooding, which powerfully and completely washed away the blood, the rotting fish, and all the bacteria. The Nile frog's reproductive period (September—October) begins at the end of the flood season (June—September). The unprecedented explosion of the frog population under God's sovereign power perhaps took place when the Nile water returned to its usual

113

health and much of the Nile fish (the predator of tadpoles) were gone. In other words, the second plague almost certainly did not closely follow the first.

FROM THE TEXT

Scholars and church leaders alike must be wary of antisupernaturalism in biblical interpretation, which can undercut the plain meaning of the text. While the scholarly trend is to produce the most convincing naturalistic explanations about this or other plagues, it is important to take literally what the text consciously presents as supernatural miracles. Many use naturalistic explanations as apologetic evidence to support the historicity of the Bible. Yet, rather ironically, such explanations, by creating a vast gap between them and the text, undermine the integrity of the biblical writers and the authority of the Bible. Undoubtedly, Yahweh can and does employ natural events and disasters as judgments, as numerous passages in the Bible clearly attest. Some of the plagues can largely be explained as a massive intensification of known natural phenomena, such as the plagues of frogs and locusts. As such, they still demonstrate Yahweh's matchless, invincible sovereignty. However, recognizing natural elements in the plague is wholly different from establishing naturalistic explanations that do not require God's supernatural power. Such explanations have more to do with an antisupernaturalism rooted in the modern European enlightenment than with a serious attempt to interpret the text on its own terms.

b. The Second Plague: Frogs (8:1-15 [7:26—8:11 HB])

BEHIND THE TEXT

In ancient Egypt, as countless frogs appeared after the annual flood inundation, the Egyptians honored the frog as an emblem of fertility. They worshipped Heqet, the frog-headed goddess of fertility and childbirth. Therefore, the second plague can be seen as Yahweh's confrontation of this goddess along with judgment upon Pharaoh for ordering the midwives to kill the newborn males (1:16).

A common domino-effect interpretation suggests that the second plague closely followed the first, taking 7:25 ("seven days passed") as a time marker indicating when the second plague began. Many hold that the frogs were forced to abandon the Nile because it was contaminated by rotting fish. The frogs then died simultaneously, having been infected by the putrefying fish.

Since the plague does involve frogs, the text begs for some naturalistic explanations. However, the particular explanation above conflicts with textual evidence. (1) The first has to do with *timing*. In the words of Yahweh with which the second plague account begins, the plague of frogs required some time for development: "The Nile *will* teem with frogs. . . . The frogs *will* come up" (8:3-4 [7:28-29 HB]). The language of 8:3 [7:28 HB] suggests a massive multiplication of the frogs in the Nile, placing the second plague at the end of October or early November, well after the flood has subsided. (2) The second textual evidence has to do with *supernatural compelling*: Aaron stretches out his hand with the staff to compel the otherwise unwilling Nile frogs to come up and cover the arid land (8:5-6 [1-2 HB]). Even the magicians use their secret arts to bring them up onto land (8:7 [3 HB]). (3) The third has to do with the remaining *frogs in the Nile*. If the Nile frogs were abandoning the contaminated river en masse, the reference to the frogs remaining in the Nile (vv 7, 9, 11 [3, 5, 7 HB]) makes little sense. (4) Lastly, there is the *supernatural ending* of the plague (→ vv 12-13 [8-9 HB]).

Some naturalistic explanation is necessary, but the supernatural causes are also undeniable. A faithful interpretation must affirm both.

IN THE TEXT

■ **1-2 [7:26-27 HB]** Similar to the first plague, Yahweh instructs **Moses** to issue a command to **Pharaoh** to release Yahweh's **people** (8:1 [7:26 HB]). The warning, **If you refuse . . . , I will send a plague** (8:2 [7:27 HB]), is given to instruct Pharaoh about the connection between the plague's cause (insubordination to Yahweh) and its effect (Yahweh's act of judgment). Through this instructive plague, the frogs are experienced not as signs of fertility and blessing but as cursed pests. The implication is that true blessing and fertility (multiplication) come only from Yahweh, not from false gods or goddesses.

■ **3-4 [7:28-29 HB]** The word "swarm" (8:3 [7:28 HB] ESV, NASB, NET, NRSV) suggests an invasion, not by a usual number of **frogs** but by millions of amphibians newly raised up. The creatures associated with fertility will not only make Egyptian life unbearable but also make fertility impossible by occupying the places of food preparation (**your ovens and kneading troughs**) and intimacy (**your bedroom** and **your bed**). The frog invasion will affect all Egyptians, ordinary people as well as Pharaoh's officials; no one will escape the plague (8:4 [7:29 HB]).

■ **5-6 [8:1-2 HB]** As in the first plague, Yahweh issues a command for Aaron to perform the sign (8:5 [1 HB]). A massive population of frogs has been growing in the **streams and canals and ponds**. An army of frogs is about to be released. The **land** here refers to the more arid area where human beings live, as opposed to the wet Nile riverbanks where the amphibians might naturally and voluntarily go. While the first plague and the subsequent flood of the Nile might have created an optimal breeding environment, the frogs' abandonment of the Nile and invasion of human habitats is entirely supernatural (v 6 [2 HB]).

■ **7 [3 HB]** The Egyptian **magicians** successfully make **frogs come up on the land** through their secret arts but fail to bring an end to the plague by removing the frogs.

■ **8 [4 HB]** Pharaoh's response to the plague indicates his recognition of an ongoing calamity that is threatening Egypt, a problem neither he nor his magicians are able to control or solve. In his appeal to **Moses and Aaron** to **pray** [*ātar*; "to make supplication," "to pray," or "plead"; a word that is always directed to God] **to the** LORD for the removal of the miserable pests, for the first time, Pharaoh implicitly acknowledges Yahweh's existence and power; Yahweh is the originator and eliminator of the plague. Pharaoh makes a sweeping but deceitful promise to release the Israelites.

■ **9 [5 HB]** Moses seems to recognize the authority of Pharaoh by letting him set **the time** for the removal of the frogs. Moses makes a distinction between the **frogs . . . that remain in the Nile** and those that occupy the human habitat. This distinction presents another reason for dissatisfaction with the naturalistic explanation, which requires all frogs to have abandoned the polluted water and then to die en masse of infectious diseases contracted from the putrefying fish.

■ **10-11 [6-7 HB]** Pharaoh loses no time, demanding that the day of deliverance be **tomorrow** (v 10 [6 HB]; *māḥār*)—which shows the urgency of the matter. The term *māḥār* could mean either "tomorrow; the next day" (e.g., 16:23) or "in due time; in the future" (e.g., 13:14). The context seems to call for the former meaning here and throughout the plague narrative (8:23, 29 [19, 25 HB]; 9:5, 18; 10:4). It will be as Pharaoh spoke, assures Moses, but he makes clear that the purpose of the removal of frogs is for Pharaoh to acknowledge that **there is no one like Yahweh our** [Moses, Aaron, and the rest of the Hebrews] **God.** Yahweh is incomparable; no other god of any nation has the power or capacity to do what Yahweh does. In Israel's tradition, **there is no one like the** LORD **our God** is a doxological statement (see similar expressions in 1 Sam 2:2; Ps 113:5; Isa 45:6). Moses' express intent is to give Pharaoh a firsthand experience of this incomparable power of Yahweh and his authority and power over Egypt and its political and religious world. In Exod 8:11 [7 HB], Moses states how Pharaoh will witness the power of Yahweh; he will remove the frogs from **you and your houses, your officials and your people; they will remain** [in their natural habitat] **only in the Nile.**

■ **12 [8 HB]** Verses 12-14 [8-10 HB] report Moses' prayer and the effective removal of frogs from the land. Leaving the palace, **Moses cries out** [*ṣ'aq* is a cry of wailing, desperately or bitterly calling for deliverance from a great trouble or danger (5:15; 14:10; 15:25; 17:4; 22:23, 27 [22, 26 HB])] **to the** LORD. Moses is seemingly desperate for Yahweh to support the promise made to **Pharaoh.**

■ **13 [9 HB]** Yahweh responds to **Moses**' cry for help by delivering what Pharaoh **asked** ("take the frogs away" [8:8 (4 HB)]) at the time Pharaoh himself set ("tomorrow" [v 10 (6 HB)]). Hence, Pharaoh could not mistake the relief as having come merely from nature running its course. Pharaoh witnesses clear evidence of Yahweh's sovereign act in direct response to Moses' intercessory prayer in accordance with Pharaoh's own prayer request (v 8 [4 HB]). Moses also receives a powerful experience of unprecedented favor from Yahweh, who did exactly what Moses asked.

■ **14 [10 HB]** The former plague made the water stink (*bāʾaš*) with dead fish (7:18, 21). Now the **land** reeks (*bāʾaš*) with dead frogs, which are **piled into** countless **heaps** (lit. "heaps, heaps").

■ **15 [11 HB]** **Relief** from the plague is followed not by Pharaoh's show of gratitude and fulfillment of his promise (8:8 [4 HB]) but with further resistance. In the absence of immediate hardship, **Pharaoh** hardens **his heart** again.

FROM THE TEXT

We can affirm the reality of "deceptive miracles" caused by demonic powers while still affirming the absolute supremacy and power of God. Besides the question of whether there are naturalistic explanations for the plagues, another challenging question of interpretation and application is how the Egyptian magicians imitated what Yahweh did. Even as a purely naturalistic explanation of the plagues does not make sense of the text, so also the magicians' acts as some kind of trick makes little sense. Although this approach sometimes is reasonable (e.g., the magicians' acts in 7:11 as a snake handling trick), it is not so for the first two plagues. The magicians' "secret arts" point to the reality of supernatural demonic power that can be associated with false religions and their practitioners. Those familiar with certain non-Christian religions and cults today can attest to this power. The Bible also warns about the possibility of "lying wonders" among false teachers, false prophets, or false messiahs (Deut 13:1-3 [2-4 HB]; Matt 24:24; Mark 13:21; 2 Thess 2:9-11; Rev 13:13-14; 16:14; 19:20). Without denying the power of other religions and their gods (or demons), the Bible, as a whole, urges us to recognize the true God's power as incomparably greater than those counterfeits.

God's demonstration of power intends the response of submission and worship from his creation. Pharaoh seems to show some willingness to concede to God's power and acknowledge God's sovereignty when he asks Moses to pray for him (Exod 8:8 [4 HB]). But when God grants his request, Pharaoh remains stubborn and claims his sovereignty over Egypt. His approach to God in this story may be paradigmatic of human tendency to turn to God for help in times of trouble, but neglect or abandon him when the crisis is over. We, like Pharaoh, make promises only to break them. We, like Pharaoh, maintain our independence and refuse to submit to God's will and authority. We, like Pharaoh, seek God's grace but do not acknowledge his sovereignty over our lives. In the end, the plague narrative shows a Pharaoh who submits to Yahweh's sovereignty, but only after paying the price that is too heavy and painful for himself and Egypt. The text invites our consistent and faithful response to God in all seasons of life.

c. The Third Plague: Gnats (8:16-19 [12-15 HB])

BEHIND THE TEXT

This is the third plague of the first triad; therefore, there is no warning given to Pharaoh. Yahweh simply carries out an act of judgment. The plural *kinnîm* is used only in the context of this plague (here and in Ps 105:31). It cannot be identified with certainty. It is variously translated into "gnats" (LXX, NIV, and most translations), "mosquitoes" (NJB), and "lice" (KJV, NJPS), to name a few. Most commentators treat it as mosquitoes that breed and proliferate quickly in stagnant waters. Such an explanation is attractive, as these insects are common in Egypt in October/November and it fits well with the domino-effect theory of the first six plagues. However, "mosquitoes" are incompatible with the text's own witness. Most notably, the text reports that the "gnats" originate from the dry dust of the ground, where mosquitoes cannot breed.

IN THE TEXT

■ **16-17 [12-13 HB]** Verses 16-19 [12-15 HB] report the plague of gnats and the magicians' recognition of God's power at work in this plague. Aaron, at the instruction of God, performs the sign. He strikes **the dust of the ground** and causes the dust to become **gnats** all over Egypt (v 17 [13 HB]). The expression **all the dust** is obviously a case of hyperbole (→ 9:6); it conveys the overwhelming nature of the plague. Aaron's act may be a prophetic, symbolic act that sets certain insects in motion. Then *kinnîm* may represent some kind of desert-dwelling, reproducing insect that Yahweh causes to increase exponentially, resulting in attacks on both humans and animals. However, the Egyptian magicians' response in 8:19 [15 HB] insists on a supernatural explanation.

■ **18-19 [14-15 HB]** In this plague, the power of the **secret arts** of the magicians reaches its limit; they fail to duplicate the plague (v 18 [14 HB]). Their statement to Pharaoh, **This is the finger of God** (v 19 [15 HB]), conveys their recognition that the source of this plague is the power that belongs to the supreme divine being. They see in this plague a miraculous, supernatural activity. They recognize that the event is well beyond human control or even what their gods could accomplish. They and their gods are no match to Yahweh.

Later, the two stone "tablets of the covenant law" are said to be written by "the finger of God," emphasizing their divine origin (31:18; see Deut 9:10). Despite Yahweh's success and the magician's utter failure, Pharaoh's heart remains unyielding. Victory is sure to come but not just yet.

FROM THE TEXT

The narrative shows that God works in unexpected ways and through unexpected people and even those who oppose God's work will ultimately recognize his work in the world. The Egyptian magicians have reached the limit of the power of their "secret arts"; they acknowledge that only the "finger of God" could have produced the transformation of dust into gnats. They also recognize that the power of God is situated in and among the Hebrews and see it at work in and through Moses and Aaron, members of the despised slave community.

In Jesus' day, by contrast, those who claim to have wisdom and the power of discernment, the Jewish religious leaders, fail to discern God's work done among them by Jesus of Nazareth. They wrongly judge that the devil, Beelzebub, is the source of Jesus' miraculous power to cast out demons (Matt 9:34; 12:24; Mark 3:22; Luke 11:14-15). Jesus answers those undiscerning accusations by identifying the source of his supernatural power as "the finger of God" by which the kingdom of God comes to earth (Luke 11:20).

Like the Jewish leaders in Jesus' day, we often fail to notice and pay attention to God's work in the world because of our strange and peculiar perception of how and when and where God may reveal his power. It is ironic that even in our world, like the magicians in this narrative, those who are outsiders to God's kingdom sometimes notice the power of God. The narrative invites its readers to be attentive to the power God manifests through the least likely people in the least likely corners of the world. Discernment of God's power at work in our midst comes not through religious wisdom and knowledge but through our willingness to see God at work in manifold ways, often through those who are at the margins of life in our world.

d. The Fourth Plague: Flies (8:20-32 [16-28 HB])

BEHIND THE TEXT

This plague is the first of the second triad. According to the pattern, Yahweh commands Moses to confront Pharaoh in the morning as he goes to the river and Yahweh initiates the plague.

For the first time, an explicit distinction is made between the Egyptians and the Israelites. The plague reportedly did not strike Goshen where the Israelites were. The name Goshen is probably Semitic, related to the Hebrew term *gûš* ("a clod" or "a lump of earth" ["scabs" (NIV), "dirt" (ESV, NRSV)], as in

Job 7:5), which also appears in a place—Gush Halav in Galilee (Sarna 2004, 32). In the OT, the name Goshen refers to three different places. (1) It refers to a region in Egypt, where Jacob and his clan migrated at the time of Joseph. This Goshen is widely held to be in the northeast part of the lower Nile, which is part of the fertile Nile Delta. (2) It refers to a "region of Goshen" (mentioned in Josh 10:41; 11:16), which lay south of Hebron, between Gaza and Gibeon in southern Palestine. (3) Goshen refers to a city (mentioned in Josh 15:51) in the mountains of Judah, probably in the region of Goshen.

IN THE TEXT

■ **20-21 [16-17 HB]** In these verses, Yahweh commands **Moses** to **confront Pharaoh** and to demand the release of the Israelites. Noncompliance will result in a plague. The Hebrew *'ārōb* occurs nowhere else, except in Pss 78:45 and 105:31, as poetic descriptions of this plague. Thus, the exact meaning of the term is unknown, but suggestions include the following: "swarms of flies" (Exod 8:21 [17 HB] ESV, KJV, NASB, NET, NIV, NRSV), "swarms of insects" (NJPS), and "wild animals" (Josephus, based on Ps 78:45 that speaks of *'ārōb* as "devouring"). The Greek translates it as the dog fly, a bloodsucking fly that attacks animals for a blood meal. The dog fly is a carrier of anthrax, an infectious disease lethal to livestock. Identifying *'ārōb* as the anthrax-carrying dog fly is favored by many commentators, since it helps to explain naturalistically the source of the massive death of the livestock in the next plague. If this LXX translation is right, then this plague involves supernaturally increased **swarms of dog flies** that invaded the houses and attacked people. Since dog flies rarely bite humans (and generally only attack in the absence of animal hosts), this widespread affliction would be a sign of divine judgment upon the Egyptians.

■ **22-23 [18-19 HB]** Yahweh announces that he will **deal differently** (*pālah*; "set apart," "distinguish") with **Goshen**; this land where Yahweh's people (**my people**) live will be exempt from the attack of the **swarms of flies** (v 22 [18 HB]). Yahweh states his purpose to Pharaoh: so that you will know that I, **Yahweh,** am in this land. Yahweh's people will experience his presence in their midst, and thus his protection, when Egypt experiences his judgment.

Although many commentators argue that the context necessitates the translation **I will make a distinction** (v 23 [19 HB]) or something similar, the Hebrew noun *pedût* invariably means "ransom, redemption." Thus, the phrase could be more literally translated *I will put a ransom between my people and your people*. This "ransom" might be in reference to the Passover lamb, the blood of which makes the ultimate distinction in the tenth plague. The redeeming benefits of the Passover are effectual perhaps both before and after the event. Or, this verse simply anticipates the Passover ransoming. Yahweh sets the time of the plague, **tomorrow**, to demonstrate his sovereign power (also in 8:10, 29 [6, 25 HB]; 9:5, 18; 10:4).

■ **24 [20 HB]** Yahweh initiates the plague. The **dense swarms of flies** pour into the **palace** and **houses** and ruin **the land**. Most likely, they contaminate everything (people, animals, food, houses, idols, sacred objects, plants), in addition to biting and transmitting diseases to human and animal hosts.

■ **25 [21 HB]** Verses 25-29 [21-25 HB] report the dialogue between Pharaoh and Moses. In v 25 [21 HB], in reverse order from the second plague (prayer request and then false promise [v 8 (4 HB)]), **Pharaoh** makes a false promise (here and v 28 [24 HB]) before asking for a prayer. Perhaps he understands that relief will not come unless he first concedes. Thus, he grants the request that the Israelites be allowed to **sacrifice** to Yahweh. But he denies the request for the people to leave Egypt.

■ **26-27 [22-23 HB]** Moses gives a rationale for the need to offer sacrifices in the wilderness away from the sight of the Egyptians. The Israelite **offerings** are an ***Egyptian abomination*** (*tô'ăbat miṣrayim*). In Deut 32:16 and Isa 44:19, *tô'ăbat* represents foreign idols. It fits the present context better to interpret *tô'ăbat miṣrayim* as representing Egyptian (abominable) deities that are symbolized in livestock, such as the bull (see Sarna 2004, 32). Moses originally may have said "sacred animal of the Egyptians" to Pharaoh. Moses raises the concern that there will be a massive revolt and killing of the Israelites if they offer sacrifices in the land. Moses insists that in order for the **sacrifice** to be acceptable to Yahweh and not offensive to the Egyptians, the Israelites **must** go **into the wilderness** as required by **the LORD** (v 27 [23 HB]; see 3:18).

■ **28-29 [24-25 HB]** Pharaoh yields to Moses' response with a condition, followed by an appeal (v 28 [24 HB]): the Israelites should **not go very far**. Pharaoh is still not sure of the intent of Moses and the Israelites. At this point his primary concern is the removal of this plague; so he appeals to Moses: **pray for me**. Moses' response to Pharaoh (v 29 [25 HB]) has two parts; he promises to pray and sets the time when the plague will end, **tomorrow**. He also appeals to Pharaoh to be true to his word and **not act deceitfully again** by retracting his decision to let the Israelites go and worship Yahweh.

■ **30-32 [26-28 HB]** Moses prays, and Yahweh does as Moses asks (as in v 13 [9 HB]). Just as the massive appearance of the flies is supernatural, so also is their complete disappearance a miraculous feat. The crisis is over; **Pharaoh** proves once again that he cannot be trusted and that he has no intention to keep his word. He hardens **his heart** and does not free the Israelites (v 32 [28 HB]).

FROM THE TEXT

The narrative reminds that prayer unleashes the power of God and makes it visible to the world. In the contest between the imperial power of Egypt and the supreme power of the God of Israel, Yahweh reveals his power through Moses. Pharaoh is powerful and deceitful. Moses is faced with a formidable power, and prayer is his only weapon against the imperial power. The narrative shows that real power is not in the hands of a powerful ruler but in the prayer of the prophet of Yahweh, and even Pharaoh admitted that truth (when he asks Moses to pray [8:28 (24 HB)]).

One of the remarkable features of this passage is the way in which the Lord acts according to the words of Moses. Both with the plague of frogs and the plague of flies, Moses daringly declares that the plague will end the next day when he prays to God. In both cases, God does as Moses asks (vv 13, 31 [9, 27 HB]). Here we have a genuine partnership between God and Moses. Moses dares to speak on God's behalf, not always waiting for explicit divine commands. Moses assumes that since he understands the general contours of his God-given mission and its purposes (to make God known to the pagan king and his pagan kingdom), he can, at times, take action that promotes God's purposes. Amazingly, God acts on behalf of Moses, because Moses is acting on God's behalf, seeking God's interest. We could say that Moses has surpassed a fearful "slave mentality" in his relationship with God. Rather, he is acting as an ambassador, or even as a son. This experience gives him confidence, not only before God, but also before the formidable opposition of the powerful Pharaoh.

In the new covenant, all Christians have the privilege and calling of being "Christ's ambassadors" (2 Cor 5:20; see Eph 6:20). This role is rooted in our identity as "children of God" who have received the "adoption to sonship" (Rom 8:14-15; see 8:23; 9:4; Gal 4:5; Eph 1:5). This identity sets us free from fear (Rom 8:15; 1 John 4:18) and enables us to draw near to God and in confidence receive all the grace and help we ever need for life, godliness, and obedience (Heb 4:16; 10:19). We can be sons and daughters who know that everything God has is ours (Luke 15:31) and, like Moses, dare to ask, dare to speak on God's behalf, and dare to believe that God hears the prayers of the righteous, however extraordinary the request be and however ordinary we might be (Jas 5:15-18).

e. The Fifth Plague: Livestock (9:1-7)

BEHIND THE TEXT

This is the second plague of the second triad of plagues. According to the pattern, the plague is announced to Pharaoh (9:1-4) before it is carried out by Yahweh (v 6). In this plague, the livestock of Egypt die. This is the first plague that brings death to living creatures. Some suggest that this loss was caused by a skin disease, cutaneous anthrax, contracted perhaps through the biting flies of the previous plague. Others suggest that it came through the animals' inhalation of anthrax spores while grazing on contaminated soil. It is possible that the plague involved anthrax or other diseases related to the previous plague of flies. Nevertheless, the sudden death of the livestock of Egypt en masse within a set time frame emphasizes the supernatural character of the plague.

The Egyptians venerated some livestock as deities, which explains why the sacrifice of livestock by the Israelites is called the *Egyptian abomination* (→ 8:26) in the previous plague account. In this plague, the animals that represent some of their chief deities are struck down (e.g., cow [Hathor portrayed as a cow, a goddess of love, motherhood, and beauty] and Apis bull [an incarnation of the pharaoh]). This plague on livestock, then, is a great blow not only on the Egyptian economy but also on their religion. Sadly, later at Sinai, the Israelites make an idol of a calf and worship it (32:4), perhaps not for the first time.

IN THE TEXT

■ **1** Verses 1-5 contain Yahweh's instruction to **Moses** to demand the release of the Israelites and announce to **Pharaoh** the plague on the livestock. Yahweh continues to identify the Israelites as **my people** and his desire for their **worship** of him.

■ **2-3** Yahweh pronounces the consequence for disobedience. The expression **the hand of the LORD** (v 3; instead of "the finger of God" [8:19 (15 HB)]) emphasizes the **terrible** and severe nature of the coming **plague**. The Hebrew term for plague or pestilence (*deber*) refers to a disease that plagues both humans and animals (e.g., Jer 21:6; Ezek 14:19, 21). Yahweh typically is the one who brings such affliction as punishment for sin.

■ **4-5** Yahweh reveals his intention to continue to make a **distinction between** those that belong to Pharaoh and those that belong to Yahweh (v 4). Yahweh also announces the arrival **time** of the plague (**Tomorrow** [v 5]; see 8:10, 23, 29 [6, 19, 25 HB]; 9:18; 10:4), making it unmistakably clear that Yahweh's sovereign power supersedes any natural law or conditions.

■ **6** Verse 6 of ch 9 reports the arrival of the plague on **the next day** and the death of **all the livestock of the Egyptians**. Later on, however, livestock are still present in the sixth (vv 9-10), seventh (vv 19-21), and tenth (11:5; 12:29) plagues. Thus, **all** here does not refer literally to every single animal, but either to most (so that what survives the plague is immaterial) or all kinds or every kind (see "all Israel" in reference to representative or most or select, be they adults, armies, or leaders [Josh 7:25; 10:15; 1 Sam 13:20; 1 Kgs 14:18; 16:16]). For a similar hyperbolic phrase used earlier, consider Exod 8:17 [13 HB]: "*All the dust of the earth became gnats through all the land of Egypt*" (NASB). Through the loss of the livestock, the Egyptians are reduced to poverty just as they have reduced the **Israelites** to slavery.

■ **7 Pharaoh** sends men to investigate the extent of the damage caused by the plague. The report of the dead livestock in Egypt comes back with an exception; there are no dead **animals** in the camp of the Israelites. The distinction Yahweh makes in judgment testifies to Yahweh's reality and power, but it does not bring about any change in Pharaoh; he is **unyielding** to Yahweh and his demand.

FROM THE TEXT

Human sins bring damage and suffering to creation itself. The effect of human sin on creation is vividly portrayed in the garden narrative (see Gen 3:17) and the flood narrative (see chs 6—9). In this Exodus passage, animals suffer because of the defiance of the political powers to God's call for the freedom of his people. In the wider plague narrative, the entire land of Egypt and its waters, animals, vegetation, and atmosphere experience destruction and death. Hosea and Jeremiah also lament over the suffering of creation because of the wickedness of God's people (Jer 12:4; Hos 4:1-3). It is as if creation itself absorbs and bears human sin and its consequences.

The Apostle Paul writes that the suffering of creation because of human sin is not in vain; "the creation waits in eager expectation for the children of God to be revealed" in the hope of the redemption of humanity and all creation (Rom 8:19). The creation's deep groans and travails alongside the people of God somehow serve the actualization of that hope in a restored creation (vv 22-23). Even in the deadly diseases and disasters and plagues that relentlessly strike down the Egyptians, the hopes of restoration and redemption remain. The hope of restoration for the nation of Egypt lies in its willingness to acknowledge and serve the creator God, rather than to serve images of created things (such as livestock).

It is the hope of the restoration of the created order—human beings existing to love and worship the creator God and human beings representing this God to the rest of creation. The plagues can be seen as the means through which the disorders (idolatry, enslavement, and defiance toward Yahweh) in Egypt are thoroughly deconstructed, in the hopes of reconstructing the proper order. The hope of redemption is also for the nation of Israel, so that Israel, too, can be reordered as a nation under the creator God, serving God's purposes.

The narrative suggests that continued human resistance to God's purpose of a restored and reordered creation can only lead to an existence marked by continued disorder for individuals, societies, and nations and for creation itself. Ultimately, God's sovereign will and purpose prevail over all the false claims of and loyalties to power and authority. Pharaohs of our world are (individual, societal, or national) powers that remain unyielding to the gracious and sovereign purpose of God for his creation. They may even be those who profess to be Christians yet resist God's good and gracious work in the world. The narrative warns them of the consequence of their actions and even their ultimate demise, if they continue to be oppressive in their dealings with others and unyielding to God's sovereign authority over his creation.

f. The Sixth Plague: Boils (9:8-12)

BEHIND THE TEXT

Within the symmetrical literary structure of the plague narrative, this is the third of the second triad. According to the pattern, this plague comes without any warning for Pharaoh, and its account is characteristically brief. Unlike the previous plague, this plague directly endangers human lives, showing that the plagues are increasingly severe.

Propp finds a parallel in an Akkadian word for "ash" that also connotes psoriasis (1999, 331). Others identify this plague as cutaneous (skin) anthrax that caused large boils, a possible extension of the last plague on livestock transferred to human beings. If such transference was the case, both human beings and animals acquired it through the biting flies (albeit a rare mode of transmission). Or, one acquired the disease by coming in physical contact with products (such as wool or hide) of affected livestock. While this naturalistic explanation is somewhat attractive, there are again reasons to doubt it. Modern medical research indicates that, when left untreated, cutaneous anthrax leads to death in 20 percent of cases for human beings, yet there is no death reported in the account of this plague in Exodus. In addition, as with other plagues, the extraordinary timing, severity, pervasiveness, and distinction between the Israelites and the Egyptians insist on a primarily supernatural explanation—even if it involved a known disease and certain discernable natural processes.

IN THE TEXT

■ **8** Yahweh's instruction and its fulfillment by Moses and Aaron in vv 8-10 follow the pattern of a symbolic prophetic act. Yahweh instructs **Moses** and **Aaron** to **take handfuls of soot from a furnace and have Moses** release it **into the air**. The ash would not have any bacteria or spores that could cause boils. Tossing ashes into the air **in the presence of Pharaoh** instructs Pharaoh that Yahweh can turn something as benign as a handful of ashes into a malicious disease.

■ **9** In v 9, Yahweh describes the plague. The ash from Moses' hands will supernaturally multiply and spread all **over . . . Egypt** and cause **boils**. The term "boils" (*šeḥîn*) elsewhere occurs along with other skin diseases (Lev 13:18-23) and in relation to Job (Job 2:7) and Hezekiah (2 Kgs 20:7; Isa 38:21), both of whom recover from the boils. Deuteronomy 28:27 mentions as one of the covenant curses "the boils [*šeḥîn*] of Egypt," distinguishing it, perhaps, as an especially dangerous and malignant strand specific to Egypt. Here, the boil is said to break out in "blisters" or "pustules" translated as **festering**.

■ **10 Moses** carries out the act of judgment **before Pharaoh**. The **boils** break out uncontrollably and engulf both **people and animals** (*behēmâ;* "animals in general," "wild animals," or "livestock") that belong to Pharaoh.

■ **11** Verse 11 describes the effects of the plague. The disease remains under Yahweh's total control; he keeps it out of Goshen (implied by the expression **all the Egyptians**). The plague afflicts even the **magicians** who were known for their power through secret arts. They are completely powerless to prevent the **boils** from incapacitating them.

■ **12** Verse 12 implies the weakening of Pharaoh's will. We find here for the first time that **the LORD hardened Pharaoh's heart**, confirming Pharaoh's predisposition to resist Yahweh (on hardening, → 7:1-7). Yahweh likely did this act in order that Pharaoh and all Egypt reap the full consequences of their sins, therefore, bringing a fuller revelation of Yahweh's true identity, character, and superiority. Yahweh also renders fallacious the notion that Pharaoh is divine, for Pharaoh has no power to prevent harm to himself, the magicians, his people, or anything in his land.

FROM THE TEXT

Even God's freedom to judge people or send plagues can be seen as an expression of God's good character. As the plagues intensify in their direct impact upon human beings, and not merely on their possessions, it prompts the question of how the loving God of the Bible can use such harsh means to judge people. Are these plague stories the product of an inferior, "OT" view of God that is replaced by a "kinder, gentler" God in the NT? Despite the popular appeal of such a view, the NT's mention of the "eternal punishment" or "eternal fire" or "eternal destruction" of the wicked (e.g., Matt 18:8; 25:41, 46; Mark 9:47-48; Luke 16:24; 2 Thess 1:9; Heb 6:2; Jude 1:7) leads to a resounding "No!" to this question. While there is some "progressive revelation" in the Bible, the fundamental character of God remains the same throughout. God is loving *and* holy, merciful *and* just, and this is manifested in all that God does. As the just and holy one, God judges sin and evil.

The plague narrative exemplifies how the judgment that falls on some (Egypt) is the very means of God's merciful salvation of the oppressed (Israel). In other words, divine judgment of the wicked is liberating, healing, and restorative for the oppressed. Even the increasing severity of judgments that fall on Pharaoh and Egypt demonstrates God's unique, merciful character. God begins with less severe plagues as a warning and call to repentance, before afflicting offenders with greater plagues for their stubbornness. However, for those who heed the warning, there is escape (e.g., the officials in Exod 9:19-

21; also 12:48), no less than the Israelites. Even God's harshest judgments are issued in the hope that they will lead people to their greatest good, to the repentance that leads to abundant life. When understood rightly, then, God's judgments are fully compatible with and integrated into God's salvific grace and love.

g. The Seventh Plague: Hail and Lightning (9:13-35)

BEHIND THE TEXT

This unit is the first of the third and final triad of plague accounts (plagues six through nine), in which Moses alone performs the acts of judgment (9:23; 10:13, 22). A clear indication of the seasonal crops mentioned in 9:31-32 places the plague between late January to early February. Like the plague of locusts, the seventh plague is an extreme intensification of natural phenomena.

This plague is part of a pattern of Yahweh bringing escalating terror and destruction upon Egypt. There are several new elements that emerge in the account of this plague: the reason for Pharaoh's present existence is made explicit (vv 15-17); Yahweh graciously grants the Egyptians an opportunity to escape the fatal effects of the plague and some of them take advantage of it (vv 19-21); some of Pharaoh's officials also harden their hearts (v 21); human lives are taken (vv 19, 25); and, Pharaoh explicitly acknowledges Yahweh's righteousness and his own human fallibility (v 27).

IN THE TEXT

■ **13** In vv 13-19, the plague of hail is announced in the form of Yahweh's direct speech to Pharaoh. The announcement begins in v 13 with Yahweh's instruction to Moses to **confront Pharaoh** presumably as he goes down to the Nile **early in the morning** (as in 7:15; 8:20 [16 HB]). Like the previous accounts, this speech also begins with the demand, **Let my people go, so that they may worship me**.

■ **14** Verse 14 announces the severity of the coming plague. The expression *all my plagues* may point to the last four plagues yet to come and the comprehensive effect of these intensified plagues (thus, **full force of my plagues**). Yahweh may also be referring to the seventh plague since it involves not just one, but four elements—thunder, hail, rain, and lightning. Either way, the plagues will serve the didactic purpose of Yahweh's self-revelation: teaching Pharaoh (and others) that **there is no one like** Yahweh **in all the earth**.

■ **15-16** Verse 15 seems to focus on the incredible power of Yahweh; the fact that the previous plagues brought only partial damage to Egypt does not mean that Yahweh is limited in his power. Yahweh makes it known to Pharaoh that he is indeed powerful enough to wipe Pharaoh and his **people . . . off the earth** with just one **plague**. He has not done so for a specific reason. He has **raised . . . up** (v 16; *'āmad* in causative is "caused to stand"; in this context the verb may mean "spared"; see NIV footnote) Pharaoh for the **purpose** of showing him his **power**, with a greater purpose and mission to **all the earth**. What Yahweh does with Pharaoh in Egypt will propel a human global proclamation of Yahweh.

■ **17** Verse 17 states the specific crime of Pharaoh that compels Yahweh to send the next plague. Pharaoh continues to exercise his control and dominance (*sālal* reflexive; "to exalt oneself up," thus **set yourself**) over Yahweh's **people** and he refuses to submit to Yahweh and set them free.

■ **18** The plague of hail is Yahweh's punishment for Pharaoh's continued defiance of Yahweh; Egypt will experience the **worst hailstorm** that **Egypt** has seen in its history. Elsewhere in the Bible, Yahweh is poetically described as stockpiling hailstones as ammunition for the day of war (Job 38:22-23) and using hailstorm, bolts of lightning, and thunder to subdue the psalmist's enemy (Ps 18:12-17 [13-18 HB]). Once again, Yahweh announces the specific time for the plague, **tomorrow** (see "tomorrow" in Exod 8:10 [6 HB]; also see 8:23, 29 [19, 25 HB]; 9:5; 10:4).

■ **19** The announcement of the plague also contains a call to prepare for the plague (9:19). Yahweh commands Pharaoh to avoid needless deaths of both humans and animals by issuing a nationwide edict. Even in the midst of a severe judgment, God shows his compassionate nature, especially for the powerless slaves and **livestock** (vv 20-21) that are under the authority of the powerful.

■ **20-21** Verses 20-21 report that some of the **officials of Pharaoh** acknowledged (**feared**) the authority of Yahweh's **word** and took action to protect their **slaves** and **livestock**, while others simply ignored (or, literally, ***did not put to the heart***) and remained loyal to Pharaoh with an unyielding heart. We do not know if those who took action to protect their property did so only to preserve their wealth or because of genuine change of heart (repentance).

■ **22-25** In vv 22-25, Moses performs another symbolic prophetic act that results in massive devastation in Egypt. At the command of Yahweh, Moses stretches out his **hand toward the sky** (v 22) and initiates catastrophic weather conditions targeting the Egyptians' **land** (v 23). Verse 23 indicates that the **lightning** (*'ēš*; "fire") continuously streamed **down to the ground** and flashed **back and forth** (v 24; the Greek *phlogizon* ["set on fire"] suggests that the lightning started fires). Accompanying thunderclaps and **hail** beating down on everything augmented the terror of the **sky**. The damage is extensive (v 25) as large hailstones killed **both people and animals** left **in the fields**, as warned, and **stripped** the trees of leaves and fruit. ***Every*** [*kōl*] ***vegetation*** (*'ēśeb*; "cereals," "vegetables," and "grass") is devastated—a great blow to the economy and future survival of the Egyptians.

■ **26** The Israelites once again experience protection from the hail in the midst of Yahweh's judgment of Egypt.

■ **27-28** In v 27 Pharaoh responds to the severity of the plague with an admission of his sin and confession of Yahweh's righteousness. For the first **time**, Pharaoh admits that he has **sinned** (*ḥāṭā'*; "miss," "offend," "sin"); God is just and **right** (*ṣaddîq*), and he and his **people** are **in the wrong** (*rāšā'*; "guilty," "ungodly"). His statements do not necessarily indicate a lasting recognition of legal and moral failures before God, with a felt need for fundamental change in his heart's attitude and behavior. Since his concession to liberate the Israelites (v 28) is short-lived, his admission of guilt is probably insincere.

But presently, pressed by the current exceedingly dire situation, Pharaoh bargains with Moses. **Pray . . . I will let you go** (v 28). It is Pharaoh's third request to pray for the end of the plague (8:8, 28 [4, 24 HB]; also see 10:17). The request indicates his acknowledgment of Yahweh's sovereign control over nature.

■ **29-30** Again, **Moses** promises a **prayer** that will end the plague so that Pharaoh **may know that the earth is the** LORD**'s** (v 29). However, Moses knows Pharaoh's apparent surrender is not genuine (v 30). Moses accurately identifies the root of the problem of Pharaoh's and his officials' obstinate heart—the lack of the **fear** of the LORD God.

■ **31** Verses 31-32 are parenthetical verses that clarify that not all grains were **destroyed** by hail, contrary to the impression given in v 25. At the time of the hail, **flax was in bloom**, but **barley** *was in the ear* (v 31; *'ābîb* means "ears," "ripe but with still soft ears," thus, not ready to be harvested for another two to three weeks, but with yellowing stems, brittle enough to be destroyed by the hail). In Egypt, this season comes in late January to early February (and these crops are harvested between February and early March; between March and April in Canaan). Flax seeds are used for oil and its fibers to make linen. Barley is used for bread, beer, and feed for livestock. The hailstorm destroyed these crops.

■ **32** Verse 32 reports that **wheat** and *emmer* (*kussemet*) were **not destroyed**. According to Sarna, while **spelt** has been found in ancient Egyptian tombs, it did not grow in Egypt (2004, 35). Rather, it was one of the main cereals in the land of Israel (Sarna 2004, 35). Barley, wheat, and emmer (a type of wheat) were three chief grains in Egypt. Therefore, the Hebrew word translated into **spelt** (*kussemet*) is best identified as emmer. The reference to wheat and emmer ripening **later** is an indication that wheat and emmer were green (and thus flexible and resilient) at the time of the hail. Therefore, the grain recovers from the storm and forms the ears later (only to be consumed by an army of locusts shortly before its harvest in March—April; in Canaan, May). The eventual destruction of all the crops of Egypt would make the economy unsustainable and life unviable.

9:26-32

■ **33-35** Away from **Pharaoh** and **the city, Moses** prays and Yahweh answers him (v 33). Thus, the text creates a pattern of contrast between the insincere, bargaining Pharaoh and the faithful, trustworthy Yahweh. As predicted by Yahweh, once the plagues are **stopped, Pharaoh** and **his officials** sin **again** by hardening **their hearts** and breaking their promises (vv 34-35).

FROM THE TEXT

Even in God's severest punishments, God's mercy is evident. The nature and manner of God's judgment on Egypt, while severe, demonstrate God's mercy toward the Egyptians and not merely toward the Israelites. (1) As v 15 hints, the Egyptians deserved nothing less than total destruction for their sins. The plagues could have been much worse than they were. Yet the Lord was patient with both individuals and nations, with Pharaoh and Egypt. (2) In addition, God allowed the severity of the plagues to escalate gradually, giving room for repentance to the Egyptians and even opportunities to avoid the brunt of the judgments (vv 19-21). (3) Furthermore, God's concern extended to the powerless slaves and livestock, who were at the mercy of the powerful. God's actions here reflect the divine character expressed elsewhere: "Do I take any pleasure in the death of the wicked? declares the Sovereign LORD. Rather, am I not pleased when they turn from their ways and live?" (Ezek 18:23). God's hesitancy to take human life is confirmed by the fact that no human deaths were reported in previous plagues, and even in this case, they were only the result of those who disregarded the Lord's warning. (4) Ultimately, God desired that they come to know and worship God, which would be to their greatest good.

The same pattern of gradually increasing severity of God's punishment appears later in Israel's history in the covenant curses (Lev 26:14-45; Deut 28:15-68). In mercy, God acts with the intention and desire that the covenant people would turn to God and repent from their sinful ways. Only when the desired change of heart and actions are not forthcoming is more severe punishment meted out. In these ways, one learns that God's judgments are not random or out of control but are purposeful and ultimately merciful. The Lord is incomparable not only in power but also in grace.

The doxological statement "the earth is the LORD's" is a powerful expression of God's ownership of the earth. The parallel statement in Ps 24:1 completes the full force of this doxology; God's ownership also extends to "all who live in it." Egypt does not belong to Pharaoh but to Yahweh, the God of Israel, the one who "created the heavens and the earth" (Gen 1:1). The doxology is also a powerful rejection of the claims of individuals or nations or special-interest groups that they have entitlement and control over the earth and its resources. This doxology warns those who would exploit, abuse, and control the earth by their technology, but comforts those who are anxious about their inability to own the land (Brueggemann 1994, 760). The claim that the earth belongs to us or that it is given to us to satisfy our unbridled desires and wants is evidence of idolatry, worship of the self, and worship of creation. The text powerfully speaks against such idolatrous claims.

h. The Eighth Plague: Locusts (10:1-20)

BEHIND THE TEXT

Within the literary structure of the plague narrative, the locust plague is the second of the final triad of plagues. While retaining the usual pattern, the plague starts with a divine speech.

The time of the plague is likely late February. Locusts are common during this time period. It allows for the time needed for the wheat and emmer ("spelt" [9:32 NIV]) and other vegetation to recover from the storm before the locust plague hits. There is also enough time for the ninth plague, the "plundering" of the Egyptians (assuming that it takes place before the tenth plague [11:1-2; 12:35-36]), and the instruction, preparation, and celebration of the Passover between the first and the fourteenth of the first month in Israelites' newly instituted religious calendar (→ 12:2).

While locusts have long been consumed as food in many cultures (see Lev 11:21-22), locust swarms have been one of the worst plagues to afflict people. Under the right conditions (following a heavy rainfall), the locust can multiply rapidly and become gregarious and migratory. A large swarm (consisting of billions of insects) can travel great distances and cover forty square miles (100 km²). On landing, such a swarm can quickly strip trees and fields and destroy crops. The eighth plague supposedly is incomparably greater in scale and more damaging than any such previous locust attacks that occurred in Egypt (Exod 10:6, 14).

Some identify "east wind" (10:13; *rûaḥ qādîm*) as *kamsin* (from the Arabic word for "fifty," as these windstorms sporadically blow over fifty days). *Kamsin* can refer to three different wind patterns. (1) Most commonly, it refers to a hot, dry, high-speed (up to 140 mph), low-level, dust/sand carried by a southerly or southwesterly wind blowing over Egypt and the Red Sea. It is unlikely that *kamsin* from the Sahara desert is involved here since it presents adverse flight conditions for the locusts. Also what lies in the southern Sahara are summer breeding grounds, which means there would not have been any locusts there yet. (2) It could refer to the easterly wind that blows over the Negev and parts of Saudi Arabia, which could be the east wind of v 13. In Egypt, it occurs annually and most frequently between March and June. When severe, it can darken the sky. The winds from the east, probably originating from Saudi Arabia, carry into Egypt the newly formed locust swarms from their winter breeding areas along the Red Sea. (3) It could also be a northerly wind, carrying cool air from the Mediterranean, which could be the wind that carries the locusts out of Egypt (see v 19).

IN THE TEXT

■ **1-2** The opening verses make explicit what Yahweh wishes to teach the Israelites through the hardening of **Pharaoh** and **his officials**. Yahweh's hardening follows rather than initiates the unyielding nature of some officials' hearts mentioned in the previous plague (9:21, 34). Verse 2 of ch 10 presents the plagues as an enduring memorial to Yahweh's righteous judgment and great power. Moses and all the Israelites are to **tell** or ***recount*** in detail the events of the exodus so that all subsequent generations (**you** is plural and collective) **may know that I am the** LORD.

■ **3** The plague is announced in vv 3-6. The announcement begins with Yahweh's question delivered by Moses and Aaron, **How long will you refuse to humble yourself . . . ?**, which is an accusation of Pharaoh's sin. Moses has already been told that it will take all the plagues (especially the last acts of judgment) to humble Pharaoh (3:19-20; 4:21-23).

■ **4** In v 4, Moses states the penalty for Pharaoh's continued arrogance and refusal to submit to Yahweh's will. Yahweh will bring ***locust swarms*** as a means of divine judgment. Later, swarms of locusts would be sent against Israel for their covenant unfaithfulness (Deut 28:38, 42).

■ **5-6** The extent of the plague is stated in these verses. Dense locust swarms will completely **cover** the land (v 5). Any vegetation that survived the previous plague and has been growing since will be utterly devoured, effectively ushering in famine. The locusts will even **fill** the **houses** (perhaps devouring stored grains, clothes, and anything made out of wood [v 6]).

■ **7** Verses 7-11 report the appeal of officials to Pharaoh to let Israel go and the negotiation between Pharaoh and Moses. The officials perceive Moses as **a snare** that caught them in a path of destruction. They recognize and remind Pharaoh that the ruined Egypt's future depends on his decision to **let the people go, so that they may worship** *Yahweh* **their God**.

■ **8-9** Pharaoh's decision to bring Moses and Aaron back for a negotiation implies the success of the appeal of the officials. Pharaoh is willing to let the people go but wants to know **who will be going** (v 8). Moses maintains his position that all Israelites and all of their livestock must leave (v 9). Moses' intention, of course, is to never come back, but he does not make it explicit (on their diplomatic bargaining, see Cassuto 1967, 124).

■ **10-11 Pharaoh** fully understands Moses' intentions and predictably responds in stormy fury. **The** LORD **be with you** (v 10) is normally a blessing, but here it is a sarcastic and angry retort. The Hebrew term (*tappekem*) that is usually translated into "little ones" (KJV, NASB, NRSV) or **children** (NIV, NJPS) most likely refers to all the noncombatants Moses listed in v 9 ("our young and our old," "our sons and our daughters"; see Gen 34:29; 43:8 for a similar inclusive usage).

Exodus 10:10 ends with Pharaoh's warning: ***Watch out, for evil is before you***. Pharaoh warns and perhaps threatens Moses and Aaron to beware and not to push him too far, lest he harm them (Cassuto 1967, 126). Pharaoh's final answer is **No!** (v 11; "Never!" [NRSV]). Releasing all Israelites is inconceivable for Pharaoh, so he makes a limited concession. **Only the men** (that is, the combatants, neither young nor old) may **go**. Pharaoh would effectively hold the rest and the livestock hostage to ensure that the men come back.

■ **12-15** At Yahweh's command, **Moses** stretches out his hand to summon the **east wind** (v 13; *rûaḥ qādîm*, see 14:21) to carry the swarms of **locusts** into Egypt. Verses 14-15 report the arrival of the locust swarms and compare it to an invasion and occupation by an indomitable army. The damage incurred from the **plague** in fulfillment of Yahweh's words (vv 5-6) is complete. All plants, grains, and fruits are destroyed. The severity not only is unprecedented but also will **never** be repeated.

■ **16 Pharaoh** summons Moses ***in haste*** "in the hope of saving something" (Cassuto 1967, 128). The onslaught of the plague appears to have humbled Pharaoh. This time, Pharaoh confesses that he has **sinned against the L**ORD and **Moses and Aaron** (**you** is plural).

■ **17** Pharaoh also begs to **forgive** his sin **once more** or "only this once" (ESV, KJV, NASB), giving the impression that he will no longer sin against Yahweh. However, his plea for a prayer comes with no promise of release of the Israelites. It appears that he is concerned only about receiving immediate relief from the **deadly plague** (simply "death" in the Hebrew).

■ **18-19** Verses 18-19 report the removal of the plague. Moses prays to Yahweh (v 18), fully aware of Pharaoh's deceitfulness. Yahweh responds by changing **the wind to a very strong *sea* wind** (v 19). The **very strong *sea* wind** may well signify the northwesterly *kamsin* wind from the Mediterranean, which blows southeastward over the **Red Sea**. The locust swarms are **carried . . . into** the Red Sea, perhaps drowning them all. Fretheim (1991, 128) sees the statement **not a locust was left** as anticipating the drowning of the Egyptian army in the Red Sea in which "not one of them survived" (14:28).

■ **20** The narrative ends with another report of Yahweh hardening **Pharaoh's heart**. Pharaoh's resistance is obviously wearing thin, but Yahweh confirms Pharaoh's stubbornness of heart, and he does not release **the Israelites**.

The OT and the NT each record one great saving act of God—the "exodus event" and the "Christ event" respectively—and call God's people of all generations to give testimony to this great saving act. One explicit purpose of the plague in this passage is that subsequent generations will know who God is and what God has done from the testimony of the preceding generations of Israelites. Those who hear, have faith, and choose to walk with God will be saved.

Throughout the OT, one finds a similar pattern of transgenerational testimony and blessing. Deuteronomy emphasizes the theme of remembrance of God's acts and commands as the key to national blessing (Deut 6:7-9). The Israelites are to take special care to remember the Lord who delivered them from slavery in Egypt when they are enjoying God-given prosperity in the land (v 12). The psalmists frequently exhort God's people to remember God's mighty saving acts. The prophets, too, persistently call the people to remember and be faithful to the national covenant that God made with them.

In the NT, likewise, there is an emphasis on witnessing to succeeding generations about God's great act, but this time, it is the act of delivering people from the bondage of sin and death through Christ (see Heb 12:1-2). Like the exodus, this great work of salvation is complete and does not need to be repeated in later generations. Rather, it is to be appropriated by faith, reenacted (in sacramental festivals and acts), and proclaimed to all people.

i. The Ninth Plague: Darkness (10:21-29)

BEHIND THE TEXT

Within the literary structure of the plague narrative noted above, this plague account is the third in the final triad of plague accounts.

The naturalistic explanation for this plague, widely accepted by most commentators, is that it probably involved intensified *kamsin* (→ Behind the Text for 10:1-20) from the Sahara desert that impaired visibility caused by a large amount of sand and dust. It seems, however, that if this plague is an extreme intensification of what Egypt occasionally experienced (as in the plague of locusts), then the plague narrative would most likely name its cause (the terms for sand, dust, and storm are not lacking in Hebrew) and would state that it came in an unparalleled way in Egypt (as in the plague of locusts). Whatever the explanation, the plague of darkness signals the Egyptians' supreme god Re's impotence and Egypt's impending doom.

■ **21** The ninth plague is **darkness that can be felt** (*mšš*). The root *mšš* in the causative, which occurs uniquely here, most likely means "cause one to grope, rummage through, or feel around" (see Stuart 2006, 257). This translation accentuates the totality of the darkness Yahweh brings (unlike the partial darkness created by a plague-level *kamsin*). Joel 2:2 also speaks of a day of clouds and thick darkness with blackness spread over the mountains. As such, darkness signifies judgment, death, and destruction, all of which are impending.

■ **22** Moses stretches out **his hand toward the sky**, supposedly releasing divine power over the atmosphere, and the plague begins (see 8:6 [2 HB]; 9:23; 10:13). Moses later uses the same motion to both part and unite the Red Sea (14:21, 27). The phrase **total darkness** conveys the absoluteness of the darkness. The blackness that enveloped **all Egypt for three days** most likely brought psychological terror to the people.

■ **23** Verse 23 reports the distinction between the land of Egypt and Goshen during the ninth plague. While the Egyptians were enveloped in thick darkness, no doubt immobilized and confined to their own houses, the **Israelites had light**.

■ **24** Again, motivated by the desire for relief from the plague, **Pharaoh** summons **Moses** and gives his consent for an Israelite exodus; all may **go**, including the dependents, but the cattle must be left **behind**. With the Egyptian livestock largely destroyed, Pharaoh appears to covet the Israelites' cattle to maintain the economic and agricultural interest of Egypt.

■ **25-26** In vv 25-26, **Moses** makes no compromise and plainly conveys Yahweh's terms. All **must** leave, including the **livestock** (v 25). Moses' reason is that the Israelites do not know what they are to **use to worship *Yahweh***. When they get to the place of worship, they will gain knowledge of Yahweh's requirements, which may include animals from their flocks and herds. Moses insists on leaving Egypt being fully prepared to worship; this seems to be a diplomatic way of saying that none belonging to Israel—and thus to Yahweh—will **be left behind** (v 26).

■ **27-28** **Pharaoh's heart** is **hardened** again, and he remains stubborn (v 27). In addition, as his bargaining is completely rejected, **Pharaoh** flies into a rage. He dismisses **Moses**, threatening him with death upon reappearance: **you will die** (v 28).

■ **29** Given Pharaoh's death threats, Moses' words **I will never appear before you again** ("I will no more see your face again" [lit.]) seems appropriate. Some suggest that Moses is only saying that he will not initiate a meeting between himself and Pharaoh. However, this verse and 11:8 together give the strong impression that Moses sincerely believed this was his last face-to-face meeting with Pharaoh, who vowed to kill Moses upon seeing him again. After the tenth plague, of course, Pharaoh seeks out Moses' "face," and Moses grants an audience with Pharaoh (12:31).

FROM THE TEXT

The Lord's power over both light and darkness demonstrates his total sovereignty over creation as the Creator of all things. The beginning of creation is marked by God's creation of light and its separation from darkness (Gen 1:3-5). Yet, in this plague, the creator God overrides the natural order—making the daytime dark for the Egyptians. By showing control over light and darkness, God manifests supreme lordship not only over the sun and stars but also over any supernatural beings that the Egyptians regarded as controlling these forces of nature. The rightful response to such sovereignty is worship.

The NT utilizes the metaphor of darkness to communicate the reality of judgment of those who reject Jesus Christ (see Matt 8:12; 22:13; 25:30) and also of the chaotic existence under the power of sin and Satan (Acts 26:18). At the same time, the NT proclaims the power of the gospel to deliver those who live in darkness into the marvelous light of God's salvation (see Matt 4:16; 1 Pet 2:9). The narrative of the plague of darkness and the NT usage of the metaphor of darkness invite us to reflect on (1) the final destiny of those who reject the good news of Jesus Christ, and (2) the evangelistic mission of those who live in the light of God's salvation to those who live in darkness—"to open their eyes and turn them from darkness to light, and from the power of Satan to God, so that they may receive forgiveness of sins and a place among those who are sanctified by faith" in Jesus Christ (Acts 26:18).

2. The Tenth Plague, the Passover, and the Exodus (11:1—13:16)

Overview

The account of the final plague is not marked by the threefold, triadic structure that marked the first nine plagues. Instead, as the most important and catalytic event that the Israelites will celebrate throughout their history, it is treated in more detail. It begins with a predictive warning account (11:1-10), followed by the institution and celebration of Passover (12:1-28). Finally, there is an account of the tenth plague itself, which leads to the climax of the exodus from Egypt (12:29-42). Further instructions on Passover exclusions (12:43-51) and three commemorative rituals (13:1-16) conclude the section.

The previous plagues make demands on Pharaoh and his officials to liberate the Israelites, which go unheeded. Yahweh demands, "Let my son go, so he may worship me" (4:23). However, Pharaoh refuses him. As a result,

Yahweh fulfills what he previously warned: "I will kill your firstborn son." The final plague of judgment produces the outcome Yahweh intends.

a. Warning of the Final (Tenth) Plague (11:1-10)

BEHIND THE TEXT

At the end of the last plague, Pharaoh ordered Moses never to seek his audience and Moses agreed (10:28-29). Yet in 11:4-8 we find Moses speaking to Pharaoh again. Commentators have offered various explanations for this apparent discrepancy. However, the difficulty is diffused simply by taking the text at its face value: with 11:1-2 as a continuation of 10:24-29 (with the Lord prompting Moses to linger before Pharaoh to deliver a last message); with 11:3 as a parenthetical editorial note; and with vv 4-8 as a continuation of vv 1-2 (Moses actually delivering the last warning, before leaving Pharaoh's presence).

This interpretation assumes that the announcement of each new plague follows the completion of the previous plague. The timing of the tenth plague ("midnight" [v 4]) does not refer to the night of the announcement, but to the designated "midnight" of the Passover meal in the near future (see "midnight" in 12:29). Before the tenth plague takes place, there must be time for the announcement of the tenth plague and the fourteen-day preparation for it (12:1-11). Moses also needs to communicate and carry out the plundering of the Egyptians (11:2).

The NIV, by contrast, interprets vv 1-2 as being out of sequence, translating v 1a with a pluperfect ("Now the LORD *had* said to Moses") and v 3 as a parenthetical note that reports the fulfillment of v 2. In this line of interpretation, the timing of the plague ("midnight" [v 4]) refers to the night of the announcement. And then the sequence of the event could be as follows: Moses gives the instructions for the Passover meal (12:1-11) and the plundering immediately after the eighth plague; the Israelites plunder the Egyptians; each family chooses a Passover lamb on the tenth of the first month (12:3); the ninth plague descends on Egypt for three days (perhaps on days eleven to thirteen); on the fourteenth, Moses announces the tenth plague to Pharaoh; and on that midnight, the plague strikes Egypt.

Whatever the exact sequence of the events, the one theological point of 11:1-10 is clear. The previous destructive signs and wonders have not produced repentance in the Egyptian king, but only more hostile resistance. Therefore, one last, absolutely devastating plague is called for. Like the first one (the Nile turning to blood), the final plague involves blood and is entirely supernatural.

IN THE TEXT

■ **1** The narrative begins with Yahweh's assurance to **Moses** that the final **plague** will compel **Pharaoh** to comply. The expression ***when he releases you altogether*** (*kešalleḥô kālâ*) means "when he sends you with everything" (LXX), that is, with "flocks and herds," which Pharaoh previously wanted to keep (10:24). After the tenth plague, Pharaoh will want a quick, complete, and irreversible departure of the Israelites. He will want nothing to do with the Israelites; thus, he will vigorously drive them **out** of **Egypt** (→ 12:33).

■ **2** Foretold in 3:21-22 and reported in 12:35-36, God tells Moses to instruct the Israelites to **ask** for **articles of silver and gold**, perhaps as a partial recompense for their years of forced servitude.

■ **3** This parenthetical verse reports the fulfillment of God's command concerning the plundering of the Egyptians (→ 3:21, 22). Through the cumulative, awe-inspiring effects of the plagues, the Egyptians' hearts are softened. The softening of the peoples' hearts contrasts with the hardening of Pharaoh's heart (Fretheim 1991, 131).

Some of **Pharaoh's officials** and **the people** regard Moses **highly**, seeing that he is indeed "like God to Pharaoh" (7:1). Moses' power and stature as the prophet of the Most High are evident to most of the **Egyptians** but evade Pharaoh and some of his officials, an indication of their hardheartedness.

■ **4** Verse 4 indicates the set timing of the plague, **midnight**, which could be the night of the announcement or in the near future.

■ **5** Verse 5 announces the plague: the death of **every firstborn** (*bekôr*; the NIV adds **son**), whether human or **cattle**, in Egypt from the highest rank to the lowest of Egypt, from the noblest to the most wretched, from the richest to "the poorest of the poor" (Cassuto 1967, 133). None will escape. The firstborn might refer to male only, given the use of the qualifying term "male" (*zākār*) in the instructions for the offering/redeeming of the firstborn in 13:13-15. However, the use of the qualifying "male" or "sons" specifically in relation to their redemption (also in 34:20) and not in relation to the plague (here and in 12:12, 29) or the consecration (in 13:2; Num 3:12-13; 8:16-17) supports the interpretation that the plague hit all male and female firstborn in Egypt. In any case, this punishment is for the crime of holding in captivity Yahweh's metaphorical firstborn son, Israel (Exod 4:22-23).

■ **6** In the middle of the night, all the firstborn of Egypt will be struck down, probably not silently so as to go unnoticed by the sleeping nation but violently as to arouse the whole household to witness the death of their beloved and cry out for help. The term *ṣeʿāqâ* (also in 12:30) could mean "the **loud** and bitter cry of **wailing**" (made by the mourners) or "the loud desperate cry for help" (made by those who are dying in great fear and pain). It most likely refers to

EXODUS

11:1-6

both. There was no other terrible cry like it before nor after this plague. Ironically, the term *ṣeʿāqâ* is used to describe the Israelites' extremely embittered and anguished cry under the Egyptian oppression and torment (3:7, 9), again highlighting the reversal of fortunes for Israel and Egypt.

■ **7-8** In great contrast, there will be no disturbance among the **Israelites** and their livestock, not even **a dog** will **bark** at them (v 7). There will be a profound peace among the Israelites. **Moses** anticipates the Egyptian officials' humble descent from the palace to Goshen, requesting Moses' royal audience (v 8). Until this point, Moses sought audience with Pharaoh either charged by God with a mission or summoned by Pharaoh in an emergency. Moses will not initiate his meeting with Pharaoh again; they will have to come, **bowing down before** Moses, begging him to **leave** Egypt (v 8). Moses, here, appears to speak on his own prophetic initiative as he has done before with Yahweh supporting him (e.g., 8:10-13 [6-9 HB]). Later, Pharaoh will summon Moses, presumably by sending his officials who conceivably bow down before Moses and beg him to come and see Pharaoh. Moses, of course, will grant Pharaoh's request for an audience with him and accepts Pharaoh's concession (12:31-32). But presently, after delivering his message, Moses, **hot with anger** (probably still enraged by Pharaoh's earlier outrage and death threat in 10:28), leaves Pharaoh's presence.

■ **9-10** Verses 9-10 are perhaps a summary of chs 7—10. What Yahweh foretold to **Moses** concerning **Pharaoh** in 7:4 has been demonstrated in the nine plagues in 7:14—10:29. Pharaoh's stubbornness was the reason for the multiplication of God's signs and **wonders** (11:9). Yahweh's hardening of Pharaoh's heart also contributed to his stubborn resistance to Yahweh's demand to **let the Israelites go out of his country** (v 10).

FROM THE TEXT

In perfect mercy and justice, God sides with the poor and oppressed and turns the tables of history in their favor. This is one of many biblical passages in which we see God restoring justice to God's people by bringing about a reversal of fortunes. The Lord brings down the rich, powerful, and arrogant and lifts up the poor, vulnerable, and humble. In the exodus, Yahweh does what the people of God celebrate poetically later in Scripture, most clearly in the songs of Hannah (1 Sam 2) and Mary (the Magnificat in Luke 1).

John Wesley is among those in church history whose theological interpretation of Scripture matches his practical concern for the poor and oppressed. In his *John Wesley's Notes on the Bible* (Wesley Center Online), he places the situation of the Israelites in 11:2 into the context of the wider biblical witness to God's justice for the marginalized:

Their masters, who had abused them in their work, would now have defrauded them of their wages, and have sent them away empty, and the poor Israelites were so fond of liberty that they themselves would be satisfied with that, without pay: but he that executeth righteousness and judgment for the oppressed, provided that the labourers should not lose their hire. God ordered them to demand it now at their departure, in jewels of silver, and jewels of gold.

Indeed, for Wesley, the gospel message of God's mercy is especially directed to the poor. In his notes on Luke 7:22, Wesley declares, "To the poor the gospel is preached—which is the greatest mercy, and the greatest miracle of all" (*Wesley's Notes on the Bible*, Wesley Center Online). In the exodus—and specifically in the plundering of the Egyptians—the Israelites experience a foretaste of the gospel that promises divine justice and mercy to those whom the worldly "principalities and powers" deprive of justice and mercy. God not only rescues us from sin and death but also adopts us as sons and daughters, making us "heirs of God and co-heirs with Christ, if indeed we share in his sufferings in order that we may also share in his glory" (Rom 8:17).

In the portrayal of God in the biblical narrative, God's judgment and mercy and his wrath and love are not opposite characteristics. Some readers may be tempted to see in this exodus narrative a violent God who threatens to take the most violent act against the firstborn of Egypt (and does so later). Such readers need to remind themselves that without such severe punishment of the powerful oppressors, the extremely oppressed people could not be liberated (→ From the Text at Exod 12:29-42). The God who unleashes wrath against the firstborn of the sinful and the defiant in the exodus story is also the God who shows supreme mercy and compassion upon the oppressed and downtrodden. Ultimately, this God is the Father of Jesus Christ who willingly gives up his "firstborn over all creation" (Col 1:15) for the dismantling of the power of sin and death and for the redemption of the world that is hostile to God (Heb 2:14-15). The message of the cross, however, does not remove the message of divine judgment of those who defy his Son (see, for example, the parable of the wicked tenants in Matt 21:33-44), lest the evildoers take advantage of divine grace and the victimized lose hope in divine justice.

b. The First Passover (12:1-28)

(1) The Institution of the First Passover (12:1-13)

BEHIND THE TEXT

This subunit institutes the commemoration of Passover and the historical-religious calendar for the Israelites. The month, in which Passover is celebrated and the Israelites come out of Egypt, marks the first month of the year (12:18; Lev 23:5; Num 9:1-5; 28:16-17; Ezra 6:19; Ezek 45:21).

Passover is first celebrated in Egypt, the night before (or on the lunar day of; → Behind the Text for Exod 12:14-20) the Israelites' liberation from Egyptian bondage. It marks the birth of the nation Israel under Yahweh. As such, the Bible records the observance of the Passover commemoration at significant (rebirthing) moments in Israel's history: (1) the first anniversary of the exodus (Num 9:1-14), following the transference of the glory of God from Mount Sinai to the tabernacle, which marked Yahweh's covenant union with Israel; (2) the Israelites' entry into the promised land (Josh 5:10-11); (3) Hezekiah's restoration of Yahweh-worship in Judah (2 Chr 30:5-14); (4) Josiah's religious reform and restoration of monotheism (2 Kgs 23:21-23); and (5) the return from the exile, when the returned Israelites and the converted people of the land celebrated the Passover together (Ezra 6:19-22). As such, the observance of Passover is a distinguishing mark of Yahweh's covenant people, who recognize Yahweh as their Father and the only God.

IN THE TEXT

(a) Israel's Religious Calendar (12:1-2)

■ **1-2** The specification of the location (**Egypt**) in v 1 where Moses and Aaron receive the instruction for Passover may indicate that the commemoration of the first Passover antedates its recording. Yahweh's instruction begins with the establishment of the **month** (***new moon***) of the exodus as the **first** in the numbering of Israel's religious calendar (v 2); the exodus thus marks a wholly new identity and life for Israel with its redeemer God. However, the seventh month (Tishri, corresponding to September/October), which is the month of atonement, marks the beginning of the agricultural year (Lev 25:9-12). The first month of the religious calendar is elsewhere called the month of Aviv (Exod 13:4; 23:15; 34:18; Deut 16:1), which means the month of fresh young barley ears (Lev 2:14), which is March/April in Palestine (→ "barley" in Exod 9:31), and is later called Nisan (Neh 2:1; Esth 3:7). Even as the civil counting of years in the West has historically referred to the birth of Jesus Christ, so Israel's reckoning of months refers to a concrete historical event of the birth (or redemption) of Israel.

(b) The Preparation and Slaughter of the Passover Lamb (12:3-7)

■ **3** The Passover preparation starts with the selection of the Passover **lamb** (*śeh*; "young goat," "young sheep"). The selection takes place on the **tenth day** of the first **month**. The tenth day of the lunar month is often set apart for a significant event in Israel, such as the Day of Atonement (Lev 16:29; 23:27), the beginning of the Jubilee Year (Lev 25:9), crossing of the Jordan River (Josh

4:19), Ezekiel's vision of the new temple (Ezek 40:1), and the beginning of the Babylonian siege that led to the fall of Judah (2 Kgs 25:1).

The selection of the lamb on the tenth day would allow for the consecration of both the Hebrews and the selected victims before the holy day (see the three-day preparation at Mount Sinai [Exod 19:10-11]). A lamb is needed for each **family** or "house of fathers"). A **household** in ancient Israel was typically made up of three or four generations (parents, sons, and their children, and children's children). Thus, "family" in this context is best understood as an extended family, rather than a nuclear family. **Each man** here refers to a representative of each household, likely a firstborn male. Passages such as Num 3:41, 45 indicate that the firstborn performed priestly duties before the installation of the priests. The actions of the male representative in this passage are clearly priestly and ceremonial in character: slaughtering the sacrificial lamb and applying its blood to the lintel and the doorposts (Exod 12:7, 21).

The Passover is to be celebrated by **the whole community of Israel** in a domestic setting. Families and neighbors (v 4) are to come together in fellowship with one another and in communion with Yahweh. The text of Deut 16:2, 5-7 envisions the Israelites in the promised land and prohibits the domestic observance of this festival and demands a pilgrimage to a centralized sanctuary (see Hezekiah in 2 Chr 30 and Josiah in 2 Kgs 23:21-23; 2 Chr 35:1-13).

■ **4** **Small** households are instructed to join **their nearest neighbor** who is also in need of more people for the consumption of the **whole lamb** in one night.

■ **5** The Passover animals (**sheep** or **goats**) must be **without defect** or "perfect" (*tamîm*; also "complete," "whole," "sound") as with the animals for the cultic sacrifices (see Exod 29:1). A defective animal with blemish or illness is not appropriate either as the Israelites' sacrificial offering to Yahweh nor as Yahweh's gracious provision to the Israelites. The Passover animals **must be year-old**, that is, "in its first year" (Lev 12:6 NRSV). An animal older than eight days (see Exod 22:30) may be chosen. They must be male. While many of the male yearlings, especially the goats, are slaughtered for their meat and coat, the more economically valuable female animals are kept for reproduction and milk. While the precise significance of **year-old** is not given, young animals were probably preferred for sacrifice, not so much for their tenderness and economic advantage, but for their ceremonial cleanness as they were not profaned by breeding or work (see Num 19:2; Deut 21:3).

■ **6-7** Verses 6-7 give instructions for the slaughter of the lamb and the application of the lamb's blood. The chosen animals must be tended for four days and kept perfect until the day of the Passover meal. The time of **slaughter** is **twilight** (*bên hā'arbāyim*; lit. "between the two [sun] settings"; see Lev 23:5; Num 9:5; Deut 16:4, 6) or between sunset and dark. **The blood** must be first drained into a basin (Exod 12:22), before it is applied to **the doorframes**.

(c) The Passover Meal (12:8-11)

■ **8** The Passover lamb/goat must be **roasted** in one piece. It must be eaten on the **same night** it is slaughtered. Roasting is the most efficient way to prepare the **meat** and drain the blood and fat.

The Passover meal includes **bitter herbs** (*merōrîm*, identified as wild lettuce or endive) to commemorate the bitter years of slavery (see 1:14). The later rabbinic traditions have allowed for the use of herbs that produce a milk-white sap (such as chicory and dandelion) and root vegetables, such as horseradish and snakeroot.

The meal also includes ***unleavened bread*** (*maṣṣôt*), rather than the bread **made** with **yeast** that takes time to rise. Unleavened bread appears to be well known among the Israelites, as it comes with no explanation of what it is (see "manna" in 16:31).

■ **9** Verse 9 prohibits eating **meat raw** or ***cooked*** [*bāšēl*] **in water** (which would require the lamb to be cut into pieces). The animal must be roasted or cooked (*bāšēl*) with fire (2 Chr 35:13). The Hebrew *bāšēl* is translated into "boil" in many passages (Exod 16:23; Num 6:19; 1 Sam 2:13-15; 2 Chr 35:13), but it may refer to "bake" (2 Sam 13:8) or "roast" (Deut 16:7). Therefore, the term is best rendered "cook," with the precise mode of cooking (boil, roast, or bake) discerned from the context.

■ **10** The sacred meal must be eaten during the designated ceremonial time and may not be eaten at any other time (see Exod 16:19-24 that prohibits storing leftover manna, except on the eve of the Sabbath). Thus, any leftover food must be burned in the **morning**.

■ **11** The Israelites must eat the **Passover** (*pesāḥ*) meal **in haste**, fully dressed for hasty departure. The most widely accepted meaning for the Hebrew *pesāḥ* is "skip or pass over," based on its usage in 12:13, 23, 27. But the Hebrew term most likely means "protect" (see Isa 31:5). The meaning "protect" serves well all of its usage, including Exod 12:13, 23, 27. The term *pesāḥ* is used in several ways in our narrative. The word is used for the Passover lamb (vv 11, 21); for the Passover sacrifice (v 27); for the Passover as an institution (vv 43, 48); and for the Lord's protection of the Israelite households that place themselves under the sign of the blood (vv 13, 23, 27).

(d) The Promise of Protection (12:12-13)

■ **12** Yahweh's **judgment** of Egyptian **gods** and all their worshippers is implicit up to this point but is now made explicit. Yahweh's judgment might involve physical destruction of the idols. Jerome (*Epistle Ad Fabiolem* 22.701) "records a legend that all temples in Egypt were destroyed during the paschal night by storms and earthquake" (Propp 1999, 400). A parallel would be Yahweh's attack and dismemberment of Dagon, the Philistines' god (1 Sam 5:2-7). Whatever the precise nature of the judgment, the Egyptian pantheon is humiliated and shown to be powerless to deliver **Egypt** from the death plague or to keep the Israelites from departing. Moses reminds the Israelites afterward, "On their gods also the LORD executed judgments" (Num 33:4 ESV). When Jethro hears of these events associated with the exodus, he confesses, "Now I know that the LORD is greater than all other gods" (Exod 18:11).

■ **13** The blood . . . on the houses is a pledge of God's mercy. **No . . . plague** from the destroyer **will touch** the Israelites. The lamb and its blood are required for the Israelites to make a clear distinction between sacred Israel and profane Egypt. The paschal lamb is most likely the "ransom, redemption" (*pedût*) mentioned in 8:23 (note that the noun *pedût* is translated into "distinction" in 8:23). The blood is **a sign for you** Israelites. The blood itself does not have any intrinsic magical power to save people. Nor does Yahweh need any signs since Yahweh already made the distinction between the Egyptians and the Israelites in previous plagues. Rather, the lamb's blood (together with the redemption of the firstborn with an animal) makes plain that their redemption is made through substitution. The animal blood stands in place not only of the firstborn in Israel but also for all Israel as God's firstborn. Further, the lamb's blood on the doorframes demonstrates the Israelites' submission to Yahweh's will and their trust in Yahweh's peculiar ways. As the Israelites obediently carry out the Passover rite, they, on a symbolic level, "participate actively in their own redemption" (Propp 1999, 401).

FROM THE TEXT

For Christians, Jesus Christ is the new Passover Lamb, and the Lord's Supper is the new Passover festival. This Christian perspective is not merely a postbiblical typological interpretation imposed on the Bible but has precedent within Scripture itself.

The OT writers already give indications that Passover festival, like the entire sacrificial system, is not a stable or adequate basis for atonement. In the original Passover, the lamb was not equal in value to a firstborn of each Israelite family. Yet, in God's grace, lamb's blood was sufficient in protecting the Israelites' homes from the destroying angel. In other words, there was an understanding that the lamb is functioning as a representative and substitute although not a perfect or equivalent one. The Passover celebration implicitly "leans forward" toward the coming sacrificial Lamb, who would be a perfect representative and substitute and thus able to make atonement for the sins not only of the Israelites but also of the whole world (see John 1:29; 1 John 2:2).

(2) The Unleavened Bread (12:14-20)

BEHIND THE TEXT

In this subunit, Yahweh instructs the Israelites to celebrate the Festival of Unleavened Bread (also in 13:3-10). The first seven-day Festival of Unleavened Bread is presumably celebrated at Mount Sinai, together with the Passover (Num 9:1-5). The statement in Exod 12:17, "It was on this very day that I brought your divisions out of Egypt," may indicate that the instruction was given not on the day of departure from Egypt, but on its first anniversary at Mount Sinai (Num 9:1-14). This festival commemorates the day the Israelites departed Egypt with unleavened dough and the subsequent days in which the Israelites ate unleavened bread (Exod 12:17, 34, 38-39). If so, this instruction is placed nonchronologically due to its literary and theological ties with the surrounding material.

The Israelites must eat the unleavened bread "from the evening of the fourteenth day until the evening of the twenty-first day" (v 18), "for seven days" (vv 15, 19). That means that the Festival of Unleavened Bread starts concomitantly with the Passover meal on the evening of the (solar) fourteenth day.

However, to some, the date of Passover and the Festival of Unleavened Bread in two other biblical texts (Lev 23:5-6; Num 28:16-17) appears to conflict with the account given here. They instruct that the Passover be held on the fourteenth day and to celebrate the Festival of Unleavened Bread on the fifteenth day. The apparent contradiction can be resolved with recognition of multiple usages of two terms: "Passover" and "day."

The term for Passover (*pesah*) may mean "the Passover lamb" (Exod 12:11, 21); "the Passover sacrifice" (v 27); "the Passover institution" (vv 43, 48); or the "protection" under the sign of the blood (vv 13, 23, 27). The "passover" (*pesah*) in Lev 23:5 and Num 28:16 is best understood as referring to "the Passover sacrifice" (rather than the institution of Passover), especially given the reference to "twilight" (Lev 23:5), which is when the Passover lamb is slaughtered (Exod 12:6; Num 9:5; Deut 16:4, 6).

The term "day" may refer to a twenty-four-hour period, which is reckoned in two different ways in the Bible (Propp 1999, 405). The solar reckoning of a twenty-four-hour day is morning to morning (e.g., the day in Gen 1) and the lunar evening to evening (→ Figure 3 below). Accordingly, the later instruction to hold the Passover on the fourteenth day and to celebrate the Festival of Unleavened Bread on the fifteenth day (Lev 23:5-6; Num 28:16-17) most likely refers to the slaughtering of the Passover (sacrifice) at the twilight of the fourteenth day and feasting on that evening (which would be the beginning of the lunar fifteenth day). If so, that instruction is not a deviation from the original instruction.

	14th	15th	16th	17th	18th	19th	20th	21st	
		1st day	2nd day	3rd day	4th day	5th day	6th day	7th day	
Lunar day: evening to evening	* #								
	14th	15th	16th	17th	18th	19th	20th	21st	
FUB	1st day	2nd day	3rd day	4th day	5th day	6th day	7th day	8th day	
Solar day: morning to morning	* #								

Figure 3: Solar/Lunar Day

* = Twilight = Slaughter and preparation of the Passover lamb
\# = Evening/Night = Passover commemoration, meal and unleavened bread
15th day morning = the exodus from Egypt
FUB = the Festival of Unleavened Bread

The exodus from Egypt then took place the day after Passover (Num 33:3), according to the solar reckoning of days, or on the day of Passover (Exod 12:17-18), according to the lunar reckoning. That later generations understood this matter is reflected in the celebration of Passover and the Festival of Unleavened Bread at the same time (Mark 14:1; Luke 22:1, 7).

IN THE TEXT

■ 14 The **day** to **commemorate** is the lunar fifteenth day, which includes Passover commemoration, the concomitant unleavened bread, and the event of the exodus from Egypt. To commemorate is more than simply remembering the past event, but is to reenact, relive, reapply the past event as part of one's own story.

■ 15 Since the festival starts in the evening of the (solar) fourteenth (or the beginning of the lunar fifteenth), the **yeast** is traditionally removed during the day on the fourteenth. The penalty for violating the ban of yeast during the **seven**-day festival is that a person **must be cut off from Israel**. The penalty of "cutting off" the guilty from Israel is applied to various cultic and sexual violations of the law. While the precise meaning and application of "cutting off" here is debated, many support "excommunication" by human agents. If this view is correct, the offenders are treated as aliens who are excluded from sacred rites.

The Penalty of "Cutting Off"

In the wider biblical context, "cut off" has serious ramifications. In Exod 31:14-15 and Lev 10:1-6, "put to death" explains "cut off." Leviticus 20 lists various offenses and their penalties that clarify what "cutting off" may mean. The penalties range from "put to death" (vv 1-6, 10-13, 15-16), burn to death (v 14), to bear the punishment for iniquity (vv 17, 19, 20), or "die childless" (vv 20-21). In Lev 20:1-6, the Lord says he will cut off the offender if his people fail (due to complacency or apostasy) to put to death the guilty (of child sacrifice). God's punishment of cutting off may involve immediate death, eventual premature death, or childlessness. Cutting off then appears to be Israel's duty to execute divine punishment on God's behalf, and it may involve capital punishment.

■ **16** On the first and the seventh day of the festival, the Israelites must **hold a sacred assembly**. A call to a holy assembly always comes with the prohibition of all regular **work** (Lev 23:7-8; Num 28:18, 25-26; 29:1, 7, 12, 35) except for the preparation of **food**.

■ **17** Each succeeding generation is to **celebrate** the festival, in a reenactment of Yahweh's redemption of Israel. The Israelite **divisions** (or "troop by troop" [see Exod 6:26 (19 HB)]) come **out of Egypt** in the morning when the curfew is over (12:22) on the fifteenth (lunar/solar) **day**.

■ **18** To help future generations of Israelites to truly remember the historic event of the exodus, the Festival of Unleavened Bread must be celebrated over the course of a whole week. **The evening of the fourteenth day until the evening of the twenty-first day** reflect the solar reckoning of seven days. They correspond to the fifteenth to twenty-first lunar days.

■ **19-20** Yahweh commands removal of **yeast** not only from bread but also from **houses** or dwelling places. Everyone, **whether foreigner** [or a non-Israelite] **or native-born** (or an Israelite), must get rid of all yeast for seven days (v 19). Any violator must be **cut off** from the people. The Passover celebration is optional for foreigners; they may choose to participate after the circumcision of males in their whole household (vv 48-49). However, the prohibition of yeast is imposed on everyone in the **community of Israel**.

FROM THE TEXT

The removal of yeast from the household and from the bread in the old covenant points to the new covenant's call to individual and communal purity and faithfulness. In this passage, the Israelites are called to eat bread free of leaven. Besides its obvious association with haste and not having time to add yeast and let bread rise, the Israelites may have already associated the elimination of leaven with purging what is unholy and incompatible with God's holiness. The process of fermentation and pungent odor involved in the use of leaven may

147

symbolize putrefaction and death. This could explain why all grain offerings are to be unleavened (Exod 23:18; Lev 2:11, etc.), being symbolically unfit as an offering to God (but see Lev 7:13; 23:17, which allows leaven in offerings consumed by humans).

In the NT, a Jewish interpreter, namely Paul, gives a symbolic understanding of leaven as sin: "For Christ, our Passover lamb, has been sacrificed. Therefore let us keep the Festival, not with the old bread leavened with malice and wickedness, but with the unleavened bread of sincerity and truth" (1 Cor 5:7b-8; also see Matt 16:6-12; 1 Cor 5:6-8; Gal 5:9). Paul also uses the imagery of leavened bread as a symbol of nominal believers who lead a pagan lifestyle (1 Cor 5:11, 13), while using unleavened bread as one of transformed, righteous believers: "Get rid of the old yeast, so that you may be a new unleavened batch—as you really are" (1 Cor 5:7a).

The OT does not explicitly interpret yeast as "malice and wickedness." But since the festival celebrates the departure from the land of enslavement, oppression, idolatry, and stubborn resistance of God's authority, the removal of yeast implies the removal of those sins. Indeed, redemption is complete once the people of God not only leave "Egypt" but also remove the "sins of Egypt" from their hearts. This cleansing is what God promises will take place in the new covenant as foretold by the prophets (Jer 31:33; Ezek 25—27). Given the transforming and sanctifying work of the Holy Spirit in the new covenant, then, there is an ethical call to choose to live in accordance with the new saintly identity that Christ has given us.

(3) The Celebration of the First Passover (12:21-28)

BEHIND THE TEXT

This subunit focuses on the observance of the very first Passover. It assumes the Israelites' complete compliance to the Passover regulations. It highlights the Passover lamb and the protective function of its blood in the tenth plague. Given its central role in the redemption of the Israelites, the Passover remains the most important celebration of Yahweh's redemptive work in Israel's and Jewish history.

IN THE TEXT

■ 21 Verses 21-22 give instructions concerning the Passover lambs, their blood, and the curfew. **Moses** summons **the elders** supposedly on the fourteenth day to give the instruction for each family representative to **slaughter the Passover lamb** for sacrifice. The word "lamb" is added to the English translation to avoid the impression that one is, rather absurdly, to slaughter the institution or day of Passover. The term "Passover" (pesaḥ) here and in 2 Chr 30:17 refers to the Passover animal. Evidently the duty of slaughtering the

Passover lamb at some point largely transferred from the family representative ("each man" in Exod 12:3) to priests and Levites (2 Chr 30:3; see Deut 16:1-6; 2 Chr 35:11; Ezra 6:20; also see 2 Chr 30:15 for an exception to this).

■ **22** A bunch of hyssop is used to apply **the blood** on the **doorframe**. Elsewhere, hyssop is used in purification ceremonies, to sprinkle the purifying liquid in a bird ritual (Lev 14:4-6, 49-52). It is also an ingredient of the formula used to prepare the red heifer ashes used for purification from sin (Num 19:6, 17-18). The psalmist uses "hyssop" metaphorically to refer to the spiritual cleansing of his heart from sin (Ps 51:7 [9 HB]).

The curfew lasts **until** the **morning** (when the Israelites depart from Egypt). Moses and Aaron are excused from the curfew, as Pharaoh summons them during the night (Exod 12:31).

■ **23** Verse 23 gives the assurance of Yahweh's protection from the destroyer. The LORD is portrayed as overseeing this last plague. Yahweh is either authorizing **the destroyer**, often understood as an angel, to carry out the destruction of the firstborn or prohibiting him from entering the Israelites' **houses**. Yahweh protects the houses with the **blood** sign. In the NT, Christ is understood as the ultimate Passover Lamb (1 Cor 5:7; see John 1:29, 36; 1 Pet 1:19; Rev 5:6). Having been justified by Christ's blood, God's people escape his just wrath (John 1:29; Rom 5:9).

■ **24** Verses 24-27 emphasize the importance of observing and passing down the Passover **ordinance** to future generations. The annual act of remembering, reenacting, and reliving Passover would function to solidify Israel's self-understanding as Yahweh's redemptive people and deepen gratitude and commitment to Yahweh.

■ **25** The term for **ceremony** (*'ăbōdâ*) is variously translated into "slavery," "bondage," "slave labor," or "work" when it is unto Egypt (2:23; 5:9), but "cultic service," "work," "observance," or "worship" when it is unto Yahweh (12:25, 26; 13:5; 35:24; 36:5; 39:42). The Passover observance is to be a joyful celebration, rather than dull work.

■ **26-27** Any strange **ceremony** arouses curiosity in **children**, which naturally becomes a teaching moment for parents (v 26). In Israel, mothers and fathers were held in high regard as teachers of the law and history (see Deut 6:7, 20 ff.). The translation **Passover sacrifice to the** LORD (Exod 12:27) conveys the idea that the Passover sacrifice was offered up to the Lord by the people. But the more literal translation *sacrifice [zebaḥ] of the* LORD's *Passover* emphasizes the Lord's provision of the lamb for the protection of the people. The term *zebaḥ* ("communion or peace offering"), used in relation to the peace offering throughout the OT (e.g., Lev 3:1; 4:10), further emphasizes the peace and fellowship between the worshippers and Yahweh, made possible by Yahweh's redemptive initiatives.

In response to Moses' Passover instruction, **the people** bow **down**, perhaps overpowered and awed by the magnitude of what will take place (both the destruction and the salvation), and worship Yahweh.

■ **28** This verse emphasizes the Israelites' total obedience, which follows true worship, arising out of the knowledge of Yahweh's just and merciful nature and unmatched power.

FROM THE TEXT

The Passover narrative invites readers to reflect on memory, tradition, and practices that are critical to the identity of the people of God and their acts of worship. The exodus narrative portrays the Passover rituals as sacred acts of worship done with precision, order, and propriety. The slaughtering of the lamb, the smearing of the blood, the preparation of the meal, and the hasty eating of the meal are acts of worship that are integrally connected to the event of the exodus. Whenever the succeeding generations remember and reenact the Passover, they identify themselves as a people whom God graciously redeemed and delivered from an oppressive power. They also proclaim that in a world that continues to decree death, they exist as a people who confess faith in God, who cares for the oppressed.

The Jewish Passover informs Christians of the importance of incorporating historical memories and traditions in their practice of worship. Contemporary Christian worship practices that fail to engage with the critical historical moments in the Christian faith through commemorative practices, such as baptism and Holy Communion, may fail to produce lasting memory and faith for succeeding generations. Where there is no living and faithful memory of the past, there is incomplete transmission of faith. The act of worship is in danger of becoming nothing more than an intellectual exercise in doctrinal matters or an emotional exercise for one's self-satisfaction.

The NT makes illuminating theological connections between Passover and the Crucifixion. Passover is the temporal context for the Last Supper (Matt 26:17-29; Mark 14:12-25; Luke 22:7-22) and Jesus Christ is the "Passover lamb" (1 Cor 5:7). Like the requirement for the Passover lamb in Exod 12:5, 46, Jesus is "a lamb without blemish or defect" (1 Pet 1:19) and his bones are not broken (John 19:36; Ps 34:20 [21 HB]). Just as the Israelites are redeemed and brought out of Egypt with God's mighty work at Passover and the tenth plague, so are the Christians "redeemed from the empty way of life . . . with the precious blood of Christ" (1 Pet 1:18-19).

Most strikingly, Jesus was crucified and died on the day of preparation for Sabbath (Matt 27:62; Mark 15:42; Luke 23:54; John 19:31). The Gospel of John clarifies that this day was also the day of preparation for Passover (19:14, 31; but see Matt 26:17; Mark 14:12). Whatever one thinks about harmonizing

John with the Synoptic Gospels' accounts, John is making a profound theological point in John 19:14. By having Jesus being led to Golgotha about noon, John makes the point that Jesus was crucified and died on the cross during the exact time when the priests were slaughtering Passover lambs in the temple courts (which in the first century was between noon and sundown). In this way, Jesus is ingeniously equated with the Passover lamb and his blood understood as redemptive. This, indeed, is the typological meaning of Passover that Christians have long recognized and celebrated. The Israelites proclaim the death of the Passover lamb when they eat the Passover lamb; Christians "proclaim the Lord's death" (1 Cor 11:26) when they take Communion.

c. The Tenth Plague and the Exodus (12:29-42)

BEHIND THE TEXT

While it may be possible to attribute some of the previous plagues to the destructive power of nature, the simultaneous deaths of all the firstborn of Egypt is wholly outside the realm of natural phenomena. In this plague, Pharaoh is given the opportunity to see clearly the direct hand of Yahweh in all of the plagues. Yahweh has forewarned him (11:4-8), and now Yahweh brings them upon Egypt. Yahweh metes out destructive, terrifying judgments to bring down the stubborn king to reluctant compliance with Yahweh's will. It is the tenth plague that finally makes the exodus possible.

IN THE TEXT

■ **29** In fulfillment of the earlier prediction "about midnight" (11:4), the plague comes at **midnight** of the first Passover. Yahweh goes through the entire land of **Egypt** and strikes **down all the firstborn**, human and animal, great and insignificant, in Egypt.

■ **30** The death plague apparently does not claim lives silently, but violently, perhaps afflicting the victims with terror and agony (→ 11:6). Or else, the thunderstorms and earthquakes that destroy the Egyptian idols (→ 12:12) keep the nation wide awake. Whatever the case, the whole of **Egypt** wakes **up during the night** to the horror and shock of watching their beloved ones die before their eyes. All Egypt loudly and bitterly mourns for their **dead**, with no one to comfort them since all suffer the same terrible fate.

■ **31-32** In vv 31-32, Pharaoh finally submits to Yahweh's demand to let Israel go. Pharaoh summons and orders Moses and Aaron: **Leave . . . Go, worship the LORD**. The **Israelites** will no longer serve Pharaoh in the land of oppression; they will serve Yahweh at the mountain of God. Pharaoh also permits all **Israelites** to leave with all of their **flocks and herds**. The previously refused demands are now granted without any restrictions. Pharaoh's request **bless me**

151

might be for the complete removal of all the curses (or plagues) that Egypt recently experienced. Or, the blessing is for future healing and prosperity, since Egypt is now largely ruined. Either way, Pharaoh is now at the disposal of Moses and his God.

■ **33** Not only Pharaoh, but the **Egyptians** are anxious to see the Israelites **leave** their **country**. The term ḥāzaq (see 4:21), repeatedly used for Pharaoh's stubborn heart, is used here to describe the Egyptians' forceful urging (with military force) of the Israelites to quickly depart Egypt (→ 6:1; 12:39). The Israelites are vigorously hurried out of Egypt at the crack of dawn, as the Egyptians fear for their lives: **we will all die!**

■ **34** The Israelites depart Egypt in such a hurry that they cannot add any **yeast** to **their dough** (see v 39). The Israelites are instructed to eat the Passover meal with unleavened bread in v 8. This verse makes sense only if the instructions for the seven-day Festival of Unleavened Bread had not been given prior to the exodus and the Israelites had fully intended to add the yeast to the dough in the morning after the Passover. Only, they could not carry out their intentions due to an unexpected, sudden departure.

■ **35** This verse represents the fulfillment of 11:2. However, the plundering of the **Egyptians** described in this verse is best understood as a rehearsal of what was done prior to the tenth plague, rather than as something being done while they are being forcefully and quickly driven out of Egypt (for the two suggestions of sequence of events, → Behind the Text for 11:1-10).

■ **36** The fact that Yahweh softened the Egyptians' hearts is already stated in 11:3. Verse 36 of ch 12 reports its effect, namely, the **Egyptians** gave whatever the Israelites demanded. The use of the term "plunder" suggests the Israelites made demands as victors of a battle, rather than begging as slaves (→ 3:21, 22). Since the Egyptians' hearts were **favorably disposed toward the people** of Israel (11:3), there was no coercion. The "plundering" of Egyptians ultimately fulfills Yahweh's promise to Abraham that the Israelites "will come out with great possessions" (Gen 15:14).

■ **37** The Israelites journey from **Rameses** (see Exod 1:11) to **Sukkoth** ("shelters" or "booths"). Sukkoth, likely still in Egypt, is the first stop the Israelites make, possibly on the very day of the exodus (→ 13:20). They bake unleavened bread there (12:39). It might be the place where Jacob and his family set up a temporary shelter when they first "arrived in the region of Goshen" (Gen 46:28). The Bible mentions another Sukkoth, which is where Jacob built shelters for his animals and a house for himself on his way from Paddan Aram to Shechem (Gen 33:17). According to Judg 8:4-5, Sukkoth on the east side of the Jordan River was a prominent city.

A large number of *strong men* (haggebārîm, which likely connotes men capable of fighting in warfare here), reportedly **six hundred thousand** (also in Num 11:21; see Num 26:51), leave Egypt. This number does not include **women and children** and, probably, the elderly men who are unable to fight.

Interpreting Large Numbers

Some have estimated the total number of the Israelites who left Egypt at two million, while others found that to be too large, interpreting 600,000 as 60,000 or as 600 clans, suggesting *'elef* here means "clan" or "chieftain," not "thousand" (see Stuart 2006, 297-303). But given its usage in combination with "hundreds" and "fifty" in the censuses of each tribe in Num 1 (the sum of which is 603,550), "thousand" seems to be the best translation for *'elef*. The unrounded number 603,550 given in Exod 38:26 (Num 1:46; 2:32; see 601,730 in Num 26:51) also indicates that the large number of men is likely literal. Given the Bible's emphasis on Yahweh's covenant with Abraham and its promise of innumerable descendants, a paranormal increase of the Israelites' population in Egypt is expected. Pharaoh's inordinate fear of the size and strength of the Israelites (Exod 1:9-10) also supports the literal reading of the rounded number.

■ **38** **Many other people** (*'ēreb rab*; "mixed crowd"; see Neh 13:3; Ps 106:35; Jer 50:37), some of whom might be fellow slaves, take advantage of the completely devastated and demoralized Egyptians and escape with the Israelites. They may be the same group of people who are later called "the rabble with them" or "mixed multitude who were among them" (NET) in Num 11:4, who are unsatisfied with manna and covet other food and stir up the Israelites to complain against Yahweh. In any case, it is clear that the people who leave Egypt are not all of one ethnicity or people group. Aaron's grandson Phinehas ("the dark skinned one" [→ Exod 6:25]) may point to Nubian (southern Egypt and northern Sudan) presence among the Israelites. Leviticus 24:10 refers to a son of an Israelite woman and an Egyptian father. Deuteronomy 29:11 [10 HB] and Josh 8:35 also record foreigners living among the Israelites. Moses' wife, Zipporah (Exod 2:21; 4:25; 18:2, 5-6) was probably an Arab Cushite, whose tribe lived in Midianite territory (Num 12:1; → "Moses' Marriage" sidebar after Exod 18:9-12).

■ **39** With the unleavened **dough** they brought out **from Egypt**, the Israelites bake and eat **unleavened bread**. The Israelites were forcefully **driven out** (→ 6:1) to ensure a quick and complete exodus. They were forced out in such haste that they had no **time** for **food** preparation. In other words, for their first meal out of Rameses, they eat unleavened bread out of circumstantial necessity, for they do not have leavened bread. Then, they continue to eat unleavened bread for seven days in obedience to Yahweh's command to do so (13:3-6).

Since the instruction to eat the Passover fully dressed and ready to travel was given (12:11), the Israelites should have expected a sudden departure. However, the people may have taken ritual only as symbolic gesture.

■ **40-41** These two verses offer a concluding historical comment about the Israelites' long sojourn in **Egypt** (v 40). The figure of **430 years**, here, is roughly similar to the figures given for the same or similar periods in Gen 15:13, Acts 7:6, and Gal 3:17. The use of the military term **divisions** (Exod 12:41) confirms that the Israelites constituted Yahweh's army (see the expression "ready for battle" in 13:18), although they may not have been trained or willing to fight (see 13:17).

■ **42** This verse explains the relationship between the two vigils: The first **vigil** is what Yahweh kept in order to protect the **Israelites** from the destroyer and compel Pharaoh to release the Israelites by striking down **Egypt** with the tenth plague; and, the second is the vigil the Israelites keep **for the generations to come** to **honor** Yahweh and commemorate Yahweh's redemptive vigil on the **night** of Exodus.

FROM THE TEXT

God ultimately subdues all human and demonic rulers that vie for supreme power, and God calls his people to participate in his victory over these powers. Pharaoh is a paradigm of the kind of powerful ruler, whether earthly or spiritual, whom only God can subdue. Pharaoh has the power to oppress the Israelites with impunity and believes himself to be invincible. Thus, the Israelites need to know that their God has power and authority over all other rulers and powers, especially one like Pharaoh. In the plagues, Israel and Egypt alike see that the Lord judges and humiliates totalitarian oppressors like Pharaoh for the evils they commit.

In our day, God is fully able to deal with powerful nations or systems that oppress and control. The objects of God's judgments today could include economic, political, and ideological systems (e.g., global capitalism, consumerism, militarism, pluralism, humanism, paganism). They may run like well-oiled machines, but these systems destroy human souls, bind people to worldly values, and compete with God for human allegiance and service. The triune God will not endlessly permit false claims to lordship from the current principalities and powers. Suffering and fearful masses can find hope again in the knowledge that the oppressive powers do not have the final word, but the God King does. As in the exodus, the God of the new covenant delivers his people from the powers that be. This happens through the power of the blood of Jesus Christ that redeems us from the powers of the world, sin, death, and Satan (see Acts 26:17-18).

The exodus narrative invites readers to ponder the question, Who speaks for God where there is bondage, oppression, exploitation, violence, and other inhumane activities? The narrative makes clear that God works through his human agents. The powerless Israelites under Pharaoh's power finally become a powerful force that Pharaoh can no longer control or oppress. Together with

Moses and Aaron, the Israelites partner with God through the keeping of the Passover and bring down the powerful empire.

The mission of the church, likewise, is to champion the cause of the powerless, speak for the voiceless, and confront the oppressors, insisting on God's demand for the freedom of the oppressed. The church, in her worship and prayer, witness, social actions, and prophetic confrontations of oppressive powers, must be the instrument of the establishment of God's justice and righteousness. The silence of the church means silent participation in the crimes committed against humanity. Churches and Christians who stood for freedom and equality during the civil rights struggle in America and the apartheid in South Africa were participants with God in bringing social and political changes; they were energized by the exodus narrative and its claim of the power of God to overcome the power of evil.

d. The Passover Exclusions (12:43-51)

BEHIND THE TEXT

This unit further regulates the Passover celebration. The primary concern here is the exclusion of those who are uncircumcised and the inclusion of the foreigners who are proselytized and circumcised. The exclusion and inclusion regulations reflect the sacredness of the festival and of Yahweh who institutes it.

Since circumcision is the physical sign of the covenant relationship with Yahweh and the covenant commitment to live under Yahweh's rule, it is for males (natives or foreigners) a prerequisite to the participation in the Passover (12:44). Those foreigners who were with the Israelites (see v 38) could only participate in the Passover festival if they were residents (v 48) and if they received circumcision; the temporary travelers, visitors, or workers did not qualify. For the Israelites in Goshen, resident foreigners would have included those Egyptians living in their midst. By receiving the covenant sign of circumcision (and by implication, entering into a covenant relationship with Yahweh), even the Egyptians in Goshen could have escaped the tenth plague.

These laws do not reflect ethnic or racial discrimination but religious. However, in the OT, there is evidence for "rigorous inclusion" that expresses not only the sacredness of covenantal rites but also Yahweh's universal saving intentions (see Lev 24:22; Num 9:14; 15:14-16; 2 Chr 6:32-33; Isa 14:1; 56:3, 6-7).

IN THE TEXT

■ **43** Verse 43 lays down the general principle that no **sons of foreigners** [*ben nēkār*] **may eat** the **Passover meal**. The subsequent verses qualify this provision. The **sons of foreigners** may refer to the literal sons of foreigners born to

155

an Israelite household or purchased as servants (Gen 17:12) or to foreigners working and living among the Israelites.

■ **44** Verse 44 of Exod 12 qualifies the general restriction of v 43, highlighting the importance of circumcision (→ vv 48-49 and 4:24-26). A foreigner who is **bought** to be a **slave** becomes part of the household and the faith community after the circumcision and, therefore, is allowed to partake in the Passover meal (see Lev 22:11).

■ **45** Those foreigners who are **temporary residents** or visitors or **hired workers** are not part of an Israelite household, so they are excluded (also in Lev 22:10).

■ **46** The meal is to be consumed in the **house** as a kind of sacred space, which is parallel to its restriction to a sacred time (Exod 12:8, 10). The reason why the **bones** are not to be broken is not stated, but it reinforces the command to roast the whole lamb (including the head; see v 9).

Unbroken / Broken Bones

The Jewish interpreters suggest that breaking the bones would be for the purpose of sucking marrow, which is bestial and unfitting for a sacred priestly meal (Jacob 1992, 356). On a symbolic level, broken bones often signify divine punishment and/or dishonorable death (1 Sam 17:46, 51; 31:9; Pss 51:8 [10 HB]; 53:5 [6 HB]; Lam 3:4) and the wholeness of the bones divine favor and protection (Ps 34:20 [21 HB]). The preservation of the wholeness of the Passover lamb's bones, therefore, very likely reflects the concern to treat with honor the sacred sacrifice, whose blood is instrumental in the redemption of the Israelites (see John 19:32-33, 36 for the unbroken bones of Jesus, which contrast with the broken bones of the others).

■ **47** The statement in v 47 reflects a kind of proto-national unity for all Israelites under Yahweh. This unity allows for the inclusion of foreigners who follow Yahweh's laws in the **community of Israel**.

■ **48-49** These verses prescribe the law of circumcision for the **foreigner** who desires to participate in the Passover. Unlike the visitors and temporary hired workers, the foreigner who came to settle down and live among the Israelites is permitted to participate in the **Passover**, provided that he and **all the males in his household** become **circumcised** (v 48). By accepting the covenant rite of circumcision, the foreigner becomes part of the covenant community with its covenant protection, privileges, rights, and responsibilities (see Num 9:14). Whether **native-born** or **foreigner** (Exod 12:49), those who do not comply with the circumcision requirement may not participate in the festival (see its repetition in Num 9:14; Lev 24:22). The fact that the **same law applies** to all people reflects the egalitarian tendencies that are often present in the Israelites' laws and notions of justice (Exod 12:49).

■ **50-51** Verses 50-51 report that the people of Israel obeyed completely **what the LORD had commanded** regarding the Passover. The phrase **by their divisions** (v 51) confirms the military character of the people (→ v 41). They come out "not like a mob of slaves escaping their masters" but "well organized" (Cassuto 1967, 157). The **day** they celebrated the Passover is also the day of the exodus. It is the lunar fifteenth day (→ Behind the Text for 12:14-20).

FROM THE TEXT

The exclusion-inclusion regulations in this text emphasize the need to maintain the integrity of the Passover by the community that experienced God's power over life, protection from death, and deliverance from the Egyptian bondage through participation in the Passover. The historical event of Passover promotes faith in the Israelites and defines them as a people redeemed by God. Therefore, the Passover celebration is not to be observed casually and without meeting the due requirements, as indicated by the exclusion regulation. Those non-Israelites who wish to embrace faith in the God of Israel and to participate in the festival must receive circumcision, as provided by inclusion regulation.

Given that the Passover is for the Israelites and for the Gentile converts through circumcision, can Gentile Christians legitimately celebrate Passover? Christians today are divided on this issue. Some believe Passover is only for Jews, combining this passage with Col 2:16-17 to imply that all Jewish festivals should be abolished from Christian practice. Others believe that Christians, who are naturalized citizens of Israel in Christ, should celebrate the traditional Passover Seder. Still others find a middle way, suggesting that Christians *can* celebrate the Jewish or OT Passover but are obliged to practice the Lord's Supper as a revised christocentric form of Passover. This last option is the most promising approach.

Since the original Lord's Supper takes place in the context of the Passover festival, it is certainly possible to harmonize the OT Passover rituals with the Christian practice of the Lord's Supper. Some form of (unleavened) bread (or rice cake) is eaten in the Lord's Supper. Christians also practice the Lord's Supper by spiritually ingesting the blood of the metaphorical Passover Lamb, Jesus Christ. Jesus' Passover meal brings to the center of the table the body (bread) and the blood (wine) of Jesus Christ as the Lamb of God, given to all from all people groups to eat.

Likewise, the "blood sign" in the original Passover in Egypt is detached from physical houses of the Israelites and is associated with the "spiritual house" that each believer in Christ represents. The blood of the Lamb marks believers, washes their robes, and makes them white, not only delivering them from the second death, but also giving them the privilege of worshipping God day and night before the throne of God (Rev 7:14-15).

e. The Festival and Commemorations (13:1-16)

This unit consists of three rituals that commemorate the day of the exodus: (1) consecration of every firstborn (13:1-2), (2) the Festival of Unleavened Bread (vv 3-10), and (3) the redemption of the firstborn male (vv 11-16). The first two instructions are most likely given on the day of the exodus, possibly at Sukkoth, their first stop (12:37). The third one is best understood as an instruction given at the time of the consecration of the Levites (to replace the firstborn) and the related redemption of the firstborn, recorded in Num 3.

IN THE TEXT

(1) Consecration of All Firstborn (13:1-2)

■ **1-2** *Every firstborn that opens every womb* of both **human** and **animal** is to be consecrated (*qādaš*; "set apart, sanctify," used also of Aaronic priests in 29:1, 9, 33, 35) to Yahweh. The firstborn is of every womb, that is, of every mother (rather than father). If a man has more than one wife, then the firstborn of each wife is to be consecrated (e.g., Peninnah and Hannah in 1 Sam 1). This ritual is the immediate and natural response to Yahweh's redemptive work.

Consecration and Redemption of the Firstborn

Israel, as Yahweh's firstborn, and every firstborn belonging to Israel are purchased/redeemed by Yahweh with the blood of the Passover lamb for the purpose of serving Yahweh (which is explicitly stated in Num 3:12-13; 8:16-17). So it is fitting that every firstborn is consecrated to Yahweh, either unto sacred sacrifice or unto sacred service (→ "firstborn" in Exod 4:23).

Following the golden calf episode (32:1-6) and the establishment of the Aaronic priesthood, however, Yahweh substitutes the Levites for all firstborn sons of Israel. The firstborn sons are released from cultic duties because the Levites are appointed to the services of the tabernacle (Num 3).

After the cultic duties are permanently transferred to the Levites, the firstborns are no longer consecrated (*qādaš*) for the sacred service. Instead, they are redeemed from such servitude. The redemption price is five shekels of silver, paid to the priest (Lev 27:6; Num 18:16). One shekel is about 0.4 ounce or 11.3 grams. Through the ransom money, the firstborn sons are "caused to pass over" to the Lord without being harmed (see Exod 30:13-14, in which every Israelite man is "caused to pass over" to safety by paying the sanctuary shekel). In this way, the redemption of the firstborn is a symbolic act in imitation of God, who first redeemed Israel (his firstborn) and every firstborn in Israel at Passover.

EXODUS

13:1-2

(2) The Unleavened Bread (13:3-10)

■ **3-4** The day of the exodus is to be remembered and celebrated by not eating anything **containing yeast**. The expressions, **this day, the day you came out** (v 3), and **Today . . . you are leaving** (v 4), point to the giving of this instruction on the very day of their departure (lunar fifteenth of Aviv; → Figure 3 within Behind the Text for 12:14-20 and In the Text for 12:1-2 ["Aviv"]), but at Sukkoth, their first stop (12:37). On the one hand, the Israelites already "came out" (of Rameses), but on the other hand, they are still leaving Egypt (since they are presently encamped in Sukkoth, within the Egyptian borders).

■ **5** The phrase **when the LORD brings you into the land** expresses the concern for the Israelites not to forget Yahweh's mighty acts of deliverance when life is good and pleasurable. The same phrase also seems to anticipate the entry into the promised land to be in the near future (that is, this verse does not anticipate the forty years of delay in the wilderness).

■ **6-7** Eating **unleavened bread** is to last for seven days (v 7; → 12:18), the last day being a day of sacred assembly and **festival** (13:6; → 12:16). The Israelites came out of Egypt with unleavened dough; therefore, they bake and eat unleavened bread (12:39) at Sukkoth (12:37). At the Lord's command, they are to continue this diet for a few more days. In future celebrations, all **yeast** must be disposed of prior to the beginning of the seven-day festival (→ 12:15).

■ **8** Verses 8-9 address the importance of keeping the historical memory vibrant, personalized, and permanently etched in the national and individual consciousness. The recent mighty acts of Yahweh must be told to and remembered by all succeeding generations. It is foundational for the formation of the children's identity, faith, and life choices based on what Yahweh has done and requires. The distant future generations who do not personally experience the event will still identify themselves with their ancestors and declare the event to their children as their own: **I do . . . for me when I came out.**

■ **9-10** The future seven-day festival **will be for you** (v 9) the occasion for recounting and instructing (**be on your lips**) and perpetuating the memories (**on your forehead**) of Yahweh's past deeds. Eliminating yeast and making and eating unleavened bread will be **a sign on** their **hand** that they are, in fact, reliving or actualizing their national history and identity.

Other OT texts use similar expressions to emphasize the importance of ingraining the law of God in children's minds (e.g., Deut 6:5 ff.; Prov 3:1, 3, "do not forget my teaching . . . bind them around your neck, write them on the tablet of your heart"; 6:20-21; 7:1-3). Some related texts appear to call for a more literal binding of the symbols of the law to one's body (Deut 6:8; 11:18; see Matt 23:5). Exodus 13:10 stipulates the annual celebration of the festival on the anniversary of the exodus as a duty to Yahweh their Redeemer.

EXODUS

13:3-10

159

(3) Sacrifice or Redemption of the Firstborn (13:11-16)

■ **11-12a** The regulations here concern the firstborn **after** they enter **the land** of Canaan. In contrast to v 2, which commands the consecration (*qādaš* onto sacred service) of all firstborn, v 12a contains commands to dedicate or *cause to pass over* ['*ābar* in causative] *every firstborn that opens every womb to Yahweh*. When "cause to pass over" is used with "through fire," it refers to the Canaanite practice of sacrifice to Molek (2 Kgs 16:3; 23:10; Ezek 20:26, 31). If this verse has the Canaanite practice in view, then, by removing "through fire" from the expression, it seeks to circumvent Israel's future imitation of Canaanite sacrifice.

■ **12b-13** Verses 12b-13 make clear the distinctiveness of Israel's practice of dedicating the firstborn (human or animal) to Yahweh. The qualification "male" represents a major alteration from the tenth plague narratives and v 2 above (→ 12:5 for the sacrifice of the male animals and the protection of the female; also → 11:5).

(1) Offer every male firstling of clean **livestock** to Yahweh (13:12b). The firstling is "caused to cross over" to Yahweh, to be used in sacred sacrifices.

(2) However, redeem unclean beasts, such as the **donkey** (v 13) with the **lamb**. If the owner does not **redeem** it, he must kill it. Since slaughtering would make it look like an acceptable sacrifice (which a donkey could never be), its **neck** must be broken. The firstling male **donkey** is dedicated **to the** Lord through the vicarious offering of the lamb.

(3) Also redeem the firstborn **sons**. The firstborn son "that opens the womb" excludes those with an older sister, since it is she who opens the womb. This may explain the rather small number (22,273) of firstborn sons counted in Num 3:43.

■ **14-16** As with the Festival of Unleavened Bread, the Israelites are called to teach their children the reason for the offering/redeeming ritual: Yahweh's killing of the **firstborn of both people and animals in Egypt** and bringing his people **out of Egypt** (vv 14-15). The ritual is a symbolic reenactment and commemoration of Yahweh's redemption of his firstborn nation Israel from **Egypt**. As such, the observance of the ritual is fundamental to the maintenance of the Israelites' identity as Yahweh's **sons** and of their historical covenant relationship with Yahweh their Father. Verse 16 further indicates the need to preserve this ritual as a living reminder, like a **sign** on the **hand** and a **symbol** on the **forehead**, of Yahweh's deliverance of Israel **out of Egypt with his mighty hand**.

FROM THE TEXT

Consistent commemoration of central, salvific events is crucial for the spiritual formation of God's people in the past and present. (1) The events of the exodus are recalled in a general way through the Festival of Unleavened Bread. In this annual festival, the Israelites remember, reenact, and even relive the epochal events of the exodus. (2) The redemption of Israel (God's firstborn) through the blood of the Passover lamb is remembered every time a firstborn son is redeemed or a firstborn male livestock is sacrificed to the Lord (13:12-13, 15). This ritual is a frequent reminder of the Lord's merciful rescue of those who worship the Lord and severe punishment for those who stubbornly resist the Lord. It also reminds the Israelites that they are the Lord's treasured firstborn sons who are called to worship and serve God as priestly people (19:6).

In the NT, the Lord's Supper, of course, is a comparable festival of remembrance. In celebration of the Lord's Supper, Christians recall, reaffirm, and appropriate Christ's incarnation and ministry, death and resurrection. In a sense, Christ is at once the Lamb of God who died for our sins and the firstborn Son of God who gives us new life.

The importance of these rituals of commemoration cannot be stressed enough. The Lord's Supper (like Passover, Unleavened Bread, and the rites of the firstborn) not only helps us to remember God's great, gracious initiatives but also gives us a context to respond in exclusive worship and thankful covenant obedience. Further, the Lord's Supper is a divine means through which God continues to administer his grace to us.

3. The Final Act at the Red Sea (13:17—15:21)

a. The Israelites' Journey to the Red Sea (13:17-22)

BEHIND THE TEXT

This unit describes the Israelites' journey from Goshen toward the Red Sea (more specifically, the Gulf of Suez; → Introduction), carefully avoiding the Philistines.

Outside the Bible, Ramesses III (r. ca. 1184-1163 BC) named *plst* (understood by some as referring to the Philistines) as one of the people groups (whom an Egyptologist named Sea Peoples). According to Ramesses III, the Sea Peoples allied themselves and invaded Egypt sometime after they invaded Amurru (that is, Amorites, the ancient Syrian people). Ramesses III claims to have defeated them and settled them in fortresses. Based on this account, some claim that the "Sea Peoples" were the Philistines who came from Crete (speculating Caphtor as Crete) and settled in Philistia. Others hold that the preexisting Egyptian mercenaries revolted but were subdued and resettled within the Egyptian borders (Erlich 2005, 786).

The first time the Philistines are mentioned in the Bible is in Gen 10:14, which traces their origin to Kasluhites, son of Mizraim (Egypt), son of Ham (Gen 10:8, 13-14; 1 Chr 1:12). Other texts (Deut 2:23; Jer 47:4; Amos 9:7) trace them to Mizraim's other son (Caphtorites) who is mentioned immediate-

161

ly after Kasluhites in Gen 10:14. It may well be that the brother tribal peoples Kasluhites and Caphtorites lived in Caphtor (likely in Mizraim/Egypt) and those who migrated and settled in Canaan were known as the Philistines.

Genesis mentions the interactions Abraham and Isaac had with the Philistines (Gen 21:32, 34; 26:1, 8, 14-15, 18). The Philistines are frequently mentioned during the periods of initial conquest, judges, and completion of conquest by King David. The Philistines resided in the southwestern coastal plains (chiefly in five city states; see 1 Sam 6:17) and were mostly in a hostile relationship with Israel. After David's time, the Philistines are seldom mentioned in the OT as an ongoing threat against Israel.

IN THE TEXT

■ **17** The **road through the Philistine country** probably refers to the Ways of Horus, which was a major trading and military route out of **Egypt** into Canaan (Propp 1999, 485). It contained a series of Egyptian fortresses, which would explain why Yahweh wanted to avoid that route! Yahweh is concerned that the Israelites will **return** to Egypt if they come under attack by the Egyptian army. When faced with war and obstacles, they may prefer slavery and bondage to death and destruction on the way to the promised land. This concern is later confirmed by the Israelites' frequent grumbling about the hardships of the desert journey, their threatening to go back to Egypt, and their romanticizing the life of servitude in Egypt's fertile land (which is largely ruined).

■ **18** Instead of the much shorter northerly route (that would take about ten days [Jacob 1992, 377]) to southern Canaan, Yahweh leads them through the much longer route that leads to the wilderness **toward the Red Sea**. Since the Israelites left Goshen **ready for battle** (→ 12:40-41, 50-51), they were probably expecting to fight and defeat either Egyptians to successfully depart Egypt or Canaanites to conquer the promised land. But the previous verse shows an apparent gap between the Israelites' outward organization as an army and the internal preparedness to battle.

■ **19** Moses, representing Israel, is faithful to the **oath** the ***sons of Israel*** swore to **Joseph** many generations before. Acts 7:15-16 indicates that they carried not only Joseph's **bones** out of Egypt but also those of his brothers.

■ **20** See Exod 12:37 for **Sukkoth**, which is the first station in the Israelites' journey from Rameses. **Etham** is the second camping site named and is described as being **on the edge of the desert**, thus, also the edge of civilization. It probably refers to the place where the Delta of the Nile ends and the harsh wilderness (of Shur) begins (→ 15:22).

■ **21-22** These verses describe Yahweh leading the Israelites by **the pillar of cloud by day** and **the pillar of fire by night** (13:22). In addition to providing clear and dependable guidance for their journey, this unusual theophany provides shade by day and light and warmth by night. With the pillars providing perhaps ideal conditions, the Israelites **could travel by day** and **night** (v 21). They walk a great distance in a short amount of time although moving with children and the elderly, not to mention large herds. Some understand these verses as a general comment about the manner in which Yahweh led the Israelites throughout their wilderness period. While that is possible, in the present narrative context, it probably describes the speed and vigor with which Yahweh led the Israelites out of Rameses (first to Sukkoth and then to Etham) and now to Pi Hahiroth, which is the next campsite. Once they are completely out of the Egyptian threats on the other side of the Red Sea, there is no need for a vigorous journey.

FROM THE TEXT

God uses the "detours" of life to accomplish divine purposes for greater human good and for the greater glory of God. God knows better than the Israelites that they are not ready for war and that war would cause them to want to return to the (false) security and familiarity of life in Egypt. So instead of leading them quickly through the shortest route to the promised land, Yahweh leads them in a longer, roundabout way. The seeming detours, however, serve specific and crucial purposes. (1) The Lord drowns the entire Egyptian army at the Red Sea (14:2-9, 23-28). (2) God humbles and tests the Israelites' faithfulness in the wilderness through hunger and thirst (15:22—16:31). (3) God brings the Israelites to Mount Sinai to worship him there to fulfil the sign he gave to Moses at the time of commissioning (3:12). (4) At Mount Sinai, God also reveals himself to the Israelites in an overwhelming theophany, gives covenant laws, and establishes a covenant relationship with them (chs 19—24). All of these steps must take place before the Israelites enter the promised land. In other words, the detours in the wilderness are an integral part of God's guiding of his people; the narrative here speaks more about God's faithful presence and guidance of his people than the preparedness of the people or their resources to successfully complete the journey through the wilderness.

In relation to the contemporary church, this account warns believers not to look for the quickest way to the attainment of God's promises but to follow God's leading carefully, even if God leads one into the "wilderness" or by "the long way." We can be assured that just as the pillars of cloud and fire accompanied the Israelites, the Great Shepherd leads us to the green pastures and waters of rest (Ps 23:2). Jesus promises, "And surely I am with you always, to the very end of the age" (Matt 28:20). Should we find ourselves in a perilous situation, when we have been faithfully following the Lord's leading (just like the Israelites caught between the Red Sea and Pharaoh's army), we should remember that our Shepherd is there even in "the valley of the shadow of death"

(Ps 23:4 KJV). Even such places of danger are part of the right path that leads to a life of complete freedom. Every challenge, when faced with faithfulness, can be an opportunity to see another aspect of the greatness and goodness of God and to grow and mature in our faith.

b. Pharaoh's Pursuit of the Israelites (14:1-14)

BEHIND THE TEXT

The events of ch 14 mark the Israelites' complete freedom. Once the Israelites cross the parted sea and the Egyptian army drown in the seawaters, the Israelites are completely free from the oppressive powers that ruled them (→ Introduction for "Red Sea").

This unit unfolds in four parts, each focusing variously on the perspectives of Yahweh (vv 1-4), Pharaoh (vv 5-9), the Israelites (vv 10-12), and Moses (vv 13-14).

IN THE TEXT

■ 1-2 Verses 1-4 reveal Yahweh's strategy. Yahweh intentionally leads the Israelites in a manner that makes them appear confused, lost, trapped, and vulnerable. Thus, Yahweh orders Moses to **turn back** (v 2). This command abruptly interrupts their journey and changes their direction. The command most likely follows 13:20 (encampment at Etham), rather than the parenthetical comment in 13:21-22 (travel day and night).

The Israelites are commanded to camp **near Pi Hahiroth** ("mouth of the gorges" or "mouth of the canals") and **Migdol** ("fortress," "tower") by the **sea** (Red Sea; likely, the Gulf of Suez; → Introduction). The meaning of Pi Hahiroth highly likely is "mouth of the rivers" or "mouth of the canals" (see Hoffmeier 1996, 170-71). The noun *pî* (construct of *peh*) means "mouth of," *ha* the article "the," and *hîrōt* refers to "rivers," "gorges," "depressed ground between hills," or "canals." The meaning of *hîrōt* is discerned from Akkadian *herû*, "to dig, dig out," applied to rivers and canals, and *harru*, "a water course" or "irrigation ditch" (ibid., 170).

If the Red Sea refers to the Gulf of Suez, then this directive to "turn back" probably involves the Israelites turning back to Egypt from Etham. Instead of journeying into the wilderness of Shur, the Israelites backtrack somewhat and then travel southward in order to camp on the west side of the Red Sea (→ Figure 2, in Introduction).

■ 3 Yahweh anticipates that the Israelites' strange itinerary will give a false impression to Pharaoh's reporters, who are supposedly observing the Israelites' movement. The observers will erroneously believe that the Israelites **are wandering around** aimlessly. The expressions **around the land** and **hemmed in**

by the desert indicate that the Israelites have not yet left the land of Egypt and have not ventured into the wilderness. Moses had announced to **Pharaoh** that they would make "a three-day journey into the wilderness to offer sacrifices to the LORD" (3:18; 5:3; 8:27 [23 HB]). Now at the edge of the wilderness, the **Israelites** would appear to be aimless or hesitant to enter the desert land. Pharaoh has no way of knowing that the Israelites' moves are highly calculated, aimed at destroying his army.

■ **4** Yahweh announces that he **will harden Pharaoh's heart** so that Pharaoh will come after the **Israelites**. Yahweh will **gain glory** for himself through the final act of judgment and deliverance at the Red Sea (vv 17-18). The expression "hardening one's heart" can be understood in terms of Yahweh giving Pharaoh over to the maximum extent of Pharaoh's own pride, arrogance, defiance, and irrationality, until Pharaoh and Egypt reap the full consequences of their century-long diabolical treatment of the Israelites (→ Behind the Text for 1:8-14).

In obedience to Yahweh's command and in awareness of its purpose, the Israelites change their course (14:2). The Israelites are willing participants in Yahweh's plan to draw Pharaoh and his army into the wilderness, to Pi Hahiroth. Sadly, the Israelites' enthusiasm for Yahweh's ingenious strategy is short-lived, since the actual sight of the Egyptian army terrifies them and throws them into great panic and protest (vv 10-11).

■ **5** Verses 5-9 describe Pharaoh's hot pursuit of the Israelites. Verse 5 seems to tell the story from the Egyptian perspective, though the narrative makes clear that events are unfolding as planned and purposed by Yahweh. **Pharaoh and his officials**, upon hearing the news about the Israelites' departure, revert to their willful defiance against Yahweh. Now that the dead are buried and the crippling effects of the tenth plague have waned, the Egyptians focus on the reality of life without the free **services** of their former slaves. Pharaoh's rhetorical question **What have we done?** is not one of contrition but of fury. Given the devastating effects of the ten plagues that the Egyptians experienced, this reversion can only be explained by a divine hardening of their hearts for the specific purpose of giving Yahweh glory through it (v 4).

■ **6-7** Pharaoh personally pursues the Israelites as foreseen by Yahweh (v 4). Pharaoh takes **all** of the **chariots (the best** and **all the other)**. The term **all** echoes Yahweh's use of the same term in v 4, emphasizing the irony of the situation and Yahweh's sovereignty over the outcome; Pharaoh sends his entire military force into a course of destruction in fulfillment of Yahweh's words (v 4).

■ **8** Pharaoh's army marches against Israel, but the show of his military might is nothing but a sign of Yahweh's hardening of **the heart of Pharaoh**. The defiant is made more defiant by Yahweh, who is determined to save his people by a mighty display of his power against the forces of Pharaoh. Though the

165

Israelites marched **out** of Egypt **boldly** (perhaps "defiantly"), their bravery is soon tested.

■ **9** Verse 9 reports that all the **horses** and **chariots** and **horsemen** and **troops** of Pharaoh **pursued the Israelites**. It probably took Pharaoh and his troops on chariots little time to overtake the Israelites encamped by the Red Sea (v 2). They present a clear danger for the Israelites. An army that has never been in a battleground is faced with the full military power of Egypt.

■ **10** Verses 10-12 provide the Israelites' perspective. The Israelites' response to the crisis in vv 10-12 is that of terror, complaint, accusation, and even complaint against Moses' failed leadership. One glimpse of the Egyptian army throws them into a great terror and panic (v 10). They are trapped between the sea, the wilderness, and Pharaoh's army. They rightly turn upward and cry out to Yahweh, their only hope.

■ **11** However, it appears that their outcry to Yahweh is not an earnest prayer, spontaneously arising out of their faith in Yahweh to deliver them out of trouble. Rather, it is a cry of bitter resentment against Moses (and implicitly Yahweh) for **bringing** them **out of Egypt** and putting them in their present state of peril. Thus, they launch a sarcastic verbal attack on Moses, accusing him of deceptively bringing them **to the desert** only **to die**. This charge is not unique to this event, for the children of Israel repeatedly complain when they are faced with various life-threatening situations, such as ruthless forced labor (5:21), lack of water in the desert (17:3), and powerful military enemies (Num 14:2-3). At this point, their worst fear is getting massacred in the desert and their bodies receiving no proper burial.

Burial of the Dead

In the ancestral period, the expression "gathered to one's kin" (e.g., Gen 25:8, 17; 35:29) is synonymous with "died" and "rested or slept with one's ancestors" (e.g., 1 Kgs 2:10; 11:43; 14:31). David spoke of going to his dead infant son (2 Sam 12:23). Barzillai wished to stay in his hometown and die near the grave of his parents (2 Sam 19:34-37 [35-38 HB]). These passages may reflect the ancient Israelite view that the dead joined one's deceased family members and relatives in the place of the dead and that reunion was facilitated through a proper burial in the proper location. Part of the reason for such burial may also have to do with the desire to be remembered and honored by one's posterity. Consequently, Abraham purchased at a high price a field for Sarah's burial (Gen 23) and the other patriarchs placed a great value in being buried in their family tomb (Gen 49:29-33; 50:25-26). The opposite of "resting with one's kin" is to receive no burial, which is one of the covenant curses: "Your carcasses will be food for all the birds and the wild animals" (Deut 28:26). This is the very fate the present Israelites fear may happen to them.

■ **12** The Hebrew text of v 12 lacks quotation marks, making it unclear exactly which words of the Israelites are from the past and which are from the present moment. However, the Israelites would not have foreseen that they would face life-threatening situations in the wilderness. Thus, only the first statement, **Leave us alone**, is what the Israelites would have said in the past while **in Egypt**. The rest of the verse is best understood as what the Israelites presently **say** to Moses: **Let us serve the Egyptians,** *for it is* **better for us to serve the Egyptians than to die in the desert.** This interpretation is supported by the fact that the Israelites' protests tend to address known or impending, rather than hypothetical or future, situations. For example, they declare that they will "die of thirst" when there is no water (17:3) and that they "will die" when terrified by theophany (20:19; also see Num 14:2, 16:34, 17:12 [27 HB] for "we will die" pronouncements). The Israelites here prefer to surrender to Pharaoh rather than put up a bloody fight so that they can be taken back to Egypt alive.

■ **13-14** In response to the complaint of the people, **Moses** gives them strong commands, which reflect a progression of attitudes (vv 13-14). They are not to be **afraid**; they are not to flee from or surrender to the enemy (v 13). Then, they must **stand firm** in faith and maintain confidence in Yahweh's deliverance, based on Yahweh's past acts of power. Moses assures the people that they **will see the deliverance** of Yahweh who **will fight for** them and eliminate the Egyptians (v 14). Therefore, they are to **be still** or be at rest, which means to expect and receive the coming salvation of Yahweh (see Pss 37:7; 46:10 [11 HB]; Isa 30:15).

FROM THE TEXT

This narrative is a prime illustration of fear of the enemy that leads to despair, and trust and confidence in God that leads to hope. This narrative contrasts the Israelites' fear of the Egyptian army with Moses' trust and confidence in God's power to save. Long before the promised land is in sight, the Israelites see the great Egyptian army racing toward them. Completely seized by terror of death, the Israelites can recall neither the mighty acts of God of the recent past, nor the great promises of God concerning the imminent future, nor the present strategy of drawing the Egyptian army out of Egypt in order to destroy them. Thus, they only see one viable option—to surrender and succumb to slavery once more. The life in Egypt is better than death en masse in the desert. This line of thinking later progresses into an intense longing for the "free" food they once had (forgetting that they were forced into free labor) and reminiscences of their supposed "better" life in Egypt (Num 11:4-5, 18). Ultimately, they will want to elect a new leader for themselves and return to Egypt (Num 14:4), which occasions Yahweh's rejection and punishment of them. Moses, on the other hand, remains confident in the power of God to deliver his people and challenges the people who are afraid for their life to "stand firm" (Exod 14:13), "be still" (v 14), and witness God's battle on their behalf.

In ancient Israel and also today, detours, insurmountable challenges, and life-threatening situations are *not* always the result of poor choices, punishment for sins, or enemies outsmarting God's people. Trying situations can become opportunities for the people of God to trust in God and witness his power at work to make a way where there is no other possible way, and for God to reveal his glory in the world through those who trust in him (see v 4). The writer of Hebrews urges us, "Let us, therefore, make every effort to enter that rest, so that no one will perish by following their example of disobedience" (4:11).

c. Deliverance at the Red Sea (14:15-31)

BEHIND THE TEXT

This unit describes one of the greatest and most incredible miracles of Yahweh. Due to its unbelievable nature, suggestions have been made by some that the Red Sea was, in fact, a shallow ford that dried out during a low tide. This suggestion, however, fails to account for the drowning of the Egyptian charioteers, since such water would still be shallow even during high tide. This supernatural event, like so many others in Exodus, simply cannot be explained away naturalistically. The text is clear that the waters were divided, with a wall of water on both sides. Unless we posit a complete fraud, we must reckon with a God of the universe who has supreme power over his creation. In this text, Yahweh does what is unnatural and humanly impossible. The creator God wills it, and the creation obeys the Creator's call.

The Bible records other miracles, in which the force of nature is temporarily suspended and supplanted by the power of God. For example, the water of the Jordan River is said to pile up "in a heap," so that the Israelites of Joshua's time can cross the river on dry ground (Josh 3:15-17). Also in response to Joshua's declaration, the sun delays going down (or the earth's rotation slows down) for a full day (10:12-14). Elijah strikes the Jordan River with his rolled-up cloak and divides the water and crosses over on dry ground (2 Kgs 2:8). After inheriting Elijah's spirit, Elisha performs the same miracle with Elijah's cloak (2 Kgs 2:14). Jesus also demonstrates God's power over nature by stilling the storm (Matt 8:26; Mark 4:39) and walking on the water (Matt 14:25-26; Mark 6:48-49; John 6:19). All these events are implausible and appear to be fraudulent to unbelieving minds, but to the eyes of the faithful, they are accurate depictions of the power and majesty of the creator God.

(1) Parting and Crossing the Red Sea (14:15-22)

■ **15** Verses 15-22 report the miracle of the Israelites walking on dry ground after Yahweh turned the sea into dry land. The narrative begins with Yahweh's question addressed to Moses: **Why are you crying out to me?** Though the preceding section does not record Moses' cry or complaint to Yahweh, it is possible that he raised a cry for help in response to the complaint of the people. Yahweh's question has in it a tinge of rebuke. Yahweh commands Moses to **tell the Israelites** not to stay frozen with fear but **move on** and continue the journey. Implied in this command is a call to trust in Yahweh, who is with Israel to protect them from the mighty forces of Pharaoh. The willingness of Israel to move on at the command of Yahweh is necessary for them to see the power of Yahweh at work at this critical moment in their journey with him.

■ **16** The command to **stretch out your hand** was previously given three times to Aaron (7:19; 8:5, 16 [1, 12 HB]) and three times to Moses (9:22; 10:12, 21; see "hand"). In these cases, stretching out their hands released Yahweh's power to initiate various plagues. In this case, it brings in a strong wind that divides the **sea** and creates **dry ground** for the Israelites' safe passage **through the sea** to the other side.

■ **17** Moses is to do his part, and Yahweh will do his part, which is to **harden the hearts of the Egyptians**. In their unwavering determination to bring back their former slaves to Egypt, the Egyptians **will go in after** the Israelites. They will be unable to reason that the one who opened the sea to save the Israelites intends to close it to destroy the Israelites' enemies.

■ **18** Through the victory over **Pharaoh** and his powerful military forces, Yahweh will **gain glory** and the Egyptians (who see or hear about this event) will gain the knowledge of Yahweh.

■ **19** This is the first mention of Yahweh's **angel** since the call of Moses. In 3:2, "the angel of the LORD" refers to Yahweh. Similarly, the angel **of God** most likely refers to Yahweh here, as it does in Gen 31:11-13 (see "angel" in Exod 23:20; 32:34). This passage reveals that all along, the angel of God has been leading **in front of Israel's army**. Now the angel and **the pillar of cloud**, in a protective move, come between the Egyptian army and the Israelite army (vv 19*b*-20*a*).

■ **20** The second part of this verse literally reads, *It was a dark cloud and it lit up the night*. Perhaps the pillar of dark cloud stood between the two camps during the day and the same pillar manifested itself in fire during the night. Or, as the NIV interpretive translation suggests, the pillar of dark cloud brought a foreboding darkness over the Egyptians (as expressed in "darkness between" in Josh 24:7) while the fire from the other side of it gave out light to the Israelites throughout the night. Perhaps the combining of the two images into "the pillar of fire and cloud" (Exod 14:24) reflects such an interpretation. The presence of God on Mount Sinai also manifested itself like a consuming fire, covered by a dark cloud (19:18; 24:16-17).

■ **21-22** Verses 21-22 of ch 14 make clear Yahweh's direct involvement in the miracle of the **sea** turning into **dry land** (v 21). He divided the waters with a fierce **east wind** (*rûaḥ qādîm*, perhaps the hot desert wind; see 10:13; Gen 41:6; Ezek 27:26) blowing **all that night** (until "the last watch of the night" [Exod 14:24]). Some scholars object that the east wind would blow directly into their faces and is, thus, unlikely. However, this concern is superficial, since they only need to have their back to the east. Elsewhere, east wind is a metaphor for Yahweh's fierce judgment (Isa 27:8; Jer 18:17) or its means (Ps 48:7 [8 HB]).

Verse 22 of Exod 14 reports that, as Yahweh promised in v 16, the Israelites **went through the sea on dry** seabed, with the divided waters forming **a wall** on either side of them. Presumably, the Israelites crossed the sea "during the last watch of the night" ($\rightarrow$ v 24), with their paths brightly lit by the fire from the pillar of cloud and fire.

(2) Drowning of the Egyptian Pursuers (14:23-28)

■ **23** In vv 23-28, the narrative focuses on Yahweh's continued actions, this time aimed toward the destruction of Pharaoh's army. Without realizing the significance of the events that were unfolding, and unaware of the danger ahead, **Pharaoh's horses and chariots** followed the Israelites **into the sea** (v 23; see 15:4). Although the text does not specify it, Yahweh appears to move the restraint from the Egyptian army (see 14:20). Since the Egyptians have been kept in nocturnal darkness and in the dark clouds/fogs that surrounded them, perhaps they did not see the miracle of the parting of the sea. They charge toward the Israelites and perhaps "they do not perceive their peril" until dawn, when the sea returns to its place (v 27; Propp 1999, 499).

■ **24-25** These verses report specific actions taken by Yahweh to prevent the Egyptian army from pursuing the Israelites. In v 24, Yahweh looks **down from the pillar of fire and cloud at the Egyptian army** and in wrath (15:7) throws them **into confusion** or divinely caused panic (also in 23:27; Deut 7:23; Josh 10:10), perhaps with terrifying thunderclaps and flashes of lightning (Ps 77:17-18 [18-19 HB]).

Night Watches

Exodus 14:24 states that Yahweh caused panic among the Egyptian army **during the last watch of the night** (lit. *in the morning night-watch*). Judges 7:19 mentions "the middle watch," which seems to imply that there were three divisions of the nighttime—the first night-watch, the middle night-watch, and the last night-watch (which is called **the last watch of the night** in Exod 14:24 and 1

Sam 11:11). The Passover narratives make reference to three phases of the night: "twilight" (*bên hāʿarbāyim*) for slaughter (Exod 12:6), "evening" (*ʿereb*) for festival (12:18; see the generic "night" [*layil*] in 12:8, 12, 30, 31, 42), and "midnight" (*baḥăṣî hallaylāh*) for the tenth plague (11:4; 12:29). With the Roman dominance, the night watches were divided into four as found in Mark 13:35: "evening," "midnight," "when the rooster crows," and "dawn."

Yahweh also causes **the wheels of their chariots** to be **jammed** (v 25), perhaps by making the ground soggy. The Egyptian army finally recognizes that Yahweh **is fighting** on behalf of his people (as announced in v 14). They try to flee, but the understanding came too late.

■ **26-28** In vv 26-28, Yahweh completes his actions through the agency of Moses. The Israelites complete their crossing, but the Egyptian army is stuck, likely in the heart of the sea. At **daybreak** the Egyptians finally perceive their impending doom, orchestrated by Yahweh (v 27). Then at Yahweh's prompt, **Moses** commands the **sea**, and the sea obeys him. The water flows **back to its place** to its original, ever-flowing state. The seawaters have been restrained from flowing and held up like a wall by the power of God. With the restraint removed, the water flows back with such a sweeping and colliding force that there is no chance of survival even for the fittest members of Pharaoh's military. The **entire** Egyptian **army** that **followed the Israelites** drowns in the raging sea, as Pharaoh and his entourage watch its destruction in utter shock (v 28). The text is emphatic that there is no survivor.

(3) Summary of the Final Deliverance (14:29-31)

■ **29** Verse 29 repeats the statement in v 22, providing a strong contrast between the protected passage of the Israelites **through the sea** and the complete demise of the Egyptian army in that same sea. This contrast points to Yahweh's power that transcends and suspends the law of nature at will. These miracles fulfill Yahweh's purposes to rescue the chosen people, demolish their foes, and gain glory for the name of Yahweh.

■ **30-31** At the Red Sea, Yahweh finalizes the deliverance of Israel from Egyptian tyranny. Yahweh's **mighty hand** (lit. "great hand") decisively shatters **the hands** [the metaphor for power] **of the Egyptians** (v 30). Now with its military power gone, Egypt cannot "stretch its hands" or exert power over the **Israelites**.

With yet another powerful experience of Yahweh's supreme power, the **Israelites** now respect and **trust** Yahweh and **Moses his servant** (v 31).

FROM THE TEXT

The crossing of the Red Sea represents complete departure from the old and entry into the new life with Yahweh. According to Paul, the Israelites were "all baptized into Moses" by being "under the cloud" and by passing "through the

14:26-31

sea" (1 Cor 10:1-2). It is symbolic of death of the old and resurrection of the new nation under Yahweh and his holy law. As such, it is a type of the baptism into the death and resurrection of Jesus Christ.

Despite such incredible experiences of God's power and mercy, however, the Israelites fall prey to temptation and apostasy. Thus, God is "not pleased with most of them" and they die shameful deaths in the desert (v 5). Paul reasons that this sobering fact is relevant to Christians, because "these things occurred as examples to keep us from setting our hearts on evil things as they did" (v 6; see v 11). Paul thus cautions participants in the new covenant to be watchful.

Paul, therefore, calls us to appropriate the power of the cross and the resurrection in our daily lives. Elsewhere, Paul declares that we have been baptized into the death of Christ and are, consequently, empowered to live a new life through participation in Christ's resurrection life (Rom 6:3-4). We are no longer slaves to sin but are slaves to the righteousness of God (Rom 6:6-7, 18). We can participate in God's holiness and maintain it through the empowering grace of God. But lest we fall into the sin of presumption, Paul goes on to warn us: "If you think you are standing firm, be careful that you don't fall!" (1 Cor 10:12). When we remain humbly dependent on God, God continues to enable us to be faithful and obedient even onto death.

d. The Victory Song of Moses and Miriam (15:1-21)

BEHIND THE TEXT

This passage includes what is known as the Song of Moses or the Song of the Sea. This victory song celebrates Yahweh's supreme power over creation and sovereign rule over political superpowers (be it the Egyptians or the Canaanites). Very thorough linguistic analysis of the song confirms its antiquity. This praise song of salvation that carries historic importance likely becomes one of the most popular songs in Israel from the time it is first composed and sung at the Red Sea.

The passage introduces the song with Moses and the Israelites as the singers (15:1), giving some the impression that Moses is the composer of the song. However, in contrast to Moses' song in Deut 31:22 (see Deut 31:30; 32:1-44), the text does not name Moses as the composer. There are compelling reasons for Miriam's authorship of the song. (1) The song is "a victory hymn, a genre associated with female rather than male musicians" (Meyers 2005, 116). There are other victory songs that are composed by women and that celebrate and memorialize significant events of salvation in the Bible, such as Deborah's song (Judg 5:1-31); Hannah's song (1 Sam 2:1-10); the women's song for David's triumph (1 Sam 18:7; see Judg 11:34; Jer 31:4); and the Magnificat of Mary (Luke 1:46-55). (2) The language of Exod 15:21 (→) indicates that Miriam is the composer of the song and taught it to all the Israelites.

This song is a poem that commemorates a historical event, artfully mixing literal and figurative language throughout. Its interpretation, therefore, must take into consideration its poetic genre and artistry.

The unit consists of an introduction to the song (v 1a), the song (vv 1b-18), a brief recapitulation of the miracle and a report of singing by Miriam and other women (vv 19-21).

The song (vv 1b-18) has an inverted chiastic parallelism, beginning and ending with praise. The opening praise is tied to Yahweh's present victory over the enemy at the Red Sea (vv 1b-5), while the ending praise pictures Yahweh's future defeat of the enemies around and in the promised land (vv 13-17). What lies in the middle (vv 6-12) is a song within the song about Yahweh's unmatched power over his enemy. Thus, the enemy's arrogant boasting in the first person is in the middle (v 9), surrounded by Yahweh's dominating response in the second person: (in the outgoing order) Yahweh's mighty breath/wind (vv 8, 10); Yahweh's incomparable majesty (vv 7, 11); and Yahweh's power ("right hand" [vv 6, 12]) that completely shatters the enemy.

a^1 Praise (v 1bc)
  b^1 Yahweh's present victory at the Red Sea (vv 1d-5)
    c^1 Yahweh's right hand (v 6)
      d^1 Yahweh's greatness in majesty (v 7)
        e^1 Yahweh's nostril blast that divides the sea (v 8)
          f The enemy's boasting (v 9)
        e^2 Yahweh's breath that makes the water return (v 10)
      d^2 Yahweh's incomparability (v 11)
    c^2 Yahweh's right hand (v 12)
  b^2 Yahweh's future victory in the land (vv 13-17)
a^2 Praise (v 18)

IN THE TEXT

(1) Introduction (15:1a)

■ **1a** This verse introduces the **song**. Overwhelmed by Yahweh's great deliverance of **the Israelites** and the annihilation of the Egyptian army, Moses and the Israelites sing a song of praise **to the LORD**. Their hasty departure from Egypt probably was not conducive for either the composition or the communal singing of a praise song to the Lord. Now on the eastern side of the Red Sea, completely safe from their former enemies, Moses and the Israelites are able to meditate on and celebrate Yahweh's nature, power, and acts.

173

(2) The Song of the Sea (15:1b-18)

(a) Opening Praise and Yahweh's Victory at the Sea (15:1b-5)

■ **1b** The song begins with praise, acknowledging and declaring that Yahweh is **highly exalted** or that "he has triumphed gloriously," as some translations have it (ESV, NET, NKJV). The reason for the praise is summarized in the rest of the verse and then reiterated in detail in vv 2-12. The Lord has done the inconceivable, parting the **sea** and then completely destroying the powerful and intimidating Egyptian chariot and its **driver**.

This verse, along with vv 2-5, describes Yahweh and his deeds in third person (**he**). This contrasts with vv 6-17, in which Yahweh is directly addressed (using "you" and "your").

■ **2** Exuberant in a joyful celebration, the song declares Yahweh as **my strength and my *song*** (*zimrâ*; "song," "song of praise," "melody"). Indeed, Yahweh is matchless in power! Finding the word "song" to be problematic, some suggest "power" or "protection" or **defense**, following the LXX. But Yahweh as "song" fits well with the context of a victory celebration and singing. The same expression occurs in Ps 118:14 and Isa 12:2, which exuberantly celebrate Yahweh's mighty acts of **salvation**. Yahweh, of course, is not a song, no more than he is a rock (Gen 49:24). **The LORD** is "my song" means, metaphorically, that the Lord is the reason for and the subject of the song.

Through the personal experience of Yahweh's salvation, the Israelites personalize the God of their ancestors (3:15) as their own God, **my God**.

■ **3** Yahweh **is a warrior** who implements the winning strategy and powerfully maneuvers nature as a weapon to defeat the foe. There is no match for him. The Israelites declare that Yahweh **is his name**, recognizing and responding to God's self-revelation as Yahweh (3:15). Yahweh's name (identity, character, and power) being known among his own people, of course, is one of the explicit purposes for divine revelation (6:7; 16:12).

■ **4** This verse clarifies that even **the best of Pharaoh's officers** were **drowned**. What the narrative describes as the action of forceful water, the poetry attributes to Yahweh. Perhaps the poet imagines the water crashing down on the chariots and drowning them as the symbolic hands of God that pick up enemy soldiers and throw them into the sea.

■ **5** The drowning Egyptians and their chariots are likened to a sinking **stone**. There is no chance of survival in a **deep**, raging sea. The archaic form of the Hebrew verb for "covered" points to the poem's antiquity.

(b) Yahweh's Sovereign Power over the Enemy (15:6-12)

■ **6** This verse begins a praise song directed to Yahweh. It celebrates Yahweh's **right hand** (also in v 12) that is **majestic in power**. "Hand" is a metaphor for power. When used of Yahweh, "hand" refers to Yahweh's acts of power that work salvation (see 3:19-20; 7:4-5; 9:3, 15; 13:3, 9, 14, 16; 14:31). It utterly shattered the power (or "hand"; → 3:8), pride, and plan of the **enemy**, namely, Pharaoh (and collectively, his army, and symbolically, any such enemy). The language evokes the image of an aggressive and skillful warrior who delivers one powerful blow with his weapon in his strong arm that instantly subdues his challenger.

■ **7** This verse proclaims Yahweh's **greatness of . . . majesty**, in which he overthrows all opponents. Yahweh is spatially, morally, and ontologically exalted above the enemy. Thus, in his exaltedness and superiority, Yahweh effortlessly destroys them as fire consumes dried **stubble**. Some interpret the language of consuming, **burning anger** as referring to the "melting" of the congealed water that drowns the Egyptian army. Alternatively, it may refer to Yahweh's actual use of lightning to strike down the chariots and set them on fire (see Ps 77:17-18 [18-19 HB]).

■ **8** The poet boldly refers to the strong east wind that divides the **waters** (14:21) as the **blast** [*rûaḥ*; "wind," "breath," "spirit"] **of** Yahweh's **nostrils**. The standing dam of water is further conceived as **congealed** or frozen water. The Jordan River is also described as piling up in a heap/**wall** to make a way for the Israelites during Joshua's time (Josh 3:13, 16).

■ **9** The poet imagines the **enemy** boasting in his military strength and in his arrogant confidence; **I will pursue, I will overtake . . . I will divide . . . I will gorge . . . I will draw my sword and . . . will destroy**. There is augmentation of evil intent with each succeeding expression. In the narrative context, the enemy would refer to Pharaoh. His original plan is to recapture the Israelites, destroy the male combatants, and bring the **spoils** (the goods and the livestock) and those women and children who can be subjected to forced labor (14:5). However, his mind changes in the face of the fleeing Israelites, perhaps because he judges that they have no intention of surrendering or serving Egypt ever again. Thus, his heart turns to unrestrained evil, to gorge himself on people, satisfying his diabolical bloodthirstiness with the utter annihilation of God's people.

Since the song also looks forward to Yahweh's destruction of the enemies both around and within the promised land, the enemy, in this verse, refers to future proud, vehement enemies. In the wider canonical context, the enemy is representative of anyone or all those who exalt themselves over Yahweh and seek to dominate or destroy God's people.

■ **10** In parallel to v 8 that celebrates Yahweh's parting of the **sea** with his *rûaḥ*, this verse marvels at Yahweh's closing of the sea with his *rûaḥ*. Yahweh completely thwarts the enemy's arrogant goals by utterly destroying the enemy's army. Although no wind is mentioned in the narrative of 14:26-28, this verse assumes it. This passage sings that Yahweh **blew** with his Spirit and caused the massive water to collapse on his enemy, who **sank like lead** into the depth of the sea.

■ **11** In parallel to v 7, the poet exults in Yahweh's majesty, **holiness**, **glory**, and powerful works. The poet stops to ask a rhetorical question, which implies the obvious answer that there is absolutely no one **like** Yahweh **among the gods**. Yahweh is supremely great in both character (holiness) and deeds; there is none like him. This is the first time in the Bible that Yahweh is referred to as "holy." Before this passage, only three events or places are identified as holy: the Sabbath Day (Gen 2:3), the ground beneath the burning bush (Exod 3:5), and the assembly during Passover/Unleavened Bread (12:16). (See also the use of "holy" in 15:13; 19:6; 26:33; 28:2, 38, 41.)

■ **12** In parallel to 15:6, Yahweh's **right hand** or supreme power is again celebrated. In the narrative, Moses is the one who "stretched out his hand over the sea" (14:21), yet the song attributes the event directly to Yahweh. The poet recognizes Yahweh as the one who works through Moses. Yahweh releases his power through Moses' obedient act. Then, like a grave, **the earth**, which includes the sea here, **swallows** Yahweh's **enemies**. The referent of the "earth" may include Sheol, the place of the dead. Others suggest that this line is a later addition referring to the unusual deaths of Dathan and Abiram (Num 16:29-34; see the use of "Sheol" in Num 16:30, 33). However, this poetic line (and others) need not and should not be taken so literally. The Egyptians were not literally swallowed by the earth or the sea any more than the people of Canaan "melt away" (Exod 15:15). The point of the entire verse is to marvel at Yahweh's magnificent power that controls his creation, causing it to behave in supernatural ways in order to execute divine justice on the enemies of God.

(c) Yahweh's Victory in the Land and Closing Praise (15:13-18)

■ **13** In parallel to vv 1b-5 and based on Yahweh's deliverance of the Israelites out of Egypt, vv 13-18 as a whole make a prophetic declaration that Yahweh will bring the Israelites into the promised land. One who utterly defeated the Egyptian powers will no doubt overcome any powers that resist the Israelites' entry into the land. From the poet's perspective, the promised land is Yahweh's **holy dwelling** even before it is conquered and occupied by the Israelites. What Yahweh has already set apart for himself is holy.

■ **14-15** The poet expects that the news of Yahweh's mighty acts of deliverance will spread rapidly to the **nations**. More specifically, the leaders and peoples in **Philistia**, **Edom**, **Moab**, and **Canaan**, whom the Israelites will need to contend to possess the land, will **hear** about the victory. The poet foresees that the inhabitants of the named territories will **tremble** in fear of death, presumably as the Israelites advance toward the land to conquer and to occupy it. They will be gripped in **anguish**, be **terrified**, and **melt away** (or faint) at the realization that the Israelites are advancing toward their own land.

■ **16** The poet pictures that **terror and dread** will grip the nations. The poet further envisions Yahweh's **arm** (that is, mighty deeds of deliverance) paralyzing the enemy nations (such as Edom and Moab [v 15]). Yahweh will make them **as still as a stone** to make a safe passageway for the Israelites, whom Yahweh **bought** by the blood of the lamb (Ps 74:2; → Exod 8:22-23; 12:13).

■ **17** The prophetic foresight takes the poet further into the time when the Israelites will have successfully penetrated into Canaan and firmly established themselves there on Yahweh's holy **mountain** (15:16-17). Some suggest that the "mountain" in this verse refers to Mount Sinai, but this is very unlikely since Mount Sinai is clearly situated outside Canaan. The whole of the promised land could be the metaphorical holy mountain of God. However, it most likely refers to Mount Moriah in Jerusalem where Abraham nearly sacrificed Isaac (Gen 22:2-14) and Yahweh made an unconditional covenant with Abraham and his descendants with a divine oath (vv 15-18) and where Solomon built the temple (2 Chr 3:1).

Of all the nations, the Israelites are treated specially, because they have been bought by a price (Exod 15:16). Further, of all the earth, the promised land is special to the Lord because it is **the place** that Yahweh chose for his **dwelling**. It is Yahweh's **sanctuary** that his **hands established**. According to this notion of the land as Yahweh's possession and sanctuary, any inhabitants of this land are only tenants who must fulfill the requirements and purposes of Yahweh as the landlord. This concept applies to the Philistines and the Canaanites (who are about to be driven out) and the Israelites (who are about to be ushered in). By implication, the tenants who defile the land will be driven out of it, whatever their covenant status before Yahweh.

■ **18** Every mighty victory of Yahweh occasions a spontaneous utterance of praise: **The LORD reigns for ever and ever**. Pharaoh's tyrannical reign over them ends. The enemies of the promised land will be subdued. Yahweh will rule and reign in his incontestable sovereignty. Not only that, but Yahweh's dominion will never come to an end. Yahweh's presence in Israel is a transmission of heaven on earth, and Yahweh's reign over Israel is an extension of Yahweh's perpetual and universal dominion over creation (19:5).

(3) Recapitulation and Miriam's Singing (15:19-21)

■ **19** This verse recapitulates the Red Sea miracle.

■ **20** The singing and **dancing** of **Miriam the prophet** and **all the women** of Israel follows the summary of v 19. This is the first time Miriam is referred to by name and called a prophet. The term "prophet" (*nebî'â*) is also used for other biblical women: Deborah (Judg 4:4), Huldah (2 Kgs 22:14), Noadiah (Neh 6:14), and Isaiah's wife (Isa 8:3). It is also used in the plural ("prophets"; e.g., Jer 23:15; Ezek 13:16). (See also Num 12, in which Miriam claims her prophetic powers as a reason for questioning Moses' unique authority.)

Miriam is introduced as **Aaron's sister**. Perhaps there is a conscious effort to deemphasize the familial ties between Aaron/Miriam and Yahweh's mediator Moses. Miriam is generally assumed to be the watchwoman of the small ark where the infant Moses was placed (2:4, 7). If this assumption is correct, then, even at a young age, Miriam's prophetic wisdom and fortitude guided her to ask pointed questions that led the unsuspecting Egyptian princess to hire Moses' own mother as a paid and protected wet nurse. If Miriam is this "girl" mentioned in 2:8, then she is some fourteen years senior to Moses (→ 2:8), thus making her an elderly woman of about ninety-five (see 7:7). In her old age, she rises in joy and strength, with *a tambourine* in her hand, to lead **all the women** in joyful singing and dancing. Women are noted as composing and singing songs, especially songs of military victory (Judg 5; 11:34; 1 Sam 18:6-7).

■ **21** Since this verse repeats the words found in Exod 15:1 almost verbatim (except for "Sing ye" [KJV] or *sing you all* instead of "I will sing"), some suggest that **Miriam sang** just the first line of the longer song of praise—perhaps as an antiphon or chorus. However, the expression Miriam sang **to them** (masc. pl.) signifies that Miriam composed and sang the entire song to all the Israelites. They likely sang after her, committing the song to their memory. If so, the first line serves as the "title" of the song, signifying that Miriam composed and taught that song to the Israelites.

FROM THE TEXT

According to John, the author of the book of Revelation, Christians are called to praise God for the saving works of Jesus Christ, the Lamb, which fulfill and extend God's saving work in the exodus. John records a vision in which "those who had been victorious over the beast" (Rev 15:2) were given harps and sang "the song of Moses the servant of God, and the song of the Lamb" (v 3*ab* KJV). John is clearly alluding to the Song of Moses in Exod 15:1-18 and in Deut 32 (see Deut 31:19, 22, 30; 32:44). John's song (Rev 15:3-4) does not quote any of the phrases found in these songs. However, several of the same themes are present in the songs of Moses and the Song of the Lamb, such as God's greatness (Exod 15:7), God's power (vv 6, 16) and God's unique holiness (v 11). In other words, the Song of the Lamb represents a thematic summary of the songs of Moses.

The song in Rev 15 is not only the Song of Moses but also "the song of the Lamb" (v 3*a* KJV). For the writer of Revelation, the Lamb—the Lord Jesus Christ—and his work are in some way included in the identity and work of the one true God of Israel. Thus, the Song of Moses and the Song of the Lamb praise the same incomparable God who redeems and delivers the people of God and judges their enemies. In the macro-narrative of the two-Testament canon, the deliverance from Egyptian bondage and subsequent conquest of the promised land (that the Song of Moses celebrates) is a type of the greater deliverance and provision accomplished by the Lamb for all who would have faith in him. Seeing the saving purposes of God in the exodus and the work of Christ, worshippers of the Lamb today may take up the themes of the Song of Moses to celebrate the new christological work of the one true God.

II. IN THE WILDERNESS: EXODUS 15:22—18:27

Overview

Onward in Part II, the Israelites are completely free from the Egyptian power. However, they face other extraordinary challenges for survival. They lack not only food and water but also leaders and preparedness for battle. Yet Yahweh meets all their needs through his miracle-working power and wisdom. Also, Yahweh uses the wilderness experience to instruct both Moses and the Israelites to fear and trust him.

This section is probably arranged not chronologically but thematically (Cassuto 1967, 187). The section consists of five units: bitter water made sweet (15:22-27), quail and bread from heaven (16:1-36), water from the rock (17:1-7), Amalekites' attack and defeat (17:8-16), and Jethro's administration of justice (18:1-27). These accounts of needs, grumblings, provisions, wars, victories, and establishments are representative of the Israelites' wilderness period (Num 11:1—27:11). As such, these stories are told for didactic purposes to remind the Israelites in the land of Yahweh's absolute faithfulness. Despite the Israelites' weaknesses and unfaithfulness, Yahweh faithfully brings them into the promised land (see Deut 9:4-7).

This unit also provides the rest of the Israelites' itinerary from Egypt to Mount Sinai: the Desert of Shur (which is called the Desert of Etham in Num 33:8), Marah (Exod 15:22-23), Elim (15:27), the Desert of Sin (16:1), Rephidim (17:1), and then the Desert of Sinai where they camp by Mount Sinai (19:1-2).

A. Bitter to Sweet Water (15:22-27)

BEHIND THE TEXT

Some insist that there was nothing supernatural about turning bitter water sweet, often claiming that a certain shrub had healing properties that sweetened bitter water. Based on the statement that "the LORD showed him a piece of wood" in 15:25, Jacob notes that no such tree has been found but considers the possibilities of the existence of such a tree at the time of Moses and that God taught Moses a natural means to sweeten the water (1992, 436). More likely, however, the wood is a symbol, rather than the means, of healing, similar to Moses' bronze serpent for the people poisoned by snake bites (Num 21:8-9) or Elisha's salt for the foul water (2 Kgs 2:19-22).

IN THE TEXT

■ **22** The **Desert of Shur** is the location of the event narrated in vv 22-27. Numbers 33:8 identifies this desert as the Desert of Etham. It appears that Shur is an alternate name for Etham. The Desert of Shur is described as located to the east of Egypt, south of the coastal plain, and north of central Sinai (Gen 25:18; 1 Sam 15:7; 27:8; Hoffmeier 1996, 188), which is where Etham also would be (→ Exod 13:20). The Hebrew noun *šûr* means "a wall" (Gen 49:22; 2 Sam 22:30; Ps 18:29 [30 HB]) and the location name Shur might be referring to the Eastern Frontier Canal embankments or where the mountain range begins (Hoffmeier 1996, 188). The people traveled for **three days** in the desert **without finding water**. The lack of water raises the following question: Will the Israelites trust Yahweh to provide for them or will they again doubt Yahweh's power, character, and intentions?

■ **23** When the people finally found water, **they could not drink** it, **because it was bitter**. The place is fittingly called **Marah**, which means "bitter." It is possible that the place already had a name equivalent to the Hebrew *Marah*.

■ **24** The Israelites, as they have done on previous occasions when they were faced with hardship, respond to the crisis of undrinkable water with their grumble **against Moses** (see 5:21; 14:10-12). The term for "grumble" (*lûn*; "to grumble," "to murmur," or "to complain") is used here and in other wilderness wandering stories (16:7, 9, 12; Num 14:27, 36; 16:11; 17:5, 10 [20, 25 HB]). It refers to Israel's doubt and rejection of Yahweh's existence, power, and promises, which result in their resentful and hostile speech and rebellious acts against Yahweh and Moses.

■ **25** In response to the crisis, **Moses** cries out to Yahweh, and Yahweh shows (*yrh*; "instruct," "teach") **him a piece of wood** (*'ēṣ*; "tree"). Yahweh evidently instructs Moses to throw it **into the water** to turn the liquid sweet.

There Yahweh sets for them a binding ordinance and puts **them to the test**, which likely refers to Yahweh's command to total obedience in v 26. Jewish tradition holds that Yahweh gave them a few basic laws, such as Sabbath, and tested their obedience there. If so, the laws are given as a foretaste of the more comprehensive body of law that is given at Mount Sinai. Yahweh's demand for and testing of total obedience in this instance anticipates further testing of their trust and obedience with specific instructions given in other trying circumstances, as found in subsequent chapters.

■ **26** The opening phrase *And* **he said** connects Yahweh's demand for absolute obedience with the previous verse, containing "a ruling and instruction" (v 25). The command to obey is followed by a promise. Yahweh promises that no **diseases** or plagues that he put on the **Egyptians** will come upon those who **listen carefully** and **pay attention** to Yahweh's commandments (be they situational instructions in their journey or abiding ordinances of Mount Sinai). Here, the relationship between obedience and well-being is made explicit. Yahweh's laws are not too difficult or overbearing (see Deut 30:11-14); thus, Yahweh's expectation on the Israelites is reasonable and his reward altogether gracious.

Yahweh proclaims his name: *I the* LORD *am your healer*. The name implies that as Yahweh healed the water, so Yahweh heals the Israelites. This healing includes not only the healing of their bodies from brutal treatments but also the healing of their souls from bitterness, unbelief, and the slave mentality that prevented them from putting their wholehearted trust in their Redeemer. The Israelites are not Yahweh's exploited and oppressed slaves; they are Yahweh's beloved "sons," whose every need God will provide.

■ **27** From Marah, the Israelites travel to **Elim**. There is a striking correspondence between the numbers here and the **twelve** tribes and **seventy** clans (represented by seventy elders, see Exod 24:1, 9; Num 11:16, 24-25). It is possible that each tribe drank from its own spring. Since this verse immediately follows Yahweh's proclamation of his name as healer, the arrival at this oasis with **twelve springs** and **seventy palm trees** could hardly be accidental. Elim represents a place of healing and restoration after an extremely arduous, perilous, and trying journey thus far.

FROM  THE TEXT

Difficult circumstances in life provide the people of God with greater opportunities to trust in and experience the power and presence of God with them and his provisions for them. After having been without water for three days, the Israelites finally run into the water of Marah. One can imagine the thirsty people and animals rushing to the waters, the pious among them even thanking the Lord for this place, only to have their hope dashed. The narrative shows that, though they have witnessed the mighty power of God that radically changed their life circumstances from slavery to freedom, they *test* the power of God to provide them with good drinking water; they raise their bitter complaint, "What are we to drink?" (15:24). They refuse to believe that the God who led them through the Red Sea is able to supply them with drinkable water. The good news of this narrative is that God does not get angry with his people for their lack of faith, but graciously provides them with water by showing Moses a piece of wood that turns the bitter water into drinkable water.

The question this narrative invites us to reflect on is this: will we trust and obey God's words/instructions when we are faced with difficult circumstances in life? Jesus models for us how to respond to difficult circumstances in life by his trust and confidence in God's presence and his resolve to obey God's word, when he was tempted/tested by the devil (Matt 4:1; Mark 1:12-13; Luke 4:1-2).

God's promise, **I am the** L<small>ORD</small> **who heals you**, *has both communal and individual dimensions*. God's promise to heal includes the restoration of his people to full health and well-being, so that they may fully participate in God's plans and purposes for them in the world. God's promise also includes the healing of the land the Israelites are about to inherit; God will remove the evil effects of sin of the inhabitants of the land, as human sin defiles the land and renders it unfruitful (see Hosea's description of the effect of sin on creation in Hos 4:3). Moreover, this promise is consistent with God's desire to bring healing and health to the whole of creation so that it may enjoy God's creational blessings (see Rev 22:2; also Rom 8:19-23). However, the narrative makes it clear that this promise can become a reality only if the people of God respond in faithfulness and obedience to God's instructions (see 2 Chr 7:14).

B. Bread and Meat from Heaven (16:1-36)

BEHIND THE TEXT

In this section, Yahweh supernaturally provides food from heaven in the form of manna and quail. Some scholars have attempted to offer possible natural explanations for the appearance of manna and an abundance of quail in the wilderness. These explanations have some value, especially in relation to quail. As with the plagues, however, the natural explanations are not sufficient to remove the miraculous elements from the account. A consistent fact remains: manna is a supernatural food given only to the Israelites during the wilderness period.

The text places literary and theological emphasis on the grumbling or murmuring of the Israelites, which starkly contrasts with Yahweh's miraculous and faithful provision of food. The word "grumble" (*lûn*) is used no less than seven times in this story (16:2, 7-9, 12). People's grumbling and Yahweh's response to it are important factors in the shape and direction of the narrative in this unit and other wilderness stories.

Some scholars take Exod 16 and Num 11 as presenting conflicting accounts of the same event. But the rabble's protest "we never see anything but this manna!" in Num 11:6 is most likely a distortion typical of complainers (rather than an accurate historical review). Also, Num 11:5-6 make it clear that manna remained long enough for the people to develop distaste for it and a craving for different foods.

IN THE TEXT

I. The Complaint (16:1-3)

■ **I** The narrative begins with the departure of the Israelite **community** (*'ēdâ* ["gathering," "assembly," "congregation"], describing both righteous and rebellious groups [Ps 1:5]) from the oasis of Elim and arrival in **the Desert of Sin**. It takes place exactly one lunar **month** after the exodus, which was on the **fifteenth** of the first month.

■ **2-3** Verse 2 picks up the theme of Israel's grumbling against Moses and Aaron. An angry mob accuses Moses of emancipating them from slavery only to **starve** them **to death** (v 3). Since the Israelites come out of Egypt with "large droves of livestock, both flocks and herds" (12:38), even if they have run out of cereal, their complaint about starving to death is absurd. Other texts make it clear that the Israelites had very large cattle, herds, and other livestock in the wilderness and at the time of conquest (e.g., 17:3; Num 20:4-11, 19; 32:1; Josh 1:14). There is no basis for their claim that their lives are threatened. Furthermore, the reader should not take their "recollection" of life in Egypt (**we sat around pots of meat and ate all the food we wanted**) as a factual account but merely as a regretful and angry mob's exaggeration of the meager slave provisions they had. It is typical of the discontented mob to twist facts in order to intensify their case against the leaders (see Num 13:32-33 for the ten fearful spies' distorted portrayal of the Canaanites as giant cannibals and the Israelites as mere grasshoppers and gnats [*kēn*] to dissuade the people from advancing into the promised land). Sadly, their excessive appetite for the native (Egyptian) food presently outweighs the benefits of the redeemed life under Yahweh.

2. Yahweh's Response (16:4-5)

■ **4-5** In vv 4-5, Yahweh responds to **Moses** concerning the Israelites' grumbling by graciously giving them **bread from heaven**. In these verses, Yahweh gives Moses the specific instruction for gathering, which will establish the seventh day Sabbath rest for Israel. However, Yahweh's instructions come with a **test**. They must trust Yahweh for daily and sufficient provision and obey him by gathering only enough for **each day**. Instructions include the provision of gathering on the sixth day **twice as much as they gather on the other days** (v 5). Some suggest that the instruction about the sixth day is given without the teaching about the Sabbath because the Israelites were familiar with a rudimentary concept of the Sabbath. If so, this familiarity may have come through hearing about God's seventh-day rest when he created the heavens and the earth (Gen 2:2-3) and the seventh-day cessation from work during the unleavened bread festival (Exod 12:16; 13:6). Moses is to instruct the Israelites **to prepare** all the manna **they bring in** on the sixth day. On the seventh day, they will cease from all work, including the preparation of food.

3. Delivery of the Divine Message (16:6-9)

■ **6-9** In vv 6-8 **Moses and Aaron** relay to the **Israelites** that they will have another opportunity to experience and receive proof of Yahweh's existence, power, and faithfulness. Thus, Moses repeatedly and almost pleadingly speaks to the unbelieving crowd, **You will know that it was the LORD . . . you will see the glory of the LORD . . . you will know that it was the LORD** (vv 6-8). Moses and Aaron strongly warn the Israelites that their excessive **grumbling** (mentioned seven times in this story [vv 2, 7-9, 12]) is not **against** them as human representatives who are ordinary men (implied by **Who are we?** of vv 7 and 8). Instead, the Israelites are complaining against a living God. What is implied in the warning is the possibility of Yahweh disciplining the Israelites if they persist in their skepticism and negative attitudes. The speech is followed by a summons to the Israelites to present themselves **before the LORD** to receive his response to their **grumbling** (v 9).

4. The Appearance of Yahweh's Glory (16:10-12)

■ **10** Verse 10 reports the appearance of **the glory of the LORD . . . in the cloud**. The cloud veils the full splendor and radiance of the glory of God (see 34:5). Elsewhere, the appearance of the glory of the Lord is likened to "a consuming fire" (24:17) or even a brilliant radiance "like the appearance of a rainbow" (Ezek 1:28). There are other instances in the Bible when all the Israelites see the glory of God, revealed in the context of divine favor or judgment (Exod 24:17; Lev 9:23; Num 14:10; 16:19; 2 Chr 7:3). Its occasional appearance to the entire community of Israel captures their attention and signals that Yahweh is about to do something of great importance. This surprise appearance of divine glory powerfully endorses Moses' case for Yahweh's existence and power (in Exod 16:7-8).

■ **11-12** From the cloud, Yahweh speaks to **Moses**. Yahweh's **I have heard** means, "I am here now to respond." Previously, Yahweh used similar expressions to indicate his responsiveness to human outcries (see 3:7-10). It is unclear how often the quail is given, while the more basic staple of manna is given every morning, except on the Sabbath. Yahweh satisfies them with **bread** (*lehem*, "food" in general [Gen 3:19; 41:54]; "bread" [Judg 8:5; 1 Sam 2:36]; "grain" [Isa 28:28]; "fruit" [Jer 11:19]). The ultimate purpose of manna is for the Israelites to acknowledge Yahweh as their God, to **know that I am the Lord your God** and be faithful to him (also in Exod 6:7; 20:2).

5. The Provision of Quail and Manna (16:13-21)

■ **13-15** Verses 13-16 narrate the provisions of meat and bread that Yahweh promised in v 12. The phrase **that evening** indicates an immediate fulfillment of Yahweh's words (v 13). Though not clearly stated in v 13, **quail** supply the meat for the Israelites. The next recorded provision of quail is nearly one year later, days after they set out from Mount Sinai (Num 11). However, in that account, Yahweh strikes the people with a very severe plague (Num 11:33), for their rejection of him and their inordinate greed, in which each gathers at least ten homers (about 100 gallons) and dries them in the sun to preserve them (see Num 11:32).

The provision of bread appears on the ground in the morning in the form of small (*daq*, **thin** or "fine") **flakes like frost** (Exod 16:14; see Num 11:9). The Israelites' question, **What is it?** (*mâ hû'*), is likely the origin of the name "manna" (Exod 16:15; see v 31). Other portions of Scripture call manna "the grain of heaven" and "the bread of angels" (Ps 78:24-25), which Israel's ancestors did not receive (Deut 8:3, 16). Moses' answer identifies this flaky substance as **the bread the Lord has given** them to eat.

■ **16** Moses proceeds to instruct the Israelites to **gather as much as they need** to eat, as **the Lord has commanded**. The instruction is most likely directed to the leader of each household (see similar instructions concerning the Passover lamb in Exod 12:3-4). The recommended amount **for each person** is **an omer**. An omer is a measurement mentioned only in this chapter of the Bible, attesting to its antiquity. This unit of measurement is evidently not used by the Israelites in the land. So an editor converts it into a measurement current to his time in 16:36.

■ **17-18** These verses report gathering of the bread by the **Israelites**; though some gather **much** and others gather **little**, when **measured** by **omer**, they find everyone having enough to meet the need of their families (v 18). No one has a lack or surplus.

■ **19** In v 19, **Moses** instructs the Israelites not to **keep** any portion of the bread overnight. Since they gather just the right amount of bread for the day, they are to consume all of it without concern for the next day. Implied in this instruction is the call to obey Yahweh's command and not to test his capacity to provide for their daily needs.

■ **20** Verse 20 reports the outcome of some of the Israelites' disobedience to Moses' instruction and his displeasure with the people. The reason for their decision to keep some **until morning** is not made explicit, but most likely, the people lacked trust in Yahweh to provide their daily bread. Their action obviously involves rationing of some sort, so that family members eat less manna than they gathered, an amount that is needed to satisfy their appetites and meet their nutritional needs. In distrust and disobedience, these individuals deprive themselves and their families of the full enjoyment of divine provision. Sadly, the portion they save for another meager meal breeds **maggots**, and it stinks.

■ **21** Verse 21 sums up the daily provision and collection of bread **each morning**. The melting of bread in the hot sun suggests its significance as a provision for the day given each morning to be received each morning. It is a gift that cannot be taken for granted just as it is a gift that cannot be hoarded. Both actions are signs of self-sufficiency and lack of trust and dependence on Yahweh each day.

6. Sabbath Regulations (16:22-30)

■ **22** Verses 22-30 deal in detail with the provision of the bread for the Sabbath and instruction for its collection on the sixth day. In v 22, the people follow the instructions and collect **two omers** on **the sixth day** (see v 5). The leaders' report to **Moses** indicates their concern for his approval of the people's action.

■ **23-24** In v 23, Moses assures them that they are in compliance and instructs that the seventh day is a **holy *complete* Sabbath** (*šabbātôn šabbat—qōdeš*), and accordingly, in v 24, the bread kept until morning stays fresh and does not rot or breed maggots. The term *šabbātôn* means "rest" or "restfulness" and is used to designate an ordinary Sabbath rest, in which one must not do any "laborious or regular work" (Sarna 2004, 66). The term is applied to the Festivals of Trumpets/New Year and Tabernacles/Booths (Lev 23:24, 35-36, 39) and the first and the seventh days of the Festival of Unleavened Bread (Lev 23:7, 8). On *šabbat šabbātôn*, "a superlative signifying the highest degree of rest" (Sarna 2004, 66), one must cease from all forms of work. The weekly Sabbath (Exod 31:15; 35:2; Lev 23:3), the Day of Atonement (Lev 16:31; 23:32), the Sabbatical Year (Lev 25:4-5) are *šabbat šabbātôn*, complete Sabbath.

This is the first text in which the noun *šabbāt* is mentioned in the Bible, although the concept is implicitly present in the Creator's rest (not least in

Gen 2:2-3). It is a day that is set apart or **holy** (*qōdeš*). Sabbath day observation is to be characterized by holiness, acknowledging Yahweh's love and provision for his people. In order to preserve the sanctity of the seventh day, Moses instructs the Israelites to cook on the sixth day the food for the Sabbath day (Exod 16:23). His instructions also include freedom given to the cook to determine whether to **boil** or **bake** it in pans as a cake (v 24; see Num 11:8) and to keep the bread **until morning**, the morning of the Sabbath day.

■ **25-27** In these verses, Moses reiterates the significance of the sanctity of the **Sabbath** day and reminds the people that Yahweh has already given them provisions for the Sabbath. He instructs them to **eat it today**, the Sabbath **day**, what Yahweh has given them on the sixth day. The Sabbath is a day of complete rest, for both Yahweh and his people. They do not need to look for bread on the seventh day; **there will not be any** (v 26). Here, the Sabbath period is morning to morning (unlike in later Judaism in which Sabbath starts Friday evening and ends on Saturday evening). This time period is similar to how a day is understood in the creation account in Gen 1, in which a day is considered morning to morning (e.g., Gen 1:5, 8). Those who defy this instruction find nothing on the ground on the seventh day (Exod 16:27). It is possible that they perceived the bread's appearance as a mysterious natural phenomenon and not as Yahweh's gracious provisions for them.

■ **28-30** These verses reiterate the importance of the Sabbath day. Yahweh's displeasure with the defiant is understandable. Even after repeated instructions, some in the community remain defiant. The phrase **How long . . . ?** expresses divine frustration (v 28). Although only "some" of the people violated divine **commands** and **instructions**, Yahweh addresses the entire community (albeit through Moses their leader). Yahweh reiterates his instructions on gathering bread for the Sabbath day on the sixth day and the importance of observing the Sabbath rest. The people finally get it; they rest **on the seventh day** (v 30). The Sabbath principle in these verses is restated in the Decalogue (20:8-11; Deut 5:12-15) as it must be instilled in the Israelites' national consciousness and practice as they take up residence in the promised land.

7. The Description and Storage of Manna (16:31-33)

■ **31** This verse identifies **the bread** by a name; **the people . . . called** it **manna**. Verse 31 also describes some characteristics of **manna**. It is like **coriander seed** (see Num 11:7) and **white** or light yellow like gum resin ("bdellium" in some English versions). It tastes good, **like wafers made with honey** and like olive oil (Num 11:8). These descriptions reveal that manna was exceptionally delicious and a delicate and special treat (since both wafers and honey are rare commodities to them).

■ **32** Moses relays, supposedly to Aaron, Yahweh's commands to preserve a sample of manna. The "bread of heaven" will presumably be supernaturally preserved for many generations to come, without being subjected to normal decay or disintegration. The sample will serve as a witness to the succeeding **generations** that Yahweh, in fact, supernaturally fed the Israelites **in the wilderness.**

■ **33** Moses further instructs Aaron to preserve **an omer** [see v 36] **of manna** in a **jar** and to place it **before** [*panîm*, "in the face of," "in front of," "in the presence of"] **the** LORD. Prior to the construction of the tabernacle, the physical location that this instruction implies is unclear. It may be referring to Moses' temporary "tent of meeting" (33:7; see "tent" in vv 7-11). Later, its home is in the ark of the covenant (16:34), the central symbol of Yahweh's presence in the tabernacle.

8. Editorial Additions (16:34-36)

■ **34** The last three verses (vv 34-36) represent later editorial additions. The instruction to **put the manna** [that is, in a jar (v 33)] *in front of the testimony* is probably added sometime after the tabernacle is constructed. The "testimony" sometimes refers to the two **tablets of the covenant law** (see 40:20), which is its intended meaning here. Other times, it refers to the ark of the covenant (probably the case in 27:21; 30:36; see also 25:21-22; 26:33-34; Num 17:4, 10 [19, 25 HB]). Hebrews 9:4 states that a golden pot of manna was placed inside the ark of the covenant.

■ **35** The editor reports that **the Israelites ate manna forty years, . . . until they reached the border of Canaan** where they gained access to "the produce of Canaan" (Josh 5:12). When they came to habited **land** where enough natural food was available to them, the manna stopped appearing.

■ **36** The editor explains what an **omer** is in relation to an **ephah**. According to v 16, an omer is evidently a dry measure, equivalent to one person's ration for a day. Based on an archaeological discovery of jars labeled "bath," which was a liquid measure equivalent to a dry measure ephah (Ezek 45:10), an ephah of cereal is estimated to be close to thirty pounds (about 14 kg). While the exact volume is undeterminable, one-tenth of an ephah (or an omer) is generally accepted as about three pounds or two quarts (1.4 kg, 2.2 L).

FROM 🜨 THE TEXT

The relationship between the gift of the bread from heaven and Sabbath-keeping in this narrative invites readers to reflect on what it means to live in freedom from anxieties of life and rest in the daily and gracious provisions of God. God provides for Israel daily in the wilderness until they arrive on the border of the land of Canaan where there is plenty of natural resources for them to survive. The wilderness, the land where resources are lacking, prompts some Israelites to live in anxiety over their daily need for food; they collect more than needed or save some until the next day or go out to collect it on the day of rest. But the narrative makes it clear that God's people survive the circumstances of scarcity not by their own restless efforts but by the providential grace and generosity of God who is present in their midst. The Sabbath is a reminder of this truth and invites us to rest in God's providential care, whether in the wilderness or in the promised land. Jesus' words—"give us today our daily bread," "do not worry about your life, what you will eat or drink," and "your heavenly Father knows" (Matt 6:11, 25, 32)—summon us to trust God and rest in his faithful provision of our daily needs. God sustains the lives of his people not by food alone, but ultimately through "every word that comes from the mouth of the LORD" (Deut 8:3; see Matt 4:4).

The Gospel writer John presents Jesus as the true bread of heaven that gives eternal life to whoever believes in him (John 6:47-57). For John and other early Christian interpreters, manna is a type of Jesus Christ, crucified and resurrected, who provides eternal sustenance. Manna in the wilderness was a short-term provision to Israel, and those who ate manna died, but the bread from heaven is offered to the whole world, and those who eat it will never die but have eternal life (John 6:49, 54, 58).

C. Water from the Rock (17:1-7)

BEHIND THE TEXT

As in the previous accounts, this incident starts with a life-threatening (real or amplified) challenge and ends with Yahweh's faithful response to the need.

Numbers 20:1-13 chronicles a similar story of Moses striking a rock and bringing water. In both accounts, the location is named Meribah (Exod 17:7; Num 20:13). Thus, some posit that the two accounts reflect the same event, only told by two different sources. Most probably, however, they are two distinct events, one near Mount Sinai at the beginning of Israel's year-long camp there and the other at Kadesh Barnea at the beginning of their thirty-eight-year camp there. This passage reports the Israelites' testing and quarreling with Moses and Yahweh. Numbers 20:1-13 tells not only of the Israelites' grumbling but also of Moses' disobedient act, which leads to Yahweh's prohibition of Moses entering the land.

IN THE TEXT

■ **1** The narrative begins with the travel itinerary of Israel. Yahweh leads them **out from the Desert of Sin**, taking them **from place to place** (namely, Dophkah and Alush [Num 33:12-14]). Yahweh commands them to camp at **Rephidim**, where **there was no water**.

■ **2** Verse 2 reports Israel's response to the lack of water at Rephidim. Though Yahweh previously turned bitter water sweet and continues to provide the supernatural bread of manna, the Israelites **quarreled with Moses**. The Hebrew expression for **quarreled with** (*ryb 'im*) carries the meaning of either disputing with someone with complaints and reproaches, or more significantly, conducting a lawsuit against someone. Thus, the Israelites' contention with Moses here is more antagonistic than those previously registered.

Moses' rebuke, given in rhetorical questions, not to quarrel with him or **put the LORD to the test** confirms that the Israelites have crossed the line. The Israelites are rejecting their leader and their God. Their demand, **Give us water to drink**, is not a humble plea from the faithful and expectant but a presumptuous test for Yahweh from the rebellious and doubtful. They are testing whether Yahweh is truly present among them (v 7), and if so, whether the Lord is sufficiently powerful and willing to produce water for them in the desert. Moses' repeated rhetorical **why** is charged with frustration and even indignation, as their behavior is truly dumbfounding, given their history with Yahweh. They have every reason to believe, but they do not.

■ **3** Israel's response to **Moses** does not change. The Israelites interpret their deliverance from **Egypt** as part of Moses' hidden agenda to destroy them in the wilderness; they accuse him of his plan to use **thirst** as the weapon of their death (see death by the army of Pharaoh in 14:11; death by starvation in 16:3; death by the sword of the Canaanites in Num 14:2-3).

■ **4** In Exod 17:4, **Moses** responds to the hostility of the **people** with another cry **to the LORD**; he feels his life is threatened by the angry mob. His words, **They are almost ready to stone me**, indicate the intensity of the anger and intimidation of the Israelites.

■ **5-6** In vv 5-6, Yahweh reveals his plan to **Moses**. Yahweh intervenes without accusation, rebuke, or frustration. He directs Moses to **go out in front of the people** (v 5), which indicates that the Israelites will arrive at the site later on (19:2; see 17:1, 8). Moses is to take the **elders** to **the rock at Horeb**. They will be his witnesses of Yahweh's miraculous provision of **water** from the rock for the thirsty, quarrelsome, and angry mob (v 6). Yahweh also commands Moses to **strike the rock** with **the staff with which** he **struck the Nile** (v 5). In the past, when Aaron struck the Nile, the life-giving water turned into toxic blood. In this instance, however, Moses with his staff is to bring water from a lifeless rock.

While some scholars speculate that Horeb is a new location, it is most likely the place where Yahweh appeared to Moses in the burning bush (3:2). Some speculate that Rephidim, the last-mentioned station before Israel's arrival at Horeb/Sinai (3:1; 33:3; Deut 1:6), was in proximity to Horeb/Sinai and that water from the rock at Horeb/Sinai flowed like a river and met the need of the Israelites and their livestock during their year-long stay at Horeb/Sinai. This speculation is perhaps based on other biblical texts that make reference to water gushing out and forming rivers through the dry deserts (Ps 105:41; Isa 48:21), or "a stream that flowed down the mountain" (Deut 9:21). The Apostle Paul seems to be referring to a rabbinic tradition about a rock that followed the Israelites in the wilderness from which they drank water; Paul typologically interprets that rock as Christ (see 1 Cor 10:4).

In the narrative itself, the precise location of the rock and the duration of the water flow are not the primary concerns. Rather, critical to the narrative is Yahweh's promise, **I will stand there before you** (Exod 17:6). Yahweh's presence indicates his direct involvement in the miracle that is about to happen. Verse 6 ends with a brief report of Moses striking the rock **in the sight of the elders of Israel**. Unlike the Israelites who refuse to trust in Yahweh's power, Moses simply trusts and obeys his command and models for the elders of Israel the proper way to relate to Yahweh. Though the text does not state what happened when Moses struck the rock, the text implies the fulfillment of Yahweh's promise, **water will come out of it for the people to drink**.

■ **7** The people tested and contended with God with the question, **"Is the LORD among us or not?"** They apparently felt the lack of water was evidence that God was not good to them or present with them. The place is given two names, **Massah** ("testing, proving, trial") and **Meribah** ("strive, contend, quarrel") for their testing of and quarreling against **the LORD**. These names are recalled in Israel's subsequent history to teach and warn against being stubborn, trying divine patience, putting Yahweh to the test, and challenging divine authority (Deut 6:16; 33:8; Ps 95:8-11).

FROM THE TEXT

The narrative calls us to trust in God as our good and faithful provider. At the same time, it warns us not to judge God's goodness and faithfulness by the criteria of earthly circumstances. The OT repeatedly affirms God as the life source who physically and spiritually feeds and enlivens his covenant people (e.g., Gen 49:24; Deut 32:18; 1 Sam 2:2; 2 Sam 22:47; Pss 18:2 [3 HB]; 19:14 [15 HB]; 78:35). The wilderness stories show that God graciously provides even for the people with a long history of rebellion. In his faithfulness and attentiveness, God orders human lives to move "from hunger to fullness, from thirst to water, from blindness to sight, from leprosy to cleanness, from poverty to well-being, and in the end, from death to life" (Brueggemann 1994, 818). However, God must not be reduced to a deity who is useful for our earthly well-being. We must not reduce our relationship with God into a "prosperity religion." The Israelites died in the wilderness not because of hunger or thirst, but because of their persistence in unbelief and rebellion. Their story warns us to trust and obey the Lord in all circumstances.

The NT, likewise, presents Jesus Christ, the Son of God, as the one who meets the physical and spiritual needs of all who hunger for food and thirst for water. He offers to all people a kind of "water" that eternally quenches one's spiritual thirst by producing in them "a spring of water welling up to eternal life" (John 4:14; see Rev 21:6). Similarly, he says to those who follow him because of the miracle of feeding, "I am the bread of life. Whoever comes to me will never go hungry, and whoever believes in me will never be thirsty" (John 6:35). While Jesus' ministry of signs and wonders and healing clearly has physical and material benefits, his kingdom ultimately "is not of this world" (John 18:36). Therefore, being "heirs of God and co-heirs with Christ" is glorious at times, while perilous at others (Rom 8:17). The narrative challenges us to be firm in our faith in Christ in wealth or poverty, health or sickness, safety or danger, life or death.

D. Defeat of the Amalekites (17:8-16)

BEHIND THE TEXT

According to Genesis, Amalek was Esau's grandson, and the term "Amalekites" appears to derive from him (Gen 36:12). Amalek became one of the chiefs of Edom (v 16). Balaam's oracle against Amalek later attests to their ancient origin: "Amalek was first among the nations" (Num 24:20). Numbers 13:29 places them south of Canaan. The hostile relationship between Israel and Amalek traces back to that of Jacob and Esau. The conflict described in this text only solidifies the preexisting hostility between the two nations. The reason for Yahweh's harsh oath in this passage (Exod 17:16) is clarified in Deut 25:18 (→ Exod 17:8). Subsequently in Deut 25:19, Moses summons the new generation of Israelites to recommit themselves to eradicating the memory of Amalek. The Amalekites continued to be one of Israel's oppressors during the time of the judges and Saul (1 Sam 15), but David subdued them (1 Sam 30; 2 Sam 8:11-12). In the biblical history, the Israel-Amalek conflict culminates in the story of Haman who was identified as an Amalekite (an Agagite, or a descendant of Agag [Esth 3:1]) who tried to annihilate all the Jews (in reversal of Yahweh's oath to completely destroy Amalek) but was killed along with his ten sons (Esth 7:10; 9:10).

IN THE TEXT

■ **8** Deuteronomy 25:17-18 provides an important detail that complements this account; when the Israelites are on their way to the promised land, the Amalek raiders launch a surprise attack, unprovoked by and unannounced to Israel. The wickedness of it has to do with the fact that they attacked not the Israelite combatants but those who were "lagging behind" (Deut 25:18), the weak, sick, and elderly. This detail is subsumed in the brief summary statement of Exod 17:8: **The Amalekites came and attacked**. This verse places Rephidim as the location of this attack against Israel.

■ **9** In v 9, Moses responds to this crisis by directing **Joshua** to muster **some** of his best **men** to **fight** the Amalekites. Joshua is mentioned for the first time in this passage, but without an introduction. Moses appoints **Joshua** the commander in chief. This becomes Joshua's and Israel's very first battle. **Tomorrow** is the specific time of God's action through Moses and Joshua to defeat the Amalekites (see "in the morning" and "tomorrow" in the plague narratives in chs 7—11). **Moses** assures them that he will watch them from the **top of the hill** and have **the staff of God in** his **hands**. What is implied is that the supernatural power of God will empower Joshua and his men to ensure victory.

Joshua, the Man of God

From other texts we know that his birth name is Hoshea ("Salvation"), but Moses names him Jehoshua ("Yahweh is salvation") or Joshua (Num 13:16). He is the son of Nun and from the tribe of Ephraim (v 8). He uniquely accompanies Moses up to Mount Sinai although not into the presence of God (Exod 24:13; 32:17) and consistently lingers in Moses' tent of meeting after Moses leaves it (33:11).

Joshua is one of the twelve spies who explore the promised land. He and Caleb (his associate spy) remain faithful when the ten spies and the rest of the Israelites rebel against the Lord (Num 13—14). They (and presumably their family members) alone, among those who are twenty and older at the time of the exodus, survive the forty years of the wilderness period and enter the promised land. At the end of the forty years, Joshua is anointed as Moses' successor (Deut 31). After Moses' death, Joshua leads the Israelites into the promised land and accomplishes the initial partial conquest of Canaan. He lives to the age of 110 (Josh 24:29).

■ **10** In v 10, **Joshua** obediently carries out Moses' orders and fights the battle. In the meantime, **Moses, Aaron and Hur** strategically station themselves on **the top of the hill**, where they can afford a plain view of the battle and lend support in prayer that will determine the final outcome.

Once again, Aaron and Hur appear together in 24:14, where Moses leaves the Israelites under their charge for forty days. Hur is conspicuously missing in the account of Aaron's creation of the golden calf in 32:1-6, perhaps attesting to his innocence in the matter. Hur is a Judahite and the son of Caleb (different from Caleb the son of Jephunneh and one of the twelve spies in Num 13—14), the son of Hezron (1 Chr 2:18-19). While the Bible does not explicitly equate Hur the leader of Israel (of Exod 17:10; 24:14) with Hur the father of Uri and grandfather of Bezalel (of 31:2-5; 38:22; 1 Chr 2:18-19, 50; 4:4; 2 Chr 1:5), Jewish traditions typically treat them as such. Their prominence and probable age seem to match and support this traditional Jewish view. Hur may mean "white" (Esth 1:6; 8:15), perhaps indicative of pale skin, or "hole, cave" (Isa 11:8; 42:22), possibly pointing to a cave-dwelling ancestry.

■ **11** Even the best of the **Israelites** chosen by Joshua are no match for the **Amalekites**, perhaps due to the Israelites' lack of experience in battle. However, this battle is not merely a natural battle, for only when **Moses** holds **up his hands** with the staff, the **Israelites** gain advantage. This circumstance makes it clear that Moses' raised hands do not merely provide psychological support but rather unleash divine power (Childs 1974, 315).

■ **12-13** These verses report Joshua's victory over the Amalekites at sunset, made possible by the raised hand and staff of Moses with the support of Aaron and Hur.

■ **14** Then Yahweh makes a kind of vow, which is rather surprising at this point. However, it is made less shocking by Deut 25:17-18, which expounds on Amalek's odious offense. Anticipating Joshua's future leadership over Israel, Yahweh tells Moses to **make sure that Joshua hears** Yahweh's will concerning the destruction of **Amalek** (Exod 17:14). At face value, the call to **completely blot out the *memory* of** appears to contradict the command to commit to writing **on a scroll as something to be remembered**. Nevertheless, the idiomatic expression **blot out the *memory* of** here means to destroy, to leave no posterity.

■ **15** Previously, naming of places memorialized the Israelites' murmuring and failure, but here **an altar** and its name, **The LORD is my Banner** (*yhwh-nissî*), memorialize their obedience, faith, and victory.

■ **16** The entirety of this verse gives the explanation of the name *Yahweh-Nissî*. The first phrase **because** [*kî*] **a hand was against the throne** [*kēs*] **of Yah** is somewhat nebulous. The NIV (and NET) reading may suggest that Moses' hands were lifted up as a prophetic act of intercession to receive and release Yahweh's power. Alternatively and more likely, the first phrase explains the cause and the second phrase the effect: because the Amalekite hand was against the rule (symbolized by the "throne") of Yahweh, Yahweh **will be at war against** them. Their lack of fear of Yahweh and their cruel treatment of Yahweh's people are parallel to raising their hands audaciously against Yahweh's throne (which is likely parallel to the contemporary idiom of "shaking one's fist at God").

FROM THE TEXT

God's covenant commitment to the covenant people includes decisive judgment upon their enemies, whether the natural enemies of Israel or the spiritual enemies of the church. In this battle, God does not act alone but calls the people of God to resist evil with God, even if it involves suffering. The Lord promised Abram that "whoever curses you I will curse" (Gen 12:3). Whether the defeat of the Amalekites in Rephidim or the thwarting of a genocidal plan in Susa, they testify to the truth that God ultimately stands against those who oppose God's chosen people. However, in both cases the victory came only as the people of God with divine grace engaged in warfare against the aggressors.

For the Israelite warriors in Rephidim, Moses' raised staff released divine power to aid them in the battle. For the Jews in Persia, the united fast of the Jews in Susa released divine favor to Esther (Esth 5:2-3), a reversal of fortunes for Haman (7:9-10; 9:24-25) and Mordecai (6:10-11; 8:2, 9-10), and power to the Jews to overcome all their enemies (see 8:11; 9:1-18).

The accounts of the Israelites in Rephidim or the Jews in the Persian Empire provide precedent for the spiritual warfare of Christians. When the spiritual enemies rage against us, we can be confident of the final outcome, for "[we] are from God and have overcome them, because the one who is in [us] is greater than the one who is in the world" (1 John 4:4). Thus, James urges, "Submit yourselves, then, to God. Resist the devil, and he will flee from you" (Jas 4:7). Those who live an obedient life and depend on God for divine vindication and authoritatively confront their spiritual enemies will overcome them.

However, our proper confidence in our authority in Christ and in our victory over evil should not be confused with triumphalism. This narrative promotes neither hatred and violence against human enemies nor demonization of human enemies as incarnations of evil in the world. Our battle as Christ followers is not with "flesh and blood" (Eph 6:12) but with the devil and his demonic minions. In relation to our fellow human beings who are hostile toward us, we gain victory over evil not through physical war and violence but through forgiveness and suffering in love like the Lamb of God. Persecution is normal and expected (Matt 10:23; 24:9-10; 1 Cor 4:8-13; 2 Tim 2:12), even while victory over evil is assured (Rev 2:10-11; 12:11). Christ impresses on us, "If they persecuted me, they will persecute you also" (John 15:20). The unjust but willing suffering of the righteous ironically is what advances the kingdom of God and manifests its victory over the world (see Matt 5:44).

E. Moses' Family Reunion (18:1-12)

BEHIND THE TEXT

This unit briefly treats the reunification of Moses and his wife, Zipporah, which is facilitated by Zipporah's father, Reuel (a proper name that means "friend of God"; → Behind the Text for 2:11-25). While visiting, Jethro (Reuel's honorific title) observes a complete lack of an efficient judicial system and helps Moses establish one (18:8-26). This sequence of the two stories indicates that the primary purpose of Jethro's visit was to restore Zipporah and her sons to Moses. Since v 27 reports Jethro's return to his homeland without Zipporah and her sons, Moses must have received Zipporah and her children back into his care (perhaps with deep gratitude to his father-in-law for taking the initiative to bring her back to him). First Chronicles 23:14-17 names Moses' sons and further descendants of Moses among the Levites, which confirms this interpretation.

It appears from Num 10:29-33 that Hobab (Reuel's son and Moses' brother-in-law) came to visit Moses as well. Perhaps he accompanied his father, as a chaperone to his sister and two nephews. While Moses releases his father-in-law to return to his own land, he persuades Hobab to stay with him to serve as a guide (for Hobab is familiar with suitable campsites in the wilderness).

Despite the chapter's current literary placement, which gives the impression that the Israelites were camped at Rephidim, the geographical setting for this chapter is Mount Sinai (→ Exod 18:5-6). Deuteronomy 1:6-19 also gives an account of Moses' appointment of judges and apparently places this event toward the end of the Israelites' encampment at Sinai.

IN THE TEXT

■ **1** News about Yahweh's mighty deliverance of Israel out of Egypt reaches **Jethro**, as it does various surrounding nations (v 1; see 15:14). Verse 1 of ch 18 does not say how Jethro hears the news; it is likely that Moses sent a messenger to him after Israel's arrival at Sinai.

■ **2 Zipporah** and her sons receive no mention after ch 4. Verses 2-4 of ch 18 reintroduce them and explain the reason for their absence and also validate Eliezer, who is introduced here for the first time, as Moses' own son. Verse 2 more literally reads **Jethro, Moses' father-in-law, took Zipporah, Moses' wife, with** ['*aḥar*] **her dowry** (*šillûḥîm*). The Hebrew term *šillûḥîm* is used in two other places in the OT and is correctly rendered "dowry" (in 1 Kgs 9:16 ESV, NASB, NJB, NJPS, NRSV) or "parting gifts" (in Mic 1:14). The fact that Moses sent Zipporah and her dowry back to Jethro implies that Moses had divorced her (→ Exod 4:24-26).

Dowry

Dowry was the property that a bride's father gave to her at her marriage (Gen 24:59-61; Judg 1:12-15; 1 Kgs 9:16). This was her inheritance from her father. Dowry also refers to the bride-price or the property that the groom brought to the bride's father at his marriage to her (Gen 24:53; 31:15; 34:12; 1 Sam 18:25). Both types of dowry were her security in the unfortunate event of divorce or the death of her husband. Genesis 31:15 appears to be a case of stolen dowry, in which Leah and Rachel display no expectation of receiving any inheritance (dowry) from Laban and accuse him of robbing the dowry Jacob paid him.

■ **3-4** The older son **Gershom** is already introduced in 2:22, but the younger **son** is only introduced in this passage. **Eliezer** means "my God is the helper."

The younger son's name acknowledges and memorializes Yahweh's active role in his safe escape from Egypt (2:11-15). The name foreshadows the divine help Moses receives in liberating the Israelites from Egypt.

■ **5-6** These verses report the arrival of **Jethro** and Moses' estranged family to where **Moses** is located. "Her . . . sons" (v 3) are now called **Moses' sons** (v 5), perhaps signaling imminent reunion. The statement **he [Moses] was camped near the mountain of God** indicates that this unit is placed nonchronologically. Jethro's visit is best understood as following the Israelites' arrival at the mountain of God (19:1-2) and most likely toward the end of the Israelites' encampment at Mount Sinai (see Deut 1:6-19). As **Jethro** and his company approach the camp, Jethro apparently sends a messenger to inform Moses that they are **coming** (Exod 18:6).

■ **7-8** Verses 7-8 focus on the meeting between the two prominent men with the woman and her children now left out of the story. Verse 7 describes the custom of formal greeting. Moses, the lesser of the two in social standing, goes **out to meet** his **father-in-law**. Moses bows **down**, probably kneeling and touching the ground with his forehead to show respect and honor to Jethro. After they greet each other, Moses gives Jethro a firsthand account of Yahweh's mighty acts in Egypt and **all the hardships** and supernatural provisions and deliverances the Israelites experienced since leaving Egypt (v 8).

■ **9-12** Verses 9-12 narrate Jethro's response to Moses' testimony of Yahweh's power and grace; a doxology in v 10, a confession of faith in v 11, and an act of worship in v 12. He praises (*bārûk*) Yahweh **who rescued** Moses and Israel **from . . . Pharaoh** (v 10) and acknowledges that ***Yahweh* is greater than all other gods** (v 11). Although he has not seen any of the mighty acts of Yahweh, Jethro declares Yahweh's supremacy and incontestable sovereignty. This faith is precisely what Yahweh desired for the Egyptians and Israelites alike through their experience of Yahweh's mighty acts in and out of Egypt; "By this you will know that I am the LORD" (6:7; 7:5, 17; 8:10, 22 [14, 26 HB]; 9:14, 29; 10:2; 11:7; 14:4, 18; 16:6, 8, 12). However, here, the great confession of faith comes from a non-Israelite who merely heard about Yahweh.

In 18:12, being a priest, Jethro's confession of faith immediately turns into worship of the God of Israel. **Jethro** prepares **a burnt offering and other sacrifices** to thank and commune with Yahweh in solidarity with those who are delivered from Egypt and cared for in the wilderness. The burnt offering is the first offering mentioned in Lev 1. The whole offering is burnt and goes up in smoke as "an aroma pleasing to the LORD" (Lev 1:9). It could serve as an act of atonement (Lev 1:4; 9:7; 16:24), for it represents the offerer's full devotion and Yahweh's total acceptance. Other sacrifices are for the **meal**, and **Aaron** and **all the elders** come to dine with Jethro. They eat the meal **in the presence of God**, which signifies that Yahweh is pleased to be present at this gathering.

18:5-12

It also connotes that the meal is a covenant meal, most likely not only between the Israelite leaders and Jethro but also between Yahweh and Jethro.

Moses' Marriage

Narratives in Exodus and Numbers show many twists and turns in Moses' personal life, including his marriage, divorce, and eventual reunion with his wife. The Bible does not tell us in what circumstances Moses divorced (or separated from) his wife, Zipporah, and sent her and their two sons back to Jethro in Midian. The most logical time for this, however, would be immediately after the attack at the lodging (4:24-26) at the beginning of their journey to Egypt (v 20). After the near-death experience, Moses likely deemed the journey too precarious for himself or his family with the possibility of not surviving the mission. Moses thus sent them back (with her dowry) to secure their safety and future, and Jethro seeing the rationale for his decision received her back.

There is another interesting twist to Moses' marriage; namely, Num 12:1 mentions Moses' Cushite wife. Exodus 2:15-22 clearly identifies Zipporah as a Midianite, which makes it seem that Moses married another woman during the two-year period of their separation, but that assumption is highly unlikely.

There is textual evidence for (nomadic) Cushites who lived near the Philistines and Arabs (2 Chr 14:13-14; 21:16; see Ps 7 for a Cush who is a Benjamite). In addition, Cushan and Midian appear to be parallel peoples in Hab 3:7, pointing to Arab Cushites. Furthermore, the Egyptian execration texts make a reference to Cushites who lived south of Israel. These texts support the identification of Zipporah as the Cushite of Num 12:1. If so, Moses did not acquire a second wife in Egypt, in the wilderness, or at Mount Sinai. Rather at Mount Sinai, Moses only received his original wife, Zipporah, an Arab Midian/Cushite, and introduced her to his family for the first time. Miriam and Aaron then subjected her to racial discrimination and Moses to severe criticism, but God vindicated both Moses and Zipporah (Num 12:4-15).

FROM THE TEXT

Moses' recounting of Yahweh's mighty acts of deliverance and gracious provision and Jethro's confession of faith and act of worship in response to Moses' testimony urge us to (1) testify God's work of salvation to new generations of the community of faith and (2) bear witness to the good news of Jesus Christ to the unbelieving world outside the church. In Mark 5:19, Jesus tells the man whom he delivered from demon possession: "Go home to your own people and tell them how much the Lord has done for you, and how he has had mercy on you." Paul emphasizes the importance of telling the gospel story when he asks: "How, then, can they call on the one they have not believed in? And how can they believe in the one of whom they have not heard? And how can they hear without someone preaching to them? And how can anyone preach unless they are sent? As it is written: 'How beautiful are the feet of those who bring good news!'" (Rom 10:14-15).

F. Judicial System (18:13-27)

BEHIND THE TEXT

In this unit, we find Jethro's advice to Moses concerning administration of justice among the Israelites. Chapter 18 is evidently placed here for thematic, rather than chronological, reasons (→ 18:5). While the establishment of the judicial system is placed before the giving of the law on Mount Sinai, Moses' recollection of Sinai events in Deut 1:6-19 places it (without reference to Jethro) after the giving of the law. Most commentators accept Deuteronomy's placement as chronologically correct.

Regardless, Exod 18 is thematically and theologically sensible, since it nicely sets up and anticipates the giving of the statutes and laws. Chapter 18 serves as a transition from a people without "law and order," prone to mob paranoia and rebellion, to a people living under the covenant law of God. Jethro's wise counsel to Moses about delegating leadership is a significant piece of Israel's judicial system, which is being established and implemented.

IN THE TEXT

1. Jethro's Observation of the Problem (18:13-16)

■ **13-14** The narrative introduces for the first time Moses' role as a **judge** for the people (v 13). The exodus narrative shows Moses' concern for justice, even before his rise to leadership (see 2:14 where an Israelite questions Moses about his self-appointed role as a judge). The problem here is not the complaint or criticism of the people, but rather an inefficient system, which results in a long delay in the judicial process; the people **stand around** the whole day for their case to be settled (v 14). Jethro appropriately recognizes the problem; his censure, **What is this you are doing . . . ?**, conveys strong disapproval of Moses alone serving **as judge** (*šāpaṭ*). He sees the weariness of Moses because of his one-judge court system as well as the weariness of the people who wait all day long.

■ **15-16** Moses' reply in vv 15-16 reveals his motivation, which, of course, is nothing less than honorable. **The people** are coming out not for mere human wisdom and decision. They are coming **to seek God's will**, divine guidance and judgment through a prophetic leader (v 15). The covenant codes are already published to the people at Mount Sinai (again, assuming that the events in this chapter follow the Mosaic covenant). However, the people may not know how to interpret and apply them. In addition, some new cases might call for receiving new **decrees and instructions** from Yahweh, which then must be taught so as to demonstrate the justness of the judgment and circumvent future offenses.

2. Jethro's Advice (18:17-23)

■ **17-19** Jethro proposes in vv 17-23 the solution to the problem; he recommends the establishment of a practical judicial system in which judicial administration is a delegated and shared responsibility of the leadership. A one-person court is ineffective (**not good** [v 17]). Jethro rightly foresees that the current system will soon fail, as the workload is **too heavy for** Moses and the waiting period is too long for the **people**. Both the judge and the people will suffer burn out (v 18).

Before laying out his plan (in vv 20-23), Jethro asserts his parental authority over Moses: *Obey me*. Jethro obviously has confidence in the soundness and effectiveness of his administrative management plan. Indeed, he expects divine endorsement and blessing (implied in **may God be with you** [v 19]). At the same time, Jethro recognizes Moses' own unique authority. Thus, diplomatically, he prefaces his advice with the recognition of Moses' call as a mediator and his duty as a judge (v 19).

■ **20-22** In vv 20-22, Jethro lays out a judicial structure. Jethro's plan involves different steps. (1) The first step in v 20 is for Moses to teach Israel the **decrees and instructions** of Yahweh and show them the righteous **way . . . to live** and their holy duties to God and to their fellow human beings. This represents a major step that would drastically reduce the legal cases. (2) The next step in v 21 is the establishment of multi-tier judicial organization with **capable** leaders who have certain indispensable qualifications: those **who fear God** and therefore **hate** bribery (→ "bribe" in 23:8) and thus are **trustworthy**. They would be appointed as legal **officials over thousands, hundreds, fifties and tens**. The numbers here probably refer not to individuals, but to families or clans. Although the existing tribal elders and tribal organization are not specifically mentioned, the Deuteronomy account does mention them: "the leading men of your tribes" (i.e., the elders) and "tribal officials" (Deut 1:15). (3) The role of these capable leaders is to **serve as judges** on a continual basis, dealing with ordinary **cases** (Exod 18:22). Only the most **difficult** cases, unresolved by their collective wisdom and counsel, are to be brought to Moses. In this way, the assistant judges will **share** and lighten the **load** for Moses.

■ **23** While Jethro makes a strong case and calls for an obedient response, he recognizes Moses' authority as the leader of the people and Yahweh's ultimate authority over the matter, **If you do this and God so commands**. Should Moses implement the plan, Jethro promises efficiency for Moses and abiding satisfaction, peace, and order for the people.

3. Moses' Implementation (18:24-26)

■ **24-26** Presumably under Yahweh's guidance and blessing, **Moses** obeys Jethro and establishes a multilevel judicial system. At a time of great need in Israel's history, Jethro's advice is accepted and implemented as Yahweh's timely provision (Childs 1974, 336). Deuteronomy 1:9-18 fills in the detail that is missing in these verses, which only contain a brief summary.

4. Jethro's Return (18:27)

■ **27** Moses releases his father-in-law from further responsibility and sends him **on his** own **way**. And **Jethro** returns **to his own *tribal territory*** (*'ereṣ*).

FROM THE TEXT

God's purpose is to distribute gifts of ministry among all of the people of God rather than having them permanently concentrated in one individual or a few leaders. Moses is a man who wears many hats—mediator, miracle worker, prophet, warrior, priest, lawgiver, judge, architect, and so forth. In this section, one sees the beginning of a process of distribution of Moses' diverse gifts and leadership functions. This narrative focuses on delegating and sharing ministry responsibility.

This process of leadership "diversification" and "democratization" is a fulfillment of Moses' own wishes (Deut 1:9-15) although Jethro first articulates its necessity and procedure. As seen in this passage, Moses shares his judicial and teaching duties with other leaders. Moses also shares his leadership position and power with the seventy elders (Num 11:16-17). Eventually, there is a greater diversification of gifts and positions in the OT, but they are still very limited. In Num 11:29, Moses wishes that all God's people could be prophets and that God "would put his Spirit on them!" His prayers, of course, are echoed in Joel's vision of the Day of the Lord, when God will pour out his Spirit on all people and empower them, including the powerless and marginalized, for service unto God (Joel 2:28-29 [3:1-2 HB]).

Joel's prophecy and the more general trend toward a democratic distribution of gifts and leadership functions are fulfilled on the day of Pentecost (see the citation of Joel 2 in Acts 2:16-21). However, the Gospels portray Jesus as already engaged in the diversification and delegation of ministry among his disciples (see Matt 10 and Luke 9—10). The book of Acts shows a greater diversification of gifts and functions within the church beginning with the day of Pentecost (Acts 6:1-6; 8:4-8; see also Rom 12; 1 Cor 12; Eph 4:11-13).

Rather than being a "pew warmer" who merely observes the professional ministers at work, every one of God's people is expected to do works of ministry by the indwelling power of his Spirit. Every member of the "body" must recognize what gifts have already been given to him or her, cultivate them, and put them into service. Every part of the body of Christ plays an essential and vital role in serving the common good in love (1 Cor 12:12-26).

III. AT MOUNT SINAI: EXODUS 19:1—40:38

A. Covenant at Mount Sinai (19:1—24:18)

Overview

The first half of the book of Exodus (chs 1—18) is primarily concerned with the accounts of Yahweh's redemptive actions on behalf of Israel. The second half of the book is concerned with Israel's response to Yahweh in proper relationship (chs 19—24) and pure worship (chs 25—40). The book of Exodus thus speaks of both divine and human sides of the covenant relationship between Yahweh and Israel.

The literary structure of chs 19—24 is marked by a generally chiastic structure: the covenant proposal (19:1-8); the theophany and the Decalogue (19:9—20:21); the covenant law (20:22—23:13); and the covenant ratification and theophany (ch 24). As a whole, the structure of chs 19—24 reflects the interdependence and inseparability of covenant and law in Israel's faith.

Yahweh told Moses that he would return to Mount Sinai with the Israelites and worship God (3:12). Now they stand at the mountain of God. Here Yahweh forges his covenant relationship with the Israelites and forever changes their identity, responsibilities, and purposes.

I. Covenant Proposed and Accepted (19:1-8)

BEHIND THE TEXT

Upon the Israelites' arrival at Mount Sinai (19:1-2), the Lord proposes a covenant with Israel (vv 3-6) and the Israelites accept it (vv 7-8). The Jewish calendar coordinates the Festival of Harvest / Weeks (23:16) or Shabuoth with the giving of the law on the sixth day of the third month.

Yahweh calls the Israelites not only to enjoy Yahweh's benefits but also to respond with obedience to divine law and fulfill their identity and calling as a "kingdom of priests." Thus, 19:4-6 provides a summary of the covenantal relation between Yahweh and Israel, which the later chapters in Exodus (and much of the Pentateuch) explain in more detail.

From the 1950s, the concept of the covenant in the Bible has been enriched by the discovery of ancient Near Eastern treaties. Especially the Hittite treaties from the second millennium BC provide a close parallel to the Sinai covenant, which can be analyzed and understood in the same format (→ the table below; see Richter 2008, 72-84).

Preamble	"I am the LORD your God . . ." (20:2).
Historical Prologue	". . . who brought you out of Egypt, out of the land of slavery" (20:2).
Stipulations	"You shall have no other gods before me" (20:3), heading the Decalogue (20:3-17) and all the other covenant laws.
Reading and Deposition	"He took the Book of the Covenant and read it" (24:7). "He took the tablets of the covenant law and placed them in the ark" (40:20; see 32:15).
Witnesses	"I call the heavens and the earth as witnesses against you" (Deut 4:26).
Curses and Blessings	"If you fully obey the LORD your God . . . all these blessings will come on you . . . However, if you do not obey . . . all these curses will come on you" (Deut 28:1-2, 15; see Deut 27:11—28:68).

Figure 4: Essential elements of Israelite treaty, which is similar to those found in ancient Near Eastern treaties.

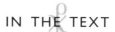
■ **1-2** Verses 1-2 give a very brief summary of Israel's travel from Egypt to the **Desert of Sinai** via Rephidim. These verses date the arrival of Israel in the Desert of Sinai and their encampment **in front of the mountain** to "the third new moon" (ESV; that is, **the first day of the third** lunar **month**) **after** their departure from Egypt. This is one and a half lunar months after the day of the exodus.

■ **3** Verse 3 does not say why Moses went up to Yahweh; the second half of v 3 implies that he did so in response to Yahweh's summons to receive his word. Verse 3 also makes clear that Yahweh's word is addressed to the people of Israel.

■ **4** Yahweh's speech starts with a summary statement of what he has done for Israel, using a metaphor of a young eaglet being **carried** on its mother's **wings**. The phrase **brought you to myself** connotes relational intimacy, like that of a bride bringing her bridegroom to a bridal chamber (see Song 8:2) or vice versa (Gen 24:67). The metaphor emphasizes Yahweh's nature as a loving parent and covenant partner.

■ **5** The initial introductory statement is followed by Yahweh's **covenant** terms and promises in Exod 19:5-6. Covenant terms primarily deal with Israel's responsibility; covenant promises primarily deal with Israel's privileged status in the world. On the condition that the Israelites completely **obey** the covenant laws, Yahweh promises Israel's privileged standing as Yahweh's **treasured possession** (*segullâ*; "personal property," "special possession"). **The whole earth** and all the **nations** belong to Yahweh and exist under Yahweh's rule in a broad sense, but only Israel is Yahweh's "firstborn" (4:22). The expression **my treasured possession** points to Yahweh's affectionate emotions, zealous protection, overabundant blessing, and liberating empowerment for firstborn Israel.

■ **6** The promise of special privileges includes Israel's standing in the world as **a kingdom of priests and a holy nation**. As the special "firstborn" of all the nations, Israel is to fulfill corporately the priestly duties of the firstborn (→ 4:23 and 13:2). The implication of this privilege and responsibility for Israel as a nation is enormous.

Kingdom of priests refers to Yahweh's kingdom made up of priestly people. The priests were mediators between God and people. Thus, Israel is to mediate between Yahweh and the nations. This interpretation of Israel's priestly role is consistent with the promise given Abram in Gen 12:3: "all peoples on earth will be blessed through you." The Israelites' careful obedience to the covenant laws and the resulting continued divine blessings upon them would show the nations the "wisdom and understanding" of the people and the law (Deut 4:6; see 1 Kgs 4:29 [5:9 HB]). Thus, Israel's priestly task is

EXODUS

19:1-6

to lead the nations into the presence of God and to teach them his laws and proper ways of worshipping God. The nations, in turn, would receive God's blessings as they enter into a covenantal relationship with God.

Such a high call requires Israel to be a **holy nation**, set apart from all that is pagan and wholly dedicated to God. The fuller implication of what it means to be a kingdom of priests and a holy nation is later revealed with the giving of the laws and regulations concerning Israel's cultic, civil, and personal life.

Israel's relationship with God is clearly a mutual one. Yahweh confers a special position and privilege upon Israel. In return, Israel is called to proclaim and demonstrate the supreme goodness and glory of Yahweh to all the nations, so that the nations might turn to Yahweh, serve Yahweh alone, and be blessed.

■ **7-8** Verses 7-8 deal with Moses' presentation of Yahweh's words to the elders, the people's response, and Moses' report back to Yahweh. The people accept the covenant offer and its terms in unison by stating, **We will do everything the** Lord **has said** (v 8). They express their commitment to obey Yahweh in every matter and thus agree to the covenant relationship with Yahweh; their response implies their commitment to be Yahweh's "treasured possession," "a kingdom of priests," and "a holy nation" in the world (vv 5-6).

FROM 🕮 TEXT

The narrative makes clear the conditional nature of God's covenant relationship with Israel. This covenant is thus unlike God's covenant with Abraham, which is made unconditional by God's self-oath, following Abraham's demonstration of his absolute love, trust, and obedience of God in (nearly) sacrificing his promised child Isaac (see Gen 22:16-18). In Exodus, God's offer to Israel of a special relationship and status with him comes with the condition, "If you obey me and fully keep my covenant" (19:5). There is no unconditional election of Israel in this text; the redeemed people of Israel are *elected* by the graciousness of God to be his faithful witnesses in the world. For that to become a reality, Israel must live in an obedient relationship with God. The same is true for the church and its vocation in the world.

Just as the Israelites are given a radically different identity and purpose as they accept the covenant relationship with God, so do our identity and purpose fundamentally change when we accept the new covenant of Jesus Christ. In his first letter, the Apostle Peter draws on the language and theme of God's covenant proposal to Israel (vv 5-6) to address the new covenant people of God, the church: "But you are a chosen people, a royal priesthood, a holy nation, God's special possession, that you may declare the praises of him who called you out of darkness into his wonderful light" (1 Pet 2:9). Peter is speaking of the glorious destiny of those who believe in Christ, in contrast to those who reject him. More radical is Peter's implication that Gentiles are now included in the special priestly position to which Israel is originally called. The church's vocation is to be a distinct community in the world on behalf of the world and to mediate the presence and blessings of God to the world. In his second letter to the Corinthians, Paul affirms that the "ministry of reconciliation" is now committed to anyone who is "in Christ" as "Christ's ambassadors" (2 Cor 5:17-20). In this way, the calling of Israel to be a blessing to all nations and peoples (Gen 12:3) is extended and fulfilled through Christ and his people who walk in truth and obedience (→ From the Text on Exod 19:9-15).

2. Theophany and the Decalogue (19:9—20:21)

a. Preparation for Theophany: Consecration (19:9-15)

BEHIND THE TEXT

Yahweh instructs Moses to prepare the people for theophany through consecration. The preparation involves ritual purity through washing of the garments and abstinence from sexual relations. These instructions set the precedence for the worship at the tabernacle (Lev 15; 22:3-4). The Lord announces that the people will be permitted to go up to the foothills at the sounding of trumpets, just as they will be invited into the courtyard of the tabernacle to worship God (→ Behind the Text for Exod 27:9-19).

IN THE TEXT

■ **9** The upcoming theophany and one of its purposes are announced here, which is the installation of **Moses** as the mediator between Yahweh and the **people**. The phrases **to you**, **with you**, and **in you** emphasize the critical need for the people to see and accept Moses as the divinely chosen prophet and leader of Israel. Yahweh's visual and audible manifestations to Moses are largely accessible to the people and should serve to quell any lingering doubt about Yahweh's existence and presence among the people and Moses' special status and authority (but see chs 32—24 and Num 12).

■ **10-11** Yahweh instructs **Moses** to **consecrate** the **people** through ritual washing. We can assume that the purpose of the external purification is to inspire internal dedication. Yahweh must not be approached flippantly but with due care and respect.

■ **12** The **mountain** is set apart for divine revelation. Any trespasser **is to be put to death**, whether by human agency or divine agency (should anyone escape human notice and execution; see vv 22, 24).

■ **13** Offenders must either **be stoned or shot with arrows**, because seizing the trespasser involves another person's violation of the restriction. The act of execution functions to instill in the executioners, not an attitude of self-righteousness, but instead a fear of the Lord that will keep them from sinning.

The limits on touching the foothill will later be lifted with the sounding of the **ram's horn** (*yōbēl*; "ram"). But the people will be allowed to **approach** only the base of the **mountain** and no further (see vv 17-25).

■ **14** Following divine commandments in v 10, **Moses** consecrates the **people**. Accordingly, the people wash **their clothes**.

■ **15** As the Israelite bride and divine bridegroom prepare themselves for the holy covenant union, they temporarily separate themselves from **sexual** pleasure. Similar to the spiritual discipline of fasting from food, both Testaments advocate sexual abstinence during times of special spiritual significance, such as during holy war (Deut 23:9-11 [10-12 HB]; Josh 3:5; 1 Sam 21:4-5 [5-6 HB]; 2 Sam 11:11) or a season of prayer (1 Cor 7:5).

FROM THE TEXT

This passage emphasizes the absolute necessity of consecration to prepare for welcoming the transcendent and holy God and becoming God's representatives. Using the imagery of a mother bird carrying her young on her wings, God speaks of his tender loving care for his people as legitimate grounds for formalizing their relationship (19:4-6). But God's motherly tenderness in no way creates a flippant or casual way of approaching and being united with God. The people must reckon with God's supreme holiness. Thus, they prepare themselves through solemn ritual. While the purification rite focuses on external purity, what is most important is the internal purification and dedication, so that God may come and dwell in their midst and God's word may be on their hearts.

Similarly, we Christians receive and rejoice in the great compassion and mercy extended to us through Jesus Christ. That grace of God demands an absolute consecration and holiness in our relationship with God and our mission to reach the unbelieving world. Since our Holy God resides in us through the Holy Spirit, our consecration through sanctification must be external and internal, physical and spiritual, contemporary and perpetual. Only then can we truly be "the righteousness of God" and "Christ's ambassadors" (2 Cor 5:21, 20).

b. Theophany (19:16-25)

BEHIND THE TEXT

Yahweh comes down on Mount Sinai, surrounded by a special entourage of visible, audible, and tangible displays of Yahweh's grandeur and might. The God King condescends to meet his subjects and make a covenant with them.

This theophany shares many elements with other theophanies in the OT (Judg 5:4; 2 Sam 22:8-14; 1 Kgs 19:11-12; Pss 29:3-9; 68:8 [9 HB]). Some explain the unusual phenomena described in this passage as the result of a volcanic eruption. However, several elements, such as Yahweh's voice and the increasingly loud trumpet sounds, cannot be explained in this naturalistic way. Yet Yahweh may harness certain natural forces (storm clouds, lightning, thunder, earthquake, etc.) as a means of divine self-revelation.

Clearly, Yahweh's presence is distinct from powerful phenomena and atmospheric disturbances that are initiated by Yahweh. Unlike the ancient Near Eastern pagans, we do not identify these events as aspects of who Yahweh is. Rather they indicate how the material world or nature itself responds when it comes in contact with the magnificent and holy presence of the creator God.

IN THE TEXT

■ **16** The theophany takes place **on the morning of the third day** (see v 1). Yahweh's appearance is accompanied by **thunder and lightning, a thick cloud,** and **a very loud trumpet** [šôfār; "horn," "ram's horn"; see "trumpets of rams' horns" in Josh 6:4] **blast**. Such blowing instruments function to sound a powerful signal for all to hear, even over a considerable distance. The trumpet sound in this passage signals that the ban on touching the mountain is lifted, in fulfillment of its provision in Exod 19:13. The people may approach the foothill (v 17).

■ **17** In v 16 God makes his appearance on the mountain; in v 17 **Moses** leads **the people** up to previously forbidden ground to **meet with God**. Verse 17 lays out the fundamental understanding of worship as the people of God approaching the holy presence of God; in awe and reverence they stand **at the foot of the mountain** to worship God, who appears on the mountain. The people are privileged to have an audience with God. Scholars (e.g., Sarna 1996, 203-4) draw attention to an interesting correspondence between the tripartite division of the tabernacle (the courtyard, the holy place, and the most holy place) and the three zones on Mount Sinai (the **foot** or foothill, the main **mountain** itself, and the top of the mountain). The Lord's self-revelation takes place in the summit, the most holy place, which is accessed by only one mediator, either Moses (v 20; 24:18) or the high priest. Only select leaders (elders or priests) are permitted to enter the holy place or the holy mountain (24:9-11). The ordinary people are allowed to access only the outer court, where the altar of burnt offering is located, or the foot of the mountain, where an altar is built (24:4).

■ **18** Verse 18 of ch 19 reports the appearance of Yahweh. He descends on **Mount Sinai . . . in fire** and in his glory and majesty, with rocks melting and **smoke** billowing **up . . . like smoke from a furnace** (Deut 4:24; 9:15; see 1 Kgs 18:38). There is also an earthquake that **violently** shakes **the whole mountain** and, no doubt, the foot of the mountain where the people stand. They witness these terrifying phenomena, in addition to hearing the ever-increasing sound of the trumpet (Exod 19:19). All such events should melt any hardness of heart and insolence in the people, instilling the proper fear of the Lord and the readiness to serve Yahweh and Yahweh alone (though the golden calf incident later shows that the theophany did not produce an abiding change of heart).

■ **19** With the people's visual, somatic, and auditory senses inundated with awe and terror, they are made ready, at least temporarily, to hear **Moses** speak with **God**. Moses initiates and the Lord responds in words audible and intelligible to all the people (Deut 4:12). This occurrence serves as an unmistakable endorsement of Moses as God's spokesperson and Moses' commandments as Yahweh's laws. The laws are not expressions of mere human wisdom or regulations but reflections of divine justice and righteousness. The Lord wishes the Sinai experience to be indelibly etched in their national consciousness, so that even later generations of Israelites would learn to put their trust in Moses and the laws given through him (Exod 19:9). Accordingly in Deuteronomy, Moses charges the Israelites, most of whom have not personally experienced the theophany at Sinai, to remember the event and obey all the commandments given to them on Sinai (Deut 4:12-15; 5:22-33).

■ **20-21** Yahweh's special meeting with Moses at the **top of the mountain** is the subject of Exod 19:20-25. Yahweh invites Moses to his very presence and issues a solemn warning to the people that they must not force their way past the set limit in order to satisfy their desire **to see** the glory of **the Lord** (v 21; even as Moses later requests to see it in 33:18). Trespassing the boundary and venturing onto the mountain beyond its foothill would result in the Lord "breaking out" and destroying **many of them**.

■ **22** Some explain the mention of the **priests** in 19:22 as a later addition, since the installation of the priests does not take place until after the construction of the tabernacle (see Lev 8). However, "priests" may also apply to those who function in priestly roles prior to the formation of the Aaronic priesthood, such as the consecrated firstborn sons (Exod 13:2) who would also be elders or the young men who carry out certain cultic duties (24:5).

■ **23** Moses' response indicates the people's understanding of the limit imposed on them. **Moses** here seems to think that the **people** have sufficient understanding that the previous injunction concerning the **limits** around the mountain is still being enforced for most of the mountain, even though they are now allowed on its base. Moses assures **the Lord** that there is no possibility of the people trespassing: The people **cannot come up**. Moses seems confident that the terror caused by the Lord is greater than any person's curiosity to see more than they are allowed to see.

■ **24** But Yahweh knows the **people** better than Moses does and thus gives Moses another warning about them. **The Lord** also commands Moses to **bring Aaron up** to the mountain. This invitation is later extended also to Nadab and

Abihu and seventy of the elders of Israel (24:1). The second warning against **the priests** points to the especially strong temptation or entitlement they might feel to climb the mountain to approach God.

■ **25** Verse 25 reports the descent of **Moses** from the mountain to deliver and carry out Yahweh's words spoken in vv 21-24.

FROM THE TEXT

This narrative presents a proper theology of worship for its modern-day readers. Worship is first and foremost our coming into the presence of God, who graciously invites us to come to his presence (v 17; see Ps 100). Moses' task here is to lead Israel to their meeting with God. There is no easy familiarity with God in this text that motivates the people to drop in at their convenience. Rather God, who is holy and majestic and transcendent, initiates this meeting. God requires that the people be holy and that they approach him with reverence and care. Everything that takes place at the top and at the foot of the mountain is regulated by God; the people come to see God, to hear him speak and give instructions for their life in the world. This is an odd way of worship for most evangelical churches in the Western world. Brueggemann insightfully comments, "Most of our worship takes place well short of the mountain, where we can seize and maintain the initiative, imagining God at our beck and call" (1994, 838). The Holy God of Mount Sinai will have nothing to do with such worship programmed, controlled, and even manipulated by the worshipping community.

God's presence and revelation come in different "packages," but they all call for worshippers' appropriate responses of recognition and acceptance. On Mount Sinai, God appears and calls Moses from the fire. There, God also appears and speaks to the Israelites in a terrifying and powerful theophany, accompanied by thick clouds, trumpet sounds, thunder and lightning, and earthquake. There, centuries later, Elijah experiences various supernatural phenomena that are similar to those that Moses and the Israelites experienced, but Elijah does not find the Lord in them (1 Kgs 19:11-13). Only in "a gentle whisper" (v 12) is his presence found. Still and small the Lord's voice may be, but it is clear and significant to Elijah (vv 13-18).

The Sinai accounts show that the presence of God comes to us in a variety of ways, whether "clothed" in a fire and violent earthquake or in quietness and gentleness. The text reminds readers to be prepared to encounter God in whatever form God might choose to employ. There are dangers of not recognizing and rejecting God's presence and work because of our hardness of heart. In the text, God comes with a sensory overloading display of power and glory, but the Israelite eyewitnesses still doubt and reject God.

In the NT, Christ in his fullness of grace and truth comes in human flesh (John 1:14), but the Jews of his time suspect and mistreat him. The Holy Spirit is now given to "all people" (Joel 2:28 [3:1 HB]; Acts 2:17), distributing various spiritual gifts according to God's pleasure (Rom 12:6-8; 1 Cor 12:4-11, 27-31; 13:13—14:1, 12; Eph 4:11-13; Heb 2:4). The church must fully acknowledge and welcome the person, works, and gifts of the Holy Spirit, along with those of God the Father and God the Son. Only then will the church be fully ready to equip all believers for works of ministry so that the whole body of Christ is "built up" and becomes fully "mature, attaining to the whole measure of the fullness of Christ" (Eph 4:12-13).

c. The Decalogue (20:1-17)

Overview

The proclamation of the Ten Commandments follows Moses' descent from the mountain (19:25) and doubtlessly the demarcation of the holy ground that must not be trespassed (v 23). Moses ascends the mountain again in 20:21. This indicates that Moses and the people receive the Ten Commandments from the foothills.

The English title "Ten Commandments" for this unit derives from the Hebrew phrase "ten words" (Greek translation *deka logous*) found in 34:28 (and also in Deut 4:13; 10:4). The content of the Ten Commandments is not entirely new in Scripture. Many of the commands are already reflected in the conscience and cultures of the people of Genesis and earlier parts of Exodus (see Gen 2:3; 4:9; 24:3; 35:2-3; 39:9; 44:4-7; Exod 2:14-15; 16:22-30). Outside of Scripture, we have evidence of similar laws in the ancient Near Eastern law codes (e.g., the Code of Hammurabi, dated several hundred years before Moses). Despite some correspondences in the non-Israelite cultural and religious environment, the Decalogue remains unique, as it demands exclusive worship of Yahweh, bans idolatry, and institutes the complete Sabbath rest. In addition, the "apodictic" ("you shall . . .") laws are relatively rare in ancient Near Eastern legal material, which typically consisted in conditional commandments and casuistic or case laws. The Ten Commandments are stated in the absolutes, as the incontestable will of Yahweh.

While scholars generally agree that there are ten commands, they debate about how to divide them. Traditionally, interpreters have divided the Ten Commandments into two "tables," with the first four commandments typically labeled as "religious" (associated with the relationship with God) and the remaining six labeled as "civil" (concerning the relationships with fellow human beings). While this division is reasonable and useful, the religious and civil aspects are interwoven. These categories have no absolute or atomistic distinction, for all civic crimes are sins before God and all sins have social implications. For example, the Sabbath law, though usually grouped with the first table of the law, is both religious (promotes honor and worship of Yahweh) and civic (regulates economy and work).

The Decalogue in Jewish, Roman Catholic, and Protestant Traditions

The Jewish tradition treats Exod 20:2 as the first commandment, whereas both Roman Catholic and Protestant traditions treat this verse as the prologue. Exodus 20:3 and vv 4-6 (prohibition against "other gods" and "graven images" [KJV]) make up the second commandment in Judaism. In the Roman Catholic tradition vv 3-6 make up the first commandment and v 7 (prohibition against the "misuse" of God's name) makes up the second commandment (v 7 is the third commandment in Protestant and Jewish traditions). The final commandment in the Protestant and Jewish traditions is broken up into ninth and tenth in the Roman Catholic tradition.

(1) Introduction (20:1-2)

BEHIND THE TEXT

The Decalogue opens with the editorial note that introduces it as God's words. Unlike other legal texts, this introduction does not name the recipient of the law (e.g., 20:22; 21:1; Lev 1:2; 4:2) and invites various interpretations. The commandments may be addressing all Israelites of all generations collectively, emphasizing the importance of communal and transgenerational obedience. At the same time, they may be addressing each individual, indicated by the use of the singular "you" throughout, underscoring one's individual responsibility. It is also possible to envision a more universal audience for these precepts, with the case laws being more culturally and religiously bound.

The editorial introduction is followed by Yahweh's proclamation of himself as the God of Israel who delivered them out of Egypt. It has been noted that this royal self-proclamation corresponds to the preamble and historical prologue of the Hittite suzerain-vassal treaty format (see Richter 2008, 84). Similar to the Hittite treaties, the covenant obligations (that is, the Decalogue) follow the historical prologue. The Israelites are asked to obey the commandments not in order to obtain divine favor but in grateful response to the unmatched grace already shown.

IN THE TEXT

■ **I** The Decalogue is introduced as **words** spoken by Yahweh the **God** of Israel. The commandments did not originate with humans. Rather, the sovereign God of the universe requires them of humans. Instead of speaking through a human agent, Yahweh himself speaks the commandments in words that are audible and intelligible to a human audience (Deut 4:12).

■ **2** Yahweh first declares himself as the **God** of Israel. Yahweh is not a product of human imagination and conceptualization, for Yahweh wholly and infinitely transcends what is human. Therefore, Yahweh must take the initiative to reveal to his people his identity and his relationship to them. Yahweh's identity, relationship, and mighty acts of deliverance establish Yahweh's unassailable, sovereign authority over his people. The people are indebted to **the** Lord, and he has every right to make binding demands on them. Since Yahweh's gracious acts of deliverance precede the giving of the laws, people's obedience is not the basis, but the desired fruit of their salvation. It is noteworthy that the expression **out of the land of slavery** presents a strong contrast to the oft-repeated "into . . . a land flowing with milk and honey" (e.g., 3:8, 17; 13:5; Num 14:8). Yahweh's demand for obedience is solely based on past deeds of power and grace, not on the hope for the fulfillment of future promises.

FROM THE TEXT

The call to obedience to the law follows God's gracious works of salvation from slavery, and this fact shows the priority of God's grace over the law and the function of the law as the administrator of the ongoing grace of God to those who are already saved. The covenant laws exist to help God's people maintain the freedom that God already gave as a gift. The call to "remember" the historical, mighty acts of God (e.g., Deut 4:10; 5:15; 7:18; 8:2, 18) therefore becomes all-important in living out a faithful and obedient covenant life. Without the ongoing grateful and joyful celebration of who God is and what God has done, keeping the covenant laws becomes burdensome.

The NT also emphasizes the priority of God's grace that works salvation over the evidence of salvation in one's obedient walk with Christ. We are rescued "from the hand of our enemies" (Luke 1:74) and cleansed "from acts that lead to death" (Heb 9:14) through God's work in the death and resurrection of Jesus Christ. One who has been forgiven much loves much (Luke 7:47) and one who loves obeys Christ's commands (John 14:15; also see Matt 5:17-20). So, just like in the old covenant, the ongoing remembrance and joyful celebration of God's acts of salvation (in the Lord's Supper, for example) fuel the love and obedience. The imperative to love, therefore, cannot become law as a means of salvation. Rather, it remains the natural fruit of salvation (see Childs 1974, 430-31).

(2) First Commandment: Exclusive Worship (20:3)

BEHIND THE TEXT

The first commandment insists on monotheism, a distinguishing feature of Israel's religion. Other cultures of the ancient Near East were generally polytheistic. Israel is not to acknowledge other "gods" as genuine. Yahweh is unique and demands absolute loyalty. The first commandment also rules out henotheism, in which one god is recognized as the supreme god among a pantheon of other lesser deities. The beings allowed in Yahweh's presence or council are angels or heavenly creatures (such as cherubim; see 25:18 ff.), not lesser deities (see 1 Kgs 22:19-20).

The first two commandments are implied in Israel's ancestors' relationship to Yahweh. The names of the patriarchs are closely and permanently tied to the very title of Yahweh, who is "the God of your fathers—the God of Abraham, the God of Isaac and the God of Jacob" (Exod 3:15; see v 16). As the ancestors belong to Yahweh, so does Yahweh belong to them. Jacob's clan's repudiation of "all the foreign gods" they had and their worship of Yahweh at Bethel (Gen 35:1-4) show that the ancestors intuitively understood the need for exclusive worship of Yahweh. In addition, Yahweh's claim on Israel as his firstborn (Exod 4:22) and Israel's worship of Yahweh in response to Aaron's words and signs (v 31) imply the beginning of a revival of monotheism among the Hebrews in Egypt.

IN THE TEXT

■ **3** The first commandment prohibits acknowledgment of anything other than Yahweh as a deity. The expression **before me** (*'al-pānāya*; or "in my presence") conveys the idea that Israel's consideration or recognition of anything besides Yahweh as its God is like carrying out the act of adultery in the plain view of one's spouse. This concept is confirmed by the fact that hearts turning after **other gods** is understood as spiritual adultery in the OT.

FROM THE TEXT

The first commandment underscores God's realistic and sober assessment of fallen human nature, not merely the weakness of Israel. This assessment is that humans have a universal propensity to worship, that humans regrettably express that need in polytheistic and idolatrous worship, and that even God's people have a tendency to forsake the invisible living God and run after "other gods." In Rom 1:18 ff., Paul indicts all humanity as universally sinful and idolatrous. He excoriates humanity for suppressing the true knowledge of God given to all through creation (vv 19-20) and for deifying images of human and created objects (which in turn would lead to deification of what those images represent).

While the salvation that Jesus offers in principle rescues us from false worship, the temptation of idolatrous or polytheistic worship remains for the people of God. The temptation can come in a form of "love of money" (1 Tim 6:9-10), normative religious pluralism (that all religions are equally true and equally mediate salvation), polytheism, or a pursuit or devotion that belongs to the triune God alone. On the level of society, Barth's Barmen Declaration continues to caution the confessing church to be alert against the popular culture that places any political leader or party in a position of veneration and devotion reserved for God alone (see Cochrane 1962, 237-42). All areas of our lives, especially economy and politics, must belong to Jesus Christ and must be scrutinized and sanctified under the lordship of Jesus Christ. Christians today must not serve any "gods of this age" or compromise their unqualified allegiance to the triune God.

(3) Second Commandment: Idolatry (20:4-6)

BEHIND THE TEXT

The second commandment is about worshipping the right God in the right way. This command forbids the production and use of idols in the worship of false gods, in the worship of Yahweh, or as a visible representation of Yahweh. This command prohibits the making and worship of the images of humans, earthly creatures, and astral bodies, which were "staples of ancient Near Eastern sacral iconography" (Propp 2006, 168).

This commandment is grossly violated by Israel throughout her history, beginning with the travesty of the golden calf incident (ch 32). In keeping with the warning and promise given with the second commandment (20:5a-6), Yahweh responds to his people with a mixture of disciplinary action and ongoing faithful love (see chs 32—34). Yahweh's perfect moral response to Israel's idolatry, however, does not deter the Israelites from plunging into idolatry and false worship, which in the end result in their exile from the promised land.

IN THE TEXT

■ **4** The second commandment bans **image** making and idol worship. The phrase **anything in heaven above or on the earth beneath or in the waters below** evokes the tripartite division of the creation into heavens, waters, and earth, with their respective animate and inanimate creatures. Yahweh is the Creator of all that exists. Yahweh is "wholly separate from the world of His creation and wholly other than what the human mind can conceive or the human imagination depict" (Sarna 2004, 81). Therefore, idols cannot represent the Creator. The people's experience of theophany at Sinai, in which they hear "the sound of words" but see no **form** (Deut 4:12), reinforces the transcendence of Yahweh and the related prohibition on making any representations of Yahweh.

The phrase **anything . . . on the earth beneath** also recalls the fact that God made humans in the divine **image** and conferred on them the privilege, authority, and responsibility of ruling over the birds of the heavens, the fish of the sea, and all the creatures of the earth (Gen 1:26). Recalling that humans are to have dominion over all earthly creatures exposes the absurdity of deifying any such creature or even associating their images with the divine.

In addition, the fact that only humans are created in the image of God implies that only they can provide the legitimate images of God to other creatures, rather than creatures providing images of God to humans. Accordingly, it is inappropriate for God's image bearers to fashion images drawn from the created realm to worship the invisible Creator. This concept starkly contrasts to the common practice in the ancient Near East (esp. Egypt) of associating or identifying deities with animals and their attributes. The use of images of humans is included in this prohibition (made explicit in Deut 4:16).

■ **5a** Yahweh's insistence on exclusive obeisance and service naturally follows the prohibition of idol making. Yahweh commands the Israelites not to **bow down** (or "bow down deeply," "do obeisance") to them, whether as a petitioner or worshipper. They are not to **worship** ('ābad; "serve," "serve as a slave," "be a slave," "perform cultic rituals for") them. This command is best understood in the context of the preceding narrative of Exodus. Yahweh brought the Israelites out of bondage where they had been forced to serve, and perhaps literally bow down, not only to Pharaoh, but also to the false gods of Egypt. They had lived as slaves then, but after the exodus, they could enjoy their status as the firstborn "son" of the living God. With mighty acts of judgment, Yahweh clearly demonstrated the inferiority of Pharaoh and all the gods of Egypt (→ 12:12), which were fashioned after the created things of heavens, waters, and earth. For the Israelites to compromise loyalty to the supreme God and return to the abominations from which they were delivered would be utterly irrational on their part and absolutely exasperating for their heavenly Father.

■ **5bc** Thus, Yahweh issues a stern warning (v 5), followed by an astounding promise (v 6), both of which flow out of Yahweh's identity as **a jealous** [*kannā'*; "jealous," "jealousy," "zealous," "zeal"] **God**. The Hebrew term for "jealous" in this verse is used exclusively of Yahweh (see 34:14), indicating that divine jealousy or zeal is qualitatively different from human jealousy, which is often subjected to insecurity, suspicion, false judgment, and other vices.

The divine jealousy has two quantitatively unequal sides, the lesser punitive nature (**punishing** [20:5]) and the incomparably greater loving nature ("showing love" [v 6]). The jealous God responds to apostasy and unacceptable modes of worship with a severe punishment. But it is limited **to the third and fourth generation of those who hate** him. A typical household in ancient Israel was made up of three to four generations, so this expression underscores the corporate nature of sowing and reaping (→ "Transgenerational Punishment" sidebar in 34:7*d*).

■ **6** By contrast, the jealous God's response to absolute loyalty and proper worship is loving and extravagant love (*ḥesed*), extended to ***thousands of* generations of those who love** (*'āhab*) and obey him. The term *ḥesed*, variously translated into "love," "lovingkindness," and "steadfast love," refers to covenant faithfulness. When applied to Yahweh, it emphasizes Yahweh's solid commitment to his covenant partner. The Hebrew term for **thousand** is plural, thus referring to two or more thousands of generations. It emphasizes the boundless extension of divine covenant love, such as was promised to Abraham (Gen 12:2-3; 18:18; 22:16-18). Such steadfast love is shown to those who affectionately, faithfully, and unreservedly love (*'āhab*) the Lord. Abraham paradigmatically expressed this kind of love in his supreme obedience and sacrifice (22:12, 18). In fact, the Yahweh-Abraham relationship epitomizes the *ḥesed-'āhab* principle, even as Yahweh swore and guaranteed *ḥesed* to Abraham (and his descendants) in response to Abraham's own faithfulness. Accordingly, the jealousy of God passionately guards the integrity of that covenant relationship by continuing to show *ḥesed* to the descendants of Abraham and by disciplining them as necessary whenever they deviate from the covenant. Thus, what truly stands out about the jealousy of God is not that he brooks no competition, but that in his enduring commitment to Israel, he is undeterred by the unfaithfulness of the covenant partner (see Exod 32—34).

FROM THE TEXT

The basic thrust of the prohibition on the human creation and worship of visual images of God stands. Idolatry seeks to meet our legitimate and deepseated human need for an object of worship in an illegitimate way, either by worshipping idolatrous images as gods or by worshipping the invisible living God through unauthorized visual representations. The OT consistently bans idolatry (e.g., Deut 4:15-16), based on the fact that God's presence had no form at Sinai (v 15). The NT condemns idolatry as one of the markers of pagan cultures (e.g., Acts 17:16; 1 Cor 5:10; 6:9-11; Rev 21:8).

(1) *Iconography versus idols.* Some Christian traditions hold that the incarnation endorses the appropriate use of icons in worship. Jesus Christ who is "the image of the invisible God" (Col 1:15) has a human bodily form in the incarnation, resurrection, and ascension (Acts 1:9-11). Therefore, God appears to finally satisfy the human desire to see God face-to-face.

Most Protestants, however, hold that the second commandment bans icons (including those of Christ) and the production and worship of images as representations or mediators of the divine. It prohibits all image or statue making, lest one also worship the artwork. Certainly, there is a human tendency not only to deify what God has made but also to idolize what humans make.

Thus, many Christians live in tension between iconoclasm and aniconism of the early church and the Reformation and the ecclesiastically legitimatized use of "icons" (be they in the forms of statues, jewelry, stained-glass windows, paintings, illustrations, flannelgraph stories, films, plays, or nativity scenes) in popular Christianity.

Certainly, fixed images (paintings and statues) are inherently problematic. God the Father, God the Son, and God the Holy Spirit cannot be captured in those representations, and visual representations of God often lead to idolatrous conceptualizations of God. For many today, Christ is forever a light-skinned, blue-eyed European, simply because that is how he has been depicted in numerous films and paintings (hanging in their church or living room).

Does this mean that no images of God can be used? Probably no. If the Christian community well understands the limitations and dangers of such depictions, the limited and cautious use of icons and other visual depictions for teaching or illustrative purposes may be helpful in communicating the historical works of God. In addition, along with the written words, the artistic representations could arouse in us the desire for real face-to-face encounters with the living God and the final unveiling of God's glory before our transformed and transfigured bodies and souls.

(2) *Visual versus mental.* Jesus insisted that he did not come to abolish the law, but to fulfill it, and that we must obey the commandments as well, not only externally but also internally. The prohibition of the second commandment then extends not only to material images of various kinds but also to mental images.

However, there are wide varieties of mental or verbal images for God the Father, God the Son, and God the Holy Spirit conveyed by the biblical writers. This juxtaposition of a ban on visual depiction but an abundant use of verbal depiction (that can easily be visualized) indicates that there is an important distinction between the visual and the mental-verbal ways of portraying God. Obviously, one can commit idolatry with one's words and thoughts too. However, mental or verbal "pictures" found in the Bible are far less susceptible to idolatry because they retain in them an element of "indeterminacy" (by humans) and of "self-determinacy" (by the Holy Spirit). When God is called a king, we must still seek understanding of God's kingship in a particular situation. But if an artist makes a statue of God as a king, that imagery gets forever locked in. All mystery is gone and God's self-revelation is reduced to one artist's interpretation and representation. Verbal images, by contrast, more readily lend themselves to illumination, interpretation, and application under the dynamic presence and working of the Holy Spirit and retain room for mystery.

(4) Third Commandment: Wrongful Use of the Name (20:7)

BEHIND THE TEXT

Abraham practiced a positive use of God's name when he made his estate manager or "senior servant" (NIV) swear by Yahweh (Gen 24:2-9). Similarly, Jacob took an oath by Yahweh (31:53). These examples of legitimate use of God's name for oaths or swearing contrast with the third commandment that prohibits wrongful or vain swearing or use. Some passages show that swearing in Yahweh's name "in a truthful, just and righteous way" brings Yahweh's blessing upon the people (Jer 4:2; also see Deut 6:13; Ps 63:11 [12 HB]; Jer 12:16). However, with the increasing revelation of Yahweh's identity and name (Exod 3:13-22; 34:5-7), Yahweh not only makes himself more approachable and accessible to people but also risks people's abuse of his name. Thus, this commandment comes with a strong warning for the violators.

IN THE TEXT

■ 7 The third commandment prohibits any false oaths (Deut 5:20; Ps 24:4; Jer 5:2; Hos 4:15; 10:4) and wrongful, worthless, or vain use or "carrying" (*nāśā'*; "to carry, lift") of the **name of the LORD**. The **misuse** of the name may refer to any speech that is false (in report, witness), idle, unnecessary, frivolous, insincere (in blessing, agreements, promises, or oaths), or fraudulent (in lawsuit). It also may include attributing the divine name to idols (Exod 32:4; 1 Kgs 12:28) or evoking the divine name in pagan rituals, incantations, magic, spells, or witchcraft. If God's name is used in an oath, it is to be invoked in love and reverence and in sincerity and truth.

Even though the offender may go unnoticed or ignored by human authorities, Yahweh will not acquit or **hold anyone guiltless** who is guilty of violating this command. Not holding guiltless is essentially equivalent to punishing (Exod 20:5; 34:7).

FROM THE TEXT

Far from being restricted to the Israel of the past or to those Christians who use foul language, the third commandment addresses us all with an urgent call to speak and live in keeping with the one whose name we bear. Our modern world, with its penchant for civil religion, and the commodification of crosses and Christian language, is steeped in the violation of this command: "There is a sense . . . in which blasphemy is the universal character of human life, nay of religious life itself" (Ephraim Radner in Braaten and Seitz 2005, 80). How often Christians flippantly take the name of the Father or the Son upon their lips even while having motivations or actions that betray those words! How easy it is for Christians to join in with the world's profanation of God's name! The prohibition stands against any form of hypocrisy, which is precisely what Jesus vehemently opposes in the scribes and Pharisees, in the religious readers and teachers of God's word. The third commandment calls us to honor God with our very existence, with our speech and actions, and with our motivations.

(5) Fourth Commandment: Sabbath (20:8-11)

BEHIND THE TEXT

The forth commandment is anticipated by the creation account. Genesis 2:3 does not necessarily establish a fixed weekly institution regulating human activity, but the fourth commandment does so in connection with Yahweh's own seventh-day rest.

Genesis 2:5, 15 indicate that work (working the ground in these texts) is the divinely assigned task of human beings. Human work in Gen 2 in a real sense is participation with God and his work of creation, by keeping the earth productive and beautiful (and thus also being the image of God in humans' relationship to the ground). The divine rest in the same way is also the pattern for human rest. "Sabbath keeping is an act of creation keeping" in that it maintains the "working/resting rhythm" that God built into the "very created order of things" (Fretheim 1991, 230). The commandment to keep the Sabbath rest (refraining from work) becomes more meaningful when we hear it in the context of work that is made more difficult due to the cursed ground because of human sin in Gen 3:17-19.

There is no parallel to a Sabbath provision elsewhere in the ancient Near East, since it is grounded not only in the imitation of the creator Yahweh but also in the Bible's concern for justice for all people, kindness to animals, and sustainability of the land. Propp notes that there is "the seven-day taboo cycle" in Mesopotamia, but given its late date, it might reflect the Israelite influence upon the Mesopotamian culture (2006, 176).

In Exodus, the Sabbath rest is observed in relation to giving, gathering, and preparing manna (16:22-30). This indicates that the Sabbath is already an established institution in Israel prior to Sinai. In the land, as the Israelites remember and imitate Yahweh's rest from creation, they also remember Yahweh's supernatural provision of manna during the wilderness period.

The Sabbath principle is extended to the seventh year as the year of Sabbath, fallowing the ground (→ 23:10-11; Lev 25:4), emancipating slaves (Exod 21:2; Deut 15:12), and canceling debts (Deut 15:9). The seventh Sabbatical Year is followed by the Year of Jubilee (fiftieth year), when those who formerly sold their property return to it (Lev 25:10-13, 28) and slaves are emancipated (vv 39-40). The years of Sabbath and Jubilee reflect the ideal state of existence in peace, rest, freedom, provision, and worship that humans enjoyed at the time of creation and will enjoy in eternity.

Keeping the Sabbath holy is inextricably related to the observance of the first three commandments. Any breach in the first three will necessarily corrupt the Sabbath worship of the creator God with idols and idolatry. Conversely, failing to remember and acknowledge Yahweh as the Creator, the giver of the Sabbath rest, and the extravagant provider, will inevitably lead to the creation and worship of idols for productivity, prosperity, and protection. Thus, the violation of the Sabbath rest is a serious breach of the covenant with Yahweh. Exodus 31:15 therefore imposes the death penalty for breaking the Sabbath.

IN THE TEXT

■ **8** The fourth commandment charges the Israelites to **remember** [or "be mindful of"] **the Sabbath day** [*šabbāt*, "to cease, desist, rest from labor"] **by keeping it holy**. This commandment assumes a kind of bondage to postfall work from which people find it difficult to extricate themselves. People need limits from working themselves and others to death, partly because of a compulsion to work due to anxiety of not having enough if one were idle (Lev 25:20). Instead, people are called to trust in the creator God's loving provision, rest, and worship Yahweh (Isa 58:13; Hos 2:11 [13 HB]), thus making the day holy.

■ **9** The Israelites are commanded to do **all** manner of **work** for **six days**. The Lord will bless and prosper his people (Deut 8:7-9), but prosperity will not come unless the people diligently work—a point reinforced in Israel's Wisdom literature (Prov 6:6-11; 10:4; 14:23; 24:33-34; 28:19; Eccl 11:6).

■ **10** The six days serve temporal concerns and pleasures, **but the seventh day** is dedicated to God. Thus, no one shall **do any work**, whether human or **animals**, **male** or **female**, old or young, free or **servant**, native or **foreigner**. "Your wife" is not mentioned, not because she alone should work, but because the command is directed to the Israelite women and men, to both the wife and the husband. God's people's prosperity in his land does not depend on human determination, endeavor, industriousness, and productivity, but on divine favor. Hosea later makes it clear that Yahweh can "take away" all blessings as a form of punishment for forgetting Yahweh even on the Sabbath days (Hos 2:9-13 [11-15 HB]). It is the acceptable **sabbath to the LORD** that releases the seventh-day blessings and holiness into all the other days, making the six days of labor fruitful, enjoyable, and satisfying.

■ **11** Yahweh set the precedent for the **Sabbath day** at the time of creation (Gen 2:2-3). Worshippers remember and celebrate the day in a jubilant imitation of the Creator of the universe who first took the Sabbath rest. As ones made in Yahweh's image, human beings are called not only to be like Yahweh (by being holy) but also to act like Yahweh (by resting and giving rest to fellow human beings and even to livestock and the land). The act of imitating God's rest becomes a merciful relief from the toilsome aspects of postfall work and an aid to sustainable productivity of the land.

FROM THE TEXT

Israel's Sabbath not only shapes their worship but also implies social justice and equality for all persons in the land and as such points to the eternal Sabbath rest. As Jürgen Moltmann observes about the Sabbath, "Men do not rest at the expense of women—parents at the expense of their children—one's own people at the expense of strangers—human beings at the expense of animals. All are meant to rest together" (2001, 281). The commandment is thus the great equalizer—no one is left out of the rest it offers. As such, the Sabbath rest is a foretaste of the eschatological justice that God will one day accomplish for all God's people and all creation to enjoy.

The Sabbath commandment invites us to bring order to our tension-filled and frenzied life, by seeking freedom from the tyranny of excessive labor, materialism, and the pleasures of life. The commandment also invites us to reflect, rest, and most of all depend on the life-giving creative work of God and his daily provisions for us. The Sabbath is thus holy, a time for celebration and praise of the creator God. The Sabbath also invites us to witness to the world of the "rest" it can find in the one who summons, "Come to me, all you who are weary and burdened, and I will give you rest" (Matt 11:28). Jesus also interprets the commandment as the "Lord . . . of the Sabbath" that "the Sabbath was made for man, not man for the Sabbath" (Mark 2:28, 27). Based on the narrative in Mark's Gospel (2:23-28), we may see in Jesus' words an invitation not only to enjoy the Sabbath but also to give the Sabbath to the hungry and the tired and the overworked in the world around us.

The writer to the Hebrews calls everyone to enter by obedient faith and faithfulness into the ultimate Sabbath rest that is "God's throne of grace" and mercy, which the promised land prefigures (Heb 4). Entering the eschatological Sabbath rest is synonymous to entering the kingdom of heaven that Christ invites us into. It is the eternal life and relationship with God that has been extended to the present life on earth through the covenant relationship with Christ. Christians can uphold this view of Sabbath rest whether they believe the fourth commandment is an abiding law (generally in the form of the Lord's Day as a Christian Sabbath) or not (based on a certain interpretation of texts such as Col 2:16).

(6) Fifth Commandment: Honoring Parents (20:12)

BEHIND THE TEXT

Respect for parents is a virtue universally valued in all cultures. The related respect for the elderly is a virtue observed in most cultures outside the modern West or westernized cultures (that value youth and information over age and wisdom). Before Sinai, the importance of upholding the honor of parents is implied in Shem and Japheth's refusal to see their father's nakedness (Gen 9:23) and in Noah's curse of Ham for exposing Noah's shame (9:25). Jacob also cursed Reuben for dishonoring him (35:22; 49:4). These stories bear witness not only to the supreme value placed on honor of parents but also to the implied God-given authority the parents have to bless or curse their children and determine the general direction of their and their descendants' lives. In cultures that value filial respect, the elders as parents of many generations under their authority receive highest respect and honor. In ancient Israel and other archaic societies, the elders also possess more wisdom and knowledge, simply by virtue of having lived long. Accordingly the elders are the rulers and legislators and chief advisers of the Israelite and Jewish communities (see Exod 3:16-18; 19:7; Num 11:16-17; Deut 22:18; 1 Sam 8:4; 1 Kgs 12:13; Ezra 6:7; Prov 31:23; Matt 26:3; Acts 5:21; 15:4) and archaic societies.

At Sinai, the filial honor is placed in the context of the covenant between Yahweh and his people. Such a placement emphasizes filial respect as a reflection of their honor of Yahweh as their Father and parental care as a reflection of Yahweh's father/mother care of his people. This law in the context of the Decalogue also explicitly resists any filial worship of parents or ancestors (see Lev 19:32; Prov 31:28).

IN THE TEXT

■ 12 The fifth commandment calls children, sons and daughters of all ages, to respect and **honor** (*kābad*) their **father** and **mother**. Besides parents, Yahweh must be approached with due honor (*kābad*; e.g., 1 Sam 2:29-30; Ps 22:23 [24 HB]; Prov 3:9; Isa 29:13). Therefore, the offender deserves the death penalty (see Exod 21:15, 17; Lev 20:9; Deut 21:18-21).

Honoring parents can be discussed in two main ways: (1) children's obedience to parents' and elders' instructions and (2) adult children's duty to the elderly.

(1) This commandment also presupposes that the father and mother are the primary instructors. In ancient Israel, the father and mother are the primary instructors and interpreters of God's covenant words (Deut 4:9-10; 6:7; 11:19; 32:46). Accordingly, the children learn and obey the laws and statutes of God under parental instructions. Therefore, obedience to parents is

essential for maintaining the wholeness of the family, religion, and society. In this context, rejection of parental instruction and discipline is tantamount to repudiation of the covenant. For this reason, this commandment is closely associated with longevity **in the land** (Deut 11:18-28; 31:13; 32:46-47). The breakdown of the family and the related breaking of the covenant laws will inevitably invite the covenant curses, lead to the eventual dissolution of the whole society, and finally result in expulsion from the land. Thus, a narrow and individualistic interpretation and application of honor of parents as guaranteeing personal prosperity and longevity is a distortion of this commandment and is detrimental to the processes of communal accountability to the divine requirements. There is a collective responsibility of the fathers and mothers toward Yahweh and to the succeeding generations, to teach the law of Yahweh. There is also a duty of the children toward the older generations who instruct and advise in the way of the Lord, to obey the law of Yahweh.

Adult children are not completely independent of their parents' instruction or authority. Thus, they are still liable to parents' disciplinary actions, and persistent extreme rebellion warrants parents handing the rebellious adult child over to the court to be judicially executed (see Deut 21:18-21).

(2) When applied to adult children, the command to honor parents includes relating to them with respect, high esteem, dignity, and deference. Thus, there are warnings against despising parents (Prov 23:22) or treating them with contempt (Ezek 22:7).

This commandment also requires kind treatment of the elderly who are no longer productive contributors to the family and thus liable to violent abuse and contempt (Exod 21:15, 17; Lev 20:9). It requires provision for the aged and protection of their estate until their death, neither seeking to seize their property prematurely nor abandoning them (Prov 19:26) nor reducing defenseless parents to poverty (28:24).

Despite the typical inseparability of honoring God and honoring parents, honor of father or mother is not above honor of the Lord. This point is made explicitly in God's prohibition of the Levitical priests and Nazirites from performing certain actions toward their family members (including fathers or mothers) that are otherwise universally observed and expected, such as mourning for the dead (Lev 10:6; 21:11; Num 6:7). Another example is the Levites' destruction of their own family members (including a father or a mother [Deut 33:9]) for their participation in the worship of the golden calf (Exod 32:27-28). Although this act may be considered abhorrent by modern sensibilities, Moses actually commends them for impartially carrying out their duties as covenant judges on Yahweh's behalf (→ 32:29; also see Deut 33:9). While the Levites' covenant vengeance provides us with an example of the priority of Yahweh's honor above filial respect, their grim acts remain confined to the Mosaic period.

FROM THE TEXT

The use of the fifth commandment in the NT shows the abiding force and relevance of honor of parents. Specifically, Jesus condemns the Jewish tradition through which adult children could avoid their obligation to provide for their parents by dedicating the money to God (Matt 15:3-6; also Mark 7:9-11). In addition, the epistle to the Ephesians cites and applies the fifth commandment to a largely Gentile audience (Eph 6:1-3), calling the minor children to obey their parents, who, in turn, are instructed not to abuse or embitter children but to nurture and instruct them in the way of the Lord.

Implicit in the Ephesian passage is the condemnation of abusive parenting. The Bible categorically condemns violent people (physical, verbal, psychological, sexual, etc.; see Eph 4:31; Col 3:8). The violent are called "evildoers" (Ps 140:1 [2 HB]) or "wicked" (Ps 140:4 [5 HB]; Prov 10:6, 11) and the Lord hates violent persons (Ps 11:5). Accordingly, many psalms cry out to the Lord to bring an end to violent persons (Pss 17:8-9; 18:47-48 [48-49 HB]; 55:9 [10 HB]; see Prov 10:31-32). In the case of abuse, the honor, dignity, wholeness, and safety of the child comes before the "honor" of an abusive or violent "parent."

Consistent with the OT, honor of God or obedience to Christ takes precedence over honor of and obedience to parents. Jesus says, "Anyone who loves their father or mother more than me is not worthy of me; anyone who loves their son or daughter more than me is not worthy of me. Whoever does not take up their cross and follow me is not worthy of me" (Matt 10:37-38).

(7) Sixth Commandment: Murder (20:13)

BEHIND THE TEXT

The sixth commandment prohibits murder and unlawful homicide. The definition of murder can vary from culture to culture. In most societies, however, murder is considered one of the most serious crimes against humanity and is therefore met by the severest forms of punishment. In the ancient Near East, the Code of Ur-Nammu from Mesopotamia (2100 BC) punished murder by the death penalty (law 1). The Code of Hammurabi (ca. 1700 BC) imposed a monetary penalty for presumably unintentional killings (laws 207-8), and intentional killings (laws 153, 209-14) required the death penalty for murder (law 153; also hinted in 206-7) and sanctioned execution of the killer's own daughter for killing another man's daughter (law 210).

The Bible treats murder with utter seriousness. In Genesis, Yahweh's condemnation of Cain's murder of Abel (4:1-16) and postdiluvian decrees concerning homicide (9:5-6) demonstrate the gravity of this crime. In the book of

Exodus, a mass murderer who decrees infanticide is punished by divine execution of all the firstborn of his nation.

IN THE TEXT

■ **13** The Hebrew term for **murder** (*rāṣaḥ*; "kill") refers to both premeditated and accidental killing of a person. The prohibition here, however, is for hateful premeditated killing (see Deut 19:11-13) and not accidental killing (see vv 4-7). Interestingly, the term *rāṣaḥ* is "never employed when the subject of the action is God or an angel" (Sarna 2004, 84). The prohibition here does not include killing in war, judicial execution, or the defense of life.

According to Gen 9:6, the sanctity of all human life is grounded in the fact that Yahweh made human beings in the divine image. While all life derives from Yahweh, and thus belongs to God, human life is incomparably valuable to Yahweh due to this special endowment or function. Yahweh therefore demands an accounting from each person who commits murder, because it is a gross violation of God's property rights (9:6). This ancient principle lies behind the requirement to put the murderer to death, most likely by the legal magistrates (or the elders of the town) seizing and handing over the murderer to the avenger of blood to die (Exod 21:12-14; Lev 24:17; Num 35:16; Deut 19:11-12). Such a judicial execution of the guilty is necessary to "purge from Israel the guilt of shedding innocent blood" (Deut 19:13) which, if left unpunished, would pollute the land. Atonement could not be made for such killing of innocent blood "except by the blood of the one who shed it" (Num 35:33). For this reason, God strictly prohibits taking any "ransom for the life of a murderer" (v 31).

FROM THE TEXT

This commandment calls us to be givers and not takers of life. Accordingly, this commandment is central to the convictions of the pro-life movement that rightfully condemns abortion as a violation of this commandment. However, this commandment, when understood theologically, calls not only for the preservation of the life of the unborn (→ Exod 21:22-25 on fatal injury to an unborn child) but also for the preservation of life from birth to death. Life is sacred from conception to death. Therefore, wherever life is in danger (due to war, violence, lack of shelter and nourishment, and lack of proper medical care), this commandment summons God's people to sustain life and to reflect on all the implications and challenges of its call.

In the NT, Jesus addresses not simply the external sin of murder but also the internal root issue that gives rise to murder, namely, anger and the verbal abuse resulting from it. Jesus addresses the common progression of anger into contempt and verbal abuse (*rhaka*; "fool," "empty head") and then into a full-blown condemnation and dismissal (*Mōre*; "you fool" or "moron" in Matt 5:22). Such anger and abuse violates the human dignity and worth of those made in the image of God (see Jas 3:9). Jesus exposes the gravity of these offenses by warning that God will punish every hateful attitude and word spoken (Matt 5:22, 26). Jesus then admonishes any offender to seek reconciliation with the offended by making any restitution needed (v 24), confess sins, and ask for forgiveness. The offended, likewise, should be quick to forgive the injury and purge any anger, contempt, or condemnation. Especially, offenders are advised to take action "quickly," before the "adversary" (ultimately, the devil) hands the guilty over to the judge (God), who is sure to impose penalties (v 25).

(8) Seventh Commandment: Adultery (20:14)

BEHIND THE TEXT

Jewish and Christian traditions uphold the conviction that God established the institution of marriage in the garden (see Gen 2:22-24). Genesis 1:28 implies procreation (through sexual relations) as one of the vocations of humans created in the image of God. The Song of Songs celebrates human sexuality and the sexual enjoyment of a bridegroom and his bride. Marriage relationship between a man and a woman at best reflects the nature of the covenant between God and Israel, which is often described in the OT using the marriage metaphor (also used by the NT writers to describe Christ and his relationship to the church). The prohibition of adultery in the Decalogue safeguards the covenant of marriage.

Condemnation of adultery is reflected in Abraham-Isaac stories in Genesis (see Gen 12:14-19; 20:1-18; 26:1-11). These accounts demonstrate the fact that the sanctity of marriage was understood in ancient Egypt and Palestine. Pharaoh recognized "serious diseases" that came on him and his household as the consequence of taking Sarai, Abram's wife, as his "wife" (12:17, 19). The Philistine kings (both named Abimelek) understood adultery as "great sin" (ESV) "that should never be done" (20:9) and as something that brings guilt upon the individual and the whole community (20:9; 26:10). Joseph also clearly expressed the idea that adultery is a sin against God (39:9). Their moral sensibility is consistent with what is found in the oldest of the ancient Near Eastern laws. Both Ur-Nammu (law 7) and Eshnunna (law 28) condemned to death an adulterous wife.

In striking contrast to Pharaoh, the Abimeleks, and Joseph in Egypt, Abraham and Isaac exhibited a willingness to compromise marital chastity in order to negotiate a perceived threat to life. Interestingly, their view is reflected in both the Babylonian and Hittite laws. Both the Hammurabi code and the Hittite laws appear to have defined adultery as sexual union between a mutually consenting man and another man's wife. They seem to have considered adultery largely a wrong against the husband but not a sin against God. In such a context, the offenders (both the adulterer and the adulteress) were punished by death, unless the offenders were pardoned at the discretion of the husband or the king (Hammurabi code 129; the Hittite law 197-98). Nesilim code, on the other hand, appears to have treated sexual union between a presumably married but mutually consenting man and woman as noncriminal (law 190). Both the Hammurabi (law 130) and Ur-Nammu (law 6) codes condemned to death a man who violated a woman betrothed to another man, while acquitting the woman (see Code of Nesilim, law 197).

In Israelite law, the definition of adultery (*nā'ap*) is widened to include any married person's consenting or forced sexual union with a person of the opposite sex. Adultery is a sin before God and not merely a violation of social or family mores. The offenders are judged based upon court proceedings with witnesses, and those found guilty are punished according to divinely sanctioned penalties (e.g., Lev 20:10). Proverbs likens the one who falls into adultery to "an ox going to the slaughter" (7:22*a*), "a deer stepping into a noose" (v 22*b*), or an easy prey (6:26).

IN THE TEXT

■ **14** The seventh commandment prohibits **adultery** (*nā'ap*). In stark contrast to other societies, the prohibition binds all Israelites, including all men, to marital chastity, whether in the normative monogamous marriages or in the few known cases of polygamous marriages (e.g., King David). The intention of the command is to prohibit all extramarital sex for married/betrothed men and married/betrothed women and all unmarried men and women.

The Hebrew term for **commit adultery** (*nā'ap*) is used for marital unfaithfulness through illicit sexual union, with either a man (Lev 18:20; 20:10; Deut 22:22) or a woman (Prov 7:5; Hos 4:13) as the subject. The verb is used in reference to an unlawful sexual union not only by mutual consent between a man and a married woman (Lev 18:20; 20:10; Deut 22:22) but also sexual consensual union between a man and another man's betrothed (Deut 22:23-24), between a married woman and a man, married or unmarried (Prov 7:5; Hos 4:13-14), and between a married man and a prostitute, as found in the expression "adulterers [masc.] and prostitutes [fem.]" in Isa 57:3.

The verb *nā'ap* can also refer to forced sexual intercourse or rape by a man against another man's betrothed woman (Deut 22:25-27), "the barren and childless woman" (perhaps divorced; Job 24:15), or the defenseless widow (v 21). The offender (in vv 15, 21) is called an "adulterer" (*nō'ēp*) probably on the basis of his marital status, that is, based on the fact that he is breaking his marital covenant with his wife.

The law imposes capital punishment on all offending (consenting or violating) parties (male and female). The above considerations show that Israel's prohibition of adultery has consistent standards for both men and women.

FROM THE TEXT

The seventh commandment reminds readers to reflect on the sanctity of marriage through faithfulness in marital relationship. Fidelity in marital relationship reflects fidelity to the covenant with God. Conversely, marital unfaithfulness is an evident sign of disrupted and unfaithful relationship with God. Adultery calls into question the integrity of God, who witnesses the covenant of marriage. The sanctity of the marriage also calls for fidelity in fulfilling sexual responsibility in marital relationship (1 Cor 7:3-5). The danger of adultery is that it destroys not only the husband-wife relationship but also relationships at the larger levels of society, including children and other families. This commandment goes beyond fidelity in marital relationships. In our understanding of this commandment today, we also need to include any form of sexual behavior or attitude contrary to the spirit of this commandment, which is fidelity in human relationships.

Jesus revisits the prohibition of adultery by addressing its root cause, which is lust (Matt 5:27-30). The tenth commandment against coveting already anticipates this approach, since it addresses the unlawful desire for another's wife that leads to adultery. There are other texts in the OT that address the root issue of lust. Most famously, the story of David's adultery with Bathsheba well illustrates this point. In the parable of the prophet Nathan, lust is likened to the traveler. In the parable, David is likened to a rich man who slaughters a poor man's only ewe lamb (namely, Bathsheba) and serves it to the traveler (namely, his lust; see 2 Sam 12:1-4). Welcoming and embracing lustful desire has dire consequences for David, his family members, and, indeed, the whole nation (v 10). The "traveler" entertained by David is apparently there to stay, wreaking havoc in his family through Ammon's rape of his half-sister Tamar (13:11-20), Absalom's violation of ten of David's concubines (16:22), and then Solomon's uncontrolled appetite for women (1 Kgs 11:1-8) that ultimately results in the divided monarchy (vv 9-13).

Jesus says that a man "who looks at a woman lustfully has already committed adultery with her in his heart" (Matt 5:28). Jesus is not denying that it is worse to commit the act of adultery than it is to lust. However, Jesus is stressing where the real problem and solution lie. As he did with his treatment of anger and murder, Jesus offers a redemptive way out of the path that leads one from lust to adultery and then to punishment; it is, namely, a radical cutting off of anything that causes one to sin (vv 29-30). In Paul's words, one is to "put aside the deeds of darkness [presumably using "the sword of the Spirit"

(Eph 6:17)] and put on the armor of light" (Rom 13:12; also see v 13). The Holy Spirit helps us walk in purity of heart and deed.

(9) Eighth Commandment: Theft (20:15)

BEHIND THE TEXT

There is general agreement in the ancient Near East and other societies that theft or unauthorized taking of another's possession is wrong. In Babylonian law, the punishments for theft varied based upon not only the value of the property stolen but also the identity of the victim. For example, in Hammurabi's laws, those who stole livestock from the temple or palace were required to pay back thirtyfold, but if they stole from ordinary people, then they repaid tenfold (to escape the death penalty; law 8). Those who stole goods from the temple or palace and those who received stolen goods were put to death (law 6). Kidnapping was punished by death (law 14). The Code of Ur-Nammu imposed capital punishment for robbery (law 2) but only imprisonment and fines for kidnapping (law 3). The Hittite laws imposed heavy fines for kidnapping (laws 19-21).

The examples from Israel's ancestral period demonstrate the apparent readiness to punish by death the crime of stealing cultic objects (Laban's household gods in Gen 31:19, 32 and Joseph's cup presented as an instrument of divination in Gen 44:8-9). Such examples show similarity with the later Hammurabi's treatment of theft involving cultic objects.

IN THE TEXT

■ **15** The prohibition against stealing is rather general. Petty theft is hardly a crime matching the severity of other crimes mentioned in the Decalogue. Therefore, Jewish scholars traditionally interpreted this law as referring to stealing from the spoils of war that are dedicated to Yahweh (e.g., Achan in Josh 7) and to kidnapping and selling the victim into slavery (see Exod 21:16; Deut 24:7). Noth sees here a prohibition against stealing human beings, especially stealing and enslaving of Israelites (1962, 166), while others include in the prohibition both persons and properties (see Childs 1974, 423-24).

However, one may interpret this prohibition as including a number of less serious forms of stealing, which are punished by fines and restitution, such as robbery (Exod 22:1-4, 7-9, 12); embezzlement (vv 7-8); and, use of dishonest weights (Deut 25:13-16). There are also passive forms of stealing: negligence (Exod 21:33-36) and keeping property that others lost (23:4).

There are other forms of stealing that especially affect the powerless and defenseless of the land. For these, Yahweh is said to act on behalf of the victims. These include defrauding or withholding the wages of a day laborer whose life depends on it (Lev 19:13; Deut 24:14-15); keeping back the tithes, by which the Levites, poor, foreigners, widows, and fatherless are supported (Deut 14:22-29; 16:9-17; 18:1-8; 26:9-13; Mal 3:6-12); and taking what Yahweh set aside as provisions for the poor (i.e., leaving some grains and fruits in Deut 24:19-22 or not harvesting at all every seventh year in Exod 23:10-11).

FROM THE TEXT

The eighth commandment prohibits the violation of the rights of others to enjoy their life and property, both of which are gracious gifts from God. Adam Clarke states in his commentary on this commandment, "All *withholding of rights* and *doing of wrongs* are against the spirit of it." If so, this prohibition indicts economic inequities in which poor children are robbed of their future, colonialism in which the developing nations are exploited, oppressed, and barred from the resources that are necessary for life through economic and military control, and human trafficking in which the poorest of the poor are robbed of freedom, dignity, and self-worth. This commandment summons God's people to arise and uphold those victims' right to enjoy God's gracious gifts of life, freedom, future, resources, property, and dignity.

The Bible differentiates stealing merely to stave off one's hunger from stealing motivated by greed. The consideration of intent and one's right to life and survival is already found in the differentiation between killing in self-defense and unlawful malicious killing. Stealing from God that is motivated by greed is most severely punished. In strong contrast, Prov 6:30 discourages people from exposing to public shame and demanding full restitution of those who steal merely to stave off hunger. The Israelite law uniquely creates equal access to food to all (through the provision of the poor tithe and numerous other provisions). This economic egalitarianism is based on the fundamental theological truth that the land belongs to the Lord. The Landlord grants the right to the produce of the land to all its inhabitants, regardless of their role in crop production. By requiring sufficient provision of food for the poor, the Lord upholds the human dignity of all.

Jesus upholds this commandment (e.g., Matt 19:18), and Paul issues a stern warning to the poor who might steal from others (1 Cor 6:10). The believers in Acts 4 shared their possessions, virtually eliminating poverty (vv 32-37). Along with such communal generosity, the NT offers working diligently, serving and trusting God for provision, being content and thankful in all circumstances, and sharing with those in need as the antidote to stealing motivated by poverty or greed (Matt 6:33; Luke 12:31; Eph 4:28; Heb 13:5). John Wesley likewise admonishes in his sermon "The Use of Money" (1980), "Gain all you can," "save all you can," and "give all you can." His exhortation helps us to give this commandment a positive reformulation and application in our community life today.

(10) Ninth Commandment: False Witness (20:16)

BEHIND THE TEXT

Truthful witness is indispensable for the administration of justice. Thus, this commandment prohibits false testimonies in a legal setting.

A false witness is universally condemned in both ancient and modern cultures. In the Code of Ur-Nammu, false witnesses or perjurers were required to pay a certain penalty set by the court, the maximum amount being equal to what the falsely accused would have paid (law 29). The Code of Hammurabi likewise imposed the death penalty for false charges of capital crimes (laws 1, 3).

The Bible describes a few cases of false witness: Potiphar's wife against Joseph that resulted in Joseph's imprisonment (Gen 39:6-20), the Amalekites' false testimony that cost him his own life (2 Sam 1:16), and Jezebel's puppet court of bribed witnesses and terrorized elders or judges who condemned Naboth to death (1 Kgs 21).

The canon as a whole commands truth-telling and condemns false testimonies. God's people are called to imitate the one about whom Samuel says, "He who is the Glory of Israel does not lie" (1 Sam 15:29). Proverbs 6:16-19 lists six things that Yahweh hates, four of which are closely related to this commandment: "a lying tongue" and "a false witness who pours out lies" that come out of "a heart that devises wicked schemes" and that may lead to shedding of "innocent blood." Such heinous crimes against humanity and sin against Yahweh should be differentiated from the "white lie" uttered in the interest of divine law and preservation of life (→ Exod 1:19).

IN THE TEXT

■ **16** In a court proceeding, both the claimant and the defendant are to produce their evidence or witness. In some cases, they might produce third-party witnesses. The court, made up of elders or other appointed leaders, would pass judgment, and the sentence would be imposed immediately (22:8-11; Deut 17:2-6). The case laws in Exodus point out various factors that would help generate **false testimony**: siding with the majority (23:2), favoritism (v 3), bribery (v 8), classism or oppression of the poor (v 6), and racism or discrimination against the foreigners (v 9).

Certain laws discourage false witnesses. Two or three witnesses are required to establish a case (Num 35:30; Deut 17:6; 19:15). Judges must make a thorough investigation (13:14 [15 HB]; 19:18). Anyone with evidence must testify (Lev 5:1), in which case, evidence against false witnesses may emerge. In addition, the false witnesses are punished with the same punishment that the accused would have suffered. Finally, the witnesses are required to be the first to cast the stones in capital cases (Deut 13:9 [10 HB]; 17:7; 19:16-21).

The scope of **your neighbor** (*rē‘a*) here and in the next verse is universal. Whereas Lev 19:17-18 may appear to define "neighbor" as one of the fellow Israelites, v 34 leaves no room for such misunderstanding; the foreigners (*gēr*) must be embraced and treated as those who are native-born; the Israelites are told to "love them as yourself."

FROM THE TEXT

The ninth commandment has broader implications than truth-telling in the court; in contrast to the ancient world where courts were able to provide protection from the miscarriage of justice, we live in a world where the court of public opinion determines the integrity of individuals, which is often manipulated and shaped by propagandas, ideological wars for political power, news media under the control of the wealthy with self-serving interests, political party loyalties, and lack of diligence given to careful examination of evidence against individuals accused of criminal action by criminal justice agencies under pressure from authorities to solve cases. The commandment reminds readers that the soundness of our public and national life depends on the commitment of its members to be truth-tellers. Lying and false testimony will lead to false accusation, character defamation (murder of the personhood), and victimization of the innocent in the society. The psalmist's prayer for deliverance from those who speak lies shows the prevalence of dishonesty even in the covenant society (Pss 5:9-10 [10-11 HB]; 12:1-4 [2-5 HB]; 27:12). This commandment calls for constructive speech and "speaking the truth in love," so that our words may become the vehicle of God's grace and justice, life and healing (Eph 4:15, 29).

For the disciples of Christ, being Christ's faithful and truthful witnesses is an important aspect of truth-telling (Acts 1:8). Christ says the reason for the incarnation is "to testify to the truth" (John 18:37), to testify for himself, even as God testifies for him (8:18). However, bearing truthful witness to his own divine identity and kingship (Matt 26:64) leads to the crucifixion, as the high priest and the whole Sanhedrin take his testimony as blasphemous (vv 65-66). So also is Stephen martyred for his bold and truthful testimony to his open-heaven vision, in which he sees Christ standing as the divine King and Judge (Acts 7:56).

Whatever the personal cost, anyone with evidence must testify (see Lev 5:1). If we have evidence that Christ is the Messiah, the Savior of the world, then we have the obligation to testify to the truth of Jesus Christ. Not to act, because of fear of rejection, persecution, or death, is to be ashamed of Jesus Christ and is to withhold the evidence that can save lives. Thus, there are numerous warnings that Christ will be ashamed of those who are ashamed of him and his words, and he will disown those who disown him (Matt 10:33; Mark 8:38; Luke 12:9; 2 Tim 1:8, 12). Paul charges us, "Join with me in suffering for the gospel, by the power of God" (2 Tim 1:8).

(11) Tenth Commandment: Covetousness (20:17)

BEHIND THE TEXT

The tenth commandment prohibits covetousness, the root of all sinful actions. The fall story in Gen 3 well illustrates the progression from ill-gotten desire to unlawful possession. Once deceived by the serpent to believe that Yahweh is withholding the best from them, the woman's judgment, focus, and desire change (Gen 3:5-6). She now falsely judges that the fruit is good for food (though it is for death). The forbidden fruit becomes the focus of her "eyes" or intense desire (blinding her to the rest that are truly good). She is engulfed by her desire to gain wisdom to be like God (forgetting that she is made in the image and likeness of God [1:26-27]). These factors lead her to commit the act, and her husband, who apparently is fully in agreement with her, follows her lead (3:6).

Achan's confession also illustrates the notion that coveting is the root sin of other crimes: "When I *saw* in the plunder a beautiful robe . . . silver and a bar of gold . . . , I *coveted* them and *took* them" (Josh 7:21).

IN THE TEXT

■ **17** Coveting is hardly a crime that can be witnessed and prosecuted. Thus, based on the action of taking implied in the usage of the Hebrew term for **covet** (*ḥāmad*) in Exod 34:24, it has been suggested that the term refers not merely to the desire but to the action. But all the other usages of the term show clear distinction between coveting and taking (see Deut 7:25; Josh 7:21; Prov 6:25; Mic 2:2). It is best to understand this prohibition as targeting internal sinful motivations and states of covetousness or lust. Coveting or the illegitimate desire to possess something or someone that belongs to another or that is prohibited can lead to the breaking of all the other commandments: theft (e.g., Josh 7:21), adultery (e.g., 2 Sam 11:2-4), false witness against and/or murder of the legitimate owner (e.g., 1 Kgs 21:8-14; also see 2 Sam 11:14-24), dishonor of parents through abandonment or dispossession (Prov 19:26; 28:24), breaking the Sabbath (e.g., Exod 16:27-29), use of God's name in vain in false witnessing (e.g., 1 Kgs 21:13), and ultimately, idolatry and worship of other gods and goddesses (e.g., Solomon [1 Kgs 11:1-6]). In obeying the first commandment, one submits to the rest. In breaking it, one is liable to lawlessness. In obeying the last commandment, one gains self-control and mastery over other sins. In breaking it, one can be mastered by the rest of sins. As such, the first and the last may be viewed as the gatekeepers of the Decalogue.

The OT offers diligent work (Prov 13:4; 28:19-20), trust in God for provision (Ps 23:1-3), godly stewardship (Prov 3:9-10; 22:9; 28:27), and contentment in what is already given (23:4-5; 30:7-9) as the antidote to covetousness.

FROM THE TEXT

Consistent with the OT, the NT condemns covetousness and shows a better way to both internal and external freedom from covetousness and attainment of righteousness. Jesus warns against covetousness, desire for abundance of possessions, greed, and envy (Mark 7:21-22; Luke 12:15). Paul treats greed as a form of idolatry and identifies the love of money as the root of all evil (Eph 5:5; 1 Tim 6:10). Likewise, James condemns covetous desire as adulterous "friendship with the world" and "enmity against God" (Jas 4:1-4). The NT message is clear; covetousness and the kingdom of God are mutually exclusive.

However, in a world beset with materialism, consumerism, and illicit sexual gratification (through pornography and sex trafficking, for example), coveting has become pandemic. Greed is at the heart of personal, interpersonal, national, and international pursuits; it plagues individuals with strife and policies that promote gain at the expense of others. Covetousness makes one blind to other people's right to life, liberty, and happiness in God. Greed makes individuals and societies ignore and lose even the most elemental concern for the humanity of the others. Coveting is the opposite of covenanting; coveting ends in unlawful acquisitions whereas covenanting leads to the caring and loving treatment of the neighbor and his or her property.

So how do we extricate ourselves from the entrapment of the world that demands our servitude and devotion? The answers are shocking when taken literally. The Apostle Paul's words, "I have not coveted anyone's silver or gold or clothing" (Acts 20:33), model for us a lifestyle free from greed. This commandment also invites the readers to seek freedom from the temptation to measure their human worth by their material possessions, and to live in freedom from the fear of scarcity, a root cause of greed and lust. The psalmist's confident statement, "The LORD is my shepherd, I lack nothing" (Ps 23:1), is the best antidote to greed and lust, which this commandment prohibits.

Paul says to be content and be thankful if our basic necessities are met (1 Tim 6:8). Beyond that, Jesus commands us to absolutely prioritize the kingdom of heaven, both receiving it for ourselves and bringing it to those who do not have it, as a true and lasting inheritance and possession. The radical obedience to such a calling, however, requires a commitment to poverty in spirit and in body, for "theirs is the kingdom of heaven" (Matt 5:3; Luke 6:20). Without deeply hungering for God and for the salvation of the lost and without radically surrendering our lives (including our finances) to God for kingdom purposes, we will not see the kingdom of God coming and manifesting in the way only Christ can bring (as in his time of ministry on earth).

The OT priests and Levites were bound to a kind of vow of poverty (with no inheritance of property). The Catholic and Orthodox churches make provision for simple (temporary) or solemn (perpetual) vows (which include the vow of poverty). Protestants affirm the priesthood of all believers; this affirmation has logical theological implications on how to manage finances and how to live the Christian life. This commandment invites readers to live, work, and interact with the world in pure devotion to Christ, in radical separation from the world, and in pursuit of the mission to advance the kingdom of God.

d. The People's Reaction (20:18-21)

BEHIND THE TEXT

This short section (20:18-21) narrates Israel's response to the divine revelation. There are similar vocabulary and themes between the theophanies in ch 20 and in Gen 15. The flashes of lightning and smoky mountain of Sinai recall the "blazing torch" and "smoking firepot" of Gen 15:17. In both cases, God is making covenant and appears in a fiery manifestation. In both texts, the fear of the Lord is a key theme. God tested Abraham (22:1) and found that he feared God (v 12); here also, God tests Israel to instill the fear of the Lord in them, so that they will be obedient (Exod 20:20).

IN THE TEXT

■ **18-19** The voice of Yahweh comes with thunderclaps and flashes of **lightning** (v 18). It appears that any fascination that the **people** have with seeing Yahweh up close is swallowed up in **fear**. It is an inappropriate fear that their lives will be lost if they remain close to Yahweh and hear his voice. Accordingly, they desire Moses' mediation (Deut 5:23-27) and Yahweh concedes to them (vv 28-31). It may well be, however, that God's ideal is for all the people to hear his voice as "prophets"—a sentiment that Moses expresses later (Num 11:24-30).

■ **20** **Moses** paradoxically tells the **people . . . not** to **be afraid** but also to have **the fear of God** with them **to keep** them **from sinning**. The people do not need to fear *for their lives* (their express concern in Exod 20:19), but they must have a holy reverence that will keep them obedient, free of sin, and close to God.

■ **21** While the **people** remain at the foothill, **Moses** ascends the mountain and draws near to the cloud where **God** is. Since the covenant relationship is not yet established, Moses is not invited into God's presence. After the covenant-making, Yahweh invites Moses into the glory cloud and they speak face-to-face (see 24:16, 18; 33:11; and 34:5, 28).

FROM THE TEXT

God comes to us and calls us to draw near, but to do so in due reverence. John Wesley understood well the difference between the improper, slavish fear of God that drives us away from communion with God and the proper, godly fear of God that drives us deeper into that holy communion. Wesley comments on this passage:

> Ever since Adam fled upon hearing God's voice in the garden, sinful man could not bear either to speak to God, or hear from him immediately. . . . We must not fear with amazement [i.e., being startled into flight from God]; but we must always have in our minds a reverence of God's majesty, a dread of his displeasure, and an obedient regard to his sovereign authority. (Wesley 1990, 81)

As we draw near to God in reverent awe and obedience, God draws near to us (see Jas 4:8). But to overcome misplaced fear, to approach the Holy God, to hear his voice, and to dwell in his presence, we need the mediator Jesus Christ, who is far greater than Moses. Without the mediation of Christ, we, too, will perish at the sight of the Holy One of Israel.

3. The Book of the Covenant (20:22—23:19)

Overview

This section (20:22—23:19) is known as the "Book of the Covenant" based upon 24:7 (see also 2 Kgs 23:2-3, 21). It contains laws concerning the altar and propriety in worship, social life, and the land. The laws are not exhaustive, but they provide general principles and guidelines for just and righteous living.

Exodus 18 shows that Moses transitions from judging every case the people brought to him (v 15) to appointing judges to share the load by settling minor cases (vv 20-22) based on the laws given. Decisions and judgments are public matters, rendered by publicly appointed magistrates based on divinely established principles. In this way, personal vengeance, societal confusion, and general anarchy are prevented and justice and order are maintained. Moses would determine only exceptionally difficult cases, perhaps due to lack of applicable precedents or general precepts (e.g., the case of the daughters of Zelophehad in Num 27:1-11 and 36:1-13).

This section can be grouped into three units: altar law (Exod 20:22-26); case laws (21:1—22:17 [16 HB]); and apodictic laws (22:18 [17 HB]—23:19).

240

a. Laws Concerning the Altar (20:22-26)

BEHIND THE TEXT

This unit with its cultic laws concerning the altar introduces the series of laws that immediately follow in chs 21—23. As such, the placement of this unit is marked by a pattern of altar laws introducing other laws also found in Lev 17 and Deut 12 (Hamilton 2011, 363).

The kind of altar mentioned here is employed for spontaneous worship and commemoration at Mount Sinai (Exod 24:4) before the creation of the tabernacle. Such a temporary altar is used elsewhere on occasion to memorialize God's mighty acts—as with the altars built by Jacob (Gen 35:1), Moses (Exod 17:15), Joshua (Deut 27:4-6; Josh 8:30-31), the Transjordanian tribes (Josh 22:10-34), Gideon (Judg 6:25-28), Manoah (Judg 13:19-20), Samuel (1 Sam 7:17), David (2 Sam 24:25), and Elijah (1 Kgs 18:30).

IN THE TEXT

■ **22** Yahweh introduces the laws with the reminder of the undeniable experience of theophany. Although the people stayed "at a distance" (v 18), they saw Yahweh and heard his voice and received the precepts to follow (Deut 5:23-33). Therefore, they cannot claim that the laws are merely Moses' laws.

■ **23** This first law, apodictic in form, is very similar to the second commandment of the Decalogue (see Exod 20:4-5), with some parallels to the first commandment (see v 3). The phrase **gods to be alongside me** is used to prohibit polytheism and syncretism.

■ **24** Yahweh commands the making of an **altar** and offering of **sacrifice**, which is fulfilled in 24:4. The Lord makes a provision for sacrifice of **burnt offerings** and **fellowship offerings** (see 18:12). The fellowship or peace offering signifies a mutual communion between the worshipper and Yahweh, with the fat portions offered to the Lord by fire and the meat consumed by the offerers in a meal. The peace offering indicates that a peaceful settlement is established between God and the worshipper (through other sacrifices, such as burnt or sin offering). Therefore, it is the very last offering to be presented in sacrifices. Yahweh promises that the acceptable altars and offerings will attract divine presence and release divine blessing.

■ **25** The **altar** is to be made with rough material such as a heap of mud (rather than mud bricks) or a pile of uncut **stones**. Human produced or re-shaped material is considered unfit for sacred purposes, perhaps because it would then be subject to human imagination like an idol that is sculpted or molded with a **tool**.

■ **26** The primary concern of this verse is that the people do not build **steps** by the **altar** since people nearby could see the nakedness of a person offering a sacrifice. Later, the priests who ministered at the tabernacle were required to wear undergarments for the sake of modesty (→ "undergarments" in 28:42). This law stands in contrast to the frequent use of steps on altars in Canaan and the widespread custom of ritual nudity among priests in the ancient Near East, as among the Sumerians (Cassuto 1967, 257).

FROM THE TEXT

God desires to be worshipped and therefore shows the proper manner in which to approach and worship him. (1) The text forbids syncretism (20:23), the worship of other gods along with worship of the one true God. So often, idols like nationalism or materialism compete for an individual's attention, stealing away loyalty that belongs only to God.

(2) The text encourages simplicity in worship, with its rejection of altars made of tool-hewn bricks. While use of artistic gifts and skills in worship is elsewhere encouraged (as in the construction of the tabernacle and its furnishings in chs 25—31), it is only in the context of clear divine direction (25:40). At least in the absence of clear divine directives for church buildings or various items used in worship, the general principle of simplicity is encouraged so as to avoid either undue ostentation or the use of human creativity in a manner that proves idolatrous (→ From the Text for 20:5-6).

(3) The text calls the ministers to modesty. This applies not only to the obvious avoidance of sexually provocative clothes but also to any ways of dressing, speaking, and acting that draw attention to oneself rather than to God (e.g., Matt 6:16-18; 1 Tim 2:9), who alone is to be the focus of our public worship.

b. Case Laws (21:1—22:17 [16 HB])

Overview

This section of the book of the covenant is composed mostly of casuistic laws addressing various legal topics. Local governing bodies of elders, chieftains, and other appointed leaders would enforce such laws. The biblical case laws both contrast with and show continuity with ancient Near Eastern case laws.

(1) Servants (21:1-11)

BEHIND THE TEXT

The judgments in this section regard the humane and merciful treatment of servants or slaves. Only two months earlier, the Israelites were slaves, subjected to exploitation and ruthless treatment. Lest they turn around and abuse their own slaves, Yahweh makes provision for just and merciful employment of slaves.

In a world in which slaves were considered a commodity or a piece of property, slaves were routinely subjected to exploitation, cruelty, and abuse. The slave laws given here, by contrast, have their ultimate theological background in the creation of every person being in the image of God (Gen 1:26-28). Accordingly, each human being, regardless of social standing, has great worth before God and shares equal standing with all other human beings. Any violation of the intrinsic value of a human being is an infringement of the divine will.

The biblical laws are generally more humane than those found in the Code of Hammurabi (e.g., law 117). More importantly, the biblical laws' ultimate ethical trajectory is more radical than mere reform of the institution of slavery. The biblical laws on slavery generally improve the institution, but they do not present a finalized ideal ethic. Rather, the biblical slave laws actually attempt to "dissuade Israelites from the practice of slavery" altogether (Hamilton 2011, 272). This is evident in many ways: the humane treatment of the Hebrew slaves as hired workers (Lev 25:40, 53), the slaves' right to Sabbath rest (Exod 20:10; 23:12), the emancipation of a Hebrew slave on the Sabbath/Jubilee Year (Lev 25:40; Deut 15:12-15), and the generous provision of livestock, grains, and seeds to prevent the cycle of poverty and slavery for the freed slave (Deut 15:13-14); and the slaves' right of redemption by another or by oneself (Lev 25:47-52). In addition, the numerous references to the Israelites' former status as slaves and Yahweh's redemption of them stigmatize the Israelite slave owners. The call to imitate Yahweh their Redeemer requires them not to be like their former slave owners (Deut 15:15) but instead to promote the freedom and well-being of all.

IN THE TEXT

(a) Male Slaves (21:1-6)

■ **1** This verse serves as a heading for the legal material that follows. The expression **And these are the laws** signals that these laws continue the Decalogue along with the commands given in the preceding chapter. Moses is **to set before them** or teach them the laws. The law is not just for the judges or legal magistrates (→ 18:20). All the people must know, discuss, understand, and implement in their lives Yahweh's laws (see "in your mouth and in your heart so you may obey it" [Deut 30:14]).

■ **2** This law requires the emancipation of **Hebrew** slaves. The term **Hebrew** (→ Exod 1:15) refers to a fellow Israelite, one born a Hebrew, or *your brother, a Hebrew (male) or a Hebrew (female)* (Deut 15:12). An Israelite could be reduced to slavery through extreme insolvency resulting from heavy court penalty. A thief convicted by law, for example, could compensate for the theft by means of labor (see Exod 22:3 [2 HB]). Those who are poor (widows, or-

243

phans, foreigners) are discouraged from selling themselves or their children as slaves. They are to be provided for through paid work (see Lev 19:13; 25:50, 53; Deut 24:14) and/or by a socioreligious welfare system (poor tithes [Deut 14:22-23, 27-29; 26:11-13] and gleaning [Lev 19:10; 23:22; Deut 24:19-21]).

The usage of the term "Hebrew" reminds the Israelites of their previous marginal status and the related economic bondage in Egypt. As newly freed citizens in a nation under Yahweh's rule, they must not keep a fellow Israelite in permanent economic bondage, but must grant freedom in the **seventh year**.

The period of debt slavery was three years in the Hammurabi code (see law 117), which can give the impression that it was more merciful than the Israelite law. However, in Israel, since unpaid debt is canceled on the Sabbatical Year (Deut 15:1-2), a debtor (who borrows money or grain, for example) would not normally be reduced to slavery. However, there is evidence in Israel's history that creditors sometimes seized the property of defaulting debtors and subjected them and/or family members to slavery (2 Kgs 4:1), a practice that the prophets vehemently oppose and condemn (Neh 5:4-5; Amos 2:6-7; 8:6). In other words, the Israelite laws ban lending / borrowing with interest / collateral and collection of unpayable debts to eliminate debt slavery of the poor (→ Exod 22:24-26 [23-25 HB]). The slaves in this verse are not debt slaves, but insolvent criminals who are sold into slavery (→ 22:3 [2 HB]). Also, in that light, the Hammurabi code's three-year term for debt slavery is lamentable.

In Israel, the maximum term of service is **six years**. Should the Year of Jubilee occur before the six-year term is completed, then the maximum term is shortened (Lev 25:40, 50). An Israelite slave has the right to be redeemed at any time during the six-year term by a relative or by himself (Lev 25:48-50). On the seventh year, an Israelite slave must be set **free, without paying anything** (ḥinnām; "without payment," "gratuitously," related to the verb "to be gracious," "show favor"). The seventh year is either the seventh year from the beginning of the servitude (Deut 15:12) or the Sabbatical Year, which is also called "the year of remission" (v 9 NASB, NRSV). The latter is more likely (→ "seventh year" in Exod 23:10-11). The rationale for emancipation or remission is the affirmation and extension of Yahweh's redemption of Israel from the land of slavery. Thus, freedom must be granted regardless of the enormity of the original debt or the creditor's perception of his future hardship without the free labor. Yahweh's historical deliverance of Israel overrides any typical human considerations or expectations.

■ **3** On the year of emancipation, all those who came to serve the master (husband, **wife**, and children) must be set **free**. Deuteronomy 15:13-14 stipulates a remarkably generous provision for those emancipated. Since they were originally reduced to slavery due to poverty (unable to pay the court-ordered fines), being sent away empty-handed would only reinforce the cycle of poverty

244

and enslavement. Therefore, in Deuteronomy, the master must provide them with a flock and enough food to last until their own harvest from their own land. The reason for such a merciful practice, unprecedented in the ancient Near East, is that Yahweh gratuitously gave the Israelites not only liberty but also property. They came out of Egypt not "empty-handed," but with droves of livestock and a great quantity of silver, gold, and clothing (Exod 3:21-22; 12:35-36, 38). Therefore, in imitation of Yahweh, they ought to emancipate their slaves and bless them with gifts. This requirement comes with the promise of continued blessing for obedience (Deut 15:15, 18).

■ **4** If the **man** came alone, he is to depart alone, leaving behind his **wife**, whom the **master** provided for him, and **her children**. Sarna draws attention to the ancient Near Eastern practice of a master mating "a slave with a foreign bondwoman solely for the purpose of siring 'house born' slaves" and keeping the woman and her children as his property (2004, 89). Although this law would allow for such a possibility, Yahweh certainly would not condone and perpetuate such a practice in Israel in light of the utilitarian view of human beings it expresses. Likely, the master arranges a marriage for the servant who could not afford the bride price out of benevolence rather than selfish intent.

■ **5** This law gives the male servant the choice to remain in bondage out of his affectionate **love** (*'āhab*; also used in 20:6), not only for his **wife** and **children** but also for his **master**. It is not clear whether the wife in such a situation is a slave whose emancipation is still to come or a foreign bondslave who is ineligible for compulsory emancipation after six years. Verse 6 seems to indicate that the wife is a bondslave, with the husband now becoming a lifelong slave along with her. Economic considerations may play a large role in his decision to remain enslaved. When freed, it might be impossible for him to save enough money to purchase his wife and children from his former master. Acquiring their freedom may not materialize even after many painful years of diligent work. These considerations and the male slave's desire to remain with his family and his master may lead him to forego his right to personal freedom and choose to become a bondslave.

■ **6** The male slave's intention to become a lifelong bondslave is solemnized through a public rite of piercing **his ear with an awl**. The ritual is most likely carried out before local authorities in a local sanctuary before God (*'ĕlôhîm*; "God," "gods").

Many English translations render *'ĕlôhîm* into **judges** because the accompanying verb is plural (also in 22:8-9 [7-8 HB]). In thousands of cases in which *'ĕlôhîm* (God) refers to Yahweh, a singular verb is used. If *'ĕlôhîm* is understood here as "gods," then one might conclude that the verse assumes polytheism. But since we have several cases in which the referent of *'ĕlôhîm* is clearly Yahweh, yet a plural verb accompanies *'ĕlôhîm* (Gen 20:13; 31:53; 35:7), it is best to conclude this verse is one of those few exceptions to the rule (also in Exod 22:8-9 [7-8 HB]).

Following a religious-legal procedure before God would prevent a master's abuse of power by detaining slaves illegally and would protect the slave's rights to freedom. Although legally allowed, his decision to change his status from temporary to permanent slave goes against God's ultimate will for the Israelites to be free from human domination; they are to be Yahweh's own servants and servants of no other (Lev 25:42; see Deut 23:15-16 [16-17 HB]). He who refuses Yahweh's freedom when it is granted must bear a mark (perhaps signifying disgrace) all his life, even if his reasons for doing so are otherwise understandable.

(b) Female Slaves (21:7-11)

■ **7** This verse could be disturbing to modern readers as it may appear to discriminate against a *female* servant (*'āmâ*) and rob her of rights to freedom. However, the subsequent verses clarify that the ultimate purpose of selling the young **daughter** as a servant is to afford her a marriage and a respectable future, which could not be secured otherwise due to financial need (i.e., no dowry, see Gen 24:59-61; Judg 1:12-15; 1 Kgs 9:16; see Hugenberger 1998, 321-22). The Hebrew term for *female* servant (*'āmâ*) is elsewhere translated into "female servant" (Exod 20:10, 17; Lev 25:6; Deut 15:17) or "female slave" (Exod 21:26, 27). Here, her status and situation is quite different from the typical slave/servant. In ancient Israel, a poverty-stricken father might sell a young daughter to a wealthy man with a preset condition of her eventual marriage, either to the master (v 8) or his son (v 9). This would secure a better future for her and provide the rest of the father's family with some extra income. Some regard the case here to be one of concubinage, rather than marriage (e.g., Hamilton 2011, 375), but v 10 (with references to her as "the first one" and to the case "if he marries another woman") dictates against the concubinage interpretation. The expression **as male servants do** does not imply that the female slaves can never go free. Rather, there are other additional circumstances that permit her redemption or freedom (see vv 8, 11).

■ **8** The law stipulates the treatment of a girl as a free woman in vv 8-11. The laws protect her from sexual exploitation and resale as a slave, should the **master** find her displeasing (*rā'â*; "wicked," "evil," "displeasing," or "unpleasant") and not take her as his wife. The Hebrew term for the expression **has broken faith** elsewhere refers to some form of marital unfaithfulness (Jer 3:8, 20; Mal 2:11). Here it refers to the master's repudiation of the prearranged marriage at the time of purchase of the potential wife as a slave. The master **must let** the unmarried girl **be redeemed** (*pādâ*; "to redeem") by her own family. The NIV and most versions translate the Hebrew *'am nokrî* into **foreigners**, but it is an ancient technical term for "one outside the nuclear family" (Sarna 2004, 91).

The master does not have the right to resell her to just anyone. Rather, either her father can redeem her or she can redeem herself (see Lev 25:47-52; Cassuto 1967, 268), so that her honor as a woman eligible for marriage is preserved.

■ **9** The girl may be designated for the master's **son**, in which case the girl is raised as his **daughter** with all the responsibilities, privileges, and **rights** of a daughter. The girl is basically treated as a free woman. The provision made for the girl in v 8 would also apply in this case, so that if the son finds her displeasing and refuses to marry her, he should let her be redeemed.

■ **10** After marrying the girl as arranged beforehand, **if he** [the master or his son] **marries another** as well, he must not reduce or withdraw the original wife's **food** [*šeʾēr*; "meat," thus fine or rich food], **clothing and marital rights**. The Septuagint translates the Hebrew term for "marital rights" (*ʿōnâ*), which is used only once in the OT, into "association, company" (*omilia*). The intended meaning here is probably the marital rights of sexual gratification and the related procreation. Having children would secure provision for the woman in her old age. Thus, depriving her of marital rights and procreation would be a heinous crime against her and against God.

■ **11** The NIV translation **these three things** suggests that this verse is referring to the provision of the "food, clothing and marital rights" mentioned in v 10. However, a more literal reading of v 11 is ***If these three he does not do for her***. Accordingly, v 11 is probably referring, not to what the husband (master or son) provides for her, but to the three previously mentioned arrangements and obligations concerning the female slave: (1) marriage to the master, with continued provision understood (v 8*b*), (2) marriage to the son, again with continued provision (v 9*b*), and (3) redemption of the unmarried girl by herself or her immediate family (v 10*b*). The failure to meet any of these obligations would result in her freedom, without having to pay a redemption price.

FROM THE TEXT

Although it is a common observation that abused people abuse other people, God expects otherwise from his covenant people. In these laws concerning slavery, God prevents those Israelites with social or political power from abusing those without such power. The laws address those with power, including economic power (to buy slaves) and gender power (e.g., the assumption that both master and the potential seller of a slave were more likely, but not necessarily, male). Further, God calls those with greater power to imitate him by extending the liberating grace and generous provision that God first extended to them. The people of Israel are not to be imprisoned in bitterness and anger over their own past experiences of abuse and exploitation or (for later generations) those of their ancestors. Rather, they are called (because they are equipped by their own experiences) to empathize with those who are treated unjustly, come to their rescue, and defend their cause. They are not to misuse their new-found freedom, power, or wealth by oppressing others. God, the Redeemer, the Healer, and the Provider, makes this kind of behavior possible, not only by setting an example of the redemptive and restorative use of power but also by providing for all their needs. God's people do not need to exploit others in order to have more material gain since God provides for them extravagantly (e.g., Deut 15:6; 28:1-14).

In our modern day as well, then, Christians are called to trust in and experience the goodness of God as he offers redemption, healing, and generosity. God desires to use our experiences of abuse or injustice as a basis for greater sympathy and understanding of others who suffer similar evils. Further, God's love breaks the cycle of abuse and empowers God's covenant people to become redemptive agents who imitate God by doing what the Father is doing.

(2) Three Capital Crimes (21:12-17)

BEHIND THE TEXT

These verses contain apodictic laws, different from the case laws of the previous unit. These laws impose the death penalty for three crimes: murder (21:12-14), great dishonor toward parents (vv 15 and 17), and kidnapping (v 16). The death penalty expresses divine and social displeasure toward the crimes and deters others from committing them. The whole local community is probably called upon to execute the guilty by stoning.

Similar kidnapping laws are found in the ancient Near Eastern laws. For the unspecified victim, the Mesopotamian Ur-Nammu code imposed a fine and imprisonment to the criminal (law 3). The Hammurabi code defined the victim as a free man's young son and stipulated the death penalty to the criminal (law 14). The Nesilim code exacted restitution for kidnapping (laws 20, 21; also see the Hittite laws 19-21).

Ancient Near Eastern laws did not apply the death penalty for abuse or dishonor of parents but imposed severe punishment instead. For example, in the Code of Hammurabi, fingers were cut off for violence (presumably by an adult child) against parents (law 195), tongues cut off for disowning adoptive parents (law 192), and eyes plucked out for abandoning adoptive parents and returning to biological parents (law 193).

(For murder in ancient Near Eastern laws, → 20:13.)

IN THE TEXT

(a) Murder (21:12-14)

■ **12** This judgment is against premeditated murder. According to other parts of the Pentateuch, the **death** sentence is carried out only on the testimony of two or more witnesses (Num 35:30; Deut 17:6; 19:15). No ransom or monetary compensation can substitute for or satisfy the demands of justice; only capital punishment can (Num 35:31; see Gen 9:5-6). Unlike other ancient Near Eastern laws, "which view murder only in terms of economic loss to the family or clan" (Sarna 2004, 91), the biblical law sees murder as a sin against Yahweh, who created humans in his image.

■ **13** If the killing is not premeditated, then it is assumed that **God** is the one who **lets it happen** (lit. "God let *him* fall into his hands"). The law implies that circumstances and the resultant death are outside human control, and thus actions of God's sovereign freedom and providence. Unintentional manslaughter is not a capital crime, and thus the law protects the killer from the "blood avenger" by providing a place of refuge. The manslayer would be tried, according to the established legal procedure to determine the case. If found innocent, he would remain in asylum until the death of the high priest, at which time he regains his freedom. If found guilty of murder, he would be put to death. In the ancient Near East, the blood avenger is typically the victim's close relative, who would dutifully seek vengeance to satisfy the familial demand for justice. This could set off a long cycle of blood feuding, however, which the Israelites' law seeks to eliminate. Divinely authorized judicial procedure and administration of punishment would ensure legal satisfaction for the death and the protection of any innocent life.

■ **14** The term **deliberately** indicates a full awareness and even careful planning. There is urgency to punish the crime of murder and purge evil from Israel and its holy place. Thus, the willful slayer must be seized even from the holy **altar** and **put to death**. The accounts of Adonijah (1 Kgs 1:50-53) and Joab (2:28-34) illustrate the assumed inviolability of the altar and related effectiveness of taking asylum at the Lord's altar. Taking sanctuary at the altar, however, did not eliminate the legal process of determining their guilt or innocence or the due penalty for the guilty. Thus, it was temporarily effective for Adonijah (1 Kgs 1:50-51) but was ineffective for Joab due to his bloodguilt (2:28-34).

Asylum at the Golden Altar

The "asylum texts" do not specifically name which altar, the bronze or the gold, is in view. However, the texts in 1 Kgs 1 and 2 show that the asylum seekers seized multiple "horns." Since the bronze altar is 7.5 x 7.5 feet (2.3 x 2.3 m) in width and length, a person could grab only one horn at a time. The golden altar of incense, on the other hand, is 1.5 x 1.5 feet (0.46 x 0.46 m), so an average person could seize two or three horns. Besides, grabbing a horn of the bronze altar with its perpetual fire would present the danger of getting burnt. Finally, according to 1 Kgs 2:28-30, Joab entered "the tent of the LORD" and grabbed the horns, thus pointing to the golden horns. For these reasons, the altar for asylum is most likely the golden altar of incense.

(b) Abuse and Dishonor of Parents (21:15, 17)

■ **15** The judgments for dishonoring parents in vv 15 and 17 are related. The Septuagint arranges them together, placing v 16 after them, which is followed here. The wording of this precept is similar to that found in v 12, except the instruction "with a fatal blow" is lacking here. The "attack" in view here is probably not a fatal blow nor a minor punch in a moment of anger (either by an adult child or a minor; see Stuart 2006, 487). It most likely refers to an adult child's severe physical abuse presumably of a defenseless, aged parent. It also may refer to an adult child who assaults ("robs" [NIV]) and heartlessly drives out his aged parents to seize their property prematurely (Prov 19:26). "Attacking" one's parent is an appalling violation of the fifth commandment to honor parents and therefore incurs the **death** penalty (→ Exod 20:12).

■ **17** While v 15 addresses physical abuse, v 17 concerns verbal or other forms of abuse. The Hebrew term for "curse" (*qll* in intensive) may mean "curse," "revile," "treat with contempt," or "treat as worthless." The opposite of such cursing is to honor (20:12) and to bless (Prov 31:28). Filial respect of **father** and **mother** is of utmost concern in Israel's religious culture, in which honor of parents mirrors reverence of Yahweh, their common Father. "Cursing" of parents is tantamount to forsaking covenant obligations to Yahweh and being given over to lawlessness. Left uncorrected, the breakdown in homes would threaten the integrity of the whole society (→ Exod 20:12). Therefore, those found guilty of this sin are **put to death** either by human agent (Deut 21:18-21) or by divine intervention (Prov 20:20).

(c) Kidnapping and Human Trafficking (21:16)

■ **16** The Septuagint substitutes **someone** with "one of the sons of Israel," but the law here is general, applying to any **victim**. Slave trade was widespread in the ancient Near East, and an abductor might have kidnapped in order to sell or keep the victim. The victim would be subjected to slavery, sexual exploitation, or both (→ Exod 20:15), either by the kidnapper or, if **the victim** is **sold**, by others. This kind of human trafficking is condemned as a monstrous, capital crime not only against those kidnapped but also against their families and friends and against Yahweh to whom they ultimately belong. Kidnappers must be put to death for the crime and for its recurrence to be averted. The severe punishment reflects the creational inviolability of human dignity and freedom under Yahweh (see Gen 1:26-27), which is expressed throughout the laws of Israel.

FROM THE TEXT

The law of capital punishment in Exod 21:12-17 clearly conveys the high value and dignity of human life. The law also emphasizes the high cost of actions deliberately taken to kill another person or to violate and abuse the helpless.

The text does not tell us whether the primary purpose of the law of capital punishment is deterrence or punishment, although both are likely involved. What is clear is that, in the ancient Israelite context, the sins of murder, severe abuse of a parent, and human trafficking were considered monstrous crimes against humanity *and against* God that they led to the forfeiture of the criminal's own life, which was itself of great value.

The contemporary reflection on these weighty laws calls for a few questions. (1) The first question for our theological and ethical reflection is: should these crimes be treated as less monstrous or less evil in our context? Perhaps the theological response to this question is, "No!," as God surely is still concerned to uphold the creational value of human life, the centrality of cogency of family for the integrity of society, and inviolability of human freedom and dignity, which are the main concerns of these laws. (2) The next question then is: should the death penalty of these laws be treated as a biblical sanction for capital punishment in our legal system? Our theological response to this question is also negative for at least a couple of factors. Most critically, the reality of scandalous mercy, outrageous forgiveness, priceless redemption, and incomprehensible love that are central to the gospel halts us from any automatic application of the death penalty, however heinous the crime. This does not mean that there never can be a legitimate death penalty carried out by a contemporary legal system. But given the demands of the gospel, the value of the criminal's life (even if it is already in theory forfeited at the time of the crime) and the concern for his or her eternal destiny must take precedence over any sense of justice in theological reflection. Another factor has to do with the unbridgeable gap between the legal system of the prophetic, theocratic society and the flawed legal system of our secular society. Whatever our conclusion about the application of these laws to our contemporary society, these laws call us to theologically reflect on ways to promote conditions that sustain the integrity of (individual and societal) life and that deter its destruction.

Human kidnapping and trafficking are crimes of the utmost seriousness. The concluding verse in this unit treats kidnapping as equally reprehensible as murder, deserving of the death penalty. When people are forcibly or deceitfully taken and transported against their will or that of their families (kidnapping) or when they are sold for a profit (human trafficking), the victims' dignity as those made in the image of God is utterly trampled upon. The victims are degraded and treated as nonhuman or subhuman. God condemns such crimes against humanity with the perpetrators deserving of death.

This admonition is certainly a wake-up call in our contemporary world with ever-increasing human trafficking and slave trading. Commercial sex exploitation, sexual slavery, forced labor, or even organ harvesting are unfortunately becoming some of the most profitable illegal activities in many coun-

EXODUS

21:12-17

tries. These heinous crimes show the great extent of humans' departure from God's perspective on the value of human life.

Victims of human trafficking are either kidnapped or deceived into their plight, and they typically have no way of escaping from their captivity. However, the God of Israel does not remain silent in these situations, but rather calls his body, the church, to lead in removing these crimes that blight our world. The church must forsake its place of personal comfort, repent from its spiritual complacency, break its apathy toward the suffering mass, and spring into godly action in imitation of Christ: "to proclaim good news to the poor," "to bind up the brokenhearted," to set the oppressed captives free, "to comfort [those] who mourn," and to provide for those who lack, to restore their beauty, dignity, and joy, and "to bestow on them . . . a garment of praise" (Isa 61:1-3) for their God and Savior Jesus Christ (Luke 4:18-19). If the church remains silent, who will "proclaim the year of the Lord's favor" (Isa 61:2) to the world in captivity? We must do our part in rescuing and restoring those subjected to human trafficking or kidnapping and in resisting, protesting, and even pulling down evil systems through prayer and godly action.

Moreover, since many are driven into selling themselves or their children into trafficking due to abject poverty, the church must respond to reduce or eliminate poverty. We cannot tolerate situations in which poor and powerless people can be bought and sold for a few meals. The church must regain its religious and humanitarian mission to the poor for their spiritual, physical, and economic freedom. The laws of Israel remind us that God takes all violations of human dignity with the utmost seriousness, and we should adopt the same view and act on it with God's grace and power that compels and empowers us to lay down our lives for Christ, who loves us and utterly gives himself up for us and for the world (Eph 5:2).

(3) Violence by Persons (21:18-27)

BEHIND THE TEXT

This unit has a collection of case laws that deal with injuries caused by violence against a free person (21:18-19), slaves (vv 20-21, 26-27), and a pregnant woman and her child (v 22) along with the related penalties and compensations.

Similar and dissimilar laws concerning bodily injuries are found in ancient Near Eastern laws. Most notably in the Code of Hammurabi, the penalty for bodily injury varied based on the victim's social standing: a literal application of "eye for eye" or "bone for bone" for injury to gentlemen, in which the same bodily mutilation was inflicted on the offender; monetary compensation for injury to freemen; and, lower monetary compensation for injury to slaves (see laws 196-201). There were peculiar literal applications of "talion law" (*lex talionis*; a Latin phrase that means "the law of like punishment" or "the law of retaliation): a creditor who struck and killed the debtor's son was punished by the death of the creditor's son (law 116; for similar laws, see laws 210 and 230). For other fatal injuries (including miscarriages), the laws extracted fines of varied amounts based on the victim's social standing (laws 207-9, 211-14).

The Hittite laws also imposed fines for bodily injuries, based on the severity of the injury and the social class of the victim (laws 7-16). Causing miscarriage was punished by fines of varying amounts based on the maturity of the child and the social standing of the pregnant woman (laws 17-18).

The later Assyrian Code of the Assura (eleventh century BC) fined those who caused miscarriage (laws I.50-51), but imposed the death penalty on a woman who aborted her own child (law I.52).

These talion laws in this unit are concerned for institutional justice, in which the nature and degree of restitution and punishment extracted by the court are proportionate to the nature and degree of damage inflicted by the offenders (see Stuart 2006, 492-94). Some understand the talion laws as expressed in Exod 21:23-25 and particularly Lev 24:19-21 as an indication that bodily mutilation was carried out in ancient Israel as an appropriate penalty for intentionally afflicting bodily injury on another. It is possible that in some especially malicious cases, such court ruling was given. However, the rest of the laws that regulate damages to human, animal, and property consistently apply the talion in terms of full restitution that the offender must make (including those laws that surround Lev 24:19-21). The heavy penalty the offender pays to the victim constitutes the "injury or blemish" that the offender suffers. In most cases, this law stands against personal retaliation and for just compensation. This point is well illustrated in this and subsequent units dealing with just compensations for various damages done. Most notably, in the case of Exod 21:26-27, the "eye for eye" and "tooth for tooth" principle does not demand that the same bodily mutilation be afflicted on the offender but that the victims receive their freedom from slavery as just compensation for the permanent bodily injury they received. The talion laws in most of the biblical laws ensure that the penalty for the offender and the compensation for the victim are appropriate, just, and satisfactory.

Of course, an exception exists regarding the cases of murder and other unlawful killings and intentions of killings (e.g., Deut 19:16-21) that require the death penalty. Since Num 35:31 prohibits ransoming the life of an unlawful killer who deserves to die and since the victim is dead and cannot be compensated, the offender is executed and pays for his crime with his own blood.

(a) Injury from a Quarrel (21:18-19)

■ **18-19** This law ensures that a full compensation is made for someone who receives a temporary injury. The offender must pay the injured person for **any loss of time** (v 19) and for any medical expenses until **the victim is completely healed**.

(b) Fatal or Temporary Injury to a Slave (21:20-21)

■ **20** A violent person who **beats** his or her **slave** (**male** or **female**) and causes his or her death **must be *avenged***. The sanctity of life, even of an economically disadvantaged person, is upheld. A slave, while economically a property of a master, is nonetheless fully human with equal worth and dignity as his or her master before Yahweh. The violent beating here appears not to be accidental, but intentional. Thus, the killing falls under the category of intentional killing. Accordingly, the death penalty is called for here (as indicated by the expression **must be *avenged***).

■ **21** However, one who inflicts a temporary injury on his or her **slave** goes unpunished. The reason for the master's acquittal is grounded in the precepts of vv 18-19. Since the slave's time and labor are the master's **property**, the master is not required to make monetary compensation to the slave. Since the master caused the injury and the loss of labor, the master must pay for any medical expenses incurred and absorb any economic loss. While this verse may appear to reflect a level of acceptance of the ancient notion that a slave is property, this verse neither describes the intrinsic worth of a slave as human nor condones the institution of slavery nor prescribes how a slave ought to be treated. Rather, this verse exposes the foolery of a bad-tempered master who suffers economic loss due to his own violent actions. The Bible generally frowns upon the institution of slavery (→ vv 12-17) and promotes the precept "love your neighbor as yourself" (Lev 19:18) as the guide of the slave laws.

(c) Injury to a Pregnant Woman and Her Child (21:22-25)

■ **22** This verse concerns a premature birth, caused by a physical blow that **a pregnant woman** suffers. While some interpreters argue that this verse addresses an accelerated miscarriage, the language of the verse dictates against that interpretation. (1) If the child is miscarried, then the usual term for "miscarry" (*škl*; also "be bereaved") is expected here (as in Gen 31:38; Exod 23:26; Job 21:10; Hos 9:14). (2) The Hebrew term for the NIV's **serious injury** (*'sôn*; "evil," "fatal injury") connotes mortal harm in all its usage (see Gen 42:4, 38; 44:29), calling for the interpretation that the "harm or injury" in this verse and the next refers to a fatal kind. (3) The Hebrew expression for the NIV's **she gives birth prematurely** is literally "her children come out." When that expression is followed by **but there is no *fatal* injury**, the logical interpretation is that a child is born prematurely, but both the birth mother and the child are reasonably healthy. Since the child and the birth mother suffer no fatal injury, the offender is punished only with a fine in the amount the **husband demands** with the court's approval. (4) The current interpretation is supported by the strong contrast the subsequent verse presents: "take life for life."

■ **23** If there is *fatal* injury ('*sôn*) to the child or the mother or both, the principle **life for life** is literally applied. Presumably the court would make a distinction between the malicious striking and killing and purely accidental hitting and killing in its judgments against the offender. That said, some have argued that the killer is punished by death only for the death of the mother while he is merely fined for the death of the child (as in some ancient Near Eastern laws). However, the biblical law punishes all murders and other un-lawful killings uniformly by the death penalty and all offenders of homicide equally with asylum, regardless of the victims' economic value set forth in Lev 27:1-8. In addition, unlike contemporary beliefs, the Bible affirms the full humanity and personhood of the child in the womb (Pss 71:6; 139:13-16; Luke 1:15, 41-44). Therefore, one cannot argue that the death of the prema-turely born child is dealt with by assessing a fine only. The penalty for killing a person (a child in the womb or an adult, free or slave, male or female, native or foreign; → Exod 21:31; see Lev 24:22) is not determined by the victim's economic value or social standing (as in ancient Near Eastern laws) but by the more fundamental truth that every human being is made in God's image and Yahweh will "demand an accounting" for every incident of human blood shed, however small that human being might be (Gen 9:5-6).

Some have raised the question whether "life for life" is carried out liter-ally, by putting to death the killer's wife and/or child (as in the Hammurabi code). However, Deuteronomy explicitly forbids that kind of practice (see Deut 24:16).

■ **24-25** If there is no fatality, but injuries occur (besides the premature birth), then the striker must make full restitution, presumably following the same principle mentioned in Exod 21:22.

(d) Permanent Injury to a Slave (21:26-27)

■ **26-27** These laws illustrate how the "eye for eye" and "tooth for tooth" prin-ciple ought to be applied. The just compensation for the injury inflicted on a slave's **eye** or **tooth** is the slave's freedom. The violent **owner** is likely expected to release the **slave (male or female)** with generous provisions, just as with the release of slaves in the year of emancipation (Deut 15:13-14; see Exod 22:2 [1 HB]). The heavy economic loss to the offending master seeks to prevent a master's physical abuse of his servants. It stands against the notion that a slave is merely property that is at the master's disposal (see 21:21). Rather, they retain a certain degree of divinely conferred rights and protection as human beings made in the image of God.

FROM THE TEXT

While the OT talion laws are concerned with seeking justice through just punishment and proportionate compensation, Jesus uses the principle of talion laws to call his disciples to relinquish their rights for the sake of the gospel. Jesus does not deny the validity of the principle of just compensation behind "an eye for an eye" or of its use in a court of law. Jesus also does not deny the right to self-defense, the need to restrain violent attackers (see Luke 22:35-38), or the obligation to mete out just punishment or extract just compensation where appropriate (see Luke 18:1-8). Jesus does not misconstrue divine grace as God's tolerance of all violent actions and attitudes.

Jesus, however, uses the talion laws to illustrate indirectly the principle of proportionate compensation in the spiritual realm. In Matt 5:38-48, Jesus calls his disciples to a radical forgiveness, meekness, mercy, and love even for an enemy or a persecutor. Such a call, of course, is for the sake of the gospel. Jesus suffers a wrongful, violent death on the cross and receives from the Father the just recompense of his own resurrection and exaltation and the salvation of the world. Our transcending the principle of the talion law in the material world for the sake of the gospel brings due compensation in the spiritual realm in the form of the salvation of enemies and persecutors or other spiritual blessings or outcomes.

(4) Violence by and Injury to Animals (21:28-36)

BEHIND THE TEXT

This unit deals with violence done by a bull (or ox) against human beings or other animals (except for 21:33-34, which deal with the injury of an animal caused by an uncovered pit). Overall, the laws in this section address the need for the owners of powerful animals to take precautions to ensure the safety of others and the punishment of the negligent.

Similar laws on fatal goring appear in ancient Near Eastern laws, in which the owner was not punished for the bull's first offense (Eshnunna law 53; Hammurabi law 250) but heavily fined for the subsequent offense (Eshnunna law 54/55; Hammurabi laws 251-52). The biblical laws impose greater penalties for the goring animal and its negligent owner than the ancient Near Eastern laws probably because the Israelites' view of human life is higher than those of the surrounding cultures.

The laws concerning a goring bull indicate the inherent dangers involved in domesticating large beasts. But the benefits of labor and meat and hides exploited from such animals apparently override any concerns raised by rare cases of injury. Instead of banning the use of a potentially violent mammal, the law provides ways to tend it with caution.

IN THE TEXT

(a) Homicidal Bulls (21:28-32)

■ **28** This verse deals with a case in which the **bull** has no history of goring, as verified by the local court. The **owner** is **not . . . held responsible** and no payment is exacted from him. His sole penalty is the loss of his aggressive bull. In a sense, such a bull bears its own guilt (in contrast to a bull bearing human guilt in Lev 4) and must be **stoned to death**. While God gave human beings the right to kill animals for food (not senseless killing), the animals become guilty for killing human beings and must account for it (see Gen 9:3-6). Stoning the violent bull must have involved tying it down first since the size and unpredictability of such a creature would make it extremely dangerous. The homicidal bull **must not be eaten** or used in sacrifice, for it is guilty of blood-guilt. Killing the homicidal bull would eliminate any possibility of additional harm. The whole community must execute the wild beast. In so doing, the community solidifies their commitment to keep their own bulls under control to uphold the sanctity of human life and to prevent losing their own valuable possessions.

■ **29** This law deals with a case in which the **owner** fails to restrain a **bull** with a known **habit of goring** humans. Since the owner is **warned** regarding the bull's violent tendencies, the owner is guilty of criminal negligence when the bull eventually kills a person (**a man or woman**; young or old [v 31]; free or slave [v 32]). Even if it is the bull's first capital offense, the owner's prior awareness of the bull's violence excludes him from receiving the gracious provision of v 28. Both the bull and the owner must **be put to death**, the bull by stoning (v 28) and the owner likely also by stoning, presumably after a due process similar to that involved in the execution of a murderer (vv 12-14).

■ **30** Whereas ransom is not allowed for the person who murders (Num 35:31), it is allowed for the one guilty of indirect killing through negligence. The victim's family probably set the ransom under the court's mediation (see Exod 21:22).

■ **31** **A son or daughter** must refer to minors (contrasting with "a man or woman" of v 29). The worth of human life does not fluctuate with age. It should be noted that the intrinsic value of human life reflected here is different from the economic worth ("your valuation, estimation") of a person based on his or her serviceability to the sanctuary (Lev 27:2-8; → Exod 21:23). The goring ox and its owner must be dealt with according to the laws of vv 28-30.

■ **32** If the victim is a **slave**, then **the owner must pay thirty shekels of silver**, which is what the Hammurabi code (law 251) imposed on the owner of an ox that killed a nobleman. By paying the ransom money to **the master of the slave**, the owner of the goring ox escapes the death penalty. The violent beast, however, must **be stoned to death**.

(b) Injury to Livestock (21:33-36)

■ **33-34** In this case, either the **pit** is in a public place or in an unfenced area of private property. Regardless, the reasonable expectation is to take precautions to properly enclose or **cover** such hazardous sites (v 33). **The one who opened the pit** is guilty of negligence and must fully compensate for the **dead animal** (v 34). The opener of the pit must give the **owner** a live animal or **pay** the full price (*šālam*; "make amends," "repay," or "restore in full") of a live animal to the claimant. The opener of the pit would keep the dead ox for its hide and meat (since there is no injunction here against eating the meat of the dead ox that died an innocent death).

■ **35** This verse returns to the case of the goring **bull** that is the subject of v 32. If a bull gores and kills another's bull and if it is the bull's first offense, the matter is considered outside the owner's control. The two owners share the loss equally. The goring bull is too dangerous to keep since its next victim may be a person. Therefore, the goring ox is sold for its meat and hide and the owners **divide . . . the money . . . equally** from the sale. They also divide the **dead** ox for meat and hide.

■ **36** If a **bull** with a **known . . . habit of goring** is not properly restrained and kills an **animal**, its **owner** is guilty of negligence and must bear all the loss. The owner of the goring bull must make full restitution to the claimant and keep the **dead animal**. Some suggest that the two owners exchange bulls. But considering the previous verse, the requirement to sell the goring bull (for meat and hide) would be all the more applicable to a bull with an established habit of goring. It would be absurd to award a violent bull to the claimant as fitting compensation. Most likely, the owner of the goring bull keeps the dead bull; the goring bull is sold (for meat and hide) and its owner keeps the proceeds; then, the owner pays the claimant the full price of a live bull.

FROM THE TEXT

God calls the Israelites and Christian disciples alike to take precaution to protect others from risks of safety or life and to hold accountable those who are negligent. These calls apply not only to negligence with dangerous animals but also with, for example, dangerous drivers or irresponsible medical personnel who can cause fatal accidents. These guidelines can also apply to defective machines or vehicles (driving with defective breaks). Negligence that causes fatal accidents must be thoroughly investigated, the guilty party held accountable, and the victim's family fully compensated to minimize the devastating impact of the sudden loss of their loved one.

Prosecuting seriously negligent persons must not be misconstrued as contradicting Jesus' call to turn the other cheek (Matt 5:38-39) or Paul's call to be wronged and defrauded in trivial matters (1 Cor 6:7). The failure to hold accountable the offender who is guilty of homicide or serious injuries or considerable property damage would lead to personal bitterness and social injustice. The threats of the offender's further destructive behavior would also cause social instability. Therefore, Christians have dual moral obligations to forgive the offender according to God's grace and to hold the offender accountable for his or her crime according to the established legal procedures. Thus, the principle of nonresistance (Matt 5:39) and the principle of "eye for eye" must be rightly interpreted and applied with wisdom.

(5) Theft (22:1-4 [21:37—22:3 HB])

BEHIND THE TEXT

These laws deal with the theft of livestock and the compensations the thief is required to make, if caught. The thief must make manyfold compensation for this premeditated crime (twofold for stealing; fourfold or fivefold for theft and sale or slaughter). This application of "life for life" principle to an animal contrasts with the case that extracts a live ox for the gored/killed ox. Thus, the intent of the offending party heavily influences the particular application of the "life for life" principle.

Many laws concerning theft of livestock are found in ancient Near Eastern laws: the oldest known law of Ur-Nammu executed the thief (law 2); the Hammurabi code demanded multiple compensation or the death penalty (law 8); the Hittite laws imposed extremely heavy fines up to fifteenfold (laws 57-70); and the Middle Assyrian Laws variously imposed the return of the stolen animal, corporal punishment, and forced labor (law C8). Compared with such laws, the penalties for theft in the Bible appear more reasonable.

IN THE TEXT

■ **1 [21:37 HB]** This verse concerns theft of livestock, followed by slaughter or sale that makes the livestock irrecoverable. Such thieves, when caught and found guilty by the court of law, must not only make full restitution for the animal but also compensate for the wrong suffered by the robbed person. The thief **must pay back** fivefold **for the ox and** fourfold **for the sheep**. The fine for the ox is heavier perhaps in recognition of the value of the ox's labor and subsequent loss to its owner. Such a heavy fine could potentially leave the thief destitute. The severe penalty reflects the theological judgment of theft not as an accidental, compulsive, or negligent act, but as a malicious, preplanned act. The heavy penalty also serves as a deterrent for the crime.

■ **2-3ab [1-2ab HB]** These verses deal with the timing of a robbery, the issue of self-defense, and the bloodguilt of the defender. What the thief is breaking into is left unspecified. It could be any enclosure for livestock, whether inside or outside the house.

The differentiation between nighttime and daytime stealing/killing may have to do with the thief's intent and the level of danger for the defender. The nocturnal **thief** may intend to kill the occupants of the house if necessary or if he is caught stealing. Also, the surprised defender may believe the intruder intends harm, so he may do anything to protect himself and his family. In addition, the defender might kill the thief accidentally due to limited visibility. In any case, the defender is not liable of bloodguilt. After the sunrise, the owner has greater visibility and lesser element of surprise and fear. Further, the owner could call for help. Significantly, the thief could be identified, seized, and brought to the court for punishment. Thus, killing the diurnal thief is unwarranted. The laws forbid not only stealing but also daytime killing of the thief, upholding the sanctity of life even for a thief.

■ **3cde [2cde HB]** This verse continues the laws concerning theft and **restitution** found in v 1 [21:37 HB]. The aforementioned **thief** must make full restitution (vv 1, 4 [21:37; 22:3 HB]). If the thief is insolvent, he is **sold** into slavery (perhaps for some fifty shekels of silver, the economic valuation of the free Israelite man in Lev 27:3). The proceeds from the sale would be considered full payment for the victim. The insolvent thief would be subjected to slavery for six years.

■ **4 [3 HB]** If the stolen animal is in the thief's custody, the stolen animal is recoverable, and the victim's loss is not as great as for slaughtered or sold animals. Thus, the penalty is lighter. The thief's motive appears to be enlarging his herd. So the thief **must pay back double**. Here and elsewhere (Exod 22:7, 9 [6, 8 HB]), the double payment might include the stolen property (yielding a net gain of 100 percent) or might be double in addition to the stolen one (a net gain of 200 percent). The thief who tries to double his livestock by theft would eventually be deprived of all (if the former) or be forced to sell other possessions to pay for another animal (if the latter).

FROM THE TEXT

Even though Jesus summons us to radical self-denial, the principles these laws promote remain instructive for our society. (1) Whether it is the rich stealing to satiate greed or the poor stealing to stave off hunger, stealing is prohibited (→ 20:15). (2) The theft laws not only punish the criminal but also make provision for proportionate restitution for the victim. (3) The victim's motive of self-defense is distinguished from any malicious intent to retaliate and gain revenge. Accordingly, the victim's right to defend himself and his property is placed within limits that respect and protect life, even that of the offender. (4) Justice must be impartial. When brought to the court, the thief must be tried and fined according to the law.

Jesus' words in Luke 6:29-30, however, call his followers to a radical detachment from worldly possessions: "If someone takes your coat, do not withhold your shirt from them. . . . and if anyone takes what belongs to you, do not demand it back." Implied in that call is the utmost concern for the person's repentance through the experience of boundless mercy and salvation through the witness of a scandalous love that accompanies the authoritative proclamation of the gospel of Jesus Christ. The Father says, "You are always with me, and everything I have is yours" (Luke 15:31). It is that truth that makes us free to be merciful.

(6) Crop Damage (22:5-6 [4-5 HB])

BEHIND THE TEXT

These verses deal with crop damage and restitution for it. The crop damage is related to the two different ways of clearing a field to make it more fertile, namely, grazing and burning. Both cases concern legitimate ways of clearing a field, which may harm an adjacent field and its crops due to carelessness or mishap.

Ancient Near Eastern laws also treated similar cases of crop damage by stray animals (Hammurabi laws 57-58; Hittite law 107) or by accidental fire (Hittite laws 105-6). In the case of crop damage caused by a neglected dike (built for irrigation) that flooded a field, the owner of the dike was required to pay in grain the equal value of the loss (Ur-Nammu laws 31-32). In a similar case, the Hammurabi code required the insolvent offender to be sold to pay for the damage (laws 53-55).

IN THE TEXT

■ **5 [4 HB]** Farmers might purposely let their **livestock . . . graze** in their own **field** or **vineyard** "to clear and/or fertilize it" (Propp 2006, 242). But if a farmer carelessly lets his livestock **stray** ("let loose" or "send away") into the adjacent field to graze, the negligent farmer **must make restitution** proportionate to the damage done to the victim's field (probably determined with the approval of the court).

■ **6 [5 HB]** This case involves a farmer who might start a legitimate, controlled **fire** to clear and fertilize the field. Perhaps due to an unforeseen strong wind, the fire gets out of control. It burns through **thornbushes** that serve as hedges and spreads into someone else's grain field. The **shocks of grain** represent an investment of the labor of harvesting and stacking. They are thus more valuable than the **standing** crop, including fruit trees yet to be harvested. The one who started the fire, even if accidental, must make restitution for the damage done.

FROM THE TEXT

The principles conveyed in these case laws continue to be relevant to our society. Whatever the context, negligence of duty and failure to take reasonable caution and care to prevent potential harm can lead to great damage of various kinds (agricultural, technical, professional, economic, medical, physical, reputational, etc.). When such damage occurs, the offending party must restore what the victim has lost. The negligence law thus calls us to faithfulness, diligence, alertness, and caution in fulfilling our duties. However, lest we toil in anxiety, fear, and restlessness, the psalmist calls us to trust in God. For all human efforts are in vain apart from God, but the Lord grants peace, security, and rest to those he loves (Ps 127:1-2; also see Ps 121:4).

(7) Breach of Trust (22:7-15 [6-14 HB])

BEHIND THE TEXT

These laws deal with the cases of death, theft, or damage to animals or goods in safekeeping. These laws on breach of trust seek to promote and maintain a level of social trust among the Israelites.

Similar to the biblical law (22:8, 11 [7, 10 HB]), Eshnunna (laws 36-37) acquitted the guardian who took an oath to testify to his innocence and to the loss of both his personal belongings and the entrusted goods through robbery. In contrast, the Hammurabi code required the guardian to compensate the owner of the entrusted goods that were stolen, making the apprehension of the thief the responsibility solely of the guardian (law 125).

In regard to the breach of trust laws for livestock, the Hammurabi laws were similar to the biblical laws. The borrower or hired worker was not held responsible for damage done by wild beasts or natural disaster (laws 244, 249, 266). However, they were required to restore equal value for any death or significant damage resulting from neglect or abuse (laws 245-46) or pay lighter monetary fines for less significant injuries (laws 247-48).

IN THE TEXT

(a) Material Possessions (22:7-9 [6-8 HB])

■ **7 [6 HB]** A person might leave valuable possessions with a guardian when there is a need for the whole family to leave home (as when making a pilgrimage). If the guardian claims that the entrusted property is **stolen** from his **house** and the **thief** is **caught**, the guardian is not held responsible. But the thief **must pay back** the owner **double** (see "double" in 22:4 [3 HB]).

■ **8 [7 HB]** But **if the thief is not found** and the guardian claims innocence, the guardian and the **owner** shall **appear before God** (*'ĕlōhîm*; "God" or "gods"; → 21:6). The case is brought before Yahweh because mere human authorities cannot settle it. This practice may reflect how the Israelites in the wilderness bring the most difficult cases to Moses to inquire of Yahweh for a divine decision. Before Yahweh and his representatives, the owner registers his charges against the guardian. Then the guardian declares his innocence under oath in Yahweh's name (20:7; 22:11 [10 HB]), pronouncing a curse upon himself should he be guilty and divine acquittal should he be innocent (see Num 5:19; 1 Kgs 8:31-32). The authorities who represent God then consult Yahweh and pronounce Yahweh's judgment. This is the likely scenario treated in this text.

■ **9 [8 HB]** This general law comprehensively deals with accusations **of illegal possession** (*peša'*; lit. "transgression"; "a breach of trust" [ESV, NASB]) of **property. Both** the accused defendant and the accusing plaintiff must appear **before God** (*'ĕlōhîm*; see 21:6; 22:8 [7 HB]) to obtain Yahweh's judgment that is mediated through a human representative or **the judges**. The one found **guilty must pay back double** (22:4, 7 [3, 6 HB]). The false accuser pays the same penalty the accused would have paid.

(b) Livestock in Safekeeping (22:10-13 [9-12 HB])

■ **10 [9 HB]** The next four verses (10-13 [9-12 HB]) deal with the safeguarding of livestock. In comparison to safekeeping silver or goods, pasturing and guarding the animals in the fields are more complex, requiring much labor and watchfulness. Thus, Sarna assumes that the guardian is paid for the job (2004, 101). The cases fall into two categories: (1) unpreventable loss for which the guardian declares his innocence under oath (vv 10-11, 13 [9-10, 12 HB]) and (2) a loss for which negligence is presumed and the guardian must make restitution (v 12 [11 HB]).

Verse 10 [9 HB] deals with three different kinds of unforeseeable mishaps that can happen to livestock in safekeeping: death, injury, and unexplainable disappearance. The Hebrew verb for **taken away** probably has the meaning of "be taken captive." Some commentators suggest that cattle raiding is implied here (see Job 1:15, 17; Cassuto 1967, 287). If so, cattle raiding is differentiated from the more common and preventable theft mentioned in Exod 22:12 [11 HB].

■ **11 [10 HB]** The guardian must take a solemn **oath** of innocence **before the LORD**, presumably involving the pronouncement of curses upon himself should he be guilty of injuring or disposing (or selling or consuming) the entrusted animal. In a culture in which people take an oath-curse not merely as a formality but as a potent reality that actually brings about deserved curses, the oath-taking is an effective means of verifying one's innocence or guilt.

Therefore, the owner must **accept** the guardian's declaration of innocence and require no **restitution**.

■ **12 [11 HB]** Since v 10 [9 HB] makes a provision for the acquittal of the guardian for unforeseeable and unpreventable situations (like raided cattle), this law must be concerned with preventable thefts that take place due to negligence. This law also assumes that the alleged thief is not found. The guardian is held responsible and is required to make **restitution**, giving **to the owner** double the kind of livestock lost.

■ **13 [12 HB]** A domestic animal falling prey to **a wild animal** is another unpreventable misfortune. The guardian must present the **remains as evidence** of the **torn animal** (*'ēd*; "witness") or as silent witness. Upon proving his innocence, the guardian is released from responsibility. If the animal carcass is not found, presumably the provision in v 11 [10 HB] would apply.

(c) Borrowed or Hired Animal (22:14-15 [13-14 HB])

■ **14 [13 HB]** Verses 14-15a [13-14a HB] probably envision a situation in which a work **animal** is borrowed free of charge and entirely for the benefit of the "borrower" (v 15 [14 HB]). Thus, the borrower is expected to take extra care to return the borrowed animal unharmed. If the damage occurs in the absence of the **owner**, then the borrower is held liable and must make full restitution. It appears that the law assumes some degree of mistreatment or negligence on the part of the borrower.

■ **15ab [14ab HB]** If the **animal** borrowed for free is harmed while the owner is "present" (v 14 [13 HB]), then the borrower is released from responsibility. It is supposed that the owner is present to supervise his own animal. So any harm that comes to it is supposed to be accidental and the supervising owner's responsibility.

■ **15cd [14cd HB]** This case concerning a **hired** animal is difficult to interpret. Various English versions render the last phrase more literally: "it came for its hire/hiring fee" (see the ESV, KJV, and NASB). With this translation, various interpretations are possible. (1) If we assume that this verse follows v 14 [13 HB] and that the accident takes place in the absence of the owner, then the verse may mean **the money paid for the hire covers the loss** and the negligent hirer is not liable for further payment. However, since this arrangement would not fully compensate for the owner's loss, this interpretation is highly unlikely. (2) If the owner is absent and some degree of the hirer's negligence or abuse is assumed (as in v 14 [13 HB]), then the just ruling would be for the owner to keep the hiring fee and the offending hirer to pay extra to fully compensate for the dead or injured **animal**.

If v 15b [14b HB] is an addendum to v 15a [14a HB], strictly concerned with incidents with the owner present, then an alternate translation proves illuminating. The Hebrew expression can literally mean **he comes out with his** *hiring fee* and its interpretation may be as follows. The gratuitous borrower of v 15*a* [14*a* HB] does not incur any responsibility; his only loss is the use of the borrowed animal. Likewise, the hirer of the animal in v 15*b* [14*b* HB] shall not incur any penalty for the animal that dies or is injured under the owner's supervision; the hirer's loss shall be only the labor of the hired animal. The hirer must not forfeit the hiring fee but recover it in order to hire another animal for labor. Since the owner, who is also the supervisor, failed to provide the animal labor for the hiring fee he received, it is only just that the owner return the hiring fee. Thus **he** [the hirer] **comes out with his hiring fee** (refunded by the owner).

FROM THE TEXT

While the specific details of these cases of property liability may be far removed from the realities of modern societies (in which few people are engaged in agriculture), borrowing or hiring someone else's property and the implied liabilities are pervasively present. Rather than borrowing a neighbor's animals, we may borrow or rent vehicles or equipment or places of residence or business. Insurance is the standard way to handle damages incurred to these various rental properties caused by acts of God, negligence, accidents, or vandalism. An elaborate legal framework exists to determine the responsibilities and liabilities of the owners and renters. Who is at fault and how losses and damages should be compensated are determined through complex legal procedures. While abuse and fraud exist, such contemporary legal frameworks reflect the concerns and intuitions about responsibility, reliability, and accountability that are found in biblical texts, including the NT (see Rom 13:1-5; 1 Pet 2:13-14), which are necessary for the integrity of society.

At the same time, however, Paul encourages believers to settle lesser cases of conflict within the church, perhaps by reliance on the wisdom of the governing authorities of the church (1 Cor 6:1-6). Paul also ultimately discourages civil lawsuits among believers over noncriminal matters. Paul is emphatic, "Why not rather be wronged? Why not rather be cheated?" (v 7). Central to Paul's concern, of course, is God's honor in the secular world displayed through the maturity of the body of Christ.

(8) Seduction of a Virgin (22:16-17 [15-16 HB])

BEHIND THE TEXT

Israelite marriage involves both an engagement period and a wedding. The girl is engaged once a man who asks for her hand in marriage receives her guardian's permission and pays her bride price (see Eshnunna laws 27-28 for a similar case). An engaged woman is legally treated like a married woman, except that she still remains under her parents' care and authority. The bride price is "paid to the father but counted among the wife's possessions" (Sarna 2004, 103). It would be the wife's security in the event of her husband's death or divorce. Otherwise, it would become her children's inheritance. Jacob worked for Laban for fourteen years as the bride-price for his two wives who later complained that Laban used up the bride-price that rightly belonged to them and to their children (Gen 31:15-16). These observations about the Israelite man's responsibility in engagement and marriage form the background for the matter of a seduced virgin in this unit.

IN THE TEXT

■ **16 [15 HB]** This case concerns the seduction of **a virgin** who is not engaged **to be married**. If the seduced woman is engaged, then she and her seducer would be guilty of adultery (20:14; Deut 22:23-24) and subjected to the death penalty. The reference to the man seducing (or "persuading" or "deceiving") points to a deception of a naive girl through insincere words of love and a promise of marriage. It may include physical coercion (as in rape; see Deut 22:28) as in the case of Amnon and Tamar (2 Sam 13:1-22). The offender **must pay the bride-price** (in the amount of fifty shekels of silver according to Deut 22:29) to the girl's father and marry the girl, whether the seducer wishes it (out of romantic attachment, as in Gen 34:3-4) or not (perhaps in contempt for the one he just wronged, as in 2 Sam 13:15).

■ **17 [16 HB]** The **father** might refuse **to give** his daughter to a man who acted dishonorably or wickedly. The father's decision might be informed by the girl's own wishes (see Rebekah in Gen 24:57-58). In the two cases of rape of a nonbetrothed virgin in the Bible (Dinah in Gen 34:2 and Tamar in 2 Sam 13:14), the virgin's brother killed the offender. Whether through persuasion or deception or coercion, the seductive act discussed in this text is extremely damaging to the girl and her family. Therefore, even if the marriage is denied, the offender must **pay the bride-price**. This is so because his crime against the virgin robs the girl of her usual opportunity to marry as a virgin and her father of his right to receive the bride-price as his daughter's future security deposit. If she does not marry the seducer, she would have the status of a divorced woman. As illustrated in the examples of widowed or divorced women remarrying (Abigail in 1 Sam 25:42 and Michal in 1 Sam 18:27; 25:44), she retains the right to remarry (which might be sought after a time of grieving and healing; see Tamar in 2 Sam 13:20).

FROM THE TEXT

This text treats premarital sex as the real, but improper formation of a marriage. Whether through seduction (leading to consensual sex) or rape (nonconsensual sex), the text regards sex between a single man and a single woman a marital union, *albeit* a premature one. As Hugenberger puts it, sexual union is a serious "marriage covenant-ratifying act" before or after public ceremonies of marriage (1998, 394).

This biblical perspective puts fornication (premarital sex) in a different perspective than the ways it is often viewed in contemporary culture, even within the church. Fornication is wrong not only because it takes sex outside of its proper context in marriage but also because it haphazardly forms a marriage without any covenant commitments and appropriate communal guidelines, recognition, and celebration that marriage should include. Moreover, since a casual sexual relationship without commitment and public recognition is often fleeting, it promotes flippancy about marriage and divorce.

The focus of this text is thus on sexual union as a marital privilege. In its ancient context, violation of this law resulted in the breakdown of social structure (the proper way to enter into marriage relationship). This law invites readers to reflect on the ways in which premarital sex contributes to the breakdown of social structure in their own cultural context. It is also important to interpret this law through the lens of the gospel proclamation of God's grace and forgiveness, and the promise of redemption to all who sin against God and others. Through repentance, those who live in violation of this law may receive victory over the sin of improper sexual desires and acts, both past and present, and freedom from guilt. The law invites readers to live a life that is pleasing to God.

Legal texts like this one reinforce the importance of honoring marriage (Heb 13:4) and retaining the proper place of sexual union within marriage. God also calls would-be husbands and wives to honor their parents in the process of coming together in marriage, by seeking their counsel, permission, and blessings. We can affirm such principles without retaining every aspect of the ancient patriarchal cultural context evident in this text.

c. Apodictic Laws (22:18—23:19 [22:17—23:19 HB])

Overview

With a few exceptions, these laws are categorical or apodictic in form, which contrasts with the preceding section that contains predominantly conditional or casuistic laws. These apodictic laws treat social and religious matters, illustrating how all aspects of life are under Yahweh's government. This final section of the book of the covenant consists of the following categories: three capital offenses (22:18-20 [17-19 HB]), justice of the disadvantaged (vv 21-27 [20-26 HB]), three obligations to God (vv 28-31 [27-30 HB]), justice for various people (23:1-13), and three festivals to Yahweh (vv 14-19).

(I) Three Capital Offenses toward God (22:18-20 [17-19 HB])

BEHIND THE TEXT

This unit addresses three abominable practices found throughout the ancient Near East that are considered capital offenses in ancient Israel. If left unpunished or tolerated, they would corrupt the Israelites. The third is a form of idolatry that would later become more common in Israel and compromise the Israelites' exclusive devotion to Yahweh and jeopardize life in Yahweh's land.

Ancient Near Eastern laws treated sorcery or witchcraft practiced by either male or female as a capital offense. Ur-Nammu (law 13), Hammurabi (law 2), and Middle Assyrian Laws (A47) subjected those accused of sorcery to an ordeal by water, treating sorcery as a capital crime.

Bestiality was practiced in Canaan before the Israelite period. Nesilim codes sentenced some offenders of bestiality to death but treated copulation with certain animals as relatively unobjectionable (laws 187, 199; also see the Hittite laws 187-88, 199, 200a).

IN THE TEXT

(a) Prohibition of Sorcery (22:18 [17 HB])

■ **18 [17 HB]** Yahweh commands the Israelites **not** to **allow** those who practice sorcery **to live**, perhaps by putting them out of business by not consulting them (Lev 19:31) or by driving them out of the land (1 Sam 28:3, 9) or by putting them to death (Lev 20:27). This law is elaborated in Deut 18:9-14 and includes male practitioners as well. The female is highlighted, however, possibly because there were generally more females practicing the occult than males (1 Sam 28:7; Isa 57:3).

A **sorceress** is one who practices magic, which was commonly practiced in the ancient Near East (e.g., Babylon in Isa 47:9, 12-13 and Nineveh in Nah 3:4). Sorcery or magic is a human "attempt to activate and manipulate to one's advantage the mysterious supernatural forces" perceived in animistic or polytheistic belief systems (Sarna 2004, 103). Isaiah sarcastically taunts the Babylonians for their use of magic in an unsuccessful and exhausting effort to obtain supernatural counsel and predictions (Isa 47:12-13).

Israelite monotheism not only insists on the exclusive worship and communion with him but also vigorously resists such occult beliefs and practices as incompatible with a holy life lived before Yahweh (Lev 19:31; 20:6). Accordingly, Deut 18:10-12 lists all kinds of abhorrent magical practices and the severe consequence (the exile) for such practices. The implication is that if the Israelites adopt these beliefs and practices, Yahweh will cast them out of the land they are about to possess. Yahweh will provide a prophet like Moses who will communicate Yahweh's will to the people (v 15). The Israelites, therefore, have no reason to turn to divination and sorcery. They are expected to adopt Yahweh's own attitude toward all magical practices and completely remove their practitioners. Sadly, the history of Israel shows that the leaders and the populace alike turned to those evil practices, until they were expelled from the land (2 Kgs 17:16-20; 21:5-6; 2 Chr 33:5-6; Isa 2:6).

(b) Prohibition of Bestiality (22:19 [18 HB])

■ **19 [18 HB]** Leviticus 18:23-24 and 20:15-16 (see Deut 27:21) also strongly condemn bestiality as a perversion and impose capital punishment on both human beings and animals alike. Bestiality violates Yahweh's order in creation, copulation, multiplication "according to its kind" (Gen 1:21-22), and the related creational institution of marriage between a man and a woman (2:22-24).

(c) Prohibition of Pagan Sacrifices (22:20 [19 HB])

■ **20 [19 HB]** This particular prohibition targets a certain pagan, communal sacrifice commonly practiced in the ancient Near East. It involved an animal slaughter and a festival celebrating fellowship between the worshipper and the deity worshipped. Pagan sacrificial fests sometimes involved sexual orgies, as seen in the Israelites' idolatrous **sacrifices** in Exod 32:6 and Num 25:1-9 (see 1 Cor 10:7-8). The penalty for such idolatry is execution. The sentence, **must be destroyed** (ḥrm), is perhaps more severe than the simple death penalty of the previous two verses. The Hebrew verb (ḥrm) means "be devoted or dedicated (to God)" for sacred service (Lev 27:28; Num 18:14; Josh 6:18-19) or for divine judgment (Josh 6:17; 7:1-26). At a minimum, the offender is executed. The penalty ḥērem may apply also to the entire household, who most likely participated in the idolatrous sacrifice, and to family property, possessions, and livestock (Josh 6:17-18; 1 Sam 15:3). Deuteronomy 13:12-17 [13-18 HB] applies the penalty of ḥērem to an entire apostate city, requiring the tribal (or national) leaders to take a military action against the city and kill all the inhabitants and their cattle and completely destroy by fire all its booty. As such, ḥērem is an execution of divine judgment for apostasy and a means of pacifying divine wrath, purifying the land, and securing continued divine mercy and blessing (Deut 13:17 [18 HB]).

FROM ⬭ THE TEXT

Death and destruction as the punishment for sorcery, bestiality, and sacrifice to other gods reflect God's uncompromising attitude toward actions that violate his call to Israel to be a holy people in the profane world. These laws call the reader to reflect on ways to honor God by a commitment to live a life of holiness, a life that follows God's creational order and purpose. The laws bundle together manipulation of the power of God, distorted sexual relations, and divided loyalties in one's relationship to God because they, individually and collectively, demonstrate one's decision to follow the path that leads to death and destruction, against the will and purpose of God for his creation to choose the path that leads to life.

The focus on holy living and life eternal is also clear in the NT's call to believers to flee from sexual impurity, idolatry, and other abominable practices (including sorcery—see Acts 8:9-11; 19:19). The NT teachings make clear that those who practice such acts "will not inherit the kingdom of God" (Gal 5:21; also see Rom 1:23-32; 1 Cor 10:7-8; Eph 4:19; Col 3:5; 1 Pet 4:3).

(2) Justice for the Disadvantaged (22:21-27 [20-26 HB])

BEHIND THE TEXT

This group of laws provides legal protection for the poor (foreigners, widows, and orphans), for those who are often mistreated, oppressed, and exploited. These laws impose basic moral obligations, calling Yahweh's people to treat the disadvantaged with compassion and restorative justice. The biblical law is unique in banning lending and borrowing money with interest and in demanding the immediate return of the pledge to the poor. Yahweh demands obedience to these moral laws centered on the fundamental theological truth that Yahweh champions the cause of the dispossessed and downtrodden but fiercely opposes the heartless oppressors, a truth he clearly demonstrates in Egypt and in the Israelite exile.

In a stark contrast to the biblical laws, the ancient Near Eastern laws did not provide any explicit protection for foreigners, widows, and orphans. The Hammurabi code, however, regulated loans, interest rates, and debt payments. The law granted the creditors the right to seize the grain of the debtor. At the same time, it penalized the creditor who seized property without the debtor's permission by demanding the return of what he seized and forfeiture of what he lent (law 113). The law also permitted the creditor to seize the nonpaying debtor and force him or his family members to work for him up to three years to pay off the debt; and, if the debtor died (a natural death) in the creditor's house, the creditor was not found guilty (laws 115-17; → 21:2).

IN THE TEXT

(a) A Foreigner, a Widow, and an Orphan (22:21-24 [20-23 HB])

■ **21 [20 HB]** Resident **foreigners** (gēr) are those who leave their homeland because of famine (Gen 45:10-11; Ruth 1:1), war (1 Sam 22:1), or bloodguilt (2 Sam 13:38) and settle in a foreign land, risking the possibility of exploitation without legal protection. Yahweh desires to protect a class of people who are not natives and are, therefore, vulnerable to abuse and discrimination.

Yahweh uses Israel's painful past status as foreigners and slaves **in Egypt** as a reason why they should not oppress other foreigners (see Deut 24:17-22).

■ **22 [21 HB]** The widows and **fatherless** are vulnerable due to the loss of legal protectors. The Israelites are allotted a share of the land by tribes and families. This means extended families or relatives settle a village. In that context, taking care of widows and orphans is a familial obligation, rather than the state's concern. Taking **advantage of the widow or the fatherless** through taking and keeping pledges, lending with interest, and then seizing property or selling them for their unpaid loans in the familial setting is an especially heinous and repulsive practice. Also, all the Israelites were recently delivered from the savage claws of their oppressors in Egypt. Therefore, Yahweh expects them to extend the same grace and generosity, which they received from him, to the needy and defenseless, rather than to prey upon them. They must preserve their fellow human beings' dignity and freedom through generous provision, which would prevent a situation of enslavement.

■ **23 [22 HB]** Yahweh is the defender of the widows and orphans and any other defenseless person. If a society deteriorates to an inhumane state of oppression, Yahweh **will certainly hear their cry** and act on their behalf. Yahweh heard the desperate cries of the Israelites under the Egyptians and responded to them by delivering them out of slavery.

■ **24 [23 HB]** Just as Yahweh opposed the Egyptians for their tyranny, so will Yahweh punish his people for their cruelty. On the other side of divine compassion and deliverance for the poor is divine **anger** and retribution toward the oppressors. Punishment takes the form of war, and the oppressors will be killed **with the sword**. The end result will be that their wives and children will become destitute like those whom they oppressed. In fact, the Israelites will suffer a worse fate (i.e., expulsion from the land) than Pharaoh and his people (who remained in their own land). The Israelites' special status as Yahweh's firstborn will not excuse their wickedness but only accentuate their guilt and need for painful discipline by their Father (see Amos 3:2).

(b) Loans and Pledges (22:25-27 [24-26 HB])

■ **25 [24 HB]** The Hebrew conjunction **if** (*'im*) here does not imply that a person can choose either to lend or not to lend to the poor. It should be translated into "when" and it connotes a fulfillment of moral obligation and divine will. The biblical law uniquely and categorically forbids lending **money** with **interest** among the Israelites (see also Lev 25:35-37). Charging heavy interest (anywhere between 20 and 50 percent annually; Sarna 2004, 106) and then seizing property or enslaving the debtor and his family were common practices in the ancient Near East. Unlike the surrounding nations, the Israelites should not **charge** interest and not harass the borrower for payments like a moneylender. Another person's misfortune must not be used as an opportunity for gain, but should occasion compassion and generosity. Since those who must borrow for basic subsistence might not be able to repay what they owe, the law requires the cancellation of debt every seventh year, the Sabbatical Year, in order that they do not permanently remain under the yoke of debt (Deut 15:6-10).

■ **26 [25 HB]** While charging interest on a loan is forbidden, obtaining a pledge is allowed, but only to return it immediately. Few biblical laws regulate the practice of taking a pledge. Deuteronomy 24:6 forbids the lender from taking as collateral a hand mill or millstones, which are used to grind grain or olives and thus essential for survival. The point is that anything absolutely necessary for life must not be taken as a pledge, or must be returned on the same day (v 13). The borrower determines what he will offer as security; the lender may not enter the borrower's house to seize property he desires as a pledge; the borrower's privacy and dignity must be respected (vv 10-11). If a **cloak** is given **as a pledge**, it must be returned to the borrower **by sunset**; Yahweh considers it a moral obligation and an act of justice to the poor (v 13).

■ **27 [26 HB]** The cloak is the poor person's **only covering** at night and one of very few possessions. They are necessary for life (such as millstones). Deuteronomy 24:12-13 makes a categorical command not to keep a poor person's pledge overnight. Thus, the poor borrower's collateral is only symbolic of his intention to repay, which serves to save his honor (Propp 2006, 261), and the creditor's return of the property by sunset amounts to no less than the forgiveness of the debt. So lenders keep the pauper's pledge for a half-day and return it by sunset and receive his blessing and divine blessing in return (v 13). If one is able to lend, it is out of abundant blessing from the Lord.

Taking and keeping the poor borrower's bare necessity as security is outrageous and will arouse divine anger (Exod 22:24 [23 HB]). If the cloak is not returned and the poor (and his family) are unable to keep warm at night, they will appeal to Yahweh with a bitter cry for justice. Yahweh will surely **hear** and respond to their deprivation and misery, for Yahweh is **gracious** (*hannûn*; **compassionate** [NIV]; see Amos's charge against the Israelites who violated this law: "They lie down beside every altar on garments taken in pledge" [Amos 2:8]). Yahweh's graciousness is one of Yahweh's essential characteristics revealed to Israel. It becomes a regular part of Israel's liturgy (→ Exod 34:6). Yahweh's graciousness that brings justice to the deprived poor is also a threat of punishment for the merciless creditor.

In many ways, the biblical teachings ultimately move toward gratuitous giving without the expectation of repayment (see Ps 112:5, 9; Prov 19:17; Matt 5:42; Luke 6:30, 34) although the borrower should do everything possible to repay what he or she owes (Ps 37:21). These moral laws are couched within the promise of the blessing of peaceful, fruitful, and prosperous life upon full obedience (Deut 15:6-10). For the community that disregards these laws, however, severe punishment such as exile is promised (Amos 6—8).

FROM THE TEXT

These laws show that God honors our right to private property insofar as we recognize the divine rights of the poor. We are but tenants of God's land. Therefore, what the land produces ultimately belongs to the master of the land and all the inhabitants of the land. God's term is clear. The tithe goes to the Levites and the poor of the land to sufficiently provide for all their needs (Deut 14:27-29; 26:10-12). In other words, at a minimum, the 10 percent of the wealth of the land belongs to the needy. It is theirs by God's decree and by their right to have the necessity of life. Any misconceived notion of right to private property that is not subordinated to the just distribution of goods must be rejected and repented of.

Furthermore, if one is rich while ten are dying of starvation, the rich is guilty of the crime of hoarding and of indirect manslaughter. The church fathers considered our excess the poor's rightful possession. Gregory the Great says, "When we attend to the needs of those in want, we give them what is theirs, not ours. More than performing works of mercy, we are paying a debt of justice" (*Pastoral Rule*, 3.21).

Jesus calls us to give our excess to the poor (Luke 12:33) and not share in the miserable fate of the rich fool (vv 13-21). Jesus calls us to "store . . . treasures in heaven" and be rich in regard to what matters to God (Matt 6:19-21). Saint Ambrose is emphatic about the just distribution of goods to the poor: "It is the hungry man's bread that you withhold, the naked man's cloak that you store away, the money that you bury in the earth is the price of the poor man's ransom and freedom" (cited in Thomas Aquinas' *Summa Theologica* II—II, q. 66, a. 6). This grace-saturated ethical framework is the context of Jesus' words in Luke: "From everyone who has been given much, much will be demanded; and from the one who has been entrusted with much, much more will be asked" (Luke 12:48).

(3) Three Duties to God (22:28-31 [27-30 HB])

BEHIND THE TEXT

These laws articulate three areas of obligations to Yahweh: do not curse but honor Yahweh and the ruler; do not withhold but give to Yahweh what belongs to Yahweh; do not eat what is defiled but maintain a pattern of holy living before Yahweh. These laws seem to be directed especially to the poor, who in desperation might curse Yahweh and the ruler, who might be tempted to withhold offerings due to their poverty, and who might resort to eating defiled meat due to hunger. It also holds accountable those who have more to lend freely to the poor (22:25 [24 HB]) and offer full poor tithes to provide for the poor in the land (v 29 [28 HB]), so that the poor are not driven to desperation.

IN THE TEXT

(a) Honor of God and Rulers (22:28 [27 HB])

■ **28 [27 HB]** This verse confronts an improper attitude of dishonor toward **God** and a God-given **ruler**. The Hebrew verb (*qll*) that means "trifle," "curse," "revile" denotes **blaspheme** when directed to God. God and a ruler (or a king) appear in parallelism in other biblical texts (e.g., "fear the LORD and the king" in Prov 24:21; "will speak contemptuously against their king and their God" in Isa 8:21 [ESV] and "For the LORD and for Gideon" in Judg 7:18). The pairing of God and the king perhaps reflects the notion that the rulers are symbols of God. God ordains the king, and the king represents divine authority. The failure of one is the failure of both, and the failure of society is attributed to both. Therefore, failure to honor a God-ordained ruler is punishable by death (2 Sam 18:14-15; ch 20; 1 Kgs 21:13), as is blasphemy (Lev 24:11-16).

Also, in close association with the preceding unit (Exod 22:21-27 [20-26 HB]) and the following (23:1-13), this verse warns the poor and the oppressed not to turn against God or the ruler, even if the people of the land fail to lend freely and return the pledge to them or to give justice. The preceding verse (22:27 [26 HB]) assures the oppressed that their desperate cries and appeals for justice to Yahweh will surely be heard and answered. However, feeling forsaken by God, the king, and the society, the deprived and oppressed may believe cursing is their "sole recourse and revenge" (Propp 2006, 263). However, this law strongly discourages the oppressed from cursing, and the previous law summons them to cry out to Yahweh for his gracious help (Exod 22:27 [26 HB]). It may be added that those who deny the poor divine justice (say, by accepting bribes from the rich and condemning the innocent poor) are guilty of trifling or blaspheming Yahweh, for they act as if Yahweh does not live and his command concerning the poor is inconsequential.

(b) Offerings of Produce and the Firstborn (22:29-30 [28-29 HB])

■ **29-30 [28-29 HB]** These two verses address three holy offerings to Yahweh: the produce of the land, the **firstborn** of the human womb, and the firstborn of the livestock. The Israelites must present their firstfruits, tithes, and **offerings** without delay from **granaries** and **vats**. The best of the cereal, wine, and oil and all firstborn livestock must be presented to the Master of the land. The rich might be tempted to withhold the offerings due to greed and the poor due to lack. Yet even the poor must **give** "in proportion to the way [Yahweh] has blessed" them (Deut 16:17). All firstborn livestock must be given to Yahweh, even if one has only one calf or only one lamb. Offering is thus both in response to Yahweh's current blessing and in trust of Yahweh's greater future blessings for obedience. The firstborn of the woman is to be redeemed (→ Exod 13:1-2, 12-13). The poor might consider it a hardship to redeem the firstborn child with five shekels of silver (Num 18:15-16). However, the observance of this law is fundamental to the maintenance of the Israelites' identity as Yahweh's firstborn and Israel's historical covenant relationship with Yahweh who brought them out of Egypt "with a mighty hand" (Exod 13:14-16).

Some associate the unqualified command to give the firstborn son to Yahweh with Ezek 20:25-26, asserting that Yahweh here is ordering the Israelites to sacrifice their infant sons. But Ezekiel makes a strong contrast between "my decrees and . . . my laws" given at Sinai by which to live (vv 11, 13) and "other statues" through which one cannot live, given in a later date as a form of punishment (vv 21-25). In addition, the context of Ezek 20 makes unambiguous that Israel's child sacrifice was part of Israel's unflinching rebellion against Yahweh and his good and life-giving laws (see vv 28, 30-31). Thus, the command to give the firstborn in Exod 22:29 [28 HB] must be interpreted as part of Yahweh's good and life-giving laws and in relation to 13:1-2, 12-13, which clarify that the firstborn sons are redeemed (see Deut 12:31 for the explicit prohibition of child sacrifice).

(c) Abstinence from Torn Meat (22:31 [30 HB])

■ **31 [30 HB]** The call to be Yahweh's **holy people** is first given in 19:6 on Mount Sinai. Leviticus 11 and Deut 14:3-21 emphasize the importance of observing dietary regulations concerning clean and unclean foods to remain holy. Animals that suffer natural death can be given or sold to foreigners (v 21), but those that are **torn by wild beasts** are not suitable for human consumption. No one, not an Israelite nor a foreigner nor one destitute, may eat the torn meat (Lev 17:15). The torn animal may be given to scavengers like **dogs** (see Lev 7:24). The poor might be tempted to act like scavengers, but the preceding laws encourage them rather to borrow. The rich of the land, of course, have the moral obligation to freely give to the poor.

FROM THE TEXT

In these laws, the individual responsibility and the communal responsibility come together, as the miscarriage of the latter can be a significant factor in the breach of the former. These laws can be interpreted as addressing especially the poor, the disadvantaged, the foreigners, and the oppressed. However, since the responsibility of ensuring the general well-being of the poor is given to the majority of the people who are better off, who have the land, who are natives, and who, thus, have more power, one may claim that these laws also hold accountable the community to fulfill their part (as described in other parts of the law). In other words, the community has the responsibility of helping the poor observe these laws, not merely by reciting the law, but by acts of just provision.

These laws are good, but if the people who have more wealth do nothing to alleviate poverty or oppression, then they are liable to the similar condemnation that the teachers of the law and the Pharisees received from Jesus (Matt 23:2-3, 13-36). Jesus excoriates them: "They tie up heavy, cumbersome loads and put them on other people's shoulders, but they themselves are not willing to lift a finger to move them" (v 4). Law without obedience or words without actions are pointless, even as James says, "Suppose a brother or a sister is without clothes and daily food. If one of you says to them, 'Go in peace; keep warm and well fed,' but does nothing about their physical needs, what good is it?" (Jas 2:15-16). A poor one might be held liable for cursing God, but the rich will be held accountable for the greater sin of causing the poor to do so (see Matt 18:6).

(4) Justice for All (23:1-13)

BEHIND THE TEXT

The following group of laws, although somewhat diverse, is united by a concern for impartial justice for all inhabitants of the land. These laws highlight Yahweh's concern for certain economic rights of the poor and the foreigners and their judicial rights that are equal to the rich natives.

While a concern to protect the weak and vulnerable is somewhat evident in other ancient Near Eastern laws, they generally mirror the highly class-conscious, hierarchical nature of ancient Near Eastern societies. The laws that explicitly promote the well-being and equal judicial rights of the poor, the enemy, and the foreigner are unique to the biblical laws and are lacking in ancient Near Eastern laws. The Hammurabi code, however, has two laws concerning a corrupt court: a false witness who testified for a bribe was punished with the penalty of the case (law 4); a judge who altered the judgment was heavily fined and removed from the office (law 5).

Some readers raise a concern for the apparent double standard between the Israelites and the foreigners in regard to the commerce law (lending money with interest to and not canceling debt for foreigners [Deut 15:3; 23:20]). Whatever the double standard, however, the radical intolerance of any poverty or oppression of the foreigners and the call to love foreigners as one of the natives, as expressed elsewhere, direct the people toward egalitarianism (see Exod 23:9; Lev 19:34; Deut 14:29). In addition, the laws of this unit express fundamental egalitarianism in regard to judicial justice. The criminal laws govern all equally, foreigners and natives alike (Lev 24:22). Thus, what is surprising with the biblical laws is not that there is a double standard in regard to a couple of laws, but rather that the foreigners are given equal rights and protections.

IN THE TEXT

(a) Judicial Justice for All (23:1-3)

■ **1** The first law of this verse prohibits spreading (*nāśā'*; "lift," "carry," "bear") **false** [*šāw'*; "worthless," "vain"] **reports** (*šēma'*; "hearing"). The second law prohibits false witness with violent intentions (see Ps 27:12 for the clear connection between the two). Together, the laws address and warn all those involved in a court case. It warns against the judges holding an unrighteous hearing (such as the leaders and elders of Naboth's city of Samaria in 1 Kgs 21:11-12), the litigants bringing false charges against the innocent, and the false witnesses giving fabricated testimonies in the court (such as the two villains who testify against Naboth in v 13). In addition, it warns against the slanderous talkers spreading rumors in private conversations (Lev 19:16). One must **not help a guilty** [*rāšā'*; "in the wrong," "guilty of crime"] **person** [such as Ahab or Jezebel in 1 Kgs 21] **by being a malicious** [*ḥāmās*; "violent," "false"] **witness**. The desired outcome of the false witnessing probably is violence against the falsely accused (e.g., the stoning of Naboth in 1 Kgs 21:13). According to Deut 17:7, in capital cases involving stoning, the witnesses are the first to throw the stones.

■ **2** This verse prohibits judicial injustice committed under the influence of the majority or of the wealthy and powerful. The Hebrew term for **the crowd** (*rābbîm*) variously means "many, much, numerous, abundant, enough" and "powerful" in influence (Job 35:9) or "great" in wealth (Lev 19:15). The two meanings converge somewhat in that the majority are usually under the influence of the rich and powerful. Justice must be upheld in all circumstances and must not be perverted due to the influence of the majority or of the rich and powerful. It calls all persons involved in judicial proceedings to an unswerving commitment to impartial justice, which must be promoted even if there is an implicit or explicit threat of retaliation from the majority or the rich and powerful or the overruled party.

Accordingly, the witnesses must **not pervert justice by siding with the crowd** or the rich and powerful. The guilty must be convicted and pay the price for their wrongdoing, and the innocent must be acquitted.

■ **3** Showing **favoritism** to the **poor**, perhaps from being moved by compassion, also perverts justice. The law instructs noble and perennial ways to show compassion and charity to the poor (Exod 22:25-26 [24-25 HB]; 23:11; Lev 19:9-10; 23:22; Deut 14:28-29; 15:7-11; 24:12-13; 26:12). The victim may choose not to press charges against a poor criminal (Prov 6:30). If the victim brings the poverty-stricken criminal to the court, however, then the court has the obligation to administer justice to the victim, even if it costs the criminal "all the wealth of his house" (v 31). The court must not allow compassion for the poor to impair either testimonies or judgments.

EXODUS

23:1-3

(b) Economic Justice for the Enemy (23:4-5)

■ **4** The neighborly obligation here has to do with preventing property loss for one's enemy. A foreign idolater, an apostate, and a hostile Israelite have been suggested as the referent of the enemy. There is no need to assume that it refers only to one kind of enemy. The law assumes that a friend naturally looks after another friend's well-being. Should one happen to **come across** the **enemy's** livestock **wandering off, . . . return it** at once. Deuteronomy 22:1-3 also prohibits keeping the lost property and instructs its immediate return; if the owner is not known, the property should be safeguarded until the owner comes looking for it. The stray animal must be returned immediately to the rightful owner; the individual must resist all temptation to enrich oneself since that would amount to stealing or to allowing the animal to remain lost, an action perhaps motivated by the desire to gain revenge on the enemy. One must not rejoice over the prospect of the enemy's loss and pain but seek his welfare as one's own. As Lev 19:16 makes explicit, loving one's neighbor (who may be an enemy) as oneself would involve overcoming one's desire for vengeance and emotions of hatred. Acts of kindness might defuse hostility and even bring reconciliation (Prov 25:21-22) so that the person in question no longer remains an enemy.

■ **5** This verse is concerned with humanitarian treatment of animals in danger, trouble, or pain: Do not let animals suffer, on the account of the ill-conceived desire to punish the owner **who hates you.**

There are two interpretive issues. (1) Many commentators assume that the owner is present with the fallen donkey and the owner is unable to set the beast of burden free from its heavy **load** or to **help** the donkey get up. This assumption has led to the emendation of the second and third '*āzab* (**leave,** "abandon") to '*zr* ("help," "assist") as reflected in the NIV translation. However, since the owner is not directly mentioned in this verse as an active agent, it seems best to assume that the owner is not present. If so, this verse continues a similar situation as in the previous verse. The fallen donkey is likely a stray donkey; his load is too heavy for him, and without his owner to set him free, he is in trouble. Another issue is the identification of the referent of **it** (the third person masc. sg. suffix in *lô* and '*immô*)—is **it** the load or the male ass? But since the humanitarian concern is toward the donkey, rather than the load, the reference to the donkey seems more likely.

If so, the command would literally read: "refrain from abandoning (the load) to it [i.e., the donkey]; leaving (after setting the donkey free), leave with it [i.e., the donkey]." Leave the load behind since the donkey apparently is not able to bear it without falling under its weight. But you must take the donkey with you, and obeying the law of Exod 23:4, immediately return the stray donkey to its owner (who happens to be your adversary). The text probably assumes that the donkey's value is far greater than that of the goods. One must restore the greater of the two to the owner and let the owner recover the lesser of the two. Beside the godly consideration of one's enemy, there is the humanitarian concern to relieve the living creature from suffering.

(c) Judicial Justice for the Poor and Foreigners (23:6-9)

■ **6** Favoring the **poor people** out of compassion perverts justice (v 3) but so does unfavorable prejudice against the poor **in their lawsuits**. Since the poor people are relatively powerless, they are more vulnerable to injustice. Instead of being an advocate for the innocent poor, the witnesses might give false testimony against the poor, and the judges (the elders and leaders of a town) might let the poor be condemned without a fair hearing. They might be motivated to do so out of favoritism toward the rich and powerful or due to bribery.

■ **7** This law warns against agreeing to be a **false** witness to bring a false charge against an **innocent . . . person**. It also prohibits the judges from condemning an **honest** person **to death**. The litigants, the witnesses, and the judges might be motivated to commit such a crime by the various issues that this section on justice is concerned with: threats from or favoritism toward the rich and the powerful (v 2); pressure from the majority (v 2); compassion for or negative prejudice against the poor (vv 3, 6); relation of animosity (which may cause the judges to deny justice in the public court [vv 4-5]); acceptance of a bribe (v 8); and legal status as a foreigner or slave (vv 9, 12). This list is by no means exhaustive, but it touches on common political, social, economic, and racial factors for injustice in both the ancient and modern worlds.

The failures or criminality of the human judicial system will not go unnoticed by Yahweh, the Judge of all. That Yahweh **will not acquit** [or "justify"] **the guilty** means he will surely punish the guilty. Yahweh will judge and punish all those who are involved in the condemnation and execution of the innocent (e.g., Yahweh against Ahab in 1 Kgs 21:17-29; Samuel's sons who "accepted bribes and perverted justice" in 1 Sam 8:1, 3; and other prophetic indictments of Israel's leaders, judges, and common people).

■ **8** This law forbids accepting **a bribe** and entering into an agreement with the briber. The bribe can cause the eyewitness to not testify or a false witness to give a fabricated testimony. It can also cause the judge to pronounce a false verdict (condemning the blameless and acquitting the guilty) or to turn a blind eye to clear cases of injustice. Isaiah 1:23 indicts such judges who "love bribes" and who do not hear the cases of the fatherless and the widow. Since the bribe can easily corrupt witnesses and judges and cause them to pervert justice, it is unequivocally condemned in the Scripture (Deut 16:19; 1 Sam 8:3; Prov 17:23; Isa 1:23; Mic 3:11).

■ **9** This general prohibition against oppressing a **foreigner** could be read in light of the preceding or the following verses. If the former, it refers especially to an unjust ruling against a foreigner, who might be poor and also considered an "enemy." If the latter, it prohibits harvesting during the Sabbath Year and depriving the poor (which would include the fatherless, widows, and foreigners) of their provision from the land. It also prohibits ruthlessly working foreigners without giving them their Sabbath day rest (Exod 23:12). The Israelites' recent experiences of injustice and oppression do not excuse them of repeating such evil. Rather, knowing **how it feels to be foreigners** should arouse in them a great empathy toward fellow human beings who are now in their former social status and economic plight. They should treat the foreigners with the same compassion and kindness that they received from Yahweh.

(d) Justice through the Sabbath Rest (23:10-13)

■ **10-11** These verses institute the Sabbatical Year. The **seventh** day rest is here extended to the seventh **year** rest (v 11). The **land**, and by implication the people and **animals**, must cease from work on the **seventh year**. The text does not specify whether everyone observes a nationwide Sabbatical Year or each farmer has an individual Sabbatical Year (analogous to the seventh year emancipation of a Hebrew slave in 21:2). But the parallel texts (Lev 25:2-8; Deut 15:1-11) establish nationwide Sabbatical Years. The first Sabbatical Year was observed on the eighth year after the entry into the promised land (Lev 25:4). Also according to parallel texts, the Sabbatical Year begins on the Day of Atonement (the tenth day of the seventh month) with the sounding of the trumpet throughout the land (vv 8-10). The Day of Atonement marks liberty from moral and socioeconomic bondages. The Sabbatical Year law institutes compulsory emancipation of slaves (Exod 21:2; Deut 15:12), cancellation of debt (Deut 15:9), and fallowing of the land (Lev 25:2-5). The sabbatical law thus prevents perpetuation of inequalities and unsustainable agricultural and ecological practices.

Agriculturally, the beginning of the Sabbatical Year falls at the completion of the ingathering of the fruits. Thus, the Sabbatical Year starts with a seven-day celebration of the Festival of Ingathering / Booths). The beginning of the Sabbatical Year also coincides with the plowing and seed-sowing season. Letting **the land lie unplowed and unused** would allow the land, the owners, and the work animals to rest and be refreshed. The permanent slaves (who are not eligible for emancipation) and the foreigners (who are hired workers) are entitled and legally required to a yearlong rest from labor. This radical call to rest presupposes perennial abundant harvests (Lev 26:10) and three years' worth of harvest on the sixth year (25:20-21) so there is enough food to last until the eighth-year harvest.

During the Sabbatical Year, there shall be no sowing and harvesting (by the landowners). They may not harvest what the land produces on its own or prune the grapevines or pick the grapes or olives. Yet **the poor** and the foreigners may eat from it. Any crop leftover will feed **the wild animals**. The violation of this law would mean overwork and oppression of the people, work animals, and the land. It would be an unlawful exploitation of the labor of the slaves, foreigners, and work animals. It is a denial of their right to rest for a full year. It also deprives the slaves, foreigners, and poor of their share from the fallowing fields and trees. The Sabbatical Year ends with the reading of the law during the Festival of Ingathering / Booths in the seventh month of the following year (Deut 31:10).

■ **12** This verse mandates a humanitarian and egalitarian practice of the **seventh day . . . rest** (→ Exod 20:8-11). All must cease from **work**, even slaves and foreigners who are **living** and working in Israel as hired workers. Exodus 34:21 stipulates that all people and animals must rest on the seventh day, even at the time of plowing and of harvest; during the time of their hardest labor, they may have a chance to "catch their breath" and be **refreshed** one day a week.

■ **13** This verse is a reminder to obey **everything** Yahweh is commanding the people to do, perhaps the entire law. Most importantly, do not **invoke** [lit. "mention," "remember"] **the names of other gods**, making sacrifices to them and looking for help from them. Rather, the people should obliterate all idols and idolatry among themselves.

If the call to faithfulness is in relation to the Sabbath laws, then it is a call to trust in Yahweh who is the creator God who owns, leases, and blesses the land. The Israelites must repudiate all other gods, the gods of rain or wine or grain. They are unable to help. The people must observe the Sabbath rest on the seventh day and seventh year, fully trusting in Yahweh who is powerful and takes pleasure in blessing and providing. They are to enjoy Yahweh's provision and worship him.

FROM THE TEXT

These laws call God's people to promote and practice universal justice for all in imitation of the righteous and gracious God of Israel. The theological reason for this universal vision is stated in the covenant proposal: the whole earth belongs to Lord (19:5). The reason Israel is chosen to be God's very first special kingly and priestly nation is so that Israel can be the mediator of God's presence and blessing to all the nations of the earth. Moreover, that calling and purpose must be lived out first at home before it is taken abroad. All people, foreigners and natives alike, must be treated with equity, justice, mercy, and generosity.

The failure to comply results in crimes and injustices committed against humans, animals, and the land, which are grievous sins against God. The injustices and sins eventually result in the breakdown of the whole society and the fracture of the Israelites' covenant relationship with God. Such breakages, of course, imply an unfulfilled mission to mediate the reality and goodness of God to the rest of the world.

There is still the need for us to relate to our fellow human beings with dignity and justice, to care for the poor with consistency and generosity, to treat animals with kindness and care, and to steward the land with faithfulness and appreciation. Exclusive loyalty and devotion to the one true God calls us to such duties toward God's creation. The fulfillment of those duties expresses the goodness of the creator God and testifies to his existence in the world. Our obedience also proves genuine our faith in and love for God. As John says, "Whoever does not love their brother and sister, whom they have seen, cannot love God, whom they have not seen" (1 John 4:20). However, "We love because he first loved us" (v 19).

(5) Three Festivals to Yahweh (23:14-19)

BEHIND THE TEXT

Yahweh institutes for Israel three agricultural festivals to be celebrated. These festivals are celebrated in the order of the harvests (see Exod 34:18-23; Lev 23; Num 28—29; Deut 16:1-17). This text does not provide fixed dates for the festivals, but a festival calendar can be established based on the dates for the Passover and the Festival of Unleavened Bread given in Exod 12:6, 15-19 and the dates for the other two in Lev 23. These agricultural festivals are celebrated concomitantly with historical-religious commemorations.

(1) The Festival of Unleavened Bread is unambiguously associated with Passover. The festival coincides with the very first of the harvests and with the historical event of the exodus, which marks the first month (Aviv/Nisan) of the historical-religious calendar and the seventh of the agricultural-civil calendar. This month is called Nisan and corresponds to the modern mid-March to mid-April.

(2) The second festival is the Festival of Harvest (Weeks), which celebrates the harvest of wheat and traditionally commemorates the establishment of the covenant and administration of the law on Mount Sinai. Although the Bible does not make an explicit connection between this farmer's festival and the Sinai covenant (but see the book of *Jubilees* 6:17, dating from second century BC), the association is perhaps natural since the giving of the law closely follows Israel's arrival at Sinai "on the third new moon" (Exod 19:1 ESV) after the exodus. This festival occurs on the fiftieth day from the first day of the Festival of Unleavened Bread in the third month of the historical-religious calendar, on the month of Sivan (May/June). Thus, its Greek name is Pentecost ("fiftieth day"). This harvest festival becomes Jewish Shabuoth.

(3) The third festival is the Festival of Ingathering. This festival follows the harvest and processing of the grapes and olives in the fifth and sixth month

respectively of the historical-religious calendar. The festival itself takes place from the fourteenth to the twenty-first on the seventh month (Tishrei, September/October) of the historical-religious calendar, which is the first month of the agricultural-civil calendar. It celebrates the harvest and commemorates the Israelites' forty-year wilderness wandering period, during which they lived in temporary shelters or Sukkoth ("booths" or "tabernacles" [Lev 23:42-43]).

Israel's Calendar

The historical-religious calendar is first introduced in the Bible at the time of the exodus. The month in which Passover/Unleavened Bread is celebrated and the Israelites came out of Egypt is unequivocally referred to as the first month of the year (Exod 12:18; Lev 23:5; Num 9:1-5; 28:16-17; Ezra 6:19; Ezek 45:21).

The evidence for an agriculture-based calendar is not as numerous but is clearly present in the Pentateuch. The first twenty-two days of the seventh month (of the historical-religious calendar) is a period of both conclusion and commencement of an agriculture-based calendar in ancient Israel. On the first day of the seventh month (September/October), the coming new year is announced (Lev 23:24; thus, the postbiblical Jewish celebration of Rosh Hashanah ["head of the year"] on the first day of the seventh month). Accordingly, the number of years is counted from this month, and the Sabbatical Year and the Year of Jubilee start with the Day of Atonement on the tenth of the seventh month (Lev 25:8-9). In this way, Yahweh juxtaposes the day that marks the spiritual freedom from sin and death with the day that declares the economic freedom from debt and slavery. The point could not be clearer; as Yahweh freely forgives the Israelites of their sins and penalties, so must the Israelites forgive their fellow Israelites of their debts and penalties. On the same month, on the eighth day of the Festival of Ingathering / Booths, "the closing assembly" is held (Lev 23:36). This marks the closing of the festival and the closing of the agricultural year (note the expression "at the end of the year" in Exod 23:16 and "at the end" in Deut 31:10). The agricultural activity then starts with the former (or early) rain that makes the grounds optimal for plowing. The planting of seeds closely follows plowing in the subsequent month.

IN THE TEXT

■ 14 This verse literally reads: *three feet to celebrate a festival to me in a year*, invoking the image of a walking pilgrimage. Other texts (Deut 16:2, 11, 15-16) also emphasize pilgrimage, insisting that the festivals should be at a place where Yahweh chooses as a dwelling for his name. The requirement for the entire household to celebrate the festivals with the Levites and the poor of their towns (see Deut 16:11, 14; 26:11) points to the celebration of the festivals at local sanctuaries (Deut 14:22-23, 28-29; 26:12), officiated by local priests living in priestly or Levitical towns all over Israel (1 Chr 13:2; 2 Chr 11:13-14;

13:9; 31:15, 19). However, later in Israel's history, there is evidence for centralized festivals in Jerusalem (1 Kgs 12:27-28; 2 Chr 30:1-27; Neh 8:15-16).

■ **15** The Festival of Unleavened Bread is celebrated concurrently with Passover (→ Exod 12:14-20 and "Aviv" in 13:4). For seven days, all must **eat bread made without yeast**, to commemorate the haste in which they departed Egypt (see 12:11, 33). The second day of the festival is "from the time you begin to put the sickle to the standing grain" of barley (Deut 16:9) and every farmer offers to Yahweh a sheaf of the first of the harvest as a wave offering (Lev 23:10-12). After the offering is made, the Israelites are permitted to eat the new grain (vv 12-14).

In the land, Yahweh blesses the Israelites with overabundance of the produce of the land, thus **no one is to appear before** Yahweh **empty-handed** (Exod 34:20; Deut 16:16-17). Each farmer is to bring a gift to honor Yahweh in proportion to the blessing received (v 17). This requirement is stipulated for all three festivals. It is a standard expression of grateful worship.

Ultimately, not only are firstfruits or token offerings made during the festivals, but a full tithe of all harvests are required. Part of it is eaten during the festivals, and part is given to the Levites and the poor (Deut 14:22-23, 27; 26:11). Every three years, the whole tithe is stored presumably in Levitical towns for the purpose of uninterrupted provision to those without property or harvests, namely, Levites, the poor, foreigners, widows, and orphans (Deut 14:22, 27-29).

■ **16a** The Festival of Harvest (Weeks/Shabuoth/Pentecost) celebrates the **firstfruits** of wheat harvest, as clarified by 34:22. From this festival, one can conclude that the ripening of wheat typically took about fifty days from the beginning of the barley harvest. Leviticus 23:15-21, Num 28:26-31, and Deut 16:9-12 give further instructions for the festival, including the types of offerings to be made, the required secession from work during this festival, and the inclusion of the Levites and the underprivileged of the society, such as the foreigners, the fatherless, and the widows.

■ **16b** The Festival of Ingathering celebrates the fruit harvest and the completion, processing, and storage of all harvests (Deut 16:13). The festival begins five days after the Day of Atonement. The expression **at the end of the year** (equivalent to "at the turn of the year" in Exod 34:22) refers to the end of the agricultural year. The Israelites are to "take branches from luxuriant trees— from palms, willows and other leafy trees—and rejoice before the LORD your God for seven days" (Lev 23:40). It is a very joyous festival with offerings and sacrifices made to the Lord each day (v 37). Everyone is to observe sabbatical rest on the first and eighth days.

■ **17** This law is repeated in 34:23 and Deut 16:16. All Israelite **men** are required to make the pilgrimage and **appear before** Yahweh to present tithes and offerings at the time of each festival. However, this does not mean that women are excluded. Other texts make it clear that all Israelites participate in the festivals (Deut 16:11, 14; 26:11; Neh 8:15-16). A woman may excuse herself for a number of reasons, including pregnancy and nursing (see Hannah in 1 Sam 1:21-23). This text may indicate that in the context of a pilgrimage to the central sanctuary, only men are required to attend.

■ **18-19** These four laws are an addendum to the three aforementioned festivals. (1) The first law concerning **yeast** (v 18) here regulates that the paschal lamb must not be slaughtered while the offerer still has yeast in the house (Sarna 2004, 113; see the parallel passage in 34:25 that specifically ties the content of the first two laws here to Passover rites). Furthermore, it requires the grain offering that accompanies the festival burnt offerings (Lev 23:12-13, 18, 37) be free of yeast.

(2) In addition to a burnt offering, other animal sacrifices are offered during these festivals. Their **fat** must be burnt before or in the **morning**. The fat of the **festival offerings** does not refer to the fat attached to the meat, but to the fat that covers kidney, liver, or intestine of the victim (e.g., Lev 3:3-5). Any leftover parts of the paschal lamb, including the fat, must be burnt up in the morning (Exod 12:10). The fat of the sin offering and fellowship offering sacrificed during the Festival of Weeks (Lev 23:19) must be removed and burned up at the altar as the share belonging to Yahweh (chs 3—4). During Sukkoth, besides the daily offerings and sacrifices, there are voluntary sacrifices of votive offerings and freewill offerings (23:38). Since no fat of an ox, sheep, or goat may be ingested at all (7:23), their fat is burnt up on the day of the slaughter and **must not be kept until the morning** (Exod 23:19).

(3) The third law requires the **firstfruits** to be offered to Yahweh. Firstfruits (*bikkûrîm* or *rē'šît* or the combination of the two terms) often refer to the firstfruits of the wheat harvest (see 23:16, 19; 34:22). Thus, the Festival of Weeks at the time of the wheat harvest is also known as the Festival of Firstfruits. But in other passages "firstfruits" refers to the first of any harvest of grains, fruits, and wool (e.g., Num 18:12-13; Deut 18:4).

(4) The fourth law appears in the context of the Festival of Firstfruits or Weeks here and in 34:26 and in the context of prohibiting consumption of unclean animals in Deut 14:21. Among various options of interpretation, it is best to regard this primarily as the prohibition of a pagan ritual in which a kid would be boiled in its **mother's milk**. There may also be a humanitarian motivation, showing sensitivity to an animal's feelings, akin to other biblical laws that prohibit slaughtering a livestock and its young on the same day (Lev 22:28), or taking the mother from the chicks or eggs (Deut 22:6), or harnessing an ox and a donkey together (Deut 22:10; Sarna 2004, 113; Propp 2006, 285).

285

FROM THE TEXT

Christians from the early church to the present have often found abiding theological significance in the festivals by observing their fulfillment in Christ and the new covenant. On a general level, the Israelite festivals emphasize the communal and sacramental character of biblical faith. The commemorative festivals mark sacred times and places of God's mighty acts of salvation or his grace-giving presence and draw celebrants into an abiding communion with him.

On a more specific level, the Israelite festivals anticipate greater fulfillment in Christ and the new life he gives. The Passover lamb typifies Christ who is slain for the salvation of the world. The unleavened bread also corresponds to Christ, the bread from heaven, who is completely free of sin and evil, symbolized in the yeast that must be purged from God's people (see Exod 13:7; Matt 16:6-12; 1 Cor 5:6-8; Gal 5:9).

It is significant that the Festival of Harvest (Weeks/Shabuoth/Pentecost) is the setting for the initial outpouring of the Holy Spirit and the launching of the church in Acts 2. Through the presence and work of the Holy Spirit, the external manifest presence of God and the law written on the tablets of stone become internal realities that are proven by the manifestation of the external "fruits." Interestingly, the Festival of Harvest, which celebrates the firstfruits, finds parallels and resonances in the NT language of firstfruits used for Jesus, the Holy Spirit, and the early believers. Jesus is the "firstfruits" of those who will be bodily resurrected (1 Cor 15:20, 23), the Spirit's work is the firstfruits that promises full eschatological adoption and redemption (Rom 8:23), and the early believers are named as firstfruits from all of God's creation (Jas 1:18; see Rev 14:4).

The final ingathering (Tabernacle/Booths/Sukkoth) and sorting of the agricultural harvest anticipates the final ingathering and sorting of the spiritual harvest to which several of Jesus' parables refer (e.g., Matt 13:24-30, 36-43, 47-50). For the NT writers, the firstfruits promise the fullness of the harvest of souls at the last ingathering.

While Christians are not obligated to celebrate the Israelite festivals (not least because of different harvest seasons in different regions around the globe), these ceremonies do instruct us to remember what God has done in the past, to celebrate what God is doing in the present, and to hope for what God will do in the future in conjunction with the person and work of Jesus Christ and the Holy Spirit.

4. Promises Concerning the Land (23:20-33)

The covenant laws conclude with various promises for the people's faithful observance. This follows the typical covenantal structure evident in some ancient Near Eastern treaties (especially Hittite treaties), in which blessings for obedience and curses for disobedience are articulated after the covenant stipulations. In this case, God promises the entry into and conquest of the promised land, as well as a blessed life within the land.

The blessings in this section (which are repeated in Deut 7) can be understood theologically as an overturn of the evil effects of sin noted in Gen 3:14-19. (1) Instead of living under the serpent's hostility against the woman and her descendants (v 15), the people of God will enjoy peace as all hostile enemies—be they nations (Exod 23:23, 27, 31), wild beasts (v 29), or deadly diseases (v 25)—will be driven out from the land. (2) Instead of suffering from miscarriages or barrenness/sterility or premature deaths (Gen 3:16), the Israelites will enjoy uncomplicated and pleasant childbearing and childrearing (Exod 23:26). (3) Instead of struggling with unyielding, cursed grounds and hostile environments (Gen 3:17-19), God's people will be lavished with extreme abundance from the fertile and fruitful land (Exod 23:25). Lists of covenant blessings are given in Lev 26:1-13 and Deut 28:1-13, which clearly show the comprehensive nature of the reversal of the evil manifestations of the postfall curses on the serpent (Gen 3:14) and the ground (v 17). Yahweh intends the Israelites' faithful covenant life in the blessed land to reflect the ideal life of the garden of Eden.

IN THE TEXT

a. Promise of an Angel (23:20-23)

■ **20** In Moses' first theophanic encounter with God, "the angel of the LORD" appeared to Moses in fire on the bush (3:2). When the Israelites came out of Egypt, the "angel of God"—presumably the same as the angel of the Lord—led and protected the Israelite army with the pillars of cloud and fire (14:19). Here the Lord promises that **an angel**, who has the divine name and has the same authority as Yahweh (23:21-22), will lead them into the promised land (v 23; repeated in 32:34). Verse 21 of ch 23 refers to this angel as a being distinct from Yahweh and the subsequent two verses identify the angel with Yahweh by using the third person ("he" or "my angel") and the first person ("I") interchangeably. In all these passages, the angel, whether it occurs alone or with the qualifying "of the LORD" or "of God," seems to refer to the revealed or manifested aspects of Yahweh that may be either visible (such as fire or cloud) or invisible (such as terror or dread). They are neither clearly distinguishable from nor easily identifiable with Yahweh (but see "angel" in 32:34).

Here, then, the **sending** of an angel **ahead** of Israel apparently is not in contrast to but in harmony with Yahweh's own accompaniment with Israel, as before (14:19). The angel will **guard** and protect from any enemy **along the way** to the promised land, even as the Israelites already experienced the angelic protection at the Red Sea (14:19-20) and divine victory over the Amalekites at Rephidim (17:8-16).

■ **21** The angel has the unique attribute of having the divine **Name . . . in him**, which means he is the manifestation of Yahweh's presence and character (see 33:19; 34:5, 14). As such, the angel has the same authority that Yahweh has. When he speaks, it is as if Yahweh is speaking. It is, thus, imperative that the Israelites obey and **not rebel against him**. In the context of covenant-making (chs 19—24), rebellion implies breaking of the covenant. Like Yahweh, the angel presumably has the prerogative to pardon (→ "forgiving wickedness, rebellion, and sin" in 34:7b). However, the angel **will not forgive . . . rebellion** against him (see the parallel phrase "will not acquit the guilty" in 23:7). Yahweh's alliance with the present generation of Israelites is contingent upon their obedience.

■ **22** Yahweh promises to **oppose those who oppose** the Israelites even as Yahweh promised to Abraham "whoever curses you I will curse" (Gen 12:3). This expression indicates that the natives have the option of abandoning the land instead of opposing and being destroyed.

■ **23** Yahweh promises to **go** before the Israelites and to destroy the native peoples of the promised land of Canaan. It is Yahweh who fights for Israel (as in Josh 23:10) even though Yahweh will use the people of Israel as an ordained instrument in such warfare (see Deut 7:2, 16 and Josh 11:11; → Exod 3:8 for comments on the list of the native peoples of the land).

b. Promise of Blessings for Faithfulness (23:24-26)

■ **24** Words from the second commandment (20:5) are repeated here: **Do not bow down . . . or serve/worship.** Yahweh absolutely prohibits worship of the **gods** of the inhabitants of the land. Israel must not adopt **their** cultic **practices** in the worship of Yahweh. The natives' **sacred stones** (or "long, standing stones") are erected in high places of sacrifice and worship. They are thought to be "the repository of a divinity or spirit" (Sarna 2004, 114). Yahweh emphatically commands: **Demolish, you must demolish them. And shatter, you must shatter their pillars.** All idols, idolatry, sacred stones, and cultic practices must be destroyed and eradicated from the land. The Israelites' violent destruction of the native cultic objects represents Yahweh's severe righteous judgment on these cults and serves as a warning against idolatry for them and their posterity.

■ **25** Following a strong command for an absolute purgation of native religions, Yahweh summons the Israelites to serve **the LORD** their **God**. Yahweh promises **blessing** upon the nation whose people are absolutely loyal to him. The blessing is collective; it is for the whole nation. Yahweh will bless the land with fertility and wholesomeness. The removal of famines, droughts, and plagues represent the removal of the postfall curse on the land (Gen 3:17-19) and reinstatement of the creational blessing of the land.

■ **26** Another manifestation of the postfall curses will be removed. The people of God will not experience barrenness that the matriarchs of Israel struggled with and overcame with divine grace. They will be extremely fruitful (see Exod 1:7, 20). God will also grant **a full life span**; there will be no infant mortality or premature deaths, whatever the cause—war, crime, capital punishment, plagues, famine, wild beasts, diseases and illnesses, or direct divine punishment. The longevity promised is not just individual but also national. The faithful people will be allowed to live in the good **land** indefinitely. Joshua 23:16 and other texts, however, warn that rebellion to the covenant will result in swift removal of the people from the good land.

c. Promise of Divine Help for the Conquest (23:27-31)

■ **27** Moses' song already prophetically and poetically described the **terror** and dread that would seize the nations upon hearing of Yahweh's exploits (15:14-16). According to Deut 2:25, when the Israelites begin to dispossess the nations on the east side of the Jordan River, then Yahweh begins to terrify the nations. The Hebrew idiomatic expression "to give the neck" used in this verse (also in 2 Sam 22:41; Ps 18:40 [41 HB]) means "to cause to **turn their backs and run**." Yahweh is an ally to his faithful people and will terrify their **enemies**. Israel later learns through a bitter defeat that when they are in rebellion, they, too, are treated as God's foes; Yahweh fights against them, causing them to turn their backs and run before their enemies (Josh 7:8, 12).

■ **28** Together with the previous verse, v 28 gives the impression that Yahweh's "terror" and **the hornet** (which are most likely synonymous parallel terms) will effectively accomplish much of the expulsion of the peoples mentioned. The Hebrew for "hornet" (ṣirʿāh; also used in Deut 7:20; Josh 24:12) is variously interpreted as the following: (1) a military invasion by a powerful nation, such as Egypt, that would cripple the natives' military power, which is unlikely, since the conquest narratives in Num 21, 25, and Joshua make no mention of any such invasion; (2) a forerunning plague of literal stinging insects that cause the native people to voluntarily abandon their land, which is possible, but unlikely since the natives and their kings, rather than abandoning their homeland, typically joined forces to defend their land and to destroy the Israelites (see Josh 10—11); (3) more plausibly, a kind of supernatural panic that God would bring upon the enemies of Israel at the battlefields as Josh

10—11 indicate. The Hebrew term for "hornet" most likely represents any unexpected physical, psychological, or strategic "blow" from Yahweh that would cause the Israelites' otherwise invincible enemies to crumble—whether it be an impenetrable wall falling down (Josh 6); inexplicable terror, dread, panic, or confusion (10:10); or a hailstorm or other natural disaster (v 11). Whatever its precise identity, it ultimately ensures Israel's overwhelming victory over the otherwise indomitable opponents.

The three native nations mentioned—**Hivites, Canaanites and Hittites**—might not be the only groups that will be affected in this way. They are likely representatives of all the peoples of the land, mentioned for their more significant size and strengths. Joshua 24:11-12 credits the expulsion of the inhabitants of the land west of Jordan (Amorites, Perizzites, Canaanites, Hittites, Girgashites, Hivites, and Jebusites) and the two Transjordanian Amorite kingdoms of Sihon and Og (see Num 21:21-35; Josh 2:10; 9:10; 24:8) to the "hornet," rather than the Israelites' military strength.

■ **29** Driving **out** the natives prematurely before there is a sufficient number of Israelites to repopulate **the land** would result in the fertile land becoming **desolate** and populated by **wild animals** that are **too numerous** (see Deut 7:22). Additional reasons for incremental conquest are given in Judg 2:20—3:4. Yahweh will test the faithfulness of later generations of Israelites by means of the Canaanites (Judg 2:22; 3:1, 4). Yahweh will also use the Canaanites to train the Israelites in the ways of warfare (3:1-2).

■ **30** This verse gives a further explanation of incremental (**little by little**) conquest: the need for population growth for full possession. Numbers 34:2-3 shows that the initial conquest and settlement took place in a much smaller territory due to Israel's small population (see Josh 12 for the initial boundaries, with explanations of the land left unconquered in 13:1-6, 13; 16:10; Judg 1:21, 27-33). But under Yahweh's blessings of fertility (Exod 23:26), the Israelites eventually increase in population and take full **possession of the land**. As in the blessings of Gen 1:28, there is an implicit connection between multiplication of offspring and dominion of the earth/land, although here the dominion includes defeat of those who oppose Yahweh.

■ **31** This verse gives a poetic sketch (**Sea to . . . Sea, desert to . . . River**), rather than "a functional geographical description of Israel's borders" as found in Num 34:2-12 (Jacob 1992, 735). The expressions **I will give into your hands . . . you will drive them out** indicate that what Yahweh grants, the Israelites must contend to possess. As the Creator and Owner of the earth, the **land** is Yahweh's to give. But unlike the exodus from Egypt, which Yahweh accomplished for Israel, notwithstanding the contributions of Moses and Aaron, the Israelites must actively conquer and possess the land. David and Solomon later take full possession of the territories promised here, but due to rebellion, that possession is short-lived.

d. Prohibition of Covenants with the Natives (23:32-33)

■ **32** The Israelites must not **make a covenant with** the natives or **their gods**. However, the Israelites later make a treaty with the Gibeonites (Josh 9). Once the covenant is made, although under deception and compulsion (without consulting Yahweh), the Israelites are bound by the covenant obligations to let the Gibeonites live.

■ **33** The idolaters must not be allowed to **live** among them. They must be destroyed or driven out of the land. Otherwise syncretism is inevitable. Tolerance of and cohabitation with the idolaters and repeated exposure to their practices will gradually wear down Israel's abhorrence for and resistance to idolatry. Ultimately they will lead to the adoption of pagan practices. This is the unfortunate reality of Israel's later history.

FROM THE TEXT

The promises in this text, though given to a people who were on their way to the promised land, remind the readers today that God is concerned with the well-being of his people, the defeat of those who wage war against them, and their security, productivity, and prosperity. However, the joining of the well-being of God's people with the defeat of their enemies in the Israelite holy war is obviously controversial in our day. Did God hate the non-Israelite peoples and wish to destroy them for that reason? Is this an instance of xenophobic violence? Does this warrant genocide in the name of God? The answer to these questions is "No!" Several observations need to be made here: (1) The destruction (of Jericho in Josh 6:24, Ai in 8:19-20, 28, and Hazor in 11:11) or displacement of the inhabitants (of all other cities; see Num 33:52) of Canaan must be located in its ancient religious and social context and interpreted through the lens of God's covenant relationship with Israel and God's theocratic reign in Israel. In particular, holy war was God's instrument of temporal judgment of the sins of Canaanites (Gen 15:16; Exod 23:33). Central concern for the expulsion of the natives was not racism or nationalism but the establishment of a theocratic, holy nation in the land. In addition, only incontestable direct command from God (which no post-Israel governing body can claim to have received) warranted the holy war during a limited period of time in Israel's early history (Num 33:52; Deut 25:19; 1 Sam 15:3). (2) The conquest of Canaan took place not through a widespread violent destruction of all the Canaanite cities in a short period of time, but through a gradual and incremental occupation (→ Introduction and Exod 23:27-31). This implies that all the inhabitants of Canaan (other than those three cities destroyed) had the choice of voluntarily abandoning their cities, instead of putting up a bloody fight and being driven out of the land. The natives of Canaan also had the opportunity to learn about the Lord and enter into a covenant relationship with him under the legal provisions for the inclusion of foreigners in the Israelite community (e.g., → Behind the Text and In the Text for 12:43-51) during the four hundred years of the period of the Judges. In other words, displacement was by no means the only option that most of the Canaanites had. (3) Israel's covenant relationship with God King comes not only with blessings for obedience but also with curses for disobedience (Lev 26:3-13; Deut 28:1-13). God denounces and punishes sin and evil not only in other nations but also in Israel—as Israel's near extinction and exile from the land demonstrate. In other words, when the tenants or occupants of the land defile the land with sin and evil, then the landlord (God) destroys or drives them out of the land, regardless of the tenants' ethnicity or covenant relationship with God (→ Exod 15:17). (4) While the wider canon confirms that those who curse Abraham's descendants will be cursed, God's intention is to bless all the peoples of the earth through Abraham's descendants (→ 19:6; also see Gen 12:2-3). (5) In light of the above points, this text, understood rightly, cannot be used to authorize or legitimize waging modern-day wars, which are often undertaken for various ideological or political or economic reasons, but often under the guise of the removal of evil powers. Rather, this text emphasizes God's opposition to and judgment of evil, God's concern for the wholeness of the land through the removal of those who defile the land, and God's boundless mercy toward the displaced Israelites (and other people groups) who recently have been rescued from a long-standing oppression.

While the promises in this passage do not apply literally to Christians today, they highlight the importance of exclusive loyalty and absolute faithfulness to God. Speaking to a people in exile, God laments the Israelites' idolatry in striking terms: "My people have committed two sins: They have forsaken me, the spring of living water, and have dug their own cisterns, broken cisterns that cannot hold water" (Jer 2:13). God is the Israelites' only source of life, but they habitually turn away from God and turn toward the world around them. Seeking to find the source of life and security in someone or something other than in the living God is futile. The Israelites only exhaust themselves in serving idols. Even if there are (deceptive) temporal successes and satisfaction in serving other gods, there is no eternal life or reward in serving them. They are "broken cisterns," and those who serve them become broken themselves.

Like the Israelites at Sinai, God calls Christians to trust in God's provision, protection, and guidance, to put away all idolatry, and abandon trust in what the world has to offer (e.g., money, pleasure, power, reputation; see Rom 12:2; 1 Cor 10:14). Distrust and unbelief lead us to make compromises or make covenants with "idols," loving, trusting, and pursuing the world and the things in the world (see 1 John 2:15-17).

5. Ratification of the Covenant (24:1-18)

a. Confirmation of the Covenant (24:1-11)

BEHIND THE TEXT

The covenant laws are followed by the covenant confirmation. There are several parallels between portions of Exod 19—20 (especially 19:3-11 and 20:18-21) and this text, some of which are noted below. Some commentators hold that both passages refer to the same incident, but there are sufficient differences between the two texts to indicate that they refer to two different covenant-making encounters with Yahweh. The events described in chs 19—20 refer chiefly to the giving of the Decalogue to the people through Moses. In contrast, this text is primarily about blood atonement, which confirms the covenant relationship that is initiated in ch 19 (vv 5-8) and makes possible communion with God, which is the ultimate goal of the covenant (Exod 24:1, 9-11).

IN THE TEXT

(1) Invitation of the Leaders to Mount Sinai (24:1-2)

■ **1** Moses is already on the mountain (20:21), so the command to **come up** involves going down and coming up again with the seventy-three, whom Yahweh invites. Joshua is conspicuously missing from the list of the invitees. Perhaps in the absence of all the major leaders from the camp, the Israelites are left under the charge of the commander of the army (see 17:9-13). Yahweh's command to come up is implemented in 24:9. **Nadab and Abihu** are Aaron's sons, first introduced in the Aaronic genealogy (6:23). Along with their father **Aaron** and brothers Eleazar and Ithamar, they are later anointed as priests (→ 28:1). The **seventy** [the number of perfection and completeness; see 1:5] **elders** are mentioned again in Num 11:16-17, 24-25 as administrative and judicial "officials" (11:16). There, they are given some of the Spirit of the Lord that is upon Moses. All seventy-four people are to prostrate themselves in awe and reverence and **worship** Yahweh.

■ **2** Although other leaders are invited to **come** up on the mountain with Moses (unlike Exod 19:23-24), **Moses alone** may **approach the Lord** and enter his presence (which Yahweh commands Moses to do in 24:12 and Moses obeys in vv 13-18). The repeated warning against the people venturing up the mountain issued in 19:21-22, 24 is once again given in 24:2, emphasizing the deadliness of a presumptuous approach toward the Lord.

(2) People's Consent to the Covenant Terms (24:3)

■ **3** This verse clearly parallels 19:8, where the people give a general consent to live under Yahweh's government. Here, the people hear all the **laws** from **Moses** and then unanimously commit to obey Yahweh and live by the laws given. Either Moses delivers a summary of all the words of Yahweh or naturally possesses a photographic memory or Yahweh supernaturally enables him to recall all the **words**.

(3) The Covenant Witnesses and Rites (24:4-8)

■ **4** Verses 4-8 summarize the covenant ratification ritual, which begins with the writing of the laws by Moses (v 4*a*). With the people's willing agreement to obey the laws, **Moses** commits to writing **everything the LORD had said**. The written laws serve as a covenant witness for or against the covenant partner Israelites. The next step in the ritual is the building of **an altar** by Moses for sacrifice to Yahweh (v 4*b*; as he has done before in 17:15). The material for the altar is not specified in either case, but Moses presumably builds it in accordance with the instructions given in 20:24-25. Later, Yahweh gives specific regulations for making a bronze altar for permanent use in offering daily sacrifices at the tabernacle (27:1-8 and 30:1-10). The making of twelve stone pillars that represent the twelve tribes follows this. The altar likely represents the divine party in the covenant, with the pillars representing the human party and Moses serving as the representative mediator between the two parties. As such, they serve as covenant witnesses that at Mount Sinai Yahweh made a covenant with the Israelites.

■ **5** The next step in the ritual is the offering of **burnt offerings** and **fellowship offerings**, carried out by **young Israelite men** sent by Moses. Burnt offerings indicate total dedication to Yahweh; fellowship offerings convey peaceful relations with Yahweh. These two offerings are mentioned together in 20:24. Such peaceful covenant communion with God is made possible only by blood atonement (24:6).

■ **6** Verse 6 indicates Moses' role as the officiating priest in the ritual of covenant-making. He puts **half of the blood** into **bowls** to use for sprinkling the people (see v 8). He splashes the other half of the blood on the **altar**. Blood is spattered on the altar elsewhere in the book of Exodus (29:16, 20, 21; also see other examples in Lev 1:5, 11; 3:2; Num 18:17; Deut 12:27). Through the blood rite, Yahweh and his people enter into a covenant union.

■ **7** Moses next reads **the Book of the Covenant**, the entirety of the laws given on Mount Sinai (Exod 24:4). This act fits the pattern of later covenant confirmation of renewal ceremonies, in which the terms of the covenant are read publicly (see Josh 24:25-27; 2 Kgs 23:2; Neh 8:5-9). Thus, the **people** of Israel hear the entire law for the second time (Exod 24:3), and they unreservedly and unanimously consent to **obey** the law without exception. Of course, it will not be long before the people fail miserably to keep the most basic and important commands of the Lord (32:1-6).

■ **8** Verse 8 reports Moses' sprinkling of blood on the people with his proclamation: **This is the blood of the covenant**. The blood speaks of the forgiving and atoning work of Yahweh that makes covenant relationship possible between holy Yahweh and the sinful people. The Sinai covenant is made **in accordance with all these words**, which means the covenant people are bound to the Mosaic legal stipulations and the curses and blessings that come with them.

(4) Covenant Theophany and Meeting on Mount Sinai (24:9-11)

■ **9-11** The covenant ratification ritual continues in vv 9-11; now, it is time for the participation of the **seventy elders** in the ceremony along with **Moses, Aaron, Nadab,** and **Abihu** (v 9). They ascend Mount Sinai in response to Yahweh's invitation (see v 1), and there they see **the God of Israel** (v 10). The description of what they see is limited to the **feet** and what lies underneath: something like an expanse or a transparent **pavement made of** precious stone, **as bright blue as the sky**. The terms and concepts used to describe the vision of God are similar to those used for Ezekiel's visions of God (Ezek 1:26). This clear and peaceful vision of Yahweh starkly contrasts with the smoke-covered and heaven- and earth-quaking theophany of Exod 19:16-19. The difference is explained by their purpose of either inducing the fear of Yahweh (20:20) or communing with Yahweh (24:11).

Anticipating the potential dangers of seeing God (see 33:20), 24:11 assures that **God did not raise his hand against** them. Exodus 33:20-23 is emphatic that no mortal can see Yahweh's face and live. Perhaps all that the **leaders** could see looking heavenward was the transparent pavement and God's "feet" above it, due to the intense radiance surrounding the manifestation of Yahweh's glory (see Ezek 1:26-28). While beholding God's self-manifestation, the noblemen partake of a meal that seals the covenant and fellowship, and then they commune with God. Perhaps they eat and drink their portion of the fellowship offerings slaughtered and sacrificed in Exod 24:5 (for fellowship offerings, → 29:19-26).

FROM THE TEXT

The brief visible appearance of the Holy God to Moses and the elders of Israel at Mount Sinai foreshadows Jesus' brief revelation of his glory to his disciples in the transfiguration, both of which are more fully realized in the abiding presence of the Holy Spirit to all those who believe in Jesus Christ. In this narrative, the "dangerously holy God" enters into the sinful world of the elders of Israel in "generous self-giving," and the only thing the elders could do is to "gaze upon God" (Brueggemann 1994, 881-83) in reverence and fear, and, presumably upon divine invitation, partake of Communion meal in amazement and gratitude.

This Sinai revelation of God's holiness finds parallel in Jesus' powerful but brief revelation of his glory in the transfiguration narrative (Matt 17:1-13; Mark 9:2-13; Luke 9:28-36). Like the elders at Sinai, the faithful disciples of

Jesus are given an intimate glimpse into the reality of God's holiness and transcendence (Brueggemann 1994, 883).

But what produces unwavering faith, an enduring transformation of heart, and radical obedience to God (which neither the elders nor the disciples who were given a glimpse of divine glory on a mountain had) is the abiding presence of the Holy Spirit. Though the steadfast presence of the Holy Spirit typically comes without the overwhelming visual manifestations of the mountains, it is he who transforms the fearful disciples into martyrs of the Gospel of Jesus Christ.

If our contemporary worship is devoid of wonderment and the mystery of God's holiness and if our Christian (individual and ecclesial) life has no evidence of radical obedience to the demands of Jesus Christ, then we must stop to wonder. Have we failed to seek and receive the glorious and abiding presence of the Holy Spirit, whom Jesus promised the Father would give to all those who ask (Luke 11:13)? Or have we shut out the holy presence of God with worship filled with human agenda? Or is the holy presence of God simply unnoticed by the worshipping community which pays little attention to the intimate, glorious, revitalizing, and transforming presence of God in their midst?

God appears to his people in a veiled form, yet in a way, God is truly known and seen by them. This passage raises an important biblical-theological question: can one see God and live? Later in the book of Exodus, God tells Moses that one cannot (33:20, 23), but in this passage, the leaders do! Which one is correct? Or can both be correct in some way? One approach is to say that God can be seen in a "veiled" form but cannot be seen (at least without harm to the one seeing) in his unmitigated, unmediated glory. In this view, every theophany in Exodus involves God appearing in a veiled, visible form, whether it is the burning bush (3:2-3), the pillar of cloud/fire (13:21-22), the fiery storm on Mount Sinai (19:16-19; 20:18; 24:15-17), the feet on a gleaming pavement (as in this passage), or the cloud over the tabernacle (40:34-38). In all these instances, God is seen in one sense, but in another sense, remains hidden, veiled, or covered by some natural element.

In Jesus' farewell discourse (John 13:18—16:33), he teaches that whoever knows Jesus knows the Father as well and whoever sees Jesus sees the Father as well (14:7, 9). Jesus Christ is the ultimate theophany, whose incarnation surpasses and fulfills all earlier theophanies. By seeing Jesus' glory (1:14), we come to know and experience God's character and ways because Jesus is in the Father and the Father is in him (14:10-11) and Jesus makes this Father known to us (1:18). However, according to Paul, our present vision and understanding of God are still partial until the day we see God face-to-face (1 Cor 13:12). Even God's self-revelation in Jesus Christ involves a veiling that accommodates human frailty. As Barth states, "In revealing Himself in this way, He also conceals Himself. He reveals His glory to faith, which sees it in this hiddenness" (Barth 1957, 55). God is both revealed and hidden, so that we may see God and still live.

b. Moses' Ascent into Yahweh's Presence (24:12-18)

BEHIND THE TEXT

Upon the completion of the covenant rites, Moses is summoned to ascend the mountain to approach the glorious presence of Yahweh to receive the tablets of stone. This unit anticipates the end of Exodus (40:34-38) in two ways: the cloud on the mountain that veils divine glory (24:15) corresponds to the cloud that covers the tabernacle, both of which serve the same purpose of veiling divine glory (40:35); and Yahweh's glory within the cloud on the mountain (24:16) corresponds to the glory that fills the tabernacle, also covered by the cloud (40:34). In both accounts, Moses is not allowed to see God's unveiled glory. Moses is permitted to encounter the glory of the Lord only as veiled by the cloud and then later shielded by the tabernacle that separates them. Yet, Moses' privilege to enter and remain in Yahweh's manifest presence in the form of a theophanic cloud underlines the uniqueness of Moses' relationship with Yahweh as the chosen and highly favored mediator between Yahweh and Israel.

IN THE TEXT

(1) Preparation to Ascend Mount Sinai (24:12-14)

■ 12 Yahweh's command to Moses to ascend the mountain and Moses' instruction to the elders to "wait here" (in v 14) assume that Moses and the seventy-three already descended the mountain after the vision of Yahweh on Mount Sinai (vv 9-11). Yahweh's words to Moses to **come up to me** and **stay here** signify special favor, intimacy, and a prolonged encounter with Yahweh. Previously, Yahweh invited Moses to the top of the mountain, but not to his presence. Now, Yahweh desires to have Moses in his presence. In such a context, Yahweh will give Moses **the tablets of stone** that contain the covenant **law and commandments**, written by Yahweh (32:16-17). Passages in Exod 34:1, 28 and Deut 10:4 make it explicit that Yahweh writes on the stone tablets nothing other than the Ten Commandments. Moses later smashes these stone tablets (Exod 32:19), but Yahweh replaces them.

■ 13 Although **Joshua** was not included among the seventy-three invitees, he alone is invited and accompanies **Moses** who **went up on the mountain**. Joshua in this way is singled out as Moses' **aide** or attendant who is given the unique privilege of witnessing Moses' extraordinary encounters with Yahweh (see "Joshua" in 33:11; also see Num 11:28; Josh 1:1). Thus, Joshua is honored and trained in preparation for his future leadership as Moses' successor.

■ **14** This verse indicates the arrangements necessary to prepare for Moses' stay on the mountain of God. Moses' comment about **Aaron and Hur** settling disputes indicates that he expects to be on the mountain for a long time based on Yahweh's command to "stay" with him on the mountain (Exod 24:12). Moses' delegation of Aaron as the chief leader in his absence accentuates Aaron's failure to govern the Israelites with authority in 32:1-6.

(2) Preparation to Enter the Presence (24:15-17)

■ **15** This verse reports the fulfillment of Yahweh's commands for Moses to come up to Yahweh (v 12). Subsequent to Moses' ascent, the **cloud** covers the **mountain**. Similar to the previous theophany of Yahweh, the thick cloud is the prelude to the descent of Yahweh's presence on the mountain (19:16, 18).

■ **16** The **glory of the** Lord settles in the **cloud**. Moses and probably Joshua who accompanies him apparently wait on the outskirts of the cloud **for six days**. Perhaps similar to the Israelites' mandatory three-day consecration before the theophany (19:10-11), Moses is required to observe a six-day consecration before being summoned into Yahweh's glory-presence **on the seventh day**. While Moses is in the Lord's presence, Joshua apparently stays on the outskirts of the cloud. Similarly, later, while Moses enters the tent of meeting to speak with Yahweh, Joshua stays at the entrance to the tent close to the Lord's presence (33:11).

■ **17** Shifting directly to the perspective of **the Israelites**, this verse reports that **the glory of the** Lord **looked like a consuming fire**. Yahweh's presence (or God's angel) and fire often appear in close association in Exodus (3:2; 13:21-22; 14:24; 19:18; 40:38). The phrase "consuming fire" is repeated elsewhere to refer to Yahweh (Deut 4:24; Heb 12:29) and, in Isaiah, God's works of judgment and purification (Isa 29:6; 30:27, 30; 33:14). Fire is an image of God's holiness in its purifying and destructive qualities.

(3) Moses in the Yahweh's Presence (24:18)

■ **18** The section concludes with a report of Moses entering **the cloud**, close to Yahweh (v 12). Moses stays **on the mountain forty days and forty nights**, in fulfillment of Yahweh's command to "stay here" (v 12). The number forty has symbolic significance for an appropriate or complete period of time (e.g., Gen 7:4; 25:20; 26:34; Num 14:33; Matt 4:2; Acts 1:3).

FROM THE TEXT

Moses' special role in the old covenant is fulfilled and surpassed only by Jesus Christ in the new covenant. This passage highlights an aspect of Moses' unique role as a covenant mediator. Previously, all of Israel's leaders saw God and met with God to ratify the covenant (Exod 24:1-11). Yet in this instance, Moses alone enters into the cloud of God's glory and remains there for an extended period. Moses enters God's presence to meet with him and to receive the word of God. Later, it is said that God spoke to Moses "face to face, as one speaks to a friend" (33:11) and that there was "no prophet" like Moses "risen in Israel" after him (Deut 34:10).

Only in Jesus Christ, the mediator of the new covenant, do we find one who surpasses Moses in intimacy and communication with God and in revelation of God. In God the Son, we have one who is at the Father's bosom and who, therefore, makes him known (John 1:18). Moses made known the words of God as enshrined in the law, but Jesus is the Word of God who administers "grace and truth" as a living revelation of God's very nature and character (vv 17-18).

B. Instructions for the Tabernacle (25:1—31:18)

Overview

The covenant is completed (chs 20—24). The Israelites have accepted the covenant that Yahweh offered, promising their wholehearted obedience to the covenant laws (24:3, 7). Yahweh is Israel's God; Israel is Yahweh's people. Now, a way must be made for Yahweh to dwell among his people. The tabernacle will be that dwelling place.

Yahweh's gracious commitment to dwell among his covenant people through the tabernacle antithetically corresponds to the expulsion of Adam and Eve from Yahweh's presence and the garden of Eden (Gen 3:23-24). Access to the garden is denied them, with cherubim guarding the entrance to it (v 24). Sinful, mortal beings do not have access to Yahweh's presence, but Yahweh now crosses such boundaries and chooses to dwell among mortals, through the re-creation of a holy ground (Enns 2000, 521-22). Only, human beings take responsibility for building the physical structure that will welcome the manifest presence of Yahweh and his blessings on the land, even as human beings were responsible for ushering in the hostile presence of the serpent and the curses on the land (vv 14, 17).

A claim of divine initiation and specification for a building project is attested in a Sumerian narration dating to 2200 BC (Sarna 2004, 120) and in another ancient Near Eastern text about temple building (Hamilton 2011, 449-50). Such parallels, however, do not detract from the singularity of Israel's tabernacle as uniquely inspired by the creator God, expressing theological ideas that are radically different from those of pagan temples.

Some believe that the Israelites built the tabernacle based on Egyptian techniques. Since the Israelites lived in Egypt for four hundred years, influencing its culture and being influenced by it, shared elements between the two cultures are expected. Although quite different from the tabernacle, a portable sanctuary is also attested in Egypt from the period of Ramesses II (ca. 1290-1224 BC; Sarna 1996, 196-200). However, based on our dating of the exodus (fifteenth century BC), it is reasonable to conclude that if such structure is evidence of intercultural influence, then the Egyptians adopted the Israelite ideas rather than the reverse.

In the instructions for the tabernacle and its furnishings, only main descriptions are given: the material to be used, the dimensions, the main structure, and the general placement of objects. Details are left out for multiple reasons. (1) These details are already committed to Moses in the vision blueprint. (2) They are left to the divinely anointed artisan's brilliant creativity, such as the intricate tapestry weaving for curtains or the decorative aspects of the metalwork. (3) There are assumed parts of the furniture, such as short feet on the ark. (4) The instructions concerning the tabernacle in Exod 25—31 and 35—40 are shaped by theological concerns that govern what is considered essential and nonessential (see Jacob 1992, 758-64).

The text balances a concern for obedient adherence to the divine instructions with a respect for an artistic freedom concerning many of the details. Where no detailed descriptions are given, one expects that artists' unique contributions were encouraged. The Spirit of God imparted divine wisdom, understanding, and abilities to the best of Israel's artists (30:3-6; 35:31-35). Thus, one can assume extraordinary ingenuity, extravagance, innovation, and invention (including new technologies or methods) were utilized that revolutionized both the Israelites and their surrounding cultures. In other words, the building of the tabernacle required far more than a mindless adherence to a set of instructions or a simple duplication of contemporary conventions from surrounding cultures.

The instructions given in chs 25—31 are fulfilled in chs 35—39.

I. Offerings for the Tabernacle (25:1-9)

BEHIND THE TEXT

The opening verses of Exod 25 connect to the end of the previous unit, 24:15-18, which reports that Moses went up to the cloud-covered mountain to be with Yahweh forty days and forty nights. At this point, Moses is still with Yahweh on the mountain. This unit reports the initial content of divine revelation Moses receives from Yahweh during those forty days.

Chapter 35 represents the fulfillment of this unit. Chapter 35 gives the accounts of Moses' invitation to the Israelites to donate the materials needed (vv 4-9), the publication of the objects to be made (vv 10-19), and the report of the generous donations given (vv 20-29).

a. The Call to Donate (25:1-2)

■ **1-2** Yahweh commands a freewill **offering** (v 2). The offering is for Yahweh (**to . . . me** and **for me**) to be used for Yahweh's tabernacle. The offering is voluntary, rather than obligatory. The only exception is that silver is required as atonement money. Every man, twenty years of age and upward, counted in the census pays half a shekel (about 0.4 oz or 11.3 g; see 30:11-16; 38:25-28). The tabernacle will be constructed through everyone's generosity (see 36:3-7). The Hebrew term for **offering** refers to lifting or heaving something from one's possession and offering it to Yahweh for sacred use. Since the tabernacle is for the benefit of the people, it is fitting to construct it with the material and labor contributed by the people. The voluntary and generous offering of material and service for the tabernacle (35:21-29) greatly contrasts with Solomon's taxation and forced labor for his temple.

b. The Materials (25:3-7)

■ **3** Verses 3-7 mention the types of material needed for the construction of the tabernacle, its furnishings, and the priestly garments: metals, yarns, fabrics, leathers, woods, oils, spices, and precious stones. Although mobile, the tabernacle is royal, thus requiring the best materials. The Israelites left Egypt with great wealth given by the Egyptians (3:22). Out of that wealth, the people are to bring **offerings** to Yahweh.

Gold, the most precious metal of the three, is listed first. It is among the most malleable of all metals and can be beaten into thin sheets. Pure gold is used for the objects closest to the presence of Yahweh. **Silver** is used for miscellaneous supportive objects inside the tabernacle and for the courtyard posts. **Bronze** refers to an alloy made of copper and tin. Bronze is hard and durable, with a high melting point. It is most suited for handling intense fire or heat and, thus, is used for overlaying the altar of burnt offering. Bronze also adorns various supportive objects for the altar, the tent, and the courtyard.

Iron, which is not mentioned anywhere in Exodus, is not required for the tabernacle, probably because it was not readily available in the premonarchic period and it was primarily for tools (Deut 19:5; 27:5) and for weapons of war (e.g., Josh 17:16, 18).

■ **4** **Blue, purple and scarlet *yarns* and fine linen *yarns*** are used to weave the inner curtains for the tabernacle (Exod 26:1, 31). Although the term "yarn" is not mentioned in the Hebrew text, it is best to take all the material mentioned here as referring to yarn—dyed woolen yarns in blue, purple, and scarlet, fine linen yarns in natural colors, and **goat hair** yarns in natural colors (see women spinning these yarns in 35:25-26; → "Weavers" sidebar in 26:1 for a discussion on various weavers).

As with the metals, the colors are mentioned in order of descending value. Like gold, the color blue is used most prominently. The blue (from marine snails) and purple (from shellfish) dyes were very costly due to the labor required for their production and were, thus, a sign of wealth and nobility, fitting a king. "Scarlet" is literally "scarlet worm," referring to the red dye obtained from dried worm powder.

Fine (lit. "twisted") linen most likely refers to linen threads spun with many fine strands, with extra luster, softness, and strength. Made from flax fibers, linen garments are exceptionally cool in hot weather. Thus, linen is well suited for clothing such as the priestly vestments (28:5 ff.). Linen is a very strong and durable natural fiber; hence, it is also used for the inner curtains along with the blue, purple, and scarlet woolen yarns (26:1, 31). It has various natural colors: ivory, ecru, tan, or light gray (modern white linen is a product of heavy bleaching). Since no color is mentioned for the linen, it was probably used in its natural colors.

■ **5** This verse lists the materials for the two layers of covering over the tent and for the frames of the tabernacle. **Ram skins dyed red** are used to make a covering for the tent (26:14; 36:19; 39:34). Placed over the ram skin cover is the outermost cover (26:14; 36:19; 39:34), made out of **another type of durable leather** (*taḥaš*; variously translated into "badgers' skins" [KJV], "porpoise skins" [NASB], "goatskins" [ESV], "fine leather" [NET, NJB, NRSV]). Elsewhere, this leather (*taḥaš*) is used as covering for the tabernacle in transit (Num 4:6-11, 25) and for sandals supposedly of the finest quality (Ezek 16:10). Whatever the exact identity of this leather, it is the outermost, protective cover of the tabernacle. The general principle for curtain/covering is that the most delicate, ornate, and splendid (tapestry) is exposed to the presence of God within, and the layers go outward in the order of descending value and ascending durability. The translation **another type of durable leather** is thus highly fitting because it mentions durability without undue speculation on its specific qualities.

■ **6** Pure **olive oil** is collected for the lamp (27:20). **Spices** (myrrh, fragrant cinnamon, fragrant calamus, and cassia) are added to pure olive oil to make the holy **anointing oil** (30:23-24). It is used to anoint and consecrate the tabernacle and everything within, the altar and the basin (Lev 8:10-11), and also Aaron and his sons and their vestments (Exod 29:7, 21). **Fragrant incense** is made with gum resin, onycha, galbanum, and pure frankincense in equal amounts (30:34). It is burnt on the gold altar.

■ **7** Precious and semiprecious stones are required. The Hebrew for **onyx** (*šōham*) is variously identified as onyx, lapis lazuli, emerald, and carnelian.

"Onyx" is mentioned as representative of precious stones found in or near the garden of Eden (Gen 2:12; 1 Chr 29:2). In Job 28:16, the adjective "precious" or "splendid" describes this precious stone. Onyx bowls and pottery, lapis jewelry, emerald jewelry, and carnelian scarabs have been found in ancient Egypt.

Two "onyx" stones with engraving of the names of the twelve tribes of Israel are **mounted on** the shoulder pieces of **the ephod** (Exod 28:9-14; 39:6-7). Twelve different kinds of **gems** are used for the high priest's **breastpiece**, each representing a tribe of Israel (28:17-21; 39:10-14).

The tribal rulers or leaders contributed the gemstones (35:27), probably not because they were the richest members of the community, but because they were the representatives of the tribes and the function of each gemstone was to represent the tribe.

c. The Purpose and the Method (25:8-9)

■ **8** The people are to **make** a **sanctuary** for Yahweh, which refers to the tabernacle. The main purpose for the tabernacle is then stated: **I will dwell among them**. Although worship and acts of atonement take place in the tabernacle, its main purpose is to be a dwelling place for Yahweh. The holy heavenly King will condescend to dwell among the sinful, earthly commoners. The royal king orders his palace to be made as a portable tent, just as his subjects dwell in portable tents. Yahweh's plan is to accompany them in their journey to the promised land. The tabernacle and the divine glory within will be the visible and perpetual sign to the people that Yahweh is with them (see 33:15-16). With the presence of God in the tabernacle, they will hopefully never doubt and test Yahweh again, asking, as they did before, "Is the LORD among us or not?" (17:7). Besides giving the assurance of Yahweh's favor, the presence of the great King will elevate Israel's status as Yahweh's treasured possession and holy, royal priests (19:6).

■ **9** In its narrower, technical meaning, **tabernacle** (*miškān*) specifically applies to the inner curtains with the cherubim woven into them (e.g., chs 26, 36). As such, the tabernacle (*miškān*) is differentiated from the cover tent (*'ōhel*), which goes over the tabernacle (26:7; 39:34). Once the tabernacle and the covers are set up, the assembled whole and all its furnishings are called the tabernacle (e.g., 40:38; Num 9:15) or the tent of meeting (*'ōhel mô'd*; e.g., Exod 27:21; 28:43; 29:4).

The creator King's terrestrial throne and dwelling place must be made according to Yahweh's own design. Thus, Yahweh gives Moses specifications and shows him a **pattern** (*tabnît*), either a model/replica of what is to be built (so in Ezek 8:10 and 1 Chr 28:11-12) or a prophetic vision of Yahweh's heavenly dwelling place, to which the earthly tabernacle will correspond (Cassuto 1967, 322). The construction of God's sanctuary cannot be left to human initiation and ingenuity, which are subject to idolatrous tendencies. Yet with

God's help, a holy place enables the otherwise unapproachable Holy Lord to dwell among the Israelites, who will approach and worship the Lord there.

FROM THE TEXT

Yahweh's promise, "I will dwell among them," is profoundly comforting to the believing community but is foolishness to the modern mind that resists the existence of God and the possibility of a transcendent God who is engaged with humanity. In fact, even to believers the prospect of God's presence in the tabernacle can in some ways be offensive to our often worldly sensibilities and values. (1) The tabernacle graciously provides the reliable place to access God's real presence. But the mode of access disturbs human control and initiative as the tabernacle must be made according to the divine (and not human) design and used entirely for divine (and not human) purposes. (2) Through the tabernacle, God's people can have a reliable, tangible, and regular contact with the holy presence of God who is willing to meet with all those who have a deep yearning for his presence (Brueggemann 1994, 891). But his presence is not something to be trifled with. The worshippers must relinquish all control and approach him only through the means and ways initiated and prescribed by God. (3) The tabernacle provides a central and legitimate place of worship, which reinforces monotheism and unity of the tribal people Israel, as their lives are ordered around right worship of the one true God. This unifying and centralizing character of tabernacle worship disturbs human desire for freedom to have diverse individual expressions in worship practices, which inevitably would lead to idolatrous worship in ancient Israelite context. Of course, there are legitimate forms of diverse local expressions for worship, but these develop under the guidance of the Holy Spirit and in ways compatible with monotheism. (4) Last but not least, the tabernacle and the presence of God that it represents disrupt the normal ways of social and ethnic groups to distinguish themselves from other groups. In Exodus, it is the tabernacle that distinguishes the people of Israel from the rest of the peoples of the world, as it is the tabernacle and the abiding presence of the God within that set them apart (33:16). After the golden calf incident, the Lord urges Moses to go with "an angel" to the promised land, but without the Lord and the tabernacle (33:2-3). But this is not sufficient for Moses, who understands the absolute necessity of the presence of the Lord for the distinctiveness of Israel's identity as God's covenant people. (5) In all these ways, the building and ongoing functioning of the tabernacle—the great visual symbol of divine presence—signify the infinite value for Israel's identity and destiny. They are to be the Lord's special people among whom the transcendent God lives.

The glorious earthly tabernacle points to the even more glorious dwelling places of God. The NT shows that the OT tabernacle was not an end in itself.

(1) The tabernacle points *up* to the eternal heavenly sanctuary. The tabernacle, with all its furnishings, is a symbolic replica of the heavenly dwelling place of God, "the true tabernacle set up by the Lord" (Heb 8:2; see 9:11, 23-24). (2) The tabernacle also points *ahead* to the historical sanctuary of Jesus Christ incarnate. Christ reconciles God and all humanity (Jews and Gentiles) in and through his body (Eph 2:11-16). (3) It also shows the purpose of humanity as a sanctuary or dwelling place for God. Thus, the believers are called the "temple" of God, with the Holy Spirit indwelling both the corporate body of Christ (1 Cor 3:16-17; Eph 2:21) and individuals (1 Cor 6:19). In the new covenant, the realities of the heavenly kingdom are expressed in and through the followers of Christ, who are the living and mobile sanctuaries of the real presence of God. Just as the presence of God within the tabernacle marked Israel as a special people of God on earth, it is the presence of the Holy Spirit in the sanctuary of a believer or of a church body that distinguishes them as holy unto the Lord.

2. The Ark of the Covenant (25:10-22)

a. The Ark (25:10-16)

BEHIND THE TEXT

Specific instructions regarding the tabernacle begin with the most important item of furniture in the tabernacle, the ark, which is elsewhere called the ark of the covenant (e.g., Num 10:33; Deut 10:8).

There are a few ancient Near Eastern parallels to the ark and its functions. There are examples of documents written on tablets kept in chests or of thrones borne by winged creatures (see Propp 2006, 516-17). These reflect three related functions of the biblical ark; as a chest to store the covenant tablets (Exod 25:16); as a witness to the covenant (v 16); and as Yahweh's footstool (1 Chr 28:2; see Pss 99:5 and 132:7), above which Yahweh's manifest presence is revealed (Exod 25:17-20).

The instructions given here are fulfilled in 37:1-5.

IN THE TEXT

■ **10** The **ark** (*'ărōn*; "coffin" in Gen 50:26; "chest" in 2 Kgs 12:10 [11 HB]) is made with **acacia wood** (*šiṭṭîm*; from the shittah tree or wild acacia, which grows abundantly south of Israel, in the Sinai desert, and in Egypt; see Cassuto 1967, 326). Despite its extreme importance, the ark is not made of pure gold, which would make it far less portable. The **cubit** (*'ammâ*) is probably the length of a forearm or about 1.5' / 0.46 m. The ark is to be 2.5 x 1.5 x 1.5 cubits (or 3.75' x 2.25' x 2.25' / 1.15 x 0.7 x 0.7 m) in length, width, and height.

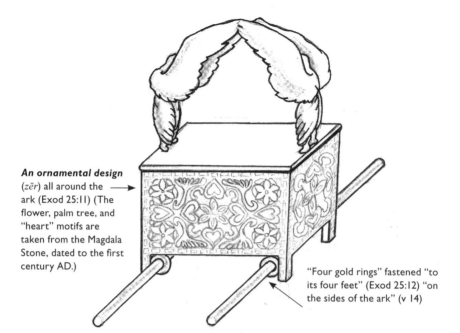

An ornamental design (*zēr*) all around the ark (Exod 25:11) (The flower, palm tree, and "heart" motifs are taken from the Magdala Stone, dated to the first century AD.)

"Four gold rings" fastened "to its four feet" (Exod 25:12) "on the sides of the ark" (v 14)

Figure 5: The ark of the covenant

25:11 ■ 11 The wooden chest is to be overlaid **with pure gold** (unalloyed and maximally purified to the Israelites' best ability). The gold turns the ordinary into the splendid, worthy of its service as the footstool for the heavenly King (1 Chr 28:2; see Pss 99:5; 132:7). Overlaying may have been achieved through nailing thin plates of gold on the wood. But since the stone tablets could easily damage thin gold plates when the ark is in transit, a rabbinic suggestion provides a very attractive alternative: two gold chests were made, one as a lining and one as a jacket of the wooden chest (Sarna 2004, 123). This rabbinic interpretation also fits well with the Hebrew expression *from without and from within*.

A gold **molding** is placed **around** the ark. The Hebrew for "molding" (*zēr*; "crown" [KJV]) is used only in Exodus in relation to the ark (25:11; 37:2), the table (25:24-25; 37:11-12), and the altar of incense (30:3-4; 37:26-27). Its meaning is debated, but a functional molding on the top, which helps to secure the atonement cover over the ark, is a well-accepted interpretation. However, in the instructions for the table for the bread in 25:24-25, "molding" (*zēr*) goes directly on the table itself. Then a "rim" (NIV; "frame" [NET]) is placed around the table with another "molding" (*zēr*) over the "rim." This suggests "molding" (*zēr*) is decorative in nature rather than structural. In view of the Septuagint's "wreaths" and an Aramaic term for "wreath, crown" (*zîrā'*; Propp 2006, 380), ***an ornamental design*** (and not the later Greek wreath) might be a good translation of the term. Since where the design should be placed is not specified (top, middle, or bottom), the whole surface is most likely in view.

■ **12** The chest is to have **four** short **feet** (*pa'am*; see Jacob 1992, 773-74) on the underside, perhaps to prevent the ark from directly touching the ground. The feet also allow for the **four gold rings** to be attached to them, underneath the ark. The rings toward the top or middle of the chest, protruding from the side, could not bear the weight of the ark, the ark cover with two solid gold cherubim statues, and the two stone tablets. The rings attached to the side would likely break off. The placement of the rings under the ark would allow the carrying poles to push up on the bottom of the ark, bearing the full weight of the ark (→ Figure 5, above). In addition to practical demands, the concern for the utmost honor of the sacred vessel might be at the center of their placement. The rings and poles under the ark would allow the objects of supreme sanctity to be borne entirely above, and not below, their human carriers.

■ **13** As with the ark, its **poles** are to be made of very durable **acacia wood**, overlaid with **gold** sheets, thick enough to bear the weight of the ark without being easily peeled away or damaged during transit.

■ **14** The **sides of the ark** here are best understood in opposition to the "front" or "back" of the ark. If so, the "sides" refer to the short sides. Together with v 12, this verse clarifies that the **rings** should be fastened to the feet on the bottom of the short sides. The inserted **poles** would then run parallel to the short sides. This would allow the front of the ark (or king's throne) to face forward when in transit (see also Jacob 1992, 774). This way of carrying the ark would well communicate the symbolic significance of the ark, namely that the God King of Israel, who is enthroned above the ark, goes before the Israelites.

■ **15** The requirement of **the poles . . . to remain in the rings** of the **ark** emphasizes the supreme sanctity of the ark and anything that touches it, including the poles. Looking ("even for a moment" [Num 4:20]), touching, or otherwise mishandling the ark in an unauthorized manner and by unauthorized personnel would result in death for the offenders (Num 4:15, 18-20; 1 Sam 6:19; 2 Sam 6:6-8). Only the authorized personnel (i.e., Aaron and his sons) can remove the poles for the purpose of covering or uncovering the ark, and only Kohathites can carry the ark and other holy objects (Num 4:4-6, 15).

■ **16** Here, the Hebrew term *'ēdût* ("testimony" or **covenant law**) is translated into **the tablets of the covenant law** (the Hebrew expression of which occurs in Exod 31:18; 32:15; 34:29) for clarification. Deuteronomy 4:13 identifies the covenant law written on the tablets as the Decalogue (see "tablets" in Exod 32:15-16; 34:1, 27-28; also see 31:18; Deut 4:13; 5:22; 9:9-11). The "covenant law" is the central content of **the ark**. Therefore, the ark and even the entire tabernacle are often evoked with the term *'ēdût* ("covenant law") attached to them; thus, "the ark of the covenant law" (e.g., 25:22; 26:33; 30:6; 39:35; Num

7:89) or "the tent of the covenant law" or "the tabernacle of the covenant law" (Exod 38:21; Num 1:50, 53; 9:15; 10:11; 17:7, 8 [22, 23 HB]). In the wider context of the Sinai covenant, the "covenant law" would refer to all of Yahweh's covenant stipulations (not only the Decalogue but also its applications as found in the book of the covenant). As such, the ark with the covenant law in it functions as Yahweh's witness to the people's repeated and solemn sworn vow to absolutely obey these stipulations. Similarly, the two stone tablets of the covenant law, written by the heavenly King-Judge, bear perpetual witness to the covenant agreement before Yahweh and the people of Israel. These witnesses call for human obedience and divine enforcement of covenant blessings and curses according to the mutually sworn agreements.

FROM THE TEXT

The ark of the covenant, the most sacred object in the old covenant, fulfills multiple functions. (1) The ark is the visible sign of God's powerful presence among his people (Num 10:36). It is the sign that God protected his people and contended against their enemies (e.g., Num 10:35; Josh 6:6-21). The ark released miraculous power according to divine will (e.g., Josh 3:9-17) and was consulted to discern divine will (1 Sam 14:18-19). Those authorized to house it received blessings (2 Sam 6:11-12). (2) As a container for the two stone tablets of the covenant law, it also functioned as a divine witness to the Sinai covenant (see Exod 25:16; Josh 8:30-33). John's vision of the heavenly ark of the covenant also hints at its function in God's rule and judgment (Rev 11:17-19). (3) Thus, several texts underline the extreme and, therefore, dangerous sanctity of the ark. When mishandled, the consequences for such infractions were dire (1 Sam 6:19; 2 Sam 6:6-7; 1 Chr 13:9-10). (4) The powerful presence of God that the ark represented was invulnerable to human manipulation. Thus, its use in war apart from obedience to God only brought a total defeat (e.g., 1 Sam 4:1-11). Unauthorized possession of it resulted in a severe punishment (1 Sam 5). Ultimately, the ark's symbolic value became devoid, as the Lord withheld his presence from the sinful people and handed them over to destruction and the exile. According to 1 Esd 1:54, the ark of God was carried away into Babylon, along with other sacred vessels from the temple. (5) Relatedly, Jeremiah speaks of a day when the ark of the covenant would no longer be spoken of or remembered (Jer 3:16). On that day, all nations will gather to honor the name of the Lord in the new Jerusalem, the new "Throne of the LORD" (Jer 3:17), on the new earth, the Eden (see Richter 2008, 127-28). Jeremiah's voice is joined by the NT, which characterizes the earthly ark as a material replica that points to superior heavenly realities (Heb 9:23-24).

b. The Atonement Cover (25:17-22)

(1) The Atonement Cover Proper (25:17)

BEHIND THE TEXT

The "atonement cover," traditionally rendered "mercy seat" (e.g., ESV, KJV, NASB, NRSV), is the most important part of the ark. Once a year, on the Day of Atonement, the high priest entered the most holy place with the blood of the bull as the sin offering for himself and then the blood of the goat as the sin offering for the people. He sprinkled the blood of each seven times on the eastern face (or the front) of the atonement cover (Lev 16:14-15). The high priest thereby made atonement for the most holy place, himself, and the people, cleansing them from all sins (v 30). This sacred rite ensured the abiding presence of Yahweh among his people.

Exodus 37:6 reports the making of the atonement cover.

IN THE TEXT

■ 17 The exact etymology of the Hebrew term (*kappōret*) for **atonement cover** is debated. It may mean simply "cover," possibly formed from the verb that means "to cover" (*kāpar*). This suggestion corresponds to its practical function. More likely, it is a technical term deriving from the verb that means "make atonement" (*kipper*) and means "a place of expiation and atonement" (thus, the LXX's *hilastērion*; "means or place of expiation"). This explanation fits well its theological function.

Due to its proximity to Yahweh's presence and its supreme theological significance, the cover of the ark is the holiest vessel in the tabernacle. Therefore, the atonement cover is to be made with **pure gold**. The size of the atonement cover is to be the same as the dimensions of the top of the ark beneath it, 2.5 **cubits** (3.75' / 1.25 m) in length and 1.5 cubits (2.25' / 75 m) in width (v 10). The omission of a measurement for the atonement cover's thickness may indicate that it is relatively thin.

FROM THE TEXT

God desires a holy place on earth where he may reveal his special presence to his people; God provides his own gracious means for dwelling among sinful people. In the old covenant, the annual animal sacrifices and their blood cleansed sin from the most holy place and made "at-one-ment" between the Holy God of Israel and the sinful Israelites; in the new covenant, Jesus Christ the Great High Priest entered the heavenly "Most Holy Place once for all by his own blood, thus obtaining eternal redemption" (Heb 9:12). The Israelites were cleansed and sanctified "outwardly" (v 13), so that the manifest presence of God may remain in the tabernacle. However, "the blood of Christ . . . cleanse[s] our consciences" (v 14) so that we may "approach God's throne of grace [or Most Holy Place] with confidence" and continue to "receive mercy and find grace" (4:16; 1 John 1:9).

(2) Cherubim Statues (25:18-20)

BEHIND THE TEXT

In the Decalogue, Yahweh strictly forbids making and worshipping graven or carved images (Exod 20:4). Following Israel's idolatry of a molten calf (32:4, 8), Yahweh makes the prohibition of molten or cast images explicit (e.g., 34:17; Lev 19:4). Constructing the cherubim, however, does not need to contradict Yahweh's prohibitions. (1) Most importantly, Yahweh, none other, commands their making. (2) The command to hammer out two cherubim avoids any perceived contradiction with the explicit rejection of making graven or molten images. (3) They are not intended for worship. No one is even allowed to see them, let alone access them, except for the high priest once a year for making atonement.

Although some composite creatures are found elsewhere in the ancient Near East (see Propp's discussion on "Griffins" in 2006, 386-88), the living cherubim are unique to biblical revelation. According to Ezekiel's visions (1:4-28; 10:8-22), these mysterious and terrifying creatures abide close to Yahweh and have some unique features. Unlike the sphinx with a face of human and a body of an animal, the living cherubim appear to have the body of a human with arms, but each with four wings and four faces of a cherub/bull, a man, a lion, and an eagle. They are covered with eyes and are associated with blazing live coals, flashes of lightning, and living wheels. Above their heads is the theophany. Thus, the cherubim statues, standing upright with their two wings spread upward, symbolize the otherwise invisible heavenly cherubim who accompany an appearance of Yahweh.

The instructions to make the cherubim are fulfilled in Exod 37:7-9.

IN THE TEXT

■ **18** Two cherubim (*kerûv*) statues are to be made by hammering the **gold** into its shape (like the lampstands in v 31), rather than by melting and casting them in a mold.

■ **19** The use of pure gold for the cover and the ordinary gold for the cherubim supports the interpretation that each **cherub** is hammered out separately, and then the completed **cherubim** are attached to the cover. The cherubim are placed on the **two short ends** of the cover. Such placement would distribute their weight appropriately on the ark's cover. Some texts refer to the statues and the cover simply as the atonement cover (e.g., 30:6; 31:7; 35:12; 39:35; 40:20; see Num 7:89).

■ **20** Cherubim's **wings** are to be **spread upward** (see Ezek 1:11), perhaps touching one another (see v 9). The wings overshadow the cover. In Ezekiel's vision, each cherub has four wings, two spread upward, touching other wings, and two covering their bodies (vv 6, 11). Here, another pair of wings for covering its body is not mentioned but is perhaps assumed to exist (see 1:6; 10:21). The cherubim statues **face each other** (each with four faces) as opposed to standing side-by-side. Also, they look down **toward the cover**, with their heads slightly bent, as opposed to staring at each other with their heads erect.

This positioning of the cherubim and their wings would create a space in between them and above the ark (→ Figure 5, following comments on Exod 25:10). That space presumably corresponds to the space in between the real cherubim, where the live coals are burning and where lightning flashes (see Ezek 1:13; 10:2, 7). Yahweh said he would meet and speak to Moses from above the atonement cover in between the two cherubim (Exod 25:22).

FROM THE TEXT

The representation of the cherubim on the atonement cover and the function of the living cherubim connect the tabernacle with the garden of Eden. In a lament over a certain rebellious cherub (which is sung over the king of Tyre for his analogous fate), the cherub is said to have dwelt "in Eden, the garden of God" (Ezek 28:13-14) and walked in the midst of stones of fire (v 14). Relatedly, Gen 3:24 describes cherubim with flaming swords as guardians of the garden of Eden. In addition, Ezekiel's vision of theophany portrays cherubim with wheels under them as a living chariot for the manifest presence of the God King (Ezek 10:1, 18-20; 11:22), who carry something like blazing coals that represent divine judgment (see 1:13-14; 10:2-7; 11:1-13).

Now the high priest's entry into the most holy place where Yahweh manifests his presence above the cherubim statues, therefore, evokes the imagery of reentry into the garden of God that is guarded by the terrifying fiery heavenly beings (see Richter 2008, 124). Only, by God's sovereign grace, the high priest is not put to death. The high priest's entry is also a reenactment of the Israelite leaders' entry into the mount of God (another symbol of the garden of Eden), where they saw God and dined in God's presence (Exod 24:9-11). There is a clear juxtaposition, therefore, of the garden of Eden, Mount Sinai, and the tabernacle. The implication is clear: the place that was once rendered inaccessible (the garden of God and the throne of God) due to disobedience is now being made accessible through covenant obedience (symbolized by the tablets of covenant law within the ark) and atonement (symbolized by the atonement cover). In addition, the promised land is an earthly extension of the celestial garden of God that is symbolized in the most holy place.

The implication of the symbolic and terrestrial reentry into the garden of God, however, is rather frightening. There is inherent danger in hosting the supremely holy presence of God in the symbolic garden of God and in living in its earthly extension. Yahweh's presence must be approached with utmost care, since his presence comes not only with blessing of the new garden but also with the threat of death (→ "jealous God" in 20:5bc and "punishment" in 34:7c, 7d) and expulsion from his garden. The prophet Isaiah addresses the terrified sinners, trembling in fear: "Who of us can dwell with the consuming fire? Who of us can dwell with everlasting burning?" (Isa 33:14). The prophetic answer is simple and clear: "Those who walk righteously and speak what is right" (v 15).

(3) The Function of the Cover: Sealing and Hosting (25:21-22)

BEHIND THE TEXT

Besides serving as a place of atonement, the atonement cover seals the tablets of covenant law (Exod 25:21). It also hosts Yahweh's manifest presence (v 22). Thus, numerous passages speak of Yahweh appearing and speaking from above the atonement cover (Lev 16:2; Num 7:89) and dwelling or enthroned in between or above the cherubim (e.g., 1 Sam 4:4; 2 Sam 6:2; Pss 80:1 [2 HB]; 99:1; Isa 37:16; see Ezek 1:1-2, 5).

IN THE TEXT

■ **21** The command to deposit **in the ark** the stone **tablets** is repeated here (see "tablets" in Exod 25:16; 32:15, 16; 34:1, 27-28). The repetition emphasizes the primary functions of the ark as the container of the covenant law and as the covenant witness (see "covenant law" in 25:16). The atonement cover seals the ark.

■ **22** Yahweh states that he will manifest himself **above the *atonement* cover between the two cherubim** statues and **over** the tablets of **covenant law**. The three elements of the ark of the covenant provide the right earthly condition for the meeting between Yahweh and his people through a mediator.

Although Moses is not the high priest, as the lawgiver and founder of Israel's cult, he stands above the regulations (Propp 2006, 393). Yahweh affirms here and demonstrates in Num 7:89 that once the tabernacle is erected, Yahweh will continue to **meet with** Moses in the most holy place, **above the *atonement* cover between the two cherubim**, and continue to give **commands** for his people.

Some interpreters, however, argue that Moses did not enter the most holy place but merely heard God's voice coming from the place between the cherubim (e.g., Jacob 1992, 887). However, this interpretation is unlikely, considering Moses' encounters with God in his tent of meeting (in Exod 33:7), their "face to face" relationship (v 11), and Yahweh's self-revelation to Moses on Mount Sinai (34:5-7).

FROM THE TEXT

The above perspectives on the ark provide a framework for understanding the relationship between (1) the holy presence of God, (2) the (symbolism of) cherubim, (3) the atonement cover, and (4) the tablets of the covenant law of God.

(1) The Holy God desires to dwell among his people, but the Lord is a jealous God, a consuming fire (e.g., Deut 4:24; Isa 33:14). (2) Cherubim on the ark's cover symbolize, among other things, God's judgment (see Ezek 10:2, 7) and God's protection of his people from that judgment. They signify the inherent dangers of God's holy presence and God's merciful shielding of the worshippers from that danger. (3) The atonement cover emphasizes the absolute necessity of expiation of sins and atonement through blood sacrifice for the ongoing, favorable presence and revelation of God. Without atonement, a holy God cannot dwell among sinful people, and so divine wrath is inevitable. (4) The tablets of the covenant law emphasize the necessity of the covenant people's obedience to those laws, if the presence of God is to abide among them. Overall, the ongoing presence of God in Israel is possible *primarily* based on God's sovereign choice (to reveal himself) and grace (expressed through the provision of atonement), rather than as a reward for human obedience. However, a level of obedience and loyalty is obviously required for the presence of God to abide in Israel. The atonement rite without obedience is ineffective for the removal of sins and guilt. Likewise, obedience without the atoning rite leaves unpurified their offenses and guilt. Thus, both obedience and atonement are required.

In the new covenant, (1) God the Son becomes flesh and comes to dwell among sinners (John 1:14). The believers, corporately and individually, are called the "temple" of God, in which the Holy Spirit dwells (see 1 Cor 3:16-17; 6:19; Eph 2:21). (2) The NT does not mention cherubim, cherubim statues no longer exist, and their symbolism has no place in Christian theology. However, we may assume their living existence in heaven and their continued function as the fearsome guardians of God's dwelling place and carriers of divine judgment. If so, God still must be approached through divinely chosen and divinely revealed means. Approaching him in any other way results in death. (3) The good news, of course, is that Jesus Christ is the Great High Priest (Heb 5:10) and our "atoning sacrifice" (1 John 2:2), through whom we can draw near to our heavenly Father and behold his glory (John 14:6-7). (4) Lest we presume upon God's grace in and through Jesus Christ, however, Christ teaches us to

25:21-22

obey the commandments (both its "letter" and its deeper intentions; e.g., Matt 5:17-20; also see John 14:15, 21). In addition, the Lord gives us the Holy Spirit, who empowers us to submit to and obey God (Rom 8:5-13), even as the Lord promised: "I will put my law in their minds and write it on their hearts. I will be their God, and they will be my people" (Jer 31:33).

3. The Table (25:23-30)

BEHIND THE TEXT

The table is always listed immediately after the ark (Exod 37:10-16; 40:4; Num 4:7-8), which might suggest its importance.

The idea of setting out food to feed and appease the deities was a practice ubiquitous in the ancient Near East (Hamilton 2011, 462). These people believed that deities required a daily presentation of food.

Against such a pagan notion, Yahweh requires the "bread of the Presence" (Exod 25:30). The Bible is emphatic that Yahweh has no need of food (see Ps 50:12-15; see Stuart 2006, 574-75). The perpetual bread, which is replaced once a week on the Sabbath (Lev 24:8), is not intended to be Yahweh's food but is explicitly for Aaron and his sons (v 9). Since God does not eat food, only the human covenant partners consume it. This weekly covenant meal is consistent with and is likely a reenactment of the covenant meal that took place on Mount Sinai (Exod 24:9-11).

The report of the making of the table is found in 37:10-16.

IN THE TEXT

■ **23** The **table** is to be made with the same materials as the ark—**acacia wood**. It is overlaid with pure gold (v 24). It is 2 x 1 x 1.5 **cubits** (3' x 1.5' x 2.25' or 0.9 x 0.46 x 0.7 m) in length, width, and height. Its height is the same as that of the ark, not including the ark's feet.

■ **24** As with the ark, the entire table is to be overlaid **with pure gold**. The top of the table is assumed to have a border around it, with an *ornamental design* (zēr; → "molding" in v 11) placed upon it.

■ **25** A functional **rim** ("border" [KJV]; "frame" [NET]) **a handbreadth wide**, that is, about 4 inches, is placed **around** the table to provide structural soundness. The rim is also beautified with an *ornamental design* (zēr) all around.

■ **26-27** These instructions specify the **four gold rings** to be **close to the rim** and on the four *feet* (regel). In the OT, the term for feet (regel [Gen 8:9; 18:4; Exod 12:11]), which is used here, is clearly distinguished from the term for **leg** (kārāʿ [12:9; 29:17; Lev 1:9]), a term not used here. Thus, no ambiguity remains as to where the rings go; they are attached to the feet, directly under the rim, which is placed at the bottom end of the table legs, with a few inches of feet left (→ Figure 6, within comments on Exod 25:29). This way, the **poles** could bear the entire weight of the table, the bread of the Presence, all the vessels, the wrapping clothes, and the durable leather cover when in transit (Num 4:7-8). If the rings protruded from the sides of the rim or legs (as in popular depictions), they would have broken away when lifted by the poles. The rings are probably attached on the short sides of the **table** (just like the rings for the ark; → Exod 25:12 for "rings").

■ **28** The sacred **table**, like the ark, must not be touched, but be carried by **poles** made with acacia wood, overlaid with a sheet of **gold**.

■ **29** The vessels associated with the table are to be made with **pure gold**. Since the text does not specify how many of each vessel to make or what their purposes are, we can only infer their uses from the wider tabernacle texts.

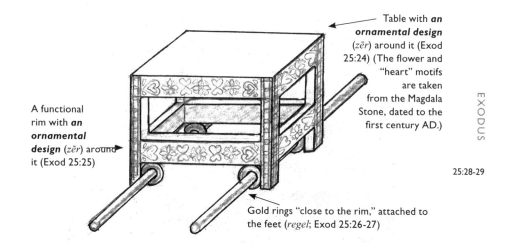

Table with **an ornamental design** (zēr) around it (Exod 25:24) (The flower and "heart" motifs are taken from the Magdala Stone, dated to the first century AD.)

A functional rim with **an ornamental design** (zēr) around it (Exod 25:25)

Gold rings "close to the rim," attached to the feet (regel; Exod 25:26-27)

Figure 6: The table

Contrary to the common assumption, the **plates** ("bowls" [LXX]) were not for the twelve loaves of bread, since the loaves were placed directly on the table (v 30; Lev 24:6). Numbers 4:5-7 suggests that the vessels were placed on top of the stacks of bread for travel only. The plates (or bowls) were likely needed for the following: (1) the grain offerings (e.g., Num 7:13, 19, 25), which were offered up daily (see Exod 29:40); (2) the storage of the unpowdered fragrant incense mix (see 30:35-36); and (3) the powdered fragrant incense mix kept next to the gold altar (30:36). No direction is given concerning the size or shape of the vessels, leaving their fashioners to make such determinations based on artistic and practical factors.

Two **dishes** (kap; "container for incense" [LXX]) were likely for pure frankincense that was set on the two stacks of bread of the Presence (Lev 24:6-7). Numbers 7 mentions twelve gold dishes (kap) full of incense offered by the leaders of Israel (see Num 7:14, 20, 26, etc.), who likely steadily supplied the incense for the tabernacle.

Pitchers and bowls were **for the pouring out of offerings**. These vessels were likely used for the following: (1) the pure olive oil needed for lighting the lamps (Exod 27:20-21; Lev 24:2-3)—the larger pitcher for holding a great quantity of oil and the small bowl for carefully refilling the lamps; (2) anointing oil, which was in the care of the high priest (see Num 4:16)—the pitcher for storage and the small bowl for rationing out "some of the anointing oil" for the anointing ceremonies (see Lev 8:12, 30); and (3) perhaps the daily libation offering of wine—the pitcher for storing and one small bowl for measuring out the daily drink offering (→ "drink offering" in Exod 29:40). Some suggest that the pitchers and bowls were for various kinds of drink to accompany the priests' weekly meal of bread from the table. If that drink was wine, such provision was repealed (Lev 10:8-9) immediately after the death of Nadab and Abihu, who offered "unauthorized fire," perhaps due to drunkenness (v 1).

There is no mention of places for storing these vessels inside the tabernacle. But likely, they were placed on the ground, on the durable leather and other fine cloth that were also used for packing (Num 4:7).

■ **30** The purpose of the **table** is a holding place to keep **the bread of the Presence . . . before** Yahweh **at all times**. It appears that the bread of the Presence is a food brought to and kept in Yahweh's presence, blessed by his presence, and consumed in his presence. The reasons for the bread are seemingly fourfold. (1) The bread (in twelve loaves, see Lev 24:5) represents the twelve tribes. As such, the bread symbolically depicts the people of Israel dwelling in Yahweh's holy presence, even as Yahweh dwells among the people. (2) As the bread is blessed by being in Yahweh's presence, the bread represents Yahweh's blessing of Israel with abundance of food and with life itself. (3) When the priests eat the bread, the meal is emblematic of the covenant fellowship between Yahweh and the Israelites. This weekly covenant meal is consistent with and is likely a reenactment of the covenant meal that took place on Mount Sinai (Exod 24:9-11). (4) The bread also points to the abundant provision in the luxuriant garden of Eden, represented in the promised land that flows with milk and honey.

FROM THE TEXT

The bread of the Presence has a rich symbolic meaning of mutual indwelling between the Lord and his people. John Wesley says, "As the ark signified God's being present with them, so the twelve loaves signified their being presented to God. This bread was designed to be . . . a token of their communion with God" (1990, 83). Surely, at its highest level, covenant is much more than an expedient contractual relationship; it is an intimate fellowship, a mutual enjoinment of life, and a united partnership. Given the complete disparity between a holy God and sinful human beings, such a relationship is made possible only through the miracle of grace. Thus, Jesus, in his High-Priestly Prayer in John 17:20-26, invokes such a grace. He prays that just as Jesus and the Father are one in mutual indwelling, so also the triune God and the believers can be one (vv 21-22). The mutual indwelling flows from the love of the heavenly Father who cares for all believers with the same love he gave to his Son Jesus Christ (v 23).

As the cultic representatives of the old covenant, the priests weekly re-enacted and celebrated the mutual covenant relationship between Yahweh and Israel. In the new covenant, all believers, as a royal priesthood (1 Pet 2:5, 9; Rev 1:6; 5:10; 20:6), partake of the covenantal meal, the Lord's Supper. The bread represents the human body and human nature that Christ assumed and perfected through perfect obedience. When such bread is consumed in remembrance of Christ, it is the "bread from heaven," the "bread of life" (John 6:32, 35) that releases the power of salvation and sanctification in us. In such ways, the bread of the Presence of Israel points beyond itself to spiritual realities that are more clearly revealed in the new covenant.

4. The Lampstand (25:31-40)

BEHIND THE TEXT

No dimensions for the lampstand are provided nor are many details 25:31-40 about its design. Many artistic and practical factors are left for Moses to communicate based upon his heavenly vision of the "pattern shown" to him (Exod 25:40) or else for the craftsmen to discern. However, judging by the descriptions given in vv 32-36, the menorah is most likely richly ornamented.

The most famous depiction of the menorah comes from the Arch of Titus in Rome perhaps, but since its tiered octagonal pedestal is decorated with "classical mythological motifs that must have infuriated pious Jews," this representation is most likely Herod's innovation (Propp 2006, 400). The recently excavated Magdala Stone from the Second Temple period depicts the menorah with the branches curving upward and supported by a sloping base (or a tripod or a quadrapod).

Although the text does not make it explicit, the lampstand may represent the tree of life. Its shaft with branches and their ornamental calyxes and flowers surely represent a flourishing tree, perhaps signifying renewal of life. If so, it finds parallels in much ancient Near Eastern and Mediterranean art, which used the tree of life as a prominent symbol of the divine power that brought about botanical fertility (see Meyers 2005, 232-35).

Of course, Scripture itself uses and develops the motif of the tree of life as the symbol of the fullness of life in the presence of Yahweh (Gen 2:9;

3:22, 24; Prov 3:18; Rev 2:7; 22:2, 14). Thus, the placement of the flourishing treelike lampstand in the holy place that is surrounded by the images of the cherubim that once stood to "guard the way to the tree of life" (Gen 3:24) is significant. Such a placement indicates that in a representative way through Moses and the priests, the people of Israel are given access to the fullness of life in Yahweh's presence.

The fulfillment of the instructions for the lampstand is reported in Exod 37:17-24.

IN THE TEXT

■ **31** The **lampstand** (*menôrâ*) is another sacred object made out of **pure gold**. The lampstand consists of the **base** and the main **shaft** (*qāneh*; "reed," which is itself called the lampstand in vv 32-36), six branches (*qāneh* [v 32]) out of the main shaft (three on the left and three on the right [v 32]), and the decorative and functional almond **flowerlike cups** (*gabî'a*), made with *calyxes* ("buds" [NIV]) and "blossoms" (v 33).

The shape of the base is not described, perhaps to be determined by the artist. But a coin from the first century BC shows a solid sloping base. But a stone tablet and the Magdala Stone from the first century BC show the menorah on a tripod or quadrapod base. Given the Hebrew term for base (*yārēk*; "thigh" or "loin"), a tripod or quadrapod may be in view.

The lampstand is not made by melting and casting but is hammered out of **one** pure gold **piece** like the cherubim in v 18. Verse 36 makes it more explicit: "the buds and branches shall all be of one piece with the lampstand, hammered out of pure gold." It is not inconceivable that the most skilled of the craftsmen, with wisdom and ingenuity, could produce such an extraordinary piece of art and craftsmanship. Yet the challenges involved in hammering the menorah, especially its decorative flowers, encourage some to favor an alternate interpretation. It is suggested that different parts of the menorah are hammered out separately and then assembled and fused into one whole.

■ **32-33** Each of the **six branches** (*qāneh* [v 32]) is to have **three cups** (v 33) in the shape of **almond flowers**, consisting of *calyxes* and blossoms—making eighteen ornamented cups in all. Since pure gold is malleable, the branches with decorative flowers can be hammered out with the right tools. The top cup on each branch is for holding the lamp (→ Figure 7 below).

■ **34-36** A flowerlike cup (v 34) is placed under each branch **pair** (v 35) that extends from the **lampstand** (that is, the main shaft). The fourth cup, on the top of the main shaft, holds the central lamp (this is not the only lamp, as some argue; see Meyers 2005, 232-33).

■ **37** **Seven lamps** are to be placed on the lampstand, one lamp per branch and one on the central shaft. The material for the lamp (a bowl of oil with a spout for the wick) is not specified, perhaps assuming either that it is gold like the lampstand or that it is ceramic as was customary. The lampstand is placed on the side opposite from the table. The spout of the lamp faces the table so as to **light the space in front of it.**

■ **38** The **wick trimmers** or scissors are for trimming the burnt wick and the tray for its removal. Even these accessories are considered so sacred that they must be made of pure gold. The word **trays** is plural. Since only Aaron is authorized to light and trim the lamps, only one tray is required. Why then is the word plural? The Hebrew term for "trays" is also translated into "firepans" (e.g., 27:3) and into "censer" (e.g., Lev 16:12; Num 16:17). One gold "tray" is made to receive trimmed wicks and probably two other gold "trays/censers" for incense burning by Moses and Aaron (Exod 40:27; Lev 16:12; Num 16:17).

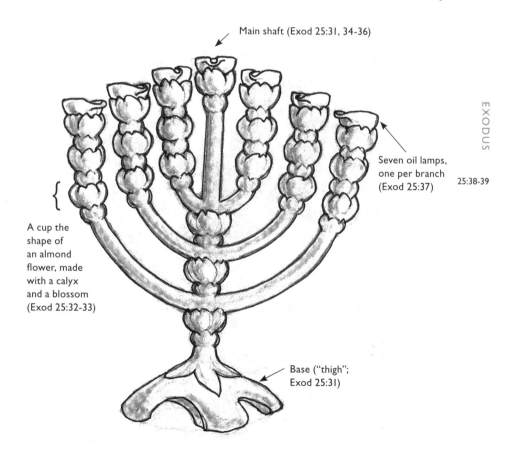

Main shaft (Exod 25:31, 34-36)

Seven oil lamps, one per branch (Exod 25:37)

25:38-39

A cup the shape of an almond flower, made with a calyx and a blossom (Exod 25:32-33)

Base ("thigh"; Exod 25:31)

Figure 7: The lampstand

■ **39** The most straightforward reading of Exod 25:37-39 is that **the lampstand** and **all** its articles (i.e., the seven lamps, its wick trimmers, and trays/

censers) are to be made of **a talent** [about 75 pounds or 34 kg] **of pure gold**. A talent is the equivalent of three thousand shekels (a shekel is about 0.4 oz or 11.3 g).

■ **40** The command to **make them according to the pattern shown** concludes this chapter and refers not only to the menorah but also to the ark and the table mentioned prior to the lampstand. Moses is to ensure that the people follow the pattern Yahweh gave him **on the mountain**.

FROM THE TEXT

If the lampstand is a symbol of life, the lamplight is a symbol of light, first of the triune God and second of God's people, both Israel and the church. (1) The lamplight represents the Lord, who is the "everlasting light" for God's people (Isa 60:19-20; also see Ps 27:1-2; Isa 2:5; 10:17; Mic 7:8; 1 John 1:5; Rev 22:5), especially in situations of darkness and danger. As such, light is an image of God as the source of a blessed life that is free of darkness (Pss 43:3; 89:15 [16 HB]). (2) The lamplight points to Jesus Christ, who is the ultimate Light of the World: "In him was life, and that life was the light of all mankind" (John 1:4). Charles Wesley famously picks up on these themes in his "Hark, the Herald Angels Sing," which declares: "Light and life to all he brings, / Ris'n with healing in his wings." Indeed, Jesus Christ, as the perfect expression and union of God and humanity, is "the light of the world," "the light of life" (John 8:12; 9:5). (3) The lamplight represents the "seven spirits" of God. It is symbolically significant that the number of lamps on the menorah is seven, the number of perfection and completeness. In his vision of heaven, John sees before the throne of God seven lamps of fire that are identified as the seven spirits of God (Rev 4:5; also see 3:1; 5:6, which variously link these seven spirits with Jesus and the Lamb). The seven lamplights may speak particularly of the illuminating and life-giving presence, manifestations, and work of the Spirit of the Lord (see Isa 11:2-5). (4) The lamplight represents Israel. As a nation that has the Lord's light and glory, Israel is a light, to which the nations will come (Isa 42:6; 60:1-3). (5) Lastly, the lamplight points to the witnesses of Christ, who are "the light of the world" (Matt 5:14; Eph 5:8). Even as Israel is called to be the light to the nations (Isa 42:6; 60:3), so are the churches called "lampstands" (Rev 1:12-13, 20). By God's own transforming presence and sanctifying work among his people, God's people display the very illuminating nature of God.

5. The Tabernacle and Its Coverings (26:1-14)

BEHIND THE TEXT

The instructions for the most important furnishings are now followed by the instruction for the tabernacle (i.e., the innermost curtain) and its three coverings. The finest textile is draped over the sacred precinct, and the strongest is the outermost layer.

The fine wool-linen used for the innermost layer is the same material used for some of the priestly garments. Being considered the most appropriate material for direct contact with Yahweh's holy presence, the wool-linen fabric is forbidden to the laity (Lev 19:19; Deut 22:11).

With the construction of the tabernacle, the glory of Yahweh transfers from Mount Sinai to the tabernacle to dwell among the Israelites. Both Mount Sinai and the tabernacle are, therefore, "divided into three distinct zones of increasing degrees of holiness and restriction of access" (Sarna 1996, 203; see the following chart).

Mount Sinai		The Tabernacle	
Section of Mountain	*Degree of Access*	*Section of Tabernacle*	*Degree of Access*
Foot	All the people	The court	All the people
Midsection	Priests and elders (and Moses)	The holy place	Priests and Moses
Top	Moses only	The most holy place	Moses and the high priest once a year

Figure 8: Zones of holiness

Exodus 36:8-19 reports the creation of the tabernacle and three coverings.

IN THE TEXT

a. The Tabernacle or the Innermost Layer (26:1-6)

■ **1** The term **tabernacle** (*miškān*) here and throughout this unit refers to the innermost curtains. Once the tabernacle is erected and covered with the three coverings, the whole structure is sometimes referred to as the tabernacle (40:36, 38). The tabernacle consists of **ten** wool-linen **curtains** (*yerî'â*; "curtain," "drape") with **cherubim** that are the ***work of a tapestry weaver*** (*ma'ăśēh ḥōšēb*; also in 36:8). The Hebrew expression translated into ***a tapestry weaver*** here (**a skilled worker** [NIV]) is also used for the curtain with cherubim, which hangs between the holy place and the most holy place (26:31; 36:35). In addition, it is used for the ephod (28:6; 39:3) and the breastpiece (28:15;

321

39:8), both of which require gold threads, in addition to the three colored woolen yarns and linen yarns in natural colors.

The term for **tapestry weaver** (*ḥōšēb*) derives from the verb (*ḥāšab*) that means "calculate, count, plan out, devise." In this context, the noun *ḥōšēb* probably refers to a person who weaves a complex, ingenious woven tapestry that requires careful planning of the pattern and counting throughout the weaving process, which is not required in simpler weaving. The plain, tightly **twisted**, thus very durable **linen** yarns were probably used as the lengthwise warps (which would not show in the finished product, as in tapestry weaving), while the expensive, colored (probably woolen) yarns were used as the widthwise wefts. The finished product would have been a splendid mixture of **blue**, **purple**, and **scarlet** with cherubim figures **woven into** the curtain. The cherubim design may have resembled the cherubim statues on the ark's cover.

Oholiab is named the chief **tapestry weaver** (*ḥōšēb*) and **skillful weaver** (*rōqēm*; "embroiderer" [NIV]) in 38:23. Since there were many tapestries to be weaved, presumably, under the supervision of the chief weaver Oholiab, other men and women weavers wove them.

Weavers

Three different terms for weavers are mentioned in the tabernacle section. The most sophisticated pieces were the **work of a tapestry weaver** (*ma'ăśēh ḥōšēb*). They were the curtains (with magnificent cherubim designs) that were closest to the most holy place or the principal and glorious priest vestments that were woven with gold. The expression **work of a skillful weaver** (*ma'ăśēh rōqēm*; "work of an embroiderer" [NIV]) is used for those pieces that required weaving with three colored yarns, along with the plain linen, such as the curtain for the tabernacle entrance (26:36; 36:37), the hangings for the courtyard entrance (27:16; 38:18), and the sash for the priest (28:39; 39:29). The pieces that required simpler weaving with one yarn, such as the robe of the ephod and the tunic, are called the **work of a weaver** (*ma'ăśēh 'ōrēg* [28:32; 39:22, 27]; **woven** [NIV]).

■ **2** The **size** of each curtain is 4 x 28 **cubits** (6' x 42' or 1.8 x 12.9 m) in length and width.

■ **3** Five . . . **curtains** are to be joined on the widest side, and **the same with the other five**, to create two large curtains. Each of the two coverings measures 20 x 28 cubits (about 30' x 42' or 9.2 x 12.8 m) in length and width.

■ **4-5** The most costly **blue** dye is used for the **loops** used to join the two large curtains to make one tabernacle. The overall dimensions of the tabernacle are 40 x 28 cubits (60' x 42' or 18.4 x 12.8 m) in length and width. When the tabernacle is draped over the frames (which is 30 x 9 x 10 cubits in length, width, and height; → 26:18-22), the tabernacle would hang 0.5 cubit (9" or 23 cm) above the ground on the north and south side. On the west side, due to socket bases increasing the overall height (even if a negligible amount), the holy tabernacle would not touch the ground directly.

■ **6** Since the inner **curtains** go directly above the holy place and the most holy place, **gold clasps** are used to join the curtains.

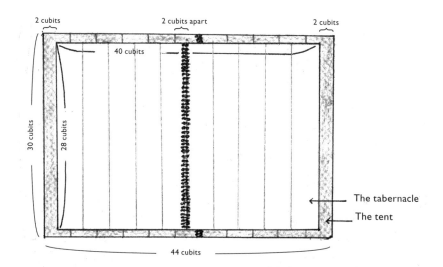

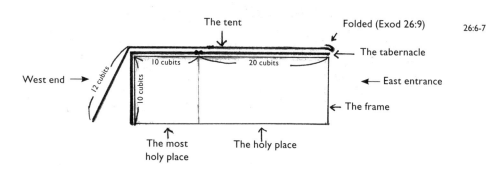

Figure 9: The tabernacle and the tent

b. The Tent of Goat Hair: The Second Inner Layer (26:7-13)

■ **7** The **tabernacle** is covered with a **tent** (*'ōhel*) made with **goat hair**. The ancestors of Israel herded sheep and goats (e.g., Gen 13:2; 26:14; 30:42-43), which supplied valuable milk, wool, meat, and leather. The Israelites left Goshen with very large herds of sheep and goats (Exod 12:38). While goat hair came in white, brown, and black, a black tent, "like the tent curtains of Solomon" (Song 1:5) or such as Arab Bedouins still make, might be the preferred color used in this instance.

■ **8** The tent is made up of **eleven curtains** of **the same size**—4 x 30 **cubits** (6' x 45' or about 1.84 x 13.8 m) in length and width—yielding 44 x 30 cubits in length and width.

■ **9** The **sixth curtain** is folded **double** and placed **at the front of the tent** (that is, the east end). It is done in a way that leaves a half curtain (2 cubits) for the west end (→ Exod 26:12). This placement of the cover ensures the joints with metal clasps do not overlap, but are spaced 2 cubits apart (→ Figure 9 above).

■ **10-11** The **loops** (v 10) were probably made from goat hair like the tent curtains. While the tabernacle is fastened together with gold clasps, the two tent curtains are joined by **bronze clasps** (v 11). When the two large tent curtains are to be joined together to form **a unit**, the tent measures 44 x 30 cubits (about 66' x 45' or 20.2 x 13.8 m) in length and width. The tent is bigger than the tabernacle, which measures 40 x 28 cubits (about 60' x 42' or 18.4 x 12.8 m) in length and width, so the tent completely covers the tabernacle.

■ **12** The **additional length of the tent curtains** (measuring 2 cubits) is to "hang over" (ESV, KJV, NET; **hang down** [NIV]) **at the rear** or on the west end, extended outward, secured with pegs, rather than pile up on the ground.

■ **13** On the north and south sides, **the tent** will be 1 **cubit** [about 1.5' or 0.46 m] **longer** than the tabernacle when draped over it. The tent is also longer than the tabernacle frames by half a cubit (about 9" or 23 cm) on the north and south sides. Assuming that the silver bases for the frames do not significantly change the overall height of the wooden structure (→ v 19), the tent extends outward, secured to the ground with pegs (like the tent on the west end).

c. The Two Leather Covers (26:14)

■ **14** This verse commands the making of two **tent** coverings, one from **ram skins dyed red** and another from some **other durable leather**. The exact identification of the second leather is difficult to discern, but since its primary function is to protect all that is underneath, "durable leather" is better than other suggestions (see "another type of durable leather" in 25:5). No measurements are given for the coverings, but one assumes that they should be big enough to cover the tent, providing complete protection against sun and rain.

FROM THE TEXT

God desired to dwell among the people of Israel, but in a way that fully expressed God's uniqueness and potentially dangerous holiness. Hence, multiple layers of various materials created and maintained an impermeable seal between God's holy place within the tabernacle and the profane world without. Only the priests, who were specifically appointed and ordained, were allowed to enter and minister in the holy place, and that, only on God's own detailed terms.

In the new covenant, by contrast, we celebrate the full access granted to all who believe in Jesus Christ into the most holy place, the heavenly throne room of God (Heb 4:16 and 10:19-22). Indeed, there is now the "open hospitality" of the God King, who invites all to approach his presence through Jesus Christ, his Son and our Mediator / High Priest. It is an invitation extended to all who stand in need of his grace, mercy, and forgiveness. The gospel of Jesus Christ promises forgiveness through repentance of sin to all who desire to enter his holy presence, and the church exists in the world as a witness of the redeeming grace and sanctifying power of God through Jesus Christ.

Not unlike the old covenant, Christians must show an appropriate concern that preserves the sanctity of God's church from the defilement and corruption of the world. In that respect, an impermeable seal (like the tabernacle coverings) that separates holiness from the sinful ways of the world must mark the true church of God. God's holy people are to be radically distinct from the world. This boundary, like the outside and inside of the tabernacle precinct, is crossed only to our peril.

6. The Tabernacle Frames and Its Curtains (26:15-37)

a. The Frames (26:15-30)

BEHIND THE TEXT

Sarna notes that critical scholars have held that the tabernacle was a "fictional retrogression of King Solomon's Temple into the wilderness wanderings" (1996, 196). The main challenge with the tabernacle was its perceived massive weight. Since the time of the Talmud, the Jewish tradition maintained that the most holy place was a perfect cube measuring 10 x 10 x 10 (half of the inner sanctuary of Solomon's temple, 20 x 20 x 20 [1 Kgs 6:20]). To achieve this measurement, each wall (not frame) was held to be 1 cubit in thickness and all eight boards of the west end assembled side-by-side. That yielded 12 cubits of width on the exterior on the west wall, but only 10 cubits in the interior, as the north and south boards took 2 cubits away from the interior measurement (see Jacob 1992, 792-93). Thus, critical scholars rightly noted the massive volume and weight problems of such a structure. Together with their solid silver bases, it was believed to weigh some twenty tons; as a result, they were not thought to be portable; thus, the structure was deemed fictional.

The text itself does not insist that the wooden structure (*qereš*) be 1 cubit thick. In fact, the text strongly resists that interpretation by not providing the thickness, which indicates its negligible size (like the atonement cover thickness). If it were to be a cubit or half a cubit or even a handbreadth (25:25), the size requirement would have been mentioned. Also, the text does not demand that the inner sanctum be a perfect cube (although one might feel

26:15-30

that the inner sanctuary of Solomon's temple and the new Jerusalem in Rev 21:16, both of which are cubes, do).

There are reasonable ways of understanding the text that uphold the structural soundness and appropriate weight of the mobile structure (suggested by Kennedy 1898 as cited by Propp 2006, 411-12 and reflected in this commentary). The following interpretation affirms the plainest measurement of the tabernacle *frames*, which is 30 x 9 x 10 cubits, with the most holy place being 10 x 9 x 10 cubits in length, width, and height (→ Exod 26:18-22, 33). We can retain much of the traditional understanding of the symmetry of the tabernacle even without positing a perfect cube for the most holy place.

The construction of the frames is reported in 36:20-34.

IN THE TEXT

■ **15-16** These verses specify the material, measurement, and design of the wooden **frames** (v 15; *qereš*; "frame," "plank") that support **the tabernacle** coverings. **Acacia wood** frames are to be made for the tabernacle.

■ **17** The more literal rendering of the first phrase clarifies how each frame is to be constructed: ***two arms*** [*yādôt*] ***of each frame are to be fitted to each other***. In other words, the frame consists of the two "arms" or vertical bars that are connected to each other with horizontal bars (the number of which is determined by Moses or the architectural engineers). If so, the parts that are inserted into the base are the bottom ends of the two "arms" (see v 11; note that many illustrations add unmentioned "feet" to the frame). This construction of the frames would make it light enough (each frame estimated at about 76 lbs or 34.5 kg; see Propp 2006, 411) both for its bases to support and for an oxcart to transport it (see Num 7:6-7).

■ **18-21** **Twenty frames** (Exod 26:18) are to be joined together to create a large frame of 30 x 10 cubits (45' x 15' or 14 x 4.6 m) in length and height for **the south** and **the north** (v 20) sides (the long sides). For each side, **forty** socket **bases** are made with **silver**. According to 38:27, they are cast in a mold and each weighs one talent (about 75 lbs or 34 kg), about the same as the weight of each frame. **Two** bases are used for each frame (26:19). Their combined weight is roughly double the weight of the frame, sufficient enough to provide stability to the frame. With the bottom end of the two ***arms*** (*yādôt*) inserted deep into the socket, the frame would be stable (the overall height would either remain the same or exceed by little).

■ **22** For the **west end**, **six** frames are joined together to form a structure 9 x 10 cubits (13.5' x 15' or 4.1 x 4.6 m) in width and height.

■ **23-24** In addition to the six frames, **two** extra frames of the same dimension are made for the **corners** of the west **end** (v 23). The extra frame faces the corner frame, parallel to each other and enjoined by **a single ring** (v 24). "One ring" may mean either one ring total that joins the two frames or more likely a single ring in five different joints where five crossbars would go through (→ "crossbars" in v 28), to provide strength and stability (→ Figure 10 below). Cassuto, however, suggests that the corner frames were a half cubit each, placed side-by-side, forming a structure of 10 x 10 cubits (1967, 356). This way, the Talmud's perfect cube (10 x 10 x 10 cubits) for the most holy place is maintained. Cassuto's suggestion is attractive, but it seems that if the size of the two extra frames were to be different, the text would have mentioned it.

■ **25** There are to be eight **frames** and sixteen **silver** socket **bases** for the west end.

■ **26-27** Crossbars (**five**, one for each **side** of the **frames**) are to be made (v 26). This is consistent with the report of its making in 36:31-32. Given the challenge of transporting a crossbar that is 30 cubits long (45' or 14 m), a crossbar that is made up of shorter pieces joined by metal socket joints (like modern tent poles) might be what is in view. Even the tabernacle and the tent are composed of two sections for practical reasons, 26:3-6, 9-11. It is assumed that each frame has the rings for the crossbars.

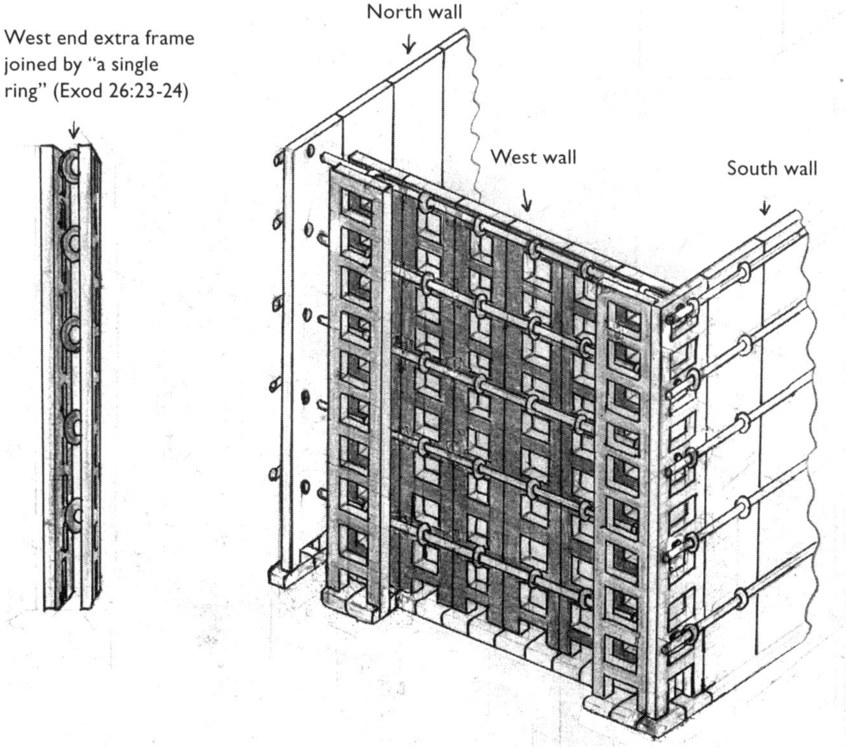

West end extra frame joined by "a single ring" (Exod 26:23-24)

Figure 10: The tabernacle frames, walls, and joints

■ **28** This verse concerns the west side. Given the symmetry of the overall structure, we may assume that the crossbars were evenly spaced across the height of the walls. The term **center** (*tîkōn*; "middle") may refer to the vertical middle position, not lower, not upper (e.g., 1 Kgs 6:8; Ezek 41:7) or temporal middle as in "middle watch" (e.g., Judg 7:19). Here, it likely refers to horizontal middle, that is, the west side, in between the north and the south sides. The center **crossbar**, then, would collectively refer to those bars that are on the west side. The expression **end to end** most likely indicates that the crossbars were longer than the width of the wall and were pegged right into the adjoining walls (see Propp 2006, 416). The expression ***through the midst*** [*betôk*] **of the frames** may refer to the crossbars going through the midst of the doubled-up frames, being inserted through the rings that adjoin those frames (→ Figure 10 above). In sum, we may envision all five crossbars extending end to end in the midst of the doubled-up frames. Such a joining of the doubled-up frames and three walls would result in a strong structure that would not easily topple.

■ **29** The **frames, gold rings**, and **crossbars** directly surround the sacred furnishings and precincts; thus, they are overlaid with the most precious metal, **gold**.

■ **30** Whatever is lacking in Yahweh's verbal instructions is supplemented by the prophetic vision Moses had from Yahweh. According to the **plan** (*mišpāṭ*; "judgment," "decision," "specifications"; but see 1 Kgs 4:28 [5:8 HB] for "charge" in the KJV and NASB) and "pattern" (*tabnît* [25:9]) Moses received from Yahweh, the Israelites will construct the tabernacle (see also 27:8).

FROM THE TEXT

In the past, critical scholars have raised serious doubts about the architectural feasibility and historicity of the tabernacle. For many, the account of the portable sanctuary in the book of Exodus is fictional. Yet, as is often the case, the supposedly indisputable results of such biblical criticism have not stood the test of time. While questions and mystery remain, internal evidence, recent archaeological finds, and ancient literary works have shown the essential feasibility of the tabernacle as a working, historical structure (see Sarna 1996, 196-200).

This evidence offers a lesson for us. Our faith in the essential reliability and trustworthiness of God's written word cannot be subjected to the shifting winds of scholarly opinion. Of course, if any texts (including the tabernacle texts) provide ample reasons to suggest that it was not intended as a historical description, then the situation becomes quite different. However, as it stands, the text points to the historical reality of the tabernacle, so we need not wait for external (e.g., archaeological) confirmation of every detail to believe it is so.

b. The Curtains (26:31-37)

This unit gives the instructions for the curtain that separates the most holy place from the holy place (26:31-35) and the curtain that separates the holy place from the tabernacle courtyard (vv 36-37). In accordance with the organizing principle of moving from the interior to exterior and from the most sacred to the least sacred in 25:10—27:19, the inner curtain is treated first, followed by the curtain that separates the holy place.

The instructions for completing the curtains and the posts are fulfilled in 36:35-38.

IN THE TEXT

(1) Curtains for the Most Holy Place (26:31-35)

■ **31** This verse gives the command to make a **curtain** and specifies its material, design, and type of weaving. The Hebrew term for "curtain" (*pārōket*; "curtain," "veil") here differs from the one used in vv 1-13 (*yerî'â*). However, this curtain is made with the same material, of the same sophisticated tapestry weaving technique by *a tapestry weaver* (*ḥōšēb*; → v 1), and the same design (**cherubim**) as those used for the tabernacle or the innermost curtains (see v 1). The dimensions for the curtain are not given, but since its function is to provide a barrier to the most holy place and the ark of the covenant (30:6), it would be 9 x 10 cubits (13.5' x 15' or 4.1 x 4.6 m) in width and height, matching the frames of the west end (→ 26:22).

■ **32** The veil between the most holy place and the holy place is to be hung **with gold hooks** from the top of **four posts**. The **hooks** or "nails" are called *vāv* in Hebrew, probably because they were shaped like the ancient letter *vāv*, which looks like the English letter Y. Cassuto envisions Y-shaped hooks on top of the posts, upon which wooden curtain rods overlaid with gold were inserted, so the veil could hang evenly (1967, 359). While the curtain rods are not specifically mentioned in association with the posts of the most holy place, they are mentioned in relation to the tabernacle entrance posts (36:38) and the courtyard posts (27:10, 11, 17; 38:10, 11, 12, 17). However, the Hebrew term for "rods" is mistranslated into "bands" in most translations (→ "bands" as "rods" in 27:10). Consistent with other furnishings and objects for the tabernacle, the posts are **overlaid with gold** and the socket **bases**, which touch the ground, are made with cast **silver**. Each silver base weighed 1 talent (about 75 lbs or 34 kg), according to 38:27. The text does not mention whether the curtain should hang in front of or behind the posts.

33 The curtain hangs from the curtain rods directly **underneath** (*tāḥāt*), rather than **from**, the gold **clasps** of the tabernacle. The curtain is placed 20 cubits (about 30' or 9.2 m) from the entrance to the tabernacle. That would leave 10 cubits to the west end. The most holy place would therefore measure 10 x 9 x 10 cubits (15' x 13.5' x 15' or 4.6 x 4.1 x 4.6 m) in length, width, and height. How the high priest is to negotiate the curtain to enter the **Most Holy Place** is not made clear. Perhaps one end of the curtain was drawn or one post moved. Or, the high priest, most dramatically, entered on hands and knees under the curtains in an expression of utmost homage.

34 Verses 34-35 clarify the proper placement of the furnishings, rather than the sequence of their placement. In 40:3-5, **the ark of the covenant** and **the atonement cover** are placed **in the Most Holy Place** probably before the curtain is hung. After the curtain is draped, the furnishings of the holy place are arranged.

35 As one enters the **tabernacle** from the east end entrance, **the table** is on the right side and **the lampstand** on the left.

(2) Curtains for the Holy Place (26:36-37)

36 The **curtain** used **for the entrance to the tent**, or holy place, is to be made from the same material used for the tabernacle (26:1) and the curtain between the holy place and the most holy place (v 31). It is the **work of *a skill-ful weaver*** (*rōqēm*; embroiderer [NIV]; → "Weavers" sidebar in 26:1). Instead of weaving a plain **linen** curtain with colors applied with needlework (embroidery), expensive colored yarns are to be used to artfully weave a patterned textile on a loom (with the finished product not showing the plain linen). The weaving here is different from the more complicated, difficult, and time-consuming weaving required for the textiles that have cherubim woven into them (→ "Weavers" sidebar in 26:1).

37 Like the **curtain** of the most holy place, the entrance curtain is most likely hung on gold-plated curtain rods. Thus, in 36:38, Bezalel makes "five posts with hooks for them" and overlays "the tops of the posts and their bands ["rods" (NJB)] with gold." The curtain "rods" rested on Y-shaped **gold hooks** (→ "hooks" in 26:32; → curtain "rods" [*ḥăšûqêhem*], in 27:10 [NJB]). The **five posts** provide the vertical support, and the hooks and curtain rods provide the horizontal support for the curtains. The socket **bases** for the entrance posts are made with **bronze**. According to 38:29-31, the total amount of bronze received and used for everything related to the tabernacle is "70 talents and 2,400 shekels" (212,400 shekels or 5,310 lbs or 2.7 tons). While the text does not specify how many talents of bronze should be used for the bronze base, it is reasonable to assume it was similar to silver bases—one talent per base (about 75 lbs or 34 kg). If so, a total of 65 talents of bronze were used for the bases (60 for the courtyard and 5 for the tabernacle entrance posts). About 5 talents and 2,400 shekels were used for all the other objects requiring bronze (the bronze altar, the bronze grating, the altar utensils, the pegs, and the clasps for the tent).

By emphasizing the rending of the curtain at the crucifixion, the NT writers emphasize the believers' confident access to God's presence based on the perfect atoning work of Christ on the cross (Eph 2:13; Heb 10:19-22). In the tabernacle, the most holy place is divided from the holy place, so that even the high priest may not unduly approach the most holy place, but draw near only at the time, through the means, and for the purposes sanctioned by the Lord.

The Synoptic Gospels mention the tearing of the veil of the temple sanctuary around the time of Jesus' death (Matt 27:51; Mark 15:38; Luke 23:45; also see Heb 6:19; 9:3; 10:19). The traditional interpretation holds that it was the inner curtain that veiled the most holy place that was torn, which is supported by Hebrews: "We have this hope as an anchor for the soul, firm and secure. It enters the *inner sanctuary behind the curtain*, where our forerunner, Jesus, has entered on our behalf" (6:19-20). This text likely refers to the heavenly sanctuary, on which the most holy place in the tabernacle is patterned. Christ entered this place as the Great High Priest on our behalf, and his atoning death made possible our entry into that same place with him (see Hamilton 2011, 473-75). Through Jesus and his atonement, we have access into God's holy presence, a way to our heavenly Father (John 14:6).

7. The Bronze Altar (27:1-8)

Offering sacrifices was common in the ancient world, and sacrifice typically included cooking on an altar. A four-horned altar of the same dimension as the bronze altar, but made of cut stones (contra 20:25; Deut 27:5), has been found in Israel (at Tel Arad). Depictions of horned altars also have been found in Hellenistic Egypt (Propp 2006, 421). Burning the sacrifice down to its ashes, however, is an Israelite religious innovation. The living God, the Creator of the universe, does not consume human food. The purpose of the Israelites' sacrifices, therefore, is not to feed the deity but to expiate sin and express worship, dedication, and gratitude.

Based on the instruction to build an altar of earth or stone in Exod 20:24, some commentators assume that the bottom half of the bronze altar was filled with stones and earth. However, the altars of earth or stone in 20:24 refer to altars erected away from the central sanctuary, which were used only once. Such stone altars were built for various commemorative or sacrificial purposes

(→ Behind the Text for 20:22-26). The bronze altar in the tabernacle needed to be hollow (27:8), fitted with doors or, more likely, short (unmentioned) feet (like the ark [25:12]) for the easy and daily collection of fatty ashes produced by daily burnt offerings and other sacrifices (Lev 6:9-10 [2-3 HB]).

The report of the construction of the bronze altar is given in Exod 38:1-7.

IN THE TEXT

■ **I** The bronze **altar** is for the burnt offering. According to Lev 6:9-13 [2-6 HB], perpetual fire is to be on the altar. Its overall dimensions are 5 x 5 x 3 cubits (7.5' x 7.5' x 4.5' or 2.3 x 2.3 x 1.4 m) in width, length, and height. Looking down from above, the altar is a **square**.

■ **2** The altar is to have a **horn** on **each of the four corners**. The function of the **horns** (bronze or golden) is not entirely clear. One purpose of the bronze horns may be practical, for tying the offering onto the altar (see Ps 118:27) or simply to hold the offering in place without need for ropes (Propp 2006, 421). More importantly, the horns are associated with religious purposes. Some of the blood of the sin offerings is put on the bronze horns, as part of the ordination or consecration rites (Exod 29:12; Lev 8:15) and the ordinary atonement rituals (e.g., Lev 4:25, 30). The atonement for priests and the annual atonement are made on the golden horns (Exod 30:10; Lev 4:7). In addition, fugitives could seek temporary asylum by taking hold of the horns of the golden altar (→ Exod 21:13-14). The holiness of the horns of the altar, however, does not ultimately shield an obvious murderer from punishment. The altar is overlaid with **bronze**, which is a hard and tough metal, appropriate for the place where sacrifices are incinerated (→ "bronze" in 26:37).

■ **3 Pots** are for removing fatty **ashes** from the altar, first to a location beside the altar, then outside the camp to a designated ceremonially clean place (Lev 4:12; 6:10-11 [3-4 HB]), on the east side of the altar (1:16). The **shovels** are for daily scraping away the fatty ashes (6:9-10 [2-3 HB]) beneath the bronze grating. The **sprinkling bowls** are for holding the blood of the sacrifices, which is subsequently sprinkled to make atonement (e.g., 1:5, 11; 3:2; 4:17; 5:9). The **meat forks** are probably for turning the sacrificial meat to aid burning. In 1 Sam 2:13, a three-pronged fork is used by a priest to retrieve his portion of meat. The **firepans** (*maḥetâ*) indicate the censer (e.g., Lev 10:1; 16:12; Num 16:16-18, 37-39, 46 [16:16-18; 17:2-4, 11 HB]).

■ **4** The firewood would be placed on the **grating** of **bronze** and the various sacrifices on top of the firewood (see Lev 1:6-8, 17; 3:5; 6:12 [5 HB]). As the offerings burn, fatty ashes would fall to the ground through the network. The rings are to be installed on the underside of the **four corners of the network** (→ Figure 11 below).

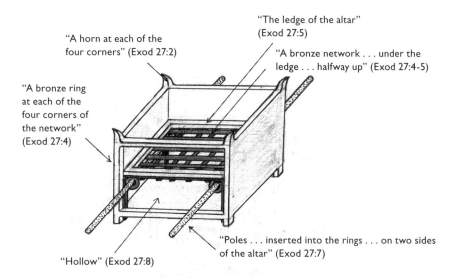

"A horn at each of the four corners" (Exod 27:2)

"The ledge of the altar" (Exod 27:5)

"A bronze network . . . under the ledge . . . halfway up" (Exod 27:4-5)

"A bronze ring at each of the four corners of the network" (Exod 27:4)

"Poles . . . inserted into the rings . . . on two sides of the altar" (Exod 27:7)

"Hollow" (Exod 27:8)

Figure 11: The bronze altar

■ **5** The referent of **it** (fem. sg.) is the network (fem. sg.). The **ledge** is built on the inside (since it is to be placed right above the network) of the **altar, halfway up**. The network, with the rings facing downward (*millemāṭṭâ*), is placed directly **under** the ledge (supposedly with unmentioned legs supporting the network). When the poles are inserted through the altar and then through the rings (which are attached to the underside of the network), the poles would push up on the altar, the network, and the ledge, effectively negotiating their heavy weight. The suggestion that the ledge was on the outside with the rings on the ledge is not convincing, as the rings could break, stressed by the massive weight of the bronze altar.

■ **6-7** The **poles of acacia wood**, overlaid with **bronze**, would be extremely strong (v 6). They are for transporting the bronze **altar**. Unlike the ark of the covenant, but like the table of the bread of the Presence, **the poles are to be inserted** only when the altar **is carried** (v 7).

■ **8** This unit ends with a command that emphasizes the importance of making each part according to instructions **shown** Moses; craftsmen do not merely rely on the verbal instructions (25:9, 40; 26:30).

FROM THE TEXT

As a place of perpetual sacrifice and burning, the bronze altar demonstrates God's wrath and repugnance toward sin and God's just punishment and merciful purging of it. Atonement, forgiveness, and purification are possible, but only through the shedding of a substitute's blood (Heb 9:22; see Rom 6:23a). In this way, the altar displays God's moral righteousness and justice.

Many Christians wish to avoid such matters as God's wrath and blood sacrifice. They affirm the righteousness of God. But they dismiss as primitive and even dangerous its implication that God deals with sin and corruption with punitive bloodshedding. But if we reject or dilute the significance of an atoning sacrifice, we may misunderstand the ministry and death of Christ. According to Paul, "God presented Christ as a sacrifice of atonement [*hilastērion*], through the shedding of his blood—to be received by faith. He did this to demonstrate his righteousness, because in his forbearance he had left the sins committed beforehand unpunished" (Rom 3:25). In this verse, Paul conjoins several ideas: (1) God is present to make reconciliation with sinners; (2) Christ embodies the place of atonement or "atonement cover" (→ Exod 25:17-22); (3) Christ made atonement "through the shedding of his blood" and, as such, he represents the perfect sacrifice and the perfect fulfillment of the altar's purpose; (4) the sacrifice of Christ demonstrates God's righteousness, the full demonstration of his wrath against sin and sinners; (5) God is forbearing in tolerating the inadequate substitutionary sacrifices of animal victims for human sin. In these ways, Jesus Christ expresses and fulfills the old covenant ministry of the altar as both the self-offering Great High Priest and the perfect and sufficient sacrificial victim. Through the cross, the mercy and justice of God are gloriously and perfectly expressed! (see Ryken 2005, 861-66).

8. The Courtyard (27:9-19)

BEHIND THE TEXT

The holy sanctuary must be enclosed, separated from the profane world outside. Thus, the tabernacle courtyard creates a kind of "buffer zone" between the holy and the common. In Exod 29:31-32, the entrance to the tent of meeting is called a "sacred place" (see Lev 6:16 [9 HB]; 7:7; 16:3, 24). Also, the consecrated bronze altar is identified as "most holy" in Exod 29:37. Such considerations indicate that the courtyard itself is a holy place. Lay worshippers, who are ritually clean, are permitted to enter this holy place to present their offerings to Yahweh (e.g., see Lev 1:11, in which the worshipper is commanded to slaughter the burnt offering on the north side of the bronze altar).

The rectangular courtyard is 100 x 50 cubits (150' x 75' or 46 x 23 m) in length (north and south sides) and width (east and west sides). The Jewish tradition envisions the courtyard as having two squares of 50 x 50 cubits with the tabernacle placed in the west square. At the center of the west square is the most holy place. The ark of the covenant, in turn, is at the center of the most holy place. In the end, the ark of the covenant, the focal point of all, occupies the center of the west courtyard (→ Figure 12 below). This arrangement remains consistent whether we maintain what seems to be the most straightforward measurement or adopt the Talmudic/Jewish resizing of the most holy place (→ Behind the Text for Exod 26:15-30).

The courtyard is built as reported in 38:9-20.

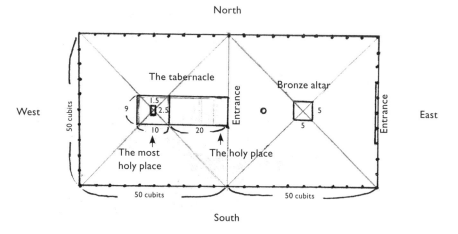

Figure 12: The courtyard

IN THE TEXT

27:9-10

■ **9** The Hebrew expression **curtains of finely twisted linen** one **hundred cubits long** may refer to individual curtains installed separately, covering one hundred cubits, or more likely, one continuous sheet comprised of many curtains sown together, using durable linen yarn in its natural color (→ "linen" in 25:4).

■ **10** The **twenty posts** are to be spaced five cubits (about 7.5' or 2.3 m) apart. In 38:17, the tops of all the courtyard **posts** are overlaid with silver. The **silver hooks** are Y-shaped (see "hooks" in 26:32). Their bottom end is probably nailed to the top of the post, and their top part is used for inserting curtain "rods" (NJB; **bands** [NIV]). The Hebrew noun translated into "band" (*ḥăšûqêhem*) derives from the verb that means "attach" or "bind." The noun in the tabernacle section is translated into "bands" (NASB, NET, NKJV) or "fillets" (ESV, KJV). Many envision solid silver bands that go around the posts, used to secure the curtains vertically. However, the noun (*ḥăšûqêhem*) is best translated as curtain "rods" (NJB) for the following reasons: (1) The same noun in 1 Kgs 7:33 means "rods" or "spokes" that connect the hub and rim of a wheel. Curtain "rods" perfectly fits the tabernacle section. (2) According to some passages, they (*ḥăšûqêhem*) were overlaid (Exod 36:38; 38:19), which implies they were made with wood. Small brackets (or bands) would not have been made with wood, but with solid silver. The amount of silver required for making solid silver brackets is sufficient for overlaying wooden rods. (3) The frequent mention of "the hooks . . . and their *ḥăšûqêhem*" (27:10, 11; 38:10, 11, 12, 17) and "their tops and their *ḥăšûqêhem*" (36:38; 38:19 in the Hebrew text) signal they belong together atop the posts. (4) In conclusion, the noun (*ḥăšûqêhem*) is best translated into curtain "rods" (NJB), upon which the curtains were fastened with cords. Practically, the posts already provide vertical support to which the curtains can be tied with cords. What the curtains really need is horizontal support, which the silver-plated wooden curtain rods provide. The **bronze** socket **bases** (see "bronze" in 26:37), each weighing about 1 talent (about 75 lbs or 34 kg), together with the pegs (27:19), would hold the posts firmly in place.

■ **11** The **north side** is to be just like the south side.

■ **12** The **curtains** of **fifty cubits** (75' or 23 m) most likely refer to one long sheet comprised of many curtains sewn together. The **ten posts** set on **ten bases** are again spaced five cubits apart. Curtain rods (see "bands" in v 10) are assumed here and for the east side in vv 13-15, and are explicitly mentioned in v 17 and in 38:17.

■ **13** The courtyard entrance faces the **east, toward the sunrise**, as does the entrance of the tabernacle.

■ **14-15** There are three **curtains** on the east **side**: two for either side of the entrance, each covering **fifteen cubits** (about 22.5' or 6.9 m), and one for the entrance in the middle (v 16), measuring twenty **cubits** (about 30' or 9.2 m).

■ **16** The **entrance . . . curtain**, according to 38:18, is five cubits high (7.5' or 2.3 m), which is the same as the rest of the curtains of the courtyard (27:18). The entrance curtain is made by the same *skillful weaver* (*rōqēm*; **embroiderer** [NIV]) with the same material and same weaving technique as the curtain for the entrance to the tabernacle (see 26:36).

■ **17-19** **All the posts** for the **courtyard are to have silver**-plated curtain *rods*, silver Y-shaped **hooks, bronze** socket **bases** (27:17), and bronze **tent pegs** (v 19). The posts will also have silver-plated tops (38:17). The curtains would be secured to the posts by ties, to the ground with guy-ropes and pegs, and to the curtain rods by insertion or by ties to prevent them from flapping in the wind.

FROM THE TEXT

The formation of Israel's tabernacle courtyard and its furniture express the distinct Israelite emphasis on the holiness of God and the approach to this Holy God through proper means. The courtyard is fenced and separated from the common area, so that the common people may not approach the holy ground apart from the rites of expiation of sin and the sanctification of sinners and the sanctuary.

Likewise in the NT, we can approach our heavenly Father only through the belief in the atoning and reconciling work of Jesus Christ and the sanctifying work of the Holy Spirit (2 Thess 2:13-14). The church, therefore, would do well to emphasize that only through the way prescribed by God, be it in the old covenant or the new covenant, can one be saved. "Jesus answered, 'I am the way and the truth and the life. No one comes to the Father except through me. If you really know me, you will know my Father as well. From now on, you do know him and have seen him'" (John 14:6-7).

9. Oil for the Lampstand (27:20-21)

BEHIND THE TEXT

This unit concerns the pure olive oil for the seven lamps of the lampstand. Pure pressed olive oil with no impurities burns without producing any smoke. An earlier mention of olive oil is found in the Ebla tablets (between 2500 and 2250 BC) of Syria, which shows Ebla as a major commerce center and olive oil as one of the major products. Since the Sinai wilderness could not supply it, it is either from Egypt or purchased from passing merchants.

Some hold that the lamps burned continually, day and night, as the only source of light in the tabernacle. This interpretation assumes that the entrance curtain was of such thickness (perhaps based on Josephus' description of the extremely thick curtain in Herod's temple) that no sunlight penetrated into the tabernacle. However, it is unreasonable to assume that the thickness of the curtains for the portable tabernacle was the same as those permanent curtains in Herod's temple that were more than double the size of the tabernacle. Since the lamp is lighted only at night, we can assume that some sunlight penetrated the tabernacle during the day.

Exodus 35:28 reports the people's donation of the oil for the light.

IN THE TEXT

■ **20** Although the NIV reads **lamps**, the Hebrew has singular "lamp," as it does for **light**. Some regard this discrepancy as a contradiction with the seven lamps (one for each branch of the lampstand) mentioned in 25:37 and Lev 24:4 (see Meyers 2005, 232-33). However, the lampstand could be viewed either as one lamp (when viewed as a whole) or seven lamps (when viewed in terms of its details). The lamps must be **kept** [*tāmîd*; "continually," that is, without ceasing, or "regularly"] **burning** regularly.

■ **21** This verse limits the duty of keeping **the lamps burning** to **Aaron and his sons**. In other places, Aaron alone is commanded to light and extinguish the lamp (Lev 24:3) and at the same time burn the incense (see Exod 30:7-8). **His sons** here most likely refers to Aaron's descendants who will succeed him and light and extinguish the lamps and trim or tend (see 30:7) the wicks.

Otherwise, it refers to his four sons who are to perform the tasks of cleaning and refilling the lamps during the day.

This verse (along with 30:7-8; Lev 24:2-4; see 2 Chr 13:11) clarifies that the lamps are lighted at twilight and kept burning through the night until **morning** (when they are extinguished or run out of oil; see 1 Sam 3:3). Keeping the lamps burning regularly is **a lasting ordinance among the Israelites**, not only because the priests represent and serve the Israelites through such activities, but also because the Israelites would supply the oil (see Lev 24:2-3). The tradition of the Aaronic priests lighting the lamps was practiced in Solomon's temple, and the tradition continued in the southern kingdom of Judah (see 2 Chr 13:10-11).

FROM THE TEXT

Just as the lamps were regularly filled with oil for regular lighting, so was Christ, who is the true Light (John 1), filled with and empowered by the Holy Spirit to carry out his mission. Likewise, for the church to carry out her mission, she must also have the oil of the Holy Spirit, namely, the presence, anointing, ministry, grace, and gifts of the Holy Spirit (Wesley 1990, 84). In this way, the lampstand of each local church (see Rev 1:20) continues to burn through any dark night it faces and shine the light of God into a dark world. Through the Holy Spirit, God's transforming and empowering presence, the church's gospel ministry has life-giving and life-transforming impact.

Just as the Israelites must regularly supply pure olive oil to the sanctuary, each believer must supply pure oil for the church. We do so by being "filled with the Holy Spirit" (Eph 5:18) and bearing "the fruit of the light," which are "goodness, righteousness and truth" (v 9). As we contribute ourselves as the pure oil to the church, it can continue to fulfill its mission to be the light of the world. Jesus' parable of the ten bridesmaids (Matt 25:1-13) strongly warns both individuals and churches against running out of oil and being rejected, like the plant among the thornbushes that never bears fruit (Mark 4:7, 18-19).

10. The Priestly Vestments (28:1-43)

a. Priestly Garments: Items and the Material (28:1-5)

BEHIND THE TEXT

Just as sacred space is separated and sanctified from common space, so sacred personnel are set apart and consecrated to minister before Yahweh. Up to this point, the head of the family or tribe, who is the firstborn male, conducted sacrificial rites (→ Exod 4:24-26). At Sinai, the Levites replace the firstborn male (Num 3:12-13, 40-45; 8:6-19; 18:2-6, 21-23; → Exod 13:2). Among the Levites, Aaron and his four sons are chosen as chief priests who will serve in the tabernacle (28:1). But before the installation of the Aaronic priesthood, Moses and certain priests and young Israelite men (likely a group of chosen firstborn sons) perform priestly duties (19:22, 24; 24:5-6, 8). Once the tabernacle is completed, Moses performs all the priestly rites (40:9-32; Lev 8:1-36). After their ordination, however, priestly duties are transferred from Moses to Aaron and his sons, to the exclusion of all others. Even so, as the prophet par excellence, the giver of the covenant and covenant laws, the installer of Israel's cult, and Yahweh's confidant, Moses eclipses the tabernacle regulations. Yahweh continues to meet and speak with Moses over the atonement cover (Lev 1:1; Num 7:89). While Moses is invited into the presence of God, wearing his common attire, the priests must wear authorized garments, without which they would die (Exod 28:43).

IN THE TEXT

■ **I** **Aaron** accompanied Moses from the beginning of Moses' ministry (4:14 ff.) and spoke as Moses' prophet (4:15-16, 30; 7:1-2). Now he is being set apart as the high priest. Further, Aaron's two older sons, **Nadab** and **Abihu**, are set apart as **priests** (→ 24:1). **Eleazar** and **Ithamar** are previously mentioned in the genealogy (6:23). Eleazar succeeds his father as high priest and serves a crucial role in dividing and assigning the land by lot to Israelite groups entering the land (Josh 19:51). Ithamar is later put in charge of the inventory of the offerings for the tabernacle (Exod 38:21); perhaps he helps direct its construction under Moses' command.

■ **2** The garments for the high priest are **sacred** (qōdeš; "holy," "set apart," "consecrated"). They give glory and beauty, **dignity and honor**, to the high priest, one who is otherwise unworthy of entering into the presence of God. Moses is adorned by God's own favor and pleasure (33:7-13; 34:9) and is granted unlimited access to the divine presence. However, the high priest must be adorned with external splendid garments.

■ **3** In v 3, the best of the weavers are commissioned to **make** the high priest's **garments**. The Hebrew expression for **skilled workers** is "wise in heart." Those who are already "wise in heart" are now "filled with the spirit of wisdom" (NET). In addition to the innate talents these artisans already have developed, Yahweh apparently gives supernatural understanding to comprehend his instructions (→ 25:40; 26:30; 27:8) and the divine wisdom and ability to make the garments according to God's design. Two such chief artists, Bezalel and Oholiab, and other assistant artisans are later mentioned (31:1-11). The provision of vestments through such Spirit-filled workers is given as God's gracious gift since they symbolically enable Aaron to approach and **serve** God without incurring the death penalty. Moreover, Israel receives divine forgiveness and benediction through the high priest.

■ **4** The high priest's vestments include the following: an **ephod** with **breast-piece** attached to it, a **robe**, a gold plate (vv 36-38), a close-fitting tunic (*ketōnet tašbēṣ*; see "tunic" in v 39), a **turban**, a **sash**, and "linen undergarments" (v 42). The ordinary priest's apparel includes a tunic (*ketōnet*), a sash, a cap (v 40), and an undergarment (v 42).

■ **5** This verse outlines some of the exquisite and expensive materials used to make the priestly garments. The costliest material is mentioned first, then the rest in the order of descending value.

FROM THE TEXT

Holy garments speak of how the priests, and especially the high priest, are entirely set apart and consecrated unto God. They receive "glory and honor" from the Lord. Their unholiness and dishonor, bearing their own sin and vicariously the sins of Israel (see Exod 28:38; Num 18:1), must be covered. The garments are a visible expression of the truth that "without holiness no one will see the Lord" (Heb 12:14). Holiness is not merely consecration. Rather, like the priest's garments, it is beautiful and glorious, partaking of the glory of the divine nature (2 Pet 1:4). Wesley says that one reason that these "glorious garments" are appointed is so "that the priests might be types of Christ, and of all Christians who have the beauty of holiness put upon them" (1990, 84). Just as the priest needed to be clothed in garments made by the work of Spirit-filled people (Exod 28:3), so also Christians need to be clothed in the holiness that only the Holy Spirit makes possible.

b. The High Priest's Garments (28:6-39)

(I) The Ephod (28:6-14)

BEHIND THE TEXT

The ephod is the outermost high priestly vestment, woven with gold wires and dyed yarns, ornamented with gold and precious stones, and joined with a resplendent breastpiece. The ephod as a whole is the principal part of the priestly garment, and the breastpiece is its crowning member.

The ephod and all its accoutrements are described individually in their making, but once all the components are completed and permanently attached, the finished whole is simply called an ephod. Thus, the ephod is often shorthand for the high priest's garments (e.g., 1 Sam 2:28; 14:3; 21:9 [10 HB]; 23:6, 9-12; 30:7-8). Using a part to refer to a whole is also evident in respect to the "ark" (the chest alone in Exod 25:10; the assembled whole in 40:21; Num 3:31) and the "tabernacle" (the innermost curtain in Exod 26:1-14; the whole tent with its furnishings in 40:38; Num 9:15).

Outside the book of Exodus, the term "ephod" typically refers to the high priest's vestments. However, based on the Israelites' idolatry in regard to Gideon's and Micah's ephods, it is widely accepted that the term sometimes refers to an idol. However, this interpretation is misleading.

The ephod is most likely somewhat stiff, from the gold wires woven into the fabric (see "gold" in Exod 28:6). For its best preservation, it is probably hung on another object when not in use. Thus, the ephod in Ahimelech's tent takes up enough space for Goliath's sword to be kept behind it (1 Sam 21:9 [10 HB]). While Gideon's and Micah's (unauthorized) ephods are intended for personal oracular purposes only (Judg 8:26-27; 18:3-6), the Israelites worship them. In Judg 17:5, Micah's ephod is draped over teraphim ("household gods" [NIV]; although plural in Hebrew, it most likely refers to a portable personal idol of varying size; see Gen 31:34; 1 Sam 19:13). As such, ephod is treated as teraphim's garment, which is the reason for "ephod" and "teraphim" (NJPS, NRSV) occurring together (in Judg 18:14, 17, 18, 20). Hosea 3:4 indicates that the Israelites continue to worship Micah's ephod and teraphim until the time of the exile. These instances highlight the idolatrous people, who turn a splendid priestly garment into an object of worship.

Another use of the term for ephod occurs in conjunction with a qualifying adjective, the linen ephod ('ēpôd bad). Samuel, the eighty-five priests at Nob, and King David reportedly wore the plain linen ephod (1 Sam 2:18; 22:18; 2 Sam 6:14; 1 Chr 15:27). These texts show that the "linen ephod" was a garment that distinguished its wearer as a priest or as priestly in some sense (see 2 Sam 6:12-19 for David assuming priestly functions and 2 Sam 7:12-13 for the establishment of the Davidic priest-king). Thus, understanding the "linen ephod" as an undergarment is an erroneous interpretation. That the priests would be distinguished by their undergarments, their most immodest piece of clothing, makes little sense. There is biblical evidence (1 Chr 24:31) for ordinary priests ministering by casting lots to render some divine decisions. Yet decisions of national importance were reserved for the high priest, paralleling the judicial administrative system of Exod 18:18-22. It is highly probable that from the judges period ephods like that of the high priest were made entirely of linen in order for the ordinary priests to carry the lots to render divine decisions.

IN THE TEXT

■ **6** The **ephod** for the high priest is to be made of intricately woven fabric, perhaps with fine designs adorning it, as suggested by *work of a tapestry weaver* (ḥōšēb; → 26:1). Besides the expensive **blue** and **purple** wool **yarn**, associated with royalty and authority, **scarlet** yarn is used. **Gold** wires or threads, likely cut from hammered-thin gold sheets, are skillfully woven into the colorful wool-linen textile. The gold thread would give the entire garment a glittering appearance and some stiffness, requiring it to be draped over another object (Van Dam 2003, 643).

■ **7** The ephod **is to have two shoulder pieces** or straps, like suspenders. They are to be sewn as one piece with the ephod, **attached** to the front of the ephod and to the **two . . . corners** of the ephod (that would be on the back when worn; see v 27). Although the material for the shoulder straps is not specifically mentioned, we may assume the same material as the ephod and the waistband, since the straps are one with them.

■ **8** The **waistband** is to be **woven** with the same yarns and same special weaving technique as the ephod itself. **Gold** threads are also used. The waistband is sewn to the ephod, over the shoulder straps, so that it is **one piece with the ephod**. Since the waistband is woven with gold wires, as with all other parts of the ephod, the rather stiff waistband would not lend itself to daily tying and untying as traditionally envisioned. The gold wires would be damaged quickly in this way. It is most likely fastened in the back by means of hooks or clasps. When fastened, it would hold the ephod and its breastpiece close to the body (29:5; Lev 8:7), preventing the breastpiece from swinging out as the high priest attends to the priestly duties (Exod 39:21).

■ **9-10** The **names of the sons of Israel** are to be engraved on **two onyx stones** (v 9). However, it is not clear which twelve names are in view: the original twelve sons of Israel (including Levi and Joseph) or the names of the later twelve tribes of Israel (excluding Levi and Joseph and including Ephraim and Manasseh). Although the majority of commentators assume the latter, several factors favor the former interpretation. (1) The word "sons" is used, rather than "tribes." (2) The book of Exodus begins with a list of "the names of the sons of Israel," the actual sons of Jacob as found in Gen 35:23-26 (see Exod 1:2-5). (3) When the "tribes" are reconfigured (for the purpose of conquest and settlement), the exclusion of the Levites is made explicit (see Num 1:47-53). Here, there is no mention of excluding the Levites.

Six names are to be carved on each gemstone, with the six oldest on one and the six youngest on the other, or the names alternating between right and left. The names are likely listed in the matrilineal **order of their birth** as found in Gen 35:23-26 and Exod 1:2-5.

■ **11** Most likely, the **names** are engraved as to make them stand out against the carved background. An engraved **seal** is attested during the Israelites' ancestor period (see Judah's seal in Gen 38:18, 25). A gemstone carving industry existed in Egypt between the sixteenth and fourteenth centuries BC (Sarna 2004, 138), which overlaps with the time of the Israelites' sojourn in Egypt. The Hebrew term used for the "fitted [*šbṣ*] tunic" in Exod 28:4 [NET] is used here for the **filigree [*šbṣ*] settings**, which is formed of woven **gold** wire.

■ **12** The two **stones** mounted on the filigree settings are attached to the shoulder straps by stitching or hooks. When worn, they would rest on the high priest's **shoulders**, symbolizing the responsibility of his office. The high priest symbolically bears the **names** of the twelve **sons of Israel** to represent the entire nation of Israel **before the LORD**. The **memorial stones** also "remind" Yahweh, as Noah's rainbow did, to continue to bestow blessings and favor upon the people and be faithful to the covenant promises made with Israel.

■ **13-14** **Two braided** or twisted **pure gold** cords (v 14; as opposed to links) are fastened to the front side of the **filigree settings** (v 13). The other ends of the cords are used to fasten the breastpiece to the front side of the ephod (see v 25).

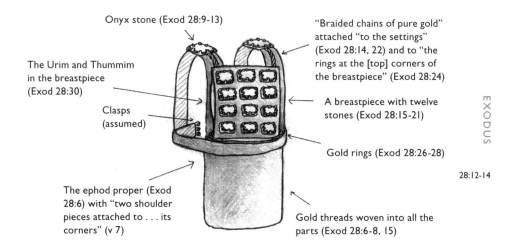

Onyx stone (Exod 28:9-13)

"Braided chains of pure gold" attached "to the settings" (Exod 28:14, 22) and to "the rings at the [top] corners of the breastpiece" (Exod 28:24)

The Urim and Thummim in the breastpiece (Exod 28:30)

A breastpiece with twelve stones (Exod 28:15-21)

Clasps (assumed)

Gold rings (Exod 28:26-28)

The ephod proper (Exod 28:6) with "two shoulder pieces attached to . . . its corners" (v 7)

Gold threads woven into all the parts (Exod 28:6-8, 15)

Figure 13: The ephod

FROM  THE TEXT

Even as the earthly tabernacle in its splendor is but a shadow of the heavenly sanctuary, so is the magnificent ephod an emblem of something much greater than itself. This glorious sacred garment and its sacred stones symbolize the magnitude of the responsibility and the burden of the office of high priesthood. The names of the tribes inscribed on the gemstones indicate the function of the priest who wears it; he brings all Israel into the holy presence of God, so that they can be reconciled to God. Likewise, Jesus the High Priest in the NT enters the heavenly sanctuary "once for all . . . to do away with sin by the sacrifice of himself" in order to reconcile the world to God (Heb 9:26; see 2 Cor 5:18-19).

The ephod also points to the great messianic King's responsibility that he shoulders with authority and power. The messianic King's governmental duties are not limited to the nation Israel but extend to the whole earth. The messianic King is glorious and splendent, not from wearing earthly garments of costly fabric, gold, and gemstones, but from his unique identity as the "Wonderful Counselor, Mighty God, Everlasting Father, Prince of Peace" (Isa 9:6). As such, there is no end to "the greatness of his government and peace" (v 7).

(2) The Breastpiece (28:15-30)

BEHIND THE TEXT

Yahweh communicates divine law, decisions, and other commands directly to the prophet Moses (Exod 18:13-16, 26; Num 27:1-11). However, Aaron the high priest and other leaders after Moses obtain divine decisions through the authorized oracular devices Urim and Thummim.

The Urim and Thummim were first entrusted to Aaron, then passed on to Eleazar (Num 20:28; 27:21), and so on, to other high priests. Many decisions of national importance were made by casting lots (Urim and Thummim); sin offerings and scapegoats (Lev 16:8-10); advancement to the promised land (Num 27:21); divisions of the land (e.g., Num 26:55-56; 33:54; Josh 14:2; 18:6-11); divine verdicts of guilt (Josh 7:14-18; 1 Sam 14:42); battle decisions (1 Sam 23:6-13; 30:7-8); and assignment of responsibilities (1 Chr 24:31; 25:8; 26:13-14). Several texts show that casting lots for divine decision was not practiced exclusively by the high priest but was widely practiced by the priests and the Levites (1 Chr 24:31; 25:7-9; 26:12-14; Neh 10:34 [35 HB]).

In the NT, Luke 1:9 shows that the various priestly offices were decided by casting lots, presumably using the Urim and Thummim. In Acts 1:26, the eleven apostles cast lots, presumably under the guidance of the Holy Spirit, to choose the twelfth apostle. They appear confident that the decision obtained reflected Yahweh's perfect will.

IN THE TEXT

■ **15** The **breastpiece** (*ḥōšen*) is so called because the high priest wears it upon his breast. It is also called the breastpiece **for making decisions** (or "breastpiece of judgment" [ESV, NASB, NRSV]) because it holds the decision-making tools of the Urim and Thummim (see Exod 28:30). The breastpiece is made from the same material as the ephod, using the same weaving technique and artistic design, suggested by the expression ***the work of a tapestry weaver*** (→ 26:1) also used for the ephod in 28:6.

■ **16** The breastpiece is to be **folded double** to form a pocket for the Urim and Thummim (see v 30). The folded breastpiece is to be a **square**, 1 x 1 span (9 x 9" or 23 x 23 cm), which would cover much of the upper body of an average-sized man. A **span** is "the maximum distance between the top of the little finger and the thumb" or half a cubit.

■ **17-20** **Four rows** of three **precious stones** are to be mounted on the breast-piece (v 17). The exact identity of many of the twelve gemstones is difficult to ascertain. The Hebrew terms for three of them—**jacinth, agate,** and **amethyst** in v 19—are used only here and in 39:12. Three other gemstones—**lapis lazuli, topaz,** and **onyx**—appear elsewhere in the Bible. Ezekiel 28:13 mentions nine precious stones (that is, all the stones except those occurring only in Exodus) as present in the garden of Eden and as ornaments worn by the cherub before his fall and expulsion from Yahweh's presence. The vision of the new Jerusalem in the book of Revelation has twelve foundations made of twelve similar gemstones with the names of the twelve apostles of Jesus Christ carved in them (Rev 21:14, 19-20).

■ **21** As with the two onyx stones, the **names of the** actual twelve **sons of Israel** are engraved on the **twelve stones, one** on **each,** likely in the matrilineal order of their birth (see Exod 28:9).

■ **22-25** The unattached **ends** (v 25) of the pure **gold** cords (v 22) already mentioned in v 14 are firmly tied to the gold **rings** (v 24) at the two upper **corners** of the **breastpiece.**

■ **26-28** These verses concern the attachment of the bottom corners of the breastpiece to the **waistband** (v 27) on the front side of **the ephod.**

■ **29** As the mediator for Israel, the high priest **will bear the names of the sons of Israel** upon **his heart** when he ministers **before the** Lord in the **Holy Place.** He is to appear before Yahweh in the interest of all people, continuing to remind Yahweh of his covenant with this people.

■ **30** Whenever he enters Yahweh's **presence,** the high priest must fulfill his responsibility of discerning Yahweh's **decisions,** thereby directing the nation's destiny. The biblical texts seem to take it for granted that the way through which Yahweh's decisions were obtained with **Urim and Thummim** was rather well-known to the Israelites. Therefore, the text provides no explanation of the procedures, techniques, or interpretations involved in decision making with these instruments. Based on biblical and archaeological discoveries in Mesopotamia, it is thought that the Urim and Thummim were made out of fairly flat stones like those used in casting lots. The names Urim and Thummim may describe their theological function rather than their physical properties. Their likely meanings, Urim ("light") and Thummim ("perfect," "complete," or "innocent"), imply that when a lot is cast, Yahweh will "perfectly illuminate Yahweh's will" (Propp 2006, 442).

The twelve gemstones on the Urim and Thummim within the breastpiece speak of the high priest's double responsibility to discern God's will for the people and to represent God's own utmost affection for the people. (1) As a mediator representing God to the people, the twelve gemstones over the high priest's heart indirectly highlight the favor and pleasure God has for the people. As allegorically celebrated in Song 8:6, Israel, as God's beloved, is placed as a seal upon God's heart. As lovers are bound to each other in affection and in covenant faithfulness, so has God bound the Israelites to himself, for better or for worse. The cost of maintaining such covenant commitment is ultimately the death of God's one and only Son, the ultimate High Priest and the new covenant Mediator. (2) As the bearer of the Urim and Thummim for divine judgments, the high priest also discerns and declares God's decisions. In his mercy and compassion, the Lord gives counsel, strategies, directions, and decisions to his people in all matters that lie beyond a human ability to know. Leaders such as David demonstrate the need to inquire of the Lord. David did not engage in a battle presumptuously, unnecessarily costing him and his men their lives. Rather, he sought and obtained the right course of action from the Lord (e.g., 1 Sam 23:1-5, 7-13; 30:7-8).

Similarly for the new covenant people, Christ has not left us as orphans but has given us the Holy Spirit and spiritual gifts that guide us into all truth (John 16:13). God has given us the word of God, godly advisers, teachers, wisdom, understanding, reason, and common sense. However, for matters beyond the reach of all these resources, we have our heavenly Father who is eager to give clear guidance for those who seek him and trust him.

(3) The Blue Robe of the Ephod (28:31-35)

BEHIND THE TEXT

Similar to the Israelite high priest, the kings and priests of the ancient Near East wore purple robes and attire with decorated hems and tassels (Propp 2006, 444-45, 523-24). In the Bible, the robe (*me'il*) is mentioned in relation to the following: cultic officials, such as Samuel (1 Sam 2:19; 15:27; 28:14) and the Levites (1 Chr 15:27); royal persons, such as Jonathan (1 Sam 18:4), Saul (1 Sam 24:4, 11 [5, 12 HB]), David (1 Chr 15:27), foreign rulers (Ezek 26:16); and other eminent persons, such as Job and his friends (Job 1:20; 2:12; 29:14). However, as a priestly garment, the blue robe of the ephod has distinct features, such as its color complete with pomegranates and gold bells on its hem. According to Josephus, the priestly robe was worn immediately under the ephod, probably extending below it, and had armholes but no sleeves (*Ant.* 3.7.4).

■ **31** The **robe** for the high priest is to be made **entirely of blue** woolen yarn. The royal **blue** color (→ "blue" in Exod 25:4) is the most expensive of the three dyes used for the tabernacle and related items.

■ **32** The **opening for the head in its center** is an **edge like a collar** that is **woven** rather than formed through cutting and sewing. Most likely, the entire robe is woven as one piece, from the top to the bottom, which is the ***work of a weaver*** (*ma'ăśēh 'ōrēg*; **woven**;→ "Weavers" sidebar in 26:1).

■ **33-34** The repetitive Hebrew expression "a golden bell and a pomegranate, a golden bell and a pomegranate" makes it clear that the **gold bells** and decorative **pomegranates are to alternate around the hem** (28:34). No purpose for the pomegranate is provided, but elsewhere, the fruit is celebrated in love songs (Song 4:3; 6:7; 8:2). Its abundance (along with other fruits) signals divine blessing and prosperity (Num 13:23; Deut 8:8), while its absence denotes divine judgment (Joel 1:12; Hag 2:19). In the ancient Near East, pomegranates were associated with rituals, such as weddings and funerals.

■ **35** **Aaron must wear** the robe, and the **sound of** his feet (thus, the **bells**) **will be heard** while serving, which will protect his life. Cassuto speculates that God would kill the high priest who enters the sanctuary unannounced without out his proper robe and without ringing of the bells (1967, 383). Since the life of the high priest is at risk when he **enters**, **ministers**, and **comes out**, however, the reason for the sound must be not only for God but also for the people. Perhaps the sound of the bells signaled to the people, twice a day, that the high priest was serving the Lord in the tabernacle, inviting them to worship the Lord from the entrance of their own tents (see a similar practice in 33:10).

FROM THE TEXT

The sound of the bells at the movement of the high priest in the tabernacle must have been a source of blessing to the worshippers without. There is an oft-repeated claim that the high priest had to enter the holy place with a rope around his ankle (or waist), so that, should he die in the tabernacle, his body could be pulled out. While this tradition is not rooted in the biblical text, the threat of death around the Lord's holy presence or sacred objects is surely real. Some biblical texts, shocking to modern readers, confirm the inherent danger involved with inappropriate encounters with God's holy presence. For example, Aaron's own sons Nadab and Abihu die when they offer unauthorized fire before the Lord (Lev 10; see the related warnings for Aaron in 16:2 ff.). God also strikes down Uzzah for his unauthorized touch of the ark of God (2 Sam 6:1-8). These frightening episodes warn against carrying out ministry to God in flippancy and presumption. However, the core message of the high priest and his bell sounds is not one denoting the threat of death. (Since wearing the prescribed robe with bells could easily avert death, we can be sure that no high priest ventured into the holy place without the robe, only to be killed by God.)

The true message is the good news that the bell sounds transmitted. The high priests' daily, vicarious service before the Lord attracted the abiding presence of God and his ever-renewed blessings of the people. Thus, the Lord prescribes the priestly blessing in Num 6:24-26: "The LORD bless you and keep you; the LORD make his face shine on you and be gracious to you; the LORD turn his face toward you and give you peace." According to early Jewish writings, the priests pronounced the blessings on the people with their hands lifted toward the people at the regular morning and evening offerings (see Lev 9:21-22).

Before his ascension, Jesus explains the Scriptures christologically, commissions his followers to preach the good news of the gospel, and promises to send the Holy Spirit to clothe them "with power from on high" (Luke 24:45-49). Further, Jesus lifts up his hands and blesses them like the priests and is "taken up into heaven" (vv 50-51). Thus, Christ's disciples are given the vestment of God's power to bring the good tidings of Jesus Christ to the ends of the earth. We dwell in the presence of the Lord; we serve the Lord, and we go into the world not with golden bells ringing from a royal robe but with the proclamation of good tidings of salvation and peace. Surely, there is no sound more beautiful and desired than the feet of those who bring such good news (see Isa 52:7-8).

(4) The Gold Plate (28:36-38)

BEHIND THE TEXT

Yahweh elected Israel to be his most "treasured possession," to be for Yahweh "a kingdom of priests and a holy nation" (Exod 19:5-6). So Yahweh chooses Aaron (and the high priests after him) to be his utmost possession, who would be for Yahweh the most holy kingly priest. Consequently, the Israelite high priest is endowed with a head ornament as a crown.

Golden rosettes on the headbands of gods and goddesses are seen in the ancient Near East (see Propp 2006, 446-47). Solomon's temple has decorative "flowers" carved on it (1 Kgs 6:18, 29). However, since Aaron's headpiece has an inscription on it, there must be a flat surface for it; thus, the NIV translation is "plate" (Exod 28:36). While the "plate" satisfies practical interpretive demands, a bare plate hardly matches the priest's outer garment in its decoration or splendor. It is, thus, best to combine the blossom motif with the plain plate. One may envision a golden plate with the inscription "HOLY TO THE LORD" and golden flower petals on top or a golden rosette in the middle to form a golden crown on his forehead, tied in the back with a blue cord (vv 36-37).

IN THE TEXT

■ **36** The high priest's forehead is to be adorned with a **plate** [*ṣîṣ* usually means "blossom" (as in Num 17:8 [23 HB]) or "flower" (as in Isa 40:7-8)] **of pure gold** that features a blossom (see *petalon* ["leaf"] in the LXX). The same object is also called a "holy crown" (ESV, KJV, NASB) or "the sacred emblem" (NIV) in Exod 29:6 and "the plate of the holy crown" (ESV, KJV, NASB) or "the plate, the sacred emblem" (NIV) in 39:30 and in Lev 8:9. The inscription HOLY TO THE LORD is raised, not inset, as seen in many ancient Near East seals.

■ **37** The gold plate is attached to the **front of the turban** with a **blue cord**, the kind also used to attach the breastpiece (Exod 28:28). This means the two ends of the flowery plate had a hole to accommodate the cord.

■ **38** With the gold plate worn over the **forehead** (see 29:6; 39:30; Lev 8:9), the high priest is exalted into the supreme priestly office and conferred with almost kingly authority over the entire nation. The explicit purpose for this consecration is to **bear *and carry away*** (*nāśā'*) the **guilt** (*'āvōn*; "sin, guilt, and the associated punishment") of the people represented in **the sacred gifts the Israelites consecrate** to Yahweh. In this way, the people and their **gifts** are made pleasing and **acceptable to** Yahweh, and Yahweh's favor and blessings are continually bestowed upon the people. The role of sin-bearing/sin-removing is elsewhere ascribed to Yahweh (→ "forgiving wickedness, rebellion and sin" in 34:7*b*). The high priest's work thus represents Yahweh's own atoning work.

FROM THE TEXT

The status and functions of the high priest emphasized in this unit foreshadow the person and work of Jesus Christ, the ultimate High Priest. This foreshadowing is evident in a number of ways: (1) In the high priest, there is the "fusing" of the priestly, prophetic, and kingly offices, although the priestly office and functions remain primary. As such, the high priest of the old covenant prefigures the perfect Priest, Prophet, and King, Jesus Christ.

(2) The high priest bears the responsibility for the people's sin and guilt (see Exod 28:38; Num 18:1; Isa 53); in this way, he is a type of Christ. Yet as a sinner himself, the high priest bears his own sins (Num 18:1; see Heb 7:27). Thus, his ministry of atonement through animal sacrifices, first for himself and then for his people, is incomplete and looks for the revelation of the sovereign redemptive work of God. Jesus Christ, who is "tempted in every way . . . , yet without sin" (Heb 4:15 NET) and is perfected through complete obedience (5:8-9), makes "perfect forever those who are being made holy" by the "one sacrifice" of himself (10:14).

(3) Since the high priest is "holy to the LORD," the Israelites, represented by the high priest, become "holy to the LORD" (Deut 7:6; 14:2, 21; 26:19).

Likewise in the new covenant, all followers of Christ vicariously participate in Christ's holiness, clothed with his nature (Rom 13:14; Gal 3:27; Eph 4:24; Col 3:10) and circumcised in our hearts by the Holy Spirit (1 Cor 6:11). Accordingly, even as the whole of Israel is ultimately called to be "a kingdom of priests" (Exod 19:6), so Christians are called to share in the priesthood of all believers (1 Pet 2:5, 9). This call involves sharing in the suffering and glory of Christ and even completing the suffering that is "lacking" in him (Col 1:24). We do so, not by aiming to repeat the completed aspects of Christ's work, but by obediently fulfilling the Great Commission given to us (Matt 28:18-20).

(4) Finally, the holiness of the high priest and Israel point to the glorious eschatological future of comprehensive sanctification. Zechariah 14:20-21 envisions a glorious messianic age in which the distinction between the profane ("the bells of the horses") and the sacred (the "bowls in front of the altar") are abrogated. The distinction is annulled because all things, including the basest vessels, are dedicated to the service of the Lord. Thus, "On that day HOLY TO THE LORD will be inscribed on the bells of the horses" (Zech 14:20) and "every pot in Jerusalem and Judah will be holy to the LORD Almighty" (v 21). So in Christ, the distinctions between the holy and the profane, the high priest and the common worshipper, and the clergy and the laity are removed. All are called to draw near to God, based on the merit of the perfect High Priest, Jesus Christ (Heb 4:16; 6:19).

(5) Tunic, Turban, and Sash (28:39)

BEHIND THE TEXT

In the Bible, the "tunic" (*ketōnet*) is often mentioned in relation to the wealthy, aristocrats, and priests: Adam and Eve (Gen 3:21); Joseph (Gen 37:3, 23, 31, 32, 33); Tamar (2 Sam 13:18, 19); Job (30:18); royal officials (2 Sam 15:32; Isa 22:21); and priests (Exod 28:4, 39, 40; 29:5, 8; 39:27; 40:14; Lev 8:7, 13; 10:5; 16:4; Ezra 2:69, Neh 7:70, 72 [69, 71 HB]).

The tunic (*ketōnet*) is translated into *chitōn* in the Greek. It may not be a mere coincidence that Jesus wore a seamless tunic (see John 19:23 ESV, NET; "undergarment" [NIV]) and that the high priest Caiaphas also wore a tunic, which he tore to express his utmost grief for the perceived blasphemy of Jesus at his trial (Mark 14:63).

Combining the descriptions of the tunic worn by priestly personnel, including Jesus, and Josephus' description of it (*Ant.* 3.7.2), one might envision the priestly tunic to be full-length, having long sleeves, relatively close-fitting, and woven as one piece without seams (which would require weaving from top to bottom, with a woven neck opening).

IN THE TEXT

■ **39** The expression **weave the tunic** (*šibbaṣta haketōnet*) and the related expression "woven tunic" (28:4; *ketōnet tašbēṣ*) occur only here and in v 4. The Hebrew term for "weave" (*šbṣ*) is variously translated into "fringe" (LXX), "broidered" (KJV), and "checkered" (NASB; NRSV). However, these are questionable translations, since the term is also used to describe "setting" or "fitting" for mounting gemstones, which suits the current context (28:11, 13, 14, 25; 39:6, 13, 16, 18; see Ps 45:14 [15 HB]). Such usage suggests that the tunic is probably "a fitted tunic" (Exod 28:4 NET), woven to hang relatively close to the body (Josephus, *Ant.* 3.7.2). The **tunic** and the **turban** are made with **fine linen**, a highly breathable material helpful for keeping the wearer cool and minimizing perspiration (see Ezek 44:18).

The Hebrew term for "turban" occurs only in Exodus (28:4, 37, 39; 29:6; 39:28, 31) and Leviticus (8:9; 16:4) and exclusively in relation to the high priest, except for one mention of a turban for an Israelite king, who wore it along with his crown (see Ezek 21:26 [31 HB]). The high priest is to wear a turban of fine linen, such as kings of the ancient Near East wore, signifying the high priest's kingly dignity and authority. According to Josephus, the turban's shape mentioned here is not conical but spherical (*Ant.* 3.7.6). Around the tunic, an intricately woven **sash**, a **work of *a skilled weaver*** (*rōqēm;* → "Weavers" sidebar in 26:1), is wrapped.

FROM THE TEXT

Ultimately, the high priestly garments point toward the priestly, intercessory ministry of the Messiah and of his people. The high priest wears special physical garments, setting him apart for his intercessory ministry on behalf of Israel. The ministry of the priest assures the continued favor and presence of God with the people. Consequently, later in Israel's history, the priests lead the way across boundaries into new territories (see Josh 3:15-17) and into battle against their enemies (see 6:4-16), symbolizing the divine presence that goes before his people and fights for them.

Isaiah predicts a time when the Lord himself takes on the ultimate intercessory and salvific work, clothing himself in a breastplate of righteousness, the helmet of salvation, and garments of vengeance and zeal (59:16-17). In Jesus Christ, this prophecy is fulfilled.

In Ephesians, followers of Christ are called to engage in spiritual warfare and intercession, clothing themselves in messianic armor that recalls the language of this chapter and Isa 59 (Eph 6:14-17). Since the atoning work of Messiah Jesus is complete, Christian intercession involves the derivative action of appropriating his work by faith as the kingdom advances into places still dominated by "the powers of this dark world" (v 12). The kingdom of God advances through powerful and effective intercessory prayer (vv 18-19) and through bold and authoritative proclamation of the gospel (vv 19-20).

c. Ordinary Priestly Garments (28:40-43)

(I) Tunics, Sashes, and Caps (28:40)

BEHIND THE TEXT

Based on the mention of the "linen sash" (Lev 16:4), which the high priest wore on the Day of Atonement in lieu of the splendid variegated sash, some suggest that the ordinary priests wore plain linen sashes. However, Exod 29:9 and Lev 8:13 indicate that only one kind of sash is used for both Aaron and his sons. Thus, Lev 16:4 is best understood as applying only to the high priest and only for the Day of Atonement. Like a dead person wrapped in strips of linen, the high priest enters the most holy place wearing linen garments only (perhaps foreshadowing Christ, who after his death "entered the Most Holy Place once for all by his own blood, thus obtaining eternal redemption" [Heb 9:12]).

IN THE TEXT

40 The high priest dons seven articles of clothing in his daily ministry in the tabernacle: an undergarment, a tunic, a sash, a blue robe of the ephod, an ephod with the breastpiece attached (Exod 28:28; 39:21), a turban, and a crown. In contrast, the ordinary priests wear four pieces: an undergarment, a tunic, a sash, and a turban. The Hebrew for "cap" (*migbā'â*) is used only four times in the OT (28:40; 29:9; 39:28; Lev 8:13) and exclusively for the priests' headwear. Related to the Hebrew word for "cup" (*gābî'a*), the term probably refers to a band wrapped around the head in an inverted cup shape. The types of material for the **tunics, sashes and caps** are already specified in previous verses. The tunic is the only garment, besides the undergarment, that the ordinary priests wear (Exod 28:40). The priestly garments give the priests glory and beauty, **dignity and honor** like that conferred on the high priest (v 2).

(2) The Command to Anoint, Ordain, and Consecrate (28:41)

BEHIND THE TEXT

In Israel, kings were appointed through anointing (Judg 9:15; 1 Sam 9:16; 10:1; 16:13; 1 Kgs 1:39; 2 Kgs 9:6; 11:12; 23:30). Divinely initiated and authorized anointing of kings raised their status, transformed their hearts, and empowered them through the infilling of the Spirit of the Lord (Saul in 1 Sam 10:6, 9-10; 11:6; see 16:14; David in 1 Sam 16:13, 18; see Ps 89:20-21 [21-22 HB]; also see Jehu in 2 Kgs 9:1-37; 2 Chr 22:7). Some prophets were

28:40

anointed as well (Elisha in 1 Kgs 19:16 and Isaiah in Isa 61:1). Whatever the office, divinely initiated anointing transmitted Yahweh's Spirit and power upon Yahweh's chosen vessel.

Some suggest that ordination or, more literally, "fill hands" (*yādām*), has to do with Moses putting the wave offering (of ram fat, fatty parts, organs, and the right thigh) on the "palms" (ESV, NJB, NJPS, NRSV; *kap*; "hands" [NIV]) of Aaron and his sons, who wave them before Yahweh (Exod 29:22-24; Lev 8:25-27; see Exod 29:1-3). Moses, however, subsequently takes them back and offers them to Yahweh by fire (29:25; Lev 8:28). Furthermore, it appears that the writer intentionally chose the term "palms" (*kap*) to avoid the facile equation readers may make between the seven-day "fill hands" (lit.) by Yahweh and Moses putting the wave offering that belonged to Yahweh on the palms of Aaron and his sons. The instructions for the ordination and consecration of Aaron and his sons are given in Exod 29 and the report of the ceremony in Lev 8—9. The rites are carried out after the tabernacle is completed and consecrated.

IN THE TEXT

■ **41** Moses is commanded to **anoint** (*māšaḥ*) **Aaron and his sons**. Apparently, the high priest is anointed by pouring oil on his head (Exod 29:7) and the ordinary priests by merely sprinkling oil on them (v 21). The priest's vestments are also anointed (vv 7, 21). Anointing symbolically (or sacramentally) confers holiness (*qādaš*; "make holy," **consecrate**) on the anointed, whether human, animal, or object (28:41; 29:21, 29, 36; 30:26-29, 30; 40:9, 10, 11, 13; Lev 8:10-12, 30; 16:32; Num 7:1). Anointing and consecration signify they are separated from the profane and common, they are consecrated to God, and they can be used for sacred purposes. Specifically for the priests, being made holy implies intimate communion with a holy God.

Yahweh commands Moses to *fill their hands* (ordain them [NIV]) as well. Elsewhere, Moses similarly says, *For seven days he [Yahweh] will fill your hands* (Lev 8:33; see Exod 29:35). The Hebrew expression "fill hands" (translated into "ordain" or "ordination" in the NIV) is used exclusively in the context of the ordination of Aaron and his sons and successors (29:9, 29-30, 33, 35; Lev 16:32; Num 3:3; 35:25; 1 Chr 29:22; see Exod 32:29). The expression "fill hands" ("ordain" [NIV]) also often occurs coupled with "anoint" (in 29:29; Lev 16:32; Num 3:3; see Exod 29:7-9).

"Fill hands" may refer to the oil literally flowing down and filling Aaron's hands, which is accompanied by the filling and empowerment by the Spirit of the Lord (in a similar manner, the kings were filled and empowered by the Holy Spirit). Since the anointing oil is sprinkled on Aaron and Aaron's sons daily for seven days (29:35; Lev 8:33), the sons are also daily filled with the presence, conviction, and empowerment of God's Spirit for their responsibilities of priesthood.

(3) Undergarments (28:42)

BEHIND THE TEXT

The prohibition of steps on altars in Exod 20:26 concerns the nakedness of the worshippers, to prevent them from inadvertently exposing their private parts to others. Since the priests were clothed with long tunics, this added concern must have been raised for another reason. As Cassuto proposes, the requirement of the undergarment is a rejection of pagan ritual nudity and ritual sexual activities (1967, 387). It is not a rejection of human sexuality in general, as Yahweh blesses sexual union between husband and wife and the procreation of new life. Rather, it is a dismissal of the pagan notion that one could have communion with the deity or deities through sexual rituals.

IN THE TEXT

■ **42** In contrast to the outer garments that are for "dignity and honor" (vv 2, 40), the **undergarments** are for modesty, covering nakedness. Thus, these garments are treated separately from the previous (glorious) vestments. They may have been like long shorts with drawstrings (see the LXX and Josephus, *Ant.* 3.7.1). The undergarment is to be made with **linen**.

(4) The Danger of Violation (28:43)

BEHIND THE TEXT

The instruction for the holy vestments is complete, but the footwear is conspicuously missing. This may indicate that the priests minister barefoot. Moses at Sinai (3:5) and Joshua near Jericho (Josh 5:15) were also ordered to take off their sandals, for they were on holy ground (→ Exod 3:5). The removal of the sandal seems to signify humility before and submission to higher authority. In 2 Sam 15:30 and Isa 20:2-4, going barefoot conveys humiliation, shame, and powerlessness.

IN THE TEXT

■ **43** The prescribed holy vestments must be worn in the **Holy Place**. Even of those who are granted permission to draw nearest to him, God requires utmost reverence and caution. Violating his institution by neglecting to wear the appointed vestments, even the underpants, will **incur guilt** and the death penalty (→ Exod 28:35).

The priestly vestments typify the righteousness of Christ, which we must put on to be made acceptable before God. In Jesus' parable of the wedding, the one without the wedding garment required for the occasion is found guilty and is expelled from the King's presence (Matt 22:11-13). Likewise, we are urged to "put off" the "old self" (Eph 4:22) like an old garment, and to "put on the new self, created to be like God in true righteousness and holiness" (v 24).

Similarly, the anointing of the priests typifies the empowerment of the Holy Spirit. Jesus "breathes" the Holy Spirit on his disciples (see John 20:22), but he also charges them to wait for the outpouring of the Holy Spirit (Luke 24:49; Acts 1:4-5, 8). Subsequently, the Holy Spirit anoints and empowers the disciples to carry on the work of Christ (Acts 2). Each generation and each individual needs a fresh infilling and empowering by the Holy Spirit. We must be "clothed with power from on high" (Luke 24:49) to carry out the Lord's ministry.

II. Installation of the Priests (29:1-46)

Overview

The instructions for the consecration of the priests are given in this passage. According to Lev 8:3-4, "[the representatives of] the entire assembly" gather "at the entrance to the tent of meeting." Since the priests are installed as mediators between God and his people to attend to all cultic matters concerning their covenant relationship, all Israel needs to be represented at the ceremony. Witnessing the rites and divine ordination would inspire in the leaders the appropriate reverence for the tabernacle and the priests. Unfortunately, Num 16 indicates that such reverence was not universal, since it records the revolt of Korah, Dathan (the Levites), and Abiram (the Reubenite) to take over the priesthood. One might speculate that they were among the "priests" mentioned in Exod 19:22-24 or the priestly "young Israelite men" in 24:5 but who were later dismissed from such duties after the installation of Aaron and his sons as priests.

No doubt, Moses, with helpers (see 19:22-24; 24:5), carries out all the priestly obligations for the actual installation ceremonies: the slaughtering, the pouring and sprinkling of blood, and the burning rites.

These instructions are briefly recapitulated in 40:9-15, and then fulfilled in Lev 8:1-36, after which Aaron and his sons begin their priestly duties.

a. Preparation of the Offerings and of the Priests (29:1-9)

BEHIND THE TEXT

The first step for the ordination of the priests is the preparation of both animal and cereal offerings and of the priests themselves. Three different animal sacrifices and three varieties of cereal offerings are to be prepared for each day of the ceremony, which will last seven days. Leviticus 8:6-12, however, indicates that there are two other steps in the ceremonies, performed between the robing and anointing of Aaron. They are the anointing and consecration of "the tabernacle and everything in it" and the anointing and consecration of the altar (vv 10-11). These events are specifically ordered to prepare the altar for the cereal and animal offerings needed for the consecration of the priests and the tabernacle, as well as for the ongoing altar ministry of the priests following their inauguration (see Lev 9).

IN THE TEXT

(1) Preparation of the Offerings (29:1-3)

■ **1** For the consecration of the **priests** to **serve** Yahweh, it requires a **young bull** as a sin offering (Exod 29:10-14) and **two rams without defect** (not "lame or diseased" [see Mal 1:8]) as a burnt offering (Exod 29:15-18) and the "ram for the ordination" (v 22).

■ **2-3** Various unleavened breads are to be made from the **finest wheat flour**, the source of which is unclear (v 2). Perhaps the flour was brought out of Egypt or purchased from merchants passing by. In any case, the fine flour later represents the fertility of the promised land, an expression of God's grace to them. The **basket** (v 3) of breads made **without yeast** (v 2) is to contain a variety of baked goods: (1) **round loaves**, (2) **thick . . . olive oil** cakes, and (3) wafer-**thin** bread **brushed with olive oil** (see Lev 2:4; 7:12; 8:26). All three kinds of flatbread are used in expressing "thankfulness" or "thank offering" (Lev 7:12). It is unclear how many of each kind of bread is required, but one of each is offered up to Yahweh as a burnt offering, along with Yahweh's portion of the ram of ordination (Exod 29:23-25). Presumably, some of the bread is for Moses and some is for Aaron and his sons (vv 32-34). The bread must be consumed "on the day it is offered" (Lev 7:15) or else incinerated the next morning (Exod 29:34).

(2) Preparation of the Priests: Washing, Dressing, and Anointing (29:4-9)

■ **4** Aaron and his sons are to be presented to Yahweh for the installation ceremony. The **entrance to the tent of meeting** refers to the entrance to the tabernacle (see Lev 8:3-4). The purification of their bodies here involves washing the entire body, either through pouring **water** on them or through immersion (Sarna 2004, 144, following Rashi). Washing by an immersion bath would require an otherwise unmentioned, large water basin (see "bronze basin" in 30:17-21).

■ **5-6** First, **Aaron** is to be clothed with holy **garments** (v 5). Although not mentioned here, perhaps because it is not an item of "dignity and honor" (28:2), an "undergarment" would still be required (28:42), without which the priest would die. Aaron presumably puts on the undergarment himself, while Moses dresses Aaron with all the outer vestments. A **tunic** (29:5) is worn against the skin, and then the sash wrapped around him. Although Aaron's sash is mentioned (almost as an afterthought) in v 9, Lev 8:7 makes it clear that the sash goes over the tunic and under the blue **robe of the ephod**. The **ephod** with its **breastpiece** is draped over the blue robe of the ephod and fastened with the **waistband**. Then, Aaron is to be crowned with the kingly **turban** (Exod 29:6) and **the sacred emblem** or "crown" (→ "plate of pure gold" in 28:36).

■ **7** Aaron is to be anointed with the fragrant **anointing oil** (30:22-33) poured **on his head** (Lev 8:12; see Exod 40:15). The oil is poured profusely, as the poetic language of Ps 133:2 indicates: "running down on the beard, running down on Aaron's beard, down on the collar of his robe." Aaron and his sons are later anointed by sprinkling of the anointing oil (Exod 29:21; Lev 8:30; see Exod 40:15). All priests are called "anointed priest(s)" (Lev 4:3, 5, 16; 6:22 [15 HB]; Num 3:3) whether through pouring or sprinkling (Exod 28:41; 29:29; → "anoint" in 28:41).

■ **8-9** Besides their undergarments, which are assumed here, Aaron's **sons** will be dressed in **tunics** (v 8), **caps** (v 9), and **sashes**. The **priesthood** is solely the burden and responsibility of **Aaron** and his descendants. The succession of the priesthood is by heredity, the point of which is reiterated in Num 18:1-7, following the revolt against Aaron and his sons in Num 17. The anointing begins the ordaining or "filling" (see "ordain" in Exod 28:41) of the priests for the responsibilities of the priesthood. Their "filling" is to continue through the entire seven-day period of ordination and consecration.

FROM THE TEXT

New Testament writers use the language and imagery of priestly ordination to speak of our being washed and anointed in the Holy Spirit for the service of God. As the priests were bathed, Titus 3:5-6 describes how "he saved us through the washing of rebirth and renewal by the Holy Spirit, whom he poured out on us generously through Jesus Christ our Savior." Just as Moses clothed Aaron with priestly vestments, Christ clothes us with himself, and with his own righteousness he wraps us with his truth and crowns us with his salvation (see 1 Thess 5:8; Eph 6:17). Moreover, as Aaron and his sons were anointed, God anoints us (2 Cor 1:21; 1 John 2:27). He, therefore, "has made us to be a kingdom and priests to serve his God and Father" (Rev 1:6; see 1 Pet 2:5, 9). God further lavishes upon us great love, revealing himself as our Father and us as children of God (1 John 3:1; Rom 8:15-17). Therefore, the writer of Hebrews beckons us to "draw near to God with a sincere heart and with the full assurance that faith brings" (Heb 10:22). We do so to love and serve the living God.

b. Three Animal Sacrifices (29:10-26)

BEHIND THE TEXT

Aaron and his sons are commanded to lay their hands on each animal immediately before the beast is slaughtered. The practice of laying on of the hands is carried out on various levels: communally, in select groups, or as individuals. The laying on of hands transmits to the recipient either something positive or something negative. The negative transmission usually relates to sin. We have examples of the transmission of sins to the animal victims used for vicarious sin offerings (by the representatives of the entire nation in Lev 4:13-15; by the entire tribe of Levi in Num 8:12; and by an individual priest or layperson in Lev 4:3-4, 22-24, 27-29, 33). On the Day of Atonement, Aaron lays "both hands on the head of the live goat and confess[es] over it all the wickedness and rebellion of the Israelites" (Lev 16:21). This act transfers all the sins of Israel "on the goat's head" for the goat to "carry on itself all their sins" (v 22). Some, however, argue that offering an animal laden with sin contradicts the requirement of the unblemished victim for the sacrifice (e.g., Averbeck 2003, 709). However, even if the sin offering is laden with another's sin, its status as the innocent victim would not be altered. When it is slaughtered, it would be suffering a substitutionary or representative punishment for the sin of another. Since the animal victim remains innocent, its blood would be acceptable for expiation and atonement. Such an offering would neither offend God's holiness nor defile the altar.

The positive laying on of hands transmits various qualities and is done on several levels as well. In Num 8:9-11, the whole Israelite community assemble and their representatives lay hands on the Levites to transfer to them the right or authority to serve at the tabernacle. In Exod 29:15, Aaron and his sons lay hands on the ram of burnt offering, probably to symbolically demonstrate their life devotion to the service of Yahweh. In Lev 3:2, 8, 13, individual worshippers lay hands on their fellowship offering. In this case, their affection and gratitude toward Yahweh is transmitted to the offering, making the offering "an aroma pleasing to the LORD" when burnt on the altar (vv 5, 16). In Num 27:18, 20, 23 (see Deut 34:8), Moses' laying on of hands on Joshua transmits some of Moses' authority and the spirit of wisdom to Joshua.

In the NT, Jesus' authority to heal or a healing power is typically communicated through the laying on of his hands, which results in healing the sick (Mark 6:5; Luke 4:40; see Acts 6:6). In other cases, the laying on of hands imparts the presence of the Holy Spirit (Peter and John in Acts 8:17) or the gifts of God (1 Tim 4:14; 2 Tim 1:6). At times, the laying on of hands refers specifically to the ordination of ministers (see 1 Tim 4:14; 5:22), to whom special graces of the Holy Spirit may also be given.

In this unit, there are three animal sacrifices, on which the priests lay their hands: the bull of the sin offering (Exod 29:10-14), the ram of the burnt offering (vv 15-18), and the ram of ordination (vv 19-26).

IN THE TEXT

(1) The Bull of Sin Offering (29:10-14)

■ **10** The priests are commanded to **lay** both **their hands on** the **head** of the **bull** of sin offering, presumably to transmit their sins to the bull.

■ **11** Since Aaron and his sons are not yet ordained for service, Moses still functions as the primary "priest." The slaughtering of the bull for the sin offering implies that the bull is accepted as a vicarious sacrifice for the sins of the priests. The bull is slaughtered **in the LORD's presence**, symbolizing how sin cannot abide in Yahweh's presence but must be judged by means of death—either of the sinner or a divinely designated substitute (like the bull).

■ **12** **Some of the bull's blood** is smeared on **the horns of the altar** to ceremonially cleanse the altar from all impurities and pollution, perhaps derived from contact with its human artisans (see "blood" in 24:6 and "horns" in 27:2). The **rest** of the blood is poured **at the base** of the altar. This act of sanctification sets the altar apart for all subsequent sacred use.

■ **13** The **fat** portions and certain **organs** are to be burnt **on the altar** as an offering to Yahweh (see Lev 4:1—5:13). The burning of **the long lobe of the liver** may portray a rejection of the pagan consultation of the liver for divination, which is mentioned in Ezek 21:21 [26 HB]. Mesopotamian clay models of the liver have been found, some of which are "divided into fifty sections and inscribed with omens and magical formulas for the use of diviners" (Sarna 2004, 145). For the Israelites, the far simpler Urim and Thummim and, occasionally, the ark (see Saul consulting the ark in 1 Sam 14:18) are the only objects authorized for the discernment of Yahweh's will.

■ **14** The rest of the bull must be burnt **outside the camp**, in compliance with the guidelines for the **sin offering**. Once the sacrificial system is in operation, the priests will consume the meat and keep the hide of individual sin offerings as their regular share. Eating the meat of the regular sin offering is part of the ritual of sin-bearing and carrying it away, thereby making atonement for the worshipper before Yahweh (see Exod 28:38; 34:7; Lev 10:17). The priests, however, do not partake of the sin offerings made to atone for the sin of a priest (Lev 4:3-12) or of the whole congregation of Israel (vv 13-21). Rather, the whole sacrifice is burnt up, Yahweh's share on the altar and the rest outside the camp at the designated clean area, where fatty ashes are poured out (vv 12, 21; see "ashes" in Exod 27:3).

(2) The Ram of Burnt Offering (29:15-18)

■ **15** This first ram is the burnt offering. The laying on of **hands** is done probably to transfer the priests' devotion of their entire lives to Yahweh.

■ **16** In contrast to the bull of sin offering, all of the **blood** of the burnt offering is splashed on the four **sides of the altar**, perhaps signifying that the priest's life, symbolized by the blood, is utterly given to service at the altar.

■ **17** The **ram is cut . . . into pieces** for better burning. **The internal organs and the legs** are washed from all impurities or anything that would produce a foul smell.

■ **18** The **entire ram** is to be offered up by fire. The expression **a pleasing aroma** is used numerous times in relation to the **burnt offering** (Lev 1:9, 13, 17), cereal offerings (2:2, 9, 12), fellowship offerings (3:5, 16), and sin offerings (4:31). The expression may indicate that the offering literally has **a pleasing aroma . . . to the LORD**. More importantly, however, it signifies that the **offering** is acceptable to Yahweh and that Yahweh accepts the worshipper. (For cases in which Yahweh rejects the aroma/stench of sacrifices due to the worshippers' persistence in sin, see 26:31; Amos 5:21-22.)

(3) The Ram of Ordination (29:19-26)

■ **19** The **other ram** is the ram of ordination, the ram of "filling" (see "ordain" in Exod 28:41). The ram of ordination is a type of fellowship offering, which is given to three parties: Yahweh through fire, the officiating priest, and the worshipper (e.g., Lev 7:29-33). In Lev 9:24, the fire from Yahweh's presence consumes the burnt offering and the fat (Yahweh's portion in this case) of the fellowship offering.

■ **20** The **blood** is to be smeared on three exposed body parts. Placing the blood on the **right** ear lobe, right thumb, and right big toe may symbolize death to the worldly affairs outside the tabernacle along with the call to hear and obey the word of God and to serve and follow Yahweh only. (See Lev 14:15, 17, 28 for a similar practice of daubing both blood and oil on the right ear, thumb, and toe of a person with a skin disease to cleanse and make atonement.)

■ **21** Some of the anointing oil is to be poured on Aaron (Exod 29:7), and a portion of it is to be sprinkled upon both **Aaron and . . . his sons and their** sacred **garments**. Moses is commanded to take **some** of the **blood** that is splashed on the altar (v 20), suggesting a very small amount, and sprinkle it on the priests, which means it was probably mixed into the anointing oil. Aaron would be, thus, anointed twice on each of the seven days of ordination (see vv 35-37) and his sons once a day. The sprinkling of the anointing oil and the blood of the ram of ordination consecrate the priests and their garments (→ "anoint" and "consecrate" in 28:41).

■ **22** The **right thigh** of a regular fellowship offering is given to the officiating priest as his share (29:28; Lev 7:32-33) and the breast is given to Aaron and his descendants as their regular share (v 31). Thus, some texts summarily state that the breast and the thigh that are waved belong to Aaron and his children (Exod 29:27; Lev 7:34; 10:14-15; see Num 6:20; 18:18). However, an exception is made in this case; the right thigh is offered to Yahweh as the officiant of the ceremony and the breast to Moses as the acting priest (Exod 29:26).

■ **23-25** The meaning of **wave** (v 24; for Heb. *nûp*) originates from the Jewish interpretive tradition that explains that the priest waved the offering to and fro, up and down. However, based on the use of the Hebrew term (*nûp*) in other passages (20:25; Deut 23:25 [26 HB]; 27:5; Isa 10:15; 19:16; Zech 2:9 [13 HB]), "lift," "elevate," or "raise" has been suggested, which fits well with the context. Whatever the exact motion, what is signified by the act is that the **offering** is **presented** to Yahweh and hence, belongs to Yahweh. Along with the three different kinds of unleavened **bread** (Exod 29:23) and the fat portions and organs (v 22), the right thigh is offered to Yahweh by fire as **a pleasing aroma** (v 25).

■ **26** The best of the **ram** (the **breast**) is raised to Yahweh for his acceptance and then given to Moses, the acting priest, since Yahweh grants that it should be his.

FROM THE TEXT

The three offerings may correspond to the Christian theological understanding of justification, mortification/dedication, and communion/empowerment (see Ryken 2005, 903-5). (1) God atones for the sin of the priests through the shedding of the blood of the bull of the sin offering. Christ, on the other hand, is sanctified by his own blood, not that of bulls and goats (see Heb 9:12 and 10:1-14). Through the perfect sacrifice of Jesus Christ, upon whom "the LORD has laid . . . the iniquity of us all" (Isa 53:6), we receive atonement for our sins, and we are justified (see Isa 53:4-5; 2 Cor 5:21).

(2) God receives the burnt offering of the first ram as a vicarious self-offering of the priest. God accepts the burnt offering as a pleasing aroma, symbolizing the priests' death to worldly affairs and total dedication to the ministry of the tabernacle. Christ, on the other hand, subjects himself to double mortification and dedication; first, he "emptied himself" [ESV, NET, NJB, NRSV] of his "equality with God," "taking the form of a servant" [ESV]; and then he lives the life of complete obedience, surrendering himself unto death (see Phil 2:6-11). Therefore, the followers of Christ are called "out of the

world" (John 15:19) to a similar crucified life, to a mortification of the flesh, and to a life of total surrender and dedication as a living sacrifice to God.

(3) God communes with the priests through the fellowship offering of the second ram. Communion with God results in the empowerment of the priests for service. Christ Jesus has a perfect union and communion with the heavenly Father (John 10:30; 14:10; 17:11, 21), which is demonstrated in his powerful ministry (14:10-11). Accordingly, Christ calls us to a mutual communion and indwelling with God the Father, God the Son, and God the Holy Spirit (vv 15-18, 20, 23), through whom we will also be empowered to do the works Jesus did and be fruitful as Jesus was (vv 12-13; 15:5).

c. Future High Priests (29:27-30)

BEHIND THE TEXT

These verses concern the provision for the ongoing institution of the Aaronic priesthood in Israel, which continues long after the death of Aaron and his sons. These verses also represent a secondary interjection or simply a necessary clarification that addresses (1) the foregoing exception (the right thigh to Yahweh and the breast to Moses) to the general rule governing the fellowship offering, and (2) the requirement of the seven-day ordination ceremony for successors to the office of high priesthood.

What remains unclear is *who* carries out the ceremony for installation of the high priests after the death of Moses. When Eleazar succeeds Aaron on Mount Hor, Moses is still living, so he removes Aaron's garments and puts them on Eleazar (Num 20:25-28). Several texts make it clear that subsequent high priests were indeed anointed (Exod 29:29; Lev 21:10, 12; Num 35:25) as shown by the anointing of Zadok (1 Chr 29:22; but with no mention of the ceremony officiant). Perhaps the prophets of God who appointed and deposed the kings, such as Samuel and Nathan, also anointed the high priests (1 Sam 10:1; 16:13; 1 Kgs 1:34, 39, 45).

IN THE TEXT

■ **27** The expression **breast that was waved and the thigh that was presented**, or something similar, also occurs in Lev 7:34; 9:21; 10:15; Num 6:20.

■ **28 From their fellowship offerings, the Israelites** must offer the fat portions to Yahweh, contribute the thigh and breast to the priests, and keep the remaining meat for themselves. This rite becomes the standard practice for the Israelites of all generations, which contrasts with the very first ordination ceremony, in which Yahweh receives the thigh and Moses receives the breast as his portion (v 26).

29:27-28

■ **29-30** The **seven**-day ordination is to be observed for Aaron's successors. The succession of the high priesthood comes through Aaron's bloodline. Thus, the **sacred garments** belong to Aaron's descendants. Eleazar succeeds Aaron (Num 20:25-28).

Priestly Succession

In Eli's time, the office of the high priest was held by Ithamar's family (Eli as a descendant of Ithamar is inferred from I Sam 14:3; 22:20; I Chr 24:3, 6). During David's reign, it is possible that two individuals served in this capacity, Abiathar from Ithamar's line, and Zadok from Eleazar's line (e.g., 2 Sam 8:17; 15:29; 20:25), possibly to achieve unity between the South and the North. Solomon removed Abiathar from the high priesthood because of his support for Adonijah's claim to kingship (I Kgs 1:5-8), and gave the office to Zadok, who supported Solomon's kingship (2:35). The high priesthood remained in the family of Zadok in Israel's later history.

While no age qualifications are given for the priests to enter service, the limits "from thirty to fifty years of age" set for the Levite men and women (→ "women" in Exod 38:8; see Num 6:2-21) for terms of service (4:3, 23, 35) may apply to the priests as well. The high priesthood may have required a life term (see 20:24-28; 35:25; Josh 22:13, 31, 32; 24:33).

FROM THE TEXT

God works through both unique, earth-quaking historical events, such as the theophany at Sinai, as well as long-standing institutions, such as the tabernacle and the priesthood. God not only reveals himself in unexpected and miraculous ways but also continually dispenses grace through less sensational, God-ordained institutions. God gives both the unparalleled covenant mediator Moses, as well as the perennial priests who maintain covenant holiness. To fulfill her calling, Israel needs both unique figures and events along with lasting institutions and recurring celebrations of given sacraments.

Likewise in the new covenant, God reveals Jesus Christ, the unique, glorious God incarnate, and also establishes the institution of the church. God accomplishes the sovereign and supernatural work of redemption in and through Christ; then he calls the church to sustain the ongoing joyful celebration of the sacraments, maintain a life of service and obedience, and faithfully fulfill the Great Commission of Jesus Christ through the proclamation and demonstration of the gospel. The kingdom of God expands in the world through the faithful routines of ministry founded on the historical and redemptive person and work of Jesus Christ.

d. The Ordination Meal (29:31-34)

BEHIND THE TEXT

After the parenthetical notes in the last unit (Exod 29:27-30), the text resumes the subject of the ordination rite for Aaron and his sons. Through Moses, Yahweh further regulates the ordination meal, which consists of three different types of unleavened bread and the priests' portion of the ram of ordination. It clarifies that Aaron and his sons are the ones who offer the fellowship offering, which is also the ordination offering in this case. Once the seven-day ordination period is fulfilled, Aaron and his sons will serve as the official priests of Israel, and thereafter will receive the regular priests' share (the right thigh and the breast).

IN THE TEXT

■ **31** The portion of the fellowship offering that the priests receive must be cooked (*bāšal*; see 12:9) **in a sacred place**. That would normally be in the courtyard (see Lev 8:31).

■ **32** The ordination meal is eaten right at the tabernacle entrance, where **Aaron and his sons** are ordered to spend the full seven days and seven nights of the ordination period (see Lev 8:33).

■ **33** The cereal offering and the fellowship ram offering effect **atonement** (*kupper*; "appease," "provide reconciliation, atonement," "cover up," "expiate"). The sins of Aaron and his sons are expiated. **These offerings** also affect consecration to (or communion with) God and ordination (or empowerment for service; → "consecrate" and "ordain" in Exod 28:41). The ***stranger*** (*zār*) here refers to any unauthorized person with respect to the ordination meal. **No one else** besides Aaron and his four sons may **eat** the **sacred** meal.

■ **34** The Israelite worshippers are permitted to eat the leftovers of the voluntary fellowship offerings on the second day. But like the Passover lamb that had to be consumed or burnt by **morning** (12:10), the **ordination . . . bread** and meat must be **eaten** on the day of the sacrifice. Any leftovers must be burnt. Each day, a new provision of cereal offerings and fellowship offerings (along with the other animal sacrifices) are made for the ordination ceremony.

FROM THE TEXT

Although they are ordinary men, God sets the priests apart to call all people into fellowship with God through them. This takes place, not by human will or strife, but by God's sovereign and gracious appointment. Through the installation of priests, God teaches Israel about the distinction between the holy and the unholy, the sacred and the profane. This is not so much to emphasize or to perpetuate the division between the sacred and the profane, but to provoke all people to a life of holiness whereby they, too, might draw near to God and be consecrated unto God.

Accordingly, the Lord makes a provision that non-Levitical men or women, if they so desire, can consecrate themselves entirely to the Lord's presence and service as Nazirites (Num 6:2-21). The complete consecration of non-Levitical Nazirites to God foreshadows the expanded vision of priesthood in the new covenant (1 Pet 2:5-9). The covenant fellowship that the priests enjoy with God, which is symbolized in the ordination meal, is extended not only to all Israelites through the fellowship offering, but ultimately to all peoples through the greatest sacrifice and priesthood found in Jesus Christ.

e. The Seven-Day Ordination Ceremony (29:35-37)

BEHIND THE TEXT

This section implies that the entire ordination rite should be carried out each day for seven days. Leviticus 8:33-36, however, makes explicit only the requirement that the priests remain on the tabernacle grounds throughout the seven days (which would make daily ordination rites possible). Exodus 29:30 expresses the seven-day requirement in terms of the high priest wearing his vestments for seven days with no other explicit rites mentioned (perhaps to avoid repetition of what has been previously stated). When Eleazar succeeds Aaron on Mount Hor, the de-robing of Aaron and robing of Eleazar are the only ceremony mentioned (Num 20:26-28). The other seven-day ceremonies (anointing and filling, sacrifices and sacrificial meal) were perhaps observed after they descended from Mount Hor. Or, since Eleazar already was consecrated through the seven-day ordination rite, the ceremony simply was not repeated. In 1 Chr 29:22, Zadok is reanointed under the new administration (from David to Solomon), which may support the view that anointing (and perhaps the related ordination ceremony) can be repeated. Whatever the case, during the seven-day period of ordination, the tabernacle (Lev 8:10) and the altar are also anointed and consecrated.

IN THE TEXT

■ **35** The number **seven** symbolizes "perfection" or "completion." They must enact the seven ordination rites daily, completing the process needed for their full consecration (see Exod 29 and Lev 8): (1) the washing and robing; (2) the anointing of the priest and the altar; (3) the sacrifice of the bull of sin offering; (4) the sacrifice of the ram of burnt offering; (5) the sacrifice of the ram of ordination and of fellowship offering; (6) the blood/oil sprinkling rite; (7) the ordination meal.

■ **36** Leviticus 8:10-17 clarifies that the anointing and consecration of **the altar** precedes the **sacrifice** of the bull of sin offering. The earlier instruction (Exod 29:10-14) focused on the procedure. This verse makes explicit one spiritual purpose for the sin offering, to make **atonement** for and **purify the altar**. This verse assumes that the altar, since human beings made it, is defiled and must be purged and consecrated before any sacred service.

■ **37** Through the seven-day consecration, the altar is made **most holy** or, more literally, a "holy of holies." This expression usually refers to the inner sanctum of the tabernacle that houses the ark of the testimony. Here, it is used "in the sense of superior, rather than superlative, holiness" (Sarna 2004, 147). The holiness of the altar is transferable. **Whatever touches *the altar*** [i.e., the sacrifices that are placed on it] **will be holy**; thus, it is offered to Yahweh by fire. Solomon observed a seven-day dedication of the temple's altar (2 Chr 7:9). Ezekiel was also told about a future restoration of the altar, for which the priest would make atonement for seven days to purify and consecrate it (Ezek 43:18-26).

FROM THE TEXT

The ordination of the priests foreshadows the priestly calling and work of Christian ministers. Consistent with the kingly priesthood of all Israelites (Exod 19:6), the new covenant affirms the priesthood of all believers. However, consistent with the election of the priests and the affirmation of the voluntary Nazirites, the NT also recognizes both the sovereign election (e.g., twelve apostles and Paul) and voluntary dedication (e.g., 1 Tim 3:1) of ministers of the gospel. For those who are chosen or volunteer to be ministers, the NT provides some guidelines for their ordination (e.g., Acts 6:3; 1 Tim 3:1-13). For Aaron and his sons, God prescribed the ceremony of glorification (through robing), justification, mortification, dedication, communion, and empowerment. This process required seven full days. Wesley notes:

> It is likewise intimated that gospel ministers are to be solemnly set apart to the work of the ministry with great deliberation and seriousness, both in the ordainers, and in the ordained, as those that are employed in a great work, and entrusted with a great charge. (1990, 86)

In the Wesleyan tradition, the ordination of such God-called individuals, both men and women, not only affirms their call but also gives them the authority to preach and teach the gospel and to administer the sacraments of the Lord's Supper and baptism.

f. The Regular Burnt Offerings (29:38-46)

BEHIND THE TEXT

The instructions for the anointing, ordination, and consecration of the priests are complete and so are the commands regarding the purification and consecration of the altar. It is, therefore, appropriate to introduce the regulations concerning the daily burnt offering, which is the primary and perpetual function of the altar (see Num 28:1-8).

Like the animal sacrifices for ordination, the daily sacrifices must be "without defect" (Exod 29:1). Offering the best of the animals is symbolic of pure devotion to God. Conversely, sacrificing "blind," "stolen, lame, and sick" animals (Mal 1:8, 13 NET) is a manifestation of the spiritual apostasy or corruption of the worshipper.

This subunit concludes with affirmations and promises concerning Yahweh's relationship with the people of Israel and the overall purpose of the tent of meeting or the tabernacle and its priests.

IN THE TEXT

(1) The Regular Burnt Offerings (29:38-43)

■ **38** Two *male* lambs (as opposed to ewe lambs) are sacrificed **on the altar**. They are fully-grown rams in their second **year** of life, before they reach their second birth season in the spring (see "lamb" in 12:3). Female sheep are not used in ritual sacrifices, being preserved for milking and breeding.

■ **39** A ram, together with a grain offering and drink offering, is sacrificed twice a day. Numbers 28:9 further requires that on the Sabbath day, additional burnt offerings of two rams, plus a grain offering and a drink offering, be given to Yahweh, essentially doubling the regular morning and twilight burnt offerings.

■ **40-41** A **grain offering** is part of the daily offering (Exod 29:41). A large amount of dough is required twice a day. An **ephah** (v 40) is a dry measure. An ephah of cereal is estimated to be close to 30 pounds (14 kg). One **tenth** of an ephah (or an omer) is about 3 pounds (1.4 kg). A **hin** is a liquid measure and is estimated to be about one quart (about .9 liter). So a **quarter** of a hin would be about a cup. A **drink offering** is first mentioned in Gen 35:14, in which Jacob erects a stone pillar in memorial to Yahweh at Bethel and pours out a drink offering on it. Here in Exod 29 it appears as part of the daily burnt offering, with **wine** being used (v 40). The text does not clarify the location for pouring the drink offering (see Num 28:7; 2 Kgs 16:13). Since it is offered up by fire as **a pleasing aroma** (v 41), we may assume that it is poured upon the cereal (and the lamb). The liquid is then optimally retained in the cereal and evaporates in fire.

■ **42** The worship of Yahweh through the **burnt offering** must be done daily and perpetually. The daily sacrifices must be made **before** Yahweh's presence in a manner acceptable to him. Approaching Yahweh through divinely prescribed, holy means yields Yahweh's gift of abiding presence, communion, and revelation.

■ **43** Yahweh promises to **meet** not only with Moses (v 42) but also with **the Israelites**. Yahweh extends the opportunity for divine communion and revelation to the whole nation. Yahweh does so by extending divine presence to the entrance to the tent of meeting, beyond the holiest place above the ark (25:22; 30:6). The concluding phrase indicates that what is consecrated through the rituals will now be consecrated by Yahweh's **glory**, appearing in the sight of the people (40:34; see Lev 9:4, 6, 23-24).

(2) The Abiding Presence of Yahweh (29:44-46)

■ **44** Through the consecration rites carried out by a human agent according to the divine prescription (Exod 29:21, 36-37; 30:29-30), Yahweh makes holy **the tent of meeting**, the **altar**, and the **priests** to Yahweh's service. Ultimately, it is Yahweh who consecrates and sanctifies them.

■ **45** By means of the holy place and holy institutions of sacrifice and priesthood, Yahweh dwells among his covenant people. The statements, **I will dwell among** them (see 25:8; Lev 26:11-12) and **be their God** (see Exod 6:7), emphasize the divine yearning to love and to be loved by those whom he chooses and redeems for the sake of love (Deut 7:7-8).

■ **46** This verse clarifies that the exodus is for the purpose of communion: **so that I might dwell among them** (see Exod 25:8). It also reaffirms the original intent of the tabernacle as revealed in 25:8. The wording of this verse implies that Yahweh's enduring dwelling among his chosen people is contingent upon their continuing acknowledgment of Yahweh as the supreme God, who delivered them from **Egypt**, punishing all who resisted him. The failure to render exclusive worship to **the LORD their God** will result in Yahweh's departure from them.

FROM THE TEXT

The covenant relationship between Yahweh and Israel is not unilateral; it is mutual. The glory of God fills the tabernacle upon its completion, calling the people to exclusive worship through sacrifices. The worship in turn welcomes the Lord's abiding presence.

In the new covenant, instead of burnt offerings, God's people approach God in continual "sacrifice of praise" (Heb 13:15) for the reconciliatory work Jesus Christ accomplished for us. As with the Israelites, the Lord desires a mutually indwelling relationship with his people. Jesus invites us: "Remain in me, as I also remain in you" (John 15:4; see v 7). Those who abide in God are "the temple of the living God" (2 Cor 6:16). Paul, therefore, issues a prohibition against forming a covenant relationship with unbelievers (vv 14-15). He even demands the breaking of any ungodly alliances (v 17). There is a sobering call for the covenant people of God to flee from all compromise and to give exclusive and absolute allegiance to the only living God. To those who respond to the call, the Lord promises, "I will receive you." And, "I will be a Father to you, and you will be my sons and daughters, says the Lord Almighty" (vv 17-18).

12. Further Instructions and the Closure (30:1—31:18)

Overview

After a long section concerned primarily with the vestments and ordination of the priests (Exod 28—29), this section completes the instructions related to the construction of the tabernacle that began in ch 25. This section includes seven instructions. The last verse (31:18) offers an ending to the account of Moses' ascent to Mount Sinai to receive two tablets in 24:12-18.

a. Altar of Incense (30:1-10)

BEHIND THE TEXT

The placement of the instructions concerning the altar of incense after the ordination of the priests, rather than including them in the section for the tabernacle and its furnishings, is unexpected. Some suggest that the reason for this literary placement is that the production of the cloud of incense is not appropriate until after the completion of the ordination of the priests. They reason that Yahweh's own glory cloud fills the tabernacle at the time of its consecration and the priests' ordination. However, one then could argue that the instructions for the lamps (25:31-40) should be in this section as well since lighting the lamps would insult the brilliant presence of Yahweh that fills the tabernacle. Most significantly, however, 40:27 makes it clear that Moses burns the daily incense from the time the tabernacle is erected. It appears there is no clear principle or theological explanation for the present placement of the instructions for the altar of incense.

Archaeological findings have confirmed the use of incense and incense altars in ancient Israel. Besides its religious symbolism, burning incense serves the practical purpose of releasing fragrance inside the tabernacle.

The creation of the golden altar is described in 37:25-28.

IN THE TEXT

■ I The **altar** of **incense** is to be made with **acacia wood**. It is also called the "gold altar" (39:38; 40:5, 26; Num 4:11), as opposed to the bronze altar of animal sacrifice.

■ **2** Looking down from above, the altar is **square**, 1 x 1 **cubit** (1.5' x 1.5' or .46 x .46 m). Its height is **two cubits** (3' or .92 m). As with the bronze altar, the altar of incense has a horn on each of the four corners (→ "horns" in Exod 27:2).

■ **3** The altar is overlaid with a sheet of **pure gold** (see 25:11) and decorated with an *ornamental design* (*zēr*; → "molding" in 25:11, 24-25).

■ **4-5** Since the exact position of the **gold** *ornamental design* (*zēr*) is not specified, we can assume that the entire altar is decorated (30:4). The cast gold **rings** and the **poles** (overlaid with gold) are placed **below** the ornamental design (*zēr*), presumably on the bottom of the gold altar (25:12, 26-27). If so, the gold altar is borne above the carrier's head (like the ark and the table).

■ **6** Of the three furnishings in the holy place of the tabernacle, the **altar of** incense is closest to the inner sanctum where **the ark** is. The description of its placement in relation to **the curtain** and the ark may emphasize the special purpose the incense plays in the manifestation of the divine presence in the most holy place.

■ **7-8** Aaron the high priest is specifically named as the one who **must burn fragrant incense . . . regularly**, that is, twice a day, once in the morning and once at twilight. It is done during the morning trimming and evening lighting of the lamp (27:21), which is also the time for daily burnt offering (29:39).

■ **9** The high priest must not present **on this altar any . . . offering** other than incense and must use only the proper kind of incense. **Other incense** refers to any unauthorized mix, besides the prescribed incense listed in 30:34-38. Nadab and Abihu, although ordinary priests, later burn "unauthorized fire," perhaps in drunkenness, and God kills them (Lev 10:1). In Num 16, a large group of rebellious people burns incense (probably using an incense different from the sanctuary blend) and are slain by Yahweh. Both unauthorized personnel and unauthorized mix incur the death penalty.

■ **10** Once a year, on the Day of Atonement, **Aaron** (and other high priests thereafter) is commanded to apply **the blood of the atoning sin offering** to the **horns** of the gold altar and sprinkle it seven times to purge the sin and uncleanness of the Israelites (Lev 16:18-19). Due to its atoning or purifying function, the gold altar is called **most holy to the Lord**, along with the most holy fragrant incense (Exod 30:36), the most holy place (26:33-34), and the most holy bronze altar and their utensils (29:37; 38:28-29; 40:10).

FROM THE TEXT

The fragrant clouds of smoke from the altar of incense may have various symbolic associations that apply to Christians today. (1) The smoke from the incense altar (Lev 16:12-13) represents the cloud that surrounds and shields the presence of the Lord (e.g., Exod 13:21; 24:16-17; 34:5; Num 12:5). Thus, the burning of the fragrant incense is an acknowledgment of the abiding presence of God in the most holy place. (2) The incense smoke also symbolizes prayers rising up to the Lord (Ps 141:2). Revelation 5:8 explicitly identifies the incense in the twenty-four elders' golden bowls with "the prayers of God's people." Another passage describes "the prayers of all the saints on the golden altar before the throne" that rise up to God, along with "the smoke of incense" (Rev 8:3-4 ESV). Since the people of God have been made worthy by the blood of Christ to serve as priests, their prayers are acceptable, holy offerings to God. (3) Ultimately, the clouds of smoke symbolize the intercession of Jesus Christ (Heb 7:25) and the Holy Spirit (Rom 8:26-27), without which no one may approach God without incurring death.

b. Atonement Money (30:11-16)

BEHIND THE TEXT

This unit deals with a mandatory census and offering of one half shekel, which is imposed upon all males above twenty years of age. Moses' one-time sanctuary tax later serves as the basis for Joash's annual tax for the repair of the temple (2 Kgs 12; 2 Chr 24:4-10). Later in Neh 10:32 [33 HB], the people commit to "give a third of a shekel each year for the service of the house of our God." According to Josephus (*Ant.* 18.9.1), in the Second Temple period, the Jews in the Diaspora had a custom of donating a half shekel annually to the temple in Jerusalem.

There are other censuses taken without the imposition of the poll tax. These censuses concern fighting men (Num 26), Levite males (3:14-39), and Levite ministers (4:1-33). Solomon counted all the foreigners and drafts them for hard labor (2 Chr 2:17-18 [16-17 HB]; see 8:8). Returned exiles were counted for the purpose of resettlement and restoration (Ezra 2:1-70; Neh 7:5-73 [72 HB]; 11:1). The above passages show that census taking in Israel was initiated by God or by civil authorities in the service of God or the nation or both. One exception to this pattern is David's census in 2 Sam 24, which was taken solely for the purpose of determining and celebrating his military power (see v 2), which therefore was punished by God.

Biblical texts related to the taking of a census may also relate to the popular superstitious beliefs of the ancient Near East, in which counting people was thought to bring the counted people supernatural danger, bad luck, or plague (see Exod 30:12). This section on the atonement money to avert a potential plague may reflect a divine initiative to dispel the fear of the people because of their limited cultural perspective or superstitious beliefs.

IN THE TEXT

■ **11-12** Yahweh commands **Moses** (v 11) to take a head **count** (v 12) of the **Israelites** and at the same time take the **ransom** money from each man counted. The term **ransom** (*kōper*) is related to the term "atone" or "atonement." Accordingly, the ransom is later called "the atonement money" in 30:16. It refers to payment made in exchange for **life** (Job 6:22; 33:24; Ps 49:7-8 [8-9 HB]; Prov 13:8). In this case, God is the one who is ransoming the men of Israel at a token ransom of one half shekel (see Isa 43:3; 47:11; Jer 31:11; Hos 13:14 for Yahweh's ransom of the people Israel). Yahweh redeems whoever pays the ransom money from some **plague** that would otherwise come upon them. This ransom payment may be a retroactive ransom for their recent redemption from Egypt and the plagues that came upon Egypt.

■ **13** Everyone must give the ransom money, which is exactly **a half shekel**. The editorial explanatory note on shekel **which weighs twenty gerahs** clarifies the value of the **offering** to the editor's contemporary readers, which remains vague to us. Exodus 38:25-28 reports that from this census, 100 talents and 1,775 shekels of silver are collected from 603,550 men making the mandatory donation (→ "silver" in 25:3 for a summary of its usage).

■ **14** Every single male from **twenty years old** and upward, that is, one who is able to serve in the army, is counted (Num 1:3, 45-46). Since the number of men counted in this census and in the census of fighting men in Num 1 is identical (at 603,550; see Exod 38:26; Num 1:46), the two accounts probably refer to the same census. The account here focuses on the ransoming and atoning effects of the census money, while the Numbers account focuses on the consecrating and commissioning aspects of the census.

■ **15** The ransom amount must not be increased or diminished based on a person's wealth or poverty. Everyone contributes an equal amount to the sanctuary, for everyone's life has equal worth before Yahweh. Yahweh probably requires what a poor man could offer without creating further hardship.

■ **16** Verse 16 indicates the proper use of the **atonement money. The service of the tent of meeting** indicates the use of this money for the tent of meeting. Some suggest that the poll tax silver supplemented the silver from the freewill offering (Exod 25:1-7; 36:3-7) and was used for the long-term upkeep and maintenance of the tabernacle (see Hamilton 2011, 510). However, Exod 38:25-28 makes it clear that the silver collected in the poll tax is what is used for the construction of the tabernacle.

The silver makes **atonement** for the **lives** of the **Israelites**. Perhaps such atonement is symbolically and perpetually memorialized in the ransom silver that is used for different parts of the tabernacle and continually exists **before** the LORD. If so, no collection of annual ransom silver would be necessary (see Hamilton 2011, 510-11, for the suggestion that Moses' poll tax is meant to be collected annually).

FROM THE TEXT

The text deals with two issues: ransom and stewardship. Atonement money is the payment of ransom for the life of every member; it reminds every Israelite that he belongs to the community of the ransomed. Membership in the community of faith has its privilege and responsibility. The responsibility in this text is the payment of atonement money (something akin to a membership fee) for the construction and/or maintenance of the place of worship. Places of worship cannot survive without the financial stewardship of those who assemble there to worship God.

In such a way, the text reminds the people of God today that their stewardship is a token of their gratitude to God for his gracious act of redemption. Stewardship does not purchase or earn atonement; nonetheless, it is a meaningful way to acknowledge our redemption through the blood of Christ. Peter reminds his readers: "For you know that it was not with perishable things such as silver or gold that you were redeemed from the empty way of life . . . but with the precious blood of Christ" (1 Pet 1:18-19).

c. Bronze Basin for Washing (30:17-21)

BEHIND THE TEXT

The bronze basin is made not from the contributions by the general public, but from the bronze "mirrors of the women who served at the entrance to the tent of meeting" (Exod 38:8; → "women" in 38:8). No dimensions are given, but the basin had to be large enough to hold the water required for washing the entire body of Aaron and his sons at the time of their ordination (→ 29:4). Presumably, the basin is used for subsequent washing ceremonies for future priests being ordained. In the daily service at the tent of the meeting, the priests use the bronze basin for washing their hands and feet before entering the tabernacle and before offering sacrifices (30:19-20; 40:31-32). The basin is placed between the tabernacle and the altar (30:18), because the priests' need to enter the tabernacle and offer sacrifices in ritual purity. The ritual purification of the hands and feet is not to be viewed as trivial, as the death penalty is meted out for the violation of this injunction (vv 20-21).

The report of the basin's construction is given in 38:8.

IN THE TEXT

■ **17-18** The shape and dimension of the **bronze basin** (*kiyyôr*) are not given. The etymology of the Hebrew term for **basin** remains unclear, although the root *kwr* (perhaps "be or make round") and thus the round shape has been suggested (Propp 2006, 480). It is securely set on a bronze stand.

■ **19** **Water from it** indicates that they do not wash their hands and feet right in the basin, but draw water from it for washing. They likely made bronze bowls for drawing water out and smaller basins for washing their hands and feet.

■ **20-21** The absolute necessity for ritual washing **with water** (v 20) every time they **approach** the tabernacle or the bronze **altar** is emphasized by repeated warnings of the penalty for violation, **so that they will not die.** There are several other warnings against death penalty infractions if priests fail to fulfill Yahweh's requirements, such as sounding bells in 28:35; wearing undergarments in 28:43; and paying the atonement money in 30:12, 16 (also see Lev 8:35; 10:6-9; 15:31; 16:2, 13; 21:1; 22:9; Num 4:15, 19-20). This ordinance of ritual washing is permanent.

FROM THE TEXT

This text focuses on purity and cleansing required of those who approach the presence of God. The Holy God requires his people to be holy in their relationship with him. Psalm 24:4 reminds readers that God requires "clean hands and a pure heart" to approach his holy presence. The need for holiness in life may be at the heart of Jesus' words to his disciples, "Unless I wash you, you have no part with me" (John 13:8). For Wesley, the daily priestly use of the bronze basin teaches us "daily to attend upon God, daily to renew our repentance for sin," and daily to apply "the blood of Christ to our souls for remission" (1990, 87). Jesus calls us to repent not only for our own sin by ourselves (Luke 18:13) but also for and with one another; we are to "wash one another's feet" (John 13:14). This act of washing, then, involves forgiving and covering a multitude of sins with grace and love. In washing others' feet, one's hands are also washed. In extending grace to others in humility, we continue to find our Father's grace (Matt 6:12).

d. Fragrant Anointing Oil (30:22-33)

BEHIND THE TEXT

The spices mentioned in this unit are expensive commodities, for they came from places as far away as Southern Arabia (for myrrh) and even India or Sri Lanka (for cinnamon). Joseph's brothers sold him to such a caravan of

Ishmaelite traders coming from Gilead on their way to Egypt, with "their camels . . . loaded with spices, balm and myrrh" (Gen 37:25). Likewise, Jacob urged his sons to take "some spices and myrrh" (likely purchased from traders) along with other gifts worthy of being presented to the ruler of Egypt (43:11). Spices reappear in 1 Kgs 10:2-3, in which the queen of Sheba arrives with large quantities of spices, gold, and precious stones. The mixing of the fragrant oil is described in Exod 37:29.

IN THE TEXT

■ **22-25** Select **fine spices** (30:23) are mixed with pure, pressed **olive oil** (v 24) to make a **sacred anointing oil** (v 25). The ingredients are listed in order of descending value. The Israelite leaders perhaps had these spices in their possession when they came out of Egypt. If not, they purchased them from various traveling merchants from India, Arabia, and East Africa. The shekel is a solid measure, which is here used for the **liquid** [or "flowing"] **myrrh** (v 23). A **hin** (v 24) is a liquid measure, estimated at about one quart or about 0.9 liter (see 29:40).

1 shekel	0.4 oz	11.3 g
250 shekels	6 lbs	2.8 kg
500 shekels	12.5 lbs	5.6 kg

Figure 14: Weights

Even as the work of textiles, carpentry, precious metals, and precious stones requires highly talented and skilled artisans, **sacred** perfumery requires an expert **perfumer**.

■ **26-30** Moses is to **anoint** (vv 26, 30) and **consecrate** (vv 29, 30) not only the priests but also the sanctuary and all its furnishings and **utensils** (v 28). This ritual makes them **holy** (v 29) and sets them apart for service to God. Everything that comes in contact with any consecrated element (such as the incense for the gold **altar** [v 28], the oil for the lamps, the bread for the table, all the gifts and sacrifices on the altar of **burnt offering**, and the water for the **basin) will be most holy** (v 29). The conveyance of holiness through touch makes the various offerings fit for God's purposes.

■ **31-33** The particular recipe for the **sacred** fragrant **anointing oil** (v 31) must never be duplicated or used on any person **other than** the **priest** (v 33). The penalty for disobeying the regulation is severe (→ "The Penalty of 'Cutting Off'" sidebar in 12:15).

The anointing of the sacred place and its furniture and Aaron and his sons with specially prepared oil that produces a pleasing fragrance renders them holy. By anointing everything and everyone directly related to the tabernacle with the sacred fragrant oil, a clear distinction between the sacred and the common, the holy and the profane, is made. It is noteworthy that holiness of the sacred personnel, place, and furniture through the anointing ritual is not bland or unnoticeable. Rather, their holiness is perpetually communicated through fragrance, a sweet smell, a scent that can be smelled by all who approach the tent.

In the NT, holy "anointing" refers to the Holy Spirit (1 John 2:20, 27) who is upon Jesus and empowers him to proclaim the good news and carry out the full gospel ministry (Luke 4:18-19). The same "anointing" of the Holy Spirit is also given to his disciples to carry on a similar ministry (Matt 10:1, 7-8; Acts 1:8). The Apostle Paul addresses "the church of God in Corinth, together with all his *holy people* throughout Achaia" and writes: "For we are to God the pleasing aroma of Christ" (2 Cor 1:1; 2:15).

The anointing by the Holy Spirit and holiness in life make the disciples of Jesus Christ not only a people separated to God but also a people who spread the sweet fragrance of Christ in the world in which they live. Readers may also infer from the text that anointing by the Holy Spirit marks their identity as a holy people with a holy mission to the world, and that any misuse or abuse of it for personal gain or satisfaction may incur God's judgment.

e. Fragrant Incense (30:34-38)

BEHIND THE TEXT

The call to contribute spices for the fragrant oil was issued earlier (Exod 25:6). This current passage lists the four ingredients for the fragrant incense. In Num 7:12-83, after the initial anointing and consecration of the tabernacle, the leaders of Israel bring their gifts, which include twelve incense dishes (→ "dishes" in Exod 25:29). Each incense dish weighs 10 shekels (4 oz or 113 g) and is filled with incense, probably the raw ingredients required to make the fragrant perfumes. The "fragrant blend of incense" includes salt. Adding salt to the sacred or common incense to boost its burning ability was a widespread practice in the ancient world. The fragrant incense mix is to be regularly powdered and kept close to the golden altar for daily offerings (30:36).

In Lev 16:12, on the Day of Atonement, the high priest is ordered to take a censer full of burning coals from the bronze altar and "two handfuls of finely ground fragrant incense," bring them into the holy place, and put the aromatic incense on the fire. This method for burning salted incense quickly produces a great cloud of fragrant smoke, creating a thick smokescreen that would conceal the atonement cover. This smoke cloud protects the high priest from seeing the intense manifestation of Yahweh's glory, thus preserving the priest's life (Lev 16:13; see Exod 33:20). Similarly, in 34:5, the cloud that descends upon Mount Sinai covers Moses and prevents him from viewing the fullness of God's glory.

Exodus 37:29 reports the fulfillment of the instructions here.

IN THE TEXT

■ **34** As with the **fragrant** anointing oil, four **spices** are used for the fragrant incense, but **in equal** quantities.

■ **35** A highly skilled and experienced **perfumer** (female or male; see 1 Sam 8:13; Neh 3:8) is required to make the **blend of incense**.

■ **36** A large quantity of the fragrant blend of incense is kept in a large bowl (→ "plates" in Exod 25:29). Aaron's sons probably carried out the duties of powdering the incense and refilling the incense dish (→ "dishes" in 25:29). Aaron alone (and other high priests after him) is authorized to burn the incense (30:7). The incense is burned **in front of the ark of the covenant** that lies behind the curtain. Because of its special function in creating the proper atmosphere for the favorable manifestation of Yahweh's glory and his communion with the people, the incense is **most holy** to Yahweh and Yahweh's people (30:37).

■ **37-38** Like the fragrant anointing oil (vv 31-33), the composition and function of the fragrant **incense** are protected. What Yahweh prescribed for holy, spiritual communion between him and the people must not be used to gratify carnal desires for pleasure. Again, the penalty for such unauthorized use is being **cut off from their people** (v 38; see v 33; → "cut off" in 12:15).

FROM THE TEXT

The holy fragrant incense ("consider it holy to the Lord*" [30:37]), like the fragrant anointing oil, is a reminder that the tabernacle is the holy place for the holy presence of God.* Some passages liken prayer to fragrant incense ascending to the Lord (Ps 141:2; Rev 5:8; 8:3-4). Such are the holy prayers of those who live in the holy presence of God. However, in Isa 1:13, God finds the incense of the worshipping community detestable (a stinking smell!) because of their wicked and unjust life. Similarly, then, our worship and prayers, accompanied by secret or unrepentant sins, are meaningless and offensive to God. But our worship and prayers, accompanied by the marks of the cross and the suffering of Christ daily born (Rom 8:17), are a pleasing aroma to the Lord; they affirm our faith in his tangible presence among us.

f. Chief Supervising Craftsmen (31:1-11)

BEHIND THE TEXT

Yahweh names the principal and assistant directors for the entire project, Bezalel, a Judahite (Exod 35:30), and Oholiab, a Danite (v 34). They are directors over all the male and female artisans, who are "skilled workers and designers" (v 35). While a team of master artists completes the construction of the tabernacle, Bezalel is specifically named as the one who makes the ark of the covenant (37:1-9). Bezalel is the master designer and craftsman in the areas of carpentry, jewelry, and artistry with metal (31:2-5). Oholiab is the master engraver, tapestry designer and weaver, and the designer and weaver of other textiles (38:23; → "Weavers" sidebar in 26:1). The Israelites' artistic abilities are most likely exploited in Egypt in the service and fame of Pharaoh and Egypt, but now as free people Yahweh consecrates these artisans and their gifts and skills for the purpose and glory of God. The public announcement and appointment of the named master craftsmen are included in 35:30-35.

IN THE TEXT

■ **1-2** **Chosen** (v 2) is literally "called by name." Out of the whole congregation of Israel, Yahweh singles out **Bezalel** for a specific purpose. **Bezalel** means "in the shadow [protection] of God." **Uri** is probably an abbreviated form of Uriah (LXX), which means "Yah is my light" (see 2 Sam 11:3). **Hur** is often mentioned in relation to Aaron (→ "Hur" in Exod 17:10).

■ **3** Already a master in his field of artistry, Yahweh fills Bezalel with **the Spirit of God**. The language used in this verse resembles words that refer to the Messiah in Isa 11:2: "The Spirit of the LORD will rest on him—the Spirit of wisdom and of understanding, the Spirit of counsel and of might, the Spirit of the knowledge and fear of the LORD." What is committed to Moses in visions and words, Bezalel is able to implement in artistic construction. He is also able to teach and direct others so that more artisans learn how to execute the work (Exod 35:34). Verse 3 connects **wisdom** (ḥokmâ), a gift from God, to one's technical knowledge and skill.

■ **4-5** These verses summarize the areas of **artistic . . . work** (v 4)—metalwork, jewelry arts, and carpentry—required for the tabernacle and its related items, except engraving and textile works, which are specifically associated with Oholiab.

■ **6** **Oholiab**, meaning "father of my tent" or "father is my tent [protection]," is appointed as Bezalel's assistant. **Ahisamak** means "my brother has supported." Yahweh gives **ability to all the skilled workers**. Yahweh adds divine knowledge, wisdom, and understanding (v 3) to their preexisting talents and skills.

■ **7-11** These verses summarize the items to be made in a slightly different order from the one found in the instructions (25:10—30:30) and from the one found in the constructions (36:8—39:32).

FROM THE TEXT

The ultimate purpose of human creativity and ingenuity is to capture and execute God's vision for divine pleasure, which, in turn, serves humanity. This understanding of art stands against art as a means of self-expression or a quest for meaning. What Jesus says to Nicodemus aptly applies to art and creative endeavors: "Flesh gives birth to flesh, but the Spirit gives birth to spirit" (John 3:6). While creativity is part of the divine image, unsanctified creativity falls short of divine glory, since the divine image in which we are created has been corrupted by sin. However, sanctified, consecrated, and anointed creativity, as part of the restored divine image in and through Christ, glorifies God.

The artists in this unit are already masters in their fields. However, Yahweh fills them with the Spirit of God for greater creativity, ingenuity, innovation, and invention. The latest and greatest techniques they possess pale in light of the divine wisdom, understanding, and abilities that the Holy Spirit imparts. The work of God requires the Spirit of God working in and through those who are willing to surrender their gifts and skills to the Spirit of God to take, bless, and use. What God envisions can only be accomplished through the power of God. When God works in and through us, he is "able to do immeasurably more than all we ask or imagine, according to his power that is at work within us" (Eph 3:20).

g. Sabbath and the Closure (31:12-18)

BEHIND THE TEXT

This unit on the Sabbath law concludes the entire section on the instructions for the tabernacle. Correspondingly, the section on the construction of the tabernacle in ch 35 begins with the Sabbath regulations. This instruction on the Sabbath, quite appropriately, is the seventh of seven divine commands concerning the tabernacle. The seven commands are each introduced by the phrase "then the LORD said to Moses" (25:1; 30:11, 17, 22, 34; 31:1, 12; see Berlin and Brettler 2004, 165, 182). The particular literary placement of the Sabbath units here and in ch 35 is clearly intentional, emphasizing the paramount importance of keeping the Sabbath holy unto Yahweh. Indeed, sacred time appears to take priority over sacred space in Israel. During the construction of the holy place of worship and communion, God's people must uphold the holy time of worship and communion.

One rationale for the Sabbath observance is found in the creation narrative in Genesis (→ Exod 20:8-11 and 31:17 below). The Sabbath also has overtones of social justice and equality that link it with other biblical laws (see 23:10-12).

The Sabbath regulations are followed by a verse (31:18) that reconnects and gives closure to Moses' ascent to Mount Sinai to receive two tablets (24:12-18). Verse 18 of ch 31 also provides a setting for what follows—the golden calf episode, in which Moses hurls down and breaks the two tablets with divine inscriptions on them (32:19).

IN THE TEXT

(1) Sabbath (31:12-17)

■ **12-13** The command to **observe** the **Sabbaths** (v 13) begins with the strong contrasting "nevertheless" (*'ak*; "however"). The text is emphatic that Sabbath must be observed. The Sabbath is a covenant **sign between** the creator God and the covenant people. The observance of the Sabbath testifies to the people's acknowledgment and worship of Yahweh as the one who created them, brought them into a covenant relationship, and made them **holy** as Yahweh is holy. The Sabbath observers become holy for entering into a time and a rest that are holy and for worshipping the one who is holy.

■ **14-15** The observance of the **Sabbath** (v 14; *šabbat šabbātôn*; "supreme rest"; → "Sabbath" in 16:23-24) involves complete cessation from work. The penalty for the violation of this requirement is severe. For **any work** done (presumably in secret), the violator will be **cut off from their people** (→ "cut off" in 12:15). Violators caught by other people (as opposed to secret violators) shall **be put to death**, that is, executed through a human judicial process (Exod 31:15). Numbers 15:32-36 records a case in which the whole assembly, at Yahweh's command, stones "to death" (v 36) a violator of this law (→ "Sabbath" in Exod 20:8-11).

■ **16-17** The celebration of **the Sabbath** (31:16) is a **lasting covenant** obligation placed on God's people. The Sabbath observance is the outwardly visible **sign** (v 17) that a community belongs to Yahweh, the creator God. The expressions **rested** and **refreshed** in relation to Yahweh are anthropomorphisms, employed for the purpose of teaching human beings the fundamental correlation between cessation from work and the revitalization of the body, soul, and spirit.

(2) The Closure (31:18)

■ **18** This verse resumes and concludes the narrative of 24:12-18, in which Moses enters the cloud on Mount Sinai to receive **the two tablets of . . . stone** (see "tablets" in 25:16; 32:15-16; 34:1, 27-28). Moses has been with **the LORD** forty days and forty nights, and he has received all the instructions for the tabernacle. Thus, in a culmination of the process, Yahweh gives Moses the two stone tablets, upon which Yahweh has written the Ten Commandments with **the finger of God** (see Deut 5:22; → "the finger of God" in Exod 8:19 [15 HB]). Due to its origin and content, the two tablets carry supreme value and importance.

FROM THE TEXT

The place of worship must be constructed by holy people who keep the Sabbath holy throughout the entire construction process. The spiritual reason for building the tabernacle is to provide a physical place for the indwelling, manifest presence of God, so that his people might approach him and worship him. Therefore, violating the Sabbath rest and worship of the Lord in favor of a speedy construction of the Lord's dwelling place would be self-defeating.

Even the Christian work of "building" the kingdom of God on earth, as important as it is, must yield to and be limited by the principle of rest or Sabbath. Whether or not this is observed as a literal seventh day of rest, the point is that our labors in the service of God and others must be carried out in the proper context of an unbroken, intimate relationship with the Lord. Only by abiding in the Lord's presence will we bear good fruit (John 15:1-8).

C. The Golden Calf: False Presence (32:1—34:35)

Overview

Israel's apostasy in worshipping the golden calf has been appropriately called "the fall story of Israel" (Fretheim 1991, 279). What precedes this rebellion in Exodus accentuates the gravity of Israel's sin, namely, Yahweh's demonstration of supremacy in Egypt, the astounding provision in the wilderness, and the profound experience of the theophany on Mount Sinai. The Decalogue given by Yahweh on Sinai further underscores Israel's willful rebellion. Israel rejects Yahweh and completely breaks her covenant with Yahweh.

The people's rebellion at Sinai (chs 32—34) interrupts the divine plan for the tabernacle. Yahweh desires to visibly and tangibly dwell among the Israelites and have them approach and worship him. The festival and worship at the tabernacle are the explicit reason for the exodus (5:1, 3, 8; 8:26-27 [22-23 HB]; 10:25-26). However, before Yahweh reveals his authorized means of perpetual sacrifice and worship to the people, they hold their own pagan festival to an idol. But there is a fundamental incompatibility between a holy God and an idolatrous people. Yahweh's holy presence among the corrupt Israelites, therefore, becomes dangerous. Thus, Yahweh's presence has to move away from the Israelites' camp and the construction and operation of the tabernacle have to be postponed until the broken covenant is renewed (chs 35—40).

I. The Golden Calf and the Broken Covenant (32:1-6)

BEHIND THE TEXT

In this unit, Aaron makes a golden calf at the foot of Mount Sinai in response to the people's urgings. Moses had left the Israelites under the charge of Aaron and Hur before he ascended Mount Sinai with Joshua (24:14). However, Hur is nowhere mentioned in this episode or afterward. Some Jewish writers have speculated that the ringleaders of the idolatry killed him for opposing them, which, in turn, forced Aaron to succumb to their menacing demands (see Propp 2006, 547).

The essential legal and theological background to this unit is the Decalogue of ch 20, which is of particular importance. As revealed in the dark events that unfold in this account, the rebellious ones violate several commands: the first command, "You shall have no other gods before me" (20:3), although some argue that it was not violated here; the second, "You shall not make for yourself an image . . . You shall not bow down to them or worship them" (vv 4-5); the third, "You shall not misuse the name of the LORD your God" (v 7); and perhaps the seventh, "You shall not commit adultery" (v 14) as suggested in revelry involving sex (32:6).

IN THE TEXT

■ **1** This verse situates the entire golden calf narrative toward the end of Moses' forty-day and forty-night stay on Mount Sinai mentioned in 24:18. The Hebrew expression for **gathered around** has a threatening tone (translated into "oppose" in Num 16:3; "gathered in opposition to" in v 42 [17:7 HB]; Exod 20:2). The people succumb to the increasing anxiety about the whereabouts and survival of **Moses** and the related uncertainty about their future travel toward the promised land.

The absence or possible death of their human mediator Moses means that Yahweh will be inaccessible to them (see the people's demand for Moses as a mediator in 20:18-21; see Deut 5:20-24). Thus, the ringleaders demand that **Aaron** produce **gods** (or "a god" [NASB, NJPS]), probably to provide a visible representation of the invisible Yahweh. In the absence of Moses as a visible mediator, they might be looking for a tangible image to become a divine mediator for them, although Yahweh intends only Moses and the provisions of the tabernacle to fulfill such mediatory roles (see Berlin and Brettler 2004, 183 on the unauthorized mediation of the golden calf).

■ **2** Some see in **Aaron**'s order to the instigators to *tear off* the treasured **gold earrings** from their **wives**, **sons**, and **daughters** an attempt to dissuade them from their evil plan. If that is Aaron's motivation, his efforts are useless. All the people, both men and women, willingly contribute their own earrings (v

3). Such jewelry is likely part of the spoils they brought out of Egypt (11:2-3; 12:35-36). Israel's false worship is funded by generous gifts.

■ **3** The expression **all the people** implicates the whole assembly in the act of rebellion. In the first chapter, Pharaoh ordered "all his people" to participate in the national crime of the infanticide of Hebrew baby boys (1:22). Yahweh, therefore, punished the whole nation of Egypt. Similarly, Yahweh threatens to destroy the whole nation of Israel for their national rebellion in 32:10.

■ **4** Perceiving that the mob is determined to pursue evil, Aaron makes a concession by casting a golden **calf** for them. Other passages attest to a **cast** or molten **idol** that is made out of carved wood or stone and then plated with gold or silver (Isa 40:19; Hab 2:19). The ox or bull was a symbol of strength, fertility, and leadership, thus, often deified and worshipped in the ancient Near East. Following the practice of the time, the young bull probably is meant to be the footstool upon which the invisible deity would stand (Sarna 2004, 155; see "the ark of the covenant" as "the footstool" of God in 1 Chr 28:2; → Exod 25:20). However, even if it is meant only as a pedestal, the ringleaders still deify the golden calf. So, they declare, **These are your gods, Israel, who brought you up out of Egypt.** In this statement, they use the plural term "gods" (*'ĕlōhîm*) with a plural verb. The use of the plural noun *'ĕlōhîm* to refer to Yahweh almost always occurs with a singular verb (with a few exceptions; see "*'ĕlōhîm*" in Exod 21:6). Therefore, this verse most likely indicates that the ringleaders are affirming two deities: the deified golden calf and supposedly the invisible deity believed to stand on it. The molten image is presented to the people not as an entirely new god, but as a symbolic representation of Israel's historical God and as a means of consulting that God for decisions and guidance. But of course, the very notion that a human-made idol can either host a deity or channel divine power and decision is thoroughly pagan and detestable to and, thus, forbidden by Yahweh. The Israelites' rebellion is both appalling and tragic in light of Yahweh's own gracious provisions for mediation (→ atonement cover in 25:22 and Urim and Thummim in Behind the Text for 28:15-30).

■ **5** Aaron's motivation for building the **altar** might be to redirect their attention from "gods" to Yahweh, so that they might worship Yahweh. Thus, **Aaron** quickly announces a **festival** to Yahweh. The set time for the festival to Yahweh is hasty: **tomorrow.** Aaron perhaps perceives that the rebels are ready to make pagan sacrifices to the idol, so he tries to provide a quick alternative. However, the alternative further baptizes blasphemy with vain and unauthorized religious activities (Hamilton 2011, 532).

■ **6** Perhaps Aaron is intending to make the sacrifices himself on behalf of Israel. However, the mob rises **early**, no doubt, to elude Aaron and to make the sacrifices themselves, including the **burnt offerings** and **fellowship offer-**

ings that only certain authorized personnel have made up to this point (18:12; 24:5). The rebels soon plunge into a celebration that involves eating and drinking (perhaps signifying a false attempt to have covenant communion with the divine, instead of an authorized meal as in 24:11 and 29:32-34). They also enjoy **revelry**, which likely involved illicit sexual activity (Hamilton 2011, 532-33). Further, they sing and dance (32:18-19), honoring the calf in a similar way as they had honored Yahweh after the exodus (15:20-21). In this manner, the festival of Yahweh, for which Yahweh brought them out of Egypt (5:1, 3, 8; 8:26-27 [22-23 HB]; 10:25-26), is dedicated to the grotesque image.

FROM THE TEXT

Whether OT or NT, the worship acceptable and pleasing to God involves love, understanding, and obedience. In the worship of the golden calf, God's people start "a new, false religion" that is similar to Yahweh's revelations of true religion given to Moses, but not yet communicated to them (see Enns 2000, 571). It is evident that this false religion includes the purported worship of Yahweh, together with remembrance of past deliverance (Exod 32:4; see 20:2), the building of an altar (32:5; see 20:24-26; 24:4-6), a festival to the Lord (32:5; see 5:1; 10:9; 12:14-20; 23:14-19), and sacrificial offerings (the burnt and fellowship offerings in 32:6; see 29:32, 38, etc.). This religious practice has all the outward trappings of obedience and conformity to Yahweh's revelation, but it violates the commandment against idolatry that rests at the very heart of true worship of Yahweh.

Unfortunately the same pattern of false religion in the name of true religion is repeated in Israel's history (e.g., Judg 8:23-27 and 1 Kgs 12:26-33, both of which have marked parallels with Exod 32). So the prophets Isaiah and Jeremiah condemn the Israelites for having the right form (sacrifices) and right words (liturgy) of worship that are offered continually, but the wrong motivation as their hearts are far from the Lord (Isa 29:13; Jer 12:2).

Christians can also be prone to idolatry. Moreover, our worship with all the right form and liturgy can be devoid of true devotion to and affection for Jesus Christ. Thus, like the church in Ephesus, we are called to renew our first love (Rev 2:4-5). Paul exhorts us to offer ourselves as "a living sacrifice, holy and pleasing to God" (Rom 12:1). How? Paul advises, "Do not conform to the pattern of this world, but be transformed by the renewing of your mind" (v 2*a*). Life lived on an altar built on our conscience involves daily self-denial and daily obedience to the word of God: "Then you will be able to test and approve what God's will is" (v 2*b*). Understanding God's "good, pleasing and perfect will" (v 2*b*), in turn, helps us to offer our lives as wholly acceptable and pleasing sacrifices to God and to remain in his love.

2. The Indignation of Yahweh and Moses (32:7—33:6)

a. Yahweh's Threat (32:7-14)

BEHIND THE TEXT

The focus shifts from the disturbing events at the foot of Mount Sinai to the disquieting conversation between Yahweh and Moses. Yahweh threatens to destroy the apostate Israelites, which is reiterated in Deut 9:12-14. Moses, however, intercedes for the people. Yahweh willingly concedes to Moses' requests and does not destroy the Israelites. While some argue that no human being can impinge upon the absolute sovereignty of Yahweh or change the course of divine action, the plain sense of the text obliges readers to a different interpretation. Moses shares the company of a few people who have found favor in Yahweh's eyes and have been given the right of friendship and whose intercession has influenced divine decision, such as Abraham (Gen 18:17-32), the Suffering Servant (Isa 53:12), and Jeremiah (Jer 7:16; 14:11).

IN THE TEXT

(1) Yahweh's Threat of Destruction (32:7-10)

■ **7** In v 7, Yahweh ends Moses' mediation on behalf of Israel because they **have become corrupt** and commands him to **go down**. We do not know why Yahweh waits until things have gone out of control to send Moses down to the people engaged in idolatrous worship. It is, however, clear that Yahweh knew what was taking place at the foot of the mountain but did not circumvent the rebellion; rather, he allowed freedom and the full intentions of people's heart to manifest. Through an act of rebellion they have rejected their special status as Yahweh's people (see "my treasured possession" in 19:5). Thus, Yahweh now treats them as Moses' people (**your people**) whom Moses **brought up out of Egypt**. Yahweh essentially disowns the iniquitous, corrupt people and puts the responsibility of deciding the fate of the people in Moses' hands, as the covenant mediator. It is significant that the words "corrupt" and "corrupted" are used to describe the earth and all "flesh" (NASB, NJPS, NRSV) before the judgment by the flood (Gen 6:12). The Israelites' degenerate condition calls for destruction.

■ **8** In this verse, Yahweh gives Moses the description of what just took place; they **made . . . an idol** and worshipped it. Despite any good intentions Aaron might have had, the Israelites did not worship Yahweh by imagining Yahweh standing on the golden **calf**. Rather, they worshipped and devoted themselves to the golden calf itself, thus, **bowed down to it and sacrificed to it**. Yahweh makes it absolutely clear the people cannot access Yahweh through an idol.

■ 9 Yahweh has been testing and observing the condition of the Israelites' hearts since their departure from Egypt. That **these people** are rebellious and stubborn is clear; **they are . . . stiff-necked**. The expression "stiff-necked" (also in 33:3, 5; 34:9; Deut 9:6, 13; Neh 9:16, 17, 29) always refers to the consummate rebellion of Israel in the golden calf incident. This expression conjures the image of rebels rejecting Yahweh and his commands and proceeding with their evil plans, unrelentingly. When Yahweh (or the people's better conscience) calls back, the rebels hold their neck stiff, refusing to turn their heads to look back and listen and obstinately pursuing their own desires (Jacob 1992, 943).

Not So Stiff-necked People

The expression "circumcised heart" (see Deut 10:16) is the opposite of "stiff-necked." Isaiah 30:21 shows what people with "circumcised hearts" are like: "When you turn to the right or when you turn to the left, your ears shall hear a word behind you, saying, 'This is the way; walk in it'" (NRSV). Should they be led astray or wander from the right path, the Lord, who remains on the right path, calls them back. Upon hearing his call, they turn their heads and see the Lord who is calling them. With their hearts palpitating with affection for the Lord and their minds filled with understanding of their misstep, they run back to him.

■ 10 The second and third commandments of the Decalogue come with the threat of punishment for idolaters and abusers of the divine name (Exod 20:5-7). Accordingly, Yahweh threatens to destroy Israel for breaking those commandments. The jealous God hates idolatry (20:5 and 34:14) and responds to it with burning **anger**. The idea "burning anger" occurs in relation to Yahweh mostly in situations of idolatry or spiritual unfaithfulness (Deut 6:14-15; 7:4; 11:16-17; 29:26-27; 31:17-18; 32:21-22; Josh 23:16; 2 Kgs 22:17). Hence, Yahweh is ready to unleash "burning anger," which would utterly consume the object of his wrath. While it is possible that the Levites did not directly participate in the idolatry (see Exod 32:26 ff.), the entire nation is treated as one entity bound together in corporate solidarity. The whole nation is guilty, and the whole nation is liable to destruction.

Previously, Yahweh told Moses to "go down" (v 7). Now Yahweh repeats a similar idea: **leave me alone**. The reason for wanting solitude is **so that my anger may burn against them**. This reason may point to the positive effect Moses' delightful (and intercessory) presence has on Yahweh. It is as if Yahweh needs Moses' consent or absence to destroy the covenant people (Ryken 2005, 987). If so, **leave me alone** is equivalent to asking Moses not to intercede on behalf of Israel, for such intercession would be effective.

But Yahweh's final intention probably is not to stop Moses from interceding or to destroy the Israelites. Rather, Yahweh leaves opportunity for Moses to intercede as a mediator and save the people of Israel (Childs 1974, 567).

Yahweh's consultation with Moses is consistent with Yahweh's disclosure to Abraham of his plans to destroy Sodom and Gomorrah, which led to Abraham's intercession (Gen 18:16-33).

Yahweh ends his speech with the offer to **make . . . a great nation** out of Moses.

(2) Moses' Intercession (32:11-13)

■ **11** Moses responds to God with a powerful speech clearly intended to bring about a change in God's attitude toward Israel (vv 11-13). He shows no interest in his own personal greatness or honor. He refuses Yahweh's offer to make him great (see Gen 12:2b: "I will make your name great"). Instead, based on **the favor of the** LORD that he already enjoys, he seeks the forgiveness of the Israelites. Previously, Yahweh referred to the Israelites as "your people, whom you brought up out of Egypt" (Exod 32:7), making them Moses' responsibility; now Moses uses the same language to put the ownership back on Yahweh. Moses appeals to Yahweh's rationality. Moses' implicit rhetorical question is: "Why should you destroy that for which you worked so hard?"

■ **12** Moses also appeals to Yahweh's reputation among **the Egyptians**, which Yahweh has established with mighty acts of power (see 7:17; 8:22; 10:2; 12:12; 14:4, 18). Moses' implied rhetorical question remains: "Why should you now ruin the reputation for which you worked so hard?" If Yahweh destroys Israel, Yahweh's name will be forever belittled and scorned among the Egyptians.

■ **13** Lastly, Moses reverently invokes Yahweh's oath to the patriarchs concerning **descendants** and the **land** (see Gen 12:2, 7; 15:5; 22:17; 26:4; 28:12-15). Moses is requesting that Yahweh fulfill that promise in his generation, rather than delay it another four hundred years, when Moses' descendants would be **numerous**.

(3) Yahweh's Concession (32:14)

■ **14** Yahweh listens to Moses and relents or changes the course of his action. The Hebrew term for "relent" (*niham*), when used of Yahweh, may mean "felt sorry, pity, or regret" (Gen 6:6-7; 1 Sam 15:11; 1 Chr 21:15) or "relent" or "change his mind" (see Enns 2000, 572 for the affirmation that God changes his mind here, and Ryken 2005, 989 for its denial). When used of human beings, the term has the additional meaning of "repent."

Yahweh is said to relent on three grounds (see Hamilton 2011, 539-40): (1) prophetic intercession, as in this verse and in Amos 7:1-6; (2) the people's repentance or change of action, either from evil to good or from good to evil (Jer 18:8-10; 26:3, 13; Jonah 3:9-10); and (3) Yahweh's free and compassionate nature (Deut 32:36; 2 Sam 24:16; Ps 106:45; Jer 42:9-10; see also Exod 33:19 and 34:6-7 below).

Yahweh is said not to relent (1) when he has taken an oath and/or made an irrevocable decree, such as the one concerning Abraham and his descendants (Num 23:19; Mal 3:6) or concerning the Davidic kingship-priesthood (Ps 110:4; see 2 Sam 7); and (2) regarding punishment for a long-standing, persistent sin (1 Sam 15:29; Jer 4:28; Ezek 24:14; Zech 8:14).

FROM THE TEXT

There is biblical evidence that in the context of an intimate relationship between Yahweh and a human being, Yahweh grants special favors in answer to prayers. So in the context of an extraordinary friendship between the sovereign Yahweh and the mortal man Moses, Yahweh allows Moses to impinge upon divine sovereignty and influence divine decisions.

However, some scholars dismiss the expression "the LORD relented" as an extreme case of anthropomorphism, while taking quite literally the counterstatement that God does not change his mind. According to Karl Barth, all biblical statements about God, including those that affirm God's unchangeableness (immutability) and those that point to God's "holy mutability" (like those who speak of "divine repentance" or relenting), teach truths about God and, therefore, must be taken with equal seriousness (1957, 496). In the context of God's self-revelation of divine attributes (34:6-7), we can affirm that God does not change in his eternal being, character, purposes, and decrees. God does change, however, in his attitudes, decisions, and actions in his interaction with humans. Barth declares boldly, "Biblical thinking about God would rather submit to confusion with the grossest anthropomorphism than to confusion with a God who is absolutely immutable and thus immobile" (1957, 496). Indeed, we should deny complete divine foreknowledge with the "open theists" who draw on texts like 32:12-14 for their views (see Sanders 1998, 53-75). We also should not deny God's sovereign freedom to choose covenantal, relational, and interactive ways of relating to his people.

God's prior choice to be with humans in covenant relationship affects the manner in which God works in the world. God does not always operate unilaterally but works with human covenant partners. God apparently invites human "friends" into divine council and allows human intercession to shape human history. Such ways of God are consistent with the divine election of and covenant with Abraham and his descendants to be the instrument of God's blessing to all nations (Gen 12:2-3). Ultimately, a God-human partnership points to the restoration of the original intention for humans to be divine representatives on earth (Gen 1:26-28), having dominion and shaping divine history. Thus, in this unit in Exodus, the future of the Israelites is not only God's call but also Moses' call. Instead of making a unilateral decision, God subjects the divine plans to the human mediator, whom God has delegated and trusted to carry out God's will and purposes.

In the NT, Jesus repeatedly says that he or the Father will do "whatever [we] ask in [Jesus'] name" (John 14:13-14; 15:16; 16:23). It is an open invitation, not for personal material blessing but for a bold advancement and establishment of the kingdom of God on earth. Jesus is inviting his disciples of all ages to become active kingdom agents who actualize divine will on earth. Jesus says, "You are my friends if you do what I command" (John 15:14; see 17:10). Those who obey and lay down their lives for Christ abide in his presence; therefore, they know what the Father's good and pleasing will is. Thus, their prayers are "powerful and effective" (Jas 5:16) for letting God's kingdom come and for allowing God's will to be done on earth as it is in heaven.

b. Moses' Punishment of the Israelites (32:15-29)

BEHIND THE TEXT

Moses' intercession averts the punishment of utter destruction, but this concession does not mean that the guilty sinners will go entirely unpunished (see Exod 20:7; 34:7). Sin and guilt remain on the people. Thus, in the unfolding narrative, Yahweh partially punishes the nation through the Levites (32:26-28) and with a plague (v 35).

This unit includes the accounts of Moses indicting Aaron as the chief leader during the Israelites' great sin and then blessing the Levites for carrying out the vengeance of the Lord. Some commentators, therefore, regard this text as a later Levite polemic against the Aaronic priesthood. However, this episode can be explained on its own terms without such speculations. Biblical figures are presented in their complexity, with their successes and failures, saintly and savage qualities, and heroic and criminal acts. So here, Aaron miserably fails, a situation that emphasizes the wideness of Yahweh's mercy in affirming his life and installing him as the high priest. And the Levites who were previously cursed for their savage quality are now blessed and consecrated to Yahweh (→ vv 28, 29). As Wesley exclaims, "The law made them priests which had infirmity and needed first to offer for their own sins" (1990, 88).

IN THE TEXT

(1) Moses' Water of Ordeal (32:15-20)

■ **15-16** Moses descends Mount Sinai with **two tablets** that carry supreme uniqueness and value (v 15). The **covenant** laws are engraved **on both sides** (see Zech 5:3 for a flying scroll that contained covenant laws and sanctions written on both sides). They are Yahweh's own **work** (Exod 32:16), perhaps in the sense of being chiseled out by Yahweh (in contrast to those cut out by Moses in 34:4). They are Yahweh's own **writing**. As such, they are incomparably more valuable than any of the sacred objects in the tabernacle, which are human-made. The dimensions of the tablets are not given. However, assuming they were placed side-by-side and laid flat in the bottom of the ark of the covenant that measured 2.5 x 1.25 cubits, each tablet would be smaller than 1.25 x 1.5 cubits (1.9' x 2.3' or 0.6 x 0.7 m).

■ **17** According to 24:13-14, **Joshua** ascends the mountain with **Moses**. How far Joshua climbed is not told, but perhaps he ventured near the outskirts of the cloud (24:18; see 33:11 for Joshua abiding in Moses' tent of meeting). Joshua apparently remains on the mountain for forty days and nights either eating manna or without eating or drinking just like Moses. This verse shows that Joshua was close enough to **the camp** that he could hear the loud **noise** arising from it. Moses and Joshua descend together and hear the noise together. Still unaware of the Israelites' idolatry, Joshua, being the commander of the Israelite army, interprets the **shouting** noises (perhaps accompanied by musical instruments) as **the sound of war.**

■ **18** **Moses**, having been informed by Yahweh, answers Joshua that the shouting is neither a **victory** chant nor the howling lament of the defeated; it is wild, cultic **singing.** This singing may be an allusion to Miriam's victory praise song that the people sang to Yahweh at the Red Sea (→ Behind the Text for 15:1-21 and In the Text for 15:21). If so, the singing highlights the extent to which Israel was building an alternative idolatrous religion.

■ **19** From the hill, **Moses** has the full view of the Israelites and their abominable idol. The personal witness of the Israelites' repulsive cultic acts stirs an intense zeal for Yahweh (see the zealous Phinehas in Num 25:7-11). Moses' righteous indignation, while justly inspired, ultimately bursts out of control. His unrestrained **anger** starkly contrasts with Yahweh's self-controlled anger (Exod 32:10; see 34:6). That said, some suggest that Moses' act of **breaking** the **tablets** may be deliberate and legal, emblematic of the covenant that is broken through the Israelites' repudiation of the covenant laws. However, Yahweh's resulting disapproval of Moses' act, "the first tablets, which you broke" (34:1), points to its irreverent and impulsive nature.

■ **20** In 32:20, Moses is no longer an intercessor, seeking Yahweh's mercy on Israel's behalf. He now acts as an indignant executor of covenant punishment. The abhorrent object—"that sinful thing of yours" (Deut 9:21), the wooden **calf** plated with gold (Exod 32:4)—is reduced to wood ashes and gold **powder** "as fine as dust" (Deut 9:21). The melted gold was likely beaten down into thin sheets and then filed into powder. The powdered state of the idol further exposes the absurdity of the Israelites' worship of it.

Moses scatters the wood ashes and gold powder into a stream of **water,** which, according to Deut 9:21, "flowed down the mountain." This is probably the part of Horeb/Sinai where Moses produced water from a rock at Yahweh's command (→ "the rock at Horeb" in Exod 17:5-6). The people are forced to drink the water with ashes and gold powder **scattered** on it. This water of ordeal for Israel's spiritual adultery is a possible model for (or at least parallel to) the later water of decision in Num 5:17, 27-28. If Moses' water is intended for decision and judgment, it would afflict and identify those who were directly involved in the rebellion, perhaps setting the stage for the Levites' execution (Exod 32:26-29).

(2) Moses' Confrontation of Aaron (32:21-24)

■ **21** Moses' question to Aaron in v 21 clearly shows Aaron's responsibility and accountability to the **great sin** of the people. His question also reflects his great anger and frustration, perhaps a reflection of Yahweh's anger toward Aaron (see Deut 9:20). **These people** may have done something to Aaron to prompt his sinful actions; however, Aaron, as a leader of Israel, is responsible for leading **them into** their sin. The expression **great sin** is used in reference to adultery in Gen 20:9 (see 39:9) and in relation to idolatry (or spiritual adultery) in this chapter (Exod 32:21, 30, 31) and elsewhere (2 Kgs 17:21; see 1 Sam 2:17).

■ **22** Although younger in age, Moses remains Aaron's superior in office and authority, even as Yahweh had declared that Moses "shall be as God to him" (Exod 4:16 ESV). In his dread of Moses' burning anger, **Aaron** responds to Moses in utmost respect, addressing Moses as **my lord**. Aaron also attempts to excuse himself by condemning the people, as being **prone . . . to evil**.

■ **23** This verse seems to be a verbatim quotation of the words of the people in 32:1; by quoting the people, Aaron may be attempting to justify himself and to hold the people accountable to their action.

■ **24** Aaron greatly abbreviates his part in the entire event and also completely removes himself from the production of the golden **calf**. Some commentators justify Aaron's excuses, saying that Aaron, as a good priest, was simply representing the will of the people (e.g., Barth 1956, 429). However, vv 4 and 35 make it clear that Aaron, in fact, made the calf. Not only that, as a priest who represented Yahweh to the people, he should have resisted the people's corrupt will. Some commentators therefore rightly emphasize Aaron's responsibility, culpability, and illegitimate self-defense (e.g., Hamilton 2011, 532, 547-48). In Moses' recapitulation of this event in Deuteronomy, Moses publicly denounces Aaron's sinful acts and articulates that "the LORD was angry enough with Aaron to destroy him" (Deut 9:20; see vv 8, 19 for the same expression used of Israel) and that only Moses' intercession saved him from death. Aaron may escape Moses' burning anger, but he cannot escape Moses' verdict that he is guilty (Exod 32:21).

(3) Execution of the Guilty (32:25-29)

■ **25** In v 25, Moses' attention returns to the **people**. Even after the breaking of the tablets of the covenant law and the drinking ordeal (vv 19-20), the people are still **running wild**. Perhaps the ringleaders or their evil influence is not completely subdued. Or perhaps the destruction of their idol causes the ringleaders to lead a riot. Whatever the case, the people are **out of control** and **Aaron** is culpable for allowing it. The restoration of order requires a drastic measure. The Israelites' shameful defection from Yahweh is about to become a subject of contempt, mockery, and ridicule among **their enemies**, especially the Egyptians. In Jeremiah, Yahweh laments over the Israelites' astonishing tendency to exchange "their glorious God for worthless idols," when no other nation ever changes gods, even though "they are not gods at all" (Jer 2:11). Yahweh or **Moses** must intervene to repair Israel's honor, which is attached to Yahweh's own honor (see Exod 32:12).

■ **26** Verses 26-29 report Moses' command and the Levites' action to punish the guilty. Moses calls out to **Whoever is for the LORD**. This call again shows that Aaron's calf and the Israelites' worship were incompatible with the true worship of Yahweh, for neither was **for the LORD**. In response to the call, **all the Levites** eagerly rally around Moses, separating themselves from the crime and the guilt. Apparently, the Levites did not join in the madness. However, **all** would be hyperbole if Deut 33:9 refers to this event and indicates that the Levites killed a few of their own tribal people who were guilty.

■ **27** In this verse, Moses delivers Yahweh's command to the Levite men, to take up a **sword** and execute the guilty. Only Yahweh can impose such a dreadful task on human agents. Later in a similar situation concerning the worship of Baal of Peor, Yahweh issues a similar command to the judges of Israel (Num 25:3-4; see also Phinehas' voluntary and spontaneous act of executing an Israelite man and a Midianite woman in the middle of their illicit sexual act, which appeases Yahweh and brings an end to the plague in Num 25:6-11). The call to kill **brother and friend and neighbor** does not mean indiscriminately, but rather setting aside all personal affections and considerations to execute idolaters (in fulfillment of Exod 22:20 [19 HB]).

■ **28** The **Levites** carry out the bloody task in their zealous response to Yahweh and his command. They slay **three thousand of the people**. The Levites no doubt target the ringleaders of the rebellion, and perhaps those engaged in ritual sexual activity (see Num 25:1-8), to end the anarchy. The guilty were likely marked in some way by the water ordeal, or the Levites targeted those whom they witnessed in their sinful acts.

The Reversal of Jacob's Curse of the Levites

Levi and Simeon attacked the unsuspecting and trusting people of Shechem for the rape of Dinah their sister (Gen 34:25). On his deathbed, Jacob cursed the tribes of Simeon and Levi, not for their indignation for the rape, but for their treachery, appetite for revenge, and cruelty. Jacob said, "I will scatter them in Jacob and disperse them in Israel" (Gen 49:7; see vv 5-7). In a fulfillment of Jacob's words, the Levites will be given no portion of the promised land for agriculture. Instead, they will be spread throughout the land. However, through the redemption of the Levites, which is evident here, they will receive a tenth of everything produced by all the other tribes (Num 18:6, 21-30; Josh 13:14), forty-eight towns to live in, and the pasturelands around the towns (Num 35:2-8; Josh 21:41). Six of the towns given to the Levites will also serve as cities of refuge for a "manslayer" (Num 35:6 KJV).

In light of the Levites' past history with violence, it is an interesting development that they are mustered in grim service for Yahweh's honor. By using their weapons of violence to execute divine punishment, the Levites ironically become peacemakers, those who bring peace between Yahweh and the people through animal slaughter and sacrifice.

■ **29** Verse 29 indicates that the killing of those guilty of idolatry is another reason for the Levites' privileged status as a group **set apart to the** LORD. **You have been set apart** is literally *fill your hands* and is a command. The expression seems related to the one used for the ordination of Aaron and his sons (→ "ordain them" or *fill hands* in 28:41). The phrase **he has blessed you this day** also might explain that the Levites' hands are filled with Yahweh's blessings. In their "preconsecration" here, their hands are symbolically emptied of violence and vengeance against people and are filled with new peacemaking responsibilities. Accordingly, they are later excluded from the census of fighting men (Num 2:32-33). Instead, they replace the firstborn in the cultic service (3:12, 45; 8:9-26; 18:6-26). As zealous guardians of Yahweh's presence, they also dwell around the tabernacle, with their tents pitched near and around it (1:53). The terms **sons** and **brothers** stand for close blood relations (see "brother" in Exod 32:27), probably referring to other Levites.

FROM THE TEXT

The sin of idolatry is treated with severity in Israel's earliest history. It is a disturbing narrative for most modern-day readers of the Bible. The degree of ruthlessness and violence reflected in the narrative raises questions about the nature of God that this particular narrative does not answer. This narrative also raises concerns about the potential for the misuse of this story to validate massacres done in the name of religion. While we cannot resolve all related issues here, the following theological considerations might alleviate some tension.

(1) First of all, the Israelites at this point are thoroughly theocratic. They live with the immanent presence of the Holy God who requires his covenant people to be holy. Relatedly, they live under divine laws enforced by divinely sanctioned judges (see 18:19-26). God sets the penalties for the violation of the laws (in this case, idolatry) and the appointed judges (in this case, the Levites) ensure their implementation. Divine immanence in Israel implies that

the perpetrators of certain heinous sins will be removed from Israel to ensure the continued presence of the supremely holy God. However, immanence and the theocratic rule of God do not mean absence of mercy and compassion for the guilty. Other features of Exod 32—34 vividly display God's supreme mercy and compassion that give hope for Israel's future.

(2) In cases in which the majority of the Israelites sin against God, incurring guilt and the death penalty for the entire nation, God the Judge personally presides over the case. God pronounces his verdict and sentence and imposes his penalty. This kind of case by nature is beyond the authority and power vested in human courts. Only God has the prerogative to judge and punish an entire nation for their corporate sin against God (such as in the golden calf episode and in a similar situation in Num 25:1-8).

(3) Also, the divine vengeance through human agents is limited to an early period of Israel's history when Israel functioned in a theocratic model.

(4) Interpreted this way, the Levites' act in no way justifies any human-initiated massacres in the name of God or religion.

c. Moses' Unsuccessful Intercession and a Plague (32:30-35)

BEHIND THE TEXT

After restoring order, Moses returns to the mountain to intercede and seek atonement for the Israelites. Moses asks Yahweh to either forgive the offenders or blot out his name from "the book" that Yahweh has written. The idea of gods keeping "tablets of destiny" is found in Mesopotamia (Propp 2006, 565). The Bible mentions three different celestial books that Yahweh keeps: (1) There are the books of divine decrees containing "lament and mourning and woe" (Ezek 2:10; see vv 9-10) or covenant laws and curses (Zech 5:1-4), according to which divine judgment is carried out. Moses is clearly not referring to this book. (2) There is a book of remembrance that records the deeds of the righteous and of the wicked. Based on this book, everyone is rewarded, each according to one's deeds (Mal 3:16-18; Rev 20:12-14; see Pss 69:28 [29 HB]; 139:16). If this book is in view, Moses may be implying, "Let there be no reward for me for bringing these people out of Egypt and leading them thereafter, since my work was in vain." (3) There is also the Book of Life that contains the names of the living and perhaps those who will live forever (see Pss 40:7 [8 HB]; 69:28 [29 HB]; 139:16; Dan 12:1; Rev 3:5; 20:15; 21:27). The names of those who sin against Yahweh are blotted out, which means they are eternally excluded from the assembly of the righteous (see Ps 1:5-6). In some texts, those whose names remain in the Book of Life (because their names were not blotted out) inherit eternal life at the time of the final judgment. Since "blotting out" appears to occur in relation to this book only, Moses is likely referring to this specific book. If so, Moses is saying either, "Let me die in place of the Israelites" (Enns 2000, 577) or "Let my eternal destiny be the same as that of the sinful Israelites."

IN THE TEXT

■ **30** The **day** after the great vengeance, order and the fear of the Lord are restored to the Israelites. There is perhaps the added fear of the Levites as well. **Moses** can leave the people to Joshua's charge and return to Yahweh. His intention is to seek forgiveness of their **great sin** (see vv 21, 31). He expresses uncertainty with the word **perhaps**, given the gravity of the offense. Yet Moses will attempt to **make atonement** (*kipper*). Twice elsewhere in the OT, a person seeks atonement and reconciliation with another offended party either through material gifts or by satisfying the offended party's demands (Gen 32:20 [21 HB] and 2 Sam 21:3; see Hamilton 2011, 553).

■ **31-32** **Back** in Yahweh's presence, **Moses** intercedes for Israel (v 31). First Moses confesses the **great sin** of Israel and then petitions for their forgiveness. Moses' plea is that Yahweh would simply **forgive** the Israelites by bearing the wrong done and suffering its consequences (v 32; → "forgiving" in 34:7); in this way, Moses hopes, Yahweh will grant atonement. In the case that Yahweh refuses Moses' petition, Moses goes on to make a daring proposal; namely, that Yahweh would **blot** him **out of the book** Yahweh has **written**. Moses' statement expresses the utmost selfless willingness to forfeit his life. Of course, Moses' hope is that Yahweh will decide to forgive the Israelites.

■ **33** Yahweh's response suggests that he does not accept either of the options that Moses presented. Yahweh does not grant forgiveness, and, if **Moses** is offering his life as atonement, Yahweh rejects it as well. Even the most righteous of Israel could not make atonement for Israel's sin. It is not Yahweh's way. Yahweh gives a reasonable and just response; **whoever has sinned**, Yahweh **will blot out** of his **book**, but he will not blot out Moses.

■ **34** Yahweh commands Moses to **lead the people** on their journey to the promised land. However, Yahweh refuses to accompany the Israelites and instead decides to send an emissary, **my angel**. The angel can be interpreted in two different ways: (1) it may refer to Yahweh's accompanying presence, yet distinguishable from the full and intense manifestation of Yahweh's glory within the cloud (→ "angel" in 23:20); (2) this angel may be a celestial being that has not yet been mentioned, one who is not so closely associated or identifiable with Yahweh (see 33:2-3). Since this angel is disassociated with Yahweh (vv 2-3) and is unknown to Moses (v 22), the latter is more likely. Yahweh's righteous anger against the unrepentant and unpardoned Israelites is apparently still present. Thus, Yahweh intends to "pay back" the Israelites at some future date. The phrase **when the time comes for me to punish** apparently indicates a temporary postponement of some or all punishment (→ "punishes" in 34:7).

It is noteworthy that there is no oath formula here, in contrast to Num 14:21, 28, which confirms that it is not an irrevocable decision to punish in the future. Yahweh can be persuaded not to punish any further, if the Israelites truly repent and maintain covenant faithfulness. Unfortunately, the Israelites do not reform their acts or intentions. They remain wholly "stiff-necked" (32:9). Eventually, Yahweh punishes them by not allowing them to enter the promised land (Num 14:22-23, 28-35). Some even consider the exile as the completion of the deferred punishment described in this verse, suggesting that had the Israelites not perpetrated the same abomination throughout their national life, they would not have been exiled.

■ **35** Perhaps as the immediate but partial fulfillment of the punishment spoken of in the previous verse, Yahweh strikes the people with a plague. By naming both the idol maker (**Aaron**) and the idol worshipper (**they**), Yahweh lays the blame equally on both parties. Yahweh's punishment is in accordance with the previous warning that Yahweh would "visit" iniquity (see 20:5; see 34:7; Num 14:18). Yahweh's smiting (*nāgap*; "strike") usually results in death, either through a **plague**, military defeat, or illness (see Exod 12:23, 27; Josh 24:5; 1 Sam 4:3; 25:38; 2 Sam 12:15; Isa 19:22). The exact nature of the plague cannot be determined, but some have linked it to the water of decision (Exod 32:20).

FROM THE TEXT

Moses' unprecedented act of intercession, offering up his own life for the sake of the Israelites, prefigures the ultimate intercession Christ makes for sinful humanity by utterly giving himself up as the atoning sacrifice. Entering into the presence of God in "the most holy place" on Mount Sinai, Moses seeks atonement, first directly from God, then through the means of his own life. However, God denies Moses' request for atonement and rejects Moses' self-offering. Christ, on the other hand, is the God-chosen guilt offering (Isa 53:10) upon whom God lays "the iniquity of us all" (v 6). As a sinless and willing victim (John 10:17-18), Christ dies for and carries away "the sin of the world" (1:29) and makes atonement and obtains "eternal redemption" for us all. Unlike Moses, Christ enters "the Most Holy Place once for all by his own blood" (Heb 9:12), reconciling us to the Father. The eternal redemption from the "second death" (Rev 2:11; 20:6; 21:8) does not abrogate temporal death (the first death) or the temporal consequences of sin (Heb 12:4-11; 1 Pet 2:20; 4:15). Yet the eternal relationship between God the Creator and Redeemer and those who are repentant is made right through the glorious atoning work of Jesus Christ. Thanks be to God!

d. Yahweh's Withdrawal of Presence (33:1-6)

This unit opens with Yahweh urging Moses to lead the Israelites to the promised land, with a greater urgency and pressure than in the previous unit. Since Yahweh has not yet granted complete pardon, tension and suspense remain. There is no known, appropriate means of atonement for Israel's sin. Even the atoning sacrificial system, if it were already in operation, would not encompass this kind of outright rebellion against Yahweh (as it largely deals with unintentional sins). Hence, should Yahweh accompany the "stiff-necked" people and should they once again provoke Yahweh's anger with their rebellion, then he may be inclined to destroy them. So Yahweh proposes that the Israelites travel without his "dangerous" presence.

IN THE TEXT

■ **1** Verse 1 displays an enormous act of Yahweh's graciousness in the midst of judgment. The reiteration of Yahweh's promise sworn to the ancestors of Israel emphasizes Yahweh's resolve to maintain that promise and give a future to the people who have broken their covenant with him.

■ **2** Perhaps to avoid the possibility of destroying them (v 5), yet still to fulfill his covenant with the ancestors, Yahweh insists on sending an **angel** (→ "my angel" in 32:34). For comments on the list of the native peoples of the land, → 3:8.

■ **3** Verse 3 contains both a command (**Go**) and a solemn statement of Yahweh's decision to be absent in the journey of Israel (**I will not go with you**). Yahweh's authority over the people still remains, even in the midst of their disobedience. Yahweh's command also indicates his commitment to complete the exodus liberation he started by leading the people out of Egypt into the land flowing with milk and honey (see 3:8, 17). The declaration **I will not go with you** may mean that while the pillar of cloud will still guide and protect them, the glory of the Lord within will not. Whatever the case, Yahweh's decision is shocking, since the very reason for the exodus and the Sinai covenant (and the instructions for the tabernacle) is for Yahweh to dwell with them. The whole proposal might be a test of the Israelites to see if they will indeed **go** for the great possession, while leaving behind the greatest "treasure," Yahweh's presence.

■ **4** The **people** are devastated and they mourn at the news. Their distraught emotions may indicate that they understood the angel of v 2 (and 32:34) as someone other than the angel of the Lord/God. Their hearts are stricken probably not with overwhelming conviction of their heinous sin against Yahweh but with new anxiety about achieving a conquest of Canaan without the im-

EXODUS

33:1-4

manent presence of Yahweh. In other words, the idea of proceeding to the land without the guarantor of the promise is too terrifying and depressing. In any case, the Israelites abandon their **ornaments** in response to Yahweh's command to take them off (v 5).

■ **5-6** What Yahweh says in v 5 chronologically comes before the report of the Israelites' reaction in v 4. The final fruit of their idolatry is the deprivation of Yahweh's presence among them. Yahweh orders the **Israelites** to **take off** their **ornaments**. It is perhaps a symbolic act of purifying themselves from the kinds of ornaments they used in making the idol (32:2-3). Genesis 35:2-4 may suggest that the gold earrings that the Hebrews wore were not simply ornamental, but cultic, probably made in the shape of an idol. If so, the removal of the ornaments in this verse intends to purify the Israelites of any idolatrous objects. Others regard the removal of ornaments as an appropriate gesture of mourning (Enns 2000, 579), but this interpretation is unlikely, since the stripping is compulsory, rather than voluntary. The stripping of ornaments, therefore, should be interpreted not as a sign of genuine repentance, but as a prompt to repent. Yahweh announces that after the Israelites have purified themselves, he will reconsider his decision to withhold his presence. (→ "Horeb" in Exod 3:1.)

FROM THE TEXT

This narrative is a powerful reminder of the faithfulness of God to keep his promises to a people who have become unfaithful in their relationship with him. The calf incident and the massive killing of the Israelites by the Levites did not end the story of God's covenant relationship with Israel. God continues to be involved in the life of Israel; Israel continues to have a place in the life of God. He still commands, he still authorizes, and he still keeps his promises. Implied in the command, "Go up to the land" (Exod 33:3), is the merciful and faithful God's willingness to forgive even those who deserve to die. This is the hope for Israel's future with God, and the hope for the future of those who hear/read this narrative today.

The presence of God is a critical issue in this narrative. On the one hand, the promise is still valid and God remains faithful to his promises; on the other hand, God threatens to remove his presence from his people who have broken their covenant with him. Israel is in danger of losing God's indwelling presence previously promised to them (29:42-45). Yahweh says, in effect, "You go to the promised land, but I am not going with you" (33:3). However, Moses and Israel know that though their future possession of the promised land is guaranteed by God's promises to their ancestors (v 1) and of "an angel" who will "drive out" the inhabitants of the land (v 2), their flourishing in the land and their distinctiveness as God's special people (see 19:5-6; 33:16) depend on his faithful presence with them. In that sense, Israel knows that the guaranteed future is hollow without the presence of the guarantor with his people. The broken covenant brings anxiety; but the awareness of the threat of the withdrawal of Yahweh's presence intensifies that anxiety (v 4). The next subsection in the narrative indicates Moses' resolve to secure the guarantee of the presence of God with his people, without which Israel's existence in the promised land will be meaningless (as Moses implies in v 16).

In the NT, we encounter the disciples of Jesus who were anxious about their survival without the presence of the risen Christ with them. The Gospel of John tells us that they went back to Galilee, to their former vocation (21:1-3). The risen Christ does not abandon them but appears to them and gives them the command, "Go and make disciples of all nations," and the promise, "I am with you always, to the very end of the age" (Matt 28:19-20). In our anxiety-filled life, we continue to hear the promise of the abiding presence of the risen Christ that makes our life and vocation as disciples of Jesus possible, fruitful, and meaningful in the world in which we live today.

3. The Friendship between Yahweh and Moses (33:7-23)

BEHIND THE TEXT

Many interpreters find it difficult to see this subunit as part of the narrative flow. Some view it as an insertion that disrupts an otherwise well-composed story. Certainly, this unit lacks temporal markers and allusions to any previous events related to the golden calf. However, nothing in the text itself suggests that the events of this unit take place at a time other than after the stripping of ornaments described in the previous unit and before the conversation between Yahweh and Moses of the next unit (Exod 33:12-23). In fact, Moses' habitual meetings with Yahweh in this unit provide the perfect context for the conversation that takes place in the next unit. We do not know the duration of the habitual meetings, but this detail is not important. The key point is that in the context of Moses' consistent intimate relationship with Yahweh, Moses secures arguably the highest favor a mortal being can receive from Yahweh; this ultimate favor becomes the basis on which Moses obtains pardon for Israel (→ 34:9-10).

a. Moses' Intimacy with Yahweh (33:7-11)

IN THE TEXT

■ **7** The **tent** is best understood as a private one, since the tabernacle has not been constructed at this point in the narrative. At the same time, the use of the **tent of meeting** emphasizes a connection with the tabernacle itself, which is frequently called by that name (fifteen times from 27:21 to 31:7). **Used to** take indicates Moses' habitual action. Whether **Moses** pitched the tent **outside the camp** even during their journey to Sinai or only since the withdrawal of Yahweh's presence is not entirely clear, but the literary placement seems to support the latter interpretation. That is, the place of meeting and Yahweh's presence are now visibly moved out of the **camp**, emphasizing the separation between sinful Israel and their Holy God.

■ **8-10** Moses (and Joshua [v 11]) alone enjoys Yahweh's presence (v 8), while Yahweh is making a final decision regarding whether to permanently withhold his divine presence from Israel (v 5*b*). The Israelites show their respect for Moses by rising to their feet **whenever Moses** goes **out to** his **tent** of meeting. The returnees from the exile also stand up to express their utmost reverence when the book of the law of Moses is read to them in Neh 8:5; 9:3. Whenever Yahweh's presence descends in **the pillar of cloud** to speak with Moses, the Israelites also worship Yahweh from their own tents (Exod 33:10). Their attitudes toward both Yahweh and Moses evidently have grown more sober and respectful.

■ **11** This verse makes a remarkable claim that Yahweh *regularly spoke* to Moses **face to face, as one speaks to a friend**. This is what makes Moses' role as a prophet and covenant mediator unique (as Num 12:6-8 and Deut 34:10 further clarify). To *see* Yahweh "face to face" is an experience Moses shares with Jacob (Gen 32:30 [31 HB]; see Judg 6:22), the Israelites at Sinai (Deut 5:4), and the seventy-three people who "saw God" and dined in his presence on Mount Sinai (Exod 24:1, 10-11). However, it is unique to *speak with* Yahweh in open and frequent dialogue as Moses does, "face to face" (33:11) or "mouth to mouth" (Num 12:8 ESV, KJV, NASB, NJPS), and be the one whom Yahweh "knew face to face" (Deut 34:10). Such intimate knowledge of Yahweh and his will and such enjoyment of Yahweh's friendship are unparalleled in the OT. (We note that there appears to be a distinction between *seeing* Yahweh's "face," which, according to the Exod 33:20 text, no one can do and live, and *speaking* "face to face.")

Previously, the future leader of Israel, **Joshua**, ascended Mount Sinai with Moses and stayed near the cloud for forty days (24:13-14). Now while at the foothill, he continues to seek Yahweh's favor by ***not departing out of the tent***, regardless of Moses' absence (33:11). However, even as Joshua did not share in Moses' encounter with Yahweh on Mount Sinai, he also does not have the revelatory experience that Moses has in his tent. Nevertheless, it is extraordinary that Joshua is allowed to be at the site of God's divine presence and revelation to Moses.

FROM THE TEXT

"Anyone inquiring of the Lord would go to the tent of meeting" (Exod 33:7) is a powerful reminder of the possibility for a sinful people to meet with God even

after they have broken their covenant with him. This meeting is made possible by the commitment of Moses to encounter the dangerously holy God and make intercession on behalf of the sinful people of Israel. Yahweh's "face to face" speaking to Moses "as one speaks to a friend" (v 11) is a manifestation of his compassion toward an idolatrous people; they can only stand in awe and amazement and worship Yahweh who graciously meets with them through Moses, their mediator and advocate.

John writes: "My dear children, I write this to you so that you will not sin. But if anybody does sin, we have an advocate with the Father—Jesus Christ, the Righteous One. He is the atoning sacrifice for our sins, and not only for ours but also for the sins of the whole world" (1 John 2:1-2). Just like the Israelites, we, too, can only worship God in awe and astonishment for graciously meeting us through Jesus Christ, our mediator and advocate.

b. Yahweh's Promise of Presence to Moses (33:12-23)

IN THE TEXT

■ **12** Verses 12-23 contain the dialogue between Moses the mediator and Yahweh the covenant God of Israel. Moses begins the dialogue with the complaint that though Yahweh has been **telling** him to **lead these people**, Yahweh has not made it known to him the identity of the one **whom** Yahweh **will send with** him to accomplish the mission. **Moses** perhaps implies that since Yahweh has not revealed who the emissary is, Yahweh himself should go with him. Just as the nation Israel is Yahweh's "treasured possession out of all the peoples" (19:5 NRSV), so Moses is Yahweh's special friend of all the Israelites. Accordingly, Yahweh knows him **by name** and favors him. In what follows, Moses leverages this special status with Yahweh in his intercession for Israel.

■ **13** Moses continues by asking for fuller revelation of Yahweh's **ways**, that is, what Yahweh is like (character) and how he works (deeds and ways). Moses cannot accept that the way of the Lord is simply to give blessings (the promised land) without his own presence. Moses has some understanding of Yahweh's character and ways but not to the extent that he is about to experience in 34:5-10. Moses desires to **know** Yahweh more intimately and seeks greater favor (*ḥēn*; "affection," "grace," "charm"), presumably to obtain pardon for the Israelites.

The request, **Remember that this nation is your people**, is essentially a prayer for Yahweh to extend the personal favor given him (33:13*a*) to the people whom Moses represents as a covenant mediator (v 13*b*). In light of the surrounding literary context, such grace involves forgiveness of sin and renewal of the covenant relationship.

■ **14** In v 14, Yahweh responds and grants Moses' request, providing an extraordinary turning point for the future of the Israelites. Yahweh's **Presence** will accompany Moses and **give** him **rest**, which in this context refers to a state of peace and security in a fertile land where all the territorial enemies have been subdued (also in Deut 3:20; 12:10; 25:19; Josh 1:13, 15; 22:4; 23:1). However, the pronoun **you** here is singular, referring to Moses. Since Moses is the representative of Israel, "you" might include Israel, but some ambiguity and tension still remain.

■ **15** The use of first person plural (**us**) in Moses' response to Yahweh indicates Moses' commitment to his people. He is "sensitive to God's omission of any mention of Israel" (Sarna 2004, 162) and immediately seeks assurance from Yahweh that he does intend to dwell and **go with** Moses *and* the Israelites and that he is no longer angry with them. As a model representative leader and mediator, Moses cannot consider himself apart from the welfare of his people (see Exod 32:10-14, 32).

■ **16** In 33:16, Moses reasons with Yahweh, as his third and final stage of intercession for the **people** (see 32:11-14, 30-32). Moses identifies himself with the Israelites and equates his own reputation with that of Yahweh's people. The distinctiveness of Moses and the Israelites does not lie in what kind of land they will inherit (which can be achieved with a powerful angel; see 32:34; 33:1-2), but entirely in their intimate relationship with Yahweh, the supreme creator God.

■ **17** Yahweh's response to Moses in this verse indicates a significant change in Yahweh's attitude toward Israel. He is moved by Moses' passion for his people. At last, Yahweh grants **the very thing** Moses has been seeking; Yahweh will return to the Israelites' camp and lead the Israelites into the promised land. By implication, Yahweh will forgive the Israelites and renew the covenant. Moses' powerful intercession, based on the extraordinary favor (**I am pleased with you**) and friendship (**I know you by name**) he has with Yahweh, turns Yahweh from "leave me alone so that . . . I may destroy them" (32:10) to "My Presence will go with you, and I will give you rest" (33:14).

■ **18** Moses has one final appeal: **Now show me your glory**. He wants to take his friendship with God to the next level. **Show me** here means "make me experience." **Glory** may refer to the intense, visible manifestation of Yahweh's presence or Yahweh's essential nature and character. Although both may be in view in this text, the second meaning of "glory" is emphasized. While Yahweh's glory can appear like "fire" (24:15-18), it can, at the same time, be captured and communicated in words as in 34:6-7. In this text, "my glory" (33:22), "all my goodness" (v 19), "I" (v 22), and the revelation of the name "LORD" (34:5-7) are essentially interchangeable (for "glory" as "Yahweh," see 1 Sam 15:29; Ps 106:20; Jer 2:11; Hos 4:7). The exchange between Yahweh and Moses is similar to Abraham's request for a sign and Yahweh's solemnization of the covenant with a covenant rite in Gen 17.

■ **19** The dialogue ends with Yahweh's response to Moses (Exod 33:19-23). In response to Moses' request, Yahweh promises to reveal his glorious nature (v 19). The essential meaning of **all my goodness** is disclosed in the declaration that follows it, **I will have mercy**. The essential content of all of Yahweh's **goodness** is Yahweh's free will to show **mercy** and **compassion** to whomsoever he chooses (→ "gracious" and "compassionate" in 34:6) so that an extension of grace exists even upon those who broke the covenant.

■ **20** After an extraordinary promise to reveal Yahweh's glory in terms of "all his goodness," Yahweh limits what Moses can **see**; he **cannot see** Yahweh's **face** (*pânîm*). Moses has been in Yahweh's "presence" (*pânîm*). He has been speaking with Yahweh "face to face" (*pânîm 'el pânîm* [v 11]). Yahweh spoke with the Israelites "face to face" on Mount Sinai according to Deut 5:4. Yahweh's "presence" has been and will accompany the Israelites into the promised land (Exod 33:14). So what is this "face" that Moses is not allowed to see? The concealed "face" of Yahweh is, by definition, the aspect of Yahweh that cannot be seen with human eyes or understood by the mortal mind without causing death. (To say more would be to attempt to explain mysteries about which the text is silent.)

■ **21-22** Yahweh promises to **cover** Moses and preserve his life during the ultimate moment of divine self-disclosure to a human being in the OT (v 22). Since the "palm" or **hand** is what covers Moses and shields him from seeing the "face," its referent is most likely the cloud that envelopes Yahweh's personal presence when Yahweh comes down on the mount (34:5; see 13:21; 16:10; 19:9; 24:16; 33:9).

■ **23** Moses is told that as the glory/goodness/LORD passes by, he can **see** the **back**, which partly refers to the effervescent afterglow of the intense fiery and eye-blinding presence of Yahweh. Moses is also allowed to "see" or understand the divine attributes proclaimed in 34:6-7 (the depth or **face** of which, of course, cannot be understood by a mere mortal). It is the revealed character, glory, or way of Yahweh that Moses seeks (33:13, 18).

FROM THE TEXT

In this story of Moses' intercession, we find a model for effective prayer. Moses prays or presses in with enormous boldness, persistence, and insistence until he receives the satisfactory answer from God. This Israelite "prayer offers much to learn for Christians, whose piety is characteristically too deferential" (Brueggemann 1994, 942) and whose prayer is often double-minded and therefore ineffective (see Jas 1:6-8).

In Luke 11:5-8, Jesus tells a parable of an annoyed man who grants his friend's request, not out of friendship, but to end his friend's "shameless audacity" (v 8; which is sure to keep awake his entire household). The point here, of course, is one of contrast to our heavenly Father, who extends to us a most loyal and selfless friendship in and through Jesus Christ and who delights in granting whatever we ask in his name (assuming we obey him and abide in his love [Luke 11:9-10; John 15:7-10]). In another parable (in Luke 18:1-6), Jesus tells of a godless and heartless judge who grants justice to a persistent widow just to end the aggravation caused by her constant pleading. Again, the point is one of contrast to the absolutely just and compassionate Judge who loves to grant justice and restore what is lost to all who come to him.

On Mount Sinai, Moses is shamelessly audacious and persistent in asking for divine forgiveness, renewal of covenant, and accompanying presence that would honor the unworthy Israelites (Exod 33:13-18). Further, based on the goodness and friendship he bestowed upon Moses, the Lord grants Moses' requests (v 19).

So Moses' story, together with Jesus' parables about prayer, calls us to seek God's gracious "face," boldly make known our requests, and wait for him. In our prayers, we are to trust and receive by faith what we request (see Heb 11:1; Jas 1:5-8), based on the friendship and mercy the righteous Father grants us through the merits of Jesus Christ.

In the mysterious veiling and unveiling of God's self-revelation to Moses and through Jesus Christ, we truly come to know God. In the very context in which God declares that "you cannot see my face, for no one may see me and live" (Exod 33:20; see v 23), the Lord gives the most powerful self-revelation in the OT (his "back"), which he allows Moses to "see" (vv 19-23 and 34:5-7). God must veil himself not only to prevent Moses' destruction but also to become visible and comprehendible to Moses in his human limitation. However, the glory revealed through the veil remains powerful enough for Moses and all generations after him to understand and celebrate the compassionate and merciful nature of God.

The divine self-revelation that Moses experienced on Mount Sinai is fulfilled in the complete self-disclosure of God in Jesus Christ, God's own Word, Son, and image (John 1; Col 1:15; Heb 1:2-3). Christ is the explanation or "the revelation of the mystery hidden for long ages past" (Rom 16:25; see 1 Cor 2:7; Eph 1:9; 3:9; Col 1:26). Yet even God's perfect and glorious self-revelation in Jesus Christ involves an element of veiling. Paul states, "Now we see only a reflection as in a mirror; then we shall see face to face. Now I know in part; then I shall know fully, even as I am fully known" (1 Cor 13:12). What we now believe and hope for in love of the one who "loved us and gave himself up for us as a fragrant offering and sacrifice to God" (Eph 5:2) will one day be fully disclosed to us.

4. The Renewal of the Covenant (34:1-35)

a. Yahweh's Self-Revelation (34:1-9)

(1) The New Stone Tablets (34:1-4)

BEHIND THE TEXT

In this subunit, Moses ascends Mount Sinai in obedient response to Yahweh's invitation to enter his presence to receive the new stone tablets. It appears that the six-day waiting period that Moses observed before being admitted into Yahweh's presence for the first time (Exod 24:16) is waved here. They are like friends (33:11), and introductory formalities are superfluous.

Moses earlier smashed the two stone tablets on which Yahweh had written the Ten Commandments. The shattered tablets symbolize the shattered covenant relationship between Yahweh and the Israelites. The renewal of the covenant, thus, requires new stone tablets. The one who broke the tablets is now required to provide the new ones. After the renewal of the covenant and the giving of the laws, Yahweh rewrites the Ten Commandments on Moses' stone tablets (34:28), formally legalizing and memorializing the renewed covenant. Upon construction of the tabernacle, the tablets are deposited in the ark of the covenant (40:20; see Deut 10:5; 1 Kgs 8:9).

IN THE TEXT

■ **1** The narrative begins with Yahweh's command to Moses to provide new tablets. Yahweh promises to write the very **words that were** engraved **on the first tablets**, which he fulfills later (Exod 34:28; Deut 10:4). The duplication of the Ten Commandments emphasizes their preeminent importance.

■ **2-3 Moses** is to **present** himself to Yahweh on the mountaintop (Exod 34:2). This time, **no one** is to accompany Moses (v 3). Joshua is excluded, presumably to keep the Israelites under control (with the sword, if necessary) in Moses' absence. Aaron played a significant role in the idolatry, so it would be foolish to leave the Israelites completely under his charge again.

■ **4** Moses carries out all the commands of Yahweh and waits for him on the designated rock (33:21).

FROM THE TEXT

The requirement of the new stone tablets for the renewal of the covenant points to the fact that the grace of the Lord is not without covenant demands. As a summary of all covenant laws, the Ten Commandments will continue to bear perpetual witness to the covenant agreement between the heavenly God King and the Israelites. The call to an obedient life is more urgent than ever before.

Likewise, in the new covenant, which is the superior covenant, the requirement of righteousness is augmented rather than reduced. The new covenant is superior also because it administers greater glory, wider grace, and better promises (Heb 8:6). In the Sermon on the Mount, Jesus makes plain the augmentation of righteous requirements. Jesus raises the bar. Jesus requires not simply the external observation of the commandments but also internal Christlikeness, without which "you will certainly not enter the kingdom of heaven" (Matt 5:20).

(2) Yahweh's Self-Revelation (34:5-7)

BEHIND THE TEXT

In this subunit, Yahweh reveals to Moses his merciful and just nature. This subunit represents the climax of the narrative of Exod 32—34. The theological problem raised by the preceding narrative—namely, how Yahweh can be present with a sinful people without destroying them—finds its final resolution in Yahweh's self-revelation of the divine name and character.

By disclosing the essential content of his name or character, Yahweh is giving Moses (and generations after him) the right to call upon his name and find grace. Thus, in another situation of national crisis, Moses quotes part of the attributes proclaimed here back to Yahweh to avert the impending destruction of the Israelites and receives some measure of grace (Num 14:18-20). Not surprisingly, the divine goodness or attributes proclaimed here become Israel's dominant confessional statement and liturgy in worship, as they are variously quoted and referred to in the OT (most prominently in Num 14:18; 1 Chr 16:34, 41; 2 Chr 5:13; 30:9; Neh 9:17, 31; Pss 86:15; 100:5; 103:8; 111:4; 112:4; 116:5; 118:1-4; 136:1-26; 145:8; Jer 32:18; 33:11; Joel 2:13; Jonah 4:2; Nah 1:3).

IN THE TEXT

■ **5** The description Yahweh **came down in the cloud** clearly distinguishes the cloud from Yahweh. Yahweh calls on the **name** of Yahweh (to show how to call on his name) and proclaims the divine attributes as found in the two subsequent verses (6-7). This is an unparalleled act of self-disclosure in the OT. As such, vv 5-7 fulfill 33:19.

■ **6a-d** In this verse, Yahweh gives a new revelation of the divine attributes or character qualities, which are expressions of the name of Yahweh. The greater revelation does not imply change in divine reality (e.g., becoming more compassionate than before) but change in the degree of human understanding of Yahweh's attributes and character.

As Yahweh passes **in front of Moses**, Yahweh proclaims, **The LORD, the LORD, the compassionate and gracious God**. The revelation of the grace and compassion promised in 33:19 is now fulfilled (but proclaimed in the reverse order). In 33:19, divine goodness is explicated in terms of divine mercy and compassion, and these are, in turn, more fully disclosed in 34:6-7. In other words, the series of qualities from **slow to anger** (v 6) to "he punishes" (v 7) explain what the phrase **the compassionate and gracious God** means. The terms "compassionate" and "gracious" are used exclusively of Yahweh, and mostly occur in the echoes of 34:6-7 (2 Chr 30:9; Neh 9:17, 31; Pss 78:38 ["merciful"]; 86:15; 103:8; 111:4; 145:8; Joel 2:13; Jonah 4:2; see Deut 4:31 ["merciful"]; Ps 112:4). An exception is the possible application of these two terms to a "righteous" person in Ps 112:4. The fact that they are generally used only of Yahweh and do not provide us with easily accessible human analogies limits our understanding of the meaning and nature of those terms. However, the derivatives of the same roots, which are used for human characteristics and relationships, show the basic range of their meaning. We can safely assume, however, that the adjectives, which are used only of Yahweh, carry a special weight in comparison to their derivatives.

The derivatives of "compassionate" (*raḥûm*) convey "deep love" rooted in a "natural" relationship, especially that of a mother and child. Indeed, the word "compassionate" and the word "womb" (*raḥam*) share the same root (*rḥm*). The etymological tie with the word "womb" may have semantic implications for the word "compassionate." The nation Israel is called Yahweh's "firstborn son" (Exod 4:22), to whom Yahweh "gave . . . birth" (Deut 32:18), and whom Yahweh protected and cared for like a mother bird would her young (Exod 19:4). The term "compassionate," therefore, suggests what might be called a "supernatural" maternal tie between Yahweh and Israel, a tie that cannot be broken. Yahweh's compassion is incomparably greater than the greatest compassion of a human mother. Lamentations 3:31-32 shows that Yahweh's covenant love and motherly compassion go hand in hand. In sum, "compassionate" expresses Yahweh's unconditional, irrevocable commitment to his people.

The derivatives of "gracious" (*ḥannûn*) suggest "to show favor" and "to act graciously." The latter meaning especially conveys the concept of unconditional bestowal of undeserved kindness. This kind of unconditional love toward Israel contrasts somewhat with Yahweh's covenant love (*hesed*) that expects obedience and loyalty from his Israelite covenant partner.

The first manifestation of divine compassion and mercy is patience, articulated in the idiom **slow to anger**. The etymological association is "long of nostrils," conveying the idea that divine anger takes a long time to build and is expressed as "the blast of nostrils" (see Exod 15:8; 2 Sam 22:16; Ps 18:15 [16 HB]).

In his patience, Yahweh does not act on a sudden surge of anger, not when Israel is making an idol (Exod 32:2-4), nor when Israel indulges in pagan revelry (v 6). Instead, Yahweh allows Moses a chance for prophetic intercession. Yahweh has self-control; he "delays the execution of his justice"; and "he waits to be gracious" (Wesley 1990, 90). Divine patience, however, does not mean sinners go entirely unpunished. It means divine punishment will be carried out with patience, self-control, timeliness, and purposefulness in order to bring out a lasting, life-affirming solution to the problem of sin.

■ **6e Abounding in love and faithfulness** comes next. Yahweh's love (*ḥesed*; "loyal love" [NET], "steadfast love" [ESV, NRSV], "lovingkindness" [NASB], "goodness" [KJV], "kindness" [NJPS]) refers to his supreme ***covenant loyalty and faithfulness***. Thus, **love** (*ḥesed*) is synonymous with "covenant" in some passages (e.g., Deut 7:9, 12; 2 Sam 7:15; 1 Kgs 3:6 ["kindness"]; Pss 86:5; 89:24, 49 [25, 50 HB; "great love"]; see Milgrom 1990, 329). The term **faithfulness** (*ĕmet*; "truth" [NASB]) points to Yahweh's absolute truthfulness and thus justice and reliability in all divine words and ways. The words often occur together, pointing to Yahweh's utter trustworthiness.

The word-pair first appears without the qualifying "great" in Gen 24 in the context of Yahweh's commitment to fulfill the promises to Abraham ("kindness and faithfulness" [Gen 24:27, 49]; "steadfast love and faithfulness" [ESV]; "loyally and truly" [NRSV]; see vv 12, 14). Accordingly, both Yahweh and Moses assume the inseparability of Yahweh's covenant "love and faithfulness" with Yahweh's covenant with Abraham (see Exod 32:13; 33:1). What is in jeopardy here, however, is not Yahweh's covenant love and faithfulness to Abraham, since Yahweh already made it clear that he would grant the material Abrahamic blessings to the Israelites (33:1-3). The critical issue is whether Yahweh will bless the current rebellious Israelites with his presence, which requires the restoration of the broken Sinai covenant. By adding the term "great [in]" or "abounding" to the word pair, Yahweh indicates that his (Abrahamic) covenant love and truthfulness are so prodigious that he will extend them even to the radically rebellious and undeserving descendants of Abraham.

■ **7a** The immeasurable greatness of Yahweh's (Abrahamic) covenant love is followed by the eternal nature of that covenant love, **maintaining love to thousands *of generations***. Deuteronomy 7:9 adds "generations" after thousands, which is implied in this passage, as well as in Exod 20:6. Yahweh's love is so "abounding" (34:6) that it will last for thousands of generations or forever. A similar expression first appears with the second commandment (→ ***thousands*** in 20:6): "showing love to ***thousands of generations*** of those who love me and keep my commandments." In this verse, the expression is altered in two ways: "showing" is changed to "maintaining," which conveys the ideas of continually watching, guarding, protecting, and preserving with fidelity; however, the qualifying clause "of those who love me and keep my commandments" is dropped in this instance. The resultant effect is lifting Yahweh's covenantal love from the legal context and revealing its true nature as ultimately independent of human merit and forever enduring. Yahweh's everlasting covenant love is poignantly captured in the words of the prophet Isaiah (Isa 54:7-8, 10).

■ **7b** The greatness and enduring nature of Yahweh's patience, covenant love, and faithfulness are intricately related to Yahweh's forgiving nature. Thus, Yahweh proclaims his attribute, **forgiving wickedness, rebellion and sin**. (1) The terms **wickedness** (*'āvōn*), **rebellion** (*pešaʻ*), and **sin** (*ḥaṭʼâ*) are standard terms linked to guilt and punishment in the OT (for *'āvōn* as "guilt" and/or "punishment," see Gen 4:13; Lev 5:1-17; 19:8; 20:17; Ezek 4:4; for *pešaʻ* as "guilt/punishment," see Dan 8:12, 13; 9:24; Ps 85:2 [3 HB]; Isa 24:20; Ezek 33:10; for *ḥaṭʼâ*, as "guilt/punishment," see Lev 19:17; 20:20; Deut 15:9; Ezek 23:49). (2) Yet these terms are also the standard terms for sins, the cause of guilt and punishment (for examples of *'āvōn* as "wickedness," see Exod 34:9; Lev 16:21; Neh 9:2; Jer 31:34; 36:3, 31; for *pešaʻ* as "rebellion," see Exod 23:21; Lev 16:16, 21; Num 14:18; Josh 24:19; 1 Sam 24:11 [12 HB]; for *ḥaṭʼâ* as "sin," see Gen 4:7; 18:20; Exod 10:17; 32:21; Lev 4:3). (3) The Hebrew term translated as **forgiving** here (*nāśāʼ*) has various literal meanings, such as "lift" (Gen 13:14; 40:13; Job 10:15; 11:15; Ps 24:4), "carry" (Gen 44:1; 45:27; 1 Sam 10:3), or "bear" (Exod 28:12; Num 5:31; 9:13; Judg 9:54; 1 Sam 14:1). (4) Thus, the whole expression means, "to bear wickedness, rebellion, and sin, thereby incurring guilt and suffering punishment, which result in forgiveness" (Milgrom 1990, 88). The term "forgiveness" (*nāśāʼ*) is elsewhere used in this same sense in reference to Yahweh (Num 14:18; Pss 32:5; 85:2 [3 HB]; Hos 14:2 [3 HB]; Mic 7:18) and also in reference to the priests of Israel (Num 18:1). Thus, the expression shows simultaneously *that* Yahweh forgives and *how* Yahweh forgives. Divine mercy comes with the satisfaction (and not at the expense) of divine justice (Wesley 1990, 90). Yahweh satisfies justice by bearing the Israelites' sin and its consequences that they cannot bear without being utterly destroyed.

Divine Sin-Bearing / Removing

In the OT the attribute "forgiving wickedness, rebellion, and sin" finds its expression in the suffering Yahweh and the Suffering Servant as found in several Isaiah passages (Isa 43:24; 50:4-9; 52:13—53:12). In the NT, the supreme expression of divine sin-bearing is found in the crucifixion of Jesus Christ. Viewed in this way, the cross of Jesus is not an entirely new revelation, but rather a logical and culminating manifestation of Yahweh's sin-bearing/forgiving and Israel's atoning sacrificial system, which are revealed on Mount Sinai.

■ **7c** Now Yahweh proclaims, **yet he does not leave the guilty unpunished**. Forgiveness (or any of the other attributes in v 6) does not mean that Yahweh overlooks the offense or entirely eliminates the punishment due to sinners. Rather, forgiveness involves divine sin-bearing, with the possibility of "pay[ing] back into the laps" (Ps 79:12; Isa 65:6, 7; Jer 32:18) of sinners any punishment warranted by a persistence in rebellion.

This statement ("he does not leave . . . unpunished") and the next statement ("he punishes the children . . .") first appear in proximity in the second and third commandments (Exod 20:5, 7). There, these two phrases together promise the surety of Yahweh's righteous judgment and vengeance on idolaters and abusers of the divine name. That "he does not leave the guilty unpunished" means that "he punishes" the guilty. The two expressions stand for the punitive side of the divine attribute of "jealousy" (→ the rewarding and punishing sides of divine "jealousy" in 20:5). The punitive quality of Yahweh warns his people not to abuse his clemency (see Num 14:11, 21-23; Jude 1:4).

■ **7d** The last proclamation is, **He punishes the children and their children for the sin of the parents to the third and fourth generation.** Furthermore, a similar expression first appears in the Decalogue (20:5). In this verse, the qualifying expression "who hate me" is dropped, but the expression "to their children" is added. The expression "to the third and fourth generation" is elsewhere used in reference to the blessing of longevity on the righteous (Gen 50:23; 2 Kgs 10:30; Job 42:16). But here, coupled with "the children and their children," it describes transgenerational, corporate punishment that can affect innocent children.

Transgenerational Punishment

On the surface, Exod 34:7d appears to contradict other biblical texts that indicate that punishment for sin falls on the sinners and not on their children (Jer 31:29-30). While the issue is difficult to resolve completely, the following considerations remove much of the tension.

(1) The elimination of the qualifying expression "who hate me" may be inconsequential. It is declared once in the Decalogue (Exod 20:5; Deut 5:9) and may be now assumed (see Deut 7:10; Ezek 18:1-20; Jer 31:29-30). The "children and their children" would apply only when they perpetuate their parents' rebellion. Hence, in Num 14, the sinful older generations are deprived of the right to enter the promised land, while the innocent younger generations are eventually granted entry.

(2) However, Num 14:31, 33 also shows that the younger generation of Israelites suffer during the forty years of punishment of the rebellious older generations. Thus, "to the third and fourth generation" points to the fact that contemporary sins and consequences inevitably bring negative effects on succeeding generations.

(3) Consistent with this concept, "the third and fourth generation" can also be understood as a reference to the entire household, which in the ancient world would consist of three or four generations (see Jer 23:34 and the punishment of Achan and his household in Josh 7:24-25). In such a setting, there is inevitable corporateness in conduct, responsibility, and consequences that affect an entire family.

410

(4) When the principle of transgenerational solidarity of "the third and fourth" is applied to a nation united as one by a covenant, the qualifying expression "who hate me" becomes irrelevant on the individual level. That is, the nation as a whole sows and reaps either good or evil consequences. Even as the righteousness of one person can bring blessing upon thousands of subsequent generations (as with Abraham) or mercy upon a whole sinful nation (as with Moses), so the wickedness of one person can contaminate and bring guilt upon the whole community (as with Achan in Josh 7 or the Israelite man in Num 25:6).

FROM THE TEXT

The name Yahweh and the attributes that accompany the name reveal something significant about the character of the God of the Bible. The frequent recurrence of the words of these verses in various parts of the OT conveys its utmost significance in Israel's confession of faith in Yahweh. In this statement of divine attributes, what is revealed at first is Yahweh's compassion, grace, patience, covenant love, faithfulness, covenant love for succeeding generations, and forgiveness of sin and rebellion. However, the reminder of his commitment to punish the guilty follows these attributes. While he lavishly displays love, mercy, and forgiveness, he also faithfully fulfills his obligation to justice and righteous judgment. While it is impossible for us humans to exhaustively comprehend how God's mercy and justice relate to each other (so the mystery of God remains), the biblical narratives do help us see how they can harmoniously converge (so the knowledge of God is gained; → Exod 34:6-7 above and the discussion on "The God of Mercy and Justice" based on ch 32—34 in Introduction). The divine self-revelation of 34:6-7 calls the contemporary communities of faith to acknowledge the multifaceted attributes of God and to affirm the whole truth about God's character (rather than selectively accepting the preferred "mercy side" only). That his name conveys both mercy and justice, both grace and judgment, warns us that his grace cannot be taken for granted. This confession of faith assures us of God's mercy but also warns us not to "live close to the margins of God's patience" (Fretheim 1991, 307). Rather, as Paul says centuries later, God calls his people to a life that is "dead to sin but alive to God in Christ Jesus" (Rom 6:11).

Just as the Israelites pray and praise God according to God's self-revealed name, Christians today pray in the name of Jesus. The name that the Lord proclaims to Moses is the essence of his core character in his being, words, and deeds. Israel's prayers, petitions, and praises rooted in God's name thus appeal to God's entire being. Calling on the name of the Lord is equivalent to the acknowledgment of the Lord's existence, words, and historical deeds, and to the worship of him. Thus, Joel declares, "Everyone who calls on the name of the LORD will be saved" (Joel 2:32 [3:5 HB]).

Likewise, praying in the name of Jesus evokes his identity as the Son of God, his character as identical to that of the Father and the Holy Spirit (John 14:16-18; 17:6), and his power over sin, death, and evil to be absolute. To pray in the name of Jesus is to pray in the name of the Father, Son, and Holy Spirit. Jesus, therefore, promises his disciples that praying in his name will result in unparalleled authority and effectiveness (14:13-14). Prayer rooted in the revealed character of the one, true, triune God is biblical prayer at its best.

(3) Moses' Worship and Intercession (34:8-9)

BEHIND THE TEXT

Divine self-revelation is followed by worship and intercession. According to Deut 9:18, Moses spends the subsequent forty days and nights in intercession, while prostrated before Yahweh. Because the prophet's heart is close to Yahweh, Moses understands and feels, perhaps like no other can, the terrifying threat of Yahweh's intense anger toward the sinful Israelites (v 19). Therefore, Moses' intercession may be just as extreme as divine wrath. Verses 23-25 record another occasion, in which Moses spends forty days and forty nights in intense intercession, following the Israelites' total rebellion at Kadesh Barnea (see Num 14:10-20).

According to the stipulations and consequences delineated in Exod 20:5, the reasonable, incontestable, and entirely just course of action would be the utter destruction of Israel. What is not an explicit part of the Sinai covenant is forgiveness. The Sinai covenant does not bind Yahweh to forgiveness as an obligation. If Yahweh forgives, it is entirely because of his sovereign freedom to do so. Here, Moses bases Yahweh's extension of such freedom to the Israelites on Yahweh's compassionate and merciful nature, which he has just revealed.

IN THE TEXT

■ **8-9** Verses 8-9 report Moses' response to Yahweh's self-revelation of his merciful and compassionate nature. He spontaneously bows **to the ground** in worship (v 8) and appeals to Yahweh on the basis of Yahweh's **favor** (or "grace") toward him to **forgive** (*sālaḥ*) the sin of Israel (v 9). The expressions **our wickedness**, **our sin**, and **us** show that Moses completely identifies himself with the Israelites and their sin. By embracing and presenting the offensive Israelites and their wickedness as his own, Moses covers them, so to speak, with the favor (or grace) he has with Yahweh. This way, Yahweh is obliged to view the guilty Israelites through the lens of grace.

The Hebrew term for "forgive" (*slḥ*) here is different from the one used in v 7 (*nāśā'*). **Forgive** (*slḥ*) refers to the "pardon" or "absolution" the priest grants after the following: (1) the sin offering that atones for unintentional sins (Lev 4:20, 26, 31, 35; 5:10, 13; Num 15:28); (2) offerings for certain crimes that require restitution be made to the victims (Lev 5:16, 18; 6:7 [5:26 HB]); (3) guilt offerings for intentional sin not deserving death (19:22); and (4) the priest's atonement for the unintentional sin of the whole community of Israel (Num 15:25-26). It also applies to divine absolution, following severe punishment for heinous sins, such as the golden calf incident (1 Kgs 8:34, 35, 39, 50; 2 Chr 6:25, 27, 30, 39; Isa 55:7; Jer 5:1; 31:34; 33:8; 50:20). In the last category, which is most relevant to the current context, "forgive" (slḥ) is the opposite of "cut off" (as clearly illustrated in Deut 29:20 [19 HB]). In these categories, the offender has to pay some kind of (light or heavy) payment for the sin committed before pardon is granted. An exception is found in Num 14:19-23, in which pardon is granted first, followed by stringent punishment of the rebellious. Yahweh's pardon (slḥ) thus appears to require some payment from the sinner. However, partial payments by sinners are not adequate to atone for their sins. Pardon (slḥ) is made possible presumably by Yahweh's commitment to the covenant and divine sin-bearing (nāśā'), which is what ultimately (or primarily) removes sin (intentional or unintentional) from his people (see Milgrom 1990, 328-29).

FROM THE TEXT

In this passage, we see a striking image of a prophetic, covenant mediator. Moses identifies with a sinful people and intercedes for God's grace on their behalf. Instead of separating and distancing himself from sinful and corrupt people, Moses completely identifies with them and owns their sin and guilt as his own and seeks God's forgiveness of the sins of his people (Exod 34:9).

The NT portrays Jesus' identification with sinners in the incarnation, baptism, and his death on the cross, and thus surpassing the ministry of Moses. As one who is "holy, blameless, pure, set apart from sinners" (Heb 7:26), he far outweighs the value of all creation and human beings and makes atonement for all. The risen Christ continues to identify with us, and represents us to the Father (v 25).

b. Yahweh's Renewal of the Covenant (34:10-28)

BEHIND THE TEXT

In this unit, Yahweh renews the covenant with the Israelites, which implies that he extends grace and grants pardon.

The covenant laws, many of which are repeated from ch 23, accompany the covenant renewal. The laws are carefully stated in view of the Israelites' recent corruption. The laws intend to counteract the specific ways they failed Yahweh and to authorize acceptable forms of worship. The laws come with appropriate warnings against further apostasy.

The pronouns "you" and "your" are singular throughout the laws, in contrast to the plural "you" in the original covenant proposal in 19:4-5. Consequently, some suggest that the renewal of the covenant is with Moses alone. However, Yahweh makes it explicit in 34:27 that he is making the covenant with both Moses and Israel. Further, it is the Israelites who need the law; Moses receives it as a covenant mediator and administrator. The use of the singular "you" and "your" is consistent with pronoun usage in the Ten Commandments and the book of the covenant. These pronouns are best understood as both personal (so each person takes the responsibility of obeying) and collective (given to all and demanding communal obedience).

IN THE TEXT

(1) Covenant Renewal, Promises, and Demands (34:10-11)

■ 10 Yahweh responds to Moses' appeal for his forgiveness of Israel's sin with offer of a new future for Israel. This future depends entirely on a **covenant** that Yahweh makes with Israel. Yahweh promises through the covenant (more appropriately, the renewed covenant) that he will **do wonders never before done in any nation in all the world**. The **wonders** may refer to such future **awesome** works of Yahweh as causing the walls of Jericho to fall (Josh 6) and causing the sun and moon to stand still (10:1-15). The expression **for you** may mean, "on your behalf," "for your benefit," "for your faith," or "for your honor."

■ 11 The covenant offer and the accompanying promise come with Yahweh's demand for Israel's obedience to the covenant laws. The demand for obedience, however, does not imply that Yahweh's accompanying presence will be removed upon the Israelites' disobedience. The repeated expression **I will** (in vv 10-11) in the context of covenant renewal implies that Yahweh now commits to personally (instead of "an angel" [33:2]) drive out the inhabitants of the land by personally performing wonders. This divine commitment is consistent with the promise Yahweh gave Moses in 33:14-17. This, however, does not remove from the Israelites the covenant requirement of obedience in order to receive the promised land. This interpretation is confirmed in Yahweh's response to the rebellious Israelites at Kadesh Barnea; instead of withdrawing his presence from the covenant breakers, Yahweh delays Israel's entry into the land until the rebellious generation dies out in the wilderness (Num 14:21-24, 28-35); upon Moses' death (which symbolizes the completeness of the death of the old), Yahweh personally brings the Israelites into the land (see Josh 1:1-6). (For comments on the list of the native peoples of the land, → Exod 3:8.)

(2) Covenant Laws and Warnings against Idolatry (34:12-17)

■ 12 Verses 12-17 convey a radical vision for Israel's life in the land of Canaan, exemplified by an alternative way of life that marks total separation from and an uncompromising attitude toward the religious, social, and cultural values of the Canaanites. Verse 12 prohibits any social alliances with the Canaanites. A similar command and warning against making treaties with native peoples is given in 23:32-33 and again in 34:15. The command **be careful not to** addresses the Israelites' will. The people have the freedom to embrace either Yahweh and the covenant life or the inhabitants of the land and adopt their ways. The latter will become **a snare**, a continual and dangerous appeal to compromise the covenant, which will result in the forfeiture of the covenant with Yahweh.

■ **13** Verses 13-14 prohibit Israel's religious alliance with the Canaanites. Yahweh stipulates the destruction of Canaanite sanctuaries and all their cultic objects because their continued existence in the land would be a snare, an alluring attraction to Israel to follow the Canaanite form of worship. The cultic objects include **altars** (see 20:25), **sacred** standing stone (made of one large stone), the wooden **poles** of **Asherah** (a leading Canaanite deity, goddess of fertility, and feminine consort of various gods, including Baal) (see Deut 12:3). Asherah worship sometimes involved male cultic prostitution (2 Kgs 23:7). Besides the biblical evidence (Judg 6:25-30; 1 Kgs 15:13; 16:33; 18:19; 2 Kgs 17:16; 21:3; 23:4), an inscription from northwestern Sinai that mentions "YHVH and his Asherah" testifies to the extent of the syncretism in Israel's religion (Sarna 2004, 165).

■ **14** Prohibition of idolatry in this verse reiterates the prohibition of religious alliance with the Canaanites. This prohibition is reinforced by the declaration of Yahweh's **name**—**Jealous**, an attribute of Yahweh already mentioned in the context of the second commandment. In both texts, Yahweh's jealousy signals the surety of divine punishment for those who turn to idolatry (→ Exod 20:5-6).

■ **15** Verse 15 continues the prohibition of social and religious alliances with the Canaanites. The warning here is clear: social alliance will lead to religious alliance (→ v 12 and 23:32-33). Again, the concern here is exclusive relation and devotion to Yahweh.

■ **16** Marriage relationship with the Canaanites is introduced in 34:16 as a prime example of how social alliance will inevitably lead to religious alliance and assimilation and idolatrous worship. While some have suggested that this text refers to the kind of cultic prostitution that existed in the ancient Near East, the phrase **prostitute themselves** (vv 15 and 16) more likely stands for idolatry and religious unfaithfulness.

■ **17** A categorical prohibition of making **any idols** concludes the various laws against idolatry.

(3) Legitimate Festivals (34:18-26)

■ **18** **The Festival of Unleavened Bread** is mentioned in 12:14-20 (→) and 23:15 (→). The Israelites celebrated a false festival to their manufactured gods who supposedly brought them **out of Egypt** (32:4-5). Thus, the repetition of the festival regulations reemphasizes the importance of celebrating only the Yahweh-authorized harvest festivals in connection with the historical events of Exodus (→ 12:2 and **Aviv** in 23:15).

■ **19-20** (For the redemption of the **firstborn**, → 13:2, 11-15.) In these verses, Yahweh reminds the Israelites of instructions they were to implement from the very beginning of their post-Exodus existence. (See "empty-handed" in 23:15.)

■ **21** The Sabbath **rest** is based both on creation (as in 20:9) and on the exodus (Deut 5:15). They are to practice the Sabbath law even during the busiest agricultural season, when one would be most tempted to work on the Sabbath day. The Israelites have been freed from slavery into freedom; therefore, they must not eagerly return to the lifestyle of a slave. Rather, they must take time to acknowledge and worship the creator God, their Redeemer and Provider. (→ Exod 20:8-11; 23:12; and 31:12-17.)

■ **22** The celebration of legitimate festivals to Yahweh can serve as an antidote to the temptation to **celebrate** pagan festivals and to sacrifice to idols. (→ **Festival of Harvest** [Weeks] and **Festival of Ingathering** in 23:16.)

■ **23** Repeated almost verbatim from 23:17.

■ **24** This verse assumes the future establishment of central or regional sanctuaries, which would require travel away from home. Yahweh will firmly establish the borders of Israel's **territory**. This may mean that Yahweh will weaken other **nations**, near and far, so that they will not take military action against Israel. This would be so even during Israel's annual festivals when the Israelite fighting men will be absent from their towns. The Israelites are to completely trust Yahweh rather than their own military strategies or strengths for their protection.

■ **25** (→ 12:10 and 23:18.)

■ **26** Repeated verbatim from 23:19.

(4) Instruction to Moses to Record the Renewal Laws (34:27)

■ **27** Yahweh commands **Moses** to **write down** the foregoing words and commands of the renewed covenant, perhaps on parchment. Moses most likely recorded the laws after descending the mountain and after delivering them to the people. These events would be consistent with the fact that Moses wrote down the previous **words** of the book of the **covenant** after he descended the mountain and recounted them to the people (24:3-4). Yahweh is the one who rewrites the Ten Commandments on the new stone tablets, even as Yahweh wrote the Ten Commandments on the original two stone tablets (24:12; 31:18; 32:16; 34:1). Previously, Yahweh did not make explicit that the Israelites were the recipients of the renewed covenant (v 10); however, at this point Yahweh does. The renewed covenant is with Moses and **with Israel**.

(5) Moses' Forty Days with Yahweh (34:28a)

■ **28a** This verse brings closure to the covenant renewal narrative that started in 34:1. It reports that Moses stayed on Mount Sinai for **forty days and forty nights without** food or **water**. In the glorious presence of Yahweh, who is the very source of life and light, Moses transcends physical needs for food and water. This anticipates Moses' radiant face that leads to his preeminent status among the Israelites.

(6) New Stone Tablets Written by Yahweh (34:28b)

■ **28b** This verse reports that Yahweh writes the Ten Commandments on the tablets, which signals the completion of the renewal of the covenant. Some commentators assert that Moses is the one who physically writes the Ten Commandments on the stone **tablets**. However, if the statement **And he wrote . . . the Ten Commandments** is supposed to be Moses' instant obedience to Yahweh's command to write, then that statement logically would have immediately followed v 27 (rather than being separated by a statement about how long Moses stayed on Mount Sinai). Also in light of 34:1 (and Deut 10:2, 4), "he" clearly refers to Yahweh (Propp 2006, 617). In addition, this unit opens with Yahweh's promise to rewrite the Ten Commandments along with Moses' call and ascent to the mountain; then the narrative concludes with the report, in the reverse order, of Moses' time on the mountain and Yahweh's (the true referent of "he") rewriting of the Ten Commandments as a fulfillment of Exod 34:1. The structure of vv 1-28 clarifies that it is Yahweh who rewrites the Decalogue on new tablets.

FROM THE TEXT

The covenant renewal offer in this text is accompanied by Yahweh's strict commands that insist on Israel's commitment to follow a way of life that is radically distinct from and free from any alliances with the world in which she will soon enter. The social, religious, economic, political, and cultural locations in which the people of God live in the world today offer attractive alternatives that often allure them to enter into "friendship" with the world. The Canaanite religion was a "prosperity" religion that offered the good life to its devotees with abundance and fruitfulness in all areas of life. In those ways, the world has not changed much since those days; the offer of the good life and friendship with the world comes to the people of God these days through corrupt political ideologies and propaganda, the hedonistic and narcissistic use of media, sex, technology and material goods, and even the message of the gospel (adulterated with the message of prosperity). James warns his readers: "You adulterous people, don't you know that friendship with the world means enmity against God? Therefore, anyone who chooses to be a friend of the world becomes an enemy of God" (4:4).

The renewal of the covenant after Israel's apostasy offers a foretaste of the forgiveness and sanctification that is the hallmark of the new covenant that God promises through Jeremiah (Jer 31:32-34). The Lord's renewal of the covenant and promise to do wonders on their behalf (Exod 34:10) are fulfilled in the history of Israel from the wilderness wandering to the entry into the promised land. However, their history in the OT testifies to their way of life marked by divided loyalty and covenant breaking through social, religious, cultural, and political alliances with the world around them.

This passage looks forward to a new covenant, which both renews the Sinai covenant and surpasses it. Jeremiah speaks of a new covenant in which the Lord will write his law on the hearts of his people and they will all know the Lord (Jer 31:31-34). Loyalty to God will no longer be regulated by external observation of laws. The laws written on human hearts point to the possibility of transformation within and internal commitment to love, obey, and worship God through an exclusive relationship with God, which the Wesleyan tradition calls entire sanctification. The Gospels proclaim the establishment of God's new covenant, not just with Israel, but with the whole human race through the death and resurrection of his Son Jesus Christ.

c. Moses' Administration of the Renewed Covenant and His Radiant Face (34:29-35)

BEHIND THE TEXT

This unit concludes the narrative of Exod 32—34. As a transitional unit, it looks both backward and forward. Looking backward, it antithetically relates to the earlier unit recounting the indignation of Yahweh and Moses. Instead of a broken covenant, broken tablets, and the angry face of Moses, the Israelites now receive a renewed covenant, new tablets, and the radiant face of Moses. Looking forward, this unit functions as a transition to the building of the tabernacle, where Yahweh's manifest presence will dwell. Moses speaking to the Israelites with his face glowing with the radiance of Yahweh's glory foreshadows Yahweh's own "radiant face/presence" dwelling in the midst of his people and bestowed upon the people through the high priest's daily blessing (Num 6:23-27).

Rabbinic tradition holds that Moses descended Mount Sinai with the two tablets on the tenth day of the seventh month; therefore, that day is regarded as the Day of Atonement (Sarna 2004, 168). This view is compatible with existing internal evidence: (1) the exodus takes place on the fifteenth of the first month, with the arrival at Sinai on the first of the third month (Exod 19:1-2); (2) the giving of the Ten Commandments and the Sinai covenant occur shortly after that date (chs 20—24; the Jewish calendar coordinates Shabuoth with the giving of the law on the sixth of the third month); (3) Moses spends forty days and nights on Mount Sinai; (4) the aftermath of the golden calf incident requires a considerable amount of time; and (5) Moses spends an additional forty days on Mount Sinai before he comes down with the renewal of the covenant. Allowing for about four months between the making of the covenant and its renewal is, thus, a reasonable timeline.

IN THE TEXT

■ **29** Moses' **face** is **radiant**, reflecting Yahweh's radiance. Habakkuk 3:4 likens Yahweh's splendor to the bright sunrise, with rays flashing from his hands. (The term for "radiant" was mistaken for the related term "horned" by Jerome in the Latin Vulgate, which yielded many Western artists' depictions of Moses with horns on his forehead.) Previously, Moses spoke **with** Yahweh numerous times, but his face did not reflect Yahweh's glory. This time is unique because Moses received a special revelation of Yahweh (Exod 34:6-7), beheld Yahweh's splendor and glory, and conversed with Yahweh in greater intimacy for forty days and nights. Previously, Yahweh made Moses like God to Aaron (4:16) and then to Pharaoh (7:1); at this point, Moses is made like God to the Israelites, with the radiance of Yahweh's presence shining through Moses' face. (→ "tablets" in 25:16; 32:15-16; 34:1, 28.)

■ **30** The natural reaction of the people to Moses' **radiant** and majestic **face** is fear; probably they are unsure whether it signifies Yahweh's favor or displeasure.

■ **31-32 Moses** calls them **near** to assure **them** of Yahweh's favor and also to deliver **all the commands** Yahweh gave **him**, which includes but is not limited to the renewed covenant commands in vv 12-26.

■ **33-35** These verses describe Moses' custom of wearing **a veil over his face** (v 33), except **whenever** he is in Yahweh's **presence** and whenever he is delivering Yahweh's commands to the people (v 34). The radiance of Moses' face perhaps indicates the symbolic presence of Yahweh's glory among his people, mediated through Moses. A reflection of Yahweh's glory has come down from the mountain through Moses, but soon its fullness will inhabit the tabernacle.

The language of these verses suggests a habitual behavior (of veiling and unveiling) occurring over an extended time period, perhaps throughout the wilderness period. The text does not explain the reason for this habit of Moses. But it does indicate that the intimate times in Yahweh's presence "recharge" or illuminate Moses' face. Perhaps the unveiling and veiling indicate that the glory of God is both welcoming and threatening; it is welcoming to those who approach God's presence with due reverence to worship him and hear him speak (thus, no veil is needed); the veiling of Moses' face protects the lives of those who may regard God's glory as something common and ordinary. The unveiling and veiling perhaps suggest this mystery of God's glory.

Even as Moses was visibly transformed by his intimate encounter with God, continually beholding God's glory transforms believers in their moral character, enabling them to become more like Christ, reflecting the perfect image of God. In 2 Cor 3:7-18, Paul asserts the superiority of the ministry of Christ and the gospel over the ministry associated with Moses, glorious though it was. The reason is that Moses' law represented the "ministry that brought death" and "condemnation" as opposed to the new covenant "ministry of the Spirit" and "righteousness" (2 Cor 3:7-9). The ministry of Moses brought condemnation, because the laws were written on tablets of stone (see Exod 31:18; 32:15-16; 34:1), unable to transform people's hearts. The Spirit, however, writes the new covenant on hearts of flesh, producing careful obedience (2 Cor 3:3, 7; see Jer 31:31-34; Ezek 11:19-20; 36:26-27). For Paul, any favor and grace that Moses and the Israelites experienced in Exodus has been surpassed and extended in scope through Christ. Paul thus states, "And we all, who with unveiled faces contemplate the Lord's glory, are being transformed into his image with ever-increasing glory, which comes from the Lord, who is the Spirit" (2 Cor 3:18; see 4:3-6).

D. Construction of the Tabernacle and the Real Presence (35:1—40:38)

Overview

With the renewal of the broken covenant, which culminates with the giving of the new covenant tablets (Exod 34:10-32), the Israelites proceed to build the tabernacle. Yahweh's compassion and mercy toward the rebellious people allow the covenant relationship to continue. Yahweh's desire to dwell among his people and be their God can now be fulfilled (25:8; 29:45-46).

The length of the sections concerning the tabernacle emphasizes the importance of the abiding presence of Yahweh in Yahweh's covenant relationship with his people. The tabernacle is the visible representation of Yahweh's real presence and continuous administration of his saving grace. As such, the filling of the tabernacle with Yahweh's glory is the culmination of the book of Exodus.

I. The Preparation (35:1—36:7)

BEHIND THE TEXT

The appointment and filling with the Spirit of the chief artisans (31:1-11) and the giving of the Sabbath regulations (vv 14-17) precede the breaking of the covenant. The Sabbath regulations (35:1-3) and the presentation of the chief artisans to the public (vv 30-35) now follow the renewal of the covenant. This literary arrangement emphasizes the priority of the covenant relationship over the tabernacle. It also emphasizes the priority of the Sabbath rest (for worship and rejuvenation) and the importance of the filling of the Spirit for the work of God. Without the covenant relationship, true worship, and the Spirit of God, the tabernacle would simply be a splendid empty shell, bereft of God's presence and grace.

In the golden calf narrative, the people made a visual representation of God. The construction of the tabernacle addresses and satisfies the people's need for something visual that would assure them of Yahweh's presence in their midst. Therefore, the people are extremely generous with their donations for the tabernacle.

IN THE TEXT

a. Sabbath Regulations (35:1-3)

■ **1-3** **Moses** summons the entire **community** of the Israelites to assemble, for everyone needs to hear the instructions and make appropriate contributions for the construction of the tabernacle (v 1).

Verses 2-3 offer a set of **Sabbath** (*šabbat šabbātôn*; "complete rest"; see "sabbath" in 16:23) regulations, a general subject that has already appeared several times in the book (16:23-29; 20:8-11; 23:12; 31:12-16). Verse 2 of ch 35 is a repetition of 31:15.

Verse 3 prohibits the lighting of **fire** on **the Sabbath day**. Although some Jewish traditions include the lighting (*'ālâ*; see 25:37; 40:4, 25; Num 8:2-3) of the lamp in the evening within this prohibition, Yahweh most likely did not intend the people to spend the entire evening/night in the dark. Most likely, lighting (*bā'ar*; "burn," "kindle") a wood fire for the preparation of food is in view. All food for the Sabbath day must be prepared on the sixth day, as indicated in Exod 16:23.

b. The Call for Contributions (35:4-19)

■ **4-9** Moses issues an invitation for the **whole Israelite community** (v 4) to voluntarily contribute materials needed to make the tabernacle, in accordance with 25:1-7. The purpose for the offering (25:8-9) is omitted here, which presupposes its prior publication and the public awareness of it.

■ **10-19** Moses now invites all the **skilled** workers (v 10; also mentioned in 31:6; 35:34-35; 36:1 ff. and 37:10 ff.) who possess God-given ability to **make** the artistic objects to volunteer. They will work under the direction of the appointed leaders Bezalel and Oholiab (31:2-6; 35:30-34; 36:1 ff.; 37:1-9; 38:22-23). Verses 11-19 of ch 35 list all the objects to be made. The instructions for these objects are probably already published.

c. The People's Willing Response (35:20-29)

■ **20-24** Armed with the knowledge and understanding of the materials needed and of the function of each object, the Israelites return to their tents (v 20), and all who are **willing** eagerly respond by contributing all the material needed for the tabernacle (v 21). Verse 22 lists the people's contribution of **gold** in the form of **all kinds** of **gold jewelry** including **earrings**, which is reminiscent of the gold earrings that all the Israelites brought to Aaron, so he could make an idol for them (→ 32:2-3). The acceptable contributions to the sacred cause have a redemptive value for the Israelites. The gold is offered to Yahweh as a **wave offering**. The gold now belongs to Yahweh and, thereby, is sanctified for sacred use. Verses 23-24 report the people's donation of various yarns and leather (→ 25:4-5) and silver, bronze, and acacia wood (→ 25:3).

■ **25-26** The **skilled** or more literally **wise-hearted** women with superior spinning skills are highlighted in these verses. Spinning is associated with women (Prov 31:19), weaving with both women and men (e.g., Exod 35:35; 2 Kgs 23:7; on weavers, → Exod 26:1), and tailoring with both women and men (e.g., 1 Sam 2:19; 2 Kgs 22:14).

■ **27-28** The **leaders** bring the precious **stones** to be **mounted** on the **ephod and breastpiece** (35:27; → 25:7). The leaders also make the costly contributions of **spices** and pure **olive oil** used for the lamp (35:28; → 27:20-21), along with the **anointing oil** (→ 30:22-33), and the **fragrant incense** (→ 30:34-38). The oil offered by the leaders of Israel may be an emblem of their consent to the priesthood of Aaron and his sons. Their offering of incense may be representing the prayers of all the tribes, especially the intercession of the tribal leaders on behalf of their tribes.

■ **29** The willingness of the offerers is reiterated in this verse (see vv 21-22), emphasizing the enthusiasm with which the Israelites make material and labor contributions.

d. Announcement of Chief Artists (35:30—36:1)

■ **30-34** These verses publicly recognize the leading artists, whom Yahweh chose previously and **filled** with the **Spirit of God** and extraordinary **wisdom** and **skills** (v 31; see 31:1-11). Now, **Moses** makes a public announcement concerning the appointment of **Bezalel** the principal artisan and **Oholiab** his assistant (35:30, 34; → 31:1-11). They are the chief craftsmen, teachers, and supervisors of all other artisans.

■ **35:35—36:1** These verses acknowledge divine gifting and empowerment of all the other artists who are also masters in their fields. The chief and assistant artists possess the wisdom and **ability** to execute the **work** according to Yahweh's design (36:1). They are not to take initiative or use creative license to make works according to their imagination (other than where it is allowed; → Overview for 25:1—31:18).

e. Overabundant Donations (36:2-7)

■ **2-7** These verses report the public appointment of the lead artists and all the artisans and the surplus of materials necessary for the construction of the tabernacle made possible by the generous donation of the people (vv 3-5). Moses issues an order to the people to refrain from any further donations (vv 6-7).

FROM THE TEXT

God's dwelling place is built by God with human participation. In this passage, the Israelites give freely and generously for the construction of the tabernacle. Later in Israel's history, the people make similarly generous contributions for Solomon's temple (2 Chr 29:1-9). When the Second Temple is constructed under Zerubbabel and others, contributions come from three sources: Jews living in Palestine, Jews living outside of Palestine, and supportive Gentiles like Cyrus (see Ezra 1:2-4). Herod's expansion and rebuilding of the temple—the temple of Jesus' day—is made possible predominantly by Gentile contributions.

These observations point theologically to an escalating level of Gentile contribution in service and participation in worship of God. Significantly, Solomon already anticipates Gentile contribution and worship at the temple (1 Kgs 8:41-43), and later Jews designate a legal domain called the Court of the Gentiles within the site of Herod's temple.

The full inclusion of the Gentiles in the assembly of the righteous and in the service of God, however, is not realized until the NT era. Christ himself and his people are seen as temples. God is the Father who seeks those who will worship him, not at a particular geographical place, but everywhere "in the Spirit and in truth" (John 4:23; see vv 19-24). In Christ, whose own body is the temple (2:19-22) or tabernacle (1:14), the worshippers, the place of worship, and the type of service shift from the ethnic, physical, and external to the spiritual and christological. God's Christ-following people are temples (1 Cor 6:19-20) and are corporately God's temple (3:16-17).

The implications for today's church are clear: "God's great building project is the church" (Ryken 2005, 1088), but what the disciples of Christ are called to build is not the physical structures, but the body of Christ. God calls us to generously contribute our finances, skills, spiritual gifts, time, and indeed life itself to God's ecclesial kingdom project. As the members of Christ's body preach the gospel of Jesus Christ in words and deeds and make disciples of all the peoples of the nations, the body of Christ grows. The goal is for God's people to offer themselves freely for God's kingdom purposes so completely that God declares, "[There is] more than enough to do all the work" (Exod 36:7)!

2. Execution of the Artistic Work (36:8—39:43)

BEHIND THE TEXT

This lengthy section accomplishes a number of important purposes in the book of Exodus, which unfold as follows: (1) most significantly, it reports the fulfillment of the instructions concerning the tabernacle (36:8—38:20); (2) it gives an account of certain precious metals (38:21-31); (3) it reports the making of the priestly garments (39:1-31); and (4) it reports the completion, inspection, and blessing of all the objects (39:32-43).

The order of items mentioned in this construction section is different from the one given in the instruction section. In the instructions (25:1—27:19), the items are mentioned in descending order of theological importance: the ark, the table, the lamp, the tabernacle (innermost curtain), the framework, the outer curtains, the bronze altar, and the court and hangings. After this, the instructions (in 27:20—30:38) appear to list items in a somewhat random way: lamp oil, vestments, gold altar, atonement silver, bronze basin, anointing oil, and fragrant incense.

The report about the construction in this section lists the items in the order of their arrangement, commanded in 40:2-8 and then carried out in 40:18-33. The tabernacle is mentioned first (36:8-38), then its furnishings in the order of descending theological value: the ark, the table, the lampstand, the gold altar, and the anointing oil and fragrant incense (37:1-29; see the order in 25:1—27:19). Then the text reports the making of the bronze altar, the bronze basin, and the courtyard (38:20).

The order in this section should not be taken as an indication that the objects were made in this particular order, one item at a time. Most likely, various artisans worked on different objects more or less simultaneously according to their skills.

This section repeatedly affirms that everything was made exactly as Yahweh commanded (36:1; 38:22; 39:1, 5, 7, 21, 26, 29, 31, 32, 42, 43). Restating the instructions as completed actions emphasizes the artisans' faithfulness. They do not deviate from Yahweh's words but completely obey them.

IN THE TEXT

a. Making of the Tabernacle and Its Furnishings (36:8—38:20)

■ **36:8-38** The **tabernacle** is built. (→ ch 26.)
■ **37:1-9** The **ark** is constructed. (→ 25:10-20.)
■ **37:10-16** The **table** is made. (→ 25:23-30.)

■ **37:17-24** The **lampstand** is made. (→ 25:31-40.)

■ **37:25-28** The **gold altar of incense** is built. (→ 30:1-10.)

■ **37:29** The **anointing oil** and **fragrant incense** are mixed. This verse is a summary of 30:22-38 (→).

■ **38:1-7** The **altar of burnt offering**, made of **bronze**, is constructed. (→ 27:1-8.)

■ **38:8** The **bronze basin** is made. This verse is a summary of 30:17-21, with additional information about the source of the material. Bronze or copper **mirrors** are made in ancient Egypt from the third millennium BC and owned by the wealthy. The **women** mentioned in this verse may have had in their possession a bronze mirror due to family wealth or perhaps due to plundering of the Egyptians (see 3:22; 11:2; 12:35-36). However they obtained it, these women willingly surrender a rare and precious possession to the Lord's service.

As for the women and cultic duties, this is one of several texts that testify explicitly that the Israelite women did participate in the ministry of the tabernacle. These women were probably Levites, the tribe chosen for the service of the tabernacle (→ 32:26-28 and 38:21).

Accordingly, this text takes for granted that the ***women cultic ministers*** [*haṣōb'ōt*] ***ministered*** [*ṣāb'û*] **at the entrance to the tent of meeting**. The verb *ṣāba'* normally means to "wage war" with the noun *haṣṣābā'* ("the war"). In the context of the tabernacle, the terms indicate holy cultic service (Num 4:3, 23; 8:25), used in relation to both women (this verse and 1 Sam 2:22) and men. Contrary to what some suggest, the terms do not indicate women ministers performed menial tasks as their sole responsibility. The terms emphasize the women's official function as cultic ministers at the tabernacle (which makes Eli's sons' sexual crime against the women cultic ministers all the more heinous [see 1 Sam 2:22]; see Propp 2006, 665-67).

Since the tabernacle is not yet constructed and functioning, **the entrance to the tent of meeting** is a case of anachronism. These women may have been serving at Moses' tent of meeting (33:7 ff.), just as Joshua remained at Moses' tent (v 11). Once the tabernacle is constructed and consecrated, these women transfer service to the entrance of the tabernacle. Alternatively, the (especially devout) women who surrender their precious bronze mirrors for service to the Lord are later appointed for ministry at the entrance to the tent of meeting. In either case, from the writers' perspective, the mirrors came from the women who served at the entrance to the tabernacle after its construction.

Women Ministers

In addition to women performing cultic functions in the tabernacle in early Israelite history, the Bible attests to Levitical women who were cultic and prophetic ministers. Heman's three daughters during King David's time were renowned temple musicians (either in vocal or instrumental music or both; see I Chr 25:1, 5-6). Men and women temple singers are also noted during Josiah's time in 2 Chr 35:25 (see 2 Chr 23:13; 29:28) and until the return from exile (in 2 Chr 35:25; Ezra 2:65, 70; 7:7; Neh 7:67, 73 [72 HB]). The roles women had in tabernacle and temple worship offer parallels to other better-known OT women who served in noncultic leadership roles related to prophetic ministry, military exploits, and religious reform (e.g., Miriam in Exod 15:20-21, Deborah in Judg 4—5, Huldah in 2 Kgs 22 and 2 Chr 34).

■ **38:9-20** Next, **the courtyard** is built. (→ Exod 27:9-19.)

b. Acknowledgment of the Leaders and Metals (38:21-31)

■ **21** Ithamar (→ 28:1 and 29:29-30) is named the chief officer in charge of the "inventory of" (NET) **the tabernacle (amounts of the material used for** [NIV]; "records" [ESV]). The public records are important for establishing the leaders' integrity; no one can charge the leaders with embezzlement (see 1 Sam 12:3-5 for Samuel's public declaration of his innocence from any kind of corruption and oppression). Under Ithamar's supervision, the Levites kept records of the material received and used. After the completion of the tabernacle, the Levites presumably continued this administrative duty (e.g., Num 7:10-88), in addition to their new assignment of care and transportation of the tabernacle (Num 4; 7:1-9).

■ **22-23** The chief artists **Bezalel** and **Oholiab** are once again acknowledged.

■ **24-31** **Gold, silver,** and **bronze** are tallied (→ Exod 25:3). Some dismiss the **29 talents** of gold as exorbitant, but given the abundance of gold in Egypt and the Israelites' plunder of the Egyptians at the time of the exodus from Egypt, the amount is not unreasonable. The monarchical period records the circulation of far greater amounts of gold (see, for example, 100,000 talents of David in 1 Chr 22:14; 29:4; Solomon's internal revenue of 666 talents per annum; → Exod 25:39 for "talent" and "shekel" and 30:11-16 for "half shekel").

c. Making of the Priestly Garments (39:1-31)

■ **1** Verse 1 reports the making of all the priestly vestments. The subsequent report highlights Aaron's **sacred garments**, as in the instructions in ch 28. The report affirms seven times that each item for the priestly vestment is made exactly as instructed by Yahweh (see 39:1, 5, 7, 21, 26, 29, 31).

■ **2-7** These verses detail the making of the ephod (→ 28:6-14). Verse 3 has additional information concerning the technique used to make **gold** thread. Sarna notes that the technique described in this verse (hammering gold into **thin sheets** over a stone and then cutting it into *strips* in spiral form) is typically Egyptian (2004, 172). Although this could suggest Egyptian influence on the Israelite artists, it could also speak of the lasting legacy of the Israelite artists and craftsmen in Egypt.

■ **8-21** The artisans also make the **breastpiece** (→ 28:15-30).

■ **22-31** These verses detail the making of other priestly garments (→ 28:31-43).

d. Completion, Inspection, and Blessing of the Work (39:32-43)

■ **32** Verse 32 reports the completion of **all the work on the tabernacle** and its furnishings. The fact that **everything** is made **just as the LORD commanded Moses** is reiterated three times in this unit (vv 32, 42, 43). The great emphasis on the Israelites' obedience and the accuracy of what is made further underscore the utter holiness and otherness of the tabernacle, rather than the creative abilities of its makers. The structure originates with God and symbolizes otherworldly realities (→ 25:9 and From the Text on 25:1-9). It is not a product of human idolatrous tendencies or imagination.

■ **33-41** Upon completion, the artisans bring **all** the items to **Moses**, as listed in these verses, to be assembled by him (presumably with Levite assistants).

■ **42-43** Moses inspects **the work** and confirms that everything is done accurately. Although Moses is the sole recipient of the visual pattern, the craftsmen execute the work according to that pattern under the instruction of Moses and the inspiration of Yahweh's Spirit. **So Moses** praises and blesses **them** for their faithful service and splendid work. Presumably, his authoritative blessing communicates to them Yahweh's own appreciation and blessing of them and their work.

FROM THE TEXT

God desires to dwell among his people and be their God (25:8; 29:45-46), *which is the ultimate purpose of the creation and redemption of the nation of Is-* *rael.* God makes Adam and Eve in order to be their God and to dwell among them. Due to their rebellion, however, they are driven out of the sanctuary, the garden of God. God, nevertheless, reinitiates and pursues divine habitation among human beings through Abraham and Sarah and their descendants. God's desire to come and dwell among human beings is about to be realized as the Israelites complete the tabernacle. It is a divinely initiated, revealed, and inspired sanctuary for God, built through human generosity and obedient, artistic work. The physical sanctuary built only by his people in such a manner is worthy of housing the abiding, manifest presence of the Holy God. Once the tabernacle is complete, God comes to abide among his people (40:34-38). It is extraordinary that God is coming to dwell with rebellious people, whom he reconciles to himself by his compassion and grace. After renewing the covenant that the apostates broke, God accepts their offerings and allows them to construct for him a holy sanctuary.

Even in the new covenant church, God initiates the giving of his presence in and through Jesus Christ. Christ loves us, comes to us, and dies for us while we are still sinners (Rom 5:8). Through God's grace and kindness, expressed in Christ's atoning work, we are reconciled to God and called into a covenant relationship with God (Gal 2:20; Eph 2:4-5). Part of that relationship is the call to build "a dwelling in which God lives by his Spirit" (Eph 2:22). That "holy temple" is the metaphorical body of Christ, which is comprised of believing members, who are "joined together . . . in the Lord" (2:21; 4:15).

However, we believers do not build the body of Christ on our own. Even as the tabernacle is initiated and designed by God, the church is "God's handiwork" (2:10). God is the builder of the church, but God does not do the work alone. God calls us to join him in the building of it and empowers us to do the work. As Paul says, "From him the whole body, joined and held together by every supporting ligament, grows and builds itself up in love, as each part does its work" (4:16). As such, like the assembled tabernacle that is filled with the glory of God, the body of Christ is filled with "all the fullness of God" (3:19).

3. Assembly of the Tabernacle (40:1-38)

BEHIND THE TEXT

Moses assembles the tabernacle and places its furnishings in proper places. In a sense, he alone can carry out this duty since he is the covenant mediator; he alone is given the heavenly vision of the tabernacle (see Exod 25:9, 40; 26:30, etc.). Yahweh determines the arrangement and the exact placement of each item. Yahweh instructs Moses in 40:2-15, and Moses carries out the command in 40:18-33.

The order found in the setup of the tabernacle and its furnishings corresponds to the order mentioned in the earlier, longer section detailing their construction (36:8—39:43). Setup proceeds from the most sacred and thus the innermost in placement to the less sacred and the outermost pieces.

Once the tabernacle is completely arranged, the glory or visible presence of Yahweh fills the tabernacle and remains on it. The book concludes with an editorial comment concerning Yahweh's visible presence in the people's wilderness wanderings.

There are striking verbal parallels between the creation account in Gen 1—2 and the tabernacle section. Just as God "finished the work" (Gen 2:2), so also "Moses finished the work" (Exod 40:33); just as God "saw" his creatures and "blessed them" (Gen 1:21-22, 28), so also Moses "saw" the work and "blessed them" (Exod 39:43). These echoes link Yahweh's creation of the garden of Eden (see Ezek 28:13; 31:9) with the human creation of Yahweh's earthly dwelling place (see Meyers 2005, 282-83). As such, the completion of the tabernacle represents the dawn of a new redemptive era in human history; the Holy God comes to dwell among sinful humankind, whom he previously exiled from his garden, in order to redeem them and their dwelling place.

a. Yahweh's Instructions (40:1-15)

(1) Assembly of the Tabernacle (40:1-8)

■ **1-2** Yahweh commands that the **tabernacle** is to be set up **on the first day of the first month** (v 2). That day is two weeks before the first anniversary of the Israelites' exodus and ten months from the day of arrival at Mount Sinai, which is "on the first day of the third month" (19:1).

No indication of the time taken to make all the objects for the tabernacle is given. However, if the tradition is correct that associates the Day of Atonement (on the tenth day of the seventh month) with the day of the renewal of the covenant when Moses came down from Mount Sinai the second time (→ Behind the Text for 34:29-35), then the Israelites had five months and eighteen days for the preparation of materials, construction, and assembling of the tabernacle.

Moses is to assemble ***the tabernacle of the tent of meeting*** (*miškan 'ōhel*, also in 40:6). The tabernacle and the tent of meeting refer to distinct aspects (→ "tabernacle" in 25:9), although sometimes the tabernacle (e.g., 40:33, 36, 38) or the tent of meeting (e.g., vv 22, 24, 32) refers to the entire structure. In this chapter, the term "tabernacle" (*miškan*), in most of its occurrences, indicates either the innermost curtains or the inner holy place. Thus, when a matter concerns the inner precincts, then the term "tabernacle" is preferred. The designation "tent of meeting" draws attention to the outer structure that covers the tabernacle curtains and its space (see vv 29, 34, 35). Thus, when a matter relates to the entire structure (and the inner precincts are not involved), then the "tent of meeting" is preferred.

■ **3-5** These verses instruct Moses to set up the furnishings and curtains that belong to the holy places.

■ **6-8** These verses concern the setting up of the furnishings inside the **courtyard** and the courtyard itself.

(2) Anointing of the Tabernacle (40:9-11)

■ **9-11** Yahweh instructs Moses to **anoint** and **consecrate all** the aforementioned items with the sacred aromatic **anointing oil** (v 9; → 30:22-33). Through the ceremony, the human-made objects are rendered **holy** (v 10), ready to receive and host Yahweh's holy presence.

(3) Installation of the Priests (40:12-15)

■ **12-15** Finally, instructions are given to install or ordain the **priests** who will serve in the tabernacle once it is set up and anointed.

The fulfillment of the instructions for the **anointing** of the tabernacle and the items within it (vv 9-11) and the installation of the priests are not recorded in this chapter but in Lev 8 (in the context of the installation and anointing of the priests). After a seven-day installation-ordination ceremony, **Aaron and his sons** begin their ministry on the eighth day. Numbers 9 records the glory of the Lord made visible to all the Israelites and the fire coming out of Yahweh's presence to consume the burnt offering (Lev 9:23-24). Such a manifestation of Yahweh's glory signals divine-human communion and union. The people, thus, shout for joy and fall facedown in worship (v 24).

b. Moses' Obedient Fulfillment of the Instructions (40:16-33)

■ **16** This verse reports Moses' fulfillment of the Lord's instructions. The phrase "just as the LORD commanded him/Moses" is repeated seven times in vv 18-33, appearing after the setup of each major item. The repetition underscores Moses' absolute obedience.

■ **17** This verse regarding the setup date fulfills v 2.

■ **18-32** These verses detail Moses' obedient, step-by-step and item-by-item assembling of the **tabernacle**. After the ordination of the priests and the consecration of the Levites, they care for and handle the tabernacle and its furnishings, instead of **Moses**.

■ **33** The unit concludes with a brief summary statement that **Moses finished the work**, which recalls the similar summary that opens the unit (v 16).

c. Yahweh's Glory on the Tabernacle (40:34-38)

■ **34** Once the tabernacle is set up, anointed, and consecrated, the **cloud** (*'ānān*) and the **glory** [*kabôd*] **of the** LORD transfer from the mountaintop to the **tabernacle**. As in 16:10, the cloud and the glory of the Lord appear together. The cloud is best understood as a visible expression of Yahweh's presence. The cloud functions to cover or shield the intense manifest glory of the Lord. Appropriately, then, the cloud covers or settles on (40:35) the external aspect of the tabernacle, that is, the tent of meeting. The cloud is seen by all the Israelites. By contrast, the glory of the Lord fills (vv 34, 35) the tabernacle, that is, the inner holy and the most holy places.

■ **35** Yahweh already has revealed that he will consecrate the **tabernacle** by his **glory** in 29:43; at this point, Yahweh fulfills his word. Moses earlier entered the **cloud** (33:9-10; 34:5) and witnessed the glory of Yahweh, albeit in a veiled form (33:18, 22). Presently, Yahweh's unveiled presence fills the tabernacle, thus **Moses** is unable to **enter** it. First Kings 8:10-11 reports a similar phenomenon of Yahweh's glory filling the temple and the cloud surrounding it, making the priests unable to perform their services.

After this initial manifestation of his glory, however, Yahweh limits his presence or glory to the most holy place. In addition, just as Yahweh called Moses from within the cloud and invited Moses into the cloud on Mount Sinai, Yahweh later calls Moses from the most holy place (Lev 1:1; see Cassuto

1967, 484). Moses then enters it, and from above the mercy seat, Yahweh continues to instruct Moses and gives additional laws (see Lev 1:1; Num 7:89).

■ **36-38** These verses indicate that the glory-cloud guided the **Israelites** through the wilderness, toward the promised land (v 36). The first time the Israelites **set out** from Mount Sinai is "on the twentieth day of the second month of the second year" (Num 10:11), which is seven weeks from the day of the assembly of the tabernacle.

It is clear that the **cloud of the LORD** (Exod 40:38) is visible to the Israelites and accompanies them **during all their travels** (first to Kadesh Barnea, and then, after thirty-eight years at Kadesh Barnea, to the plains of Moab). The manifest, glorified presence of Yahweh is an ongoing, central feature of Israel's covenant life with Yahweh.

FROM THE TEXT

The culminating theme of Exodus, the presence of the one true God among the people of God, is not only the goal of Israel's story, but also the goal of the Christian story. Through the tabernacle, the Lord is with his people. The promise "I will be with you" first spoken to Moses is now confirmed to the whole nation as God's firstborn. The reality and future promise of the ongoing presence of God among his people is the culmination of the great events of the book of Exodus. Every major part of the book leads up to this conclusion and cannot stand on its own without this goal being fulfilled. The goal of the exodus from Egypt is not simply to liberate the Israelites from oppression but also to grant them a covenant life in the Lord's presence in the promised land. The desert travel and provisions teach people to trust in God's daily provision and, therefore, to observe the Sabbath rest, which has significant implications for the people's longevity in God's land. The theophany at Sinai and the Decalogue powerfully demonstrate the supreme holiness and utter otherness of their God, instilling in the people the fear of God necessary for the covenant life with him. The Sinai covenant and the laws show God's righteous requirements for the people to live a holy life that is pleasing and acceptable to the Lord who dwells in their midst. God's dealings with the apostate Israelites (in the golden calf episode) underscore the centrality of divine grace that not only initiates the covenant relationship with sinful human beings but also maintains it even in the face of his covenant people's unfaithfulness. In addition, God's express readiness to destroy the entire nation for their apostasy warns that such destruction still remains a possibility in the case of repeated rebellion. The instructions for the tabernacle reinforce the reality of God's supreme holiness that requires obedience, reverence, and care in approaching God's real presence. With the covenant renewed and the tabernacle completed and assembled, the Lord comes to dwell with his people. God expects his people to move with him as his cloud moves (Exod 40:36-38), at least until there is a more permanent dwelling place for both God and people in the promised land.

The later history of Israel shows that it was not so easy for the Israelites to live in a way that allowed for the continued presence of God in their midst. They not only violate the law in blatant and serious ways but also fail to maintain proper worship in the tabernacle and later temple. Yet, various writers and prophets reassure God's people that there will come a time when Israel's faithful God will again dwell among his covenant people who are contrite and faithful (see Isa 7:14; 57:15; 66:1-2).

The presence of God with his people was a significant theme in the NT. Jesus Christ, Immanuel, is "God with us" (Matt 1:23). Through the incarnation, he dwelt ("tabernacled") among us, thereby revealing "his glory" (John 1:14). The Holy Spirit, as God's presence, came upon Jesus at baptism and remained on him (Luke 3:22; 4:1, 14). Through his death on the cross, Jesus accomplished once-and-for-all atonement that made possible fellowship between God and sinners, now extending the covenant blessings even to the Gentiles who believe in him.

The Holy Spirit is the presence or glory of God that fills the "temple." Yet "temple" is now redefined as the individual and corporate people of God, rather than any physical structure or building. The people of God can become God's resting place or dwelling place. The triune God lives within the followers of Jesus who love and obey him (John 14:21-23). Jesus gives his glorious presence to his followers so that they would be one with the Father and one with one another. Such unity will supremely demonstrate to the world that God sent Jesus (17:22-23). In fact, the creation itself eagerly waits for the revelation of the children of God in unity with the Father and with one another. It is then that the creation itself is set free from the curses that came by human disobedience.

Ultimately, the fullest meaning of the tabernacle is fulfilled in the new heaven and the new earth. God will dwell among his holy people in his holy dwelling place, the new Jerusalem (Rev 21:2). God's Holy City will be filled with God's own glorious light (22:5). The faithful "will be his people, and God himself will be with them and be their God" (21:3). We all will see him face to face (1 Cor 13:12; Rev 22:4). Further, as kingly and priestly people, we will serve and worship him and "reign for ever and ever" (22:5). Until then, and even beyond the ushering in of the new Jerusalem, the exodus narrative reminds readers that God's abiding and indwelling presence will accompany "by day, and . . . by night" all those who walk with God "during all their travels" (Exod 40:38).